תנ״ך

ArtScroll Tanach Series®

A traditional commentary on the Books of the Bible

Rabbis Nosson Scherman/Meir Zlotowitz
General Editors

Yehoshua

Yehoshua

THE BOOK OF JOSHUA / A NEW TRANSLATION WITH A COMMENTARY ANTHOLOGIZED FROM TALMUDIC, MIDRASHIC, AND RABBINIC SOURCES.

Published by

Mesorah Publications, ltd

Translation and Commentary by
Rabbi Reuven Drucker

Overviews by
Rabbi Nosson Scherman

FIRST EDITION
First Impression . . . January 1982
Second Impression . . . January 1989
Third Impression . . . November 1993
Fourth Impression . . . March 1994

Published and Distributed by
MESORAH PUBLICATIONS, Ltd.
4401 Second Avenue
Brooklyn, New York 11232

Distributed in Europe by
J. LEHMANN HEBREW BOOKSELLERS
20 Cambridge Terrace
Gateshead, Tyne and Wear
England NE8 1RP

Distributed in Israel by
SIFRIATI / A. GITLER — BOOKS
4 Bilu Street
P.O.B. 14075
Tel Aviv 61140

Distributed in Australia & New Zealand by
GOLD'S BOOK & GIFT CO.
36 William Street
Balaclava 3183, Vic., Australia

Distributed in South Africa by
KOLLEL BOOKSHOP
22 Muller Street
Yeoville 2198, Johannesburg, South Africa

YEHOSHUA / JOSHUA

ISBN
0-89906-087-0 (hard cover)
0-89906-080-9 (paperback)

Typography by CompuScribe at ArtScroll Studios, Ltd.
4401 Second Avenue / Brooklyn, N.Y. 11232 / (718) 921-9000

Printed in the United States of America by Moriah Offset
Bound by Sefercraft, Quality Bookbinders, Ltd. Brooklyn, N.Y.

ספר זה מוקדש לזכר נשמת חברתנו

חנה מרים מוסקט ע״ה

שנקטפה באיבה בי״ד שבט תש״מ.

אשת חיל לבעלה, בנתה לו בית נאמן בישראל;

אמא אהובה לבנותיה, נטעה בְּקִרְבָּן אהבת תורה וישראל;

חברה יקרה ונאמנה, פנתה דרך לקהילתה.

This volume is dedicated

by the friends of

Ann Moscot ע״ה.

She remains in our memories always.

יהי זכרה ברוך

The following friends of the Moscot family have supported the publication of ספר יהושע:

DR. AND MRS. MARVIN S. BLUSH
DR. AND MRS. ROBERT DUBLIN
DR. AND MRS. YEHUDI FELMAN
MR. AND MRS. IRVING FORMAN
MR. AND MRS. AVERY GROSS
DR. AND MRS. ALLAN D. NOVETSKY
MR. AND MRS. MELVIN H. ROSENBERG
MR. AND MRS. ABRAHAM ZYLBERBERG
MR. AND MRS. ARI EIGER
MR. AND MRS. BENJAMIN LEIFER
RABBI AND MRS. AARON MIRSKY
DR. AND MRS. FRED NAIDER
DR. AND MRS. JOSEPH TAITELBAUM
MR. AND MRS. JOSEPH WEISS
MR. AND MRS. ARNOLD ARONOWITZ
MR. AND MRS. JOSEPH BARATZ
MR. AND MRS. MARTIN BECKER
MR. AND MRS. JAY GOLDBERG
MR. AND MRS. BERNARD KAPLAN
MR. AND MRS. ROBERT LEVINE
RABBI AND MRS. YAAKOV MARCUS
RABBI AND MRS. YITZCHAK PESSIN
MR. AND MRS. ALEXANDER REICH
MR. AND MRS. JACK SIEGEL
DR. PAUL SLATER
DR. AND MRS. JOSEPH STRAUSS

◈§ *Table of Contents*

Maps and Illustrations

מכתב ברכה

RABBI JACOB I. RUDERMAN
400 MT. WILSON LANE
BALTIMORE, MD. 21208

יעקב יצחק הלוי רודרמן
באלטימאר, מד.

כ"ט אייר תשמ"א

לכבוד הרב המאור הגדול בתורה ויר"ש
הרה"ג ר׳ ראובן דרוקער שליט"א,

כמה מאושר אתה להיות מן החולקים בראש במוקדשים בהטפת טל תחיה על ארץ יבשה אין כל, כשכמה וכמה מאחינו בני ישראל צמאים לדבר ה׳ כי יקר הוא בימיהם, ויודעים לרוות צמאונם רק אם מגישים להם בשפה המובנת להם – ואלה נאמרים בכל לשון.

והנה דור דור וספריו דור דור ולקוטיו. וכמה מן העדינות וההבחנה נדרשת למשש דופק הדור ולהבין צרכיו. ועל הכל להיות מזוין בלשון למודים למצוא השביל המוביל אל לבותיהם של הצעירים ומובילם הלאה לקראת בוראם שכשמכירים תורתו מכירים גם את מי שאמר והיה העולם.

וכבר אמר שלמה המלך בני אם חכם לבך ישמח לבי גם אני. והנה זכית להתחיל ולסיים פרוש על ספר יהושע וזכות הרבים תלויה בך. ובפרט הגדלת לעשות בברור שמות המקומות והעיירות המכביד כ"כ על מי שרוצה להיות בקי בספר זה. ויישר כחך על העמל הכבד שהשקעת בעבודה חשובה זו. ואני תקוה שמכבוש יהושע תעלה מעלה לכבוש ע"י עזרה מקודש גבולים גדולים ורחבים שלא תבטל לעולם וכאשר מסרת לצעירים תזכה עוד להיות מן המוסרים לזקנים כאות נפשך וכאות נפש הכותב וחותם לכבוד התורה ולומדיה,

יעקב יצחק הלוי רודרמאן
נר ישראל
ראש הישיבה

מכתב ברכה

מרדכי גיפטער
ישיבת טלז
RABBI MORDECAI GIFTER
28570 NUTWOOD LANE
WICKLIFFE, OHIO 44092

ב״ה - ב׳ שמות, תשמ״ד

מע״כ ידי״נ הרה״ג ר׳ מאיר זלאטאוויץ שליט״א, ראש תכנית „ארטסקרול״, יחד עם כל הצוות אשר עמו, יחיו, שלום וברכה נצח!

ואחדשה״ט באהבה,

מה נכבד היום בהופעת [illegible] אור יקרות, פרי יגיעתו ועמלו של ידידי האברך הנעלה הרב ר׳ ראובן דרוקער נ״י, הוא תרגום וביאור ס׳ יהושע, שהנהו [illegible] טבלת [illegible]. [illegible] של [illegible] תרגום וביאור נביאים וכתובים כפי התכנית שהתויתם לעבודתכם בתכנית „ארטסקרול״.

הספר יהושע הנהו לא רק הראשון לספרי נביאים אלא שיושבו מעין המשך לתורת משה [illegible] תלמידו הנאמן - יהושע משרת משה - [illegible] ״א, א׳, שמעו הגבורים הוא שורש בספרו של יהושע [illegible] ספר תורת אלקים והוא [illegible] התוספתא ביחס להמשנה. מלחמת הכיבוש דתחלת קדושת הארץ יש בה [illegible] המשך ישיר לכיבוש סיחון ועוג ע״י מרע״ה. והשתלשלות דבכי ימי [illegible] ה׳ שרשה במנהגה יהושע כממשיך דרכו של מרע״ה, ויאורו של משה לנצח ישראל [illegible] במעשה יהושע [illegible] פני משה כפני חמה פני יהושע כפני לבנה.

ולכן דרושה זהירות יתירה בהגשת ספר יהושע לפני קהל המעיינים הרחוקים משפת המקור, לשון הקודש. וזהירות דרושה הן בתרגום הן בביאור. וידעתי שידידי ר׳ ראובן נ״י השקיע בעבודה זו רב עמלו במשך כמה שנים [illegible] הוציא מתח״י [illegible] נאה ומתוקן, ואין [illegible] [illegible] ספק [illegible] הרבים שיהיה זה לתועלת רבה, וכל המעיינים ימצאו בספר מלא כל נחת.

ויה״ר שתזכו להמשיך בעבודת הקודש ומתרחבת [illegible] שאין השמחה להגיד כמה משפטי הביאורים [illegible] [illegible] [illegible] ברכה [illegible] בהוצאת ארטסקרול [illegible] לב [illegible] ותוציאו לאור תשבחות [illegible] אלה [illegible] בהצלחה, והיינו בברכה.

הנני בזה אוהבכם תמיד, דורש שלומכם כל הימים,
מרדכי גיפטער

Author's Preface

To each Jewish soul corresponds one of the six hundred thousand letters in the Sefer Torah (Megaleh Amukos *186).*

'Much ink has been spilled and many quills have been broken' in attempting to reconcile this statement from the 'hidden chambers' of Torah with the reality that there are precisely 304,805 letters in a Torah scroll. R' Reuven Margolios *suggests (based on* Jerusalem Shekalim *6:1) that in addition to the 304,805 black, visible letters inscribed on the parchment, the Torah contains invisible 'white letters' in the spaces between the black letters and the words which they form. It is to these letters that our Sages refer when they state that the Torah is 'white fire written upon black fire.' These are the elusive three hundred thousand letters which complete the count of six hundred thousand letters in the Sefer Torah.*

In the totality of Jewish life, there are those of our brethren whose role in Torah life is less visible than others because their knowledge of Torah is faint. But every Jew is a 'letter' in the Torah, and no Torah scroll is valid if even one letter is missing. Those who have been fortunate enough to be educated in their share of Torah have the responsibility to share their good fortune with others and make the Torah's riches accessible to all. Comprehensive, inspiring Jewish education is the only solution to the reclamation of this precious segment of our people.

It is a great privilege for me to contribute to the ARTSCROLL TANACH SERIES, *which has proven to be a significant and effective source of Torah knowledge not only for those who have received extensive Jewish education, but also for those who wish to become more aware of their rich heritage. I am indeed thankful for being granted the opportunity to make my small contribution to this form of Jewish education and to address the entire spectrum of 'letters' in our Holy Torah,* להגדיל תורה ולהאדירה.

INTRODUCTION AND PREFATORY REMARKS

In the Introduction *I endeavored to provide the historical and philosophical perspectives which I felt were essential to understanding the* Book of Joshua. *It is my hope that these words, together with the* Prefatory Remarks *appearing before each chapter, provide direction and allow some of the real religious issues of our often misunderstood Prophets to come into view.*

COMMENTARY

Not until one writes his Torah thoughts does he begin to realize the implication of our Sages' reminder that the Torah is literally infinite (see Eruvin *21a). This* Commentary *is perforce limited; however, I have attempted to present both the major opinions concerning the surface meaning of the text and additional material which provides greater depth. On occasion a personal insight was included and stated in brackets. I have also suggested sources for readers interested in further investigation.*

For an elegant treatment of the halachic nature of Joshua, *the reader is referred to the original and scholarly volume* Nachlas Shimon, *authored by my friend and colleague, Rabbi Shimon Krasner.*

TRANSLITERATION OF NAMES

Most proper nouns appear in their transliterated form in the Translation (e.g., Menashe, Divon). However, English names which are commonly substituted for the Hebrew original have been included to enhance readability (e.g., Jerusalem, Hebron, Simeon).

GEOGRAPHY

Since almost one-third of the Book of Joshua *deals with the geography of* Eretz Yisrael, *it has been a 'closed book' to all but those who have done extensive research outside the classical commentaries. The classical commentators did not intentionally refrain from providing geographical information about* Eretz Yisrael. *Their unfamiliarity with* Eretz Yisrael's *topography was a sad, inevitable result of our bitter Exile and of their inability to travel to the Land. We do find that whenever authorities, such as R' Eshtori HaParchi* (Kaftor V'Ferach) *and* Ramban *(see for example,* Bereishis *35:16), were able to ascend to* Eretz Yisrael, *they carefully researched its geography and related it to their understanding of Torah and even halachah.*

Upon approval of the Editorial Board I have based the geographical portions of the Commentary *and maps primarily on* T'vuos HaAretz, *written by Rabbi Yehoseph Schwarz (1801-1865). This is by far the most comprehensive work on the geography relating to the* Book of Joshua, *and it ranks with* Admas Kodesh *(Rabbi Yitzchak Goldhor) as a classic in its field. All geographical references in the* Commentary *and maps, unless attributed to another source, are based on the research of* T'vuos HaAretz.

As evidenced by his writings, R' Schwarz was a man with an extraordinary love of Eretz Yisrael, *and he devoted a good portion of his life to researching and discovering the modern day equivalents of the cities mentioned in Tanach and Talmud. He naturally reported his results in the Arabic nomenclature, and this method was preserved in the* Commentary. *He had an encyclopedic grasp of every Torah reference pertaining to geography — be it a Tosefta, a Mishnah in*

Taharos, or an arcane reference made by a Prophet — and he employed it to deduce the location of many cities mentioned in Joshua. *Within seven years his work was translated into both German and English, together with the map which he constructed of the Land. Readers of the English edition of* T'vuos HaAretz *are cautioned that there are discrepancies between it and the original Hebrew.*

A Geographical Index *was included to aid readers in locating the cities in the* Commentary. *It is hoped that the information provided will also prove useful to students of other books of Tanach as they seek clarification of geographical references.*

MAPS

At first glance it would appear relatively simple to generate a map which would delineate the borders of the territory allocated to each tribe. One would simply draw lines between the cities mentioned in the text and obtain the outline. Several factors nullify this approach. First, many cities mentioned in the text are completely unknown today. Second, the cities that can be identified are not always on the border (cf. Rashi *to 15:21), and it is not always clear from the text which cities are along tribal boundaries. Third, there is much evidence to indicate that the borders between tribes were not like the distinct territorial borders which divide modern states. Rather, corridors of land belonging to certain tribes penetrated the territories of other tribes, often for many miles (see* Zevachim *118b and* Commentary *to 19:10 and 19:12). Fourth, the interpretation of verses describing borders can be unclear (see especially* Commentary *to 16:6 and 18:14), thus causing the position of the border to be a matter of conjecture. Fifth, other verses in Tanach may describe a city as belonging to a certain tribe, but from the borders mentioned in the* Book of Joshua *it may not be contained within that tribes' border (see* footnote *to 16:5). Sixth, many tribes owned territory within another tribe's boundaries (see* Commentary *to 19:10).*

Given these complicating factors, it is understandable that there are many opinions regarding the details of the maps. Since it would be burdensome to the reader, if not impossible for the author, to illustrate every point in contention, it was deemed appropriate to follow one unified view, based on the conclusions of T'vuos HaAretz.

Although T'vuos HaAretz *constructed maps of* Eretz Yisrael, *they do not include territorial borders, nor do they include the great bulk of the geographical identifications which he made in his masterwork. The borders shown on the maps, as well as the placement of certain cities, were constructed from the verbal descriptions given by* T'vuos HaAretz *and are, therefore, only reasonable estimates. In some cases, interpolations and judgments were required to account for all the information he presented (see, for example,* Commentary *to 19:40).*

Therefore, it cannot be overemphasized that the maps included in this volume are only approximations and are at times speculative. For the sake of clarity, however, the Editorial Board felt that these approximations were advisable.

ACKNOWLEDGMENTS

I would like to take this opportunity to express my gratitude to some of the many people whose counsel and personal example have had a profound effect on my growth and development.

To my dear parents, MR. and MRS. MURRAY DRUCKER, *whose self-sacrifice, foresight, and encouragement have been mainstays throughout my life, I am eternally grateful. I would also like to express my appreciation to my mother-in-law,* MRS. EVELYN COHEN, *for her help and encouragement. May they all be blessed with good health, long life, and much nachas from their children and grandchildren.*

I have been privileged to spend the past ten years at YESHIVAS NER YISRAEL *under the tutelage of the world renowned gaon and Rosh HaYeshiva,* מרן הרב הגאון רב יעקב יצחק הלוי רודרמאן שליט״א, *whose very presence has served to motivate and inspire me. I wish to thank him for all his guidance and support throughout the years and for the enthusiasm with which he launched me on this project. May the Almighty grant the Rosh HaYeshiva many more years of good health so that Klal Yisrael may continue to benefit from his 'Light to Israel' which he prophetically kindled in America almost fifty years ago.*

HARAV HAGAON MORDECHAI GIFTER שליט״א, *the Telshe Rosh HaYeshiva, has been a source of guidance, inspiration, and encouragment to me and my wife, and we are forever grateful to him and to his dear Rebbitzen. I am deeply moved that he has so generously given his* Michtav Brachah *to be included in this volume, for he truly was the source of its coming to fruition. May the Rosh HaYeshiva and his family be granted many more years of good health* להגדיל תורה ולהאדירה.

From the moment I came to the yeshiva, HARAV NAFTOLI NEUBERGER, *Menahel of* NER YISRAEL, *showered me with his sincere, personal concern and help. His selfless, unstinting dedication to the needs of Klal Yisrael and his abundant chesed have served as a model for me, a fraction of which I would only hope to accomplish in my own lifetime. May Klal Yisrael continue to benefit from his wisdom and goodness for many more years. To Rabbi and Mrs. Neuberger, I extend my most heartfelt thanks.*

I am deeply indebted to HARAV MOSHE EISEMANN *for his precious friendship and valuable assistance. It is he who launched me on this project and encouraged me along the way. His extensive notes on* Yehoshua *and* Shoftim *have been a great aid to me, and many of his thoughts have been incorporated into the* Introduction. *May he and his family be granted* אריכת ימים טובים ושלום *so that Klal Yisrael may continue to benefit from the so very much they contribute.*

Words cannot express my appreciation to RABBI BORUCH BORCHARDT *for his uncanny wisdom, guidance, friendship, and hospitality. He and his wonderful family have a very special place in my heart.*

I would like to give special thanks to RABBI AARON BRAFMAN *for his*

precious friendship and counsel. May he and his dear family be blessed with His Goodness.

I am profoundly grateful to my colleagues in the NER YISRAEL KOLLEL. *They are* talmidei chachamim *of the first order, and their Torah accomplishments never cease to be an inspiration to me. In particular, I would like to thank Rabbis Eliezer Gibber, Chaim Gibber, and Yisroel Moshe Janowski.*

I wish to express my thanks to my colleagues of the ETZ CHAIM CENTER FOR JEWISH STUDIES *in Baltimore, who so graciously allowed me to attenuate my teaching commitments during the preparation of this volume.*

I would like to acknowledge my appreciation to MISS FAIGE ZILBERMINC *of the Library of Congress for her ever-pleasant and professional assistance in helping me obtain sources which have proven so valuable for the writing of the* Commentary.

I am especially grateful to ArtScroll editors, RABBI MEIR ZLOTOWITZ *and* RABBI NOSSON SCHERMAN, *not only for giving me the opportunity to contribute to the ArtScroll series, but also for allowing me to make their valued friendship. Their wise suggestions have improved the quality of this volume immeasurably. It is my hope and blessing that they be enabled to complete the* ARTSCROLL TANACH SERIES, *which is truly a monumental service to Klal Yisrael.*

The production of this book involved many technical challenges which were all met with grace, good cheer, and elegance by my good friend REB SHEAH BRANDER. *His clear and tasteful construction of more than twenty-five maps and diagrams enhances the sefer immeasurably and provides a textual clarity that could not otherwise have been achieved. He is a craftsman and artist par excellence and has rightfully earned the appreciation of the ArtScroll readership. To* REB SHEAH *go my sincerest thanks.*

I wish to thank my friend RABBI AVIE GOLD *of Mesorah Publications for his meticulous reading of the manuscript. By dint of his erudition, he noted areas requiring clarification and correction and offered a host of invaluable suggestions for the improvement of the text. I am forever indebted.*

I wish to take this opportunity to mention the following people whose kindness has left an indelible mark on my development:
RABBI MENDEL KAUFMAN, DR. NAFTOLI LEVI, DR. YEHUDAH SORSCHER, MR. AVRAHAM BESS, RABBI ELIYA GALUPKIN, RABBI ZEV LEFF, RABBI AARON LEVITANSKY, RABBI SHMUEL GLAZER, *and* RABBI YISROEL REZNITZKY.

Mesorah Publications is indeed fortunate to have such a professional, competent, and cheerful staff — MR. STEPHEN BLITZ, YOSEF TIMINSKY, MRS. SHIRLEY KIFFEL, MRS. FAIGIE WEINBAUM, LEA FREIER, CHANEE FREIER, EDEL STREICHER, *and* ESTHER GLATZER. *I have truly appreciated all their efforts.*

Finally, I would like to thank my wife, HILARY. *During the preparation of the manuscript, she has admirably doubled as a supportive wife and as a superb style editor, and she made invaluable improvements in the clarity and readability of the text. May we and our*

children, Shira, Dovid, Devorah, Aviva Miriam, and Yaakov Eliyahu, forever fulfill the charge that was urged upon Yehoshua himself:

לא ימוש ספר התורה הזה מפיך והגית בו יומם ולילה למען תשמר לעשות ככל הכתוב בו כי אז תצליח ואז תשכיל.

As I conclude I wish to pay homage to Him who has provided all, and declare:

ברוך אתה ה׳ למדני חוקיך
אמן אמן אמן סלה ועד

Reuven Drucker
Baltimore, Maryland
מוצש״ק פרשת ויחי חזק
January 9, 1982

Mesorah Publications *adds its tribute to the memory of* **Ann Moscot** ע״ה *in whose honor this sefer was dedicated. That her family and so many of her friends chose Torah as the vehicle to keep alive what she stood for is a reflection not only of her ideals and faith, but of the devotion she kindled in others. May the study of Joshua be a merit for her soul and a source of comfort to her family and all who treasure her memory. Their names may be found on the dedication.*

We are deeply grateful to **Dr. Allan D. Novetsky** *who was instrumental in arranging this dedication. As a well-honed tool of the Supreme Healer, one of the architects of a model Jewish community, and an early friend of the ArtScroll Series, he has won the admiration of all who know him.*

Yehoshua

◆§ The Overviews

*An Overview/ Prophets and Prophecy**

תָּנוּ רַבָּנָן אַרְבָּעִים וּשְׁמֹנָה נְבִיאִים וְשֶׁבַע נְבִיאוֹת נִתְנַבְּאוּ לָהֶם לְיִשְׂרָאֵל וְלֹא פִּחֲתוּ וְלֹא הוֹתִירוּ עַל מַה שֶּׁכָּתוּב חוּץ מִמִּקְרָא מְגִילָּה ... תַּנְיָא הַרְבֵּה נְבִיאִים עָמְדוּ לָהֶם לְיִשְׂרָאֵל כְּפַלַּיִם כְּיוֹצְאֵי מִצְרַיִם אֶלָּא נְבוּאָה שֶׁהוּצְרְכָה לְדוֹרוֹת נִכְתְּבָה שֶׁלֹּא נִצְרְכָה לֹא נִכְתְּבָה

*The Rabbis taught: Forty-eight prophets and seven prophetesses prophesied for Israel; they neither subtracted from nor added to what is written [in the Torah] except for [the commandment of] reading the Megillah ... It was taught: Many prophets arose for Israel — twice as many as those who left Egypt — but a prophecy that was needed by future generations was written [in the twenty-four books of Scripture] and what was not needed was not written (*Megillah 14a).

The word *navi* [נָבִיא], which is commonly translated *prophet,* is one of the most basic to the study of Scripture — and one of the most misunderstood.

The prophecies of only fifty-five people were recorded because only theirs were 'needed by future generations' — what constitutes a 'needed' prophecy?

What is he and what is his function? If the prophets added and changed nothing, why were they needed? The prophecies of only fifty-five people, forty-eight men and seven women, were recorded because only theirs were 'needed by future generations' — what constitutes a 'needed' prophecy? And what did the other prophets do? If there were 'twice as many as those who left Egypt,' we have a grand total of at least 1,200,000 — what sort of

*This Overview is based primarily on *Mevo HaShe'arim* by Rabbi Klonimos Kalmish Schapiro הי״ד and *Nevi'ei Emes* by Rabbi Avraham Yitzchok Klein ז״ל.

prophecies did they receive and what teachings did they deliver? In short, virtually everyone who has ever studied Scripture has used the words *navi* and prophet countless times without much reflection on what they mean. Let us try to achieve some clarity in a welter of misconception.

I. What is a Prophet?

The Cover and the Book

Very often in human experience we tend to confuse what someone does with what someone is.

Very often in human experience, perhaps especially in the study of spiritual matters, we tend to confuse what someone *does* with what someone *is*.

What is a great *rosh yeshiva* [seminary dean]? Many people would describe his characteristic garb, the fact that he lectures regularly on the Talmud, administers a yeshiva, frequently performs public functions and so on. What is a chassidic *rebbe?* He, too, has a characteristic garb, he is the primary factor in the life of his disciples, has a distinctive life style, presides at functions and so on. These descriptions are accurate, but they fall far short of the truth, because they are limited to appearance rather than essence. If the *rosh yeshiva* or *rebbe* is truly great, his outstanding scholarship, piety, and unremitting efforts at self-improvement will have made him a superior human being. He will have become the sort of person whom *Chazon Ish* describes as 'an angel in the garb of mortal man.' It is his *inner* worth that qualifies him for whatever communal and institutional responsibilities and honors he is given.

In terms of his public posture, he can be described as the performer of a long list of tasks, but such definition is superficial.

In terms of his public posture, he can be described as the performer of a long list of tasks, but such a definition is as superficial — and therefore as inaccurate — as it is to say that happiness is to smile or a train is a means of transportation.

The Hebrew word for angel is מַלְאָךְ — literally an *agent* or *messenger* — the same word that is applied to a human agent. The fact is that the word מַלְאָךְ has no spiritual connotation whatever, but it is used for an angel because the language has no words to capture the essence of angels. They are totally

spiritual beings whose existence is known to us only because Scripture relates how they occasionally assumed various guises when they appeared to people and because the Sages teach that they are God's 'agents' in carrying out the functions of nature (see *Rambam, Hil. Yesodei HaTorah* 2:7). We do not know what angels *are*, so we describe them according to their tasks: Raphael is the angel of healing [רפא=*heal*], Gabriel is the angel of power [גבר=*strength*], and the generic name for angel is מַלְאָךְ, *agent*, because we know nothing more about this spiritual being than that it serves God.

We do not know what angels are, so we describe them according to their tasks.

There is an ancient fable about blind men coming across an elephant for the first time. One clutches his ear and says an elephant is a fan. Another gropes along his huge side and says he is a wall, and so they continue, each feeling a different part of the beast. His tusk — an elephant is a spear! His leg — he is a tree! His tail — he is a rope! His trunk — he is a snake! All the blind men have felt the elephant and all know something about him, but even the combination of all their perceptions does not tell them what an elephant is, because they lack the sense of sight, the one sense that will make a coherent whole out of all the parts.

Different Roles

The word נָבִיא, prophet, is another example of a descriptive noun, one that describes what the person does.

The word נָבִיא, *prophet*, is another example of a descriptive noun, one that describes what the person *does*. Scripture uses it for a prophet because ordinary people cannot comprehend his essence. As *Rashi* writes *(Exodus* 7:1), the word נָבִיא is derived from נִיב שְׂפָתַיִם, *utterance of the lips (Isaiah* 57:19), because a prophet 'announces and causes the nation to hear words of admonition.' *Rashi* concludes by translating this function of a prophet with the Old French word for 'preacher.' In other words, the familiar word נָבִיא is intended to indicate the prophet's role only when he is given a Divine message to transmit to others. Accordingly, *Abarbanel* explains the Sages' statement *(Sanhedrin* 93b) that Daniel was not a נָבִיא as a reference to his particular mission rather than to mean that he had

not heard the word of God. Daniel *was* a prophet in the sense that God spoke to him directly, but none of his prophecies were to be transmitted to the people. Technically speaking, therefore, he can be referred to only as a חוֹזֶה, one who receives a חָזוֹן, *vision,* but not as a נָבִיא, *preacher,* to the nation.

There was a period in Israel's history when prophecy had become relatively rare. Of the youth of Samuel, we are told וּדְבַר ה׳ הָיָה יָקָר בַּיָּמִים הָהֵם אֵין חָזוֹן נִפְרָץ, *the word of HASHEM was precious in those days, 'vision'* [of God] *was not widespread (I Samuel* 3:1). During those days, even the few existing prophets were very seldom dispatched to reprove the nation. Then, the main function of a prophet was to help people find solutions to questions that were beyond human intelligence. So it was that when Kish, the father of Saul, lost his donkeys and Saul sought them unsuccessfully, he was advised to seek the help of the prophet Samuel *(ibid.* 9:1-6). Clearly, Saul was not seeking a spiritual message, a proclamation of the word of God. He sought Samuel's guidance in a very mundane matter indeed — "Where can we find my father's lost donkeys?" Scripture itself expresses this distinct nature of the prophetic role as it had evolved in Samuel's day:

Then, the main function of a prophet was to help people find solutions to questions that were beyond human intelligence.

> לְפָנִים בְּיִשְׂרָאֵל כֹּה אָמַר הָאִישׁ בְּלֶכְתּוֹ לִדְרוֹשׁ אֱלֹהִים לְכוּ וְנֵלְכָה עַד הָרֹאֶה כִּי לַנָּבִיא הַיּוֹם יִקָּרֵא לְפָנִים הָרֹאֶה
>
> *Previously in Israel, so spoke a man when he went to inquire of God: 'Come let us go to The Seer,' for what is now a navi* [*preacher*] *was called previously 'The Seer'* (I Samuel 9:9).

Before Samuel's maturity, when prophecy was not widespread and it was rare that God sent a prophet to chastise the people, prophets were called 'Seers,' a very accurate term because it described them as people who were privileged to see Godly visions and hear Divine messages. From Samuel's day onward, when prophecy became more common, and especially in later years when the spread of idolatry and sinfulness required that God send such great

Before Samuel's maturity, when prophecy was not widespread, prophets were called 'Seers.'

men as Elijah, Elisha, Hoshea, Isaiah, Jeremiah, and Ezekiel to chastise the nation and influence it to repent, people began to differentiate: one who delivered God's message to Israel was called a נָבִיא, *preacher;* while one who merely received communications from God might still be called a רֹאֶה, *seer,* or חֹזֶה, *visionary (Chasam Sofer, Even Ha'ezer* II, *responsa* 40).

II. A Different Kind of Person

The Prophet as Forecaster

For most people in modern times, the word 'prophet' conjures visions of someone who foretells future events.

For most people in modern times, the word 'prophet' conjures visions of someone who foretells future events. True, Scripture tells us of many prophets who made such predictions and the most common way in which an alleged prophet proved his authenticity was by making predictions that came true in every detail. Although the sorcerers of ancient times, like those who surrounded Pharaoh and challenged Moses, had a knowledge of impure, evil forces that enabled them to make predictions, they could achieve only *general* accuracy, but could not predict correctly every detail of an event. Their prophecies were likened to grain mixed with straw; the kernel of truth was there but it was mixed with falsehood and foolishness. The genuine prophets, however, were truthful in every detail, like winnowed, sifted grain, from which all impurities and foreign matter have been removed. An even greater proof of a prophet's authenticity would be his performance of miracles like those performed by Moses and Elijah, but such feats were not required; it was sufficient if he demonstrated a consistent ability to predict the future in accurate detail *(Hil. Yesodei HaTorah* 10:1-3).

The prophet's ability to foretell events is only incidental to his primary function.

That the prophet's ability to foretell events is only incidental to his primary function is apparent from Scripture's introduction of the institution of prophecy as a vital factor in Israel's national fabric:

וַיֹּאמֶר ה׳ ... נָבִיא אָקִים לָהֶם מִקֶּרֶב אֲחֵיהֶם

כָּמוֹךָ וְנָתַתִּי דְבָרַי בְּפִיו וְדִבֶּר אֲלֵיהֶם אֵת כָּל אֲשֶׁר אֲצַוֶּנּוּ

> *HASHEM said ... I will set up a prophet for them from among their brethren like you* [i.e. Moses]; *I will place My word in his mouth and he will tell them* [i.e. Israel] *all that I will command him (Deuteronomy* 18:17-18).

Israel's possession of prophecy derives from its need to have a 'spokesman' of God.

Clearly, though the prophet may predict events and perform miracles, those are not his primary tasks, nor are they the reasons why God allowed His voice to be heard and His visions to be seen by mortal men. Israel's possession of prophecy derives from its need to have a 'spokesman' of God, who will direct the people in His ways and inform them of His commands. In this role of the prophet, the verse calls him נָבִיא, literally *preacher.* As we have seen, however, and as we shall discuss in further detail below, there are other aspects of prophecy.

The Prophets' Essence

We began our discussion by noting that one should not confuse the responsibilities and activities of a prophet with his caliber as a human being. Very few people gain designation as a 'prophet,' and the fact that someone becomes one is the most eloquent testimony of his worth.

Rambam begins his discussion of the institution of prophecy with a description of the sort of person who can become a prophet:

Among the foundations of the religion is to know that God makes people prophets.

> Among the foundations of the religion is to know that God makes people prophets. Prophecy can rest only on a scholar who is great in wisdom, powerful in character, whose inclination cannot subdue him in any matter on earth. Rather his intellect always conquers his inclination, and he possesses vast and exceedingly reliable wisdom. A person filled with all these traits, who is sound in body — when he enters the 'orchard [of hidden wisdom]' and continues in those exalted subjects, and attains the reliable wisdom needed to

understand and grasp, and he continues sanctifying himself and withdraws from the attitudes of the common people who conform to the darkness of the times, but instead continuously prods himself, training his soul not to give a thought to any vain matters or to the vicissitudes and conspiracies of the time; rather, his mind is always free for higher things ... concentrating on the wisdom of the Holy One, Blessed is He ... recognizing His greatness — thereupon, the holy spirit will rest upon him. And when that spirit rests upon him, his soul will be sweetened by the loftiness of the angels ... He will become transformed into a different person and understand with his own intellect that he is not what he was before, but has risen above the level of other wise human beings, as it is written with regard to Saul *(I Samuel* 10:6): *You will prophesy with them and be transformed into a different person (Hil. Yesodei HaTorah* 7:1).

And when that spirit rests upon him, his soul will be sweetened by the loftiness of the angels.

Proof of Achievement

Rambam makes very clear that the essence of prophecy is the attainment of an unusually high degree of holiness, not by some magic formula, but by hard, unrelenting efforts at sublimating oneself. In his Introduction to Mishnah, *Rambam* writes that even the breathtaking miracles of Elijah, Elisha, and other prophets were not performed to prove themselves — their reputations were already well-established. Rather they had their own good reasons for wishing the respective miracles to happen, *and so great was their closeness to God that He fulfilled their wishes.*

In summary, the essence of the prophet's task is to remove the material, physical barrier that separates him from God.

In summary, the essence of the prophet's task is to remove the material, physical barrier that separates him from God. If he is successful, he can aspire to prophecy; his attainment of that spiritual peak is attested to by his hearing God's voice. It is *that*

accomplishment that is basic to prophecy; predictions are secondary.

How can man approach the angels if he must carry with him the baggage of style, ideology, and passion that drags him back?

In his attempts to reach God, the ordinary man is repulsed by his human urges, his tendency to rationalize, the intellectual environment that demands conformity to its whims and dictates. How can man approach the angels if he must carry with him the baggage of style, ideology, and passion that drags him back? But if he divests himself of his earthliness, making his body the ministering host of his soul, he has the right to expect that God's spirit will rest upon him to a commensurate degree. How can he and his comrades know how successful he has been? The spirit of prophecy is proof — he would not have it if he had not fashioned himself to be an appropriate vessel, any more than a container with less than a gallon's capacity could hold more than a gallon of fluid. The miracles performed by Joshua or Elijah were great because they testified to the enormous striving of the prophet who performed them. Having made himself — all of himself, body as well as soul — a sacred being, he could command the obedience of material objects and forces.

That God rested His spirit upon such people had the further effect of assisting them toward their goal of attaining ever higher spiritual elevations, for the Holy Spirit enabled them to perceive secrets of the Torah so that they knew how to direct their lives toward higher plateaus of holiness.

This aspect of the Jew's service continues even today in the absence of prophecy.

This aspect of the Jew's service continues even today in the absence of prophecy, for we remain with the challenge of subduing our animal passions and self-delusive inclinations. Today, as three thousand years ago, God asks us to lead our bodies after our souls, not vice versa. In ancient times, the reward could be prophecy, today it is a lesser aspect of holiness, but the fray is the same and so is the goal. Then, the temptation was to idolatry; today it is to whatever vices are fashionable in various social and economic strata, intellectual circles, or countries. And just as the spiritual victor in ancient times became transformed into a new person, so today's

saint is as removed from the sinner as Elijah was from Ahab *(Shaarei Kedushah* of *R' Chaim Vital).*

Man's spiritual achievements give him power to alter the destiny of man and nature alike.

The Scriptures and the Sages teach repeatedly that man's spiritual achievements give him power to alter the destiny of man and nature alike. Over and over, the Torah declares that Israel's adherence to the commandments will guarantee peace, prosperity, and even military dominance. Speaking about the Messianic king, Isaiah (11:4) says, *he will strike the earth with the rod of his mouth and with the breath of his lips he will slay the wicked* — Isaiah spoke not of Messiah's army, but of the power of righteous words. When appointing the young and reluctant Jeremiah as His prophet, God told him, *'See I have set you today over nations and over kingdoms, to uproot and to smash, to destroy and to dismantle, to build and to plant' (Jeremiah* 1:10). Jeremiah neither had nor would ever have an army or the power of government at his disposal, but God addressed him as though he were a mighty potentate, for, indeed, the bearer of God's word is stronger than the mightiest ruler.

Such promises must be understood in the sense of the Sages' teaching that, for example, honest judges and observers of the Sabbath become God's partners in the creation of heaven and earth. Since He had a reason for bringing the universe into existence, it stands to reason that people whose deeds achieve God's goal are indispensable to Him.

Although only God can bring into being, only Israel can make His handiwork endure.

In this light, *R' Chaim Vital* explains how God speaks to Israel and the prophets as though *they* had the power to create and destroy, to plant and uproot. Although only God can bring into being, only Israel can make His handiwork endure, because the continued existence of the universe depends on man's fulfillment of God's will as expressed in the Torah. Therefore, the concept of prophecy was a necessary part of creation: there had to be a means to bring God's word into man's life to provide him with inspiration and guidance regarding the will of the Creator.

Proximity to Greatness

When people spend time in the proximity of a company of people sincerely dedicated to spiritual striving and self-improvement, they too change for the better.

Just as man can turn the animal and vegetable world into implements of holiness — tefillin, mezuzos, shofars, Torah scrolls, sacred books — so prophets and great people can influence and elevate their neighbors. When people spend time in the proximity of saintly individuals or with a company of people sincerely dedicated to spiritual striving and self-improvement, they too change for the better; sincerity and dedication rub off, and so does personal sanctity. When Saul joined the company of prophets, he astonished all who knew him by prophesying along with them *(I Samuel* 9:10-12).

Nevertheless, not all people respond identically to a spiritual stimulus. A hundred people can spend an evening with a scholar or saint. They will be inspired by him, moved by him, informed by him. They will all recognize that they have been in the presence of greatness, but each one will be affected differently. Some may resolve to change their lives while others may go away with nothing more than a conversation piece and an anecdote or two. Some will marvel at the content of the great man's words and others will discuss his vocabulary. Some will ponder his spiritual breadth and others will discuss the extent of his eloquence and the quality of his rhetoric. With such matters we are all familiar; we have lived through similar experiences many times. But there is another layer of difference that is beyond our realm of experience.

Although Torah scholarship is a prerequisite of prophecy, a prophet's Torah knowledge is not qualitatively different from that of other scholars.

Let us imagine that we could go three thousand years into the past and stand in the presence of a prophet. If he expounded upon the Torah in an elementary way, perhaps we might grasp his trend of thought. Although Torah scholarship is a prerequisite of prophecy, a prophet's Torah knowledge is not qualitatively different from that of other scholars. *Rambam (Intro. to Mishnah)* takes pains to stress that prophecy does not confer halachic authority on a prophet. The Halachah can be decided only on the basis of the halachic tradition and the principles of Talmudic reasoning and analysis. Consequently, scholars of post-prophetic eras might

understand the *halachic* discourse of a Samuel or an Elijah.

Rambam (ibid.) writes: 'Whatever Joshua or Phineas might attempt in matters of analysis and deciding the law is exactly what Rabina and Rav Ashi (the redactors of the *Gemara)* would do.' Prophecy is not equivalent to scholarship. A prophet has no authority to decide matters of law on the basis of Divine inspiration — in fact, a prophet who claims to have received a revelation deciding a halachic dispute is automatically declared to be a false prophet and liable to the death penalty *(Hil. Yesodei HaTorah* 9:4).

A prophet has no authority to decide matters of law on the basis of Divine inspiration.

However, though we might understand the prophet's intellectual teachings, we would not be able to enter his spiritual, prophetic world. None of us would become capable of prophesying in a prophet's presence as did Saul. In all probability we would not even sense that we were in a prophetic presence. Since prophecy has not been part of the Jewish experience for twenty-four centuries, we are not attuned to sense it. Among the masses who watched Elijah on Mount Carmel, even the commonest folk, the simplest idolaters, had been exposed to such men of the spirit and were capable of recognizing the difference between the Prophet of God and the rabble of impostors masquerading as prophets. They lived in an age of prophecy. They knew prophecy as well as we know cars, but we know as little about prophecy as they did about the internal combustion engine.

Some Aspects of Prophecy

It is axiomatic that the absence of prophecy for so many centuries makes it impossible for us to comprehend what that spiritual phenomenon was. Nevertheless, some of the principles of prophecy are discussed by *Rambam (Hil. Yesodei HaTorah* ch. 7-10), *Ramchal (Derech Hashem* part III ch. 3-5) and others. We will offer a few highlights.

Prophecy and רוּחַ הַקֹּדֶשׁ*, Divine Inspiration, are not synonymous, although both are forms of Godly assistance.*

Prophecy and רוּחַ הַקֹּדֶשׁ, *Divine Inspiration* [lit. *Holy Spirit*], are not synonymous, although both are forms of Godly assistance enabling man to receive

influences that are beyond normal human capacity. 'Divine Inspiration' enables man to achieve a perception of things or events that are ordinarily accessible to the human intellect, but Divine Inspiration will enable him to know them *more clearly* than otherwise possible. Or Divine Inspiration may bring him a step further and teach him regarding future events or hidden secrets — matters that are beyond the grasp of unassisted human intellect. Whatever the form of this Divine Inspiration, its recipient will know that he has been Divinely inspired. This inspiration, however, is inferior to prophecy.

Whatever the form of this Divine Inspiration, its recipient will know that he has been Divinely inspired.

One who experiences prophecy actually feels an attachment to God, as it were, an attachment that is tangible and unmistakable to him, as if he were touching an object. Obviously, no human being — even Moses — can attach himself *directly* to God or 'see' him as if He were a human being. Prophecy is transmitted through intermediaries which filter and obscure God's holiness until it can be perceived by the mortal prophet. How clearly an individual prophet can 'see' the prophetic vision depends on his own stature. Thus, the prophecy of a Samuel was infinitely 'clearer' than that of his many students, and even clearer than that of most prophets whose words are recorded in Scripture. Another factor can enhance the degree of an individual's perception: the needs of the nation. The classic example of this was Moses. Because of his pivotal role in the genesis of Israel's nationhood, he was granted a clarity of vision and an accessibility to God's word that were in a class by themselves. Moses' level of prophecy was unprecedented and would never again be equaled by anyone, even if he were to attain Moses' degree of righteousness. But though they could not aspire to the pinnacle of Moses, other prophets were granted visions in proportion to their own fitness and the needs of Israel.

Though they could not aspire to the pinnacle of Moses, other prophets were granted visions in proportion to their own fitness and the needs of Israel.

The intermediaries that convey prophecy are described by the Sages as אַסְפַּקְלַרְיוֹת, *mirrors* (also translated as *lenses).* Given the fact that no one can

'see' God, a prophetic vision is likened to something reflected by a series of mirrors. The more 'mirrors' are involved and the less clear they are, the more blurred the vision will be. Moses' prophecy is described as אַסְפַּקְלַרְיָא הַמְּאִירָה, *a clear mirror*, that is, his perception of God was as unobscured as any prophecy can ever be. Lesser prophets, however, will perceive their visions infinitely less clearly, though the degree of obscurity will vary from prophet to prophet. We can visualize the difference between prophecies by looking at ourselves in a brightly polished mirror and then viewing ourselves through the last in a series of dusty, dirty mirrors reflecting from one to another. Moses' prophecy was like the first looking glass. Others' prophecies were like the last reflection in the series. In both cases, the prophet did not see God — he saw only a reflection of the reality that was the source of his vision, but the clarity of the visions were not comparable to one another. Nevertheless, every prophet, even the least accomplished, was granted a full awareness of whatever prophecy God wanted him to receive. Even the most inferior prophecy, however, is far superior to Divine Inspiration, because even a dull prophecy involves an actual attachment to God.

Lesser prophets will perceive their visions infinitely less clearly, though the degree of obscurity will vary from prophet to prophet.

Since prophecy involves a degree of real attachment to God, the human body is an impediment. The animal part of man — even after he has sublimated it — cannot tolerate the 'glare' of revelation. Therefore, all prophets with the exception of Moses lost control of their senses during their prophetic experiences; they might lose consciousness and fall into a trance or they might have their visions in a dream. Only Moses could receive prophecy while he was wide awake.

All prophets with the exception of Moses lost control of their senses during their prophetic experiences.

Some prophets received messages to be transmitted to the entire nation or to individuals. Others were granted private visions that served only to elevate their own levels of spirituality. Some prophets were shown only visions and devised their own words to express what they had seen. Others were given the exact words that they were to relay; even when this

happened, however, the words chosen by God were suited to the individual nature and experience of the prophet. Sometimes, especially in the early stages of a prophet's development, he would not be aware that a spiritual experience was actually a prophecy. This occurred when Moses first saw the burning bush and when the young Samuel first heard God's voice — in both cases, they did not realize at first that they were receiving prophecies.

Sometimes, especially in the early stages of a prophet's development, he would not be aware that a spiritual experience was actually a prophecy.

Sometimes, the words conveyed to a prophet can have nuances that are not revealed to him, even though God allows him to know everything that is required for the fulfillment of his mission. Jonah, for example, was sent to Nineveh with a message that the city would be overturned. He understood this to mean physical destruction. As events developed, the Ninevites repented to such an extent that the Divine decree was withdrawn — but this was not a contradiction of Jonah's prophecy. Nineveh had *indeed* been overturned — but in the spiritual rather than the physical sense of the word.

It must be understood, however, that when we speak of a prophet 'hearing God's voice,' we do not imply that God has organs of speech or even a voice, any more than the statement that Moses saw the image of God (*Numbers* 12:8) means that God has a physical form. Rather, God causes the human ear to hear sounds audible to it just as he causes the eye to see visions comprehensible to it. The essence of God is infinitely beyond man's power of comprehension, but by means of prophecy He allows man to receive whatever messages He deems appropriate.

We do not imply that God has organs of speech, rather, God causes the human ear to hear sounds audible to it.

III. The Scriptural Prophets

Had Israel Not Sinned

What was the primary service *to the nation* of the prophets? We do not speak of the profound influence on the individual recipient of God's spiritual gift of prophecy. As *Rambam (Hil. Yesodei HaTorah* 7:7) and all commentators stress, prophecy can be a *private* gift, one that the prophet earns, but

that is conferred to enrich his own development without any apparent benefit to the nation (with the understanding, of course, that since Israel is the sum of its individual members, the quality of national life is enhanced in proportion to the spiritual growth of its individual components). But what of the *direct* benefits to the nation — what was the role of the primary prophets and how, if at all, was it supplemented by their colleagues who are not mentioned in Scripture?

In a sense, the recorded teachings of the prophets should be regarded as a necessity that reflects poorly on the state of Israel's spiritual development.

In a sense, the recorded teachings of the prophets should be regarded as a necessity that reflects poorly on the state of Israel's spiritual development. 'Had Israel not sinned, it would have been given only the Five Books of Moses and the Book of *Joshua*, which contains the boundaries of *Eretz Yisrael' (Nedarim* 22a). Had Israel not sinned, we would surely have had many more *prophets*, because prophecy is a spiritual dimension associated with very high degrees of righteousness, but we would not have had *books* of prophecy. That most books of Scripture — eighteen out of twenty-four — were required, as the Sages taught, because of Israel's sins suggests that *recorded* prophecy is intended to combat national downfall. *Rashi* makes this point explicitly in explaining why the prophecies of the forty-eight men and seven women are called נְבוּאָה שֶׁהוּצְרְכָה לְדוֹרוֹת, *prophecy that was needed by future generations. Rashi* says their prophecies were needed לִלְמוֹד תְּשׁוּבָה אוֹ הוֹרָאָה, *to teach repentance or laws* [lit. *teaching*] *(Megillah* 14a).

Rashi's few words require clarification, however. Even a cursory glance at Scripture shows many, many chapters that do not qualify as teachings of either repentance or law. Some books consist almost exclusively of narrative, predictions, and praises of God's greatness or miraculous interventions. Why is the special gift of prophecy a prerequisite to chastisement of the people — is that not a task that any wise *tzaddik* can carry out? Conversely, can it be that none of the unrecorded prophets had anything to say about repentance or law?

Can it be that none of the unrecorded prophets had anything to say about repentance or law?

In any era, a generation has only a limited number of people who can be considered its greatest leaders. The rest of the nation will look to them for guidance, but be unable to see them, hear them, understand them. Their personalities and messages will be too sophisticated, too lofty for most people. Consequently, mediators are needed. There will be teachers, scholars, interpreters, and leaders of varying degrees of competence. Assuming that conditions are ideal, the availability of such people will enable the influence and message of the leaders to filter to all strata of society. So it was in the age of prophets. Only fifty-five prophets and prophetesses are mentioned in Scripture, but hundreds of thousands of unknown prophets exerted a profound influence on the nation.

Only fifty-five are mentioned in Scripture, but hundreds of thousands exerted a profound influence.

The fifty-five recorded prophets must be understood as the primary bearers of God's words to Israel. Their teachings related not only to every member of their own generation, but also to every Jew to this day. Their teachings were valid for as long as Israel would require people to lead and teach it, so their prophecies were made part of the Written Torah. But, like the teachings of each era's leaders, they had to be translated somehow into the heart-talk of every troubled Jew, interpreted to fit the unique situation of every family, understood in the perspectives of new generations. The experiences recorded in the Book of *Judges* applied to the nobility in Isaiah's time, and Samuel's insistence that Israel had no need for a king because *HASHEM your God is your King (I Samuel* 12:12) applied equally to the Jerusalem of Zedekiah, when Jeremiah and Ezekiel tried vainly to salvage a vestige of the monarchy. But how were a prophet's contemporaries to understand all the layers of his message and how were unborn generations to know how it applied to their own changed circumstances? For this, thousands upon thousands of other prophets were needed. They interpreted and applied, explained and reiterated. In a sense they may be described as spokesmen and commentators rather than bearers of new messages.

How were a prophet's contemporaries to understand all the layers of his message and how were unborn generations to know how it applied to their own changed circumstances?

Therefore, their teachings were not recorded.

But what of the countless Scriptural passages that do not discuss admonition or law — why were they recorded?

The Prophet as Interpreter

God spoke to people so that they could provide illumination concerning many vital areas of life.

We are mistaken if we think that fiery messages that burn our ears and fill our hearts with remorse are the only calls to repentance, or if we think the only valid 'teachings' are those that send us scurrying to library shelves. God spoke to people so that they could provide illumination concerning many vital areas of life.

It is characteristic of people that they wish to see themselves in a good light. Decent people cannot live with the idea that they are evil or callous. Inevitably therefore, they interpret situations in accord with their own deep, inner needs and condition. Impatient people will see everywhere calls for decisive action; diffident souls will counsel deliberation and delay. Some will find evil under every rug and others will justify every lapse. At times when legions of wise and sincere people line up behind every point of view, how are we to know where a people has *genuinely* gone wrong? Scripture, especially when it is leavened and enriched by the traditions and interpretations of the Sages, is filled with instances of confusion and dispute where strong cases could be made for every point of view. Who is right? If we were there, we might have thrown up our hands in despair and said, "Only God knows!" True — only God knew, but He sent His prophet to tell *us,* not just for the sake of the people living through the dilemma, but so that future generations would know as well.

Even when the prophet appears in Scripture as a miracle worker, there is a vital lesson for the future.

Even when the prophet appears in Scripture as a miracle worker, there is a vital lesson for the future. Since we know the supreme spiritual effort that is needed to turn an ordinary mortal into an exalted being touched by God's presence, we know the source of his ability to alter nature. That a prophet could bring prosperity to destitute widows, resuscitate a dead child, or cure leprous generals is

possible because his righteousness made him a 'partner' of the One Who created nature. The prophet could suspend natural law as Joshua did by stopping the sun in Gibeon (10:12) because he had made himself superior to nature. Knowing that, each experience with a prophet's ability to perform a miracle reaffirms our faith in the Torah's message that observance of the commandments is the only assurance of prosperity and reward. When tragedy was salved by God's emissary, those who suffered could not help but recognize that 'no one injures his finger below unless it was decreed upon him from above' *(Chullin* 7a).

Perhaps most important, the prophet interprets events for people.

Perhaps most important, the prophet interprets events for people. As the Overview and Commentary to *Ezekiel* set forth graphically, people can easily misinterpret history, with often tragic results. Ezekiel's generation knew that a large segment of Jerusalem's scholars and disciples had been transported to slavery in Babylon — but the remaining Jerusalemites prided themselves on being the *deserving* remnant whose future was secure because they were the guardians of the Temple. Ezekiel taught them — though many would not believe — that the exiles were the builders of the Jewish future while the survivors were doomed to be destroyed together with the Temple whose holiness had already been stripped by the sins of its supposed adherents. Deborah's victory over Sisera, like many other miraculous victories in Scripture, could surely have been explained by natural causes. Deborah's song put the entire era into its true perspective.

Let us not delude ourselves that the spiritually blind saw more clearly in ancient times than they do today.

Let us not delude ourselves that the spiritually blind saw more clearly in ancient times than they do today. In our daily prayers we thank God *for Your daily miracles with us and for Your wonders and favors at all times,* but if we were to ask someone to tell us about the most recent miracle he has witnessed, he would probably look at us as if we were dangerous. The prophets, with their pronouncements, predictions, threats, and praises gave perspective and interpretation to events, letting

people know when miracles had occurred and how their own deeds, good and bad, affected events.

And now, we have lost prophecy; all we have left are the chronicles of forty-eight men and seven women.

Why Prophecy was Removed

Harav Gedaliah Schorr explained why the gift of prophecy was removed from Israel. In the early days of the Second Temple era, the Men of the Great Assembly feared for Israel's future. They knew what destruction had been caused by the passion for idolatry in the period of the Judges and the First Temple. If Israel in its new commonwealth were to be subject to the same desire, the resultant destruction would be too terrible to contemplate. The Sages prayed that God remove the passion for idolatry, and He granted their request.

The Sages prayed that God remove the passion for idolatry, and He granted their request.

Modern man studies the Scriptural chapters on idolatry with an incomprehension bordering almost on disbelief. We read of our ancestors worshiping clods of clay, statues of wood and gold. How could they be so foolish, we wonder. Even *we* — without the benefit of a Temple, God's tangible Presence, and prophets — know that idolatry is ludicrous. How could *they* be so misguided? The question is a good one. That we have so little belief in, even curiosity about, idol worship is the greatest proof that the prayer of the Sages was successful. In ancient times, even some great men could not resist the lure of idols, while to us they are not even worthy of notice, because the passion for them was removed by Divine intervention.

Life on earth is a system of delicate balances, and when one thing goes, another is affected.

But life on earth is a system of delicate balances, and when one thing goes, another is affected. In order to permit man to choose freely between good and evil, God must allow evil to have an appeal strong enough to deceive sensible people. If the cause of good is compelling beyond doubt and evil is ludicrous beyond temptation — then man's choice of good is no more free than is the choice between drinking fresh water and rancid poison. Idolatry had been appealing because its adherents could point to

its 'prophets' and *their* 'miracles,' to its 'philosophies' and results. If that were removed, but God's righteous, true prophets still walked the earth, how could anyone ever doubt the truth? And if the truth was so obvious, why should anyone deserve to be rewarded for following its dictates?

With the removal of idolatry as a serious force in Jewish life, prophecy had to be removed as well. Thus was the balance preserved.

Therefore, with the removal of idolatry as a serious force in Jewish life, prophecy had to be removed as well. Thus was the balance preserved. Undoubtedly, the price was heavy, but its fairness was determined by the One Who balances human intellect and inclination.

The prophets are not with us, nor are their disciples who, touched by God's presence, interpreted their words. But, as the Sages teach:

מִיּוֹם שֶׁחָרַב בֵּית הַמִּקְדָּשׁ, אַף עַל פִּי שֶׁנִּיטְּלָה
נְבוּאָה מִן הַנְּבִיאִים מִן הַחֲכָמִים לֹא נִיטְּלָה

From the time the Temple was destroyed, even though prophecy was removed from prophets, it was not removed from Torah scholars (Bava Basra 12a).

Just as prophecy is God's gift, so the proper use of the intellect is a gift.

Just as prophecy is God's gift, so the proper use of the intellect is a gift. The world suffers grievously from people who are brilliant but not wise. By allowing Israel's wise men to glimpse the wonders of His Torah and glean its teachings, God filled the vacuum left by the absence of prophecy in its ancient form (see *Maharal, Chiddushei Aggados).* The balance is intact, because humanity has any number of philosophies and scholars competing for our attention with the Torah's teachings. But we have Scripture and the Oral Torah, and we have our Sages past and present to illuminate their meaning.

An Overview/ Joshua — Disciple and Luminary

לֹא יָרְשׁוּ בָנָיו שֶׁל מֹשֶׁה מְקוֹמוֹ אֶלָּא יְהוֹשֻׁעַ, ,,וְשֹׁמֵר אֲדֹנָיו יְכֻבָּד״ זֶה יְהוֹשֻׁעַ שֶׁהָיָה מְשַׁמֵּשׁ אֶת מֹשֶׁה בַּיּוֹם וּבַלַּיְלָה, וּלְפִי שֶׁשִּׁימֵּשׁ אֲדֹנָיו זָכָה לְרוּחַ הַקֹּדֶשׁ זָכָה לִנְבוּאָה.

Moses' sons did not inherit his position, only Joshua. He who safeguards his master will be honored (Proverbs *27:18) — this refers to Joshua who served Moses day and night. Because he served his master, he earned the holy spirit; he earned prophecy (Bamidbar Rabbah* 12:9).

I. From Attendant to Leader

With Moses

Moses stands alone, but Joshua can hardly be mentioned, much less understood, unless he is associated with Moses.

If Israel's quintessential teacher is Moses, its quintessential disciple is Joshua. Moses stands alone, but Joshua can hardly be mentioned, much less understood, unless he is associated with Moses. Only in terms of their relationship can we understand Joshua's greatness and his monumental role in Jewish history.

Toward the end of his last will and testament to Israel, Moses said to his people: *'For I know that after my death you will become corrupt and depart from the path in which I instructed you' (Deuteronomy* 31:29). *Rashi* notes that Israel did *not* stray as soon as Moses died, for Scripture testifies that the people continued to serve God as long as Joshua lived *(Joshua* 24:31), and he survived his teacher by many years. From Moses' statement we learn, *Rashi* teaches, that

תַּלְמִידוֹ שֶׁל אָדָם חָבִיב עָלָיו כְּגוּפוֹ. כָּל זְמַן שֶׁיְּהוֹשֻׁעַ חַי הָיָה נִרְאֶה לְמֹשֶׁה כְּאִילוּ הוּא חַי.

A person's disciple is as beloved to him as himself. As long as Joshua was alive it seemed to Moses as if he himself were still alive.

Moses knew that he would still be 'alive and with' his people even after his mortal body was interred.

Or HaChaim attaches this concept to Moses' earlier expression בְּעוֹדֶנִּי חַי עִמָּכֶם, *while I am still living with you* (31:27). Moses knew that he would still be 'alive and with' his people even after his mortal body was interred. The 'life' of Moses survived his flesh and blood, for as long as his teachings illuminated Israel's path, *he* would still live in the person and leadership of Joshua. Indeed, the corrupting influence of the Canaanite peoples had no effect on Israel until after Joshua died — for it was not until then that the most serious effects of Moses' absence were felt. Until then, the teacher's influence lived on through his disciple.

Very soon after the Exodus from Egypt, we find Moses relying on Joshua in a time of great national crisis. When Amalek attacked Israel, Moses called upon Joshua to choose warriors and lead them in battle, while he, Moses, ascended a hill to pray and inspire Israel with faith in God [*Exodus* 18:8-11]. That incident shows us that Joshua was Moses' trusted right hand, and the Torah, the Sages, and the commentators shed light on the characteristics that made Joshua great enough to become Moses' successor.

Moses went to the mountain. Before ascending it, Moses charged all except Joshua to remain behind.

After God transmitted the Ten Commandments to Israel, Moses prepared to climb Mount Sinai for the forty days and forty nights during which God would teach him the Torah with all its laws and principles. Accompanied by Aaron, Hur, the elders, and Joshua, Moses went to the mountain. Before ascending it, Moses charged all except Joshua to remain behind and serve as the leaders and judges of the people until he returned. Then he and Joshua went on until the point beyond which only Moses was permitted to advance *(Exodus* 24:13-15).

As *Ramban* notes, Joshua was not only Moses' loyal disciple, who accompanied his master as far as God allowed, he was superior to any of the other

elders. Unlike them, Joshua was worthy of 'visions of God and every prophecy.' Moses ordered Aaron, Hur, and the elders back to the camp, but he excluded Joshua from the command because he knew that Joshua would remain on the slope of Sinai, loyally awaiting the return of his teacher. Indeed, Joshua maintained his lonely vigil for all forty days of Moses' absence. When Israel built its Golden Calf and obscenely, raucously danced around it, Joshua did not even know what had happened (*Exodus* 32:17), for he had not gone back to the camp.

When Israel built its Golden Calf and obscenely, raucously danced around it, Joshua did not even know what had happened.

Nor was it presumptuous of Joshua to separate himself from the people as though only he felt Moses' absence. In the Wilderness, a Jew's proper place could be determined by where his portion of manna fell each morning. It happened that two men disputed the ownership of a slave, one claiming that he had purchased him and the previous owner denying that the sale had been completed. The two claimants came to Moses for a ruling. His decision was that the question would be settled the next morning: if an extra portion of manna appeared at the tent of the alleged purchaser, it would prove that the slave was now part of a new household; but if manna appeared at the tent of the original owner, it would be proof that the slave was still his (*Yoma* 75a). While Joshua camped on Mount Sinai, his portion of manna fell for him there (*Yoma* 76a), proving conclusively that he belonged as close to Moses as he could possibly be.

While Joshua camped on Mount Sinai, his portion of manna fell for him there proving that he belonged close to Moses.

This intimacy continued throughout the forty years in the Wilderness. After Israel disgraced itself with the Golden Calf, Moses pitched his tent outside the main body of the camp. Then, anyone who sought to hear his teaching or to visit the holy presence of the prophet would leave his tent and walk to the home of Moses. Such a person was called a מְבַקֵּשׁ ה׳, *seeker of* HASHEM. He had to exert himself by leaving his everyday surroundings if his quest was to be successful (*Exodus* 33:7-10). And where was Joshua?

וּמְשָׁרְתוֹ יְהוֹשֻׁעַ בִּן נוּן נַעַר לֹא יָמִישׁ מִתּוֹךְ הָאֹהֶל

And his servant Joshua son of Nun, the youth, would not depart from within his [i.e., Moses'] *tent (ibid v.* 11).

The unchanging pattern had been established. Joshua would not leave Moses. Joshua was his student. But so was every other Jew: whenever Moses received a new commandment or teaching from God, he taught it first to Aaron, then to Elazar and Issamar, the sons of Aaron, then to the seventy elders and finally to all the people *(Eruvin* 54b). Every Jew was Moses' student, but only Joshua was his disciple and servant.

Every Jew was Moses' student, but only Joshua was his disciple and servant.

Joshua Develops

By his uninterrupted presence at Moses' side, Joshua was fulfilling the dictum גְדוֹלָה שִׁמּוּשָׁהּ שֶׁל תּוֹרָה יוֹתֵר מִלְּמוּדָהּ, *to serve Torah* [*scholars*] *is more important than to study it (Berachos* 7b). As the commentators explain, the knowledge of Torah embraces more than an understanding of specific laws and principles. Not only what one does but how he does it, the kinds of tone and expression with which one greets people of different backgrounds and how he relates to their problems, one's reaction to provocation and how he exercises self-control, how he eats, loves, chastises — all these and myriad more are part of the total Torah personality and they can best be learned only by studying the behavior of God's elite. Joshua chose this course, and not only was it rewarding to him, it provided Israel with the successor to the greatest of all leaders. When the Torah describes Joshua as Moses' servant *(Exodus* 24:13, 33:11), its purpose is certainly not to denigrate him or even to report a fact, rather it is to inform us of the trait that led to his future greatness.

Toward the end of his life, Moses asked God to designate his successor as the leader of Israel. He was hoping that one of his own sons would be found worthy to succeed him — an understandable ambition, but one that was not fulfilled. Instead, God told him to elevate Joshua to the post *(Numbers* 27:15-23), a command that Moses carried out with a full measure of generosity. Why Joshua? God

He was hoping that one of his own sons would succeed him. Instead, God told him to elevate Joshua to the post.

explained: 'He served you exceedingly and honored you exceedingly ... Since he served you with all his ability, it is fitting that he serve Israel, for he should not forfeit the reward due him. Designate Joshua son of Nun, to fulfill what is written (*Proverbs* 27:18), *He who guards the fig tree will eat its fruit'* (*Bamidbar Rabbah* 21:14).

Since he served you with all his ability, it is fitting that he serve Israel, for he should not forfeit the reward due him.

Lest we think that God assigns Israel's leaders like a king or president apportioning plums to devoted courtiers, the Midrash (21:15, see also 12:9) explains further. Why is the Torah likened to a fig rather than other fruits? the Midrash asks. The fig has no waste, all of it is edible and delicious; similarly every part of the Torah is significant and true. There is another similarity to the fig, a similarity that sheds light on Joshua's greatness. In the case of other species in *Eretz Yisrael,* all the fruits on an individual tree become ready for picking at roughly the same time; a farmer can harvest the crop of that tree and put it out of mind until next year. Figs, however, ripen at different intervals even on the same tree. Each fig must be examined and picked separately. The study of Torah, too, requires careful attention to each law, and it requires the patience to meditate and question. A proper understanding of the laws, their nuances, and corollaries will not come all at once; as one's perceptions ripen his comprehension deepens, his fund of knowledge expands, and even what he once thought he knew takes on new dimensions and releases new meanings and applications. To this, Solomon alluded when he said, *He who guards the fig tree* [i.e., the tree of Torah] *will eat its fruit.*

Joshua not only perceived the total perfection of the Torah's fruit, he applied himself to Moses, the source of Torah knowledge.

Joshua not only perceived the total perfection of the Torah's fruit, he applied himself to Moses, the source of Torah knowledge, unremittingly for forty years, never leaving his side, never letting a word of the teacher escape the ear of the disciple, seeding his fertile mind with Moses' pregnant thoughts. Joshua knew that the fruits of Torah ripen at different times, so he was always ready to pluck them lest he miss even one fruitful teaching through inattentiveness or absence. It is in this sense that we must

understand the reward given Joshua for his loyal attentiveness to Moses' needs, utterances, and actions. By listening and applying himself to his master's teachings, Joshua made himself Israel's greatest repository of Moses' Torah; by serving and studying his master's mode of living, Joshua absorbed the lessons of Moses, the Godly *man.*

By serving and studying his master's mode of living, Joshua absorbed the lessons of Moses, the Godly man.

In tracing the chain of authoritative transmission of the Torah, the Sages *(Avos* 1:1) teach that Moses accepted the Torah from Sinai and transmitted it to Joshua, who, in turn, transmitted it to the elders from whom it went to the prophets and so on. *Rambam,* in his introduction to Mishnah, gives the line of tradition in more detail: Moses to Joshua to Phineas to Eli to Samuel to David and so on until the time of the Mishnah. In assessing Joshua's standing in this listing, two things are noteworthy: first, the Sages in *Avos* mention only Moses and Joshua by name, the others — even the great Samuel and David — are included only among the general categories; and second, *Rambam* cites only Joshua as the direct heir of Moses, even though such luminaries as Elazar, Phineas, Caleb, and Asniel son of Kenaz were Joshua's contemporaries. Clearly, his distinguished peers not withstanding, Joshua stood out. The guardian of the fig tree had indeed made himself worthy of enjoying its fruit, *all* its fruit.

As mentioned above, when Moses asked that his successor be chosen, he inwardly hoped that the mantle might fall upon his children, but God chose otherwise, telling him, as the Midrash *(ibid.)* relates, that his sons had not applied themselves diligently to the study of Torah. But the Scriptural account (*Numbers* 27:19-23) indicates that even Joshua could not step into Moses' shoes immediately. Moses had to bless him and invest him with his own majesty.

If even Joshua required blessings to make him worthy of leadership, why could not the same blessings be conferred upon Moses' children?

Avnei Nezer wonders: if even Joshua required blessings to make him worthy of leadership, why could not the same blessings be conferred upon Moses' children so that they could succeed him just as Aaron's sons followed him in the priesthood? *Avnei Nezer* explains that the blessings of a great

man are like the flow of any priceless substance. If one pours gold coins into a torn purse, they will tumble to the ground; if one pours vintage wine onto a silver nugget that has never been shaped into a cup, it will trickle away and be lost forever. Like gold and wine, spiritual blessings must be poured into a proper receptacle or they are wasted. True, Moses' blessings were available to every Jew — children, disciples, and strangers alike — but there was only one receptacle in Israel capable of receiving those precious blessings and becoming a Joshua. The nation possessed no one, not even Eliezer or Phineas, who was as well-formed a vessel as Joshua. And what had formed him? No advantages of birth or position, only his own forty-year commitment to learn from Moses by study and service.

There was only one receptacle in Israel capable of receiving those precious blessings and becoming a Joshua.

Everyone's Potential

The Jew's responsibility to emulate Moses did not end with the sealing of Scripture. *Rambam* writes:

כָּל אָדָם רָאוּי לִהְיוֹת צַדִּיק כְּמֹשֶׁה רַבֵּינוּ.

Every person potentially can be as righteous as Moses our Teacher (Hil. Teshuvah 5:2).

Rambam's sweeping dictum seems to state unequivocally that the humblest, least-endowed Jew has the capacity, and hence the *obligation*, to attain the stature of Moses, but our experience cries out that this cannot be. Surely the stature of Moses is beyond our most strenuous efforts!

Rabbi Elchonon Wasserman explains that *Rambam* refers not to the accomplishments of Moses but to his dedication to serve God to the utmost of his ability. Though it is true that we cannot match Moses' greatness, we *can* equal his zeal to serve God with all our capacity. Scripture calls Moses עֶבֶד ה׳, *the slave* or *servant of HASHEM (Joshua* 1:1). The commentators explain that Moses' utter devotion to God was such that Moses ascribed to himself no personal rights or possessions. He existed only to serve his Master with absolute selflessness, like a slave who has no personal rights under law. It is axiomatic that man's every talent and resource was

Though we cannot match Moses' greatness, we can equal his zeal to serve God.

assigned him by God for a purpose and to whatever degree required to achieve that purpose. If a person of intellectual brilliance were expected to score grades no higher than those of his hard-working, mediocre colleague, then why did God endow him with superior capacity? Did God give someone great business acumen merely to afford him a home for every season and a wardrobe for every occasion? In many cases in where Temple offerings are required, the Torah provides that a poor person bring a much less expensive sacrifice than his wealthy neighbor, but each achieves the same degree of atonement because he did what was expected according to his ability. In this sense, every Jew can be 'as righteous as Moses,' though not his equal in caliber of accomplishment. Moses was a giant because God endowed him with spiritual, intellectual, and physical gifts beyond our imagination — but Moses himself — not God — made the decision to devote himself to God like a slave to his master. Such a decision is within everyone's grasp, and, by making it, the humblest Jew can equal Moses' righteousness *(Kovetz Maamarim)*.

Did God give someone great business acumen merely to afford him a home for every season?

The *Chofetz Chaim* made a similar point with a parable: A great monarch decided to tour his entire kingdom. In the big cities, masters, lords, and rulers came out to greet him. As he advanced to the countryside, mayors and lower-ranking officers offered homage. When he made his way to isolated alleys and tiny villages, the highest official he would see might be a part-time justice of the peace or an aging constable. But the insignificant policeman would hardly dare say that anyone below the rank of dukes and marshals is not fit, and therefore not required, to honor the king. To the contrary, every citizen must show allegiance according to his authority and ability. The minor constable has the same degree of responsibility for his alley or intersection as the powerful governor has for his province. All must honor the king, each in his way. Similarly, no Jewish generation can absolve itself of its duty to serve God by arguing that it cannot attain

The minor constable has the same degree of responsibility for his alley or intersection as the powerful governor has for his province.

the spiritual pinnacles of yesteryear. We are not required to *surpass* the mystics of medieval Safed, the Tosafists of France and Germany, or the Sages of the Talmud. But we are required to exert our best effort to serve God, just as they did.

In fulfilling this responsibility, Joshua was extraordinary and in the process he crafted himself into the vessel that was capable of receiving Moses' majesty and holding his staffs of leadership.

II. Sun and Moon

Moses' Reflection

One of the best-known statements about Joshua is the evaluation made by his contemporaries, the elders who knew both Moses and Joshua. They said:

פְּנֵי מֹשֶׁה כִּפְנֵי חַמָּה פְּנֵי יְהוֹשֻׁעַ כִּפְנֵי לְבָנָה

The face of Moses was like the face of the sun; the face of Joshua is like the face of the moon (Bava Basra 75b).

On the surface, the comparison seems most uncomplimentary and even unfair to Joshua. Moses' level of prophecy was unequalled by *any* prophet. When God rebuked Aaron and Miriam for criticizing Moses, He told them that Moses' degree of prophecy was so supreme as to be incomprehensible even to his own brother and sister, who were prophets in their own right *(Numbers* 12:6-9). In the concluding verses of the Torah, after stating that Joshua was *filled with the spirit of wisdom because Moses had placed his hands upon him* [in blessing], Scripture makes plain that there would never be a prophet like Moses *(Deut.* 34:9-12). As *Sfas Emes* points out, Moses' *essence* was so lustrous that his face always shone and he had to wear a mask when he was with the people (34:29-35). Other prophets, on the other hand, looked no different from other people and reached a state of exaltation only when they experienced a prophetic vision.

We make a mistake if we see in the sun-moon comparison only a derogation of Joshua.

But we make a mistake if we see in the sun-moon comparison only a derogation of Joshua. How many other 'moons' did Moses have? None. Only Joshua

was capable of receiving Moses' blinding spiritual light and reflecting it to the people of Israel. To say that Joshua was not a Moses is to see only the dark side of the moon. There was only one Moses, but there was only one Joshua. Joshua was Moses' greatest student, his sole successor, his only 'moon.'

There was only one Moses, but there was only one Joshua. Joshua was Moses' greatest student, his sole successor, his only 'moon.'

This uniqueness of Joshua helps explain a decision of Moses. When he dispatched the twelve spies to gather information about *Eretz Yisrael,* Moses singled out Joshua for a special blessing. His name had been הוֹשֵׁעַ, *Hoshea,* but Moses added the letter י, making his name יְהוֹשֻׁעַ [Yehoshuah], *Joshua (Numbers* 13:16). With that added letter, Joshua's name began with the letters יה, the spelling of one of God's Names. Thus, Moses implied the prayer יָהּ יוֹשִׁיעֲךָ מֵעֲצַת מְרַגְּלִים, *May God* [*Yah*] *save you from the conspiracy of the spies (Sotah* 34b).

Why did Moses pray only for Joshua? If he knew prophetically that the evil intentions of the other spies were beyond the influence of his prayer, why did he not add a prayer for Caleb, who *did* remain above the conspiracy?*

Gur Aryeh explains that Moses was especially concerned with the behavior of his closest student. Ordinarily it is improper for a person to seek Divine intervention to influence someone's freedom of choice, but, had Joshua sinned, people would have taken it as a reflection on Moses' teaching. Critics would have said, 'Had his master taught him properly, Joshua would not have demeaned God's promised land. Surely the seed of the corruption was implanted in Joshua by Moses himself!' Moses had a right to seek God's help in protecting his own reputation, especially since such an imputation against Moses would have diminished the authority of the Torah he taught in the Name of God.

Moses had a right to seek God's help in protecting his own reputation.

Arvei Nachal adds that since Joshua was destined to lead Israel into *Eretz Yisrael,* his integrity had to be preserved. While it is true that Moses did not know

*[The very difficult question of why the once-righteous spies went wrong and why the nation followed their counsel instead of heeding Moses, Aaron, Joshua, and Caleb, will be discussed in the Overview and Commentary to the *sidrah Shelach.*]

at the time that, more than thirty-eight years later, Joshua would succeed him, his prophetic instinct undoubtedly perceived that Joshua would be a major player in Israel's destiny and the people's needs required that he not be besmirched, even if his freedom of choice was compromised by Divine assistance in avoiding sin. That Joshua's freedom had to be so restricted was a mark of honor; it meant that he had become too important to be risked. He was one of only two people in history to be placed in that category. The first was Moses.

That Joshua's freedom had to be so restricted was a mark of honor; it meant that he had become too important to be risked.

When Freedom is Withdrawn

In a fundamental dissertation in his introduction to *Exodus, Meshech Chochmah* discusses what can justify such tampering with this most basic spiritual freedom. One of the principles of Judaism, the seventh of *Rambam's* Principles of Faith, is unswerving belief in the prophecy of Moses. No testimony nor miracle on earth is strong enough to contradict or raise doubts concerning his prophecy *(Hil. Yesodei HaTorah* 8:3). But the Sages teach that הַכֹּל בִּידֵי שָׁמַיִם חוּץ מִיִּרְאַת שָׁמַיִם, *Everything is in Heaven's power except for fear of Heaven (Berachos* 33b), meaning that while God controls everything from the cosmos to the amoeba, He does not determine whether someone will be virtuous or sinful. Human freedom of choice is at the very basis of creation and God does not interfere with it. But if so, then *Moses* had to retain the freedom to sin — even the freedom to give up his faith ח״ו. That someone becomes a prophet does not guarantee that he will never rebel against God, as illustrated by the case of Chananiah ben Azur, who rebelled and became a false prophet *(Jeremiah* 28:2-10; *Sanhedrin* 69a). If so, how could God require Israel to believe forever in Moses' prophecy while the possibility existed that he would kick over the traces and become an apostate? Were that to happen and he decreed commandments of his own fancy, were the people to be required as an article of faith, to believe that every heresy that he uttered was commanded by God? Or if they realized that he had become tainted,

That someone becomes a prophet does not guarantee that he will never rebel against God.

wouldn't they naturally doubt everything he had ever told them?

Moses' freedom of choice had to be removed from him. This did not mean that he could never sin; only that no transgression could cast doubt on his integrity.

There was only one way out of this dilemma. Moses' freedom of choice had to be removed from him. This did not mean that he could never sin; only that no transgression of his could be serious enough to cast doubt on his basic integrity. Moses lost his chance to enter *Eretz Yisrael* because he struck the rock instead of sanctifying God's Name by speaking to it (*Numbers* 20:7-13; this subject will be discussed in the Overview and commentary to *Chukas*). Although his striking of the rock was reckoned as a serious error for a man *of his stature*, it was clearly an error in judgment rather than a sin in the common understanding of the word. Though the major commentators offer a wide variety of interpretations of the sin, the consensus is unanimous that only someone of Moses' awesome greatness could have been taken so much to task for it. The people of Israel, too, knew that though Moses had erred he retained his stature as a prophet *nonpareil*.

Joshua, too, was an 'author' of the Torah — not like Moses, but too much to permit his prophecy and teachings to be questioned.

Joshua, too, was an 'author' of the Torah — not like Moses, of course, but too much to permit his prophecy and teachings to be questioned. According to R' Yehudah, Joshua wrote the last eight verses of *Deuteronomy* (the narrative that follows Moses' death); and (in chap. 20) he recorded God's commandment that the six cities of refuge be formally designated and begin to function (*Makkos* 11a). R' Yitzchok says on behalf of Rav that one of the requirements of circumcision is derived from *Joshua* 5:2 (*Yevamos* 71b). Furthermore, *Nedarim* 22b teaches that אִלְמָלֵא חָטְאוּ יִשְׂרָאֵל לֹא נִתַּן לָהֶם אֶלָּא סֵפֶר תּוֹרָה וְסֵפֶר יְהוֹשֻׁעַ בִּלְבָד, *Had Israel not sinned, only the Torah and the Book of Joshua would have been given to them; the Book of Joshua* would have been given because it contains the boundaries of the tribal portions of *Eretz Yisrael* — information that is of Divine origin and is essential to the nation. From the above citations it is plain that Joshua is in the category of Moses. Consequently the nation could not be placed in the predicament of

receiving basic teachings from a prophet who might conceivably go astray in an essential matter.

What Made Them Worthy?

The removal of choice is no small matter because it violates the principle that man be free.

The removal of choice is no small matter because it violates the principle of creation that man be free to choose between good and evil. There is a reason for that freedom: unless man *could* choose to sin, his performance of good deeds would be no better than the efficient functioning of a robot. What does he prove if he performs what he was programed to do? But the greater an individual becomes, the more he rids himself of freedom — by his *own* choice. As he comes to feel the spiritual bliss of acting in accordance with God's will and the foolishness of the transitory pleasures that once enticed him, his choices become so clearly between black and white that there is no longer room for doubt. When that happens, he has reached the level of the angels, of spiritual beings that exist only to serve God. Sometimes a person, or even an entire people, can reach that status temporarily, as Israel did at Sinai. The sight and sounds of revelation and the inner awareness of God's Presence made them all angel-like prophets, but such exaltation could not last, though its aftereffects remain with Israel forever. God alluded to this irrepressible tug of man's humanity that does not let him remain too long in spiritual heights: after revealing Himself and pronouncing the Ten Commandments, God told Israel, שׁוּבוּ לָכֶם לְאָהֳלֵיכֶם, *return to your tents (Deut.* 5:27). By this command, God meant that Israel had to descend from the zenith and return to their everyday lives. True only a great nation could scale such heights even temporarily, but man cannot live with the angels forever *(Shabbos* 87a).

Only a great nation could scale such heights even temporarily, but man cannot live with the angels forever.

Moses was different. To him God said, וְאַתָּה פֹּה עֲמֹד עִמָּדִי, *but you are to remain here with Me (Deut.* 5:8). He would forever remain in the state of holiness that precluded the temptation to sin, because he had raised himself above the physical limitations that still gripped his fellow Jews (see *Rambam, Hil. Yesodei HaTorah* 7:6). It is true, as explained above, that

Moses' role required him to be stripped of most of his freedom to choose sin, but God assigned him that task only because he had already won the battle against his Evil Inclination. Because he was capable of remaining at the level of Sinai, he was invited to do so; because he had transcended the flesh, God made his prophecy inviolate for all time. Conversely, had Moses not attained this spiritual plateau, God would not have deprived him of his free will and He would not have declared Moses' prophecy to be supreme no matter what might happen in the future.

Like Moses, Joshua could not have won this position unless he had won the war against temptation.

Joshua — though nowhere near Moses' level of prophecy — had a similar position as an author of portions of Torah verses and law. As such, his teachings, too, had to have permanency, primacy. Like Moses, Joshua could not have won this position unless he had won the war against temptation; like Moses, his role and his victory made it possible for God to remove his freedom of choice. This is why Moses could pray that God save Joshua from the conspiracy of the spies and why he could imply before his death that as long as Joshua was alive, it was tantamount to Moses himself still being with Israel (as explained at the beginning of the Overview). This also explains why God assured Joshua that he would make him as great as Moses in the eyes of the people (3:7).

The Elders Err

Most indicative of how lightly he was held, the elders compared Joshua to Moses as a moon to a sun.

Though Joshua was in the front rank of Israel's greatest figures, his stature was not as appreciated as it should have been. Apparently, even Moses did not regard Joshua as his heir-apparent, and it was necessary for God and Moses to demonstrate publicly during Moses' lifetime that Joshua was worthy of his role. Most indicative of how lightly he was held, the elders compared Joshua to Moses as a moon to a sun.

In making their unfavorable comparison of Joshua to Moses, the elders said 'אוֹי לָהּ לְאוֹתָהּ בּוּשָׁה, אוֹי לָהּ לְאוֹתָהּ כְּלִימָּה, *Woe for this shame, woe for this humiliation.'* Most commentators explain their plaint more or less as *Rashi* does: 'In such a brief time, the

glory [of Israel's leadership] became so diminished! — for though Joshua was a prophet and leader like Moses, he could not attain Moses' glory.'

However, *Mabit (Beis Elokim)* offers another, telling, insight. This failure to evaluate him properly should not be surprising; the moon is never noticed before the sun sets. As long as Joshua was Moses' loyal, self-effacing servant, his personal luster paled beside the brilliance of his master. Who sees the moon at high noon? But when Moses died, the elders, who should have had an insight into the real Joshua, finally realized that all along a 'moon' had lived among them — Israel's closest reflection of Moses' greatness — and they never realized! Chagrined at their own blindness they exclaimed, *'Woe for this shame, woe for this humiliation.'*

A 'moon' had lived among them — Israel's closest reflection of Moses' greatness — and they never realized!

III. Master of Torah

בְּשָׁעָה שֶׁנִּפְטַר מֹשֶׁה לְגַן עֵדֶן אָמַר לוֹ לִיהוֹשֻׁעַ, שְׁאַל מִמֶּנִּי כָּל סְפֵקוֹת שֶׁיֵּשׁ לְךָ. אָמַר לוֹ, רַבִּי כְּלוּם הִנַּחְתִּיךָ שָׁעָה אַחַת וְהָלַכְתִּי לְמָקוֹם אַחֵר?

At the time when Moses passed away to the Garden of Eden, he said to Joshua, 'Ask me about all your questions.' [Joshua] answered him, 'My master, have I left for even a moment and gone elsewhere?' (Temurah 16a)

The Transition

Joshua's role as an author of Torah went beyond his participation in recording certain commandments or the boundaries of *Eretz Yisrael. R' Tzadok HaCohen (Mach'shevos Charutz)* comments that the Book of *Joshua* inaugurated a new era in the nature of Torah knowledge. The Torah of Moses was given directly by God, but Joshua wrote his own book. It was the first of the prophetic books that were composed by human beings (see *Bava Basra* 15a for the authorship of the books of Prophets and Writings).

Joshua's book was new in another way. It begins

with the word וַיְהִי, a term that always alludes to sadness or affliction. In Joshua's case, the sadness was the death of Moses, both the fact of his death and the tragedy caused by his passing. During the period of mourning for him, many hundreds of laws were forgotten *(Temurah* 16a). Moses' loss was made even more poignant by that illustration that the period of absolute clarity of knowledge was beginning to recede. Simultaneously, however, a new era of Torah knowledge was beginning — that of the Oral Law, by means of which the Written Torah is expounded and applied, and laws are derived from it. As the Talmud *(ibid.)* teaches, Asniel ben Kenaz utilized the principles of hermeneutical derivation to recall those forgotten laws.

Moses' loss was made even more poignant by that illustration that the period of absolute clarity of knowledge was beginning to recede.

Joshua's first days as leader were a period of transition, and all such periods are difficult. Joshua was the successor, but he had not yet come into his own as a great leader; his young authority was still fragile, based on Moses' blessing and God's commandment that he be obeyed. Joshua had not yet proven his own prowess and, had the influence of Moses been shut off completely, no one can know how well Israel would have survived the trauma. But God in His mercy kept the changeover from being unbearably abrupt, like the setting sun whose rays bend over the horizon even after it sets. The last eight verses of the Torah — written by Joshua (according to R' Yehudah in *Makkos* 11a) — carried the glow of the Written Torah into the period of Joshua. Those verses tell that Joshua was filled with wisdom because Moses had placed his hands upon him and that Israel obeyed him and continued to heed all that God had commanded Moses. Thus, like every period of twilight, there was a mixture of light and darkness: the light of Moses' Torah relieved the darkness of his passing and the forgetfulness it caused.

God in His mercy kept the changeover from being unbearably abrupt.

The phenomenon of the manna was a further manifestation of this transitionary stage. Throughout the forty years in the Wilderness, the manna had fallen in Moses' merit. It was a spiritual

food, *the food of angels* (see *Psalms* 78:25), and it was entirely fitting that such food should be provided to the flock of Moses, who was himself more angelic than human. When Moses died, the manna stopped falling, but the last day's supply lasted for five weeks, until Joshua had led the people into *Eretz Yisrael* and they were able to gather the produce of the Land. Again, Moses' influence sustained Israel until Joshua was able to assert himself independently.

In God's first vision to Joshua, He stressed that day-and-night study of the Torah was the key to Israel's success in all areas.

Both as disciple of Moses and as leader of Israel, Joshua was responsible to carry on Moses' task of making the study and knowledge of the Torah the very essence of Jewish existence. In God's first vision to Joshua, He stressed that day-and-night study of the Torah was the key to Israel's success in *all* areas, for Israel is the bearer of God's spiritual message on earth (1:7-8). *Arvei Nachal* gives this concept a profound application to Israel's physical conquest of the Land. The Sages taught that God used the Torah as the 'blueprint of creation,' for He looked into the Torah, as it were, and created the universe in consonance with the Torah's teachings and demands. By telling Joshua, on the threshold of the war of conquest, that Israel must maintain its diligence in Torah study, God was implying that knowledge of the Torah was the key to the conquest. If Torah is the blueprint, then we may assume that every part of creation corresponds to a law, a thought, a teaching, a principle of the Torah. This is especially true regarding *Eretz Yisrael,* because it is the world's seat of holiness, the place from which God's influence emanates to the rest of the world (see *Ramban, Deut.* 11:12). By its allegiance to the *mitzvos* corresponding to a particular portion of the Land, Israel assured its conquest of that portion — not only the conquest, but the miraculous intervention that brought victory without any casualties (except in the case of Ai, where Israel was found unworthy due to Achan's sin. See chapt. 7 with comm.).

By its allegiance to the mitzvos corresponding to a particular portion of the Land, Israel assured its conquest of that portion.

Arvei Nachal maintains that the hundreds of laws that were forgotten during Moses' period of

mourning were the cause of Israel's inability to conquer some parts of *Eretz Yisrael;* the forgotten laws corresponded to the unconquered places. But, as the Talmud relates *(Temurah* 16a), Asniel ben Kenaz restored those laws through his scholarship. It is not coincidental, therefore, that Asniel then became the conqueror of Devir (15:15) — having mastered the blueprint, he won the city.

Joshua's Twin Responsibilities

As Rambam says: Moses had three primary disciples; but it was to Joshua 'who was Moses' disciple' that he transmitted the Oral Law.

The responsibililty to transmit the Oral Law faithfully, and for a chosen few of Israel's greatest scholars to be responsible for its maintenance and interpretation in each generation, began with Moses' own successors. As *Rambam* says in his Introduction to the Mishnah, Moses had three primary disciples: Joshua, Elazar, and Phineas, but it was to Joshua 'who was Moses' disciple' that he transmitted the Oral Law and whom he commanded to preserve it. This is further indicated by the very first *mishnah* in *Avos,* which states clearly that Moses passed on the Torah to Joshua.

Rambam's source for his assertion that responsibility for the *Oral Law* was placed particularly in the hands of Joshua may be *Sifrei (Pinchas).* There we are told, that when Moses was commanded to designate Joshua as his successor, he was commanded: צַוֵּהוּ עַל דִּבְרֵי תַלְמוּד, *instruct him concerning the 'Talmud.' Rambam* interprets this as a clear reference to the Oral Law. This would explain why Israel was so incensed when Joshua forgot hundreds of laws that there were some who threatened to kill him *(Temurah* 16a)! Why the wrath against Joshua alone when there were myriad other scholars and elders in the nation who were equally guilty? Because, as leader of the people, Joshua had been made responsible for the preservation of the Oral Law. Everyone should have remembered all the laws, but their preservation was Joshua's responsibility *(Harav Yitzchok Zev Soloveitchick).*

Everyone should have remembered all the laws, but their preservation was Joshua's responsibility.

The Talmud notes a discrepancy between Moses' description of Joshua's function and God's Own

Moses said, 'For you will accompany this people,' implying that Joshua would not dominate the elders, but would consult with them.

charge to him. Moses said, חֲזַק וֶאֱמָץ כִּי אַתָּה תָּבוֹא אֶת הָעָם הַזֶּה אֶל הָאָרֶץ, *Strengthen yourself and persevere, for you will* **accompany** *this people to the Land (Deut.* 31:7), implying that Joshua would not dominate the elders, but would consult with them — *accompany* them — as they jointly entered the land. In effect Joshua would be the 'first among equals.' Later in the same chapter, however, God Himself charged Joshua (*v.* 23, see *Rashi)* saying, כִּי אַתָּה תָּבִיא אֶת בְּנֵי יִשְׂרָאֵל אֶל הָאָרֶץ, *for you will* **bring** *the Children of Israel to the Land,* implying that Joshua would be the uncontested leader, with the authority and obligation to impose his will — *bring* — against their wills if need be. The Talmud explains:

אָמַר ר׳ יוֹחָנָן, אָמַר לוֹ מֹשֶׁה לִיהוֹשֻׁעַ אַתָּה וְהַזְּקֵנִים שֶׁבַּדּוֹר עִמָּךְ. אָמַר לוֹ הקב״ה טוֹל מַקֵּל וְהַךְ עַל קָדְקֳדָם, דַּבָּר אֶחָד לְדוֹר וְאֵין שְׁנֵי דַבָּרִים לְדוֹר

R' Yochanan said: Moses told Joshua, 'You and the elders of the generation with you [*shall lead the people jointly*]*.' The Holy One, Blessed is He, told* [*Joshua*], *'Take a stick and swat their skulls — a generation can have a single leader; there cannot be two leaders of a generation' (Sanhedrin* 8a).

On the surface, it would seem that God contradicted Moses; Moses assigned a cooperative-type of leadership to Joshua while God gave him sole authority. Such an interpretation is most difficult, however, for Moses spoke as God's prophet — how can it be that he failed to convey what God had told him?

Moses had the status of a king and he was also the head of the Sanhedrin, Joshua, too, held both positions.

Rabbi Yitzchok Zev Soloveitchick explains that two separate functions of leadership were conveyed from Moses to Joshua — Moses referred to one function while God referred to the other. Moses had the status of a king and he was also the head of the Sanhedrin, the high court composed of himself and the seventy elders. Joshua, too, held both positions. The president of the Sanhedrin is indeed a *member* of a deliberative, decision-making body. As such, he

consults with the others and they make their decision jointly based on the rule of the majority. Moses addressed himself to this role when he implied that Joshua would act in consultation with his colleagues. This representation was accurate but it failed to take note of Joshua's other function, and by omission it implied that Joshua had no authority other than his collegial one. Therefore, God charged Joshua to be cognizant of his duty to exercise the strong authority of kingship — in addition to his presidency of the Sanhedrin, he had to exercise the strong, coercive, unilateral authority of the king. As such, he had to lead, and there can be only one leader. [For a partial discussion of the differences between king and Sanhedrin, see Overview to *Ruth* pp. xxviii — xxxvi.]

God charged Joshua to be cognizant of his duty to exercise the strong authority of kingship.

IV. The Leader for the Time

Uniting Force

After being told that he would soon die, Moses asked God to appoint his successor. He said:

> *May HASHEM — God of the spirits of all life — appoint a man over the congregation. One who will go out ahead of them and will come in ahead of them, who will lead them out and bring them back. Let not the congregation of Israel be like sheep without a shepherd (Numbers 27:16-17).*

Or HaChaim explains Moses' reference to 'God of the spirits' and to the need for a leader who will go and come 'ahead of the people, and lead them out and bring them back.' The nature of human beings makes it almost impossible for any man to exercise leadership in such a way that he will satisfy everyone and win unanimous allegiance. People's drives, natures, and perceptions are different. Their needs are different. For this reason, God commanded each tribe to have its own judges and officers of the court, and this is why each town and hamlet had its own authorities. Officials who are close to the people can better understand the special needs of their fellow tribesmen and neighbors. Moses was unique in that

Officials who are close to the people can better understand the special needs of their fellow tribesmen and neighbors.

he could divinely understand each person and find the way to reach his heart and satisfy his deepest inner needs. This is an almost supernatural trait, it is this characteristic that Moses sought in the next leader of Israel when he addressed God in His manifestation of *God of the spirits of all life.* Just as God understands every man's own spirit, so should His deputy, the leader of Israel. Such a man must love his people so much that he *will go out ahead of them and will come in ahead of them,* and he must inspire such love and confidence in them that they will follow him trustingly, willingly, allowing him to *lead them out and bring them back.*

Just as God understands every man's own spirit, so should His deputy, the leader of Israel.

To Moses' plea, God responded that he should take Joshua, *a man in whom this spirit is present* (ibid. 27:18). Then, to strengthen Joshua's innate ability, God commanded Moses to place his hand upon him, infusing the disciple with the master's spirit, and He commanded Moses to do this in the presence of the entire congregation so that they would all realize the greatness of the man whom they had tended to overlook because he had paled in the glare of Moses' brilliance.

The Sages teach that the temperaments of a leader and his generation tend to match one another.

The Sages teach that the temperaments of a leader and his generation tend to match one another. Whether the generation makes the leader or the leader makes the generation, Divine Providence provides each generation of Israel with the leader who can channel to it the Divine emanations suited to its collective personality and unique needs *(Arachin* 17b). This concept is found over and over again in the teachings of the Sages. The greatness of Moses is ascribed to the needs and merit of Israel, but when Israel erected the Golden Calf, God told Moses, 'Descend from your greatness,' because Israel's own level of sanctity had fallen precipitously *(Exodus* 32:7, see *Rashi).* Such relatively minor judges as Yiftach are equated with Samuel, the greatest of the judges: Yiftach in his generation is equal to Samuel in his generation *(Rosh Hashanah* 25b). The two were by no means of equal stature, but each corresponded to the condition of the people he led.

Once the Sages heard a heavenly voice [בַּת קוֹל] saying: 'There is one among you who is worthy that the Divine Presence should rest on him as it did upon Moses, but his generation is not deserving.' Those who heard the voice all looked at Hillel the Elder (*Sotah* 48b).

In perhaps the most illustrative and astounding statement of this concept, the Sages say, 'If Aaron were still alive, Ezra would have been greater than him *in his time' (Koheles Rabbah* 1:4). By no stretch of the imagination was Ezra greater in absolute terms than Aaron, but the generation of the Exodus needed Aaron and the generation that built the Second Temple needed Ezra. Neither leader would have sufficed for the generation of the other.

The generation of the Exodus needed Aaron and the generation that built the Second Temple needed Ezra.

Joshua's Time

Joshua's time had come. The Midrashim relate that the spirit of prophecy left Moses and (to a lesser degree of course) rested upon Joshua. To God's choice of Moses for one generation and Joshua for the next, *Sfas Emes* applies the Talmudic dictum:

הָרוֹאֶה אוּכְלוּסֵי יִשְׂרָאֵל אוֹמֵר בָּרוּךְ חֲכַם הָרָזִים שֶׁאֵין דַּעְתָּן דּוֹמָה זֶה לָזֶה וְאֵין פַּרְצוּפֵיהֶן דּוֹמִין זֶה לָזֶה.

Whoever sees huge numbers of Jews [600,000 or more (Rashi)] should say, 'Blessed is the Wise One [*Who knows*] *the secrets'* [*within the minds of all people (Rashi)*], *for their ideas are dissimilar just as their features are dissimilar (Berachos* 58a).

God permits each person to receive his share of holiness in accordance with his own capacity and how well he has perfected it. The Sabbath is a sacred day, for example, but not all people are equally equipped to perceive and make use of it. All of God's gifts are dispensed similarly: the entire community of Israel is allotted a general — and generous — portion, but within the community each individual receives the share to which he is entitled. *Eretz Yisrael* as a whole is the inheritance of all Israel, but the Land was subdivided among the tribes, the

The Sabbath is a sacred day but not all people are equally equipped to perceive and make use of it.

families, the individuals. The Sages teach that not only was the Land apportioned by lots, but each lot 'spoke,' as it were, proclaiming to whom it was awarding the portion described upon it. Moses was the collective soul of the entire Jewish nation; he represented קְהִלַּת יַעֲקֹב, *the community of Jacob.* Joshua was the leader suited to a different function: the requirement that the nation be subdivided, each family settled in its own homestead.

Moses reigned at a time of unity while Joshua reigned at a time of dispersion.

In this sense, *Sfas Emes* understands the descriptions of Moses and Joshua as sun and moon. Moses was like the fiery sun, concentrating all light within itself and dispensing it equally in all directions. Joshua, however, was like the moon, which shares the dispersed light of evening with the stars. Moses reigned at a time of unity while Joshua reigned at a time of dispersion.

His enactments were all designed to facilitate the functioning of a harmonious society, one in which people would surrender property rights for the common good.

Against this background of Joshua's role — that he was a leader who could understand individual needs and inspire a sense of unity and loyalty *(Or HaChaim),* and he was the leader uniquely suited to separate the people into their appropriate parts of the Land where they would carry out their separate roles for the future *(Sfas Emes)* — we can perhaps appreciate the task Joshua took upon himself to smooth the rough edges of society. Inevitably, the general good would conflict with individual rights. The shepherd wants to graze his sheep wherever he finds grass, but has he the right to lead them into a private forest? Should the forest-owner keep the shepherd from using grass for which he, the owner, has no use? Who is entitled to use spring water? May farmers cut off their neighbor's excess branches for replanting? The Talmud *(Bava Kamma* 80b-81a) describes ten conditions Joshua imposed upon the Jewish people when he divided *Eretz Yisrael* among them. His enactments were all designed to facilitate the functioning of a harmonious society, one in which people would surrender property rights for the common good, but which would prevent the multitude from infringing unfairly upon the individual. [See Comm. to 25:25.]

יְהוֹשֻׁעַ לֹא קָרָא עַצְמוֹ עֶבֶד והקב״ה קְרָאוֹ עֶבֶד
Joshua did not call himself a servant [*of God*], *but the Holy One, Blessed is He, called him a servant (Sifrei, Va'eschanan).*

Joshua became leader of Israel with the elders bemoaning the humiliation of a pale moon replacing the setting sun. The first verse of his book describes Moses as עֶבֶד ה׳, *the servant of HASHEM*, and Joshua as nothing more than מְשָׁרֵת מֹשֶׁה, *the attendant of Moses*. But his years of dedicated, effective leadership vindicated God's choice of him. When his life was over, he had taken his place in the galaxy of Israel's greatest leaders, the architect of a Jewish society that fashioned the miracle of bringing Godliness into the plowing and harvesting of material life.

At his death God described Joshua just as he had described Moses.

And what was God's Own assessment of Joshua? At his death God describes Joshua just as he had described Moses — וַיָּמָת יְהוֹשֻׁעַ בִּן נוּן עֶבֶד ה׳, *Joshua son of Nun the* **servant of HASHEM** *died* (24:29).

The disciple had joined his master.

Rabbi Nosson Scherman
טו״ב טבת תשמ״ב

◆§ *Introduction*

An Introduction / The Denouement of Destiny

And He said to Abram, 'Know with certainty that your offspring shall be aliens in a land not their own, they will serve them, and they will oppress them four hundred years. But also upon the nation which they shall serve will I execute judgment, and afterwards they shall leave with great possessions ... And the fourth generation shall return here ...' (Genesis 15:13, 14, 16).

As the *Book of Joshua* begins, we find the nation of Israel stationed on the east bank of the Jordan River, anticipating their entry into *Eretz Yisrael*. Some four hundred years earlier God had promised Abraham in the Covenant Between the Parts that although his children would be exiled from the Land of Israel, the *fourth generation would return (Genesis* 15:16). This multitude stationed on the east bank represents the fourth generation of Abraham's descendants calculated from Jacob's descent to Egypt *(Rashi)*. They are about to return to the Land, in fulfillment of the Divine promise.

Even understood outside the context of the covenant, this event is most remarkable from the perspective of human history. When has a group of people coalesced and emerged as a nation outside a geographic state? When has a nation been able to display its entire corpus of social legislation before the state's halls of justice have ever been occupied? Several generations earlier, seventy Israelites descended to Egypt. Now, several million Jews who share the same language, values, and mores stand ready to cross the Jordan to live together as a people. Their resolve for unity was unlike that of any other nation's, for it was forged in an alien and perverse country — in Egypt — and nurtured during forty years of wandering in a wilderness. They were even able to transfer their vision of nationhood to their children, for those who had initially become inspired were unable to realize their goals (see *Prefatory Remarks* to Chapter 2). (How unusual it is that parents are able to bequeath their

newly acquired life's visions to their offspring. How often children develop ambitions of their own.) On their entry to the Land the Jews were able to display the entire set of laws which would govern their newly formed state until the advent of the Messiah. When they built the altar at Mount Eval (8:22), they meticulously etched the entire Torah on its stones, thus vividly underscoring the significance of this historical exception. All other political states were formed over a period of years; only afterwards was national legislation promulgated. The Jewish state, however, was Divinely mandated and governed by a pre-existing Divine code, the Torah.

If, moreover, we consider this event in the context of the covenant, it is truly astounding. Never have so few words left their mark on so much of Scripture. The thirty Hebrew words which record God's decree for Abraham's descendants have guided Israel's destiny as portrayed in four and one-half books of the Pentateuch.

□ *Your offspring shall be aliens in a land not their own.* In *Genesis* we read that Isaac was commanded to sojourn through the Land and that Jacob traveled to the land of Ham. Jacob's sons, unknowingly fulfilling the Divine plan for Jewish history (see *Maharatz Chayes* to *Shabbos* 10b), sold Joseph down to Egypt. Jacob and his seventy descendants later joined him there as a result of a ubiquitous famine. From that time until the beginning of the *Book of Joshua,* the Israelites did not live in *Eretz Yisrael.*

□ ... *they will serve them, and they will oppress them ... But also upon the nation which they shall serve will I execute judgment.* In *Exodus* we read that Egypt was later ruled by a new king, who was unaware of Joseph's service to the Egyptians. This king enslaved the Israelites and made their life bitter. God heard the Israelites' cries and brought the ten plagues upon the Egyptians in order to punish them and to demonstrate to the Jews that God not only created the world, but also controls its every event.

□ *And afterwards they shall leave with great possessions. HaKsav VeHaKabballah* notes that *great* in this context refers to greatness in quality, rather than in quantity. Thus, the spiritual wealth which the Israelites received was the Torah at Mount Sinai.

□ *And the fourth generation shall return here.* Jacob's children and grandchildren perished in Egypt. His great-grandchildren left with the Exodus and stood at the foot of Mount Sinai. Because they sinned by believing the slanderous report of the reconnaissance mission dispatched to survey *Eretz Yisrael,* they were condemned to

die in the Wilderness. It is this generation which is portrayed in the greater portion of *Exodus*, and in *Leviticus*, *Numbers*, and *Deuteronomy*. Their children, who represent *the fourth* generation, are portrayed in the *Book of Joshua*.

The last three words of the Covenant Between the Parts, *and the fourth generation shall return here*, are about to be fulfilled. *Abarbanel* explains that it was for this very reason that the *Book of Joshua* was included in Scripture.

> The narratives of the *Book of Joshua* are not merely genealogical or historical accounts ... The *Book of Joshua* holds the unique distinction of bearing testimony to the fulfillment of God's prophecies made to the Patriarchs Abraham, Isaac, and Jacob, and to Moses concerning the conquest and settlement of *Eretz Yisrael*. All the promises were realized without exception, and it was for this reason the *Book of Joshua* was written. At the end of his life, Joshua himself testified to the fulfillment of all of God's promises: *You know with all your heart and with all your soul that not one of all the good things that HASHEM your God has told you has fallen short. All have come about for you, not one word of it has fallen short* (*Joshua* 23:14).

Divine Promises to Moses

God reiterated His promise to Moses to give *Eretz Yisrael* to the Israelites just before the Exodus from Egypt, *'I will bring you into the land which I swore to give Abraham, Isaac, and Jacob'* (*Exodus* 6:8). In addition, He disclosed more details about its acquisition. The fulfillment of these guarantees are also mentioned or alluded to in *Joshua*. Some of them will be briefly described.

Israel suffered only thirty-six casualties in the entire conquest of the thirty-one Kings of Canaan. Had Achan not sinned by taking some of the booty of Jericho (see *Commentary* to 7:1), there would have been no losses. This quiet miracle of Divine protection was made to Moses when God forgave the sin of the Golden Calf and reestablished His covenant with the Jews with the issuance of the Second Tablets: *'Observe that which I command you this day:* See *I drive out before you the Emorites, Canaanites, Hittites, Perizzites, Hivvites, and Jebusites'* (*Exodus* 34:11). Moreover, Moses was promised a spectacular Divine intervention when Israel routed its foes in *Eretz*

Yisrael (see *Prefatory Remarks* to Chapter 3), *'I will do marvels such as have not been done in all the earth nor in any nation' (Exodus* 34:10). The sun and moon stopped in their orbits as the entire world learned of Joshua's greatness (10:12). Hailstones descended from the heavens to foil the escape of the Gibeonites' attackers. God's presence in Israel's efforts was truly extraordinary.

An angel appeared to Joshua (5:13-15) to lead the Israelites through the gauntlet of Canaanite opposition in fulfillment of the promise: *'For My angel shall go before you and bring you to the Emorites, Hittites, Canaanites, Perizzites, Hivvites, and Jebusites, and I will cut them off' (Exodus* 23:23).

The Jews were promised developed cities, planted fields and fully furnished houses as soon as they entered *Eretz Yisrael.* Through a complex concatenation of events, Divine providence arranged that the Canaanites would abandon their possessions and fight in unison against the invading Israelites (see *footnote* to 7:5). When the Canaanites were vanquished in battle, the Israelites stepped into *great and good cities which* [*they*] *did not build, and houses full of good things which* [*they*] *did not fill, and hewn out wells which* [*they*] *did not dig, vineyards and olive trees which* [*they*] *did not plant (Deuteronomy* 6:10-11).

Transition to a Torah Perspective — Appearance versus Reality

All human knowledge is haunted by the ghost of illusion, for things often appear much different than they really are. Funhouse mirrors can make their onlookers appear monstrously grotesque, inordinately plump, or diminutive of form. How can man be certain that the judgments he has formed about the nature of things are correct? After all, these judgments are based on perceptions which are *sometimes* incomplete. For example, we would be grossly inaccurate if we were to estimate an iceberg's size by its tip.

Even more disturbing, our interpretations will be entirely false if we fail to recognize the true causality of events and place the cart before the horse. The *Talmud (Sotah* 49b) predicts that the Messiah will come in a generation 'when the face of the people will be as that of a dog.' *R' Yisrael Salanter* explained that if we see a dog trotting before its master, it appears as though the dog charts the course and the master obediently follows. In reality, however, it is the master

who decides the direction; the dog constantly turns its head backward in order to anticipate its master's next move so that it can retain a lead of several steps. At the time of the Messiah, explained *R' Yisrael,* we will experience a breakdown of authority. Torah leaders will no longer determine the course of the Jewish nation; rather, the masses will assume the power of leadership and those who have assumed the leadership positions will run ahead of them as a dog dashes before its master.

The *Chofetz Chaim,* however, explained that the Messianic prediction not only describes the Jews' situation at the 'end of days,' but also offers a recommendation for their response to it. If a stick is hurled at a dog, commented the *Chofetz Chaim,* the animal will immediately pounce upon the stick and bite it. To the dog, the stick appears to cause the pain, rather than the man who threw it. The generation before the advent of the Messiah will fail to understand the true causality of events, and hence their interpretation of events will be unreliable.

But how are we to achieve a true understanding of causality so that our interpretation of events is correct? How are we to insure that we will not be the ones to attack the stick instead of he who threw it? As Jews, our answer is simple. God would not have cast us upon the sea of life without providing us with buoys to find our course. Therefore, He gave us the Torah.

Torah: The Key to Causality

The *Midrash* tells us, 'God looked into the Torah, and then created the world.' The implications of this statement are staggering. An entirely new perspective of life is demanded. By revealing that, the Sages indicate that the ultimate causality for everything lies in the Torah. Just as the architect's plans for the World Trade Center determined the location of every brick in its towers, so the Torah's precepts and spiritual purposes determined the location of every atom in the universe. The physical world is merely the design which follows the Architect's plans concerning the spiritual necessities of life.

Many admire the beauty of the Torah's precepts. How nicely the Jewish son and daughter are required to treat their parents. What a high regard the Torah places on personal property, through its exacting laws concerning stealing and borrowing goods. These statements are true on one level, but do not go far enough, for the

Torah was not given on Mount Sinai to be *superimposed* on our lives. To the contrary, everything we find in our lives is a result of the Divine blueprint. It is *because* the Torah mandates honoring one's parents that men are brought into the world through the union of male and female. God certainly could have created each individual from dust as He did Adam, but He created a world in which each person has parents so that the spiritual benefits of honoring them in accordance with the Torah's precept could accrue to man. Similarly, man could have been created without the desire for material acquisition, but the spiritual demands of observing the Torah's precepts concerning personal property necessitated it. The Torah did not merely address man's condition; rather, man's condition was created because of the Torah's spiritual antecedents.

We must be humble, therefore, in our attempts to fathom the causality of any event that we find mentioned in the Torah. We must cast aside the models of analysis which modern pundits of interpretive history have foisted upon us. If we analyze an event in Scripture from the standpoint of its antecedent economic, political, or social condition, then we suffer from myopia, for we must search instead for the underlying spiritual demands which necessitated the event we wish to understand. We must not be guilty of attacking the stick.

The Conquest— The Revolutionary Concept of War

Israel's enemies present spiritual threats, not merely physical ones. True, Scripture is filled with accounts of real battles fought with real weapons; but, as *Michtav M'Eliyahu* explains, each enemy which threatens Israel actually represents a particular spiritual defilement which challenges the sanctity of the Jewish nation. When Israel combats its enemies, the true battleground escapes the eye's detection, for the true battleground is located in the recesses of the Jewish soul. It is in this invisible arena that the forces of sanctity battle the challenging forces of defilement. To the extent that Israel succeeds in its spiritual conflict, it will succeed in the material one, for the physical battleground only *reflects* the metaphysical one. Only if Israel is able to extirpate the defilement foisted upon it will it be able to vanquish its military foes.

Nearly one-half of the *Book of Joshua* contains descriptions of battles and the preparations for war. According to *Meiri* (Introduction to *Psalms)*, a book of Tanach was assigned to the Prophets only if several conditions were met. One prerequisite was that the prophet must have been sent either to admonish the Israelites to repent of their evil ways or to guide them in matters of war. One justification for canonizing the *Book of Joshua* in the Prophets, writes *Meiri*, was that Joshua provided the Israelites with guidance for their victories over their enemy.

Although it might seem that a general would be the commander most likely to insure military success, God assigned a prophet to lead the Jews in their campaign against the Canaanites. Clearly, a war which requires a prophet is a war of the soul, not of the state. Let us, then, investigate the spiritual challenge which Joshua faced.

The License to Kill

Value is a relative concept. It has been said that if the human body, ninety per cent of which is composed of water, were reduced to its constituent chemicals, it would be worth $3.86 before inflation. That, of course, is from the point of view of the cold-eyed chemist. A person's boss may estimate his employee's worth by calculating how much it would cost to hire and retrain his replacement. To the person's family he is invaluable.

From the Torah's point of view, however, each man is of infinite value. If faced with the ghastly choice of killing another person or letting oneself be killed, the Torah demands passivity. The *Talmud* succinctly states, 'Who says that your blood is redder (i.e., of greater value)? Perhaps his blood is redder!' Even in a situation where the inhabitants of an entire city can save their lives only by sacrificing the life of one of their fellow citizens, the Torah mandates passivity, even if all will die as a result. Since the Torah places infinite value on each individual, by definition the value of several persons cannot exceed the value of one. One infinity and one thousand infinities are equally large.

Yet, the *Book of Joshua* chronicles the wholesale slaughter of the Seven Canaanite Nations. How can the Torah countenance, let alone command, such destruction of human life? How can this campaign of extermination be reconciled with the principle of sanctity of human life?

The answer is that a life has value only insofar as it bears the imprint of the Divine. Man was created in the *image of God,* and it is this *image* which confers value upon the substance of his body. If an individual is irrevocably entrenched in behavior which denies the very existence and authority of the Divine, he reverts to a mere clod of chemicals. Thus, *Ramban (Genesis* 34:13) explains, Simeon and Levi were justified in their decimation of Shechem after that city countenanced the violation of their sister Dinah. Since the city of Shechem was rife with idolatry and licentiousness, *Ramban* writes, *the blood of its inhabitants was considered as water.* The inhabitants of Shechem, like the Canaanites, were regarded chemically because they had degraded themselves spiritually.

> *Therefore, it shall be, when* HASHEM *your God has given you rest from all your neighboring enemies in the Land which* HASHEM *your God gives you for an inheritance ... you shall blot out the remembrance of Amalek from under the heaven (Deuteronomy* 25:19).

Amalek and the Seven Nations

Israel was charged with three mitzvos upon entering the Land: appointing a king, destroying the seed of Amalek, and building the Holy Temple *(Sanhedrin* 20b). According to the *Midrash (Pesikta Rabbasi* 12), Joshua planned to fulfill the mitzvah of exterminating Amalek, but was told by God to refrain, for this mitzvah was reserved for King Saul, who would encounter Amalek in the future. Joshua's assignment was limited to destroying the Seven Nations — the Hittites, Girgashites, Emorites, Canaanites, Perizzites, Hivvites, and Jebusites — in fulfillment of the Biblical commandment, *'You shall utterly destroy them' (Deuteronomy* 7:2). The Torah repeats this commandment in *Deuteronomy* 20:17 and adds a negative commandment: *'You shall not let any* [*Canaanite*] *soul live' (Deuteronomy* 20:16). From the verse in *Deuteronomy* which discusses the mitzvah of destroying Amalek, it would appear that the campaign against Amalek was to commence only after the threat posed by the Seven Nations had been removed. *'When ... God has given you rest from all your neighboring enemies (the Seven Nations) ... you shall blot out ... Amalek.'* What spiritual threats did these nations pose, that they needed to be subdued before Amalek?

The Torah itself explains why it is imperative to exterminate the Seven Nations: *'that they do not teach you to do all their abominations which they have done to their gods' (Deuteronomy* 20:18). *Rambam (Sefer HaMitzvos)* identifies these Seven Nations as 'the root of all idolatry' in the world. They denied the existence of God and were guilty of inhuman practices. The Jews who were charged with destroying them were the children of the generation which stood at the foot of Mount Sinai. Although they themselves had personally experienced God's protection and miraculous sustenance in the Wilderness, their faith in God could not be relied upon to protect them from the idolatrous influences and the ungodly ways of the Canaanite nations. Living in their vicinity carried high risks — they could become influenced. The Jews physical proximity to idolaters would have bred spiritual propinquity. Mingling with the Canaanites, they would have lost sight of their lofty historical mission and God's 'lamplight unto the nations' — the Jews — would have been extinguished. Even such a generation of spiritual giants could not have remained indefinitely immune to the attitudes and philosophies about them, for osmotically, alien philosophies trespass values. As *Rambam* rules, if a person lives in a country where the inhabitants exhibit reprehensible conduct, he is required to move to a better environment. If none is to be found, he must even live in isolation in a cave or a wilderness *(Hil. De'os* 6:1).

The Jews would have been particularly vulnerable to idolatrous influences because their emergence as a nation had taken place in the murky environment of Egypt, whose blood and demon cults had left an imprint upon them. Having become habituated to idolatry, the Jews were constantly tormented with the desire to return to it even though they had experienced the verity of God at Mount Sinai. To dwell among idolaters in *Eretz Yisrael* could therefore have posed a challenge beyond their ability to withstand.

In fact, Joshua was not entirely successful in routing all the Canaanites (see *Commentary* to 13:1), and successive generations of Jews suffered because of it. *Ha'amek Davar (Deuteronomy* 31:16) isolates two distinct periods of idolatry in Israel's history: the period of the Judges and the period of the monarchies in Israel and Judah. The Jews' participation in idolatry during the period of the Judges was directly attributable to the influence of the Seven Nations. Allegorically, he explains that:

> Israel is often compared to a woman ... There was once a woman who truly loved her husband, and her husband

returned her love and provided for all her needs. But, because she had previously been morally loose, she occasionally succumbed to her former habits when she saw her friends do the same. Naturally, her husband became infuriated, distanced himself from her, and withdrew his support. Since her husband remained distant from her, she felt that he was not merely reacting to her provocation, but that indeed he hated her. This, in turn, prompted her to continue her unfaithful ways. Of course, she should have explained to her husband that her weakness in the face of temptation was due to her association with immoral friends, and asked his forgiveness for her improprieties. However, since she interpreted her husband's aloofness as hatred, she expanded her infidelity, claiming that she was a victim of her husband's callousness.

Thus it was in the days of the Judges. The Jews' original involvement with idolatry was due to their proximity to the Seven Nations, for the people did not heed Joshua's admonition, *And now remove the strange gods which are among you (Joshua* 24:23). Their infidelity to God was comparable to marital infidelity, and God distanced Himself from the Jews. This, however, even led the Jews to practice the idolatry of the people not in the Seven Nations.

Joshua's conquest of the Land was to be followed by the second stage in the Jew's extirpation of evil: the elimination of Amalek. It is important to analyze the spiritual challenge which this nation posed to the Jews.

Amalek

Just before receiving the Torah, the Jews were attacked by the nefarious nation of Amalek, and Moses appointed Joshua to lead Israel's defense. Scripture observes: *When Moses held up his hand, Israel prevailed; when he let his hand down, Amalek prevailed (Exodus* 17:11). Pondering the import of Scripture's observation, the *Mishnah (Rosh HaShanah* 29a) incredulously asks, 'Was it Moses' hands that won or lost the battle?' The reply is, 'As long as Israel looked heavenward and subjugated their heart to their Father in Heaven, they would prevail; but when they did not, they would fail.'

Although military strategy would dictate that soldiers should not divert their eyes from the battleground, Israel looked to Heaven, directing prayers to God *(Chasam Sofer).* They were not oblivious to the danger before them; they understood that the challenge which their enemy presented was fundamentally spiritual.

Amalek, *R' Hirsch* explains, delighted in the military might and prowess of other nations, for their systems of defense paid implicit tribute to Amalek's own philosophy, which exalted the unfettered exercise of physical power. Amalek believed the world is governed solely by the power of the sword, and he attempted to impose his power and his philosophy on all mankind. By attacking the Israelites soon after the Exodus, Amalek not only sought to prove his military superiority over Pharoah (who had suffered defeat at the hands of the Jews), but he also intended to discredit the Jewish principle of Divine providence. Amalek and his heirs abhor the Jews precisely because the Jews do *not* believe in the power of the sword. Amalek recognized that the Jewish people who appealed to God, a power far above the sword's reach, utterly scorned the basis of his *Weltanschauung.* To protect his world view, he unleashed his might in an unprovoked conflict at a time when the Israelites were most vulnerable.

For the Israelites to have defended themselves in a conventional military manner would have been a vindication of the very ideology which Amalek personified, for Amalek held that God cannot intervene in human affairs and that man's own actions and physical force are always efficacious. Amalek challenged Israel on one of the cardinal points of its faith, for Judaism propounds that God not only created the world, but is also continuously involved in its affairs. God, not the sword, therefore, determines the outcomes of wars. To implant this tenet of Judaism in Israel's soul, God unleashed Amalek as His agent upon the Jews. Israel needed to internalize that their success in temporal affairs was entirely dependent upon God.

Amalek descended from Esau, who will remain Israel's archenemy until the days of the Messiah. Amalek shared his progenitor's traits, the most salient of which was articulated by the sightless Isaac when he sought positive identification of Esau, before bestowing his blessings upon him. To identify Esau, Isaac understood that one must test the hands: *'The voice is the voice of Jacob, but the hands are the hands of Esau' (Genesis* 27:22).

How one regards the results of his labor is a critical religious issue. For example, when a person starts a business, and it becomes very

successful, does he say, *'My power and the might of my hand have gotten me this wealth' (Deuteronomy* 8:17)? Or, does he recognize his success as an expression of God's will and see his own efforts merely as a prerequisite for the fulfillment of the Divine decree? Esau and Amalek lived by the sword because they denied God's intervention in the world. They lived by the sword because they believed that man's might alone forged his destiny.

Moses, however, instructed the people to look heavenward and prayed for God's intervention. He sought to topple Amalek's *Weltanschauung* through the very instrument Amalek regarded as the source of his success — his hands. Moses' hands were raised in supplication, in the attitude of a slave beseeching his master. He recognized that human hands are merely instruments by which God can express His will. To be victorious over Amalek, the Jews needed to internalize this belief. When they did, their physical threat vanished.

The Essence of Judaism

The *Rishonim* (early commentators) attempted to distill Judaism to its essence. What is a Jew required to believe? *Rambam* listed thirteen principles of faith which a Jew must believe in order to have a share in 'the Torah of Moses.' His list became popularized, forming the basis of the synagogue hymn, *Yigdal.* R' Yosef Albo, in his *Sefer HaIkkarim,* cites opinions of other authorities, some of whom claim that there are twenty-six tenets, and others who argue that there are only six. He, however, crystallized three principles of faith: God exists, He directs the world and metes out reward and punishment, and He authored the Torah. *Sefer HaIkkarim* contends that, in principle, *Rambam* may agree to his abstract, they only differ on how to identify a main tenet from a derivative.

These three essentials correspond to the three blessings which form the heart of the longest prayer of the yearly cycle, the *mussaf* of Rosh HaShanah:

□ The Blessing of Kingship is based on the first principle — the existence of God. Included in this blessing is the Aleinu prayer, the second paragraph of which expresses our desire to see God revealed on earth in all His splendor and to witness the elimination of idolatry so that all mankind will recognize only His sovereignty.

□ The Blessing of Remembrance is based on the second principle — God's providence and reward and punishment. God did *not* withdraw after He created the world, allowing it to run on its own. Rather, He remains immanent, constantly aware of man's behavior. He directs the course of history and reacts, so to speak, to man's deeds by meting out reward and punishment. 'Remembering,' in this context, does not mean the opposite of 'forgetting,' since God is omniscient. Rather, 'remembering' means judgment; God considers all the actions of each individual and acts on that information by deciding the nature of his next year.

□ The Blessing of Shofaros (ram's horns) is based on the third principle — God's authorship of the Torah. God disclosed His design and plan for mankind by revealing His will at Mount Sinai. Since that event was orchestrated with a unique and deafening shofar blast, the blessing is called Shofaros. The main part of this blessing is the narrative of the Torah's transmission as recorded in Scripture.

The forces in man to rebel against these principles beat hard within the human breast; the Seven Nations and Amalek represent these forces. The Seven Nations constituted 'the root of idolatry' in the world, for they denied the supremacy of God. Joshua's mission in the conquest was, in the words of the Aleinu prayer, 'to rectify the world [in its understanding] of God's sovereignty so that all mankind call [God] by His Name, and all the wicked of the earth turn to [Him].' Joshua articulated this sublime objective when he composed the Aleinu prayer during the Conquest (see *footnote* to 6:15).

Establishment, Then Perfection

The Midrash declares that אֵין שְׁמוֹ שָׁלֵם וְאֵין כִּסְאוֹ שָׁלֵם 'Israel's perception of His Name and the majesty of His throne could never be complete until Amalek was erased from the face of the earth' (*Pesikta Rabbasi* 12). Amalek's sin was not a denial of God's existence, for that would have totally obscured Israel's vision of His throne. Rather, it was a denial of God's ability to intervene in the world. One who lives in an abandoned castle, no matter how regal it may be, is not concerned about abusing the interior if he feels certain that the king will never return. Amalek felt no need to restrain his aggressiveness, for he

believed that he could never be held accountable for his behavior. Joshua, who was the first to encounter Amalek under Moses' auspices, planned to obliterate Amalek's presence in the Land as soon as the Israelites entered. However, the *Midrash* says he was told by God to concentrate on the Seven Nations. God's throne had *first* to be established, *before* it could be made complete. The Seven Nations must be leveled before Amalek.

Three Proclamations Denied

But even the Seven Nations which lay in the quagmire of idolatry were given the opportunity to lift themselves and reestablish their connection with the Divine image. Before Joshua entered *Eretz Yisrael,* he sent three proclamations to the Canaanites. The first announced that the Land's inhabitants were at liberty to flee *Eretz Yisrael* to avoid the Jews' imminent onslaught. In fact, the Girgashites fled to Africa, and some other Canaanites escaped to Germany *(Radak, Obadiah* 1:20). His second communique informed the Canaanites that those who wished to remain in the Land could do so if they were willing to become servants to the Israelites. None of them chose to do so, although the Gibeonites had a change of heart after they witnessed the Israelites' successes; then they devised an elaborate ruse in order to join Israel's ranks (see Chapter 9). The third proclamation announced that the Jews were about to enter the Land and that the only course open to the Canaanites at this point was to fight in battle *(Rambam, Hil. Melachim* 6:5).

As Rachav reported to the spies (2:12), all the Canaanites had heard how God had protected the Jews at the Sea of Reeds and had enabled them to defeat the mighty kingdoms of Sichon and Og. The Canaanites were terrified of Israel, yet they chose to go to their death clutching their idols rather than to admit the existence of the true God. Their blood remained water.

'Do not ask,' writes *Sefer HaChinuch,* 'why God created these evil nations, if their end was to be wiped off the face of the earth. Everyone is capable of becoming either righteous or evil; God does not create him that way. Since these nations became so egregiously wicked, they deserved death and obliteration.'

'Man's true enemy,' writes *Chovos HaLevavos,* 'lies beneath his ribs.' In the first half of the *Book of Joshua,* Joshua was simultaneously engaged in two battles, although there was only one battleground. Faced with the challenge of the Seven Nations,

The Real Conquest

Joshua had to combat any slight desire or inclination for idolatry that might exist within the nation. As king of the Israelites (see *footnote* to 1:7), Joshua's spiritual struggles had repercussions that stretched far beyond the perimeter of his own soul. In explaining the special strictures which the Torah imposes upon the Jewish king, *Rambam* writes: 'the heart of the king is the collective heart of the entire congregation of Israel' *(Hil. Melachim* 3:6). To the extent that Joshua succeeded in his attempts to uproot any inclination that would deny the existence of God, the entire spiritual level of the Israelites would be lifted, and the enemy, both within and without, would fall.

From his very birth man has been drafted into war, the war between his passions and the fear of God. God programed man with many natural fears. The infant recoils at a loud noise, the child at the sight of a large animal, and an adult at an uncontrolled blaze.

Every Man A 'Warrior'

These instinctive reactions serve to protect man from harm. However, God did not instill in man an innate fear of the *spiritually* harmful, for this would have removed man's free will; then, he would have had no choice but to perform God's will *(Kochvei Ohr).*

We may not understand the overwhelming desire that man once had for idolatry; we have been saved from that war through the foresight of the Sages, who prayed for the removal of those urges from Israel's heart. Before the era of the Second Temple, however, the proclivity for idol worship was very strong. Consequently, Joshua's war against the ideology of the Canaanites represented a formidable spiritual challenge to the Jewish nation.

This Book of Torah is not to leave your mouth (1:8). This refers to the *Book of Deuteronomy* which was the

signet of Joshua. At the time that God appeared to Joshua, He found him sitting with the *Book of Deuteronomy* in his hand. God said to him, *'Strengthen yourself, Joshua, persist Joshua, this Book of Torah is not to leave your mouth' (Bereishis Rabbah* 6).

The *Midrash* relates that before God charged Joshua to implement the long awaited Divine plan for bringing the Israelites into the Land and uprooting its inhabitants, Joshua was deeply immersed in Torah study; his text, the *Book of Deuteronomy.* Joshua was preparing for the real war he was about to fight.

Deuteronomy: Lodestar of the Soul

The *Book of Deuteronomy* is different from the other books of the *Pentateuch.* In Hebrew, *Deuteronomy* is called *Devarim,* because it contains words of expostulation *(divrei tochachah)* whose purpose is to bind the hearts of Israel to the Torah.

The impact of this *Book* has been compared to the tefillin worn on the arm, for it contains the essence of the four prior *Books,* just as the tefillin of the arm contains one compartment with four scrolls. And as the tefillin of the arm is bound across from the heart, so the *Book of Deuteronomy* draws the Jewish soul more immediately to God, more immediately than the other *Books* of the Pentateuch *(Chidushei HaRim).* Moses' poignant pleas and ringing revilements served as Joshua's source of spiritual fortification, his *sefer mussar.* As Joshua studied the *Book of Deuteronomy,* he perfected the armaments with which he would wage war on behalf of the first principle of faith — the existence of God. God then appeared and bade Joshua to strengthen himself for the upcoming war and to retain the fear of God which he had acquired through studying the *Book of Deuteronomy.*

Behold I send My messenger, and he shall clear the way before Me; and the Lord Whom you seek shall suddenly come to His temple (Malachi 3:1).

The Messiah will come when the obstacles in his path are removed, when the evildoers perish *(Rashi).* The task of clearing the Messiah's path was assigned to the tribe of Joseph. Joseph,

as the extension of his father Jacob, sought to use this world as a vehicle for the sanctification of God's Name, not unlike an individual who designates an ordinary animal as a sacrifice to be offered in the Holy Temple and raises its status from the profane to the sublime. (This concept has been discussed in greater depth in the ArtScroll Overviews to *Sidrah Vayeishev* and *Vayigash, Bereishis,* Volumes 5 and 6.)

Messiah's Vanguard

In the Covenant Between the Parts, the Israelites were condemned to exile and were promised redemption. Later, Joseph became viceroy in Egypt; and, as a result of his policies during the famine, he was able to subjugate the entire Egyptian population, thereby paving the way for Israel's domination over Egypt at the time of the Exodus and the fulfillment of the promise, *They shall leave with great possessions (Genesis* 15:14). Similarly, it was Joshua, Joseph's descendant through Ephraim, who was called upon to prepare Israel for the final Redemption by fighting Israel's first battle, which was against Amalek, Esau's grandson. *Ramban (Exodus* 19:9) explains that the manner in which Moses and Joshua dealt with Amalek in that encounter will be repeated by Elijah and Mashiach ben Yosef (the Messiah from Joseph's line) in the Jews' ultimate encounter with Esau's seed.

Had Joshua been successful in his efforts to destroy the Seven Nations, the second stage of redemption would have been fully prepared so that King Saul could have revealed the perfection of God's throne by destroying Amalek, the nation who denies God's intervention in man's affairs. This would have cleared the path for the Messiah of Judah's line. But since Joshua and King Saul did not accomplish these goals, we must await the descendant of Joseph who will finally clear the path of its obstacles; then, *the Lord whom* [*we*] *seek shall suddenly appear in His temple.*

Rabbi Reuven Drucker
ר״ח ניסן תשמ״א

לזכר נשמת אחד מחברינו
הרב אריה ליב בן דוד ז״ל
שנקטף בדמי ימיו
י״א ניסן תשמ״א
והשאיר אחריו ברכה
יהי זכרו ברוך
ת.נ.צ.ב.ה.

לעילוי נשמת
ראובן שלמה בן פרידעל פישמאן הי״ד
נקטף בדמי ימיו ע״י רוצחים שונאי ישראל
כ״ו אייר ה׳ תשל״ח
נעשה קדוש בחייו, ונקרא קדוש במותו
בא ללמוד ונמצא מלמד
שקדן, למדן, עובד ה׳
יהי זכרו ברוך
ת.נ.צ.ב.ה.

לזכר נשמת הרבנית החשובה
מרת גאלדע פייגע רודרמאן ע״ה
בת הרב הגה״צ רב שבתי שפטיל קרמר זצוק״ל
אשת מרן הגאון שר התורה ראש הישיבה
דישיבת נר ישראל
חכמת נשים בנתה ביתה.
וחכמה ועמלה הצליחה לעזור לבעלה
מרן ראש הישיבה שליט״א
להקים אחד ממקומות התורה החשובים בעולם.
ת.נ.צ.ב.ה.

ספר יהושע

I

TRANSITION *is the prominent motif of the first chapter of the* Book of Joshua.

The scepter of Israel and the splendor of prophecy have passed from Moses to Joshua. This first chapter of the Prophets continues the Pentateuch's chronicle of the Jewish people and their quest for the Holy Land. Indeed, because Joshua *is the sequel to the Pentateuch, this chapter was selected as the* haftarah *reading for* Simchas Torah, *the holiday which marks the annual completion of the synagogue readings of the Pentateuch (see* Tosafos, Megilla *31a, s.v.* למחר).

The text could not be more explicit in building this theme of transition. In addition to the verses in the first chapter which exactly parallel verses from Deuteronomy *(vs. 3,4,5,9), the theme of transition is apparent from the chapter's hammering leitmotif* חֲזַק וֶאֱמָץ, Strengthen yourself and persevere, *which is urged upon Joshua three times by God and once by the tribes of Reuben, Gad, and Menashe. God's three exhortations are reminiscent of the three times Moses exhorted Joshua with the same words to realize his true potential (*Deuteronomy *3:28; 31:7; 31:23).*

But the connection between Deuteronomy *and* Joshua *is more profound than the repeated use of similar words. In fact, the words themselves connote the essential thematic transition.* Arizal *notes that the numerical value of the word* חֲזַק *(115) is one-third the value of Moses (*מֹשֶׁה *= 345). God's thrice-repeated command (*חֲזַק*) summoned Joshua to marshal all his spiritual resources in order to become like Moses, the nation's leader and prophet. As* Rambam (Hil. Teshuvah *5:2) explains:*

> *Do not think ... that God decrees upon a man's conception whether he will be righteous or evil ... merciful or brutal, etc. This is not so. Every man can be as righteous as Moses or as evil as Jeroboam ...*

When Moses died, Israel lost the quintessential Leader and Prophet of all time, the one who brought God's Torah from the Heavenly spheres to man on earth. And it was Moses who was told directly by the Almighty the spiritual course on which to lead Israel through the Wilderness. Who could replace him?

As explained in the Commentary *to 1:1 (s.v.* משרת משה*), Joshua was particularly well-suited to fill Moses' national position. The Midrash (*Bamidbar Rabbah *21) cites a verse to explain God's reason for choosing Joshua:* He who guards the fig tree eats of its fruit (Proverbs *27:18). This citation implies that Joshua had proven his worthiness by displaying such a dedication to Torah that no avenue of service was beneath his dignity. Thus, it was Joshua who straightened the chairs in the house of study and tended to all the needs of his teacher Moses.*

*One who attempts to absorb the totality of Torah solely through study is limited by the powers of his insight. Joshua studied diligently, but he also supported Torah with a pure devotion which transcended intellectual finitude, for a burning soul knows no limits (*R' Tzadok).

This is the Joshua whom God chose to convey His Word to the Jewish people. This is the Joshua whom the Jews accepted as their king (1:18).

א וַיְהִי אַחֲרֵי מוֹת מֹשֶׁה עֶבֶד יהוה וַיֹּאמֶר יהוה אֶל־יְהוֹשֻׁעַ בִּן־נוּן מְשָׁרֵת מֹשֶׁה

☙ God Appears to Joshua

1. וַיְהִי — *And it was.*

Rashi and *Metzudos* remark that the prefix ו, *and*, indicates that this passage is appended and directly related to the end of *Deuteronomy* which recounts the details of Moses' death: Because Moses had died, God spoke to Joshua, instructing him to assume the leadership of Israel. *Abarbanel* adds that the linking of these chapters informs us that Joshua received prophetic vision only upon Moses' demise. The verse would then be understood, *And it was* [only then] *upon the death of Moses that HASHEM spoke to Joshua ...*

[However, see *Ramban* to *Deuteronomy* 31:19 who indicates that Joshua became a prophet during Moses' lifetime.]

Radak maintains, however, that the ו is merely a convention of composition in the Hebrew language and does not necessarily signal a connection between passages. Otherwise, he argues, it would not always be possible to explain why many other books of Scripture begin with a ו.

אַחֲרֵי — *After.*

[Scripture uses two expressions for the adverb 'after,' אַחַר and אַחֲרֵי. *Rashi (Genesis* 15:1; 39:7) explains that the word אַחַר means *immediately following,* whereas the word אַחֲרֵי, as in our verse, means *following at some later time.* Hence, there was an interval between Moses' death and Joshua's first prophetic vision.]

[*Rashi* bases his translation on *Bereishis Rabbah* 44; however, the *Midrash* also cites a second opinion which contends that these definitions of אַחַר and אַחֲרֵי should be reversed. This would imply that the first prophecy of Joshua came immediately after the death of Moses.]

אַחֲרֵי מוֹת מֹשֶׁה — *After the death of Moses.*

Based on the chronology given in *Kiddushin* 38a, *Radak* (3:2) asserts that there was a thirty day interval between Moses' death and God's command to Joshua that Israel was to cross the Jordan, corresponding to the thirty day mourning period after Moses' death (see *Deuteronomy* 34:8). Accordingly, our verse should be understood, *after the mourning period for Moses had elapsed.* Following the Rabbinic dictum (*Shabbos* 30b) that the Divine Presence does not rest on a person while he is sad or distressed, it was not possible for Joshua to receive a prophecy until the mourning period had concluded.

Moses died on 7 Adar (*Megillah* 13b; *Kiddushin* 38a). [The year was 2488 after creation.] As given by *Kiddushin* 38a, and explained by *Rashi* and *Tosafos* there, the chronology of the major events is as follows:[1]

1. This chronology follows *Tosafos'* concluding explanation of *Rashi's* opinion. *Tosafos* reasons that a full thirty day mourning period was observed between Moses' death and the Divine communication to Joshua. Thus, since Moses died on 7 Adar, the thirty days (which include the day of Moses' death) ended on 7 Nissan. [This computation assumes that Adar had twenty-nine days, as is generally the case.] Israel crossed the Jordan on 10 Nissan (3:19). Therefore, when the marshals commanded the people to prepare themselves, *'Because in another three days you will cross this Jordan'* (v. 11), the implication could not be three *full* days of preparation with the crossing on the fourth day, for if so, the crossing would have taken place on 11 Nissan. This would contradict 3:19, which dates the crossing on the tenth. *Tosafos* explains, however, that the verse, *It was at the end of three days ...* (3:2), actually means at the close of the *second* day, which is, in reality, the beginning of the third day. *Tosafos* maintains that such usage is idiomatic in the Hebrew language, as found in the explanation given in *Arachin* 33a to the verse in *Jeremiah* 34:14. [Thus, in our case, the *end of three days* refers to the beginning of the third and last day of the three day period, i.e., the close of the second day.]

Tosafos cites a second opinion that God spoke to Joshua on 7 Nissan, the thirtieth day of the

1
1 [1] *And it was after the death of Moses, servant of*
HASHEM, that HASHEM said to Joshua son of

7 Adar	Moses died and the mourning period began.
6 Nissan	Reconnaissance mission (2:1) was dispatched [cf. first opinion of *Ralbag (v.* 10), *Vilna Gaon (v.* 11), and *Malbim (v.* 10)].
7 Nissan	Mourning period ended [*cf. Vilna Gaon (v.* 11) and *Sefer HaMiknah (Kiddushin* 38a) who contend that the mourning ended on 6 *Nissan*].
8 Nissan	God spoke to Joshua. Marshals told people to ready themselves to cross the Jordan in three days *(v.* 11).
9 Nissan	Joshua told the people to prepare themselves (3:5).
10 Nissan	Jews crossed the Jordan (3:19).

עֶבֶד ה' — *Servant of HASHEM.*

Radak notes that the term *servant of HASHEM* is reserved for those people who direct all their energies and mold all their motivations toward the service of God, even in the realm of mundane matters. Others so described are Abraham *(Genesis* 26:24) and David *(II Samuel* 3:18).

The word עֶבֶד literally means *slave.* In common parlance the title 'slave' is the lowest designation a person could receive, since it implies that he has lost that which separates man from the animals — namely, his free will. In regard to his relationship with God, however, it is the most noble of titles, for it indicates that the person has risen to the loftiest of spiritual levels and realizes that he is totally dependent upon God *(Daas Sofrim).*

Sifri [*Deuteronomy* 34:5] states in regard to Moses: The title of עֶבֶד, *servant,* is not a derogatory appellation; on the contrary, it is a citation of rare merit. Thus we see the earlier prophets were called עֲבָדִים, *servants,* as it says: *Surely HASHEM will do nothing, without revealing His secret to His servants, the prophets (Amos* 3:7).[2]

Malbim suggests that Moses is called

mourning period. This is in accordance with the Talmudic principle that part of a day can be considered as equivalent to an entire day in some cases *(Pesachim* 4a). [This principle is commonly followed in the practices of mourning. Thus, the initial period of mourning is concluded on the morning of the seventh day.]

Sefer HaMiknah notes, however, that this view is difficult in light of the verse in *Deuteronomy* 34:8: *And the days of weeping and mourning for Moses were ended.* The word וַיִּתְּמוּ, *were ended,* derives from the word תְּמִים which means *whole* or *complete* (see *Menachos* 66a on *Leviticus* 23:15). This would imply that thirty full days had elapsed. To reconcile this discrepancy he postulates that Adar had thirty days that year instead of the usual twenty-nine, as had originally been assumed by *Tosafos.* According to *Sefer HaMiknah* the thirty day mourning period concluded on 6 Nissan and Joshua received his prophecy on 7 Nissan.

When the marshals told the people, *'In another three days you will cross this Jordan (v.* 11), three *full* days are implied (8, 9, 10 Nissan). However, when Scripture says that Joshua spoke to the people three days after his prophetic vision (3:2), the three days include part of the day on which he received God's communication. [See *Rashi* to 1:10 who seems to concur with *Tosafos'* second explanation *(R' Simchah MiDessau).*]

2. *R' Yitzchak Hutner* explains this *Sifri* according to the *Talmud (Berachos* 34b):

After R' Chanina ben Dosa successfully prayed for the health of R' Yochanan ben Zakkai's son, R' Yochanan ben Zakkai, who was the leader of his generation, declared that if he had put his head between his knees the entire day and prayed, he would not have been answered. His wife asked him, 'Does that mean that R' Chanina is greater than you?'

He replied, 'No, he is like a servant before the king, and I am like a minister before the king.'

Rashi explains: A minister's official position subjects him to the restraints of protocol and formality. He cannot speak to the king whenever he pleases nor can he make unprompted

א ב ² לֵאמֹר: מֹשֶׁה עַבְדִּי מֵת וְעַתָּה קוּם עֲבֹר

God's servant even after his death, because a righteous person who has worked his whole life for the sake of his own and future generations is credited with all the future achievements that result from his original effort.

Meshech Chachmah notes that the Pentateuch describes three people as *My servant* — Abraham, Calev and Moses. The common denominator among them is that they never referred to any man as 'my master' or to themselves as 'your servant.' Joshua, however, is not entitled 'My servant,' because he referred to Moses as אֲדֹנִי מֹשֶׁה, *my master Moses (Numbers* 11:28). Aaron, too, referred to Moses as *my master (Numbers* 12:11).

יְהוֹשֻׁעַ — *Joshua.*

In *Numbers* 13:8,16 the Torah relates that Joshua had originally been named הוֹשֵׁעַ, *Hoshea.* Upon dispatching him as one of the spies who were sent to survey *Eretz Yisrael,* Moses added the letter י to Hoshea's name, changing it to *Yehoshua.* The best known reason for this addition is that given by *Rashi (Numbers* 13:16) citing the *Midrash. Rashi* explains that the י is connected with the next letter, ה, and spells one of God's names יָהּ. The remainder of Joshua's name (שֻׁעַ) means *salvation.* Before Joshua embarked on his assignment, Moses prayed: 'May God save you from sinning along with the spies.' [For a full explanation of this comment and for other explanations of Moses' change of Joshua's name, see commentaries to *Numbers* 13:16.]

בִּן־נוּן — *Son of Nun.*

[Joshua was a descendant of the tribe of Ephraim (see *Numbers* 13:8).]

Usually, the Hebrew word for 'son' is vocalized with a *segol,* בֶּן [*ben*], but in reference to Joshua we always find the word vocalized with a *chirik,* בִּן [*bin*]. Since both *bin* and *Nun* are words of a single syllable, they would inevitably be run together and pronounced like a single word. That being so, the *segol* [*ben*] was changed to a *chirik* [*bin*] to simplify the pronunciation; *bin-nun* is easier to say than *ben-nun (Radak).*

Ramban (Exodus 33:11) comments that *bin* was used so that the very pronunciation of Joshua's name could be understood as a title of honor for Moses' most outstanding disciple. The words *bin Nun* sound like the single word בִּינוּן, *binun,* which is synonymous with נָבוֹן, *understanding one,* as if to say that Joshua was unsurpassed in understanding. Alternatively, the pronunciation was meant as a prayer for Joshua: may this person who is בִּן [a short form of בִּינָה], *understanding,* be נוּן, *remembered forever* [from נִין, *a descendant*].

[According to this explanation it could be more easily understood why the name of Joshua's father is pronounced as Nun throughout Scripture, while in *I Chronicles* 7:27 it is pronounced *Non.* The verse in *Chronicles* speaks about the father, Non, and his name is therefore vocalized according to its true pronunciation. Everywhere else in Scripture, however, the reference is to

requests. A servant, however, by virtue of his lower status, has unlimited access to the king, even to his private chambers. The informality of his relationship enables him to speak to the king in ways and about things that a minister cannot. Consequently he — and someone like R' Chanina — can beseech the king for special favors at times when a minister cannot gain admittance.

Moses, despite his position as leader of Israel, was unique in that his access to God was unlimited. Accordingly, when the *Sifri* proclaims that the title עֶבֶד, *servant,* is not a derogatory expression, it means that the title *servant* does not denigrate Moses' princely piety or holiness. Rather, it refers to his ability to prophesy in the sense that he had unrestricted access to God and to the guarantee that God would not turn His eyes away from him.

When Moses died and this level of prophecy was withdrawn from mankind, the title 'servant' became an appellation of eminence and distinction *(Pachad Yitzchak, Shaar Chodesh Aviv).*

1 *Nun, Moses' attendant, saying,* [2] *'Moses My servant*
2 *has died. Now, arise! Cross this Jordan, you and all*

Joshua, and it is pronounced as the title of honor, which is homophonous with the *one who understands.*

On the basis of *Ramban's* explanation we can better understand why Joshua is never referred to as בִּן נוּן, *the one who understands,* before the giving of the Torah (see *Exodus* 17:9-14), for true understanding is possible only through Torah.]

מְשָׁרֵת מֹשֶׁה — *Moses' attendant.*

[Although Joshua is referred to as עֶבֶד ה', *HASHEM's servant,* in the final chapter of *Joshua* (24:39), here he is referred to as מְשָׁרֵת מֹשֶׁה, *Moses' attendant.*]

Because Joshua devotedly served Moses, he merited both prophetic vision and the highest position of national leadership[1] *(Malbim).*

לֵאמֹר — *Saying.*

According to *Radak,* the expression לֵאמֹר indicates that the prophecy which follows should be said to the nation of Israel. Thus, our verse should be understood: *HASHEM said to Joshua, 'Say to the nation of Israel that Moses My servant ...'*

Ramban (Exodus 6:10) argues, however, that many verses could not be reconciled according to this explanation. For example, *HASHEM spoke to Moses,* לֵאמֹר, *saying, 'Speak to the people of Israel and say to them.'* (See further, 20:1.) If the word לֵאמֹר, *saying,* implies 'to Israel' then the second stich is redundant. *Ramban* contends that *saying* means that God spoke to Joshua with perfect clarity, without mere hints or vague expression (cf. *R' Bachya* to *Exodus* 13:1; see also ArtScroll *Bereishis* 1:22).

Vilna Gaon contends that the expression *saying* is merely Scripture's way of beginning a direct quotation.

2. מֹשֶׁה עַבְדִּי מֵת — *Moses My servant has died.*

Why was it necessary to include a universally known fact in a prophetic revelation?

Rashi considers this phrase to be a preface, indicating that Joshua was a second choice for leading the mission. The force of the statement is: *Moses My servant has died,* but had he been alive I would have preferred him for this assignment.

Ralbag comments that Moses would have been preferable because he was able to completely vanquish his enemies (e.g., Sichon and Og), whereas Joshua was unable to do so (see *Commentary* to 13:1). Moses could not be the Israelites' leader at this time because of God's decree to the contrary when Moses hit the rock *(Numbers* 20:11-12). Additionally, the Israelites were no longer worthy of Moses' leadership due to the sin they committed by accepting the slanderous report of the reconnaissance mission (see *Prefatory Remarks* to Chapter 2).

Malbim identifies these words as a causative phrase. Only because Moses is no longer alive could Joshua lead Israel into *Eretz Yisrael.* While Moses was living, there were two reasons why Joshua could not do so: (a) Joshua could not assume leadership during Moses' lifetime; (b) even if Joshua had been able to replace Moses, Israel could not have entered the Land because God had made an oath that Moses could not cross the Jordan [see *Numbers* 20:12, 13]. Upon Moses' death both impediments to Joshua's mission were removed.

מֵת — *Has died.*

The verb מֵת has been rendered in the past perfect tense: *has died.*

Scripture uses two ways to express the past tense: the future tense of the Hebrew verb [e.g., יָמוּת, *he will die*] preceded by the conversive ו [וַיָּמָת]

1. The *Talmud (Berachos* 7b) declares that serving a scholar whose total character is molded by Torah (a *talmid chacham)* is more important than the study of Torah itself. *Maharsha* explains that while students may learn from their teachers many *halachos* regarding theoretical

אֶת־הַיַּרְדֵּן הַזֶּה אַתָּה וְכָל־הָעָם הַזֶּה אֶל־ א
הָאָרֶץ אֲשֶׁר אָנֹכִי נֹתֵן לָהֶם לִבְנֵי ג
ג יִשְׂרָאֵל: כָּל־מָקוֹם אֲשֶׁר תִּדְרֹךְ כַּף־

denotes the simple past [*he died*]; the past tense of the Hebrew verb [מֵת,] denotes the past perfect tense [*he has died*] (see *Rashi, Genesis* 4:1; *Malbim,* v. 12).

וְעַתָּה קוּם — *(And) now, arise!*

According to *Abarbanel,* this exclamation *'arise!'* should be taken literally, for Joshua had been seated in a position of mourning. By saying, *'Now, arise!'* God commanded him to end the mourning period because one may not mourn for more than thirty days.

Radak, however, contends that the verb קוּם should be understood idiomatically as an expression of exhortation and as connected to the imperative which follows: 'Rise up and cross this Jordan.' [Based on this interpretation the word *now* cannot refer to the immediate present, since we find in verse 11 that Joshua commanded the officers to inform the people that they would be leaving within three days. Surely, if God commanded that they must cross immediately, Joshua would not have delayed! So the command must have been: *And 'soon' rise up! and cross this Jordan.* We find other places where the word עַתָּה means *soon.* For example, *Then HASHEM said to Moses,* 'עַתָּה *you shall see what I will do to Pharaoh, for with a strong hand he will let them go ...' (Exodus* 6:1). In this verse the word עַתָּה cannot mean 'now' for he did not release them until almost a year later.]

הַיַּרְדֵּן — *(The) Jordan.*

The Jordan received this name because the source from which this river *descended* was in the territory of *Dan.* יַרְדֵּן [*Yardein*], *Jordan,* is a contraction of two words: יָרַד [*yarad*] which means to *descend,* and דָּן, the tribe of *Dan (Bechoros* 55a).

[In Scripture things are often named on the basis of events which do not occur until later. Thus, the Jordan received its name even before the birth of Dan (see *Commentary* to 19:47. See also *Kesubos* 10b; *Genesis* 13:10-11).]

הַזֶּה — *This.*

The adjective *this* does not necessarily indicate that the Jordan was visible to Joshua at that moment. The word 'this' can also refer to something that is in close proximity. For example, Moses asked to see *this mountain (Deuteronomy* 3:25). The Sages say (see *Rashi)* that *this mountain* refers to Jerusalem, which Moses certainly could not see from across the Jordan *(Sefer HaShorashim* from *Sfas Emes).*

Others understand *this* as a demonstrative adjective referring to something well-known, though not necessarily present (see *Rashi* to *v.* 4).

אַתָּה — *You.*

Even though Joshua was included in a general command to all the people, he was singled out and mentioned first, in accordance with the charge that God gave Moses in *Deuteronomy* 3:28, *'And you [Moses] should command Joshua*

situations, it is only when they observe their teachers' daily behavior that they understand how the Torah's precepts are brought to life. From *Maharsha's* explanation, it would follow that Joshua was well-qualified for leadership, because for many years he had been in attendance while Moses rendered halachic decisions.

However, this would not explain why Joshua attained the level of prophecy. *R' Mordechai Gifter* comments that one can be considered a true student of Torah only if he has subjugated his personal will to God's will. One who learns Torah and does not serve תַּלְמִידֵי חֲכָמִים, *Torah scholars,* has not subordinated himself to God because he has not absorbed the requirements of God's will as they are applied to everyday situations. By serving Moses, Joshua became a true student of Torah, and consequently could be a vessel for communicating God's words.

1 *this people, to the Land which I give to them, to the*
3 *Children of Israel.* [3] *Every place upon which the sole*

... *that he should cross before this people.'*

The *Yalkut* (7:5) declares: If [Joshua] will pass before them, they will possess the land, and if he will not, they will not possess it. Therefore, when Joshua remained [in the camp] and dispatched some of the people to campaign against Ai, the enemy killed thirty-six men.

אָנֹכִי נֹתֵן — *I give.*

According to *R' Hirsch* (see *Genesis* 7:4), the two pronouns for 'I', אָנֹכִי and אֲנִי, have different connotations: אָנֹכִי implies an intimate relationship, whereas אֲנִי implies a more distant one. [Since our verse refers to God by the more intimate form of 'I,' it could imply that even though the people received their inheritance through wars and battles, they were accompanied by a highly visible degree of Divine direction and guidance.]

[The pronoun אָנֹכִי can have another nuance. We find sometimes that it has a restrictive sense *I, and I alone,* such as *I am HASHEM, your God (Sforno, Exodus* 20:2). Therefore the force of this phrase would be, *I, and only I, am giving them this land.* Even though you are about to conquer the indigenous nations by military means, you should realize that it is only because of Me that you will be victorious.]

לָהֶם לִבְנֵי יִשְׂרָאֵל — *To them, to the Children of Israel.*

Since the leader of a conquest usually assumes ownership of newly acquired territory, God emphasized that the land would be given to the *entire nation (Malbim).*

Abarbanel explains that the phrase implies that the land would be given *to them* only so long as they are worthy of the title, *Children of Israel.*

Ramban in his commentary to *Exodus* 35:5 cites this verse as one of several examples in Scripture where a pronoun is immediately defined by a noun, and hence is not considered redundant in the Hebrew idiom. See *Exodus* 2:6, וַתִּרְאֵהוּ אֶת־הַיֶּלֶד, *she saw him, the child,* and *Jeremiah* 27:8, אֹתוֹ אֶת־נְבוּכַדְנֶאצַּר, *him, Nebuchadnezzar.*

The word עַם, *people,* is a generic term which includes both Jews from birth and converts. *Eretz Yisrael,* however, was divided only among Jews from birth. Accordingly, the qualification *to the Children of Israel* limits the word *them* to indicate the recipients of the inherited land *(HaRav Gifter).*

3. כָּל־מָקוֹם אֲשֶׁר תִּדְרֹךְ כַּף־רַגְלְכֶם בּוֹ — *Every place upon which the sole of your foot will march.*

Alshich comments that God said: 'I realize that you will not be able to acquire the entire outlined territory, but I assure you that in the future you will surely extend to these reaches.' In fact, this occurred during the reign of David.

The verse seems to imply that the boundaries of *Eretz Yisrael* were dependent upon the initiative of the Israelites. Why then does the next verse explicitly detail the land and its borders? *Rashi, Radak,* and *Abarbanel* offer three different approaches to reconcile this apparent contradiction.

Rashi comments that this verse could not refer to *Eretz Yisrael* proper, since the following verse defines the land's exact boundaries; therefore, this verse serves (a) to equate the sanctity of the territory outside of *Eretz Yisrael* that Israel might eventually conquer, with the holiness of the land itself; and (b) to give Israel a legal claim to the ownership of this additional territory.[1]

Radak understands the boundaries mentioned in verse 4 as defining the territory mentioned in this verse. 'Now

1. It was not permissible, however, to conquer territory outside *Eretz Yisrael* until the entire land itself had been conquered *(Sifri).* This is why Sumaria, the territory which King David conquered before the entire land had come into Jewish possession, did not receive the sanctity of the Holy Land. (See also *Tosafos, Gittin* 8a, s.v. כבוש יחיד.)

א רַגְלְכֶם בּוֹ לָכֶם נְתַתִּיו כַּאֲשֶׁר דִּבַּרְתִּי
ד אֶל־מֹשֶׁה: ד מֵהַמִּדְבָּר וְהַלְּבָנוֹן הַזֶּה וְעַד־
הַנָּהָר הַגָּדוֹל נְהַר־פְּרָת כֹּל אֶרֶץ הַחִתִּים
וְעַד־הַיָּם הַגָּדוֹל מְבוֹא הַשָּׁמֶשׁ יִהְיֶה

that you are about to cross the Jordan, I will give you the strength to conquer the entire land; any part of *Eretz Yisrael* upon which you set foot will be yours. And what are the boundaries of that land? *From the desert and this Lebanon to ...'*

Abarbanel suggests that this verse does not intend to define the boundaries of Israel's future territory. Rather, from the previous verse one might have thought that God would fight all the battles necessary for the acquisition of the land and that the people would not need to exert any effort. Therefore, it was necessary to inform them that they must proceed with utmost alacrity because their success *depends upon their* participation.

לָכֶם נְתַתִּיו כַּאֲשֶׁר דִּבַּרְתִּי אֶל־מֹשֶׁה — *I have given to you, as I have spoken to Moses.*

[This statement refers to *Deuteronomy* 11:24: *Every place upon which the sole of your foot will march will be yours.* Moses employed the future tense, *will be yours,* whereas God's prophecy to Joshua used the past tense, *I have given to you.* The reason for the difference lies in the nature of the territory being discussed. The territory included in *Eretz Yisrael* proper was described to Abraham (see *Genesis* 15:18, with *Ramban)* with prescribed borders. Moses, however, informed the people that their boundaries could be extended as God's reward for scrupulous observance of the commandments. Thus, in addition to the land given Abraham, the nation would be permitted to annex territory that would then acquire the legal status of the original borders (see *Ramban, Deuteronomy* 11:24). In *Deuteronomy* the future tense is used because that is the first time such annexed territory is mentioned. Since here God refers to the promise already given to Moses, He uses the past tense.

Perhaps the change of verbs from *be* to *give* can be explained in a similar fashion. Whenever mention is made of the land promised to Abraham, the verb *give* is used because title to that territory had already been given to Abraham; it remained only for Israel to conquer it. In the case of additional territory, the land had not been *given* but could *be* a part of *Eretz Yisrael* depending on the judgment of the monarch and the concurrence of the Sanhedrin.]

4. מֵהַמִּדְבָּר וְהַלְּבָנוֹן הַזֶּה — *From the desert and this Lebanon.*

The desert refers to the Desert of Kadesh, also called the Desert of Tzin, on the *southeastern* border of Israel, through which the people entered the Land *(Rashi).*

Radak, however, suggests that this is the Desert of Sin which forms the southern border of the Land. *Haamek Davar (Deuteronomy* 11:24) maintains that this is the eastern boundary.

This Lebanon refers to a known area [in the north of] *Eretz Yisrael (Radak). This* implies that they were in close proximity to this region, which is clearly not the case since they were still stationed on the eastern flank of the Jordan River. *Radak* suggests that the demonstrative adjective *this* is employed either because the Lebanon region was visible from the Israelites' encampment or because it was a well-known place, not necessarily within view.

Vilna Gaon, however, contends that *Lebanon* was located in the southeastern section of *Eretz Yisrael* where the Israelites were stationed, and thus Scripture refers to it as *this.*

T'vuos HaAretz questions *Vilna*

1 *of your foot will march I have given to you, as I have*
4 *spoken to Moses.* [4] *From the desert and this Lebanon*
to the great river, the Euphrates River, all the land of
the Hittites to the Mediterranean Sea westward will

Gaon's comment, for he never found any reference mentioning that the Lebanon mountains were located in the southern section of *Eretz Yisrael.* He suggests that the word *this* modifies Lebanon since it was relatively closer to Joshua's position than the Euphrates River, which is mentioned further in the verse.

Metzudos explains that Lebanon is the name of a forest where cedar trees grew. He conjectures that the name comes from לְבָנָה, *white,* describing the color of the wood.

The locations mentioned in this verse [*the desert ... the Mediterranean Sea*] proceed from south to north and from east to west. [The directions were given relative to the position of the Israelites, who were then just outside the southeastern corner of the Land.]

It is not clear whether the boundaries mentioned in this verse refer to the boundaries of *Eretz Yisrael* proper *(Sifri; Rashi; Ramban)* or to the boundaries of the territory outside of Israel which they were permitted to acquire *(Haamek Davar, Deuteronomy* 11:24 and *Abarbanel;* see *Commentary* to v. 3).

According to the former opinion, the continuity of the verses is as follows: You may conquer land outside of the Land of Israel *(v.* 3) on the condition that the Land of Israel which is defined by the following borders *(v.* 4) is conquered first *(Malbim, Deuteronomy* 11:24). According to the latter opinion: You may conquer that territory outside of *Eretz Yisrael (v.* 3) which is circumscribed by the locations mentioned in verse 4.

הַנָּהָר הַגָּדוֹל נְהַר־פְּרָת — *The great river, the Euphrates River.*

This describes part of the *northern* border *(Rashi; Vilna Gaon).*

Rashi (Shavuos 47b) explains that the Euphrates was actually the smallest of the four rivers mentioned in *Genesis* 2:14, but in honor of its proximity to *Eretz Yisrael* it is called 'great' (see also *Rashi* to *Genesis* 15:18 and *Deuteronomy* 1:7).

כֹּל אֶרֶץ הַחִתִּים — *All the land of the Hittites.*

This formed *the northeastern* boundary of the Land *(Vilna Gaon).*

The land of the Hittites is not mentioned in the parallel verse in *Deuteronomy* 11:24. *Abarbanel* explains that the borders had to be detailed more precisely here for Joshua than for Moses, since Joshua would actually conquer the Land. For the same reason, the latter phrase *westward* (see below) was added to this verse.

וְעַד־הַיָּם הַגָּדוֹל מְבוֹא הַשָּׁמֶשׁ — *To the Mediterranean* [lit. *the great*] *Sea westward* [lit. *toward the going down of the sun*].

The Mediterranean Sea forms the *western* boundary of the Land.

The western boundary was not the coastline, however. According to the Sages (*Gittin* 8a), certain islands in the Mediterranean Sea are part of the Land. To ascertain which islands are included in the Land an imaginary line is drawn from the most northwesterly point of the Land (Turi Amanon) to the most southwesterly point (the River of Egypt). [The exact identity of these places is disputed; see ArtScroll *Yechezkel,* 47:15-19 for a discussion of the various opinions.] This line cuts through the Mediterranean, and any island between the line and the concave coast of *Eretz Yisrael* is considered part of the Land. [Perhaps the phrase *toward the going down of the sun* indicates that the Land continues westerly past the coast of the Mediterranean.]

Both the Euphrates and the Mediter-

א
ה־ז

ה גְּבוּלְכֶם: לֹא־יִתְיַצֵּב אִישׁ לְפָנֶיךָ כֹּל יְמֵי
חַיֶּיךָ כַּאֲשֶׁר הָיִיתִי עִם־מֹשֶׁה אֶהְיֶה עִמָּךְ
ו לֹא אַרְפְּךָ וְלֹא אֶעֶזְבֶךָּ: חֲזַק וֶאֱמָץ כִּי
אַתָּה תַּנְחִיל אֶת־הָעָם הַזֶּה אֶת־הָאָרֶץ
ז אֲשֶׁר־נִשְׁבַּעְתִּי לַאֲבוֹתָם לָתֵת לָהֶם: רַק

ranean Sea are called *great* in this verse, whereas in *Deuteronomy* 11:24 (which is almost identical to this verse) these adjectives are omitted. *Abarbanel* explains that in Joshua's eyes these bodies of water were large, but in Moses' eyes they were small.

The Mediterranean is called *the* **great** *sea* in order to distinguish it from the other seas in *Eretz Yisrael,* such as the Dead Sea and the Kineret *(Radak).*

5. לֹא־יִתְיַצֵּב אִישׁ לְפָנֶיךָ — *No man will challenge* [lit. *stand before*] *you.*

God promised Joshua not only that no one else would become the leader of Israel during his lifetime, but also that no one would even challenge his leadership[1] *(Malbim),* as Korach challenged Moses' and Abshalom challenged King David's *(Alshich).*

According to *Sifri (Deuteronomy* 11:25), this verse is a guarantee that not only would no man challenge Joshua, but also no country, family, or sorcerer. The word *man* is employed to denote that even a man like Og, King of Bashan, [who was more of a threat than an entire nation *(Emek Netziv)*] would be no challenge.

Abarbanel observes that this promise reminded the people that the victory foretold in the previous verse would result from God's intervention, not from Israel's military prowess. No enemies would present a threat because He instilled them with a fear and dread of the Israelites. This is similar to *Deuteronomy* 11:25 where Moses was promised that as long as Israel observed the Torah *their* enemies would fear *them.* Furthermore, the promise was addressed specifically to Joshua, for only during his time — but not later — would the Canaanites fear Israel.

כֹּל יְמֵי חַיֶּיךָ — *All the days of your life.*

Abarbanel understands this expression to have emphatic stress. Only during his lifetime would Joshua be unequaled as a leader, but after his death, others would equal him. In regard to Moses, however, Scripture said *another such prophet would not arise in Israel (Deuteronomy* 34:10).

כַּאֲשֶׁר הָיִיתִי עִם־מֹשֶׁה אֶהְיֶה עִמָּךְ — *As I was with Moses so will I be with you.*

My Divine Presence will be manifest upon you through miracles and wonders, just as it was upon Moses *(Malbim).* [See *Commentary* to 3:7.]

As has been noted above, verses 3, 4, and 5 are similar to *Deuteronomy* 11:24-25. By repeating to Joshua the words He had spoken to Moses, God implicitly compares the two men and thereby renders great tribute to Joshua. Joshua and Moses were similar in that both clearly recognized that their salvation in war came only from God *(Abarbanel)*

[The comparison between the two becomes more vivid when we consider that the very expression אֶהְיֶה עִמָּךְ, *I will be with you (Exodus* 3:12) was said to Moses when God guaranteed him that he would be successful in his mission to

1. The *Talmud* [*Sanhedrin* 8a commenting on *Deuteronomy* 31:23] relates that God instructed Joshua to exercise great authority, saying, *For you shall bring them into the Land,* [even against their will; everything depends on you alone *(Rashi, Deuteronomy* 31:7)]; if necessary take a stick and beat them over the head. There can be only one leader of a generation, not two.

1
5-6

be your boundary. 5 No man will challenge you all
the days of your life. As I was with Moses so will I be
with you; I will not let you part from Me nor will I
abandon you. 6 Strengthen yourself and persevere
because you will cause this people to inherit the Land
which I have sworn to their fathers to give to them.

Pharaoh; see *Rashi ibid.*, second interpretation.]

Included in this promise was the guarantee that Joshua would live as long as Moses, 120 years. Because of Joshua's sin, ten years were deducted. [See *Commentary* to 23:1.]

לֹא אַרְפְּךָ — *I will not let you part from Me* [lit. *I will not let you get loose*].

The translation follows *Rashi (Deuteronomy* 4:31) who understands this verb to be in the *hiphil* [causative] conjugation, literally meaning *I will not allow you to get loose from me.* [In our context, this is God's assurance that He would continue His firm support of Joshua's efforts.]

The *Vilna Gaon* interprets this as a promise that Joshua will be victorious in war.

וְלֹא־אֶעֶזְבֶךָּ — *Nor will I abandon you.*

If you sin, I will distance myself from you, but I will never abandon you *(Haamek Davar, Deuteronomy* 31:6).

Even after the war is over, My heavenly protection will be with you *(Sforno, ibid.)*.

Malbim understands these last two phrases respectively as reinforcements of the two promises made earlier in the verse.

◆§ Joshua is Exhorted

6. חֲזַק וֶאֱמָץ — *Strengthen yourself and persevere* [lit. *have courage*].

The translation follows *Malbim* who defines חֲזַק as a command to motivate oneself, while אֱמָץ charges one to translate his convictions into action.

According to *Vilna Gaon*, חֲזַק refers to strengthening the body and וֶאֱמָץ refers to strengthening one's emotions so that there is no fear.

Verses 6, 7, and 9 all contain this expression of exhortation. Here *Rashi* explains that God appealed to Joshua to exercise strong leadership in temporal affairs, such as the division of *Eretz Yisrael* among the tribes. *Abarbanel* points out that land division can be a very sensitive process, as we see in the case of the sons of Joseph (17:14).[1]

Malbim refers this command back to the first promise made in the preceding verse, that no man would challenge Joshua's authority. Joshua is told to *strengthen* himself because God's help will be commensurate with his own attempt to implement the Divine promise.

Abarbanel suggests that this verse qualifies a different part of the preceding verse: *as I was with Moses so will I be with you.* Lest Joshua think that even his level of prophecy would equal Moses', he is now told that his Divine assistance would equal that afforded Moses only to the extent needed to conquer the Land.

תַּנְחִיל — *Will cause ... to inherit.*

[This means that Joshua will distribute the Land.]

לַאֲבוֹתָם — *To their fathers.*

Fathers refers to the Patriarchs of the Jewish nation — Abraham, Isaac, and Jacob — since the oath mentioned in this verse was made to them.

7. רַק — *O that* [lit. *only*].

[The word רַק can have several

1. Moses' admonition to Joshua (see *Deuteronomy* 31:7) is almost identical to the one given here. *HaRav Gifter* based on *Rashi* to *Exodus* 19:24 notes that one needs encouragement and inspiration both before and during the fulfillment of a commandment.

א חֲזַק וֶאֱמַץ מְאֹד לִשְׁמֹר לַעֲשׂוֹת כְּכָל־
ח הַתּוֹרָה אֲשֶׁר צִוְּךָ מֹשֶׁה עַבְדִּי אַל־תָּסוּר
מִמֶּנּוּ יָמִין וּשְׂמֹאול לְמַעַן תַּשְׂכִּיל בְּכֹל
ח אֲשֶׁר תֵּלֵךְ׃ לֹא־יָמוּשׁ סֵפֶר הַתּוֹרָה הַזֶּה

meanings. Here it seems most appropriate to translate it as an introduction to a blessing, which is the way that *Ibn Janach* understands this expression in verse 17.]

Metzudos interprets רַק more literally: *Only strengthen yourself,* i.e., only if you strengthen yourself by keeping the Torah will you be an effective leader.

חֲזַק וֶאֱמָץ — *Strengthen yourself and persevere.*

Strengthen yourself in Torah study *(Maharsha)* and *persevere* in the performance of good deeds *(Berachos* 32b).

According to *Malbim* this verse refers to the second promise made in verse 5 *as I was with Moses so will I be with you,* which guarantees Joshua a close relationship with God. Great self-discipline was required of Joshua in order to be worthy of such intimacy.[1]

לִשְׁמֹר לַעֲשׂוֹת — *To observe* [lit. *to guard*], *to do.*

לִשְׁמֹר — *to observe* the negative commandments;

לַעֲשׂוֹת — *to do* the positive commandments *(Vilna Gaon).*

כְּכָל־הַתּוֹרָה — *According to all of the Torah.*

Your observance should not be according to your *personal understanding,* but rather according to the dictates of the Torah *(Malbim).*

אַל־תָּסוּר מִמֶּנּוּ — *Do not deviate from him.*

The difficulty in translating this expression lies in identifying the antecedent of מִמֶּנּוּ, a masculine pronoun that may mean either *from him* or *from it.* [In Hebrew the neuter pronoun does not exist; 'it' is either masculine or feminine, depending on the gender of the antecedent.] From the context, the antecedent would seem to be *Torah;* however, *Torah* is feminine.

The translation follows *Radak* who suggests that מִמֶּנּוּ means *from him,* and refers to Moses who set an example for Joshua. Alternatively, *Radak* and *Malbim* render *from it,* suggesting that מִמֶּנּוּ refers to the Book of the Torah; the masculine noun *book* is in ellipsis.[2]

1. *Abarbanel* observes that more self-discipline in the face of physical desires was required of Joshua than of the rest of the people. [The explanation might lie in the fact that Joshua was king as well as prophet. *Rambam (Hil. Melachim* 3:6) explains why a king is particularly enjoined against excessive familiarity with women: The Torah was concerned lest the king's heart be distracted, as it says ולא יסור לבבו, *so that his heart shall not be turned away (Deuteronomy* 17:17), for the heart of the king is the collective heart of the entire congregation of Israel. Therefore, the Torah exhorted the king more than all others to concentrate his heart on Torah study all the days of his life. (See *Overview* to ArtScroll *Tehillim, p. 36.)*]

The commentators disagree whether Joshua had the status of a king. For those who hold Joshua was king, see: *Rashi, Yoma* 73b; *Rambam, Hil. Melachim* 1:3, 3:8; *Hil. Sanhedrin* 18:6; *Ramban, Deuteronomy* 33:17. For those who disagree see *Ran, Droshos* 11 and *Rashi, Succah* 27b.

2. *HaRav Gifter* suggests that the exhortation refers to Moses' methodology for resolving problems according to Torah directives and priorities. When a disciple first assumes a position of leadership his natural tendency is to pioneer new modes of conduct that he had not learned from his teacher. Therefore, God strongly cautioned Joshua with the additional word מְאֹד, *very much,* so that he would fully comprehend that even in these matters he is required to subjugate his understanding to Moses. Only by doing so would Joshua become enlightened in his understanding and incorporate all the essentials of Torah into his rational faculties.

1
7-8

[7] *O that you will strengthen yourself and persevere
very much in order to observe, to do, according to all
of the Torah that Moses My servant has commanded
you. Do not deviate from him to the right or to the
left, that you may succeed wherever you may go.*
[8] *This Book of the Torah is not to leave your mouth.*

יָמִין וּשְׂמֹאול — *To the right or to the left.* According to the interpretation that the subject of this part of the verse refers to the Book of the Torah, straying to the *right* would mean adding positive commandments to the Torah and straying to the *left* would mean subtracting negative commandments *(Vilna Gaon).*

לְמַעַן תַּשְׂכִּיל — *That you may succeed.* The rendering of the word תַּשְׂכִּיל as *that you may succeed,* follows *Rashi* and *Radak.*

Metzudos comments that תַּשְׂכִּיל, literally *understand,* is used for *succeed* because people generally impute wisdom to successful people.

Vilna Gaon translates תַּשְׂכִּיל more literally as *in order that you understand:* through your observance of the commandments you will achieve understanding and judgment which will help you in battle.

8. לֹא־יָמוּשׁ סֵפֶר הַתּוֹרָה הַזֶּה מִפִּיךָ — *This Book of the Torah is not to leave*[1] *your mouth.*

Radak comments that the simple meaning of the verse follows R' Yishmael *(Menachos* 99b) who interprets this as a negative commandment forbidding one to refrain voluntarily from Torah study. The verse continues with the positive commandment that one dedicate himself to Torah study.

In the view of R' Shmuel bar Nachmani *(ibid.),* however, this is not a commandment, but a blessing. God blessed Joshua that forgetfulness would not cause his Torah knowledge to *depart from* [his] *mouth.*[2] The use of the term יָמוּשׁ in the blessing is meant to allude to the trait that earned Joshua this blessing: so loyal was he to Moses that לֹא יָמִישׁ מִתּוֹךְ הָאֹהֶל, *he* [Joshua] *did not depart from the tent* [of Moses] *(Exodus* 33:11).

The *Midrash (Shemos Rabbah* 21:15) relates that Joshua's dedication to Torah extended beyond actual study. He

1. The custom to grasp the handle of the pole to which the Torah Scroll is affixed, at the time of its reading, derives from this verse, *This ... Torah is not to leave your mouth.* [*This ... Torah* implies that he was holding it in his hand at the time *(Mishnah Berurah* 36).] Similarly, the custom for the entire congregation to exclaim חֲזַק, *Strengthen yourself,* at the conclusion of the reading of each book of the Pentateuch derives from verse 6 *(Rama, Orach Chaim* 139:11), for at the time that God appeared to Joshua he had just completed the *Book of Deuteronomy (R' Zalman Sorotzkin)* [see further in *Commentary*].

2. [On the verse *(Job* 28:17): *Gold and glass cannot equal it; neither shall the exchange of it be for vessels of fine gold,* the Sages comment: These are the words of Torah which are hard to acquire like vessels of fine gold, but are easily destroyed (forgotten) like vessels of glass *(Chagigah* 15a).

Likewise they said *(Avos d'Rabbi Nosson* 31): The words of Torah are compared to clothes of fine linen, just as those clothes are hard to come by and easily torn, so are the words of Torah.

The *Talmud (Megillah* 6b) states: R' Yitzchok said, If a person tells you 'I labored (in Torah) but I did not find,' do not believe him; 'I did not labor and I found,' do not believe him. 'I labored and I found,' believe him. This is said only with one respect to understanding the complexity of Torah, but with respect to how well he remembers his learning, he is dependent upon Heavenly assistance.

It was this Divine blessing of recall that was given to Joshua.]

א מִפִּיךָ וְהָגִיתָ בּוֹ יוֹמָם וָלַיְלָה לְמַעַן
ט תִּשְׁמֹר לַעֲשׂוֹת כְּכָל־הַכָּתוּב בּוֹ כִּי־אָז
ט תַּצְלִיחַ אֶת־דְּרָכֶךָ וְאָז תַּשְׂכִּיל: הֲלוֹא
צִוִּיתִיךָ חֲזַק וֶאֱמָץ אַל־תַּעֲרֹץ וְאַל־
תֵּחָת כִּי עִמְּךָ יהוה אֱלֹהֶיךָ בְּכֹל אֲשֶׁר

would go to the study hall early and stay late, as well as arrange the benches and spread the mats.

Malbim regards this verse as delineating a second condition on the promise made in verse 5, *as I was with Moses so will I be with you.* In order for Joshua to gain such intimacy with God, he required not only self-discipline *(v. 7)*, but also a total immersion in the study of the Torah's laws and commandments.

Abarbanel comments: Since Joshua had been urged (in the previous verse) to *observe* and *do* the commandments, he was now advised to study the Torah constantly, for study leads to performance [*Kiddushin* 40b].

סֵפֶר הַתּוֹרָה הַזֶּה — *This Book of the Torah.*

This Book refers to the *Book of Deuteronomy*, which was before him at the time of this prophecy *(Rashi)*. [See *Introduction*.]

According to *Metzudos, 'this' Book of Torah* refers to the *entire* Torah which was mentioned in the previous verse.

Abarbanel comments that verse 6 referred to the obligation to observe the commandments, while this phrase requires Joshua to take note of the moral and ethical teachings derived from the Torah's narratives.

וְהָגִיתָ בּוֹ יוֹמָם וָלַיְלָה — *You should contemplate it day and night.*

The translation of *contemplate* follows *Rashi*.

Radak, however, suggests that וְהָגִיתָ means *you should talk.* This part of the verse is meant to add emphasis to the earlier prohibition against neglect of study. *Day and night* does not mean uninterrupted speech, but rather an involvement with Torah study during any free moments, day and night.

Despite his many obligations concerning the conquest and division of the Land, Joshua was still required to immerse himself in ongoing Torah study *(Daas Sofrim)*.

לְמַעַן תִּשְׁמֹר לַעֲשׂוֹת כְּכָל־הַכָּתוּב בּוֹ — *In order to observe, to do, all that is written in it.*

Even your observance of the oral tradition will be only according to what *is written in it*, because after penetrating study, it will be found that even the Oral Law can be derived from the Written Law, either through applying the hermeneutic principles of Torah exegesis or through scrutinizing the language of the verses *(Malbim)*.

Not until the Jews crossed the Jordan were they able to observe *all* the commandments of the Torah, for living in *Eretz Yisrael* is a prerequisite for the performance of some, such as tithing the grains. Thus, Joshua was admonished to observe the *entire* Torah at the first point in Jewish history when it was possible *(Beis Elokim* 3:37).

כִּי־אָז תַּצְלִיחַ אֶת־דְּרָכֶךָ — *For then you will make your ways successful.*

The translation follows *Radak's* primary interpretation that תַּצְלִיחַ is a transitive verb in the causative voice.

The success of a man's activity can never be guaranteed, because it depends on factors beyond his own control. Only by keeping the commandments and earning the reward for their fulfillment can a person be said to *make his ways successful (Radak)*.

In *Radak's* second interpretation, the verb is intransitive. *You will be suc-*

1 *You should contemplate it day and night in order to*
9 *observe, to do, all that is written in it. For then you*
will make your ways successful, and then you will
become understanding. 9 *In truth I commanded you,*
"Strengthen yourself and persevere." Do not fear
and do not lose resolve because HASHEM, your
God, is with you wherever you may go.'

cessful in your ways.

דְּרָכֶךָ — *Your ways.*

Radak notes that although the word דְּרָכֶךָ is written in the singular form [without a י] it is [as indicated by the vocalization] really plural, דְּרָכֶיךָ, *your 'ways.'* [Were it singular it would be pronounced דַּרְכְּךָ.]

וְאָז תַּשְׂכִּיל — *And then you will become understanding.*

That is to say, you will understand how to make yourself successful *(Vilna Gaon).*

Malbim comments that תַּצְלִיחַ implies success which comes from good fortune while תַּשְׂכִּיל implies success resulting from wise decisions. When one studies the Torah, he changes his fortune for the better, and, in addition, he acquires the insight needed to make correct choices.

9. הֲלוֹא — *In truth.*

This translation follows *Ibn Janach* (see *Sefer HaRikmah,* p. 102). He notes that the prefix ה is used as in this verse to establish a fact and declare its veracity.

Radak understands this as a phrase of exhortation.

[Usually the prefix הֲ is understood as introducing a question הֲלוֹא צִוִּיתִיךָ, *Did I not command you?* But in this context it is difficult to suggest such a translation, since the force of the last three verses is quite imperative and powerful.]

צִוִּיתִיךָ — *I commanded you.*

Rashi explains that this command was given in *Deuteronomy* 31:23: *And he* [Moses] *commanded Joshua son of Nun, and he said, 'Strengthen yourself and persevere because you will bring the Israelites to the Land which I swore to them, and I will be with you.'*

חֲזַק וֶאֱמָץ — *Strengthen yourself and persevere.*

— In war, as the verse continues: *Do not fear and do not lose conviction (Rashi).*

[As *Rashi* explains, the thrice-repeated phrase refers to three different responsibilities: division of the Land, Torah observance, and war. Since these were Joshua's major tasks, he received a separate exhortation for each one.]

The extreme difficulties involved in achieving these three goals become evident when we realize that despite Joshua's best efforts, the conquest of the Land was not completed in his time, and he was unable to remove all the obstacles to Torah observance *(Daas Sofrim).*

אַל־תַּעֲרֹץ וְאַל־תֵּחָת — *Do not fear and do not lose resolve.*

Targum renders תַּעֲרֹץ as *fear* and תֵּחָת as *broken.* According to *Metzudos,* however, both verbs express *fear.*

Malbim identifies these verbs as antonyms of the thrice-repeated expression *be strong and persevere.* תַּעֲרֹץ is the antonym of *strength,* hence *weakness because of fear,* and תֵּחָת is the antonym of *perseverance,* hence *loss of resolve.*

כִּי עִמְּךָ ה׳ אֱלֹהֶיךָ — *Because HASHEM, your God, is with you.*

Scripture includes many verses where God refers to Himself in the third person.[1] For example, *And to Moses He said, 'Come to HASHEM,'* rather

1. [It may be that God does not refer to Himself, as it were, but to the way in which He would

י תֵּלֵךְ: וַיְצַו יְהוֹשֻׁעַ אֶת־
יא שֹׁטְרֵי הָעָם לֵאמֹר: עִבְרוּ | בְּקֶרֶב הַמַּחֲנֶה
וְצַוּוּ אֶת־הָעָם לֵאמֹר הָכִינוּ לָכֶם צֵדָה
כִּי בְּעוֹד | שְׁלֹשֶׁת יָמִים אַתֶּם עֹבְרִים
אֶת־הַיַּרְדֵּן הַזֶּה לָבוֹא לָרֶשֶׁת אֶת־

than, *'come to Me'* (*Exodus* 24:1; *Radak*).

Malbim, however, understands this entire verse to refer back to Moses' declaration to Joshua (*Deuteronomy* 31:8): *HASHEM your God goes before you; He will be with you.* Consequently, God does not refer to Himself in first person, because He alludes to Moses' assurance to Joshua.

◆§ The Marshals Inform the Nation

10. וַיְצַו יְהוֹשֻׁעַ — *And Joshua ordered.*

... on the last day of the mourning period for Moses (*Rashi*). [*See footnote* to Chronology cited in verse 1. *Rashi's* comment here appears to corroborate *Tosafos'* second explanation of his interpretation in *Kiddushin.*]

[As in verse 1, the ו has been translated *and,* in order to show that it was because of the prophecy which Joshua received that he gave these orders to the marshals.]

Before God commanded Joshua to cross the Jordan and take possession of the Land, Joshua had doubted his own ability to lead the Israelites. Because of his apprehension, he had instructed the tribes of Gad and Reuben to prepare themselves for battle. Joshua's insecurity had also prompted him to dispatch a reconnaissance mission into the Land to aid in planning for its conquest. However, after God spoke to him (*vs.* 2-9), Joshua was reassured. Therefore, he decided to proceed with the initial preparation for the invasion of the Land without waiting for the mission's return (*Malbim*).[1]

manifest Himself. This would explain the use of third person: God was telling Joshua 'I shall be with you in My roles of HASHEM and ELOHIM.'

As *R' Hirsch* explains (*Genesis* 2:4), the development of human history is guided by two factors: (a) The unchanging laws of nature — represented by ELOHIM; and (b) the modifications in God's guidance that are caused by man's behavior — represented by HASHEM.

Accordingly, God now told Joshua that although Israel's conquest of the Land was rooted in the natural order of creation, their success would be contingent on their personal merit.]

1. Exactly when did Joshua dispatch the reconnaissance mission and when did he give the marshals their orders?

Ralbag calculates that the reconnaissance mission must have been dispatched before Joshua gave this order to the marshals. He reasons that the spies spent three days in the mountains (2:22) and returned to Joshua on the fourth day (2:23). On the fifth day Joshua moved the people from Shittim to the Jordan (3:4), and this marked the end of the *third day* on which the marshals had been circulating through the camps (3:2).

Ralbag also suggests a second possible chronology which would lead to the conclusion that the spies had been dispatched on the same day that Joshua told the marshals to inform the people of the imminent crossing. The reasoning is as follows: The day that Joshua ordered the marshals to inform the people is not one of the three days mentioned in verse 11 because there the verse employs the expression בְּעוֹד שְׁלֹשֶׁת יָמִים, implying *three days after this one.* Therefore, it was not until the beginning of the fifth day after this order that the full three days had ended. Moreover, we can assume that the reconnaissance mission reached Rachav's house on the same day it was dispatched. The spies slept there that night (2:1). When 2:22 states that they stayed in the mountains three days, it means *until* the third day of their mission. The word *until* is understood. [This construction is found throughout Scripture as in *Deuteronomy* 25:3, *He may give him forty lashes,* which means *up to* forty lashes, i.e., thirty-

1
10-11 [10] *And Joshua ordered the marshals of the people,*
saying, [11] *'Circulate within the camp and command*
the people, saying, "Prepare yourselves provisions
because in another three days you will cross this
Jordan to come to inherit the Land which HASHEM,

שֹׁטְרֵי הָעָם — *The marshals* [lit. *officers*] *of the people.*

They were appointed to inform the people of Joshua's directives and to enforce them *(Metzudos).*

11. לֵאמֹר — [*And the marshals commanded the people*] *saying.*

The interpolation follows *Vilna Gaon,* who explains that the word לֵאמֹר, *saying,* of verse 10 introduces Joshua's command to the marshals, and the same word in verse 11 introduces the order that the marshals actually transmitted.

[The verb וְצַוּוּ can mean *and command* (in the imperative form) or *and they commanded. Vilna Gaon* follows the second meaning.]

הָכִינוּ לָכֶם צֵדָה — *Prepare yourselves provisions.*

Provisions in our verse refers to any supplies and weapons needed for the crossing. Ordinarily, צֵדָה refers to provisions of food, but the Israelites had no need to prepare food because they were still eating manna. The Sages taught *(Kiddushin* 38a) that the manna stopped falling with the death of Moses on 7 Adar, but the manna remaining in the Israelites' vessels was not depleted until 16 Nissan, when they began using the produce of the Land, as we find (5:12) *when the manna was depleted the following day* [after the first day of Passover] ... *they ate from the aged grain of the Land (Rashi).*

Radak renders צֵדָה as provisions of food. Although they still had manna, they prepared *other* foods [that they purchased from local merchants *(Metzudos)*]. *Radak* notes further that the simple meaning of 5:12 implies that the manna was still falling daily at this point, or they may have had manna left from Adar, as the Sages taught.

Malbim adds that the *provisions* could indeed refer to the manna, which they were instructed to grind or otherwise prepare for future use.

According to the *Midrash (Yalkut Shimoni* II, 1:7), this verse refers to spiritual provisions, not physical ones. The Israelites were charged to repent so that they could enter the Land.

כִּי בְּעוֹד שְׁלֹשֶׁת יָמִים — *Because in another three days.*

There is a difference of opinion regarding the interpretation of this expression. *Targum* and *Rashi* render בְּעוֹד as *at the end of,* which would imply three *full* days. *Tosafos* (see *footnote* to Chronology in *v.* 1), however, contends that it means *within* three days. According to this opinion, two days and a fraction elapsed before the Israelites crossed the Jordan.

לָבוֹא לָרֶשֶׁת אֶת־הָאָרֶץ — *To come to inherit the Land.*

The verb יָרַשׁ is understood differently by the commentators. According to *Targum* and *Radak (Sefer HaShorashim*

nine. *Count fifty years, (Leviticus* 23:16) which means *up to* fifty years, i.e., forty-nine.] On the fourth day they returned to Joshua (2:23), so the fifth day coincided with the end of the third day on which the marshals had been circulating through the camps (3:2).

Vilna Gaon (v. 11) is of the opinion that the mourning period for Moses ended on 6 Nissan (this is in agreement with *Sefer HaMiknah,* cited in the *footnote* to the Chronology in v. 1), and the reconnaissance mission was dispatched that day. They arrived at Rachav's house the same day and left that night (7 Nissan) for the mountains. They remained there for three nights (7, 8, and part of 9 Nissan), and during the night of 9 Nissan they returned to Joshua. On the morning of the ninth, Joshua arose early and led the Israelite camp to the bank of the Jordan (3:1). There the nation spent the night of the tenth, and the next morning, the tenth, they crossed the Jordan.

א
יב־יד

הָאָרֶץ אֲשֶׁר יְהוָה אֱלֹהֵיכֶם נֹתֵן לָכֶם
יב לְרִשְׁתָּהּ: וְלָרְאוּבֵנִי וְלַגָּדִי
וְלַחֲצִי שֵׁבֶט הַמְנַשֶּׁה אָמַר יְהוֹשֻׁעַ
יג לֵאמֹר: זָכוֹר אֶת־הַדָּבָר אֲשֶׁר צִוָּה
אֶתְכֶם מֹשֶׁה עֶבֶד־יְהוָה לֵאמֹר יְהוָה
אֱלֹהֵיכֶם מֵנִיחַ לָכֶם וְנָתַן לָכֶם אֶת־
יד הָאָרֶץ הַזֹּאת: נְשֵׁיכֶם טַפְּכֶם וּמִקְנֵיכֶם

s.v. ירש) it means 'to inherit,' which is the usual translation. *Ibn Janach,* however, argues that it may also be translated 'to conquer.'

Deuteronomy 1:8 uses a similar expression: בֹּאוּ וּרְשׁוּ אֶת־הָאָרֶץ, *Come and inherit the Land.* There *Rashi* comments: No one will contest the matter, and you will not need to wage war. In that context, ירש means *inherit,* and thus *Rashi* appears to adopt the view of *Radak.*

לְרִשְׁתָּהּ — *As an inheritance* [lit. *to inherit it*].

The translation follows *Targum* and *Radak* in *Sefer HaShorashim* (s.v. ירש).

12-18. We find in *Numbers* (32:1-42) that the tribes of Gad and Reuben had very large herds of cattle. They asked Moses if they could have the newly acquired territory of Sichon and Og, because it was spacious and excellent for cattle grazing. In exchange, they were willing to relinquish their portion in the land of Canaan. Moses thought their request was motivated by fear of fighting the Canaanites and that such an attitude could infect the other tribes as well. To prove their faith and trust in God, and their loyalty to the rest of the nation, Gad and Reuben pledged to lead the other tribes in battle *(Ramban, Numbers* 32:2). Later, part of the tribe of Menashe joined in the bargain *(Numbers* 32:33, see *Ramban).*

Moses agreed, on the condition that they take part in the conquest of the Land along with the other tribes. He gave them the cities of Ataros and Divon and several other cities. The large remainder of their request would be theirs if they fulfilled their pledge *(Ramban, Numbers* 32:29). They pledged not only to participate in the conquest of the Land, but also to remain in *Eretz Yisrael* until the Land had been divided among their brethren (see *Prefatory Remarks* to Chapter 22).

◆§ Reuben, Gad, and Menashe are Reminded of their Promise

12. The context of this verse and the apparent assumption of the commentators seem to indicate that Joshua himself now addressed the two and a half tribes that had taken their inheritance on the eastern side of the Jordan. *Rif,* however, comments that this message, too, was transmitted by the marshals.

וְלָרְאוּבֵנִי ... אָמַר יְהוֹשֻׁעַ — *And to* [*the tribes of*] *Reuben ... Joshua had said.*

Joshua had spoken to the two and one half tribes before he received God's charge (*v.* 10) and instructed the marshals. In Scriptural usage, past perfect is indicated, as it is in this verse, by placement of a noun before the verb and by the use of a simple past-tense verb, as explained by *Rashi* to *Genesis* 4:1 Had Joshua spoken to these tribes only *after* the previously given event, the verse would have read וַיֹּאמֶר יְהוֹשֻׁעַ, *and Joshua said,* stating the verb first and using the future tense יֹאמַר with the conversive ו [ו׳ הַמְּהַפֵּךְ] *(Malbim)*

The suffix י to the name Reuben and Gad as well as the prefix ה to the name Menashe are devices used by Scripture to denote genealogy. Hence, לָרְאוּבֵנִי means to all

1 *your God, is giving you as an inheritance.'' '*
12-14 [12] *And to the tribes of Reuben and Gad and part of*
the tribe of Menashe Joshua had said, [13] *'Remember*
that matter which Moses, servant of HASHEM,
commanded you, saying, ''HASHEM your God gives
you rest, and He will give you this land.'' [14] *Your*
wives, your children and your cattle will reside in the

members of the tribe of Reuben (see *Numbers* 26:5 ff; *Mateh Binyamin).*

וְלַחֲצִי שֵׁבֶט הַמְנַשֶּׁה – *Part* [lit. *half*] *of the tribe of Menashe.*

Of the eight families that composed the tribe of Menashe (*Numbers* 26:29-32), only Machir and Gilead, which were the two families with the fewest members *(Ramban, Numbers* 32:33), received land on the eastern bank of the Jordan (*Numbers* 32:39-42). Hence, חֲצִי, *half,* cannot be taken literally, and must be understood as *part.* (See *Ibn Janach, s.v.* חצה, that חֲצִי can mean either *half* or *part.)*

13. ה' אֱלֹהֵיכֶם מֵנִיחַ לָכֶם ... *HASHEM your God gives you rest ...*

The term *gives you rest* refers to the conclusion of the division of the Land, when each family can rest in its own inheritance. In *Numbers,* Moses required that Reuben, Gad, and Menashe remain with their brethren only until the *conquest* was complete. Although in *Numbers* 32:18 they had voluntarily offered to remain until the divison was complete, Moses did not make their acquisition of the eastern bank conditional on staying so long. But in *Deuteronomy* 3:20, he added as a moral requirement that they stay until after the division.

Here Joshua repeats Moses' words and offers two reasons why it is fitting that they remain in *Eretz Yisrael* until the Land is finally divided:

First, *HASHEM gives you rest;* your wives and children are established in their cities and need not continue wandering homelessly, as do the rest of the tribes' families. Second, *HASHEM gave you this land* which you requested *(Malbim).*

Abarbanel suggests a different interpretation of the two reasons advanced by Joshua. *HASHEM ... gives you rest:* since Sichon and Og are not attempting to recapture their homeland on the east bank, you are free to join your brothers in conquering their territory. And since you did not have to fight for your own homeland because God gave it to you, it would not be equitable for you to remain while your brothers go to war.

וְנָתַן – *Will give.*

This is in the future tense according to *Targum* וְיִהַב. Had it been past tense, *Targum* would have rendered ויהבת. [*Abarbanel* and *Malbim* (mentioned in the previous note) understand this verb to be in the past tense; although territory had *already* been given to the two and a half tribes much of their inheritance was held back until they fulfilled their promise to remain in Canaan during the years of conquest and division (see *Ramban* cited in preface to *vs.* 12-18). By translating *will give, Targum* could be referring to that remainder of land which they would receive in the future.]

14. נְשֵׁיכֶם טַפְּכֶם וּמִקְנֵיכֶם – *Your wives, your children and your cattle.*

[This order is significant. When the tribes of Gad and Reuben asked Moses for their portion of land across the Jordan, they displayed a warped sense of values by speaking of their possessions before their children: '(let us) *build corrals for our sheep here and cities for our children' (Numbers* 32:16). Moses rejoined, *'Build cities for*

א טו־יח

יֵשְׁבוּ בָּאָרֶץ אֲשֶׁר נָתַן לָכֶם מֹשֶׁה בְּעֵבֶר
הַיַּרְדֵּן וְאַתֶּם תַּעַבְרוּ חֲמֻשִׁים לִפְנֵי
אֲחֵיכֶם כֹּל גִּבּוֹרֵי הַחַיִל וַעֲזַרְתֶּם אוֹתָם׃
טו עַד אֲשֶׁר־יָנִיחַ יהוה | לַאֲחֵיכֶם כָּכֶם
וְיָרְשׁוּ גַם־הֵמָּה אֶת־הָאָרֶץ אֲשֶׁר־יהוה
אֱלֹהֵיכֶם נֹתֵן לָהֶם וְשַׁבְתֶּם לְאֶרֶץ
יְרֻשַּׁתְכֶם וִירִשְׁתֶּם אוֹתָהּ אֲשֶׁר | נָתַן לָכֶם
מֹשֶׁה עֶבֶד יהוה בְּעֵבֶר הַיַּרְדֵּן מִזְרַח
טז הַשָּׁמֶשׁ׃ וַיַּעֲנוּ אֶת־יְהוֹשֻׁעַ לֵאמֹר כֹּל
אֲשֶׁר־צִוִּיתָנוּ נַעֲשֶׂה וְאֶל־כָּל־אֲשֶׁר
יז תִּשְׁלָחֵנוּ נֵלֵךְ׃ כְּכֹל אֲשֶׁר־שָׁמַעְנוּ אֶל־
מֹשֶׁה כֵּן נִשְׁמַע אֵלֶיךָ רַק יִהְיֶה יהוה
יח אֱלֹהֶיךָ עִמָּךְ כַּאֲשֶׁר הָיָה עִם־מֹשֶׁה׃ כָּל־

your children and corrals for your sheep' (ibid. 32:24).][1]

אֲשֶׁר נָתַן לָכֶם מֹשֶׁה — *Which Moses had given to you.*

This land included the cities of Ataros and Divon as well as the other cities mentioned in *Numbers* 32 *(Ramban, Numbers* 32:29).

חֲמֻשִׁים — *Armed.*

The translation follows *Rashi (Exodus* 13:18).

Yalkut Shimoni [1:227] perceives a connection between the word חֲמֻשִׁים, *armed,* and the similar word חָמֵשׁ, *five.* The warriors were armed with five weapons [sword, bow, shield, lance, and spear *(Zeis Raanan)*].

כֹּל גִּבּוֹרֵי הַחַיִל — *All the mighty warriors.*

All the mighty warriors among them were to participate *(Rashi).*

1. A person's values become blinded when he starts to view his wealth as of his own making for his own purposes. The blindness that Gad and Reuben demonstrated in the reversal of their priorities of children and cattle is an illustration of how far even the most perfect people can stray from the proper path when the material world becomes the focus of their attention. [See also *footnote* to 22:25.]

The tribes of Gad and Reuben were never criticized by our Sages for relinquishing their portion in *Eretz Yisrael* in favor of more suitable grazing land across the Jordan [cf., however, *Bamidbar Rabbah* 22:6]. Since God blessed them with such large herds of cattle, it was obvious that their wealth was intended for a noble, sacred purpose. Therefore, it was their responsibility to maintain and develop their wealth by seeking the optimal conditions for their cattle.

The difficulties one encounters with the sanctification of the mundane are in certain ways more challenging than those encountered in strictly spiritual pursuits. One always runs the risk of becoming ensnared by the allures of the material world, but this is especially true when the focus of one's service to God lies in amassing wealth for the sake of Heaven.

Even though it was apparent that the tribes of Gad and Reuben needed the land across the Jordan for their cattle, they should have waited for a command from God to acquire this land. Had their sole motive been to fulfill God's purpose in having given them this wealth, they would have had enough trust in God to wait for Him to provide them with suitable land. Instead, they demonstrated an unworthy personal desire to maintain their wealth *(Michtav MeEliyahu).*

land which Moses had given to you across the
Jordan. Then you will cross over, armed, before your
brothers — all the mighty warriors — and you will
help them, 15 *until HASHEM gives your brothers rest*
as He has given you, and they also take possession of
the land which HASHEM, your God, gives them. Then
you may return to the land of your inheritance and
inherit it — that which Moses, servant of HASHEM,
gave you across the Jordan on its eastern side.'
16 *And they answered Joshua saying, 'All that you*
have commanded us we will do, and wherever you
send us we will go. 17 *As fully as we listened to Moses*
so shall we listen to you. O that HASHEM, your God,
be with you as he had been with Moses! 18 *Any man*

[About 40,000 men from the tribes of Reuben, Gad, and part of Menashe entered the war against Jericho (see 4:13). In *Numbers* 26 when the eligible combatants were counted, there were from the tribe of Reuben 43,700, from Gad 40,500, and from the whole tribe of Menashe 52,700. Apparently, not all the warriors from these tribes were fit or needed for this battle. See *Commentary* to 4:13.]

15. עַד אֲשֶׁר־יָנִיחַ ה׳ לַאֲחֵיכֶם — *Until HASHEM gives your brothers rest.*

I am not asking more of you than was demanded of your brothers when they helped you conquer *your* territory. Furthermore, the conquest of the Land will not require much of your time, because it is God Who will give your brothers rest, and who could possibly oppose Him? *(Abarbanel).*

You should remain until the Land is divided so that your brothers will have their inheritance as well as the rest from their enemies, just as you do *(Malbim).*

וִירִשְׁתֶּם — *And inherit it.*

See *Commentary* to verse 11.

אֲשֶׁר נָתַן לָכֶם מֹשֶׁה — *Which Moses, ... gave you.*

Remember that He gave you this Land on the condition that you participate with your brothers *(Malbim).*

בְּעֵבֶר הַיַּרְדֵּן מִזְרַח הַשָּׁמֶשׁ — *Across the Jordan on its eastern side* [lit. *from the rising of the sun*].

The translation follows *Rashi.*

Even though they were presently located on the *eastern* side of the Jordan, they called that area 'across the Jordan,' because in the future, the Israelites would settle on the western side and this would then be considered 'across the Jordan' *(Mahari Kara).*

◆§ The Affirmation of Joshua

16. כֹּל אֲשֶׁר־צִוִּיתָנוּ — *All that you have commanded us.*

We will not limit ourselves only to that which we promised Moses, because we are also obligated to obey *your* commands *(Malbim).*[See *Commentary* to 22:2.]

וְאֶל־כָּל־אֲשֶׁר תִּשְׁלָחֵנוּ נֵלֵךְ — *And wherever you send us we will go.*

We will follow you across the Jordan and even to the ends of the earth, if you so command *(Abarbanel).*

17. רַק יִהְיֶה ה׳ אֱלֹהֶיךָ עִמָּךְ — *O that* [lit. *only*] *HASHEM, your God, be with you.*

The translation of רַק follows *Ibn Janach* who contends that it is used in

א יח

אִ֠ישׁ אֲשֶׁר־יַמְרֶ֨ה אֶת־פִּ֜יךָ וְלֹֽא־יִשְׁמַ֧ע אֶת־דְּבָרֶ֛יךָ לְכֹ֥ל אֲשֶׁר־תְּצַוֶּ֖נּוּ יוּמָ֑ת רַ֖ק חֲזַ֥ק וֶאֱמָֽץ׃

this context to introduce a short prayer (see *Sefer HaShorashim*). [See *Commentary* to v. 9.]

Radak interprets this phrase: You should follow Moses' ways so that God will be with you as He had been with Moses.

Metzudos renders the word רַק more literally: We will listen to you *only* if God is with you as he was with Moses.

You will be considered our teacher if God is with you as He was with Moses (*Malbim*).

Even though your prophecy is not equal to that of Moses, [the word רַק has a limiting sense] if you will only follow Moses' ways, God will be with you as He was with Moses (*Rif*).

18. אֲשֶׁר־יַמְרֶה ... וְלֹא־יִשְׁמַע — *Who will rebel ... or will not listen.*

Metzudos traces the word יַמְרֶה to the root מרי, which means *rebel* as we see in the case of בֵּן סוֹרֵר וּמוֹרֶה, *a wayward and rebellious child* (*Deuteronomy* 21:18).

To rebel means to act contrary to a command and *to not listen* means to fail to execute a command. Each constitutes an act of treason against the king (*Malbim*).

[*Rambam* (*Hil. Melachim* 3:8) rules that if a king commands one of his subjects to go to a certain place or not to leave his house, and the person does not heed his directive, the king is empowered to impose the death penalty. Again we see that acts of omission and commission are both punishable offenses.]

HaRav Gifter points out that the tribes of Gad and Reuben are reaffirming Joshua's kingship, which the entire nation had previously accepted [*and the Israelites listened to him* (*Deuteronomy* 34:9)]. [*Radvaz* (*Hil. Melachim* 3:8) emphasizes that one has the legal status of a king only if he is appointed by a prophet or if the entire nation accepts his authority; if, however, one assumes the throne by force, the people are not required to follow him. In the case of Joshua we find both: he was appointed by Moses (*Deuteronomy* 31:7, 23) and accepted by the people.]

לְכֹל אֲשֶׁר־תְּצַוֶּנּוּ — *In* [lit. *to*] *whatever you may command him.*

— Even a trivial command (*Malbim*).

יוּמָת — *Will be put to death.*

From this verse, the *Talmud* (*Sanhedrin* 49a) derives the law that one who rebels against the king is liable to the death penalty by sword.

רַק — *O may* [lit. *only*].

It would appear that all are required to follow the king's directives, even if he orders an act forbidden by the Torah. However, the word *only* has a limiting force: *only if* the king's commands comply with the Torah is one obligated to follow (*Sanhedrin* 49a). Thus, King Saul's servants refused to slay the Kohanim at his bidding (*Rashi* to *I Samuel* 22:17).

חֲזַק וֶאֱמָץ — *Strengthen yourself and persevere.*

Strengthen yourself so that your leadership will be in accordance with the Torah, for if you tell us to transgress even one of its laws, we will not obey you, since both you and we must guarantee Torah observance (*Ralbag*).

[According to this interpretation, *strengthen* implies the king's special responsibility to study the Torah. More than any other citizen, the king must maintain a constant awareness of the Torah and its teachings. *Rambam* rules (*Hil. Melachim* 3:1): At the time a king ascends to the throne he must write a Torah scroll for himself, even if he has inherited one from his forefathers ... if he has not inherited a scroll from his forefathers, or it was ruined, he must write two scrolls. One he puts into storage, and the second he always keeps with him ... when he goes out to war, the scroll must be with him, when he comes back, it must be with him, when he sits in judgment, it must be with him ...]

Ralbag offers a second interpretation:

1 *who will rebel against your utterance or will not*
18 *listen to your words, in whatever you may command*
him — will be put to death. O may you strengthen
yourself and persevere!'

Take very firm control of the leadership of the nation, because it cannot exist without a strong reign.

Metzudos understands רַק חֲזַק to mean: Be strong to punish rebels and do not forego the respect that is your due.

II

Before the Jews were about to ascend to Eretz Yisrael, *Moses acquiesced to the people's request that he send a reconnaissance mission* (Rashi) *to gather strategic and descriptive information about the Land. This mission miscarried, resulting in one of the most disastrous episodes in Jewish history; because the nation believed the scouts' slanderous report concerning the Land's conditions, God decreed that most of the nation would die in the Wilderness (see* Numbers *13).*

Since Joshua was one of the scouts dispatched by Moses to reconnoiter the Land, he was keenly aware of the mission's calamitous consequences. Nevertheless, approximately thirty-nine years later, he implemented a similar plan to gain information about the Land. This chapter, which describes the second reconnaissance mission, is traditionally read as the Haftarah to Parshas Shelach, *the portion that contains the account of the earlier mission. As mentioned earlier* (Commentary *1:2), if the Jewish people had not dispatched a mission to survey the Land, God would have permitted them to enter* Eretz Yisrael *without meeting resistance and without requiring weapons. It is therefore important to understand why the Jews deserved the punishment of having to plan military strategies in order to gain their inheritance. What sin had been committed by dispatching these scouts?*

*The instructions that Moses gave the scouts before their mission reveal the purpose behind the operation: He directed them to ascertain whether the Land's inhabitants were strong or weak, numerous or few (*Numbers *13:18), and to determine the physical layout of their encampments (*ibid. *13:19). Since the Israelites erroneously believed that acquisition of the Land would be dependent upon military efforts, they viewed the amassing of strategic information as a necessity. By acting according to this fundamental misconception, Israel indicated that it had lost sight of its manifest destiny.*

As R' Hirsch *explains, the Torah was given outside* Eretz Yisrael *in order to underscore the difference between Israel and the other nations. While all the other nations of the world first developed a geographical state and then enacted a social contract, Israel first received its Law, the Torah, and then proceeded to occupy its land. The Torah was not created as a response to the social needs of a political state; rather, the political state served as an arena for the observance of the Law. The acquisition of* Eretz Yisrael, *therefore, was a prerequisite for the complete fulfillment of the Torah.*

To the degree that one trusts in God's help, one receives it. Had Israel recognized this, their faith in Divine Providence would have been strengthened, and they would have realized that their conquest was not dependent on military planning and prowess — thereby obviating the need for spies and military reconnaissance. Because the Jews failed to rely on His intervention, they were subject to a diminution of Divine Guidance, resulting in the obligation to participate actively in securing their inheritance. As a result, Israel had to shoulder weapons and gird its loins.

ב א וַיִּשְׁלַח יְהוֹשֻׁעַ בִּן־נוּן מִן־הַשִּׁטִּים שְׁנַיִם
א אֲנָשִׁים מְרַגְּלִים חֶרֶשׁ לֵאמֹר לְכוּ רְאוּ

Joshua's issuance of a reconnaissance mission was enacted in a completely different spirit. He intended both to rectify Israel's past error and to inculcate the Jews with the proper attitude toward entering the Land — an attitude of trust in God. By ordering the spies into the Land, he intended only to ascertain whether the proper moment had arrived for Israel's march. [Although God commanded Joshua to cross the Jordan, He did not specify a time.] Joshua reasoned that if the Land's inhabitants feared Israel, it would be a sign that Divine Providence had arranged the scene for Israel's entry to the Land (Lev Aharon). *To learn this, the spies traveled to Rachav's house. Since travelers from all parts of the Land passed through her inn, she was continually aware of the national mood. When she announced that the hearts of the people had melted* (v. *11) upon hearing of the miracles God performed for Israel when they left Egypt and of their victories over the powerful nations of Sichon and Og, the spies could report with confidence that the time had come to initiate their attack.*

Joshua's gesture of dispatching the reconnaissance mission demonstrated to Israel that the outcome of their attempt to conquer the Land was a function of Divine Providence. Their bearing of arms and mounting of military compaigns would be only token gestures of participation in the fulfillment of their national destiny; since God had still remained in their midst, they would not require brute physical strength to be victorious. Thereby, Joshua rectified the failure to recognize that the inheritance of Eretz Yisrael *was an essential element in Israel's destiny and would be engineered by Divine Providence, rather than by human efforts.*

◆§ Joshua's Reconnaissance Mission

1. וַיִּשְׁלַח יְהוֹשֻׁעַ בִּן־נוּן — *Joshua son of Nun dispatched ...*

As was mentioned in the *Prefatory Remarks,* Joshua was well aware of the tragic consequences of the reconnaissance mission dispatched by Moses, yet he decided to order a similar mission.

The problem is further complicated according to the view mentioned in the *footnote* to 1:10 that Joshua had dispatched the spies *after* he received his first prophecy. The question then arises: Why did he not trust in Hashem's assurance *do not fear and do not lose resolve* (1:9)? The commentators offer three approaches to explain his decision:

□ *Radak* suggests that Joshua intended to raise the morale of the people by launching a mission which would be successfully completed. Therefore, the spies were sent *secretly;* even if they failed, there would be no loss in *esprit de corps.* [If they were successful, however, all would be informed.] *Alshich* comments that their morale was low because their encampment in Shittim reminded them of the abominable national sin of *Baal Pe'or,* which occurred during the days of Moses (see *Numbers* 25:1).

Ralbag remarks that their spirits would be lifted by hearing that the Canaanites were alarmed by Israel's strength. Thus, when the spies returned, they said, *'All the inhabitants of the Land have melted because of us.' Lev Aharon* explains that their joy stemmed from the fact that the Divine Providence which had paved the way for their invasion had not departed from Israel after Moses' death.

This view also explains why Joshua sent the spies, according to the view that their mission took place before his first prophecy. Knowing that sinfulness on the part of the Jews could have caused postponement of their entry into the Land, Joshua was doubtful whether the proper moment for launching their conquest had arrived. Therefore, he decided to probe the country for a sign which would indicate whether

2
1

¹ Joshua son of Nun dispatched two men — spies — from Shittim and secretly ordered them, 'Go

Divine Providence favored their plans.

□ A second approach is offered by *Abarbanel* who contends that Joshua's mission differed from Moses' mission in a very basic way. The people in Moses' time intended to use the results of the report to decide whether or not they should follow God's command to secure *Eretz Yisrael.* Joshua, however, was determined to obey the Divine command. He ordered the mission only to determine the best method of approaching the Land.

Malbim notes that the verse specifically mentions that the spies left from Shittim, which is geographically close to the Land. This demonstrates that they were already prepared to enter *Eretz Yisrael.* In contradistinction, we find that Moses dispatched his mission when the people were in Paran, which was distant from the Land. Secondly, *Meam Loez* observes that Joshua sent only two spies, while Moses sent twelve, one from each tribe. In Moses' time, each tribe desired first-hand knowledge in order to decide whether to participate in the conquest; in this case, however, only Joshua, who was leading the attack, needed to know the topography of the enemy.

□ *Nachalas Reuven* offers a third resolution of Joshua's actions. Joshua's reconnaissance mission was not dispatched to gain information for Israel, but was rather a ploy to beguile the Canaanites. Joshua sent spies to Rachav's house, located at a crossroads for travelers, so that they would be highly visible. He reasoned that the kings of Canaan would learn of their presence and infer that Israel no longer merited Divine intervention and now needed to rely on its own military skill. Realizing that they were militarily superior, the kings would unite to destroy Israel. Had they feared Israel, however, they would have dispersed to the corners of the Land. Joshua preferred to launch a single battle against a united Canaanite command, rather than to wage individual battles against separate kings throughout the Land.

מִן־הַשִּׁטִּים — *From Shittim.*

The letter *hei* preceding Shittim may be a part of the name, as in the case of the city of Ai, הָעַי (see 7:2). Or, perhaps, it is the demonstrative adjective *the,* which connotes that Shittim was well known, either because it was the last of Israel's encampments in the Wilderness or because Moses died nearby on Mount Nevo *(Mateh Binyamin).*

Because Moses died nearby, Scripture calls Shittim, אָבֵל הַשִּׁטִּים *(Numbers* 33:49) 'Mourning of Shittim' *(Mateh Binyamin)* [See *Rashi* to *Genesis* 14:6.]

שְׁנַיִם אֲנָשִׁים — *Two men.*

Radak comments that these were men of integrity, unlike the majority of those in Moses' mission, who strayed when they left the company of their master. [See *Rashi* to *Numbers* 13:3.]

As a point of grammar, Scripture should have employed the adjective שְׁנֵי, *two,* rather than the noun שְׁנַיִם, *two. Lev Aharon* suggests that שְׁנַיִם connotes they were equal in their piety and righteousness, i.e., the two [were equal as] men. He also observes that their faithfulness and purity of purpose can be seen from the fact that Scripture calls them מְרַגְּלִים, *spies,* even before they actually were charged with their mission. This appellation denotes that they were unswerving in their dedication to the mission from beginning to end.

These two men were Pinchas and Calev *(Bamidbar Rabbah* 16:1).

Musar HaNeveim remarks that their names were not explicitly mentioned in the verse to spare them the indignity of being associated with a harlot. The Sages revealed their identities, however, because Rachav later became such a righteous person.

When Israel was among the Ammonites

ב א
אֶת־הָאָ֖רֶץ וְאֶת־יְרִיח֑וֹ וַיֵּ֨לְכ֜וּ וַ֠יָּבֹאוּ בֵּֽית
אִשָּׁ֥ה זוֹנָ֛ה וּשְׁמָ֥הּ רָחָ֖ב וַיִּשְׁכְּבוּ־שָֽׁמָּה׃

(see *Numbers* 21:32), Moses had dispatched another reconnaissance mission that conquered their small villages. According to *Targum Yonasan (Numbers* 21:32), Calev and Pinchas participated in this mission. Thus, they had had experience together in such missions before being dispatched by Joshua.

Their identities may be inferred from the words חֶרֶשׁ לֵאמֹר. The word חֶרֶשׁ means *silence;* it alludes to Calev, who silenced Israel's murmurings during the calumnious report of Moses' first reconnaissance mission (see *Numbers* 13:30). The word לֵאמֹר, which means *saying,* refers to Pinchas, who, as the anointed priest of war, would publicly proclaim before battle that the troops should have no fear, since God would help them in their efforts *(Poras Yosef).*

חֶרֶשׁ לֵאמֹר — *Secretly ordered.*

[חֶרֶשׁ is normally translated as *silent* and לֵאמֹר as *saying;* however, the combination is difficult to understand. Some commentators divide the expression, some deal with it as one unit. We have chosen to translate this phrase according to *Radak* (see further).]

It is not clear whether *Rashi* treats these words as one unit. He understands חֵרֵשׁ as an adjective describing the spies: *deaf spies.* They were to feign deafness so that the Canaanites would not hesitate to mention secrets in their presence. *Alshich* follows this understanding of חֵרֵשׁ and explains these words as one expression. He comments that the purpose of their 'deafness' was to get people to speak, לֵאמֹר.

Radak also understands these words as one expression, but in an entirely different sense. He renders according to *Targum* בְּרָז לְמֵימָר which means *secretly commanded. Radak* explains that the spies were sent in secrecy so that the Israelites would not be frightened that Joshua feared Canaanite power and resorted to dispatching a reconnaissance mission.

Malbim suggests that the expression be divided: חֶרֶשׁ describes the manner in which the spies were sent, i.e., *in silence,* and לֵאמֹר introduces Joshua's command to *go observe the Land.*

Mateh Binyamin, however, contends that according to the cantillation of these words, it appears that they should be read together.

Lev Aharon reads the three words מְרַגְּלִים חֶרֶשׁ לֵאמֹר together. He interprets חֶרֶשׁ to mean *thoughts,* as in אַל־תַּחֲרֹשׁ עַל־רֵעֲךָ רָעָה, *do not devise evil against your neighbor (Proverbs* 3:29). The entire phrase would mean: spies of thoughts who could get the Canaanites to verbalize what they were thinking.

The *Midrash* states, 'What does חֶרֶשׁ לֵאמֹר mean? Rabbi Yehudah says that they (the spies) had lumbermen's equipment on hand. [This is a play on the word חֶרֶשׁ, which can also mean 'woodcutter'.] Rabbi Nechemiah says that they made earthenware pots and barked, 'Pots for sale,' so that no one would suspect them (*Bamidbar Rabbah* 16:1). [When חֶרֶשׁ is vocalized חֶרֶשׂ it means *pottery.*] *Minchas Shai* points out that this *Midrash* does not mean to imply that the correct reading of the word is חֶרֶשׂ. Since vowel points are omitted in scrolls of Scripture written for synagogue use, homiletic interpretations based upon alternative vocalizations are commonly found in midrashic literature.

לְכוּ רְאוּ אֶת־הָאָרֶץ — *Go observe the Land.*

In regard to Moses' spies, the Torah states וַיִּשְׁלַח אֹתָם מֹשֶׁה לָתוּר, *Moses sent them to scout (Numbers* 13:17). The word לָתוּר connotes 'observing with the intent to judge.' They sought to determine *whether* the Jews should conquer the land (see *Malbim* and *R' Hirsch* to *Numbers* 13:2). This was not the case with Joshua's mission. They were sent merely to *observe* [רְאוּ], rather than to form judgments about the merits of the Land. Their observations were

2 *observe the Land and Jericho.' So they traveled and*
1 *came to the house of a woman innkeeper named*
Rachav, and they slept there.

intended only to help develop a strategy of entry *(Malbim).*

אֶת־הָאָרֶץ וְאֶת־יְרִיחוֹ — *The Land and Jericho.*

Even though Jericho is a part of the Land, it was singled out because it was more difficult to capture than all the other cities combined, since it was located on the border [and border cities must be particularly well defended] *(Rashi* from *Sifri). Meam Loez* comments that Jericho's strength derived from the fact that it was surrounded by seven walls and had an army composed of troops from all the Canaanite kings.

Other commentators maintain that Jericho was distinguished because it was such a large city *(Radak).*

Often Scripture makes a general statement and then cites one specific case in order to indicate that the specific case alone is equivalent to the general one. For instance, when Yoav returned from following Avner, he gathered his people together, but *there were nineteen of David's servants missing and Asa'el (II Samuel* 2:30). Even though Asa'el was one of the nineteen missing, he was singled out because he was as important as the other eighteen *(Rashi, ibid.).*

From this chapter it seems that the spies were not able to complete their double mission of scouting the Land and Jericho and that in this respect, their mission was not successful. However, *Lev Aharon* remarks that the spies' sole purpose was to visit Jericho, Canaan's strongest fortification. If they could ascertain that Jericho was alarmed by Israel's close presence, this would indicate that the moment had arrived to make their invasion (see *Prefatory Remarks),* and it would not be necessary for them to travel the remainder of the Land. In this sense, Jericho was equal to all the other cities of Canaan.

Poras Yosef contends that they were commanded to traverse the entire land first and then to enter Jericho, so that its inhabitants would not be able to discern that the spies originated from Israel's camp.

Malbim agrees that this phrase connotes two distinct missions, but disagrees in regard to journeying the entire land. He understands אֶת־הָאָרֶץ to refer only to the outskirts of Jericho.

יְרִיחוֹ — *Jericho.*

The city received this name because fragrant trees grew there; the Hebrew root רֵיחַ means 'to smell' *(Rashi, Berachos* 43a).

Others suggest that its name stems from יָרֵחַ, *moon,* a reference to the pagan cult of moon worship which was deeply entrenched there *(Ahavas Yehonasan).*

For an explanation of the variant spellings of יְרִיחוֹ (sometimes יְרֵחוֹ), see *R' Bachya (Deuteronomy* 32:49).

וַיֵּלְכוּ וַיָּבֹאוּ — *So they traveled and (they) came to.*

Poras Yosef continues: *so they traveled,* refers to their journey through the entire country; *and they came,* refers to their stop in Jericho.

The phrase וַיֵּלְכוּ וַיָּבֹאוּ is not redundant (see *Rashi's* comment to *Sotah* 35a on *Numbers* 13:26).

בֵּית אִשָּׁה זוֹנָה — *To the house of a woman innkeeper.*

Targum renders זוֹנָה as פּוּנְדְּקִיתָא which literally means *a seller of foods. Rashi* understands *Targum* literally, but *Radak* argues that *Targum* translated euphemistically; just as a food merchant will sell his products to anyone, so will a harlot sell hers. *Abarbanel* suggests that there is no contradiction between the two views. Typically, a woman who sold food [in an inn] was a harlot. [Cf., *Rashi's* comment to verse 15; he seems to reverse his interpretation and understands זוֹנָה as *harlot.*]

Malbim suggests that the spies purposely went to Rachav's house in

ב

ב־ג

ב וַיֵּאָמַ֗ר לְמֶ֣לֶךְ יְרִיח֔וֹ לֵאמֹ֑ר הִנֵּ֣ה אֲ֠נָשִׁים
בָּ֣אוּ הֵ֧נָּה הַלַּ֛יְלָה מִבְּנֵ֥י יִשְׂרָאֵ֖ל לַחְפֹּ֥ר
ג אֶת־הָאָֽרֶץ׃ וַיִּשְׁלַח֙ מֶ֣לֶךְ יְרִיח֔וֹ אֶל־רָחָ֖ב
לֵאמֹ֑ר הוֹצִ֨יאִי הָאֲנָשִׁ֜ים הַבָּאִ֣ים אֵלַ֗יִךְ

order to maintain a low profile. Since the people in Canaan understood that harlotry was abhorrent to the Jews, they would never have suspected these two men of being from the Israelite camp.

Alshich explains that the spies chose Rachav's house because she was the paramour of the thirty-one Canaanite kings[1] *(Zevachim* 116b) and was therefore privy to their thoughts.

Abarbanel, however, claims that the spies exercised poor judgment in visiting Rachav's house; since their mission was to survey the Land, they should not have entered any houses. He maintains that because of this mistake they were punished by being detected and pursued.

וּשְׁמָהּ רָחָב — *Named* [lit. *and her name*] *Rachav.*

According to the Sages, Rachav was the most infamous of harlots:

☐ There was not one prince or ruler who had not visited Rachav the harlot (*Zevachim* 116b).

☐ *Her house was in a wall ... and in the fortification she lived* (2:15) — She offered her services to the inhabitants within the city and to the robbers without *(Sifri Zuta, Numbers* 10:29).

☐ She was twelve years old when Israel left Egypt, and she was a harlot for the forty years that Israel lived in the Wilderness (*Zevachim* 116b).

However, the *Midrash* teaches that when the expression *his name* follows a person's proper name in Scripture, this indicates that he was an evil person (e.g., *Naval is his name — I Samuel* 25:25). When the expression *his name* precedes a person's name (e.g., *his name was Elkanah — ibid.,* 1:1), this indicates that he was righteous *(Esther Rabbah* 6:2). Why, then, does this verse state *and her name was Rachav,* which would seem to imply that Rachav was righteous?

The Sages explain that when the two spies came to Rachav's house that night, she abruptly repented of her sins and totally refashioned her entire being. By virtue of her perfect repentance, that very same evening she attained to the lofty level of *ruach hakodesh,* a spiritual level close to prophecy. The *Midrash (Ruth Rabbah,* Ch. 1) and *Sifri* (to *Deuteronomy* 1:24) deduce this from the fact that Rachav was able to predict that the search party would return after three days. The verse, *the young maidens love You* [God] *(Song of Songs* 1:3) refers to Rachav *(Rashi, ibid.).*

Her prediction is found in verse 16. Verse 22 indicates that they did indeed give up the search after three days.

Rachav later converted to Judaism and married Joshua (*Megillah* 14b; see 6:25 and *Commentary).*

The *Midrash* (*Tana deBei Eliyahu Zuta,* Ch. 22) relates that she was called רָחָב [lit., *wide*] because she gained 'extensive' merit in that

1. How could Pinchas and Calev rely on their own righteousness and moral self-discipline and risk being tempted by this seductive harlot?

The *Midrash (Bamidbar Rabbah* 16:1) explains that there is no one more beloved to God than an agent who is sent to perform a *mitzvah* and who totally dedicates himself to his mission. The *Midrash* notes that no agents were ever more dedicated to their holy mission than those dispatched by Joshua. The *Talmud (Sotah* 21a) declares that even though an individual is protected from external harm while performing a *mitzvah,* he is not protected from the influence of his own evil inclination. This explains why Moses' spies, who were engaged in performing a *mitzvah,* fell prey to the dictates of their evil inclination. Joshua's spies, however, were afforded additional protection by virtue of their stalwart dedication and devotion to their mission *(Mussar HaNeveim).*

2 *It was told to the king of Jericho as follows,
'Behold! men have come here this evening from the
Children of Israel to investigate the land.'*
3 *The king of Jericho thereupon sent to Rachav,
saying, 'Deliver the men who have come to you, who*

her descendants included eight prophets: Nariah, Baruch, Serayah, Machsayah, Jeremiah, Chilkiah, Chanamel, and Shalom (*Megillah* 14b; *Ruth Rabbah* adds Ezekiel and his father Buzi; see *Commentary* to v. 11, s.v. כי ה', and *footnote* 1 to verse 15).

וַיִּשְׁכְּבוּ־שָׁמָּה — *And they slept there.*

This informs us that the spies remained there for less than one night; they left while it was still dark *(Radak)*. [Perhaps, *Radak* derived his interpretation from the fact that Scripture employed the word *slept*, instead of the more common usage for spending the night וַיָּלִנוּ, *they lodged* (see 3:1).]

As soon as they arrived, the spies feigned fatigue from travel and went to sleep, so that their lack of interest in Rachav would not cause her to suspect them of being spies *(Minchah Ketanah)*.

2. וַיֵּאָמַר — *It was told.*

This term connotes the relating of an astonishing message *(Mateh Binyamin)*.

There are two words in Hebrew which are equivalent to the English 'was told' — וַיֻּגַּד and וַיֵּאָמַר. The verb וַיֻּגַּד is used when the message related would not surprise its recipient because he would expect such an event to ultimately come about (see *Genesis* 31:22, *Exodus* 14:5), whereas וַיֵּאָמַר [the *niphal* form] is used when the message would startle its recipient because the news was unpredictable. Jericho was so well-fortified against Israel's entry that the king never feared an infiltration. Therefore, *it was told* (וַיֵּאָמַר) to the king *(Mateh Binyamin)*.

The word הִנֵּה, *behold*, is used to introduce the message because this expression also connotes surprise *(Mateh Binyamin)*.

מִבְּנֵי יִשְׂרָאֵל — *From the Children of Israel.*

The inhabitants of Jericho concluded that the men were spies on the basis of three facts stated in this verse (*Malbim*):

(a) *men have come* — They were able to penetrate a fortified city where no one enters or leaves.

(b) *here* — Had they been merchants they would have lodged outside the city gates in order to get an early start in the morning; they would not have come *inside* Jericho.

(c) *this evening* — Travelers normally enter a city *before* nightfall.

לַחְפֹּר — *To investigate.*

Rashi renders לַחְפֹּר as לְרַגֵּל, *to spy*. However, *Malbim* distinguishes between the words לְרַגֵּל and לַחְפֹּר. While לְרַגֵּל means to survey and view a broad expanse, לַחְפֹּר, from the root חָפַר, *to dig*, connotes an in-depth search in one area. The spies wished to determine the attitude of the entire country by delving into the thoughts of the inhabitants of Jericho.

[This word analysis supports *Lev Aharon's* comment to verse 1, concerning *The Land and Jericho*.]

3. הוֹצִיאִי — *Deliver.*

[The king's messengers asked Rachav to surrender the men and did not immediately storm her house to apprehend them.]

Ahavas Yehonasan explains that Rachav's house was also a center for pagan worship, and the prevailing custom of that time was that miscreants were granted asylum in such places until the religious functionary agreed to their surrender. Hence, the messengers were not empowered to enter without permission.

Abarbanel (v. 4) advances that women locked their doors at night. [Presumably, she listened to their request through her closed door.]

Meam Loez suggests that by seeking her cooperation, the messengers implied that they felt she was not deliberately harboring them.

אֲשֶׁר־בָּאוּ לְבֵיתֵךְ כִּי לַחְפֹּר אֶת־כָּל־
ד הָאָרֶץ בָּאוּ: וַתִּקַּח הָאִשָּׁה אֶת־שְׁנֵי
הָאֲנָשִׁים וַתִּצְפְּנוֹ וַתֹּאמֶר כֵּן בָּאוּ אֵלַי
ה הָאֲנָשִׁים וְלֹא יָדַעְתִּי מֵאַיִן הֵמָּה: וַיְהִי
הַשַּׁעַר לִסְגּוֹר בַּחֹשֶׁךְ וְהָאֲנָשִׁים יָצָאוּ לֹא
יָדַעְתִּי אָנָה הָלְכוּ הָאֲנָשִׁים רִדְפוּ מַהֵר

הוֹצִיאִי הָאֲנָשִׁים הַבָּאִים אֵלַיִךְ — *Deliver the men who have come to you.*

You will not be held responsible for harboring these men, because we know that they have deceived you by saying that they were interested in harlotry. The verb *to come* also has the connotation of living together *(Lev Aharon).*

אֲשֶׁר־בָּאוּ לְבֵיתֵךְ — *Who have entered your house.*

The translation follows *Targum.* The commentators explain that the phrase *who have entered your house* is not redundant.

Lev Aharon continues: The men came to your house in order to gather intelligence about our country through all the people who are at your inn.

Abarbanel suggests that the king wanted her to produce all the visitors of her inn, both those who came for immoral reasons and those who came for lodging. *Daas Sofrim* also understands this as a compound expression, but interprets it slightly differently, to mean: all the visitors and future visitors of your inn (הַבָּאִים), and particularly those spies who have recently come (... בָּאוּ).

Alshich interprets the second phrase *who have entered your house* as an explanation of the first expression *the men who have come to you.* Since the first expression could be understood to mean that they came for immoral reasons, the messengers clarified their words to exclude such an interpretation.

4. וַתִּקַּח הָאִשָּׁה — *The woman had taken.*

She had already hidden the spies before the king's messengers arrived *(Radak).*

Radak asserts that the prefix ו not only reverses the tense of the verb, but can also indicate the past perfect tense (cf. *Commentary* to 1:2).

Lev Aharon argues that the verb וַתִּקַּח, *she took,* cannot refer to leading or conveying people. Rather, it should be understood reflexively as 'she took the side of the men.' *Onkelos* sometimes (e.g., *Numbers* 16:1) understands the verb לָקַח, *to take,* when it refers to people, to taking sides (See *Rashi ad loc.* and *Ramban).*

וַתִּצְפְּנוֹ — *And had hidden them* [lit. *him*].

Rachav concealed both spies, although וַתִּצְפְּנוֹ literally means she hid *him. Targum* also translates this word in the plural, rather than literally.

Rashi comments that it is not unusual for Scripture to refer to the plural as the singular. In this case, Rachav hid them hurriedly and in a narrow place that was suitable for only one man.

Rashi offers another explanation according to which the singular form is used to imply that each spy was concealed separately. *Radak* adds that each spy was hidden separately so that if he was able to escape to the roof, his hiding place would not be as noticeable since the hollowed-out section in the flax where he was hiding would have been large enough for only one man. *Metzudos* contends that it was easier for Rachav to conceal them separately.

The *Midrash* explains, however, that Rachav actually hid only one spy, while the other spy hid himself (*Bamidbar Rabbah* 16).

have entered your house, for they have come to spy
out the entire land.'
4 *The woman had taken the two men and had*
hidden them. She said, 'It is true, the men did come to
me, but I did not know from where they came. 5 *At*
dark, when the city gate was about to close, the men
left; I don't know where they headed. Pursue them

Others suggest that Rachav did not hide Pinchas and Calev. Rather, she planned a deception by hiding another man and leaving Pinchas and Calev in open view (*Meam Loez).*

Lev Aharon and *Alshich* understand וַתִּצְפְּנוֹ as *she hid it* — i.e., Rachav did not reveal her knowledge of their presence. *Poras Yosef* points out that this interpretation resolves the apparent inconsistency between וַתִּצְפְּנוֹ (verse 4) and וַתִּטְמְנֵם (verse 6), for the former is taken as a reference to Rachav's concealing her knowledge and the latter to her physically hiding the spies.

Rashi cites *Tanchuma* that Rachav had to conceal only Calev; Pinchas, however, was like an angel, which is invisible.[1]

כֵּן בָּאוּ אֵלַי — *It is true,* [*the men*] *did come to me.*

[Rachav's response seems puzzling since the king's messengers never asked if they had come, but rather demanded their presentation.]

Lev Aharon comments: Yes, it is as you said [see *Commentary* to verse 3]; they deceived me by feigning interest in me, but I was not able to find anything about their past.

Alshich continues: Yes, they came, to me. And if there were only two that came I would have been able to find out where they came from. However, just as these two (she points to Calev and Pinchas to imply that they are obviously not those in whom the kings' messengers are interested) have come and I do not know their past, so many others have come whose origin I do not know. [This is in accordance with the view in the previous note that Rachav did not hide Pinchas and Calev.]

וְלֹא יָדַעְתִּי מֵאַיִן הֵמָּה — *But I did not know from where they came.*

If she had known, she would have been culpable for not delivering them to the king on her own initiative *(HaRav Gifter).*

5. וַיְהִי הַשַּׁעַר לִסְגּוֹר בַּחֹשֶׁךְ — *At dark, when the city gate was about to close.*

The word הַשַּׁעַר, *the gate,* refers to the gate of the city, which was closed at evening *(Metzudos).* However, *Abarbanel* suggests that it could refer to the gate at Rachav's house: When I was about to close my gate at night, these men fled. Only then did it become apparent that these visitors were not ordinary lodgers, but spies *(Malbim).*

לֹא יָדַעְתִּי אָנָה הָלְכוּ הָאֲנָשִׁים — *I don't know where they headed.*

Just as I never learned where they came from, I did not find out where they were going. This is another indication that they were spies *(Malbim).*

רִדְפוּ מַהֵר אַחֲרֵיהֶם כִּי תַשִּׂיגוּם — *Pursue them quickly for you can overtake them.*

1. The question arises: In what respect did Pinchas resemble an angel? *Be'er Moshe* suggests that Pinchas was similar to an angel in that he was innocent of any impure thoughts, even while in the presence of Rachav. The *Talmud (Taanis* 5b) declares that Rachav was so irresistibly alluring that one who merely uttered her name twice was unable to control his desire for her. [As *Mesillas Yesharim* explains, one who does not have the desire for sin is on a higher spiritual plane than one who desires but refrains. Thus, Pinchas appeared as an angel in comparison to Calev.]

ו אַחֲרֵיהֶם כִּי תַשִּׂיגוּם: וְהִיא הֶעֱלָתַם
הַגָּגָה וַתִּטְמְנֵם בְּפִשְׁתֵּי הָעֵץ הָעֲרֻכוֹת
ז לָהּ עַל־הַגָּג: וְהָאֲנָשִׁים רָדְפוּ אַחֲרֵיהֶם
דֶּרֶךְ הַיַּרְדֵּן עַל הַמַּעְבְּרוֹת וְהַשַּׁעַר סָגָרוּ
אַחֲרֵי כַּאֲשֶׁר יָצְאוּ הָרֹדְפִים אַחֲרֵיהֶם:
ח וְהֵמָּה טֶרֶם יִשְׁכָּבוּן וְהִיא עָלְתָה עֲלֵיהֶם
ט עַל־הַגָּג: וַתֹּאמֶר אֶל־הָאֲנָשִׁים יָדַעְתִּי כִּי־

Rachav said this to divert the messenger's attention so that they would neither search her house nor remain in the city. Their leaving the city would allow her enough time to lower the spies from her window [which overlooked the outside of the city] *(Lev Aharon).*

6. וְהִיא הֶעֱלָתַם הַגָּגָה — *She had brought them up to the roof.*

After Rachav directed the king's couriers away from her house, she brought the men up to the roof for fear that the messengers might return *(Malbim).*

וַתִּטְמְנֵם — *And had hidden them.*

Verse 4 mentioned that Rachav concealed the men. At this point, Scripture recounts the details of their concealment *(Radak).*

[According to *Lev Aharon* and *Alshich* (see *Commentary* to v. 4), Scripture now discusses the concealment of the spies for the first time.]

Metzudos understands this to connote a *second* hiding; Rachav now hid the men in a safer location. Others explain that Rachav heaped so much flax on the men that no onlooker would be able to detect them *(Abarbanel).*

בְּפִשְׁתֵּי הָעֵץ — *In the stalks of flax.*

Ben Poras Yosef suggests that Rachav hid them in flax to indicate to them that the Canaanite forces had become as dry as wood.

Radak explains that the words are inverted and should be understood as עֲצֵי פִּשְׁתִּים, *stalks of flax,* meaning that the flax fibers had not yet been separated from the stalks.

Alternatively, the plant may have been *cotton,* rather than flax *(Malbim).*

הָעֲרֻכוֹת לָהּ עַל־הַגָּג — *That were methodically stacked [for her] on the roof.*

While *Radak* and *Targum* understand הָעֲרֻכוֹת, *methodically stacked,* as describing the previous arrangement of the flax, *Metzudos* understands it as describing the way in which she now arranged the stalks on top of the men.

Radak explains that the flax was arranged on the roof to facilitate its drying.

7. וְהָאֲנָשִׁים רָדְפוּ אַחֲרֵיהֶם — *So the men pursued them.*

Duped by Rachav's ruse, the messengers rushed out, thinking they were pursuing the spies *(Radak).*

עַל — *To* [lit. *on*].

The translation follows *Targum. Radak* notes that עַל, usually translated 'on,' can also mean *until,* as in *and his border will be* עַל, *until Zidon (Genesis* 49:13).

Minchas Shai observes that there are nine such cases in *Tanach.*

הַמַּעְבְּרוֹת — *The fords.*

Thinking that the Israelites would return to their encampment, the king's couriers headed for the part of the Jordan which bordered the plains of Arvos Moav and was easy to cross *(Rashi).*

וְהַשַּׁעַר סָגָרוּ — *They closed the gate.*

Malbim interprets: 'they [the messengers] closed the [city] gate after themselves.' He maintains that the final

2
6-9

quickly for you can overtake them.' [6] *She had
brought them up to the roof and had hidden them in
the stalks of flax that were methodically stacked on
the roof.*

[7] *So the men pursued them in the direction of the
Jordan to the fords. They closed the gate soon after
the pursuers had gone out after them.*

[8] *They had not yet gone to sleep when she came up
to them on the roof.* [9] *And she said to the men, 'I*

word of the verse, אַחֲרֵיהֶם, should be connected with סָגָרוּ. Thus, the king's messengers closed the city gate from the other side to thwart the Israelites escape, in case they had not yet left the city. Others say that it was the gate keeper who closed the city's gate (*Metzudos*). [According to this view the word אַחֲרֵיהֶם is in its proper place.]

Alshich, however, suggests that it was not the city gate which the king's couriers locked, but Rachav's gate, on the chance that the spies might still be in the house. If, after pursuing them, the couriers were not able to find the Israelites, they could return and thoroughly search Rachav's house. This also explains why she had to let the spies out through the window.

אַחֲרֵי כַּאֲשֶׁר — *Soon after.*

The construction אַחֲרֵי כַּאֲשֶׁר is problematic because the letter כ, appears to be superfluous. See *R' Yishaye HaRishon* and *Sefer HaRikmah* who assert that it is, in fact, unnecessary.

Radak explains that if Scripture had stated אַחֲרֵי אֲשֶׁר, it would have connoted that the gate was closed after some time (see *Commentary* to 1:1, s.v. 'After'), and if it had stated כַּאֲשֶׁר יָצְאוּ, it would have meant immediately after. [Thus, the כ serves to identify the approximate time, in this case, *soon after* the pursuers had left. See *Exodus* 11:4, כַּחֲצֹת הַלַּיְלָה, *about midnight.*]

Rif, however, maintains that the king delayed closing the city's gate so that the escaping Israelites would not be trapped within the city, but would be able to flee. They would then be handily met by their pursuers.

The people inside Rachav's house did not close the gate as soon as the king's couriers left, for they felt that this would have led the messengers to suspect that the spies were hiding in the house (*Radak*).

Rachav's people shut the gate to assure privacy so that no intruding lodgers would discover that the spies were still in the house (*Abarbanel*).

☙ Rachav's Plea

8. טֶרֶם יִשְׁכָּבוּן — *They had not yet gone to sleep.*

This indicates that the spies slept there that night, despite their great peril. Their composure during this crisis attests to their deep trust in God's protection (*Kli Yakar*).

עֲלֵיהֶם — *To* [lit. *on*] *them.*

Scripture includes other instances in which עַל (usually translated 'on') means 'to.' *I Samuel* 2:11, for example, states, *Elkanah went to Ramah* עַל *'to' his house* (*Radak*).

Malbim translates עֲלֵיהֶם literally as *on them.* He understands the verse to mean that Rachav climbed on top of the pile of flax stalks in order to remove them so that she could talk to the Israelites.

Alshich also understands עֲלֵיהֶם literally, but suggests that Rachav went to the roof of a room which was *above* the roof the spies were on. This way she was able to talk to the men out of earshot of the other guests and did not

נָתַן יהוה לָכֶם אֶת־הָאָרֶץ וְכִי־נָפְלָה
אֵימַתְכֶם עָלֵינוּ וְכִי נָמֹגוּ כָּל־יֹשְׁבֵי הָאָרֶץ
י מִפְּנֵיכֶם׃ כִּי שָׁמַעְנוּ אֵת אֲשֶׁר־הוֹבִישׁ
יהוה אֶת־מֵי יַם־סוּף מִפְּנֵיכֶם בְּצֵאתְכֶם
מִמִּצְרַיִם וַאֲשֶׁר עֲשִׂיתֶם לִשְׁנֵי מַלְכֵי
הָאֱמֹרִי אֲשֶׁר בְּעֵבֶר הַיַּרְדֵּן לְסִיחֹן וּלְעוֹג
יא אֲשֶׁר הֶחֱרַמְתֶּם אוֹתָם׃ וַנִּשְׁמַע וַיִּמַּס
לְבָבֵנוּ וְלֹא־קָמָה עוֹד רוּחַ בְּאִישׁ

appear too forward, as she would have if she had climbed next to the men.

9. יָדַעְתִּי כִּי־נָתַן ה׳ לָכֶם אֶת־הָאָרֶץ — *I know that HASHEM has given you the Land.*

This is a general statement. Rachav then indicates the two facts upon which her conclusion is based: (a) *Fear of you has fallen upon us,* and (b) *all the inhabitants of the Land have melted because of you (Malbim).*

According to *Abarbanel,* Rachav made three observations in this verse and traced the underlying reason for each one in the following verse. This statement is her first observation. She deduced it from the miracle that God performed for the Israelites by drying up the water of the Sea of Reeds, mentioned in verse 10 (see *Abarbanel* further).

וְכִי־נָפְלָה אֵימַתְכֶם עָלֵינוּ — *Fear of you has fallen upon us.*

We are terrified because of your greatness *(Malbim).*

According to *Abarbanel,* this is Rachav's second observation: The king of Jericho and his princes were terrified by the Israelites; the great effort which they expended to capture the spies attests to this. In verse 10, she cites the defeat of the Emorite kings as the cause for their fear.

וְכִי נָמֹגוּ כָּל־יֹשְׁבֵי הָאָרֶץ מִפְּנֵיכֶם — *And all the inhabitants of the Land have melted because of you.*

They have melted for fear of the evil that you will perpetrate against them *(Malbim).*

Abarbanel explains that this is Rachav's third observation: Not only the royalty, but also the Land's other inhabitants are afraid, for they saw how you utterly destroyed Sichon and Og (mentioned in *v.* 10).

10. כִּי שָׁמַעְנוּ אֵת אֲשֶׁר־הוֹבִישׁ ה׳ אֶת־מֵי יַם־סוּף — *For we have heard how HASHEM dried up the water of the Sea of Reeds.*

According to *Abarbanel (v.* 9), this expression constitutes the evidence for Rachav's statement (*v.* 9) that God has given the Land to the Israelites. If God can fashion such a miracle as happened at the Sea of Reeds, then surely He can give you this land.[1]

1. What is the connection between the miracle of the drying of the Sea of Reeds and the inheriting of *Eretz Yisrael,* and why did Rachav single this out from among the many miracles that took place at the Splitting of the Sea?

The *Midrash* provides a perspective for understanding the significance of this particular miracle (see *Gevuros Hashem,* 40).

R' Meir teaches that The Holy One, Blessed is He, said to Adam, 'For you, My one and only, I will make the seas into dry land, as it is written, *Let the waters gather (Genesis* 1:9). For a holy congregation, I should certainly do the same!' *(Mechilta* to *Exodus* 14:15.)

To provide Adam with a dwelling place, God disregarded water's tendency to spread out, and partially withdrew the seas from the face of the earth. This was a gesture not of חֶסֶד,

know that HASHEM has given you the Land. Fear of
you has fallen upon us, and all the inhabitants of the
Land have melted because of you. 10 *For we have*
heard how HASHEM dried up the water of the Sea of
Reeds for you when you came out of Egypt and what
you did to the two Emorite kings across the Jordan —
to Sichon and Og — whom you utterly destroyed.
11 *When we heard, our hearts melted — no spirit is*

מִפְּנֵיכֶם — *For you* [lit. *from before you*].

The miracle at the Sea of Reeds was performed by God out of His great love for the Israelites. Had it been merely as a punishment for Pharoah and his troops, there would have been no need to make such an involved miracle as the parting of the waters and the crossing on dry land *(Chida).*

וַאֲשֶׁר עֲשִׂיתֶם לִשְׁנֵי מַלְכֵי הָאֱמֹרִי — *And what you did to the two Emorite kings.*

Abarbanel continues: For this reason, the royalty of Jericho is alarmed at your presence.

Since you dealt so harshly with the two Emorite rulers, the royalty of Jericho fears that you will do the same to them *(Abarbanel).*

11. וַנִּשְׁמַע וַיִּמַּס לְבָבֵנוּ — *When we heard, our hearts melted.*

Rachav's statement is a clarification of her previous remark, *Fear of you has fallen upon us (v.* 9). The Canaanites did not fear Israel itself, but the mighty God who had chosen them. Therefore, Rachav proclaimed *that HASHEM your God, He is ... (Abarbanel).*

When the people of a country hear that a distant attacker is approaching, they are usually filled with trepidation. When the enemy has arrived at their boundary, however, their natural impulse is to rally and to ward him off. This was not so in the case of the Canaanites. Even when the Jews arrived, the Canaanites remained paralyzed with fear, for they realized that it was impossible for them to withstand God's might *(Malbim).*

וְלֹא קָמָה עוֹד רוּחַ בְּאִישׁ מִפְּנֵיכֶם — *No spirit is left in anyone* [lit. *man*] *because of you.*

Their energies are sapped to the extent that they have lost their sexual desire *(Rashi).*

[*Rashi's* comment is based on *Zevachim* 116a, which is in consonance with the statement of the *Talmud (Sotah* 36a) mentioned in the *Commentary* to 24:12. The hornet which preceded Israel's entry to *Eretz Yisrael* (see *Exodus* 23:28) was sent to blind the Canaanites. According to the *Talmud (Sotah* 36a), the poison ejected by the hornet also sterilized the Canaanites. For this reason, therefore, the men became sexually effete, no longer interested in procreation.]

kindness, but of דִין, *strict justice* or *necessity,* for without dry land, man would perish and God's goals for Creation would not be realized. Therefore, in describing God's ingathering of the seas to expose dry land (Genesis 1:9), Scripture uses ELOHIM, the Name that alludes to Him as Judge. God's original purpose was to have been fulfilled by Adam and all his offspring. In the aftermath of Adam's sin and the failure of succeeding generations to be worthy of this calling, the mission passed to Abraham and his offspring, Israel (see Overview to *Yechezkel,* part IV and *Derech HaShem,* Part II, Chapter 4).

When Israel was freed from Egypt, the nation was prepared to receive the Torah and go on to *Eretz Yisrael,* the land of holiness, which is perfectly suited to the fulfillment of God's goal for man. As the primeval gathering of waters had paved the way for Adam's mission, so the receding of the Sea of Reeds paved the way for Adam's standard bearer, the nation of Israel.

Thus, Rachav related to the spies that Israel's unique relationship with God found its most graphic demonstration in the gesture that had once been shown Adam — the drying up of the sea. Therefore, the Canaanites recognized that they could not stand in Israel's way.

מִפְּנֵיכֶם כִּי יְהוָה אֱלֹהֵיכֶם הוּא אֱלֹהִים
יב בַּשָּׁמַיִם מִמַּעַל וְעַל־הָאָרֶץ מִתָּחַת: וְעַתָּה
הִשָּׁבְעוּ־נָא לִי בַּיהוָה כִּי־עָשִׂיתִי עִמָּכֶם
חָסֶד וַעֲשִׂיתֶם גַּם־אַתֶּם עִם־בֵּית אָבִי
יג חֶסֶד וּנְתַתֶּם לִי אוֹת אֱמֶת: וְהַחֲיִתֶם אֶת־

Radak and *Metzudos* understand this expression more literally, i.e., 'everyone's spirits are low and depressed.'

כִּי ה׳ אֱלֹהֵיכֶם הוּא אֱלֹהִים בַּשָּׁמַיִם מִמַּעַל וְעַל־הָאָרֶץ מִתָּחַת -- *For HASHEM your God He is God in the heavens above and on the earth below.*

Rambam (Hil. Yesodei HaTorah 1:8) finds evidence in this verse for a fundamental belief of Judaism — that God is non-corporeal. Since Scripture asserts that God is both in the heavens and on earth, it would be impossible for him to possess a body, since no body can be in two places at the same time.

In the short span of that evening, Rachav achieved an understanding of God which eclipsed that of any other convert. The *Midrash (Yalkut Shimoni* 247:10) relates that Jethro said, *'Now I know that HASHEM is greater than all gods' (Exodus* 18:11) ... Na'aman acknowledged God more, saying, 'Behold, I know that there is no other God on all the earth besides Israel's *(II Kings* 5:15) ... But Rachav surpassed their understanding when she said, *'For HASHEM your God He is God in the heavens above and on the earth below.'* The Holy One, Blessed is He, said to Rachav, 'I understand your recognition of Me on *the earth below,* but how could you possibly have accepted My existence *in the heavens above* which you cannot see? By virtue of this, your descendant [Ezekiel] will see what the other prophets were not able to see, as Scripture states *(Ezekiel* 1:1), *It was in the thirtieth year ... the heavens opened, and I* [*Ezekiel*] *saw visions of God.'* [See *Commentary* to v. 1, s.v., *'Rachav.'*]

Kli Yakar infers from this that although Rachav may have surpassed Jethro's and Na'aman's understanding of the Almighty, Moses surpassed hers, for Moses said not only *because HASHEM is God in the heavens above and on the earth below,* but also, *there is nothing else (Deuteronomy* 4:39).

12. וְעַתָּה — *Now.*

Malbim explains that Rachav means: Now that I have converted, I can claim exemption from the Biblical command, *no soul may you let live*[1] *(Deuteronomy* 20:16).

1. *Malbim's* insights into Rachav's plea are based on *halachah* and require some preliminary explanation.

Upon entering *Eretz Yisrael,* the Jews were required to fulfill the commandment לֹא תְחַיֶּה כָּל־נְשָׁמָה, *no soul may you let live (Deuteronomy* 20:16). *Sefer HaChinuch* (425, 525) explains that the seven indigenous nations of the Land (Canaanite, Perizzite, Hivvite, Jebusite, Hittite, Girgashite, and Emorite) were to be totally eradicated from the face of the earth, because they had become so inextricably entrenched in pagan practices that they were loathsome to God. Israel was charged with their destruction in order to insure the religious purity of the Holy Land and in order to impress upon the Jews the egregiousness of such idolatrous acts and the severe punishments incurred by idolaters.

Everyone descending from these seven nations was included in the Biblical decree of destruction. However, *Tosafos (Sotah* 35b) explains that the decree went into effect only after the first war had been fought in the Land. Before then, the descendants of these seven nations could convert to Judaism and be exempted from the Biblical decree (cf., *footnote* to 2:13). Our Sages tell us that upon Rachav's extraordinary recognition of her Creator, she converted (*Commentary* 2:1 and 2:11; cf. *footnote* 1 to 2:13). Thus, the decree of destruction no longer applied to her. [See 2:13, *footnote* 1, which suggests that Rachav's family also converted.]

left in anyone because of you, for HASHEM your God,
He is God in the heavens above and on the earth
below. 12 *Now, I beseech you, swear to me by*
HASHEM — since I have done you kindness —that
you too will do kindness with my father's house and
give me a countersign. 13 *Keep alive my father,*

הַשָּׁבְעוּ־נָא לִי — *Swear to me.*

Because Rachav initiated the oath, once the spies agreed to abide by it, they could never revoke their pledge (*Malbim*).

Although there is a legal procedure by which a person may annul an oath, this procedure is not effective under certain conditions. Two of these conditions are that: (a) The oath was initiated by another person (*Ran, Nedarim* 65a) and (b) the oath was taken in response to a kindness which a person had done for him (*Radvaz,* to *Hil. Shavuos* 6:7). In either of these cases, dissolution of the oath can take place only with the consent of the other person. [Thus, Rachav incorporated both of these advantages: she initiated the oath, and she mentioned that it was to be taken in response to the kindness which she had shown them.]

נָא — *I beseech you.*

This is an expression of entreaty (*Rashi, Genesis* 19:18).

בַּה' — *By [the name of] HASHEM.*

Rachav included God's Name in the oath because an oath taken with such a Name, or a descriptive title, is more serious (*Malbim*).

[Only the violation of such an oath incurs the penalty of flogging (*Rambam, Hil. Shavuos* 2:3).]

כִּי־עָשִׂיתִי עִמָּכֶם חָסֶד — *Since I have done you kindness.*

As noted above, an oath sworn to a person who had done a kindness cannot be dissolved unilaterally.

חָסֶד — *Kindness.*

Kindness refers to an act of mercy which one is not obligated to perform. Since Rachav had performed a *kindness* by saving the spies' lives, she asked that they reciprocate her kindness by swearing to spare the lives of her family whom they had no obligation to save. Rachav does not mention herself, however. Because she had saved their lives, to spare her would not be deemed an act of *kindness (Radak)* but of *truth (Vilna Gaon,* verse 14), for *truth* denotes the fulfilling of an obligation or repayment of a debt.

אוֹת אֱמֶת — *Countersign* [lit. *sign of truth*].

The translation follows *Rashi* who understands this term as a physical sign that Rachav could show to the Israelites upon their invasion so that they could recognize her and spare her.

Radak, however, contends that this sign was supposed to serve as a token that the spies intended to keep their promise to Rachav.

Ben Poras Yosef suggests that Rachav was requesting a sign (אוֹת) which would demonstrate that she had converted to the true faith (אֱמֶת). This sign would prove that she had converted before the first battle and was therefore not subject to the Biblical injunction of Canaanite eradication.

13. From this verse it appears that Rachav made two distinct requests of the spies — that they should *spare* her family and that they should *save* them.

According to *Malbim,* Rachav's first request was that the spies spare her family from physical harm; her second request was that they be spared from spiritual oblivion by being permitted to convert to Judaism.

[According to the *footnote* to this verse, Rachav's requests may be interpreted as the two-stage plan she devised for the physical salvation of her family. First she asked the spies to

ב °אַחְיוֹתַי ק׳ אָבִי וְאֶת־אִמִּי וְאֶת־אַחַי וְאֶת־°אחותי
יד־טו וְאֵת כָּל־אֲשֶׁר לָהֶם וְהִצַּלְתֶּם אֶת־
יד נַפְשֹׁתֵינוּ מִמָּוֶת: וַיֹּאמְרוּ לָהּ הָאֲנָשִׁים
נַפְשֵׁנוּ תַחְתֵּיכֶם לָמוּת אִם לֹא תַגִּידוּ
טו אֶת־דְּבָרֵנוּ זֶה וְהָיָה בְּתֵת־יְהוָה לָנוּ אֶת־
הָאָרֶץ וְעָשִׂינוּ עִמָּךְ חֶסֶד וֶאֱמֶת: וַתּוֹרִדֵם
בַּחֶבֶל בְּעַד הַחַלּוֹן כִּי בֵיתָהּ בְּקִיר

temporarily spare her family when they returned to vanquish Jericho so that her family would have the opportunity to convert to Judaism. Then she asked that upon their return to Jericho, the spies should convert her family to Judaism so that they would not be subject to the decree of Canaanite extermination.]

וְהַחֲיִתֶם אֶת־אָבִי — *Keep alive my father.*

Since Rachav was a harlot, she did not have a husband or children and therefore asked for the welfare of her family of origin *(Abarbanel).*[1]

וְאֵת כָּל־אֲשֶׁר לָהֶם — *And all that they have.*

[From *Abarbanel's* next comment, it appears that he understands this phrase to refer to the offspring of Rachav's relatives, not to their material possessions.]

וְהִצַּלְתֶּם אֶת־נַפְשֹׁתֵינוּ מִמָּוֶת — *And save us from death* [lit. *save our souls from death*].

I am not asking that you save our property or our money, but only our lives *(Abarbanel).* You may take all our wealth *(Meam Loez).*

☙ The Spies' Promise

14. נַפְשֵׁנוּ תַחְתֵּיכֶם לָמוּת — *Our life for yours* [lit. *our lives are in your stead*] *to the death.*

If anyone attempts to kill you, we will sacrifice our lives to save you *(Radak).*

This expression indicates the spies' acceptance of the oath which Rachav proposed *(Radak, v.* 17).

1. [As has been explained previously (*footnote* to 2:12), there is a Biblical injunction to kill all the inhabitants of the Land who descended from the seven Canaanite nations. A double-edged question arises: how could the spies make an oath to Rachav in violation of this commandment? And if for some reason the commandment to kill the Canaanites did *not* apply to Rachav and to her family, then why was it necessary for the spies to take an oath not to kill them? *(HaRav Gifter* also raises this question.)

Mizrachi (Deuteronomy 20:18) asserts that it would be ludicrous to assume that the commandment to kill the Canaanites could apply to converts to Judaism. He puzzles rhetorically, 'How could the Torah have commanded the Israelites to kill Jews?' (Note that this does not agree with *Tosafos* mentioned in *footnote* to 2:12.)

Accordingly, Rachav did not request to be spared because it was understood that her life was not in jeopardy, since she had recently converted. However, she was concerned that her family would be in peril when the Israelites returned to storm Jericho. Feeling certain that her family would convert, Rachav implored the spies to take an oath which would allow her family enough time to convert to Judaism and thereby avoid extermination.

Thus, we see in 6:23 that after Jericho fell, the spies entered and removed Rachav and her family, and, *they brought out all her families and situated them outside the camp of Israel. Radak* explains that they converted outside the camp and were then permitted inside to reside among the Israelites.

According to this explanation, this was the fulfillment of the spies' oath! They delayed in exposing Rachav's family to the Israelites, who would have been obligated to kill them. This delay was not a nullification of the extermination decree, but rather a delay until it was no longer applicable to Rachav's family.]

mother, brothers, sisters, and all that they have and save us from death.

14 *And the men said to her, 'Our life for yours to the death, if you do not reveal this discussion of ours. And it will be when HASHEM gives us the Land, we will deal with you in kindness and truth.'*

15 *And she lowered them by the rope through the window, for her house was in a wall of the*

אִם לֹא תַגִּידוּ אֶת־דְּבָרֵינוּ זֶה — *If you do not reveal* [lit. *tell*] *this discussion of ours.*

The spies' oath was made on the condition that Rachav and her family keep the countersign secret from the other inhabitants of Jericho. The spies feared that if the sign became generally known, other Canaanites whose houses were in the wall of the city would make use of it, pretending to be members of Rachav's family *(Radak; Ralbag).*

Ahavas Yehonasan, however, understands that *this discussion,* refers to the *halachah* that a Canaanite who converts to Judaism is not subject to the Biblical injunction of Canaanite extermination. If Rachav and her family were to publicize this *halachah,* all the Canaanites might convert, in which case, many insincere proselytes would flood the ranks of Israel.

Poras Yosef interprets *this discussion* as the conversation which the Israelites had with Rachav. If it were revealed to the king, he would know they were spies and would order a full scale search to apprehend them. While the spies felt secure that God would save them from the king, they stipulated that they would be exempt from their oath if any members of Rachav's family were indiscreet.

חֶסֶד וֶאֱמֶת — *Kindness and truth.*

Rachav's plea for *kindness* concerned the saving of her family; her plea for *truth* referred to their sparing of her *(Vilna Gaon).* (See *Commentary* and *footnote* to 2:13.)

◆§ The Spies Return to Joshua

15. וַתּוֹרִדֵם בַּחֶבֶל — *And she lowered them by the rope.*[1]

Rachav used the same window and rope for the spies as she had used for the licentious men who had visited her. She proclaimed contritely, 'God, with these I have sinned; with these I ask forgiveness' *(Rashi).*[2]

Mateh Binyamin suggests that *Rashi* derived his comment from the definite article 'the' before rope and window. The definite article indicates that these objects possessed a prior significance.

בְּעַד הַחַלּוֹן — *Through the window.*

Because the gates of the city were

1. We learn from this incident that even while engaged in the performance of a mitzvah, a person must be careful to perfect every detail of his behavior.

We find that after Jeremiah was cast into a pit on treasonous charges, he was later rescued by Eved Melech by means of a rope *(Jeremiah* 38:6). The *Midrash (Yalkut Shimoni* 326) relates that Jeremiah, suffering from the arduous ascent, asked for a ladder. God responded, 'You ask for a ladder! Just as your grandmother (Rachav; see *Commentary* to v. 1, s.v. 'Rachav') lowered them [the spies] with a rope, so will you be retrieved with a rope.'

Even though Rachav saved the lives of the Israelites, she disregarded their comfort by forcing them to escape in this uncomfortable fashion. Because of this oversight, her descendant Jeremiah suffered similarly some 800 years later *(Be'er Moshe).*

2. A repentant sinner should use the medium by which he sinned as the vehicle for his repentance [see *Kitzur Shulchan Aruch* 151:7].

Perhaps this can be explained by the Talmudic dictum, 'In the place where penitents stand, righteous people cannot stand' *(Berachos* 34b). A man is composed of two inclinations, one

טז הַחוֹמָה וּבַחוֹמָה הִיא יוֹשָׁבֶת: וַתֹּאמֶר
לָהֶם הָהָרָה לֵּכוּ פֶּן־יִפְגְּעוּ בָכֶם הָרֹדְפִים
וְנַחְבֵּתֶם שָׁמָּה שְׁלֹשֶׁת יָמִים עַד שׁוֹב
יז הָרֹדְפִים וְאַחַר תֵּלְכוּ לְדַרְכְּכֶם: וַיֹּאמְרוּ
אֵלֶיהָ הָאֲנָשִׁים נְקִיִּם אֲנַחְנוּ מִשְּׁבֻעָתֵךְ
יח הַזֶּה אֲשֶׁר הִשְׁבַּעְתָּנוּ: הִנֵּה אֲנַחְנוּ בָאִים

closed, Rachav lowered the spies through her window which faced the outside of the city *(Metzudos).*

The spies left through the window, not through the door, so that the neighbors would not detect their escape from the sound of the door bolt unlocking *(Radak).*

[According to *Alshich* cited in *Commentary* to verse 7, Rachav lowered them through the window because her gate had been bolted from the outside by the king's messengers.]

כִּי בֵיתָהּ בְּקִיר הַחוֹמָה — *For her house was in a wall of the fortification.*

The translation follows *Targum.* The *fortification* refers to the large, protective wall around the entire city.

Vilna Gaon explains that Rachav's dwelling was composed of two parts. One part was a three-sided structure located within the city limits and utilized the city wall as its fourth side. The city wall was very thick; part of its thickness was carved out to serve as an extension to Rachav's house. Her window to the outside of the city was located in this extension. This explains how Rachav, who lived in the wall, was not affected when the walls collapsed miraculously (6:20), for at that moment she was in the part of her house that was within the city. *Vilna Gaon* understands the phrase *in a wall* as referring to the part of her house which was adjacent to the city wall.

וּבַחוֹמָה הִיא יוֹשָׁבֶת — *And in the fortification she lived.*

This verb can mean either 'to dwell' or 'to sit.' *Vilna Gaon* understands it in the first sense (see above note). She sometimes dwelled in the extension of the house which was carved out of the city wall — e.g., when she lowered the men by the rope.

Abarbanel, however, interprets יָשַׁב according to its second meaning 'to sit.' After Rachav lowered the men, she sat in the wall, and said to them, *Go to the mountain (v.* 16).

16. עַד שׁוֹב הָרֹדְפִים — *Until the pursuers return.*

From this comment, the Sages derive that Rachav was granted prophetic vision (רוּחַ הַקּוֹדֶשׁ), for we see in verse 22 that the pursuers did in fact return to Jericho on the third day.[1] (See *Commentary* to *v.* 21.)

which motivates him to do good acts and one which seduces him to do evil ones. One difference between the inclination to do good and the inclination to do evil is that the latter results in behavior which is more impassioned. When a person repents and refashions his evil act into a mitzvah, he takes all the very energies which had produced the evil act and rechannels them. Thus, his mitzvah is performed with greater intensity and fervor than it would have been had the person never sinned *(Mussar HaNeveim).*

[In light of *Be'er Moshe's* comment cited in the previous *footnote,* we would need to qualify the opening statement. A repentant sinner should use the medium by which he sinned as the vehicle for his repentance if, by so doing, he does not show insensitivity to another's needs.]

1. God does not allow the righteous to remain in distress for more than three days, as it says, *In the third day He will raise us up (Hoshea* 6:2).

☐ Joseph, who had accused his brothers of being spies, allowed them to return to their

fortification and in the fortification she lived. [16] *She*
said to them, 'Go to the mountain lest your pursuers meet you. Hide there three days until the pursuers return; then, you may go on your way.'

[17] *The men said to her, 'We are absolved from this oath of yours which you made us swear.* [18] *Behold,*

Radak, however, contends that Rachav was merely making a reasonable estimate when she predicted that the pursuers would return in three days. She calculated that they would follow the spies back to their encampment across the Jordan, which was about a day's journey from Jericho. Allowing another day for their search, and a day for the return trip, Rachav predicted that they would be back in three days.

17. נְקִיִּם אֲנַחְנוּ – *We are absolved* [lit. *innocent*].

The spies were saying that their oath was conditional on their request that Rachav display the countersign upon their return to Jericho. If she did not comply, they would not be held responsible to keep their oath *(Rashi).*

The spies understood the importance of completely fulfilling an oath, and they realized that according to Rachav's wording it would be impossible. She asked that her entire family be spared, to which the spies could not agree, since they could not identify *all* her relatives. Agreeing to *her* oath would be tantamount to violating the commandment of Canaanite extermination, since the spies would not be able to kill *any* Canaanite lest he be a relative of Rachav. Thus, they agreed to spare only those relatives who would be in her house upon their return to Jericho *(Ralbag).*

Malbim, however, understands this statement as a revocation of their oath in verse 14. Although oaths cannot be annulled arbitrarily, the spies claimed that their oath was not binding because Rachav had exacted it from them under duress, when their lives were in her hands (see *Nedarim* 20b). Nevertheless, they agreed to take a second, conditional oath (see *Malbim* to verse 18 and verse 20). The second was not made under duress, because they were outside her house at that time.

According to *Meam Loez,* the spies intended to tell Rachav that even without their oath, they would fulfill her wishes out of an enormous sense of gratitude for all she had done for them.

מִשְּׁבֻעָתֵךְ הַזֶּה – *From this oath of yours.*

Grammatically, the word *oath* is feminine and should therefore be modified by the feminine adjective הַזֹּאת, *this,* and not the masculine הַזֶּה, *this.*

Alshich explains that Rachav actually presented two oaths to the spies. One oath was her plea for the Israelites to spare her (cf. *footnote* to 2:13), and the other was her plea for them to save her family. It was this second oath that the spies refused to make when they said *we*

father after detaining them for three days *(Genesis* 42:18).

□ Jonah, who was caught in the entrails of a large fish, was spewed forth on the third day *(Jonah* 2:1).

□ Esther, after fasting three days, entered the inner court of the king's chamber in order to implement her plan to save the Jews (*Esther* 5:1).

And because of what merit are the righteous freed from their distress on the third day? The Sages said because of the merit of the Torah which was given on the third day of preparation *(Exodus* 19:16). R' Levi said because of the merit of the *Akeidah*, the binding of Isaac, which took place on the third day of Abraham's journey [*Genesis* 22:4] *(Bereishis Rabbah* 56:1).

בָּאָרֶץ אֶת־תִּקְוַת חוּט הַשָּׁנִי הַזֶּה תִּקְשְׁרִי
בַּחַלּוֹן אֲשֶׁר הוֹרַדְתֵּנוּ בוֹ וְאֶת־אָבִיךְ
וְאֶת־אִמֵּךְ וְאֶת־אַחַיִךְ וְאֵת כָּל־בֵּית
יט אָבִיךְ תַּאַסְפִי אֵלַיִךְ הַבָּיְתָה: וְהָיָה כֹּל
אֲשֶׁר־יֵצֵא מִדַּלְתֵי בֵיתֵךְ | הַחוּצָה דָּמוֹ
בְרֹאשׁוֹ וַאֲנַחְנוּ נְקִיִּם וְכֹל אֲשֶׁר יִהְיֶה
אִתָּךְ בַּבַּיִת דָּמוֹ בְרֹאשֵׁנוּ אִם־יָד תִּהְיֶה־
כ בּוֹ: וְאִם־תַּגִּידִי אֶת־דְּבָרֵנוּ זֶה וְהָיִינוּ
כא נְקִיִּם מִשְּׁבֻעָתֵךְ אֲשֶׁר הִשְׁבַּעְתָּנוּ: וַתֹּאמֶר
כְּדִבְרֵיכֶם כֶּן־הוּא וַתְּשַׁלְּחֵם וַיֵּלֵכוּ
כב וַתִּקְשֹׁר אֶת־תִּקְוַת הַשָּׁנִי בַּחַלּוֹן: וַיֵּלְכוּ
וַיָּבֹאוּ הָהָרָה וַיֵּשְׁבוּ שָׁם שְׁלֹשֶׁת יָמִים

are absolved, and it was this oath to which they were referring when they said *this.* 'This' in the masculine, הַזֶּה, has the numerical equivalent seventeen (ה=5, ז=7, ה=5), the number of words in verse 13 which was Rachav's plea for the saving of her family. [See *Alshich* cited in *Commentary* to 6:23.]

18. אֲנַחְנוּ בָאִים — *When we come* [lit. *we are coming*].

The translation follows *Metzudas Zion,* who interpolates the word *when.*

תִּקְוַת חוּט הַשָּׁנִי — *Scarlet cord.*

Targum renders 'a border of a red cloth.' *Rashi* renders 'a line or rope.'

Radak, however, understands this as a line twisted from fibers of scarlet linen.

Malbim views this as a provision of the spies' vow: 'We will abide by our new oath on the condition that you signal us with this string.'

תִּקְוַת — *Cord.*

The word תִּקְוַת is cognate to תִּקְוָה, *hope.* This *line* was Rachav's only 'hope' for salvation *(Kli Yakar).*

R' Yishaye, however, contends that it is related to the word מִקְוֵה, *gathering.* The *line* used for the countersign was a 'collection' or ball of red threads.

הַזֶּה — *This.*

Radak asserts that the demonstrative adjective is employed because Rachav had shown the Israelites the string before she lowered them from her window.

Metzudos contends that the very string with which she lowered the men was to serve as the countersign.

תִּקְשְׁרִי — *You shall bind.*

You shall bind it as a signal to us that you have assembled your entire family *(Mateh Binyamin).*

Alshich, however, understands the rope as a sign to the Israelites that they should not enter Rachav's house during their conquest of Jericho.

אֲשֶׁר הוֹרַדְתֵּנוּ בוֹ — *From which you lowered us.*

This phrase refers to the window. In this case, בוֹ, which literally means 'in it,' means 'through it' *(Metzudos).*

19. דָּמוֹ בְרֹאשׁוֹ — *His blood will be on his head.*

This is an idiomatic expression which connotes responsibility. Anyone who leaves Rachav's house will become responsible for his own life; however, the spies will accept responsibility for safeguarding the lives of all the relatives

2
19-22

when we come in the Land, you shall bind this scarlet
cord in the window from which you lowered us; your
father, mother, brothers, and all your father's
household you are to gather together in the house.
19 *Then it will be that anyone who leaves the doors of*
your house, his blood will be on his head; we will be
absolved. Anyone who remains with you inside the
house, his blood will be on our head, if a hand is laid
on him. 20 *And if you reveal this discussion of ours,*
we will be absolved from the oath which you have
made us swear.'
21 *She replied, 'As you say, so it will be.' She sent*
them away, and they went; and she tied the scarlet
cord to the window.
22 *And they went, and they came to the mountain*
and stayed there three days until the pursuers

who remain inside Rachav's house during the conquest *(Rashi).*

20. וְאִם־תַּגִּידִי אֶת־דְּבָרֵנוּ זֶה — *And if you reveal this discussion of ours.*

Malbim continues (see verse 17): Our new oath to save you and your family is contingent upon your promise not to reveal our discussion.

זֶה — *This.*

This refers to the countersign of the scarlet thread *(Metzudos).*

21. כְּדִבְרֵיכֶם כֶּן־הוּא — *As you say, so it will be* [lit. *As your words*].

While the expression כֶּן הוּא, literally indicates the present tense 'so it is,' it can also denote the future *so it will be (Ramban, Genesis* 44:10). The expression marks Rachav's acceptance of the conditions imposed by the spies in their second oath.

Abarbanel, however, understands this expression to mean 'so it is.' According to this view, Rachav tersely replies, 'It is true that you are not obligated to uphold the first oath, since you accepted it under coercion.'

וַתְּשַׁלְּחֵם — *(And) she sent them away.*

She did no physical act to send them away; she merely said, 'Go in peace' *(Radak).*

Radak maintains that Scripture does not mean to imply that Rachav tied the thread at *this* moment; rather she attached the string later, at the time of the Israelites' return. According to *Radak,* this verse merely informs us that Rachav obeyed the Israelites' command.

Abarbanel, however, suggests that Rachav actually tied the string immediately, fearing that if she waited until the Israelite conquest, her neighbors would suspect that she was signaling to the Jews and would kill her.

22. וַיֵּלְכוּ וַיָּבֹאוּ — *And they went, and they came.*

As *Alshich* explains this seemingly redundant expression, the spies ascended (וַיֵּלְכוּ) the mountain, but then left their encampment to determine if any Canaanites were lying in ambush. When they felt secure, the spies returned (וַיָּבֹאוּ) to their mountain encampment.

עַד־שָׁבוּ הָרֹדְפִים וַיְבַקְשׁוּ הָרֹדְפִים בְּכָל־
כג הַדֶּרֶךְ וְלֹא מָצָאוּ׃ וַיָּשֻׁבוּ שְׁנֵי הָאֲנָשִׁים
וַיֵּרְדוּ מֵהָהָר וַיַּעַבְרוּ וַיָּבֹאוּ אֶל־יְהוֹשֻׁעַ
בִּן־נוּן וַיְסַפְּרוּ־לוֹ אֵת כָּל־הַמֹּצְאוֹת
כד אוֹתָם׃ וַיֹּאמְרוּ אֶל־יְהוֹשֻׁעַ כִּי־נָתַן יהוה
בְּיָדֵנוּ אֶת־כָּל־הָאָרֶץ וְגַם־נָמֹגוּ כָּל־יֹשְׁבֵי

וְלֹא מָצָאוּ — *But did not find.*

Of course they did not find the spies who were hiding in the mountains! The intention of the verse, however, is to indicate God's intervention on behalf of the Israelites: even though the pursuers diligently searched the countryside for the slightest lead as to the whereabouts of the spies, they were not able to obtain any information *(Kli Yakar).*

23. וַיָּשֻׁבוּ שְׁנֵי הָאֲנָשִׁים — *The two men returned.*

They returned to their journey, for they had been in seclusion for three days in the mountains *(Radak).* [The spies followed the counsel that Rachav gave in verse 16.]

According to *Alshich's* interpretation (see verse 22), 'and they returned' refers to the spies' return to the temporary encampment from which they had departed in search of potential assailants. After hiding for three days, they descended the mountain and began the journey back to the Israelite camp.

שְׁנֵי — *Two.*

Upon their descent from the mountain, the spies traveled separately so that they would not be recognized. When they reached the Jordan, however, they reunited and concluded their journey *(Rif).*

וַיַּעַבְרוּ — *They crossed over.*

They crossed over the Jordan *(Rashi).*

וַיָּבֹאוּ אֶל־יְהוֹשֻׁעַ — *And (they) came to Joshua.*

This took place on the night of the ninth of the month of Nissan, according to *Vilna Gaon.* (See *footnote* to 1:10.)

The spies did not appear before the entire congregation (as did the reconnaissance mission which Moses had dispatched), but only before Joshua *(Daas Sofrim)* [who had dispatched them].

24. כִּי־נָתַן ה׳ בְּיָדֵנוּ — *For HASHEM gave HASHEM gave all the Land into our hands (Radak).*

The reason why everything we just mentioned to you occurred to us is that *HASHEM gave us all the Land (Radak).*

On what did the spies base their conclusion that God had given them the Land?

Malbim suggests that the Israelites knew from the fact that He had saved them from the Canaanites in such a miraculous way.

Lev Aharon, however, contends that their knowledge was based on the information stated in the latter part of the verse, *all the inhabitants of the Land have melted because of us,* for they recognized from the fact that the inhabitants were so alarmed that Divine Providence had prepared their entry (see *Prefatory Remarks* to this chapter and *Commentary* to verse 1, *Radak).*

Alshich notes two difficulties in this verse: (a) The evidence for their statement occurs after their statement rather than before, as it logically should have; (b) the second half of the verse seems to be disconnected from the first half; וְגַם, *(and) also,* seems to be introducing a second thought, rather than presenting evidence for the first statement. *Alshich* suggests that the spies did not want to present any sort of evidence for their belief in God's promise that Israel would inherit the Land (1:3), for they had complete faith in His word. Therefore, they stated, *HASHEM gave all the Land.* After this declaration, they mentioned the Canaanites' fear as an indication that the Israelites' imminent entry

2
23-24 *returned. The pursuers searched the entire way but did not find.*

23 *The two men returned and descended from the mountain; they crossed over [the Jordan] and came to Joshua son of Nun and told him all that happened to them.* 24 *They said to Joshua, 'For HASHEM gave all the Land into our hands; also, all the inhabitants of the Land have melted because of us.'*

into *Eretz Yisrael* would be successful. The second part of their declaration thus follows from the first, but the first part does not depend upon the second.

נָמֹגוּ — *Have melted.*

Nachalas Reuven suggests that the spies were able to determine the Canaanites' alarm from the fact that the king dispatched a contingent to investigate the report concerning strangers in the land. If a country is strong, it does not scrutinize every newcomer; if a nation feels insecure, however, every stranger represents a potential threat.

[Rachav's remarks in verses 9-11 also indicated the extent of the Canaanites' fear.]

III

Israel had been waiting forty years. After receiving the Torah on Mount Sinai, they were to make an eleven day journey to Eretz Yisrael *to acquire the land in which their destiny would unfold. Then, tragedy befell them; the generation that experienced Sinai was doomed to death in the Wilderness (see* Prefatory Remarks *to Chapter 2) and their offspring were charged with the fulfillment of their mission. After forty years and forty-two encampments in the Wilderness, they arrived at the eastern bank of the Jordan, within view of their goal. Abruptly their new momentum stalled, and they were commanded to camp for three long days of preparation before crossing (1:11).*

These three days were patterned after the three days which the Jews had spent at the foot of Mount Sinai before the Revelation (see Exodus *19:15). Just as the Jews who encamped at the foot of the mount had been required to cleanse themselves* (Exodus *19:10), so did Joshua order their offspring to cleanse themselves before they crossed the Jordan (3:5). As they stood before Mount Sinai, the Jews had reached an extraordinary level of fellowship: 'they were as one man with one heart' (see* Rashi, Exodus *19:2); similarly, their progeny attained a miraculous unity between the staves of the Holy Ark (3:9, see* Commentary) *before their entry into Eretz Yisrael.*

The Holy Ark plays the predominant role in this chapter. It is called אֲרוֹן בְּרִית־ה׳, the Ark of the Covenant of HASHEM (3:3), *because it contained the Two Tablets of the Law received from the Almighty by Moses. The word* בְּרִית, covenant, *derives from these tablets, which are referred to as* שְׁנֵי לוּחוֹת הַבְּרִית, the Two Tablets of the Covenant (Deuteronomy *9:15). Thus, to understand the significance of the Ark and its contents it is necessary to examine the import of the covenant which forms a part of its name.*

A covenant denotes a binding relationship between two parties in which each party makes a certain guarantee. In his recounting of the history of the Wilderness, Moses told his people, 'HASHEM, your God, made a covenant with us at Horev [*Mount Sinai*]' (Deuteronomy *5:2).*

א הָאָרֶץ מִפָּנֵינוּ׃ וַיַּשְׁכֵּם יְהוֹשֻׁעַ
בַּבֹּקֶר וַיִּסְעוּ מֵהַשִּׁטִּים וַיָּבֹאוּ עַד־הַיַּרְדֵּן
הוּא וְכָל־בְּנֵי יִשְׂרָאֵל וַיָּלִנוּ שָׁם טֶרֶם
ב יַעֲבֹרוּ׃ וַיְהִי מִקְצֵה שְׁלֹשֶׁת יָמִים וַיַּעַבְרוּ
ג הַשֹּׁטְרִים בְּקֶרֶב הַמַּחֲנֶה׃ וַיְצַוּוּ אֶת־הָעָם
לֵאמֹר כִּרְאֹתְכֶם אֵת אֲרוֹן בְּרִית־יהוה

In this pact, Israel guaranteed their observance of the entire Torah (Exodus *24:8*) *in exchange for a unique kind of Divine intervention in their history as it is written* (Exodus *34:10*)*:* And He said, 'Behold, I am making a covenant with you; before all your people, I will do marvels such as have not been done in all the earth, nor in any nation. All the people around you will see the work of HASHEM which I do with you, that it is awesome.' *(See* Or HaChaim *to* Deuteronomy *5:2.)*

Malbim (Exodus *34:10*) *identifies three principles in this relationship: (a) The miracles performed for Israel will be open and revealed so they are not mistaken for natural occurrences; (b) they will be unparalleled in history; (c) and they will be made public for all to see. These Divine promises were made in regard to the Jewish conquest of* Eretz Yisrael, *for Scripture continues,* Observe that which I commanded you this day: behold I drive out before you the Emorites and the Canaanites and the Hittites, and the Perizzites and the Hivvites and the Jebusites (Exodus *34:11*) [*see* Malbim, Joshua *10:2*].

The Ark, then, served as visible evidence of Israel's contract with the Almighty. Israel pledged Torah loyalty; the Almighty, wondrous protection in Eretz Yisrael. *To demonstrate its worthiness of the Divine protection promised in the covenant, Israel needed to renew its dedication to Torah observance as God had admonished Joshua (1:8)* [*see* Commentary *to 3:14*)]. *This renewal contained the same elements present at the original acceptance of the Torah by their forefathers at Mount Sinai: cleansing of the body, strong national fellowship, and three days of preparation.*

In the Wilderness, the Ark had traveled behind the standards of Judah and Reuben, but the Ark was placed at the head of Israel's procession across the Jordan (Sotah *33b*)*. It was as if the Ark had emerged from concealment when the Israelites approached the Land and renewed their Sinaitic pledge. As they entered the Land, they presented the Ark as their 'passport.' With the Ark in the forefront they were confident of receiving Divine aid* such as [has] not been done in all the earth (Exodus *34:10*).

◄§ The Crossing of the Jordan

1. וַיַּשְׁכֵּם יְהוֹשֻׁעַ בַּבֹּקֶר — *And Joshua arose early in the morning.*

This is one of several instances in which Scripture informs us of Joshua's early rising (see further 6:12; 7:16; 8:10). Rising early is in consonance with the Talmudic dictum that one should be prompt to perform a mitzvah *(Pesachim* 4a).

According to the *Midrash,* Joshua arose early to pray, just as the Patriarchs had done, because the early morning is a time for Divine kindness and prayers are more acceptable then.

Chida points out that the *Talmud* derives this principle from Abraham, for Scripture states in regard to Abraham's preparation for the sacrifice of his son, Isaac, *And Abraham arose early in the morning (Genesis* 22:3). It is not coincidental, *Chida* observes, that Scripture uses the expression in regard to Joshua. The Sages have stated that the waters of the Jordan parted because of the merit of Abraham, who was willing to sacrifice his son. (See *Commentary* 3:11.)

וַיַּשְׁכֵּם ... וַיִּסְעוּ — *And Joshua arose ...*

3
1-3

1 *And Joshua arose early in the morning, and they journeyed from Shittim and arrived at the Jordan, he and all the Children of Israel, and lodged there before they crossed.*

2 *It was at the end of three days that the marshals circulated within the camp.* 3 *They ordered the people, saying, 'When you see the Ark of the*

and they journeyed.

Although the first verb in the verse is singular, the second verb is plural; with this sentence construction Scripture indicates the implicit trust Israel had in Joshua's leadership, for when Joshua arose early in the morning to approach the Jordan, the entire nation followed *(Alshich).*

These events occurred on the ninth of Nissan (see Chronology, *Commentary* to 1:1).

וַיָּלִנוּ שָׁם — *And lodged there.*

The nation did not cross the Jordan on the night of the tenth, but rather waited until morning. There were three reasons for the delay. God wanted the splitting of the Jordan River to take place during the day so that (a) the miracle would have maximum visibility and therefore inspire Israel to have greater faith in both God and Joshua [see *v.* 3:7]; (b) the Canaanite kings would become terrified at the sight of the miracle; and (c) Israel would have time to prepare and cleanse themselves for the imminent miracle *(Ralbag).*

2. וַיְהִי מִקְצֵה שְׁלֹשֶׁת יָמִים — *It was at the end of three days.*

According to the Chronology proposed in Chapter 1, the expression *the end of three days* is idiomatic and actually means the end of the second day. It is referred to as *three days* because the close of the second day is, in reality, the beginning of the third day. Thus, when Scripture refers to the conclusion of this time period, it actually means the third day *(Tosafos Kiddushin* 38a).

[This verse is the fulfillment of Joshua's order to the marshals in verse 1:11.]

◆§ Joshua's Orders for Crossing the Jordan

3. וַיְצַוּוּ אֶת־הָעָם — *They ordered the people.*

The marshals relayed to the people the order which Joshua had received in his first prophetic vision (*v.* 1:1) [cf., however, *Alshich* on this verse].

כִּרְאֹתְכֶם ... — *When you see ...*

Malbim notes that two new procedures are introduced in this verse: (a) the Holy Ark would now lead Israel's procession across the Jordan, whereas, in the Wilderness, the Ark had been transported behind the standards of Judah and Reuben[1] and (b) the Kohanim would carry the Ark, whereas in the Wilderness the Levites had carried it *(Numbers* 4:15; see also *Ramban B'Tanach, Ch.* 3, footnote 2*).

1. According to *Tosafos (Eruvin* 63b), there were two Arks, one made by Betzalel *(Exodus* 37:1) and the other made by Moses before he received the Second Tablets *(Deuteronomy* 10:3). The Second Tablets, as well as the shards from the first Tablets, were placed in this Ark until Betzalel constructed his. At that time the Second Tablets were placed in Betzalel's Ark. It was Betzalel's Ark which had remained behind the standards of Judah and Reuben when the Israelites traveled through the wilderness and which emerged to lead their procession into *Eretz Yisrael. Numbers* 10:33 which states that the Ark proceeded the Israelites' journey through the Wilderness refers to the Ark made by Moses, the one which contained the broken Tablets *(Rashi, ibid.).*

When Israel journeyed through the Wilderness, the Divine Presence could not lead Israel's

אֱלֹהֵיכֶם וְהַכֹּהֲנִים הַלְוִיִּם נֹשְׂאִים אֹתוֹ ג
וְאַתֶּם תִּסְעוּ מִמְּקוֹמְכֶם וַהֲלַכְתֶּם אַחֲרָיו: ד
ד אַךְ | רָחוֹק יִהְיֶה בֵּינֵיכֶם וּבֵינָו כְּאַלְפַּיִם
אַמָּה בַּמִּדָּה אַל־תִּקְרְבוּ אֵלָיו לְמַעַן
אֲשֶׁר־תֵּדְעוּ אֶת־הַדֶּרֶךְ אֲשֶׁר תֵּלְכוּ־

The commentators have suggested additional reasons for the Ark's prominence when Israel crossed the Jordan (cf. *Prefatory Remarks* to this chapter):

□ *Alshich* continues (from *verse* 1) that Joshua wanted to rechannel Israel's implicit trust in him into trust solely in God. Therefore, he issued a directive that Israel's future journeys would be signaled by the movement of the Holy Ark.

□ *Chida* explains that the Ark would serve the function of the Clouds of Glory which surrounded Israel during their journey through the Wilderness (see *Exodus* 13:21). Upon Moses' demise, the Clouds departed (*Taanis* 9a), and the Jews sought a substitute to 'light their way.' In addition, the clouds symbolized God's great affection for Israel and the Ark represented this same relationship.

אֲרוֹן — *The Ark.*

[The Ark served as the container for the Two Tablets of the Law which Moses received on Mount Sinai (*Deuteronomy* 10:5).]

The word אֲרוֹן derives from the word אוֹר 'light' since the Torah which it contained is referred to (*Proverbs* 6:23) as 'light' (*R' Bachya, Exodus* 25:10).

ה׳ אֱלֹהֵיכֶם — *HASHEM your God.*

See *footnote* to 1:9.

וְהַכֹּהֲנִים הַלְוִיִּם — *And the Kohanim Levites.*

They are called Kohanim-Levites because the Kohanim, or priestly class, descended from the tribe of Levi (*Rashi*).

Ramban (gloss to *Sefer HaMitzvos* of *Rambam*, Section III) apparently understands the phrase כֹּהֲנִים הַלְוִיִּם to mean Kohanim and Leviim.

There are three places in Scripture where the Kohanim were charged with carrying the Ark: (a) during the crossing of the Jordan, (b) when Israel encircled Jericho, and (c) when the Ark was returned to its place as described in *II Samuel* 15:29 (*Sotah* 33b) [cf., however, *Rashi, Sotah* 33b].

4. אַךְ רָחוֹק יִהְיֶה — *But maintain a distance ...* [lit. *but distance there will be*].

The people were required to distance themselves from the Holy Ark out of respect for the Divine Presence which surrounded it (*Rashi*).

בֵּינֵיכֶם וּבֵינָו — *Between yourselves and it.*

The word is spelled as if it were pronounced וּבֵינוֹ, *and between it*, but the Mesorah [traditional reading] tells us to pronounce it וּבֵינָיו, *and between them. Rashi* explains the Mesorah by suggesting that there were two Arks: one contained the Tablets and the other contained Joseph's bones.

However, if there were two Arks, why spell ובינו in the singular?

The *Talmud* (*Sotah* 13a) states: During the years that Israel journeyed through the Wilderness, two Arks traveled together, one containing Joseph's bones and the other containing the Tablets, which served as the focus for the Divine Presence. When it was asked whether it is customary for a corpse to procession, since the land outside of *Eretz Yisrael* lacks sanctity. Rather, it dwelled in holiness among the standards of the twelve tribes. Upon Israel's entry to *Eretz Yisrael*, however, the Divine Presence was able to leave the confines of the nation and lead the Jews' entry. At this point, the Holy Ark was required to emerge from Israel's ranks and become a more intense focal point for the Divine Presence. Because the Ark had acquired additional holiness, it could be carried only by the Kohanim (*Maharsha, Sotah* 33b).

3 *Covenant of HASHEM your God and the Kohanim —*
4 *Levites carrying it, then you shall move from your*
place and follow it. ⁴ *But maintain a distance between*
yourselves and it of two thousand amos *in*
measurement; do not approach it so that you may
know the way on which you will travel, for you have

travel with the Divine Presence, the response was, 'this one [the corpse] fulfilled what was written in the other one,' i.e., Joseph was so righteous that he fulfilled the entire Torah. (See *Rashi* to *Sotah* 13b.)

Mussar HaNeviim suggests that since Joseph constantly bent his will to the will of the Torah, the two 'Arks' were actually one. Hence, the singular is employed by Scripture.

כְּאַלְפַּיִם אַמָּה בַּמִּדָּה — *Two thousand* amos *in measurement.*

The laws of the Sabbath prohibit the Jew from walking a distance of two thousand *amos* (approx. 3750 ft.) outside his encampment (see *Exodus* 16:29) [cf. *Chayei Adam* 76:2]. Since Joshua realized that Jericho would be besieged on the Sabbath, he told the marshals to urge the people not to distance themselves more than this measurement so that they could pray before the Holy Ark[1] *(Rashi* from *Midrash).*

[The meaning of this verse, according to *Rashi,* is that the Jews were to keep their distance from the Ark, but not more than two thousand *amos.*]

Although the Jews were admonished not to encamp *more* than two thousand *amos* from the Ark, Scripture does not state how far they were to distance themselves from it as a gesture of respect. *Abarbanel* notes that it was permissible to come within this two thousand *amos* limit as evidenced later (4:5) when Joshua sent twelve men to pick up the stones from the feet of the *Kohanim* who were carrying the Ark. (Cf. *Radak* on this verse.)

כְּאַלְפַּיִם — *Two thousand.*

The prefix כ is employed by Scripture when an approximate number is mentioned (see *I Samuel* 13:15). In this case, the כ could also signify that the number mentioned is precise, not approximate, since the word *measurement* is used following the number *(Radak).*

לְמַעַן אֲשֶׁר־תֵּדְעוּ — *So that you may know.*

[This expression presents a difficulty, for if the Ark were to serve as the guide on their journey, their distancing themselves from it would cause the people to lose their way.] *Rashi,* therefore, interprets this phrase to refer to the last stich of verse 3, *and [you shall] follow it ... so that you know the way.*

Malbim notes that *Rashi's* interpretation is contradicted by the cantillation. Since the ֑ *esnachtah,* or mid-verse pause, is on the word בַּמִּדָּה, it seems unlikely that only part of the latter half of the verse refers to verse 3. *Malbim,* therefore, explains the verse according to the interpretation of *Radak* and *Ralbag.*

Radak, on the other hand, understands the expression in its context — i.e., as an explanation for the distance. He explains that a certain distance was required between the Ark and the people so that they would gain perspective concerning the Ark's path and would be able to follow it in an orderly fashion.

1. *Mussar HaNeviim* suggests that although the Jews were not allowed to approach the Holy Ark on weekdays, they were permitted to approach it on the Sabbath. He bases his explanation on the verse, *And God blessed the Sabbath day and made him* [normally translated 'it'] *holy (Genesis* 2:3). *R' Saadiah Gaon* interprets 'him' as a reference to the person who keeps the Sabbath: 'he' [i.e., the Sabbath observer] becomes holy. Thus, since the Jews become holy on the Sabbath, they were permitted within the two thousand *amos* of the Holy Ark; during the rest of the week, however, they needed to remain outside this boundary.

בָהּ כִּי לֹא עֲבַרְתֶּם בַּדֶּרֶךְ מִתְּמוֹל
ה שִׁלְשׁוֹם: וַיֹּאמֶר יְהוֹשֻׁעַ אֶל־הָעָם
הִתְקַדָּשׁוּ כִּי מָחָר יַעֲשֶׂה יהוה בְּקִרְבְּכֶם
ו נִפְלָאוֹת: וַיֹּאמֶר יְהוֹשֻׁעַ אֶל־הַכֹּהֲנִים
לֵאמֹר שְׂאוּ אֶת־אֲרוֹן הַבְּרִית וְעִבְרוּ
לִפְנֵי הָעָם וַיִּשְׂאוּ אֶת־אֲרוֹן הַבְּרִית
ז וַיֵּלְכוּ לִפְנֵי הָעָם: וַיֹּאמֶר יהוה
אֶל־יְהוֹשֻׁעַ הַיּוֹם הַזֶּה אָחֵל גַּדֶּלְךָ בְּעֵינֵי
כָּל־יִשְׂרָאֵל אֲשֶׁר יֵדְעוּן כִּי כַּאֲשֶׁר הָיִיתִי
ח עִם־מֹשֶׁה אֶהְיֶה עִמָּךְ: וְאַתָּה תְּצַוֶּה אֶת־
הַכֹּהֲנִים נֹשְׂאֵי אֲרוֹן־הַבְּרִית לֵאמֹר

כִּי לֹא עֲבַרְתֶּם בַּדֶּרֶךְ — *For you have not passed this* [lit. *the*] *way.*

You need guidance in your journey, because you have never traveled in this fashion *(Rashi). Radak* explains this different fashion to refer to the dividing waters of the Jordan; however, *Rif* explains it to refer to the following of the Ark.

מִתְּמוֹל שִׁלְשׁוֹם — *Before.*

This expression should be understood idiomatically as referring to both the immediate and the distant past, since the Israelites never before pursued this course. In the Hebrew language, an expression referring to a short interval of time often denotes a much longer interval. For example, *When your son asks you tomorrow ... (Exodus* 13:14) actually refers to the distant future *(Mateh Binyamin).*

5. הִתְקַדָּשׁוּ — *Prepare yourselves.*

The translation follows *Targum. Radak* explains: prepare your utensils and necessities for crossing. *Metzudos,* however, understands this expression to refer to spiritual preparation. *Mateh Binyamin* contends that the expression should be understood according to its root קדש, *holy.* Thus, the Jews were told 'to sanctify themselves.'

כִּי מָחָר — *For tomorrow.*

Radak comments that common sense, rather than Divine communication, led Joshua to predict the miraculous crossing of the Jordan. When he was commanded to cross the Jordan (1:2), he deduced that there would be accompanying miracles, since the waters of the river clearly reached its banks [making it impossible for the Israelites to cross in a natural way].

נִפְלָאוֹת — *Wonders.*

Wonders appears in the plural because there were actually six miracles associated with the crossing of the Jordan: (a) the waters parted; (b) they returned to their place; (c) after the waters had returned, the Ark flew across the waters, carrying its bearers *(Sotah 35a),* (d) all Israel gathered between the staves of the Ark (3:9); (e) the day they crossed the Jordan the Israelites traveled to Mount Gerizim and back, a total distance of 120 *mil;* (f) all witnesses were overcome with fear *(Kli Yakar).*

6. וַיֹּאמֶר יְהוֹשֻׁעַ אֶל־הַכֹּהֲנִים *And Joshua said to the Kohanim.*

This occurred on the morning of the tenth of Nissan, the day they crossed the Jordan *(Rashi).*

not passed this way before.'
[5] *And Joshua said to the people, 'Prepare*
yourselves, for tomorrow HASHEM will do wonders
in your midst.' [6] *And Joshua said to the Kohanim,*
'Carry the Ark of the Covenant and advance to the
head of the people.' And they carried the Ark of the
Covenant, and they went to the head of the people.
[7] *And HASHEM said to Joshua, 'This day I will in-*
augurate your greatness in the sight of all Israel that
they may know that as I was with Moses so will I be
with you. [8] *And you shall command the Kohanim*
that bear the Ark of the Covenant saying, "When

וְעִבְרוּ לִפְנֵי הָעָם — *And advance to the head of the people* [lit. *and pass before the people*].

Malbim notes that this is the execution of the new procedure introduced in verse 3, i.e., that the Ark will no longer travel behind the standards of Judah and Reuben, but will lead the Israelites' procession into *Eretz Yisrael.*

This verse marks the conclusion of the first *sidrah* of the *Book of Joshua* according to the Mesorah, or traditional division of the text. While the printed texts of *Joshua* are typically divided into twenty-four chapters, the Mesorah divides the text into fifteen, each division marked by a blank space of at least nine letters in the hand-written text.

[Most printed texts follow the division of Scripture established by the Gentiles who translated it into Latin *(Vulgate)* in the fourth century. Even though in many instances it does not conform to the meaning of the text, their system was widely adopted by Jews of the Middle Ages to facilitate researching Scriptural citations during the disputations in which the Jews were forced to participate. For a further discussion of this chapter division, see *footnote* to ArtScroll *Yechezkel,* p. 442.]

7. וַיֹּאמֶר ה' אֶל־יְהוֹשֻׁעַ — *And HASHEM said to Joshua.*

Note the lack of the expression לֵאמֹר 'saying' (see *Commentary* to 1:1).

As in the case of Moses in the Pentateuch, most of God's communications to Joshua are not prefaced by לֵאמֹר (see 5:2, 5:9, 6:2, 7:10, 8:1, 8:18, 10:8, 11:6; Cf. 1:1, 4:1, 4:8, 4:15, 20:1). For an explanation, see *Lev Aharon* cited in *Commentary* to 5:1.

אָחֵל — *I will inaugurate.*

The translation follows *Metzudos. Mateh Binyamin* renders *confirm.*

כַּאֲשֶׁר הָיִיתִי עִם־מֹשֶׁה אֶהְיֶה עִמָּךְ — *As I was with Moses so will I be with you.*

[This verse is the fulfillment of the promise which God made to Joshua in 1:5.]

The commentators differ as to which miracle would reveal the similarity between Joshua and Moses (see *Commentary* to 1:5).

Just as I parted the waters of the Sea of Reeds before Moses, so will I part the waters of the Jordan before you[1] *(Radak).* [Strong support for this

1. It was clearly unnecessary for the waters of the Jordan to part in such a miraculous manner. When David fled from Abshalom *(II Samuel* 17:22), he was able to cross the Jordan on foot. Similarly, Jacob declared, *With my staff I crossed this Jordan (Genesis* 32:11) [c.f., however, *Rashi, ibid.*].

God performed this miracle, however, in order to allay the Israelites' fears that they would

ג
ט־יא

כִּבְאֲכֶם עַד־קְצֵה מֵי הַיַּרְדֵּן בַּיַּרְדֵּן
ט תַּעֲמֹדוּ: וַיֹּאמֶר יְהוֹשֻׁעַ אֶל־
בְּנֵי יִשְׂרָאֵל גֹּשׁוּ הֵנָּה וְשִׁמְעוּ אֶת־דִּבְרֵי
י יְהוָה אֱלֹהֵיכֶם: וַיֹּאמֶר יְהוֹשֻׁעַ בְּזֹאת
תֵּדְעוּן כִּי אֵל חַי בְּקִרְבְּכֶם וְהוֹרֵשׁ יוֹרִישׁ
מִפְּנֵיכֶם אֶת־הַכְּנַעֲנִי וְאֶת־הַחִתִּי וְאֶת־
הַחִוִּי וְאֶת־הַפְּרִזִּי וְאֶת־הַגִּרְגָּשִׁי וְהָאֱמֹרִי
יא וְהַיְבוּסִי: הִנֵּה אֲרוֹן הַבְּרִית אֲדוֹן כָּל־

interpretation lies in the verse, *And they believed in HASHEM and Moses his servant (Exodus* 14:31). After witnessing the miracles at the Sea of Reeds, all the Jews declared their firm belief in Moses as God's servant! HASHEM now promises that the miracle at the Jordan will have a similar effect on the people's belief in Joshua. (See further, *Beis HaLevi, Parshas Bereishis,* p. 7).]

Alshich suggests that the miracle of the entire people being encompassed between the staves of the Holy Ark (verse 9, see *Commentary)* brought Joshua equal status with Moses in the eyes of the people. It was reminiscent of the miracle which Moses performed when the entire nation gathered within four *amos* of the rock (see *Numbers* 20:10).

Others suggest that the great distance which Israel traveled in one day (from the Jordan to Mount Eval) was similar to the miraculous journey which occurred when Moses led the Jews between Ramses and Succos, (a roundtrip distance of 120 *mil)* in a short time *(Poras Yosef.* [See *Prefatory Remarks* to this chapter.]

8. עַד־קְצֵה מֵי הַיַּרְדֵּן — *To the edge of the waters of the Jordan.*

There is a difference of opinion as to the side of the Jordan on which the *Kohanim* were to plant themselves. *Rashi* understands this expression to refer to the eastern side of the Jordan, where they entered, but *Radak* interprets this to mean the far side of the Jordan [near the west bank].

בַּיַּרְדֵּן תַּעֲמֹדוּ — *Plant yourselves in the Jordan.*

Remain in the Jordan until the people pass to the other side *(Rashi),* for when the Ark leaves the water, the water will return to its place *(Malbim).*

9. גֹּשׁוּ הֵנָּה — *Come here.*

Joshua told the people to approach and gather around him at the Ark *(Radak).*

The *Midrash (Bereishis Rabbah* 5) indicates that the entire nation miraculously gathered between the two staves of the Ark. This is one of the several places in Scripture where a small area contained a large number of people (see *Prefatory Remarks* to this chapter).

Be'er Moshe explains the significance of this miracle according to the *Midrash (Yalkut Shimoni, Tehillim* 719). When

not be able to conquer the Land. They understood that in order to conquer the formidable Canaanites they would need Divine Protection. While Moses was alive, the people felt assured that they would receive this supernatural protection, for they had benefited from the miracles that God wrought through Moses' hands. When Moses died, however, the Israelites worried that the miraculous protection they had received would be lacking, leaving them vulnerable in their efforts to vanquish the Canaanites. Therefore, God provided them with miraculous entry into *Eretz Yisrael* to demonstrate that although Moses died, the Jews would still enjoy Divine protection *(Meam Loez).*

you come to the edge of the waters of the Jordan,
plant yourselves in the Jordan." '
9 *And Joshua said to the Children of Israel, 'Come*
here and listen to the words of HASHEM your God.'
10 *And Joshua said, 'By this you will know that the*
Living God is in your midst and that He will chase
out from before you the Canaanites, the Hittites, the
Hivvites, the Perizzites, the Girgashites, the Emorites,
and the Jebusites. 11 *Behold, the Ark of the Covenant*
of the Ruler of all the earth is passing before you in

the Almighty was apportioning land to all the nations of the world, each nation was given territory twice the size of *Eretz Yisrael.* When He hinted to the Jews to choose *Eretz Yisrael,* they were reluctant because it was the smallest of all countries. Therefore, He forcibly thrust it upon them, as it says: *I will give you a pleasant land (Jeremiah* 3:19).

God demonstrated here that even though *Eretz Yisrael* is the smallest of all countries, a small area can contain a large number of people.

10. בְּזֹאת תֵּדְעוּן — *By this you will know.*

[It is unclear which miracle Joshua is referring to by this statement.]

Rashi suggests that *this* refers to the miracle described by the *Midrash* (see *Commentary* to verse 9), in which all Israel gathered between the two staves of the Ark. *Radak,* however, argues that if this were Joshua's reference, the previous verse would have explicitly mentioned this miracle. Therefore, he interprets Joshua's statement as a reference to the parting of the Jordan's waters, mentioned in verse 13. Upon witnessing this event, the people would realize *the Living God is in your midst.* (See *Commentary* to verse 11.)

אֵל חַי — *The Living God.*

The commentators do not explain the significance here of this infrequently used name for God. It is used in only two other places: *Psalms* 42:3 and 84:3. For explanation, see *Commentary* to verse 11.

בְּקִרְבְּכֶם — *In your midst.*

Targum renders 'that His Divine Presence will be among you.'

וְהוֹרֵשׁ יוֹרִישׁ — *He will chase out.*

The translation follows *Metzudos.*

11. אֲרוֹן הַבְּרִית אֲדוֹן כָּל־הָאָרֶץ — *The Ark of the Covenant of the Ruler of all the earth.*

[The commentators understand this unusual expression in different ways.]

Targum renders: 'The Ark of the Covenant *of* the ruler of all the earth.'

Radak [presumably following *Targum's* translation] comments that the prepositional phrase 'of the Ruler ... earth' could refer either to the Ark or to the Covenant.

Rashi interpolates the word *God* and explains: 'The Ark of the Covenant [of God who is the] Ruler of all the earth.'

Radak also cites other commentators who understand this expression as a dual title of the Ark; אֲדוֹן כָּל־הָאָרֶץ is in apposition to the Ark. The Ark was also known as the *Ruler of all the earth* according to this interpretation, because it was a focal point for the Divine Presence.

[In previous verses, the Ark is merely referred to as *the Ark of the Covenant.* The fact that in this verse it is given the additional title, *Ruler of all the earth,* can be explained in light of the *Midrash (Pesikta d'Rav Kahana* 15). Scripture

יב הָאָרֶץ עֹבֵר לִפְנֵיכֶם בַּיַּרְדֵּן: וְעַתָּה קְחוּ
לָכֶם שְׁנֵי עָשָׂר אִישׁ מִשִּׁבְטֵי יִשְׂרָאֵל
יג אִישׁ־אֶחָד אִישׁ־אֶחָד לַשָּׁבֶט: וְהָיָה כְּנוֹחַ
כַּפּוֹת רַגְלֵי הַכֹּהֲנִים נֹשְׂאֵי אֲרוֹן יהוה
אֲדוֹן כָּל־הָאָרֶץ בְּמֵי הַיַּרְדֵּן מֵי הַיַּרְדֵּן
יד יִכָּרֵתוּן הַמַּיִם הַיֹּרְדִים מִלְמָעְלָה וְיַעַמְדוּ
נֵד אֶחָד: וַיְהִי בִּנְסֹעַ הָעָם מֵאָהֳלֵיהֶם

uses the word 'Ruler' (אֲדוֹן) to indicate that inhabitants will be uprooted and others will take their place. The source of this concept is the verse *The Ark of the Covenant, Ruler of all the earth (Joshua* 3:11). The Canaanites were uprooted and Israel entered.

Israel's legal right to take ownership of *Eretz Yisrael* and to displace its inhabitants is based on the promise God made to Abraham almost 500 years earlier in *Genesis* 15:18. Thus, the dual title of the Ark can be understood as a reference to the two promises God made to the Jewish people. *Ark of the Covenant* (as explained in the *Prefatory Remarks* to this chapter) refers to the extraordinary Divine assistance that God promised the Jews when they entered the Land. According to the *Midrash, Ruler of all the earth* is a reference to God's promise that Abraham's seed will inherit *Eretz Yisrael.* (Thus, verse 10 which promises the inheritance of the land by mentioning only the seven nations [see *Commentary, ibid.*]) parallels *Genesis* 15:18, where God promises *Eretz Yisrael* to Abraham by referring only to these seven nations.) When the Ark passed through the Jordan, Israel would witness simultaneous fulfillment of *both* promises. It is this point Joshua is emphasizing to the people through the additional title he affixed to the Ark.

According to this explanation, Joshua's reference to God as 'Living' (verse 10) can also be understood. This term was used in reference to the parting of the Jordan's waters *(Radak,* verse 10). Since the Israelites' extraordinary entry into the land depended upon the fulfillment of both promises God had given Israel, Joshua assured the Jews *the Living God is in your midst.* The God of Israel is not like the gods of the heathens, which are products of *wood and stone (Deuteronomy* 4:28). Rather, He is a *Living God* who can and will fulfill His previous promises.]

עֹבֵר לִפְנֵיכֶם — *Is passing before you.*

The Ark will enter the Jordan before your entry *(Rashi).*

◆§ Testimony for the Miracle

12. קְחוּ לָכֶם שְׁנֵי עָשָׂר אִישׁ — *Take for yourselves twelve men.*

In verses 4:2-3, Joshua received a prophecy that twelve men should remove twelve stones from under the feet of the Kohanim. The question arises among the commentators whether these twelve men that Joshua designated in this verse were supposed to carry out the order he issued in Chapter 4. No mention is made in this verse what function these twelve men were to serve.

Malbim comments that Joshua on his own accord chose these twelve men to bear testimony to the miracle of the parting of the Jordan, *not* to collect the twelve stones from the river bed (mentioned in 4:3). *Alshich* explains that a witness was needed from each tribe to inform his brethren that the Jordan's waters parted only *after* the Ark entered. Since the nation traveled in

3 *the Jordan.* 12 *Now, take for yourselves twelve men*
12-14 *from the tribes of Israel, a man for each tribe.* 13 *And*
it shall come to pass, that as the soles of the feet of the
Kohanim, bearers of the Ark of HASHEM, Ruler of all
the earth, shall rest in the waters of the Jordan, the
Jordan's waters will be cut off — the waters
descending from upstream — and they will stand as
one column.'
14 *It came to pass, when the people moved from*

a formation 12 *mil* by 12 *mil,* it was not possible for all to witness the miracle personally; they might have assumed that the waters had parted even *before* the Ark's entry, thereby weakening the proof mentioned in verse 10 (see *Radak, ibid.).*

According to *Malbim,* when Joshua received his prophecy (in Chapter 4) to remove the twelve stones from the Jordan's bed, he decided to use the same twelve men he had earlier designated to testify to the miraculous parting of the Jordan *(Commentary* to 4:4). In *Malbim's* view, Joshua received his prophecy about the stones when the Israelites had completed their crossing of the Jordan.

Rashi (see *HaRav Gifter's* remark to 3:12), however, maintains that Joshua received his prophecy concerning the stones *before* the Israelites entered the Jordan. It was for this reason that Joshua designated one man from each tribe. He did not, however, tell them what their mission would be *(Radak). HaRav Gifter* explains that Joshua delayed in informing the men of their mission so that their curiosity would be aroused, and they would consequently accept their orders with a fullness of spirit. In *Rashi's* view, from the break in 4:1 (see *Commentary* to 4:11) Scripture flashes back and explains Joshua's prophecy which he received before the crossing of the Jordan.

13. וְיַעַמְדוּ נֵד אֶחָד — *And they will stand as one column.*

The waters which flowed from upstream collected at one site, and the successive waters vertically stacked themselves upon this invisible dam *(Rashi)* in order to prevent the backed up waters from inundating the surrounding areas *(Radak).*

Malbim notes that since the waters of the Jordan flowed with a current, it was sufficient to cut them off upstream from the Jews' crossing. The waters of the Sea of Reeds, however, did not flow with a current; therefore, they needed to be blocked on both sides of the people's crossing. *Malbim* further explains that the waters of the Jordan which flowed downstream from the site of the miracle continued in their normal fashion.[1]

◆§ The Miraculous Entry to the Land

14. מֵאָהֳלֵיהֶם — *From their tents.*

[It is noteworthy that Scripture mentions this seemingly insignificant detail — where the Israelites were located before they crossed the Jordan. Perhaps, *tents* does not refer to the

1. [Although nature *seems* to operate automatically, Judaism teaches that God continuously intervenes to provide the natural order which we have come to expect. From *Malbim* (see text) we can gain remarkable insight into the concept of God's control over nature.

We all view the events of the world according to the theory of cause and effect. However, one of the cardinal points of Torah belief is that God is the antecedent cause for *all* events. Were it not God's Will, no apparent cause in the world would create its typical effects; if it *is*

לַעֲבֹר אֶת־הַיַּרְדֵּן וְהַכֹּהֲנִים נֹשְׂאֵי הָאָרוֹן
טו הַבְּרִית לִפְנֵי הָעָם׃ וּכְבוֹא נֹשְׂאֵי הָאָרוֹן
עַד־הַיַּרְדֵּן וְרַגְלֵי הַכֹּהֲנִים נֹשְׂאֵי הָאָרוֹן
נִטְבְּלוּ בִּקְצֵה הַמָּיִם וְהַיַּרְדֵּן מָלֵא עַל־
טז כָּל־גְּדוֹתָיו כֹּל יְמֵי קָצִיר׃ וַיַּעַמְדוּ הַמַּיִם
הַיֹּרְדִים מִלְמַעְלָה קָמוּ נֵד־אֶחָד הַרְחֵק
מְאֹד °באדם הָעִיר אֲשֶׁר מִצַּד צָרְתָן °מֵאָדָם ק׳
וְהַיֹּרְדִים עַל יָם הָעֲרָבָה יָם־הַמֶּלַח תַּמּוּ
יז נִכְרָתוּ וְהָעָם עָבְרוּ נֶגֶד יְרִיחוֹ׃ וַיַּעַמְדוּ
הַכֹּהֲנִים נֹשְׂאֵי הָאָרוֹן בְּרִית־יהוה
בֶּחָרָבָה בְּתוֹךְ הַיַּרְדֵּן הָכֵן וְכָל־יִשְׂרָאֵל

Israelites' dwelling places but rather to their בָּתֵּי מִדְרָשִׁים, *houses of study* (see *Genesis* 25:27; *Rashi; Numbers* 19:14, *Midrash).* As was mentioned in the *Prefatory Remarks* to this chapter, the miraculous protection which God had promised to the Jews was predicated on their commitment to Torah study and observance in order to be worthy of His miraculous intervention. What would be a more appropriate preparation before plunging into the Jordan and experiencing the miracles than to be occupied in the study of Torah!]

15. בִּקְצֵה הַמָּיִם — *In the edge of the water.*

See *Commentary* to verse 8.

וְהַיַּרְדֵּן מָלֵא ... — *And the Jordan is full ...*

According to most commentators, this half of the verse is to be understood in connection with verse 16.

גְּדוֹתָיו — *Its banks.*

Rashi explains that the sides of the Jordan were high.

The Jordan reached to the top of its banks because it had received additional water from the snows which melted during the spring *(Radak).*

Malbim interprets: Even though the Jordan is so full that it overflows its banks during the harvest season, it still rose up in one column.

Daas Sofrim [citing the *Talmud (Sotah* 34a)] comments that although the Jordan was so full that it would normally have overflowed its banks, the river did not flood during the Jews' crossing. Rather, the excess water rose in one column and towered over that section of the river bed through which the people crossed.

See *Radak* to 4:18.

כֹּל יְמֵי קָצִיר — *All the days of the harvest season.*

This event took place during Nissan, which is the time of harvest *(Rashi).*

16. וַיַּעַמְדוּ הַמַּיִם — *The waters ... stood.*

The *Talmud (Sotah* 34a) records two opinions in regard to the height reached

God's Will, any effect can be created even if it is unrelated to a traceable cause. Verse 13 serves as a reminder that nature is under direct Divine control. Normally, water gushing downstream gradually slows down unless it is constantly propelled by the waters upstream. At the Jordan, however, the waters which were cut off (i.e., below the site of the miracle) continued to flow despite the interrupted flow of the current. Although the apparent cause for their continued flow was removed, the Jordan's current was not affected for God, the true cause of its flow, had decreed that it continue! (See *Rashi* to *Chullin* 7a, s.v. רְצוֹן קוֹנִי.)]

3 *their tents to cross the Jordan, the Kohanim bearers*
15-17 *of the Ark of the Covenant, were at the head of the*
people. 15 *Upon the arrival of the bearers of the Ark*
at the Jordan and the feet of the Kohanim, bearers of
the Ark, were immersed in the edge of the water —
and the Jordan is full on all its banks all the days of
the harvest season — 16 *the waters descending from*
upstream stood, they rose up in one column, far from
the city of Adam which is near Tzarsan; and those
descending to the sea of the plain, the Dead Sea,
ceased flowing; they were cut off, and the people
crossed opposite Jericho. 17 *And the Kohanim,*
bearers of the Ark of HASHEM, stood in the Jordan on

by the column formed by the upstream waters. One opinion was that the column rose 12 *mil;* the other, more than 300 *mil.*

מֵאָדָם הָעִיר — *From the city of Adam.*

The translation follows *Rashi,* who understands *Adam* as the name of a city. The *Midrash* views *Adam* as a reference to Abraham [whom Scripture *(Joshua* 14:15) describes as *the great man (Adam) among giants*], for it was because of his merit that the waters of the Jordan divided [see *Commentary* to verse 11].

צָרְתָן — *Tzarsan.*

[In *I Kings* 7:46 we read that the brass vessels which Chiram made for King Solomon were cast in the plain that ran from Succos to Tzarsan. If this is the same city as the one mentioned in our verse, then it was located approximately forty miles north of the site where the Jordan's flow was interrupted, for *T'vuos HaAretz* locates Succos southeast of Beis Shean.]

וְהַיֹּרְדִים — *And those descending.*

The water did not approach the nearby city of *Adam,* because the Jordan's waters arose in a column and did not inundate the surrounding areas *(Radak).*

עַל — *To* [lit. *on*].

See *Commentary* to 2:7.

תַּמּוּ נִכְרָתוּ — *Ceased flowing, they were cut off.*

When the waters downstream from the site of the miracle continued on their course until they emptied into the Dead Sea *(Rashi),* the downstream waters ceased to flow since they were cut off from those upstream *(Malbim).* As a result, the river bed downstream was dry and the people could cross easily *(Radak).*

17. בֶּחָרָבָה — *On dry ground.*

Even the little puddles in the uneven surface of the Jordan's bed evaporated; therefore, the river bottom was completely dry. Upon witnessing this miracle (see *Prefatory Remarks* to this chapter), the Kohanim entered the Jordan *(Alshich).* Thus, the sense of the verse should be understood as follows: the Kohanim stood on dry land which prepared the way for all Israel to cross the Jordan since they dispelled any possible fears of being overtaken by the water.

[Just as God made dry land appear to provide Adam a dwelling place so that he could carry out his mission, so He later caused dry land to appear for the Israelites at the parting of the Sea of Reeds to symbolize that Adam's mission was transferred to the Jews (see *footnote*

ד עֹבְרִים בֶּחָרָבָה עַד אֲשֶׁר־תַּמּוּ כָּל־הַגּוֹי
א א לַעֲבוֹר אֶת־הַיַּרְדֵּן: וַיְהִי כַּאֲשֶׁר־תַּמּוּ כָל־

to 2:10 for a further discussion of this concept). The drying up of the Jordan's bed is a second confirmation of this reinvestment of Adam's role in Israel. Perhaps, this is the reason that Scripture relates that the Jordan's waters split *far from Adam,* i.e., this occurred long after the lifetime of the original man, Adam. Even though the parting of the Jordan occurred about 2488 years later than the removal of water from parts of the earth's surface (mentioned in *Genesis* 1:9), Adam's universal mission continued in Israel.

And perhaps, it is for this reason that Scripture in discussing the Jews' universal mission refers to the Israelites in this verse as גּוֹי which is a more universal term for *nation* than the word עַם which specifically connotes the *Jewish* nation. (See *Commentary* to 4:1).]

הָכֵן — *Firmly.*

The Kohanim were standing opposite one another *(Rashi)* [since it would be disrespectful for them to turn their backs to the Ark].

עֹבְרִים — *Crossed.*

The *Talmud (Sotah* 34a) cites two opinions regarding the manner in which Israel crossed the Jordan. Israel's camp was in the shape of a square, 12 *mil* on a side. One opinion is that the camp moved *en masse* across the Jordan through a 12 *mil* channel. According to the second opinion, they proceeded in single file, one man following the next *(Sotah* 34a, *Rashi,* see *Maharsha).*

IV

When the Ark entered the Jordan, Israel secured visible evidence that God would fulfill His guarantee to guide the Jews with a miraculous Providence in Eretz Yisrael *(see* Prefatory Remarks *to Chapter 3). The vigorous flow of the Jordan was suddenly interrupted; its waters were stacked to towering heights, and the river bed dried up to allow the Ark and the Israelites passage into* Eretz Yisrael. *This chapter focuses on the stone memorial which God commanded the Jews to construct so that all future generations would know* that the waters of the Jordan were cut off before the Ark of the Covenant of HASHEM (verse 7) *and* that HASHEM your God dried up the waters of the Jordan before you until you crossed (verse 23).

Although the general command to build this stone memorial had been given in Deuteronomy 27, *not until verses 2 and 3 of this chapter does God inform Joshua of the precise details of the memorial's construction: (a) how many stones should be used; (b) where they should be obtained; (c) how many men should select them; and (d) where they should be placed.*

The command in Deuteronomy *required that the Israelites inscribe every verse of the Pentateuch on these stones* (Ramban) *immediately upon their entry to* Eretz Yisrael *to emphasize that it was the power of the Israelites' Torah observance which would destroy Israel's enemies* (R' Bachya).

According to Abarbanel, *a conquering nation customarily erected a monument on the soil of its defeated adversary; the monument would bear an inscription stating the year of the conquest and the name of the victorious king.* Abarbanel *observed that in his time the markers which the Roman legions had placed in Italy and Spain were still standing. He suggests that by commanding the Jews to erect a stone monument with a Torah inscription, God wished to elevate this general custom to a mitzvah which would raise the banner of Torah, instead of the glory of the conquering king.*

4 *dry ground firmly. All Israel crossed on dry ground*
1 *until the whole nation completed crossing the Jordan.*
[1] It was when the entire nation had completed

There is a second reason for God's command that the Pentateuch be inscribed on the Jews' memorial. Although territorial aggrandizement is an activity common to all nations, the inscription from the Torah emphatically underscores the vast difference between Israel's victories and those of other nations. Israel's conquest was Divinely justified, for the Jews were not snatching what did not rightfully belong to them. Rather, they were taking possession of the gift which God had bestowed upon their patriarch Abraham, a gift which was clearly described and frequently alluded to in the very Torah inscribed on these stones.

On a deeper level, the Torah inscription indicated that the entire corpus of Israel's social and moral legislation could be placed in full view of all mankind, from the day they first set foot on the Land. All other states were formed over a period of years; only afterwards was national legislation promulgated. The Jewish state, however, was Divinely ordained and governed by a pre-existing Divine code (see R' Hirsch cited in Prefatory Remarks to Chapter 2).

Although this chapter does not explicitly mention that such an inscription took place, Rashi understands from the Talmud (Sotah 36a) that on the same day the nation crossed the Jordan (10 Nissan), they traveled to Mount Eval (a distance of 60 mil, or approximately 42 miles), built an altar from the stones, plastered them, inscribed the Torah on them, offered sacrifices on this altar, ate, drank, rejoiced, uttered the blessings and curses and returned to Gilgal to lodge for the evening. The fact that Joshua first relates the events on Mount Eval in 8:30-35 is not problematic, for the events recorded in Scripture are not always written in chronological order (Pesachim 6b).

Haamek Davar (Deuteronomy, 27:2 ff) suggests a different interpretation which preserves the sequence of the text. Through a careful analysis of the passage in Deuteronomy, he concludes that Israel was actually required to make two inscriptions of the Torah. The first inscription was to be written in Hebrew as a testimony for the Jews. According to Malbim (8:30), this writing took place in Gilgal on the day Israel crossed the Jordan. The second inscription was to be written in seventy languages in order to instruct the Gentiles in the Noachide laws. It was this writing which took place later on Mount Eval and is described in Chapter 8.

Certainly the miraculous journey across the Jordan would not have been forgotten, even without the stone memorial which the Jews were commanded to build. Fathers would have recounted the miracle to their children for generation after generation, and Scripture itself records the event. Thus, the memorial was not needed to preserve this historical fact. Rather, it served to teach generations of Jews a vital lesson concerning their history. Just as a sample of the manna which had sustained the Jews in the Wilderness was kept (Exodus 16:33) to teach later generations the challenge of trust in God, so the twelve stone memorial was erected by Joshua to teach future generations that their life in Eretz Yisrael depended upon their Torah observance. Their covenant with God ensured their continued existence in the Land only so long as they followed the precepts of the Torah.

Two major opinions have been detailed regarding when Joshua received the prophecy mentioned in verses 1-10 (see Commentary to 3:12). Malbim contends that Joshua received this prophecy after the Israelites had crossed the Jordan, as verse 1 implies. Rashi, however, maintains that verses 1-10 constitute a flashback, detailing a prophecy which Joshua had received before the Israelites crossed the Jordan.

ד הַגּוֹי לַעֲבוֹר אֶת־הַיַּרְדֵּן וַיֹּאמֶר
ב־ד
ב יהוה אֶל־יְהוֹשֻׁעַ לֵאמֹר: קְחוּ לָכֶם
מִן־הָעָם שְׁנֵים עָשָׂר אֲנָשִׁים אִישׁ־
ג אֶחָד אִישׁ־אֶחָד מִשָּׁבֶט: וְצַוּוּ אוֹתָם
לֵאמֹר שְׂאוּ־לָכֶם מִזֶּה מִתּוֹךְ הַיַּרְדֵּן
מִמַּצַּב רַגְלֵי הַכֹּהֲנִים הָכִין שְׁתֵּים־
עֶשְׂרֵה אֲבָנִים וְהַעֲבַרְתֶּם אוֹתָם עִמָּכֶם
וְהִנַּחְתֶּם אוֹתָם בַּמָּלוֹן אֲשֶׁר־תָּלִינוּ בוֹ
ד הַלָּיְלָה: וַיִּקְרָא יְהוֹשֻׁעַ אֶל־
שְׁנֵים הֶעָשָׂר אִישׁ אֲשֶׁר הֵכִין מִבְּנֵי

1. כָּל־הַגּוֹי — *The entire nation.*

Scripture uses the word גּוֹי, *nation* [instead of its synonym עָם] to include even the Gentiles who followed the Israelites *(Poras Yosef)* such as the water carriers and wood cutters [who had appeared before Moses; see *Deuteronomy* 29:10; *Rashi*], thereby signifying that the waters of the Jordan parted even for those who merely affiliated themselves with the Jewish people *(Alshich)* [cf. *Chullin* 7a].

◆§ A Memorial for the Miracle

וַיֹּאמֶר ה׳ — *HASHEM said.*

According to the Mesorah (traditional reading of the text), the beginning and end of this verse are disconnected. The beginning of the verse, וַיְהִי ... אֶת־הַיַּרְדֵּן which introduces the account of Israel's experience after crossing the Jordan, is interrupted from ויאמר ה׳ until verse 11, where this account is continued. There are thirty such cases of פִּיסְקָא בְּאֶמְצָעוּת פָּסוּק, *interrupted verses,* in Scripture, two of these occur in *Joshua* (see 8:24; cf., however, *Minchas Shai* there).

In *Radak's* and *Rashi's* view (see *Rashi* to 3:12 and *HaRav Gifter's* remark there), the expression וַיֹּאמֶר ה׳ introduces a ten verse flashback explaining the details of prophecy which Joshua had received prior to entering the Jordan. Scripture signals this flashback by interrupting the verse *(Meam Loez).*

In *Malbim's* view, verses 1-10 appear in their correct chronological sequence. He does not explain the significance of the interruption in this verse.

2. קְחוּ לָכֶם — *Select* [lit. *take for yourselves*].

As mentioned in the *Commentary* to 3:12, *Rashi* is of the opinion that the selection of the twelve men spoken of in this verse had already been mentioned in the last chapter. There, however, Scripture did not relate the nature of their mission; this is explained below in verse 3. *HaRav Gifter* comments that Joshua delayed in informing the men of their task in order to arouse their curiosity and motivate them to fulfill their assignment with dedication.

מִן־הָעָם — *From the people*

According to *Malbim* (as noted in the *Commentary* to 3:12), Joshua had personally commanded these twelve men to serve as witnesses to the Ark's effect on the Jordan. Now he gives them an additional mission, commanded by God: they are to gather the stones from the Jordan.

This second mission was given after the twelve men had already crossed the Jordan *(Poras Yosef).* They were not told to gather the stones while they were crossing, so that they could gain

4
2-4 *crossing the Jordan, HASHEM said to Joshua, [2] 'Select*
twelve men from the people, a man from every tribe,
[3] and command them, saying, "Lift from this place,
from the Jordan, from the place where the Kohanim's
feet stood firmly, twelve stones and carry them across
with you and set them in the lodging place where you
will lodge this evening".'
[4] Joshua summoned the twelve men whom he had
designated from the Children of Israel, a man from

additional reward for the added inconvenience of returning to the Jordan *(Lev Aharon). Abarbanel* explains that according to this [*Malbim's*] view, the second half of verse 4:1, וַיֹּאמֶר ה׳ is *not* out of chronological order, as *Rashi* had suggested. (See *Commentary* to verse 1.)

3. וְצַוּוּ — *And command.*

The *Talmud (Kiddushin* 29a) declares that Scripture employs the word צַו, *command,* as an exhortation to the individual to whom the command is addressed. In this instance the twelve men ordered to reenter the Jordan to gather the stones needed additional encouragement, because they feared that the column of water might break on them, since the entire nation had already crossed *(Alshich).*

מִזֶּה — *From this place.*

The interpolation of the word 'place' follows *Rashi (Genesis* 42:15) who understands 'from this' as *from this place.*

God pointed, so to speak, to the place from which the stones should be removed *(Malbim).*

מִמַּצַּב רַגְלֵי הַכֹּהֲנִים הָכִין — *From the place where the Kohanim's feet stood firmly.*

Metzudos comments that the *Kohanim* lifted their feet, and the men removed the stones from the river bed.

[These stones were to be a memorial testifying to the miracle which occurred at the Jordan, as Scripture relates in verses 6 and 7. Perhaps God's command to remove the stones from beneath the Kohanim's feet was to serve as a remembrance of one aspect of that miracle — the *drying* of the floor of the Jordan (see 3:17 and *footnote* to 2:10). This interpretation is further supported by verses 22 and 23, which explain that the purpose of the stone memorial was to make future generations of Jews aware that God *dried* the bed of the Jordan.]

שְׁתֵּים־עֶשְׂרֵה אֲבָנִים — *Twelve stones.*

Several Rabbis of the *Talmud* reported that they had stood on these stones; they estimated that each stone fragment weighed at least forty *seah (Sotah* 34a). The fact that one man could lift and carry such a heavy rock to Mount Eval (according to *Rashi's* view) was truly a miracle *(Meam Loez).*

וְהַעֲבַרְתֶּם אוֹתָם עִמָּכֶם — *And carry them across with you.*

... as Moses commanded *(Rashi).* The *Talmud (Sotah* 36a) states that on the day that the nation crossed the Jordan [10 Nissan], they traveled to Mount Eval, built an altar from stones, plastered the stones, inscribed the Torah on them, offered sacrifices on this altar, ate, drank, rejoiced, uttered the blessings and curses, and returned to Gilgal.

4. אֲשֶׁר הֵכִין — *Whom he had designated* [lit. *prepared*].

Those men that Joshua had previously designated to be witnesses (see *Commentary* to 3:12) were chosen to carry out God's command to build the stone memorial *(Malbim).*

יִשְׂרָאֵל אִישׁ־אֶחָד אִישׁ־אֶחָד מִשָּׁבֶט׃
ה וַיֹּאמֶר לָהֶם יְהוֹשֻׁעַ עִבְרוּ לִפְנֵי אֲרוֹן
יהוה אֱלֹהֵיכֶם אֶל־תּוֹךְ הַיַּרְדֵּן וְהָרִימוּ
לָכֶם אִישׁ אֶבֶן אַחַת עַל־שִׁכְמוֹ לְמִסְפַּר
ו שִׁבְטֵי בְנֵי־יִשְׂרָאֵל׃ לְמַעַן תִּהְיֶה זֹאת
אוֹת בְּקִרְבְּכֶם כִּי־יִשְׁאָלוּן בְּנֵיכֶם מָחָר
לֵאמֹר מָה הָאֲבָנִים הָאֵלֶּה לָכֶם׃
ז וַאֲמַרְתֶּם לָהֶם אֲשֶׁר נִכְרְתוּ מֵימֵי הַיַּרְדֵּן
מִפְּנֵי אֲרוֹן בְּרִית־יהוה בְּעָבְרוֹ בַּיַּרְדֵּן
נִכְרְתוּ מֵי הַיַּרְדֵּן וְהָיוּ הָאֲבָנִים הָאֵלֶּה
ח לְזִכָּרוֹן לִבְנֵי יִשְׂרָאֵל עַד־עוֹלָם׃ וַיַּעֲשׂוּ־
כֵן בְּנֵי־יִשְׂרָאֵל כַּאֲשֶׁר צִוָּה יְהוֹשֻׁעַ

5. עִבְרוּ לִפְנֵי אֲרוֹן ה׳ — *Pass before the Ark of HASHEM.*

[The following comment conforms to *Rashi's* view, mentioned in *Commentary* to 3:12 (cf., *Malbim* to 3:12).]

At the crossing of the Jordan, Joshua remained on the eastern side and sent the entire nation ahead to assuage their anxiety that the waters of the Jordan would return to their place. They would more easily believe that the tower of water would not descend upon them if Joshua had not yet crossed. When Joshua was about to cross, he commanded the twelve designated men with him to enter the Jordan and gather the stones *(Radak).*

6. This verse and verse 21 seem almost identical, for they both anticipate questions which *your children* will ask concerning the purpose of the stones lifted from the Jordan, but *Malbim* contends that the two questions are addressing two entirely different issues. *Malbim* explains that in verse 6, Joshua is referring to the memorial's significance *for you,* i.e., for the generation which experienced the miracle at the Jordan. In verse 21, however, Joshua refers to questions which his generation's descendants will ask *their fathers* concerning the memorial's significance to these future generations of Jews.

Alshich, however, interprets the question differently. He explains that the children of the twelve men selected by Joshua (3:12) to witness the miracle will ask their parents, 'Why were *you* commanded to choose the stones from the Jordan?'

אוֹת — *Sign.*

The stone memorial served as a *sign* for the generation which experienced the miracle at the Jordan, testifying that the Jordan split in deference to the holiness of the Ark and the Tablets which it contained (see *Prefatory Remarks* to Chapter 3; *Malbim).*

כִּי־יִשְׁאָלוּן בְּנֵיכֶם מָחָר לֵאמֹר — *For in the future when your children ask, saying.*

The children of the generation that experienced the miracle will ask their parents, 'Why do you need a memorial for the miracle? You were there!' *(Malbim).*

מָחָר — *In the future* [lit. *tomorrow*].

The translation follows *Metzudos,* who understands מָחָר as a figurative

each tribe. 5 *And Joshua said to them, 'Pass before*
the Ark of HASHEM *your God into the Jordan. Raise*
every man one stone upon his shoulder, according to
the number of tribes of the Children of Israel, 6 *so*
that this will be a sign among you. For in the future
when your children ask, saying, "What is the
meaning of these stones for you?" 7 *you shall tell*
them, "That the waters of the Jordan were cut off
before the Ark of the Covenant of HASHEM; *when it*
passed by the Jordan the waters of the Jordan were
cut off." And these stones shall be a memorial for the
Children of Israel forever.'
8 *And so the Children of Israel did, just as Joshua*

expression signifying the future. [See *Commentary* to end of 3:4.]

7. וַאֲמַרְתֶּם — *You shall tell.*

In verse 22, Joshua says, 'וְהוֹדַעְתֶּם, *You shall* **inform** *them,'* whereas here he says, *'You shall* **tell** *them.' Malbim* observes that this change supports his interpretation that verse 7 is a response to the children of the Jews who experienced the miracle at the Jordan and were consequently familiar with its details. Thus, they needed only to be *told* that the Jordan split on account of the Ark. Verse 22, however, is Joshua's response to future generations who would not be so familiar with the details of the miracle and would therefore need to be *informed* of the details as well.

Alshich continues (from 6): Since we twelve men were the witnesses to the Jordan's parting, we were chosen to collect the stones which will serve to bear witness to the miracle forever.

[The entire nation was not able to see the waters part as a result of the entry of the Holy Ark. These twelve witnesses were designated to report to their tribes that indeed, because of the Holy Ark, the waters divided.]

אֲשֶׁר נִכְרְתוּ מֵימֵי הַיַּרְדֵּן ... מֵי הַיַּרְדֵּן — *That the waters of the Jordan were cut off ... the waters of the Jordan.*

R' Saadiah Gaon (cited by *R' Bachya* to *Exodus* 7:24) distinguishes between the two Hebrew expressions for *waters of:* מֵימֵי and מֵי. The word מֵימֵי is used for water which is fit for drinking, and מֵי is used for water which is not fit for drinking.

On the basis of this explanation, *Chida* explains the apparent redundancy in this verse (twice Scripture says *the waters of the Jordan were cut off*) and the two expressions מֵימֵי and מֵי.

As soon as the Ark appeared on the river bank all the waters near the surface of the Jordan which were fit for drinking parted while the deeper, murky waters remained in their place. When the Ark actually entered the Jordan, the deeper waters also divided.

The sense of the verse is: *You shall tell them, 'The (deeper) waters of the Jordan were cut off before the Ark of the Covenant of HASHEM; (when) it passed by the Jordan, the (surface) waters of the Jordan were cut off.'*

לְזִכָּרוֹן לִבְנֵי יִשְׂרָאֵל עַד־עוֹלָם — *(For) a memorial for the Children of Israel forever.*

In addition to being a memorial for this generation, it will also be a memorial for future generations. Joshua elaborates on the latter function in verses 21 through 24 *(Malbim).*

ד
ט־י

וַיִּשְׂאוּ שְׁתֵּי־עֶשְׂרֵה אֲבָנִים מִתּוֹךְ הַיַּרְדֵּן
כַּאֲשֶׁר דִּבֶּר יהוה אֶל־יְהוֹשֻׁעַ לְמִסְפַּר
שִׁבְטֵי בְנֵי־יִשְׂרָאֵל וַיַּעֲבִרוּם עִמָּם אֶל־
ט הַמָּלוֹן וַיַּנִּחוּם שָׁם׃ וּשְׁתֵּים עֶשְׂרֵה
אֲבָנִים הֵקִים יְהוֹשֻׁעַ בְּתוֹךְ הַיַּרְדֵּן תַּחַת
מַצַּב רַגְלֵי הַכֹּהֲנִים נֹשְׂאֵי אֲרוֹן הַבְּרִית
י וַיִּהְיוּ שָׁם עַד הַיּוֹם הַזֶּה׃ וְהַכֹּהֲנִים נֹשְׂאֵי
הָאָרוֹן עֹמְדִים בְּתוֹךְ הַיַּרְדֵּן עַד־תֹּם כָּל־
הַדָּבָר אֲשֶׁר־צִוָּה יהוה אֶת־יְהוֹשֻׁעַ לְדַבֵּר
אֶל־הָעָם כְּכֹל אֲשֶׁר־צִוָּה מֹשֶׁה אֶת־

8. כַּאֲשֶׁר צִוָּה יְהוֹשֻׁעַ ... כַּאֲשֶׁר דִּבֶּר ה׳ — *As Joshua commanded ... as HASHEM had told Joshua.*

Malbim explains these seemingly repetitive phrases. God's command to Joshua (verses 2 and 3) did not mention that each man should select one stone, and Joshua's command to the men (verses 4 and 5) did not mention that the stone memorial should be erected where they would lodge that evening. Consequently, Scripture states that each man took one stone, as Joshua commanded, and brought it to Israel's lodging, as God commanded.

אֶל־הַמָּלוֹן — *To the place where they lodged.*

They encamped in Gilgal that evening *(Rashi).*

9. וּשְׁתֵּים עֶשְׂרֵה אֲבָנִים — *And ... twelve stones.*

Joshua took another set of twelve stones *(Rashi)* upon Divine command *(Radak)* and inserted them under the feet of the Kohanim, where the first twelve stones had been removed, as a memorial commemorating the actual *site* of the miracle [of the splitting of the Jordan] *(Malbim).* He first built up a mound of soil on the river bed in order to allow the stones to project above the surface *(Meam Loez).*

[It should be noted that these second twelve stones are *not* the stones mentioned in the command in *Deuteronomy* 27; the memorial for which the first set of stones was used is explained in *Prefatory Remarks* to this chapter.]

הֵקִים יְהוֹשֻׁעַ — *Joshua erected.*

Joshua personally labored to erect these stones to demonstrate to his twelve appointees that he had not assigned them to lift the boulders from the Jordan's bed in order to wield power over them and to spare himself the toil involved. Rather, Joshua's sole motive was his desire to fulfill God's command *(Meam Loez).*

תַּחַת מַצַּב רַגְלֵי הַכֹּהֲנִים — *In* [lit. *underneath*] *the place where the feet of the Kohanim stood.*

Joshua placed these stones *in the place* where the Kohanim had stood, but not literally beneath their feet, for the priests had left the Jordan after Joshua related his message to the nation, as verse 10 states: *The Kohanim ... remained standing in the Jordan until the completion of the entire message which HASHEM had commanded Joshua to convey. Abarbanel* infers that the Kohanim remained in the Jordan only until Joshua fulfilled God's command to him; they did not wait there while Joshua finished erecting the twelve

*commanded and lifted twelve stones from the Jordan
as HASHEM had told Joshua, according to the number
of the tribes of the Children of Israel, and carried
them to the place where they lodged and placed them
there.* 9 *And Joshua erected twelve stones in the
Jordan in the place where the feet of the Kohanim,
bearers of the Ark of the Covenant, stood. They are
there to this day.* 10 *The Kohanim, bearers of the Ark,
remained standing in the Jordan until the completion
of the entire message which HASHEM had comman-
ded Joshua to convey to the people, according to all
which Moses commanded Joshua. The people*

stones mentioned in this verse, for he did this on his own initiative. [Cf., however, *Radak* to verse 10.]

Kli Yakar cites a comment which we do not have in our texts in which *Rashi* suggests that these stones were placed under the feet of the Kohanim while they were still in the Jordan so that their feet would not become soiled by the mud in the river bed. *Kli Yakar* rejects this interpretation, however, because verses 22 and 23 explicitly state that the floor of the Jordan miraculously became completely dry. *Lev Aharon* justifies *Rashi's* comment by suggesting that these stones were needed while the Kohanim were placing their feet in the water *after* it split and *before* the river bed dried.

עַד הַיּוֹם הַזֶּה — *To this day.*

Metzudos explains that wherever *until this day* appears in the Prophets, it means 'forever' because at whatever point in history one reads this expression, he will read 'until this day.'

10. **עַד־תֹּם כָּל־הַדָּבָר ...** — *Until the completion of the entire message.*

According to *Radak*, the Kohanim remained in the Jordan until the stones were placed at their feet and until the other set of stones which was the memorial for this event discussed in *Deuteronomy* 27 was erected at Gilgal (verse 20).

Abarbanel, however, maintains that the Kohanim did not remain in the Jordan while Joshua placed the stones *in the place where* [*their*] *feet stood* (see *Commentary* to verse 9).

☙ What was the message?

As they crossed, Joshua admonished the people, 'Always remember that you are crossing the Jordan in order to take possession of *Eretz Yisrael*, as it states, *You shall uproot all inhabitants of the Land from before you (Numbers* 33:52). If you strive to uproot them, all will be well. But if you do not, these waters will come and wash you away' (*Sotah* 34a).

Abarbanel suggests that while they were in the Jordan, Joshua related to the entire nation the content of his first prophecy (given in 1:2-10).

Joshua told them: Just as the waters of the Jordan split before you, so will the Canaanite nations fall before you *(Meam Loez)*.

כְּכֹל אֲשֶׁר־צִוָּה מֹשֶׁה אֶת־יְהוֹשֻׁעַ — *According to all which Moses commanded Joshua.*

This statement refers to Moses' command in *Deuteronomy* 27:2: *On that day when you cross the Jordan ... (Radak).* [See *Prefatory Remarks* to this chapter.]

ד
יא־יד

יא יְהוֹשֻׁעַ וַיְמַהֲרוּ הָעָם וַיַּעֲבֹרוּ: וַיְהִי
כַּאֲשֶׁר־תַּם כָּל־הָעָם לַעֲבֹר וַיַּעֲבֹר אֲרוֹן־
יב יְהוָה וְהַכֹּהֲנִים לִפְנֵי הָעָם: וַיַּעַבְרוּ בְּנֵי־
רְאוּבֵן וּבְנֵי־גָד וַחֲצִי שֵׁבֶט הַמְנַשֶּׁה
חֲמֻשִׁים לִפְנֵי בְּנֵי יִשְׂרָאֵל כַּאֲשֶׁר דִּבֶּר
יג אֲלֵיהֶם מֹשֶׁה: כְּאַרְבָּעִים אֶלֶף חֲלוּצֵי
הַצָּבָא עָבְרוּ לִפְנֵי יהוה לַמִּלְחָמָה אֶל
יד עַרְבוֹת יְרִיחוֹ: בַּיּוֹם הַהוּא
גִּדַּל יהוה אֶת־יְהוֹשֻׁעַ בְּעֵינֵי כָּל־יִשְׂרָאֵל

וַיְמַהֲרוּ — *The [people] hastened.*

According to *Radak,* the people hastened to build the stone memorial in the Jordan. *Metzudos* explains that they worked rapidly because of their reverence for the Holy Ark which was waiting in the Jordan while the nation completed its task and crossed. [*Radak* here is consistent with his view cited in the *Commentary* to the beginning of this verse; cf., however, *Abarbanel.*]

◆§ The Crossing is Completed

11. According to *Rashi,* the flashback which relates the details of Israel's crossing of the Jordan has now ended. The beginning of this verse, which is almost identical to the beginning of verse 1, continues the interrupted flow of the chapter. [See *Commentary* to verse 1.]

וַיַּעֲבֹר אֲרוֹן־ה׳ וְהַכֹּהֲנִים — *That the Ark of HASHEM and the Kohanim passed over.*

[The sequence of events mentioned in this verse seem to indicate that first the Israelites left the Jordan followed by the Ark with the Kohanim. The difficulty with this interpretation is the last two words of the verse לִפְנֵי הָעָם, literally, 'before the people,' which imply that the Kohanim departed from the Jordan first.]

Rashi (based on *Sotah* 35a) preserves the sequence of events indicated by the verse which implies that the Israelites left the Jordan first. He explains that the Kohanim did not cross in the same manner as the rest of the people. They retreated to the eastern bank, and the waters of the Jordan returned to their place. Miraculously, the Ark lifted them up and carried them across the Jordan so that they could be reunited with the rest of the people. The final two words of the verse, which imply that the Kohanim left the Jordan first, *Rashi* interprets as 'in the sight of the people.' Thus Scripture is emphasizing that this miracle took place in full view of the Israelites.

R' Bachya (Exodus 25:10) notes that the verb form supports this interpretation, for וַיַּעֲבֹר literally means **it** *passed over,* indicating that the Ark crossed with the Kohanim as a single unit. Had both crossed in the usual fashion, it would have stated וַיַּעַבְרוּ, **they** *passed over.*

Radak argues that if such a miracle had happened, Scripture would not have refrained from recording it. *Radak* preserves both the chronological sequence of the verse as well as the literal meaning of 'before the people.' He suggests two alternative interpolations of the verse: (a) '... when the people had completely crossed, the Ark of HASHEM and the Kohanim [who were previously] before the people crossed.' (b) '... when the people had completely crossed [they waited on the shore of the Jordan until] the Ark of HASHEM and the Kohanim passed before the people';

hastened and crossed.
11 *It was when the entire people had finished crossing that the Ark of HASHEM and the Kohanim passed over in the sight of the people.* 12 *And the tribes of Reuben, Gad, and part of Menashe went across armed before the Children of Israel, as Moses had said to them.* 13 *About forty thousand armed combatants went across before HASHEM to do battle, to the plains of Jericho.* 14 *On that day HASHEM exalted Joshua in the sight of all Israel, and they*

[the people then followed the Ark]. It would be incorrect to argue that *Radak* ever attempted to invalidate the *Talmud's* interpretation, for he remarks that, '[The Rabbis of the *Talmud*] knew what they were saying, for their wisdom is far superior to ours.' [Presumably what he means is that his interpretation is closer to the simple meaning of the text.]

12. חֲמֻשִׁים — *Armed.*

In 1:14, this word was translated *armed. Malbim* suggests that it may also be understood according to its cognate, חֲמִשִּׁים, *fifty,* for these tribes went to war in platoons of fifty men.

כַּאֲשֶׁר דִּבֶּר אֲלֵיהֶם מֹשֶׁה — *As Moses had said to them.*

Scripture relates that the tribes of Gad, Reuben, and part of Menashe kept the promise which they had made to Moses in *Numbers* 32 and which they later confirmed to Joshua (1:16) [see *Prefatory Remarks* to 1:13].

Alshich remarks that the tribes of Gad, Reuben, and Menashe chose precisely this moment to appear before their brethren in order to indicate that they were not afraid to participate in the war against the Seven Nations. [Thus, they demonstrated the faith they had gained from the miracle at the Jordan, and their faith served as a model for the rest of the people, especially since these two and half tribes would not even benefit by gaining any territory in *Eretz Yisrael* for their efforts.]

13. כְּאַרְבָּעִים אֶלֶף חֲלוּצֵי הַצָּבָא — *About forty thousand armed combatants.*

Chida comments that although these tribes contained many more able-bodied men (see *Commentary* to 1:14), only the strongest among them participated now, just as Joshua required, *all the mighty warriors* (see 1:14).

Kli Yakar suggests that the more than one hundred thousand able combatants from these two and one-half tribes crossed over the Jordan in order to fulfill their promise to Moses. When they witnessed all the miracles at the Jordan, however, many concluded that since God would certainly insure Israel's success, their presence was unnecessary. Therefore, they returned to the east of the Jordan.

לִפְנֵי ה׳ — *Before HASHEM.*

Targum renders 'before the people of HASHEM.'

14. גִּדַּל ה׳ אֶת־יְהוֹשֻׁעַ — *HASHEM exalted Joshua.*

Here God fulfilled the promise which He had made to Joshua in 3:7: *'This day I will inaugurate your greatness in the sight of all Israel.'*

[According to *Alshich* and *Poras Yosef* mentioned in the *Commentary* to 3:7, God had confirmed Joshua's greatness with other miracles. However, they would probably understand that God *began* to raise Joshua's status with the other miracles and *completed* this process with the miracle at the Jordan.]

ד
טו־כ

וַיִּרְאוּ אֹתוֹ כַּאֲשֶׁר יָרְאוּ אֶת־מֹשֶׁה כָּל־
טו יְמֵי חַיָּיו׃ וַיֹּאמֶר יהוה אֶל־
טז יְהוֹשֻׁעַ לֵאמֹר׃ צַוֵּה אֶת־הַכֹּהֲנִים נֹשְׂאֵי
יז אֲרוֹן הָעֵדוּת וְיַעֲלוּ מִן־הַיַּרְדֵּן׃ וַיְצַו
יח יְהוֹשֻׁעַ אֶת־הַכֹּהֲנִים לֵאמֹר עֲלוּ מִן־
הַיַּרְדֵּן׃ וַיְהִי °בעלות הַכֹּהֲנִים נֹשְׂאֵי
אֲרוֹן בְּרִית־יהוה מִתּוֹךְ הַיַּרְדֵּן נִתְּקוּ
כַּפּוֹת רַגְלֵי הַכֹּהֲנִים אֶל הֶחָרָבָה וַיָּשֻׁבוּ
יט מֵי־הַיַּרְדֵּן לִמְקוֹמָם וַיֵּלְכוּ כִתְמוֹל־
שִׁלְשׁוֹם עַל־כָּל־גְּדוֹתָיו׃ וְהָעָם עָלוּ מִן־
כ הַיַּרְדֵּן בֶּעָשׂוֹר לַחֹדֶשׁ הָרִאשׁוֹן וַיַּחֲנוּ
בַּגִּלְגָּל בִּקְצֵה מִזְרַח יְרִיחוֹ׃ וְאֵת שְׁתֵּים

°כַּעֲלוֹת ק׳

וַיִּרְאוּ אֹתוֹ — *And they feared him.*

Mateh Binyamin observes that the construction וַיִּרְאוּ אֹתוֹ, *and they feared him,* refers to a fear inspired by awe, while the construction ...וַיִּרְאוּ מִ refers to a fear of punishment.

כָּל־יְמֵי חַיָּיו — *All the days of his life.*

Kli Yakar comments that *his life* could refer to either Joshua or Moses: either the people feared Joshua as they had feared Moses all the days of Moses' life, or the people feared Joshua all the days of Joshua's life as they had feared Moses.

15-18. According to *Rashi* and *Radak,* verses 15 through 18 constitute a flashback explaining the details of the Kohanim's departure from the Jordan (which Scripture mentions in verse 11). *Malbim,* however, preserves the chronological sequence of the verses by maintaining that verse 11 does not refer to the Kohanim's departure from the Jordan; he contends that verse 11 merely describes how the Ark moved from its position near the western bank of the Jordan toward the eastern bank.

Malbim asserts that the language of Scripture supports his view, for verse 11 states [*they*] *passed over,* whereas verse 16 states *they should ascend,* implying that the Kohanim now ascended from the depths of the river bed to the bank of the Jordan.

16. אֲרוֹן הָעֵדוּת — *Ark of Testimony.*

The Ark has many appellations, each signifying one of its functions (see *Prefatory Remarks* to Chapter 3 and *Commentary* to 3:11). This appellation, *Ark of Testimony,* indicates that the Ark bears witness to the Divine Presence which dwells in Israel (*R' Bachya, Exodus* 25:10). [Perhaps Scripture refers to the Ark by this title precisely after the miracle at the Jordan, because Israel had just secured visual proof of God's presence and of His providential intervention in Israel's history.]

וְיַעֲלוּ — *That they should ascend.*

Rashi (in support of his interpretation of verse 11) explains that Scripture did not mention that the Kohanim should *cross* the Jordan, but that they should 'rise up.' Since they were situated just off the eastern bank to 'rise up' would imply that they did not cross the river, as did the other Israelites; rather, they waited on the eastern bank until the nation crossed.

4
15-20

feared him as they feared Moses all the days of his
life.
15 *HASHEM spoke to Joshua saying,* 16 *'Command*
the Kohanim bearers of the Ark of Testimony that
they should ascend from the Jordan.'
17 *And Joshua commanded the Kohanim saying,*
'Ascend from the Jordan.'
18 *It was when the Kohanim, bearers of the Ark of*
HASHEM, ascended from the Jordan and the soles of
the Kohanim's feet were uprooted to the shore, the
waters of the Jordan returned to their place and
stretched to all its banks as before.
19 *And the nation ascended from the Jordan on the*
tenth day of the first month and encamped at Gilgal
on the eastern side of Jericho. 20 *Those twelve stones*

Since Joshua had previously commanded them to remain in the Jordan (3:5), the Kohanim were not permitted to ascend from the river bed until they were commanded to do so *(Malbim).*

18. הֶחָרָבָה – *The shore* [lit. *dry land*].

The translation follows *Malbim,* who cites two meanings for this word: either (a) inundated land which has completely dried or (b) land which has never been inundated, but is moist or muddy (e.g., shore). The shores of the Jordan had always remained muddy since the miracle of the river bed drying had not occurred there.

וַיָּשֻׁבוּ מֵי־הַיַּרְדֵּן – *The waters of the Jordan returned.*

The waters gradually returned to their former position so that they would not spill over the river banks and flood the nearby shores *(Radak).* [Cf. *Commentary* to 3:15.] This was an extraordinary miracle because water which falls from such a height (see *Commentary* to 3:16) normally spills over the sides of its container *(Meam Loez).*

19. לַחֹדֶשׁ הָרִאשׁוֹן – *Of the first month.*

This is the month of Nissan.[1] The Pentateuch always refers to a month by the number which designates its position in the twelve month cycle (see *Ramban* to *Exodus* 12:12).

בַּגִּלְגָּל – *At Gilgal.*

This is the lodging place mentioned in verse 3 *(Rashi).*

Scripture explains the significance of the name Gilgal in 5:9.

1. Rabbi Levi said: The merit of Israel's first *Pesach* offering benefited them at the Jordan, for Scripture states, *On the tenth day of this month every man shall take a lamb ... (Exodus* 12:3), and *Joshua* 4:19 also states, *And the nation ascended from the Jordan on the tenth of the first month (Yalkut Shimoni).*

Israel fulfilled God's command concerning the *Pesach* lamb at great risk, for the lamb was worshiped by the Egyptians' pagan cults, and anyone who injured a lamb was executed as a heretic. Since the Israelites conquered their natural fears on the tenth of Nissan in order to fulfill the command concerning the *Pesach* lambs, they were rewarded with a miraculous (supernatural) passage across the Jordan on the tenth of Nissan *(Mussar HaNeveim).*

ד
כא־כד

עֶשְׂרֵה הָאֲבָנִים הָאֵלֶּה אֲשֶׁר לָקְחוּ מִן־
הַיַּרְדֵּן הֵקִים יְהוֹשֻׁעַ בַּגִּלְגָּל׃ וַיֹּאמֶר אֶל־ כא
בְּנֵי יִשְׂרָאֵל לֵאמֹר אֲשֶׁר יִשְׁאָלוּן בְּנֵיכֶם
מָחָר אֶת־אֲבוֹתָם לֵאמֹר מָה הָאֲבָנִים
הָאֵלֶּה׃ וְהוֹדַעְתֶּם אֶת־בְּנֵיכֶם לֵאמֹר כב
בַּיַּבָּשָׁה עָבַר יִשְׂרָאֵל אֶת־הַיַּרְדֵּן הַזֶּה׃
אֲשֶׁר־הוֹבִישׁ יהוה אֱלֹהֵיכֶם אֶת־מֵי כג
הַיַּרְדֵּן מִפְּנֵיכֶם עַד־עָבְרְכֶם כַּאֲשֶׁר
עָשָׂה יהוה אֱלֹהֵיכֶם לְיַם־סוּף אֲשֶׁר־
הוֹבִישׁ מִפָּנֵינוּ עַד־עָבְרֵנוּ׃ לְמַעַן דַּעַת כד
כָּל־עַמֵּי הָאָרֶץ אֶת־יַד יהוה כִּי חֲזָקָה

☙ The Memorial is Erected

20. הֵקִים — *Erected.*

Although verse 8 states that the stones were *placed* in Gilgal, here Scripture states that Joshua *erected* a monument from them. *Malbim* explains that the stones which were gathered from the Jordan served both as a *sign* to the children of the generation which had experienced the miracle and as a *memorial* for future generations. [See *Malbim* to verses 6 and 7.] The *sign's* function could be fulfilled merely by placing the stones in Gilgal, but the memorial's purpose could only be accomplished by erecting a monument.

בַּגִּלְגָּל — *At Gilgal.*

Gilgal was selected as the monument's site because it served as the Jewish capital for the nation's first fourteen years in *Eretz Yisrael (Meam Loez).*

Ralbag suggests reasons why these stones were erected in public view instead of being placed in the Tabernacle as a remembrance for the miracle at the Jordan, just as the flask of manna was placed in the Tabernacle during Moses' lifetime *(Exodus 16:33)*: (a) The stones were so large that they would have occupied too much space in the Tabernacle; (b) Joshua did not want it to appear that he was equating his own stature with that of his teacher Moses by ordaining such a similar form of remembrance; (c) the miracle at the Jordan was not performed with these stones themselves, whereas the manna was intrinisically miraculous.

21. אֲשֶׁר יִשְׁאָלוּן — *When [your children] ask.*

Here Joshua refers to the question which *future generations* will ask when they see the monument *(Malbim).* [See *Commentary* to verses 6 and 7.]

Alshich understands this as two questions: (a) Why were stones chosen for the monument? and (b) what is the significance of the number twelve?

22. וְהוֹדַעְתֶּם — *You should inform.*

According to *Alshich* (see verse 21), the answers to their questions are that stones were selected because stones symbolize tribes; twelve were ordered because there were twelve tribes. Similarly, before lodging at Mount Moriah (see *Genesis* 20:11 and *Rashi*), Jacob[1] placed twelve stones around his

1. The splitting of the waters of the Jordan is another fulfillment of the principle, 'Everything that happened to the Patriarchs is a portent for the children' (see *ArtScroll Bereishis*, pp. 379-

4
21-24

which they had taken from the Jordan, Joshua
erected at Gilgal.
[21] *He spoke to the Children of Israel, saying,*
'When your children ask their fathers in time to come
saying, "What are these stones?" [22] *You should*
inform your children, saying, "On dry land Israel
crossed this Jordan." [23] *For HASHEM your God dried*
up the waters of the Jordan before you until you
crossed, as HASHEM your God did to the Sea of
Reeds, which He dried up before us until we crossed.
[24] *So that all the peoples of the earth know the hand*

head to represent the twelve tribes which would descend from him.

23. אֲשֶׁר־הוֹבִישׁ — *Dried up.*

[It was not sufficient for Joshua to merely mention that *On dry land Israel crossed this Jordan* (verse 22); he also needed to compare the miracle of the Jordan's dry river bed with the similar event at the Sea of Reeds. As has previously been noted (see *footnote* to 2:10), the miracle of dry land at the Sea of Reeds revealed to mankind that Adam's mission in this world was to continue only through the nation of Israel. The reenactment of this miracle at the Jordan reconfirmed this investiture of Adam's mission in Israel, thereby indicating that the sins which Israel had committed in the Wilderness had been forgiven (see *Aruch LeNer, Yevamos* 72a) and that their mission was to unfold in *Eretz Yisrael.*]

מִפְּנֵיכֶם ... מִפָּנֵינוּ — *Before you ... before us.*

Joshua's words were addressed to those who had left Egypt and had personally experienced the miracle of the Sea of Reeds *(before you).* To those who were born in the wilderness and did not experience the miracle at the Sea of Reeds, Joshua said, *'Before us,'* i.e., before those of us who were at the Sea of Reeds (excluding you who were not yet born) *(Radak).*

24. לְמַעַן ... לְמַעַן — *So that ... so that.*

Jews and Gentiles are expected to have different degrees of awareness of God's providence and of His powers. *Haamek Davar* suggests that the first purpose for the monument mentioned in this verse *(so that all the peoples of the earth know the hand of HASHEM that it is mighty)* is addressed to the Canaanites, who should derive a general understanding of God's strength from the miracle at the Jordan and desist from idolatry.

The second purpose for the monument, however, is that the Jews should derive a *continuous* fear of God from the miracle at the Jordan. That this fear should be continuous is indicated by the phrase *all the days.* This was not stated in regard to the Gentiles, for non-Jews only need occasional resolve in order to refrain from idolatry, not continuous inspiration. Jews, however, are constantly occupied with the performance

384). The *Midrash (Bereishis Rabbah* 76:5) states: In the Torah, Prophets, and Writings we find that Israel crossed the Jordan on account of Jacob's merit. In the Torah it says, *for with my* [*Jacob's*] *staff I passed over this Jordan (Genesis* 32:11). In the Prophets it says, *You should inform your children saying, 'On dry land Israel* [i.e. *Jacob*] *crossed this Jordan' (Joshua* 4:22). And in the Writings it says, *The sea saw it and fled, the Jordan was driven back ... at the presence of the God of Jacob (Psalms* 114:4-6).

ה הִיא לְמַעַן יְרָאתֶם אֶת־יְהוָה אֱלֹהֵיכֶם
א כָּל־הַיָּמִים: א וַיְהִי כִשְׁמֹעַ כָּל־
מַלְכֵי הָאֱמֹרִי אֲשֶׁר בְּעֵבֶר הַיַּרְדֵּן יָמָּה
וְכָל־מַלְכֵי הַכְּנַעֲנִי אֲשֶׁר עַל־הַיָּם אֵת
אֲשֶׁר־הוֹבִישׁ יְהוָה אֶת־מֵי הַיַּרְדֵּן מִפְּנֵי
°עָבְרָם ק׳ בְּנֵי־יִשְׂרָאֵל עַד־°עברנו וַיִּמַּס לְבָבָם

of mitzvos; thus they must maintain an ongoing awe of God in order to perform the precepts properly.

Poras Yosef comments that the Canaanites derived their understanding of God's *strength* from the stacking (3:16) of the waters of the Jordan, which could even be seen by those living a great distance from the river. Israel, however, derived its *fear* of God from the miracle in which the Ark carried the Kohanim across the Jordan (see *Commentary* to 4:11); this could only be seen by the Israelites.

יְרָאתֶם — *Will fear* [lit. *feared*].

Although the verb *fear* is in the past tense, it actually refers to the fear which will be inspired by witnessing the monument in the future. In Scripture, a verb in the past tense often refers to the future *(Radak)*.

V

The Redemption from Egypt (which the Israelites had experienced forty years earlier) was not complete until the Jews entered Eretz Yisrael (Ramban, Introduction to Exodus). *When God promised Moses that He would deliver the Israelites from Egypt, He concludes,* 'And I will bring you to the Land (Exodus *6:8*). Sifri *explains that it was because the Jews performed the rite of circumcision and sacrificed the Pesach offering that they merited freedom from the Egyptian bondage. Significantly, circumcision and the Pesach offering, both described in this chapter, were the first mitzvos the Jews performed when they entered* Eretz Yisrael.

The Redemption, then, consisted of two stages: leaving the pernicious effects of the Egyptian culture and entering the sanctified land of Eretz Yisrael. *This dual theme, which the Psalmist expressed as,* Turn from evil and do good (Psalms *34:15*), *is reflected in the two mitzvos which accompanied both stages of redemption.*

The mitzvah of circumcision involves a two-step process (see Commentary *to verse 2, s.v. 'For a second time'). According to* Beis HaLevi (Lech Lecha), *the Jews scrupulously adhered to the mitzvah of circumcision while they were enslaved in Egypt. However, since the second step of the ritual was not required by the Torah until Joshua's time* (Yevamos *71b*, Ramban), *the Jews only performed the first step. According to* Beis HaLevi, *these two stages of circumcision have different underlying meanings. The first stage removes the individual's non-Jewish status, whereas the second stage infuses him with sanctity and gives him the full status of an Israelite. When the Jews entered the Holy Land, they positively affirmed their status as Israelites by performing this second step in the process of circumcision.*

Similarly, there are two meanings ascribed to the Pesach offering. Since the lamb figured prominently in the idolatry practiced by the Egyptians, slaughtering it represented a denial of the Egyptian's paganism (Shemos Rabbah *15*). *Future generations of Jews, however, sacrifice the Pesach offering in order to remember all the miracles God performed for the Jews in Egypt* (Sefer HaChinuch, Mitzvah 5). *Thus, it was appropriate that upon entering* Eretz Yisrael *and experiencing the*

5 *of HASHEM, that it is mighty, so that you will fear*
1 *HASHEM your God all the days.'*

[1] *It was when all the Emorite kings on the western side of the Jordan and all the Canaanite kings on the Sea heard that HASHEM had dried up the Jordan's waters before the Children of Israel until they had crossed, their hearts melted, and there was no longer*

fulfillment of God's promise of deliverance, the Jew's commemorated the miracles with which God had initiated their Redemption from Egypt.

[*This chapter (verses 5:2 to 6:1) has been chosen as the* Haftarah *selection for the first day of Passover.*]

1....וַיְהִי — *It was...*

This verse provides the backdrop for the entire chapter. Because the Canaanites became effete with fear, the Israelites lost no military advantage by delaying their conquest several days in order to perform the mitzvah of circumcision *(Malbim).*

וַיְהִי כִשְׁמֹעַ כָּל־מַלְכֵי הָאֱמֹרִי — *It was when all the Emorite kings ... heard.*

Although the Canaanites were able to see the huge column of water which rose from the Jordan (3:13), they were *not* able to see the drying of the Jordan's floor. This fact constituted the additional information which they only *heard* about *(Poras Yosef).*

There is a dispute between the earlier authorities concerning the powers of the prophets. *Rambam (Moreh Nevuchim* 2:35) argues that of all the prophets, only Moses was able to perform a miracle which could be witnessed by multitudes. [Hence all the Canaanites only *heard* of Joshua's miracle at the Jordan, as this verse relates.] *Ramban (Deuteronomy* 34:11), however, maintains that Moses was not unique in *this* respect, and that other prophets were also able to perform miracles in the sight of many people. He asserts that the splitting of the Jordan was as public as the splitting of the Sea of Reeds. This verse, he contends, merely attests that even the Canaanites located in the western region of *Eretz Yisrael* were aware, through word of mouth, of the miracle at the Jordan.

מַלְכֵי הָאֱמֹרִי...מַלְכֵי הַכְּנַעֲנִי — *Emorite kings ... Canaanite kings.*

[The commentators do not explain why these two kingdoms in particular are mentioned. Perhaps Scripture cited the closest and the furthest kingdom from the Jordan to indicate how far the Canaanites' awareness of the miracle extended.]

אֲשֶׁר־הוֹבִישׁ — *That* [*HASHEM*] *had dried up.*

[See *footnote* to 2:10 which explains the significance of the drying up of the Sea of Reeds. The drying up of the Jordan has the same meaning: the fact that God had invested the nation of Israel with the sacred mission formerly entrusted to Adam.]

עָבְרָם — *They had crossed.*

According to the traditional reading of the text (Mesorah), this word is written עָבְרֵנוּ, *we crossed,* but pronounced עָבְרָם, *they crossed. Radak* explains that Joshua, using the first person, wrote *we crossed.*

וַיִּמַּס לְבָבָם — *Their hearts melted.*

[Rachav (2:11) announced to Joshua's reconnaissance mission that the Canaanite kings became fearful of Israel because of the drying up of the *Sea of Reeds,* but Scripture states here that their fear was based on the drying up of the *Jordan.* This apparent contradiction can be resolved according to *Yalkut Shimoni (Exodus* 67).

After Israel crossed the Sea of Reeds, Moses led the nation in a song of praise to the Almighty for the miracle which He wrought. Moses sang, *Fear and*

ה וְלֹא־הָיָה בָם עוֹד רוּחַ מִפְּנֵי בְּנֵי־
ב־ג ב יִשְׂרָאֵל׃ בָּעֵת הַהִיא אָמַר
יהוה אֶל־יְהוֹשֻׁעַ עֲשֵׂה לְךָ חַרְבוֹת צֻרִים
ג וְשׁוּב מֹל אֶת־בְּנֵי־יִשְׂרָאֵל שֵׁנִית׃ וַיַּעַשׂ־

dread shall fall upon them [Canaanites] */.../ till your people pass over, HASHEM/till this people pass over* (*Exodus* 15:16). *Yalkut* understands the repetition of *pass[ing] over* to refer to two different crossings, the crossing of the Sea of Reeds and of the Jordan (cf. *Targum, Exodus* 15:16). Thus, *Joshua* (2:11 and here) contains the realization of Moses' prediction that *both* crossings would frighten the Canaanites.]

וְלֹא־הָיָה בָם עוֹד רוּחַ — *And there was no longer spirit within them.*

Metzudos comments that the literal meaning of this phrase is hyperbolic. Therefore, we have translated it figuratively: the Canaanites became so terrified that they lost their spirit.

☙ The Circumcision

2. This verse attests to Israel's dedication to the performance of God's precepts, for even though they were exhausted from their journey, they were still willing to undergo circumcision (*Chida*).

בָּעֵת הַהִיא — *At that time.*

While the Jews were in Gilgal, God appeared to Joshua (*Abarbanel*).

There are several reasons why *that time* was particularly suitable for the performance of the mitzvah of circumcision:

□ While recuperating from circumcision, the Jews would not be able to defend themselves against attackers. Since the Canaanites feared the Jews after the miracle at the Jordan, however, Israel need not fear any attack during their three day recuperation period (*Malbim*).

□ The circumcision was required for the upcoming Pesach offering. This offering may not be eaten by anyone who is uncircumcised or whose sons are uncircumcised. Therefore, the circumcision on 11 Nissan (which was the day after their crossing) afforded a three day recovery period before the time of the Pesach sacrifice on 14 Nissan (*Alshich*).

□ Israel had just crossed the Jordan and circumcision was required for entry into *Eretz Yisrael*. The *Midrash* explains that when God promised Abraham *Eretz Yisrael*, He made a condition. *Genesis* 17:8-9 states: *I am giving you and your children after you ... all of the land of Canaan* on the condition that *you and your children after you guard my covenant* [i.e., circumcision] (*Bereishis Rabbah* 46).

אָמַר ה׳ אֶל־יְהוֹשֻׁעַ — *HASHEM said to Joshua.*

Lev Aharon asserts that the phrase לֵאמֹר, *saying*, is only used in regard to a command which was previously unknown to the people. Since everyone was aware of the mitzvah of circumcision, this Divine communication was only directed to Joshua; hence, Scripture does not use the word לֵאמֹר.

עֲשֵׂה לְךָ — *Make (for yourself).*

It would be unreasonable to assume that Joshua single-handedly circumcised all the Israelites. Nevertheless, this command is addressed to Joshua in the second person singular לְךָ, *you*, because Joshua had the responsibility for supervising the circumcision (*Radak*).

Metzudos (verse 4), however, maintains that only Joshua knew the skill involved in circumcision, because he had been present at the mass circumcision in Egypt forty years earlier and that he, in fact, circumcised the entire nation unaided. He was told to prepare one thousand knives so that he would not be delayed between circumcisions when one blade became blunt (*Meam Loez*).

spirit within them because of the Children of Israel.
[2] *At that time HASHEM said to Joshua, 'Make sharp knives and return and circumcise the Children of Israel a second time.'* [3] *And Joshua made sharp*

חַרְבוֹת צֻרִים — *Sharp knives.*

Targum renders *sharp knives. Mateh Binyamin,* however, traces the word צֻרִים to the word צוּר, *stone.* Therefore, he translates *stone knives. Rambam* translates: *hard stone (Moreh Nevuchim* 1:16). [Cf. *Targum Onkelos* to *Exodus* 4:25.]

Joshua prepared one thousand knives *(Minchah Ketanah).*

As *Rambam (Hil. Milah* 2:1) states, our custom today is to perform circumcision with a metal knife, although all sharp instruments are permissible.

וְשׁוּב ... שֵׁנִית — *And return ... [a] second [time].*

The translation follows *Rashi,* who understands this verse as referring to the second collective circumcision of the people. (The first mass circumcision had taken place forty years earlier on the night preceding the exodus from Egypt.) Because the male children born in the Wilderness had not undergone circumcision, they were required to do so at this time.

The *Talmud (Yevamos* 71b) offers two reasons why the Jews did not circumcise their children in the Wilderness:

☐ It had been considered potentially dangerous to circumcise the males in the Wilderness for fear they might have to endure the hardship of travel in a weakened condition. (The Jews never had advance knowledge concerning the duration of their encampments in the Wilderness, but made and struck their camps according to Divine decree.) Thus, they were never sure that the nation would remain in any one camp long enough to recuperate from circumcision.

☐ The salubrious northerly wind was absent in the Wilderness, thus making circumcision a threat to life. This wind did not blow, either because Israel did not merit it after the sin of the reconnaissance mission *(Tosafos, Yevamos* 71b) [see *Prefatory Remarks* to Chapter 2], or because the Clouds of Glory surrounding Israel's encampment would have been dispersed by this wind. *Aruch LeNer (Yevamos* 71b) explains that these reasons are complementary. Together they explain why the wind was absent before the sin of the reconnaissance mission which occurred in the second year in the Wilderness (because the Clouds of Glory would have been dispersed) and why the wind did not return until the tenth of Nissan forty years later, even though the Clouds of Glory permanently departed from Israel's camp on the seventh of Adar of the fortieth year when Moses died (because they were not forgiven for their sin until they entered *Eretz Yisrael).* [Cf., however, *Ritva, Yevamos* 71b.]

Radak, however, maintains that the phrase *for a second time* connotes repetitive action: Joshua needed to circumcise the Jews without interruption until the entire nation had been circumcised.

The *Talmud (Yevamos* 71b) interprets this phrase in yet a third manner to mean a *second* circumcision for those who had already been circumcised in Egypt (the word שֵׁנִית means *second*). The commandment of circumcision involves a two-step process. First, the foreskin is excised (מִילָה); second, the thin membrane adhering to the glans is folded back (פְּרִיעָה). Moses was given this commandment, but it was first to be effective when the Jews entered *Eretz Yisrael (Ramban, Yevamos* 71b). Therefore, those men who had been circumcised in Egypt needed to undergo the second process (פְּרִיעָה) when they entered *Eretz Yisrael.* [According to *Tosafos' (Yevamos* 71b) version of *Pirkei De R' Eliezer,* the Jews circumcised their children in the Wilderness. However, they did not perform פְּרִיעָה. The question then remains why Joshua was commanded to prepare sharp knives if only the second stage of circumcision needed to be performed. According to *Rambam (Hil. Milah* 2:2), only the fingernails are needed to perform this procedure. See the explanation given by *Achiezer, Responsa III,* 65:12.]

ה לוֹ יְהוֹשֻׁעַ חַרְבוֹת צֻרִים וַיָּמָל אֶת־בְּנֵי
ד־ו ד יִשְׂרָאֵל אֶל־גִּבְעַת הָעֲרָלוֹת׃ וְזֶה הַדָּבָר
אֲשֶׁר־מָל יְהוֹשֻׁעַ כָּל־הָעָם הַיֹּצֵא
מִמִּצְרַיִם הַזְּכָרִים כֹּל | אַנְשֵׁי הַמִּלְחָמָה
מֵתוּ בַמִּדְבָּר בַּדֶּרֶךְ בְּצֵאתָם מִמִּצְרָיִם׃
ה כִּי־מֻלִים הָיוּ כָּל־הָעָם הַיֹּצְאִים וְכָל־
הָעָם הַיִּלֹּדִים בַּמִּדְבָּר בַּדֶּרֶךְ בְּצֵאתָם
ו מִמִּצְרַיִם לֹא־מָלוּ׃ כִּי | אַרְבָּעִים שָׁנָה
הָלְכוּ בְנֵי־יִשְׂרָאֵל בַּמִּדְבָּר עַד־תֹּם כָּל־
הַגּוֹי אַנְשֵׁי הַמִּלְחָמָה הַיֹּצְאִים מִמִּצְרַיִם

3. גִּבְעַת הָעֲרָלוֹת — *The Mound of Aralos* [lit. *foreskins*].

The name of this site commemorates the event that occurred there: so many people were circumcised that a mound of foreskins (עֲרָלוֹת) was formed *(Ramban, Yevamos* 71b).[1]

4. וְזֶה הַדָּבָר — *This is the reason* [lit. *this is the thing*].

Ramban (Leviticus 10:3) understands זֶה הַדָּבָר as *the reason* why this circumcision was commanded: because the children born in the Wilderness had not been circumcised, as mentioned in verse 5 *(Radak).*

Rashi, however, interprets דָּבָר as 'word,' rather than 'thing.' He comments that Joshua convinced the people to be circumcised by saying the following words: 'Do you think that uncircumcised men can inherit the Land? Did not God tell Abraham, *"You shall keep my covenant* [circumcision] ... *and I will give you and your children after you* [*Eretz Yisrael*]"?'

Metzudos follows *Ramban's* interpretation, but contends that Scripture is explaining why Joshua *in particular* was commanded to circumcise the people. As the second half of the verse indicates, no one else knew the skill involved, for those present at the circumcision in Egypt were no longer living. Hence, Joshua was given this responsibility.

כָּל־הָעָם ... מִמִּצְרָיִם — *The entire nation ... (from) Egypt.*

[The second half of this verse requires explanation because the reference to those who had been circumcised in Egypt and died in the Wilderness has no apparent connection with the beginning of the verse.]

Radak explains that the end of verse 4 and the beginning of verse 5 (which relate that those men who left Egypt

1. Bilaam alluded to this episode in Jewish history when he said, *From the top of the rocks* (צֻרִים) *I see him, and from the hills* (גְּבָעוֹת) *I behold him (Numbers* 23:9). The rocks he envisioned were the rocks Joshua used to circumcise the Israelites, and the hill was the mound of foreskins mentioned in this verse *(Meiri, Yevamos* 71b). The *Midrash (Pirkei De R' Eliezer,* Chapter 29) states that these Israelites covered their circumcised foreskins with earth from the Wilderness. Because of the merit which Israel gained from this act, Bilaam was incapable of cursing them; therefore he exclaimed, *'Who can count the dust of Jacob?' (Numbers* 23:10). This incident prompted the Rabbis to declare that the blood and the foreskin from the circumcision should be covered with earth. *Shulchan Aruch (Yoreh Deah* 265:10) codifies this practice as one of the laws of circumcision (cf., *Yam Shel Shlomo, Yevamos,* Chapter 8 for a different explanation of this practice).

knives and circumcised the Children of Israel at the
Mound of Aralos.
4 *This is the reason why Joshua circumcised: the*
entire nation that left Egypt — the males, all the men
of battle — had died in the wilderness on the way
during their exodus from Egypt. 5 *All the people that*
left were circumcised, but all the people that were
born in the wilderness on the way during their
exodus from Egypt were not circumcised, 6 *because*
forty years the Children of Israel journeyed in the
wilderness until the death of all the nation — the men
of battle — who left Egypt and did not hearken to

were circumcised) indicate that the fact that these children had not been circumcised in the Wilderness does not mean that their parents were negligent. On the contrary, their willingness to undergo circumcision in Egypt establishes that they were dedicated to the performance of the Torah's precepts. Rather, it was for the reasons mentioned in the *Commentary* to verse 2 (s.v. 'And return ... a second time') that circumcision was postponed in the Wilderness.

Lev Aharon comments that the second half of this verse and the following verse explain why Moses and Joshua had not circumcised the people before this time: those who left Egypt had already been circumcised and those born in the Wilderness could not be.

כׇּל אַנְשֵׁי הַמִּלְחָמָה — *All the men of battle.*

This term refers to the men who were between twenty and sixty years old, for only they were eligible for military service *(Radak).*

5. כִּי־מֻלִים הָיוּ — [*They*] *were circumcised.*

Some commentators contend that the Jews in Egypt were remiss in regard to the mitzvah of circumcision. However, all agree that on the night prior to their exodus from Egypt they did perform this mitzvah *(Radak).* (Cf., *Beis HaLevi* cited in *Prefatory Remarks* to this Chapter.)

לֹא־מָלוּ — *Were not circumcised* [lit. *did not circumcise*].

See *Commentary* to 5:2 for the reasons why the children were not circumcised in the Wilderness.

Despite the risks involved, the Levites did circumcise their children. Moses praised them for this, saying, *'And Your covenant* [*circumcision*] *they* [*the Levites*] *kept' (Deuteronomy* 33:9; *Rashi).*

6. כִּי אַרְבָּעִים שָׁנָה — *Because forty years.*

Chida comments that Scripture would not make a derogatory remark about the generation of the Wilderness without a reason. He explains that here Scripture intimates that the generation of the Wilderness was indirectly responsible for the circumstances which led to their inability to perform the mitzvah of circumcision on their sons. Since they had not listened to God, they were sentenced to die in the Wilderness where they were unable to circumcise their children. The generation of the Wilderness therefore incurred a certain degree of guilt for not circumcising their sons. In order to spare their deceased fathers punishment in the after-life on this account, Joshua pleaded with the Israelites at this time to submit to circumcision. If they had refused, their parents would have been held indirectly responsible for this sin.

אֲשֶׁר לֹא־שָׁמְעוּ בְּקוֹל יהוה אֲשֶׁר נִשְׁבַּע
יהוה לָהֶם לְבִלְתִּי הַרְאוֹתָם אֶת־הָאָרֶץ
אֲשֶׁר נִשְׁבַּע יהוה לַאֲבוֹתָם לָתֶת לָנוּ
ז אֶרֶץ זָבַת חָלָב וּדְבָשׁ: וְאֶת־בְּנֵיהֶם הֵקִים
תַּחְתָּם אֹתָם מָל יְהוֹשֻׁעַ כִּי־עֲרֵלִים הָיוּ
ח כִּי לֹא־מָלוּ אוֹתָם בַּדָּרֶךְ: וַיְהִי כַּאֲשֶׁר־
תַּמּוּ כָל־הַגּוֹי לְהִמּוֹל וַיֵּשְׁבוּ תַחְתָּם
ט בַּמַּחֲנֶה עַד חֲיוֹתָם: וַיֹּאמֶר
יהוה אֶל־יְהוֹשֻׁעַ הַיּוֹם גַּלּוֹתִי אֶת־חֶרְפַּת
מִצְרַיִם מֵעֲלֵיכֶם וַיִּקְרָא שֵׁם הַמָּקוֹם

לֹא־שָׁמְעוּ בְּקוֹל ה׳ — *[They] did not hearken to (the voice of) HASHEM.*

The Jews experienced God's glory and miracles in Egypt and in the Wilderness. Nevertheless, they demonstrated their lack of confidence in God by failing ten trials of faith in the Wilderness *(Derech Chaim* to *Avos* 5:4).

אֲשֶׁר נִשְׁבַּע ה׳ — *Which HASHEM had sworn.*

This oath is mentioned in *Numbers* 14:21-23.

לָתֶת לָנוּ — *To give us.*

Joshua, author of the *Book of Joshua,* frequently employs the first person plural *(Mateh Binyamin).*

זָבַת חָלָב וּדְבָשׁ — *Flowing with milk and honey.*

This refers to the milk of goats and the honey of dates *(Rashi, Exodus* 13:5).

7. וְאֶת־בְּנֵיהֶם הֵקִים — *But their children He raised.*

The translation follows *Radak* who understands that it was God who sustained the children born to the generation of the Wilderness [with manna, water, and protection].

It was these children who were born in the Wilderness whom Joshua circumcised *(Rashi).*

תַּחְתָּם — *In their stead.*

According to *Targum* this should be understood 'after them'; our translation, however, follows *Radak* who renders 'in their stead.'

כִּי־עֲרֵלִים הָיוּ — *Since they were uncircumcised.*

They had all the halachic restrictions of uncircumcised males. For example, they were not permitted to eat sacrificial offerings *(Tosafos, Yevamos* 71b).

בַּדָּרֶךְ — *On the way.*

According to the opinion [cited in the *Commentary* to 5:2, s.v. 'And return ... a second time'] that the Israelites did not perform circumcision in the Wilderness because of the hardship of travel, this phrase could be interpreted to mean 'because of the journey' rather than simply *on the way,* for it was the fact that the Jews had to travel which precluded them from circumcising their children in the Wilderness *(Maharsha, Yevamos* 71b).

8. כָּל־הַגּוֹי — *All the nation.*

Scripture employs the Hebrew word גּוֹי for *nation* rather than its synonym עָם, to imply that even the slaves captured in Moses' time in the battle with Midian were circumcised on that day *(Meam Loez).* [See also *Commentary* to 4:1 and 5:10.]

לְהִמּוֹל — *Being circumcised.*

Some suggest that this chapter

HASHEM, about whom HASHEM had sworn that He would not show them the Land which HASHEM had sworn to their forefathers to give us, a land flowing with milk and honey. 7 *But their children He raised in their stead — those Joshua circumcised since they were uncircumcised because they did not circumcise them on the way.* 8 *It was when all the nation had finished being circumcised, they remained in their place in the camp until they recuperated.*

9 *And HASHEM said to Joshua, 'Today I have removed the reproach of Egypt from you.' He called*

contains eight references to circumcision as an allusion to the Biblical command of circumcision, which takes place on the eighth day after the child's birth.

וַיֵּשְׁבוּ תַחְתָּם — *They remained in their place.*

They remained in their places and did not besiege Jericho *(Rashi).*

עַד חֲיוֹתָם — *Until they recuperated.*

They remained in their places until they recovered from the ordeal of circumcision *(Rashi).* The recuperation lasted three days *(Meam Loez).*

Maharsha (Yevamos 71b) infers from this phrase that this was the *first* time in forty years that they were able to recuperate from the wound of circumcision. He suggests that this inference supports the opinion [cited in *Commentary* to 5:2, s.v. 'And return ... a second time'] that the Israelites did not perform circumcision in the Wilderness because of the absence of the salubrious northerly wind.

9. חֶרְפַּת מִצְרַיִם — *Reproach of Egypt.*

Reproach of Egypt refers to the foreskin. It acquired this name because of historical reasons. Before the Exodus, the Egyptians would taunt the Jews by saying, 'They are uncircumcised, just as we are.' Hence, the foreskin became a source of shame *(Metzudos).*

On the basis of *Midrashim, Beis HaLevi (Parshas Shmos)* demonstrates that the Jews tenaciously adhered to the mitzvah of circumcision in Egypt. He explains, however, that in order to avoid antagonizing the Egyptians by appearing dissimilar from them, the Jews concealed their circumcisions by stretching the prepuce over the glans. [This led the Egyptians to say 'You are uncircumcised just as we are,' as *Metzudos* comments.]

Through astrology, Pharaoh had a vision that the Jews would encounter blood in the Wilderness. This blood was considered an evil omen, a symbol of death; thus, the Egyptians taunted the Jews that God was taking them out in order to spill their blood in the Wilderness. In fact, when Israel sinned in the Wilderness with the Golden Calf, God did consider, so to speak, killing the entire nation. Upon Moses' entreaty, however, He relented and decreed that the Jews' blood would be 'shed' through circumcision rather than through Divine punishment. When the Jews were circumcised at Gilgal, they realized that Pharaoh's vision of blood was being fulfilled with the blood of circumcision. Then the taunt (or *reproach*) of the Egyptians was finally removed from them. (See *Rashi, Exodus* 10:10.)

HaRav Gifter suggests that *reproach of Egypt* refers to the Jews' statement in the Wilderness (after hearing the spies' slanderous report about *Eretz Yisrael), It would be better for us to return to Egypt (Numbers* 14:3). As a result of

ה י הַהוּא גִּלְגָּל עַד הַיּוֹם הַזֶּה: וַיַּחֲנוּ בְנֵי־
י־יא יִשְׂרָאֵל בַּגִּלְגָּל וַיַּעֲשׂוּ אֶת־הַפֶּסַח
בְּאַרְבָּעָה עָשָׂר יוֹם לַחֹדֶשׁ בָּעֶרֶב
יא בְּעַרְבוֹת יְרִיחוֹ: וַיֹּאכְלוּ מֵעֲבוּר הָאָרֶץ

their murmuring, they no longer merited the salubrious northerly wind. Once this wind stopped, they could not perform circumcisions (see *Commentary 5:2).* When God commanded Joshua to circumcise the nation at Gilgal, it became apparent that their sin of murmuring *(reproach of Egypt)* had been expiated (removed), and the northerly wind was reinstated.

Ralbag interprets חֶרְפַּת מִצְרַיִם as the pernicious influences of Egypt: sexual immorality and pagan beliefs. These influences were removed from the consciousness of the Israelites by circumcision and the Pesach sacrifice. *Lev Aharon* comments that the site of this mass circumcision should have been named Gal instead of Gilgal, for it is derived from the word גַּלּוֹתִי. He suggests, however, that according to *Ralbag's* interpretation the double appellation Gilgal was affixed because two influences were removed from the Israelites there: sexual immorality and pagan beliefs.

וַיִּקְרָא — *He called.*

Since an anonymous person gave Gilgal its name, Scripture employs the third person singular; similarly, *Genesis* 48:29 states *'And he said to Joseph,'* when the identity of the person who spoke to Joseph is unknown *(Match Binyamin).*

◆§ The Pesach Sacrifice

10. בְּנֵי־יִשְׂרָאֵל — *Children of Israel*

In verse 8, the Jews were referred to as גּוֹי, a term which generally connotes a heathen nation, whereas Scripture now calls them בְּנֵי יִשְׂרָאֵל, *Children of Israel. Poras Yosef* comments that גּוֹי was used before they were circumcised for then the Jews were not visibly different from the other nations. After circumcision, however, when it became evident that they are part of the Covenant of Abraham, the Jews are called *Children of Israel.*

בַּגִּלְגָּל — *At Gilgal.*

In our times, the Torah forbids us to sacrifice the Pesach offering anywhere except at the site of the Holy Temple (see *Deuteronomy* 12:8-14). [We are unable to, however, because we do not know the exact site of the altar.] After the Jews left the Wilderness, before the Holy Temple was erected in Jerusalem, however, the Pesach offering could be sacrificed on public altars. When the Jews crossed the Jordan, they erected a public altar at Gilgal; this was used until the public altar was moved to Shiloh, fourteen years later. (See *Prefatory Remarks* to Chapter 18.)

וַיַּעֲשׂוּ אֶת־הַפֶּסַח — *And (they) made the Pesach sacrifice.*

They made the Pesach offering at this time, because until now they were uncircumcised. In *Exodus* 12:48, the Torah explicitly prohibits an uncircumcised male from eating the Pesach offering *(Malbim).*

Tosafos (Kiddushin 37b) expresses two different opinions concerning the status of the Pesach offering brought by the Jews at this time. One opinion contends that the command to bring the Pesach offering was applicable only after the Jews had conquered and divided the Land. Hence, this Pesach offering was ordained by special Divine Decree, rather than by the injunction in *Exodus* 12:6. [Scripture, however, does not indicate that Joshua was given a special command to make the Pesach offering.]

The second opinion holds that the command regarding the Pesach offering was

5
10-11

the name of that place Gilgal until this day. [10] *And*
the Children of Israel encamped at Gilgal and made
the Pesach sacrifice on the fourteenth day of the
month at evening in the plains of Jericho. [11] *They ate*
from the aged grain of the Land on the day after the

operative from the time the Jews received the Torah on Mount Sinai. The Jews in the Wilderness could not offer it, though, since they were uncircumcised. [Consequently, Scripture here records the second Pesach offering the Jews made in their history as a people. (Cf. *Tosafos. Yevamos* 72a, s.v. משום.)]

בָּעֶרֶב — *At evening.*

Evening refers to the time after mid-day, when the sun begins to sink in the west *(Metzudos).*

◆§ Eating from the Grain of the Land

11. According to Biblical law, Jews are forbidden to eat from newly grown grains (i.e., wheat, oats, rye, barley, and spelt) until 16 Nissan (or, nowadays 17 Nissan) when the Omer sacrifice is offered.[1] This prohibition, *chadash* (חָדָשׁ) applies whether the grain is eaten raw, roasted, or ground (see *Leviticus* 23:14 and *Menachos* 70a). When Moses died on 7 Adar (about a month before the crossing of the Jordan), the manna ceased *(Kiddushin* 38a), but the Jews had a five-week supply stored away.[2] When their supplies dwindled on Passover (which begins 15 Nissan), they were forced to eat from the grain of the Land. [There is a dispute in the *Talmud* whether the prohibition of *chadash* commenced immediately upon their entering the Land *(Kiddushin* 37b, 38a) or fourteen years later *(Yerushalmi, Challah* 2:1). The majority view that the prohibition began immediately upon Israel's entry to the Land will be followed here.]

וַיֹּאכְלוּ מֵעֲבוּר הָאָרֶץ — *They ate from the aged grain of the Land.*

Verse 12 states that Israel ate from תְּבוּאַת אֶרֶץ כְּנַעַן, *the grain of the Land of Canaan,* while this verse states that they ate מֵעֲבוּר הָאָרֶץ, *from the aged grain of the Land. Malbim* distinguishes between the two terms: מֵעֲבוּר הָאָרֶץ — from עבר, *to pass* — refers to grain grown in the previous growing season; since this did not fall under the prohibition of *chadash,* it could be eaten even before 16 Nissan.

The term תְּבוּאַת אֶרֶץ כְּנַעַן refers to the grain grown in the present growing season, which could only be eaten after 16 Nissan.

Malbim's distinction is in accordance with his interpretation of מִמָּחֳרַת הַפֶּסַח, as explained in the following note. However, according to *Rashi* and *R' Yitzchak* (who are also cited in the following note), this distinction is unnecessary.

1. According to *halachah,* the Omer offering could only be brought from barley which grew in a field owned by a Jew. Although the Israelites had just entered the Land, they were still able to bring the Omer, for the barley — which had already grown to one-third of its mature size while being tended by the Canaanites — miraculously grew to full maturity in the six days that the Israelites occupied the Land. This two-thirds growth met the requirement that the barley grow in a field owned by a Jew *(Kli Yakar).* [See *Rosh HaShanah* 13a.]

2. In the Wilderness, if an individual attempted to hoard manna for fear that a fresh supply might not fall the next day, the manna would miraculously spoil (see *Exodus* 6:20). On 7 Adar, however, when the manna stopped falling, a special miracle occurred: God allowed the Jews to store manna for the future. *Alshich* explains that this miracle enabled the Jews to go directly from the sanctity of the manna to the sanctity of the grains of the Land, without having to profane themselves by eating the ordinary produce of Arvos Moav.

מִמָּחֳרַת הַפֶּסַח מַצּוֹת וְקָלוּי בְּעֶצֶם הַיּוֹם ה
הַזֶּה: יב וַיִּשְׁבֹּת הַמָּן מִמָּחֳרָת בְּאָכְלָם יב
מֵעֲבוּר הָאָרֶץ וְלֹא־הָיָה עוֹד לִבְנֵי

מִמָּחֳרַת הַפֶּסַח — *On the day after the Pesach sacrifice.*

R' Tam (to *Kiddushin* 37b) contends that this term is always used in the Pentateuch (see *Numbers* 33:3) to refer to the first day of Passover, 15 Nissan,[1] although the literal translation would imply that it means the day after Passover. In this context, Pesach does not refer to the first day of the holiday, but to the day *before* the holiday, when the Pesach offering was prepared. Hence, 'the day after Pesach' is actually the first day of the holiday.

According to this interpretation, the Israelites abided by the prohibition of *chadash* — which was in effect until 16 Nissan — by making the matzos for their Passover observance from grain which they had purchased from Gentile peddlers *(Radak).* [Whether grain grown in a field owned by a Gentile is included in the prohibition of *chadash* is the subject of a dispute among the halachic authorities. See *Tur* and *Shulchan Aruch, Yoreh Deah* 293.]

According to other commentators, the prohibition of eating new grain was not an issue, for they render מִמָּחֳרַת הַפֶּסַח literally, as ' the day after [the beginning of] Passover,' i.e., 16 Nissan (*Rashi* and *R' Yitzchak*, in *Tosafos, Kiddushin* 37b).

Following the view that *chadash* was not prohibited until fourteen years after Israel's entry to the Land, *Rashi (Kiddushin)* explains that Israel waited until after Passover to eat from the grain of *Eretz Yisrael* because they preferred eating manna. *Daas Sofrim* remarks that although Israel was initially contemptuous of the manna (see *Numbers* 21:5), they eventually found it dear and holy.

מַצּוֹת — *Matzos.*

Only grain which has the potential to become *leavened,* is kosher for the baking of matzos (*Pesachim* 35a). The Jews could not use the manna which they had stored, since that could never become leavened. Therefore, they used the aged grain from the Land *(Lev Aharon).*

1. The festival of Shavuos is unique among the holidays commanded by the Torah in that the precise date of its observance is not explicitly mentioned in Scripture. Rather, the Torah tells us to calculate the day of its observance by counting *from the morrow after Shabbos, the day you brought the omer offering, seven full weeks* (*Leviticus* 23:16). In the days of the Second Temple, a vitriolic dispute arose between the Sadducees and the Sages of the *Talmud* concerning the interpretation of the word *'Shabbos,'* the day from which Scripture commands us to reckon the holiday of Shavuos.

The Sages of the *Talmud* had an oral tradition from Moses that *'Shabbos'* (in this context) actually refers to the first day of Passover. Accordingly, Shavuos would always be observed on the same day of the week as the second day of Passover.

The Sadducees, however, did not believe that the Oral Tradition (which explains the Written Law) had also been given to Moses by God on Mount Sinai. Therefore, they interpreted the word *'Shabbos'* literally, as meaning the seventh day of the week. Thus, they began their fifty day count from the Sabbath after the first day of Passover. Obviously, according to this interpretation, Shavuos would be observed on a Sunday, no matter which day of the week Passover started.

The argument of the Sadducees was revived by the Karaites in the times of the Geonim, but the Geonim and other Jewish sages throughout the ages marshalled evidence from Scripture itself in support of the Oral Tradition. One such proof is offered by *Rambam (Hil. Tamidim U'Musafim* 7:11) and is based on our verse וַיֹּאכְלוּ ... מִמָּחֳרַת הַפֶּסַח.

Israel is prohibited from eating the new grain of the Land until the Omer offering is brought (*Leviticus* 23:14); yet *Rambam* notes, Scripture records here that Israel ate of the new grain on the day after Passover. [It is evident that *Rambam* understands this verse as do *Rashi* and *R'*

5
12

*Pesach sacrifice, matzos and roasted grain, on this
very day.* [12] *When the manna was depleted the
following day, they ate from the aged grain of the
Land. The Children of Israel did not have manna*

[See *Tosafos (Kiddushin* 38a) s.v. אקרוב.]

וְקָלוּי — *Roasted grain.*

Rashi (Leviticus 2:14) explains this term to refer to roasted grain which is milled into flour. *Malbim* comments that they used this grain for appetizers.

בְּעֶצֶם הַיּוֹם הַזֶּה — *On this very day.*

This very day refers to 16 Nissan, the second day of Passover, which is also called *this very day* in the Pentateuch (see *Leviticus* 23:14). The verse is thus divided: They ate matzos from the aged grain of the Land on Passover, and the next day *(this very day)* they ate [newly grown] roasted grain *(R' Tam, Kiddushin* 37b).

[According to *Rashi* and *R' Yitzchak*, there is no need to divide the verse.]

12. וַיִּשְׁבֹּת הַמָּן — *When the manna was depleted* [lit. *ceased*].

According to the *Midrash (Mechiltah Shmos* 16:35), the manna stopped falling when Moses died on 7 Adar. At that time, the people stockpiled a five-week supply of the manna. Therefore, this phrase can only be understood as 'when their supply of manna was depleted' and not 'when the manna stopped falling' *(Metzudos). Ralbag,* however, cites an opinion that the manna actually fell until this day.

מִמָּחֳרַת — *The following day.*

This refers to the day after the day which was mentioned in the previous verse; since verse 11 refers to the fifteenth of Nissan, the day on which Passover begins, this verse is referring to the sixteenth of Nissan *(Malbim).*

Radak, however, interprets מִמָּחֳרַת to mean the same day mentioned in the previous verse, 15 Nissan (which was the day *following* the Pesach offering mentioned in verse 10). He explains that the manna was not needed on 15 Nissan, since they were then eating from the aged grain of the Land. *Malbim,* however, understands that only their matzos were made from the aged grain, but the remainder of their meal was prepared from the manna.

בְּאָכְלָם — *They ate.*

Rashi argues that they only ate from the produce of the Land because their supply of manna had been depleted. He would therefore interpret the beginning of this verse: 'Since their supply of manna had been depleted, they ate from the grain of that year' *(Meam Loez).*

Malbim remarks that the manna ceased *because* they began to eat from the grain of the Land.

Yitzchak, cited in *Commentary.*] Hence, it is the day after Passover begins when the Omer offering is made, and it is this day which Scripture mentions *(Leviticus* 23:16) as the starting point for the fifty day counting. *Rambam* further explains that it is untenable to assume that the Passover mentioned in our verse occurred on the Sabbath (in which case the reckoning of the Sages and the Sadducees would yield identical results), since Scripture indicates that their sanction for their eating was merely dependent on Passover (מִמָּחֳרַת הַפֶּסַח) and not the Sabbath. (See also *Ibn Ezra, Ramban* and *Abarbanel* to *Leviticus* 23:11, *Kuzari* (3:41), and *Kol Yehudah, ibid.)*

[According to the *Midrashim* which recount the day of Moses' death, Passover could not have occurred on the Sabbath that year. Moses died on 7 Adar. One *Midrash* states that 7 Adar occurred on the Sabbath in which case Passover would have fallen on Monday. The other *Midrash* fixes 7 Adar on Friday, in which case Passover would have fallen on Sunday, for in the year Moses died, Adar had only 29 days (cf., however, *Sefer HaMiknah* cited in Chronology to 1:1). Since the Karaites did not believe in the authority of the Oral Law, however, *Rambam* could not have used these *Midrashim* to identify the date of Passover that year. He therefore needed to justify his claim from Scripture itself.]

ה יִשְׂרָאֵל מָן וַיֹּאכְלוּ מִתְּבוּאַת אֶרֶץ כְּנַעַן
יג יג בַּשָּׁנָה הַהִיא: וַיְהִי
בִּהְיוֹת יְהוֹשֻׁעַ בִּירִיחוֹ וַיִּשָּׂא עֵינָיו וַיַּרְא
וְהִנֵּה־אִישׁ עֹמֵד לְנֶגְדּוֹ וְחַרְבּוֹ שְׁלוּפָה

וְלֹא־הָיָה עוֹד לִבְנֵי יִשְׂרָאֵל מָן — *The Children of Israel did not have manna anymore.*

Thus ended a remarkable period in the history of Israel. During the forty years in which the Jews were miraculously sustained by the manna, the entire nation was relieved of the burden of earning a living so that the people could immerse themselves in the study of Torah *(Daas Sofrim).*

In the future, the manna will return *(Yalkut).*

וַיֹּאכְלוּ — *They ate.*

Metzudos renders: they began to eat.

אֶרֶץ כְּנַעַן — *The Land of Canaan.*

[In the Pentateuch, the Land of Israel is called either *Land of Canaan* or simply *Land.* Not until the Prophets is the appellation *Eretz Yisrael* used (see *Ezekiel* 40:2, 47:18 and *II Chronicles* 22:1.]

Several reasons have been offered to explain why the Torah calls *Eretz Yisrael 'Canaan.' Rashi (Exodus* 13:5) suggests that its name derives from the former inhabitants of the land; they are collectively referred to as Canaanites, since their father was Canaan (*Ramban, Exodus* 13:5). The *Midrash* relates that Canaan merited having *Eretz Yisrael* named for him because he (i.e., the Girgashites [*Malbim*]) willingly vacated the Land when he heard that the Jews were about to enter *(Mechiltah, Bo,* 18).

Others believe that the name Canaan was derived from the Hebrew word for business and trade, since *Eretz Yisrael* was a hub for commercial activity *(Kaftor V'Ferach).* A similar use of the word is found in *Isaiah* 23:8 ... *whose merchants are princes, whose traffickers* (כִּנְעָנֶיהָ) *are the honorable men of the earth.* [See also *Rashi* and *Ibn Ezra* to *Genesis* 38:2.]

It is also possible that the name comes from the Hebrew cognate *humility* (הַכְנָעָה), for *Eretz Yisrael* was given to those who would humble themselves before God and perform His will *(Chida).* Some explain that the association of *Eretz Yisrael* with humility is hinted at in the verse *(Numbers* 13:18) *See the Land, what it is. 'What'* (מַה) refers to humility, as in *Exodus* 16:7: וְנַחְנוּ מָה, *what are we? (Divrei Emes).* [See *Prefatory Remarks* to Chapter 13.]

בַּשָּׁנָה הַהִיא — *That year.*

Malbim interprets this phrase as modifying *the grain of the Land;* i.e., 'they ate from the newly grown grains, from the grains which had been grown *that year.'* He argues that *that year* cannot refer to *when* they ate, for they ate from the grains of the Land every successive year, also.

The Appearance of the Angel

13-15. [The curious encounter between Joshua and the angel with which this chapter concludes is interpreted by the Sages (see *footnote* to 5:14) as a castigation of the Israelites for temporarily forsaking Torah study. Even though the people were engaged in preparations for the siege of Jericho, they should not have been remiss in their dedication to Torah study. Their neglect of this mitzvah represented a failure to recognize that Torah study was the source of their success. Just as the Torah study preceded the miracle at the Jordan (see *Commentary* to 3:14), so it must precede the miracle at Jericho. This is in accordance with the covenant that Israel made with God at Mount Sinai (see *Prefatory Remarks* to Chapter 3).]

5 anymore; they ate from the grain of the Land of
13 Canaan that year.

[13] *It was when Joshua was in Jericho that he lifted up his eyes and saw, and behold! A man was standing opposite him with his sword drawn in his*

13. בִּירִיחוֹ — *In Jericho.*

Since it would be absurd to think that Joshua was inside Jericho, this verse must mean that Joshua was on the outskirts of the city, which are often referred to by the name of the city proper (*Rashi;* see *Nedarim* 56b). Joshua had moved to the outskirts of Jericho after the circumcision and Pesach offering took place at Gilgal (*Radak*).

[According to *Rambam* (cited in the following note), the entire scene described in the next three verses was a prophetic vision; thus, Joshua *could* have envisioned himself as being in the city itself.]

וַיַּרְא וְהִנֵּה־אִישׁ — *And saw, and behold! A man.*

As explained in the following verse, this was actually an angel who appeared in the form of *a man* (*Radak*).

In *Rambam's* view (*Moreh Nevuchim* 2:42), whenever Scripture mentions that an individual 'saw' an angel, the epiphany took place in a prophetic vision or dream. *Rambam* maintains that this verse is referring to a prophetic vision.

Ramban (*Genesis* 18:1) agrees with *Rambam* that no one can literally 'see' an angel, and that Scripture uses the word 'see' to denote a dream or vision. However, *Ramban* does not believe that this experience is necessarily an act of prophecy, as *Rambam* asserts. Unlike *Rambam, Ramban* contends that when Scripture ascribes human form to an angel [as in our case], the angel *can* be visible to man.

Joshua was able to recognize that he was an angel, because he did not gradually approach from a distance, as a person would, but rather appeared suddenly. Joshua also realized that he was the only person who could see the apparition (*Meam Loez*).

עֹמֵד לְנֶגְדּוֹ — *Standing opposite him.*

Joshua realized that this man was really an angel, and he understood that the angel's drawn sword was symbolic of the prophecy which Joshua was about to receive concerning the battle against Jericho which would be fought with a sword. However, he did not understand why the angel was standing *opposite him.* Joshua reasoned that if the angel were going to lead Israel in battle against their enemy, he should have been facing the enemy rather than facing Israel.

Malbim explains that the direction of the angel's face symbolized the kind of Divine aid Israel would receive in the battle against Jericho. Had the angel faced the enemy, Joshua would have surmised that God would fight the battle for them. Since the angel was facing Israel, Joshua realized that God would instead grant the Israelites the strength to fight their own battle.

וְחַרְבּוֹ — *(And)* [*with*] *his sword.*

Lev Aharon perceives the sword as symbolic of Torah study. The Torah is sometimes referred to as a double-edged sword, as in *Psalms* 149:6: *a double-edged sword in their hand.* Whenever Israel is occupied in Torah study, it is as if they bear a double-edged sword which will save them from all danger and enemies. Since Israel neglected Torah study that night (see *footnote* to verse 14), the angel's sword signified that the Jews should resume their studies immediately in order to be victorious over Jericho.

Abarbanel comments that the *sword* was a sign that Israel would be victorious in the battle against Jericho.

שְׁלוּפָה — *Drawn.*

The translation follows *Metzudos.*

Numbers 2:23 and *I Chronicles* 21:16 are among the many instances in Scripture in

ה בְּיָדוֹ וַיֵּלֶךְ יְהוֹשֻׁעַ אֵלָיו וַיֹּאמֶר לוֹ הֲלָנוּ
יד אַתָּה אִם־לְצָרֵינוּ: יד וַיֹּאמֶר | לֹא כִּי אֲנִי
שַׂר־צְבָא־יְהוָה עַתָּה בָאתִי וַיִּפֹּל יְהוֹשֻׁעַ
אֶל־פָּנָיו אַרְצָה וַיִּשְׁתָּחוּ וַיֹּאמֶר לוֹ מָה

which an angel bears a drawn sword *(Mateh Binyamin).*

הֲלָנוּ אַתָּה — *Are you for us?*

Targum renders: Have you come to support us?

Have you come merely to strengthen us in our own military efforts? *(Malbim).*

Metzudos, however, renders more literally: Have you come to help us?[1]

אִם־לְצָרֵינוּ — *Or for our enemies?*

Metzudos continues: Or have you come to aid our enemy?

Or have you come to take over the task of fighting our enemies? *(Malbim).*

14. וַיֹּאמֶר לֹא — *And he said, 'No ...'*

[The angel's response to Joshua's question presents a difficulty because although he had not been asked a yes-or-no question, he responded 'No.']

Radak interprets the angel's reply as follows: *No,* it is not as you think; I am not a man who has come to wage war, but I am an angel sent by God.

Metzudos suggests: *No,* I have not come to aid your enemies, for I am the guardian angel of the Israelites.

Malbim continues: *No,* do not remain in doubt, for I have not come by myself. There are myriads of heavenly hosts to assist you in your wars against your enemies and *I am the commander of the Host of Hashem.*

שַׂר־צְבָא־ה' — *Commander of the Host of* HASHEM.

Rashi identifies this angel as Michael, of whom Scripture says, *Michael your prince (Daniel* 10:21). He is an angel of kindness whose primary function is to bring forgiveness. After Israel sinned with the Golden Calf and was forgiven, God sent Michael to lead Israel through the Wilderness. (Previously God had led the Jews directly with the Pillar of Cloud and the Pillar of Fire.) God intended to withdraw His immediate presence from the people in punishment for their sin. Through prayer, however, Moses persuaded God to suspend this Divine decree until the times of Joshua *(R' Bachya, Exodus* 23:20).

The *Midrash* identifies the angel as Matatron, who guided the Jews on their journeys and who will accompany the Messiah. Others identify him as Gabriel, who fights Israel's battles in a fierce manner [Gabriel was the angel who destroyed Sodom during Abraham's time *(Bava Metzia* 86b)] or as the Angel of Redemption[2] *(Ramban, Exodus* 23:22). [See *Prefatory Remarks* to Chapter 10 for further elucidation.]

צְבָא־ה' — *Host of HASHEM.*

This phrase *Host of HASHEM* refers to the nation Israel, which is HASHEM's host. Thus, this angel is called 'Angel of Israel' *(Rashi).*

Malbim interprets *Host of HASHEM* as a reference to the myriads of angels who will aid Israel in their conquest of the Land. Thus, the angel who came to

1. When the angel drew his sword, Joshua was uncertain if he had come to aid the Israelites or oppose them. However, when the angel drew his sword before King David *(I Chronicles* 21:16), David immediately knew that the Israelites were in danger. *Rashi (ibid.)* explains that King David saw the sword perched over Jerusalem, which symbolized impending doom. However, Joshua's situation was ambiguous. Joshua was standing with his back toward his enemies and did not know if the angel was drawing his sword against the inhabitants of Jericho or was forecasting doom for the Israelites. Hence he asked, *'Are you for us or for our enemies?'*

2. [It is noteworthy that when individuals encounter angels in Scripture, some ask the angel for his name, but others do not. Jacob *(Genesis* 32:28) and Manoach *(Judges* 13:7) did not

5
14

hand. Joshua went to him and said to him, 'Are you
for us or for our enemies?'
14 *And he said, 'No, I am the commander of the*
Host of HASHEM; now I have come.'
Joshua fell before him to the ground and prostrated himself and said to him, 'What does my

speak to Joshua is their commander.

עַתָּה בָאתִי — *Now I have come.*

I tried to come in the days of Moses, your teacher, as *Exodus* 23:20 states, *Behold, I send an angel before you ...,* but Moses did not accept me. *Now,* however, *I have come* to lead you in battle against the seven Canaanite nations dwelling in *Eretz Yisrael,* thereby fulfilling the promise made in *Exodus* 23 *(Tanchuma, Mishpatim* 18).

The *Midrash* understands this statement as a reproach to Joshua for the Jews' lack of diligence in Torah study.[1]

אֶל-פָּנָיו — *Before him* [lit. *on his face*].

The translation follows *Radak.*

וַיִּשְׁתָּחוּ — *And prostrated himself.*

want the angel to depart without giving his name, yet Joshua (5:14) and Gideon *(Judges* 6) made no effort to learn the angel's name.

Perhaps the difference lies in the fact that both Joshua's and Gideon's encounters with an angel were foreshadowed in the Pentateuch in the blessing that Jacob gave to his grandsons Menashe and Ephraim: *the angel who redeemed me from all evil* [i.e., the Angel of Redemption] *bless the lads ... (Genesis* 48:16). Two details of this blessing are significant: (a) Menashe and Ephraim are referred to as *lads* and (b) Jacob asked that they be blessed by an intermediary rather than by God Himself.

The Torah refers to both Joshua *(Exodus* 33:11) and Gideon *(Judges* 6:15) as '*lads.*' Joshua descended from Ephraim and Gideon from Menashe *(Niflaos M'Toras Hashem).* After they realized that an angel had approached them, they understood that it must be the Angel of Redemption, in fulfillment of Jacob's blessing; thus they did not need to ask the angel's name.]

1. With a drawn sword in his hand symbolizing reproachment, the angel said, '*No, I am the commander of the Host of HASHEM.*' According to the *Talmud (Eruvin* 63b), the angel continued, 'Yesterday you did not offer the afternoon sacrifice, and today you are not engrossed in Torah study.'

Joshua asked, 'For which of the two misdeeds have you come to chastise me?'

The host replied, '*Now I have come*' [for tonight's transgression of not studying Torah].

The night that the angel admonished them, the people were not able to study Torah because they were lying in wait around the city of Jericho.

The Holy Ark, normally stationed in Gilgal, remained with the Israelites outside Jericho. In addition to the reproachment for indolence in Torah study, Joshua was punished [by not being given male offspring (see *Megillah* 14b)] because he had deprived the Israelites of conjugal relations this one evening. Rabbi Abba Bar Pappa continued, 'We have a tradition that when the Holy Ark was not in its proper place, the people were forbidden to have marital relations.'

□ From this *Midrash* it becomes apparent how important it is for a leader to take into account the entire spectrum of the nation's needs. Joshua did not inadvertently leave the Ark outside its resting place. He purposely kept it with the people lying in ambush of Jericho to afford them the Divine protection that it guaranteed. However, since he only considered the needs of war and did not give proper weight to the mitzvah of 'Be fruitful and multiply' he was rigorously judged and not granted a son *(Mussar HaNeviim).* Thus, he was punished measure for measure by not being granted fulfillment of the commandment 'Be fruitful and multiply' which requires that a man father both a boy and a girl *(Maharsha).*

□ *Be'er Moshe* deduces from this *Midrash* that one is not exempt from Torah study, even under the most tumultuous conditions of war. '*Now, I have come,*' replied the angel, on your forsaking Torah study. All moments of one's life have to be regarded as '*Now,*' the only time left for study. As the *Mishnah (Avos* 2:4) says, 'Do not say when I have time I will learn, for maybe you will never have time.'

ה טו אֲדֹנִי מְדַבֵּר אֶל־עַבְדּוֹ: וַיֹּאמֶר שַׂר־צְבָא
טו יהוה אֶל־יְהוֹשֻׁעַ שַׁל־נַעַלְךָ מֵעַל רַגְלֶךָ
ו כִּי הַמָּקוֹם אֲשֶׁר אַתָּה עֹמֵד עָלָיו קֹדֶשׁ
א א הוּא וַיַּעַשׂ יְהוֹשֻׁעַ כֵּן: וִירִיחוֹ סֹגֶרֶת

According to Jewish law, one is forbidden to prostrate himself to an angel, for this constitutes an act of idolatry. However, it is permissible to bow as a mark of respect because the angel is a messenger of God (*Sefer HaIkkarim* 2:28). This must have been Joshua's intention.

According to *Abarbanel*, the angel did not come to aid Joshua in his battles, but rather to take full charge of the Israelites' army. By prostrating himself, Joshua showed that he was subordinating himself to the angel's role as commander.

מָה אֲדֹנִי מְדַבֵּר אֶל־עַבְדּוֹ — *What does my lord say to his servant?*

Make your request, and I will fulfill it as a slave who follows his master's orders (*Metzudos*).

15. שַׁל־נַעַלְךָ — *Remove your shoe.*

The *Midrash* states that the Divine Presence became revealed whenever the angel Michael appeared, and it is forbidden to wear shoes where God's presence is revealed (*Abarbanel*).

Malbim understands the removal of Joshua's shoes as an act of preparation for Joshua's next prophecy.

נַעַלְךָ ... רַגְלֶךָ — *Your shoe ... your foot.*

Joshua was required to remove only one of his shoes, whereas Moses was required to take off both shoes at the Burning Bush (see *Exodus* 3:5). *Abarbanel* explains that the incident at the Burning Bush demanded a greater display of respect because God himself appeared to Moses, whereas only an angel, God's messenger, appeared here to Joshua.

Malbim (Exodus 3:5), however, understands the removal of one or both shoes as symbolic of the difference between Joshua's and Moses' prophecy. No matter how ethereal a life a man leads, shoes remind him of his physicality. The pure soul requires two elements of physicality ('shoes') in order to exist in this world: it requires a body, which serves as a dwelling place, and a mind, which serves as the intermediary between the soul and the body. However, these two external needs of the soul act as barriers between it and the Creator. In the case of all prophets other than Moses, only one barrier (shoe) was removed so that the Divine communication could penetrate the prophet's soul. In Moses' case, however, both impediments (shoes) were removed in order to allow a perfect union between Moses and the Divine word.

כִּי הַמָּקוֹם ... קֹדֶשׁ הוּא — *For the place ... is holy.*

According to the most literal understanding, this phrase refers to the ground where the angel appeared. However, *Daas Sofrim* suggests a broader interpretation. Actually all of *Eretz Yisrael* is holy ground, and it would be appropriate for you to remove your shoes whenever you walk on it. Since this is not humanly possible, however, let this gesture remind you of the Land's sanctity so that you retain this awareness during all your wanderings in *Eretz Yisrael.*

VI

The campaign against Jericho launched the Jews' conquest of Eretz Yisrael. *As this chapter indicates however, Scripture's concept of war is entirely different from the mechanistic, military model with which we are familiar. The physical threat*

5 *lord say to his servant?'*
15 [15] *And the commander of HASHEM's Host said to*
Joshua, 'Remove your shoe from your foot, for the
place upon which you stand is holy.' And Joshua did
6 *so.*
1 [1] *Jericho had closed its gates and was barred*

which Israel's enemies pose is secondary to the spiritual menace which they represent to the world as a whole.

As a bastion of idolatry, Jericho constituted a source of spiritual defilement within the Holy Land (Ahavas Yehonasan), *and it was this evil influence which the Jews were commanded to destroy. The conventional elements of military strategy and armaments are utterly irrelevant in such a confrontation between the forces of holiness and the forces of desecration. Spiritual preparation and 'weapons' are essential however. Thus, God commanded that seven Kohanim (priests) blowing shofars should encircle the walled city one time each day for six consecutive days. The Kohanim were to be preceded by the ablest soldiers and followed by the Holy Ark. On the seventh day, this procedure was to be repeated seven times; then the Jews were to shout in unison, and the city would be given to them (see* Commentary *to 6:5).*

To insure that the forces of holiness would be victorious, the Jews had to prepare themselves for a spiritual war. This task was facilitated by the blowing of the shofar, for — as Rambam *explains in regard to the practice of trumpeting the ram's horn on Rosh HaShanah* (Hil. Teshuvah *3:4) — the shofar inspires repentance. Only if each Jew could remove every vestige of inner defilement would the nation be able to conquer the external threat (Jericho) which embodied spiritual defilement* (Michtav M'Eliyahu).

The encircling of the city of Jericho was symbolic of the means by which an individual should excise inner impurities: as they marched around Jericho, the Jews were circumscribing the unworthy elements of their own personalities. When this process was completed on the seventh day, their defilement was uprooted. Consequently, the wall of Jericho — which signified the inner obstacles to repentance — lost its metaphysical foundation and fell 'by itself' (Michtav M'Eliyahu).

The shofar blast also served another purpose. Baal HaTurim (Exodus *19:13) remarks that the same shofar which caused the destruction of Jericho's wall orchestrated the transmission of the Torah on Mount Sinai; it had originally been taken from the ram offered in Isaac's stead at the* Akeidah (Genesis *22:13). Thus, the shofar evoked the powerful memories of trust and belief in God which these two events had inscribed in the collective heart of Israel. Faith in God was especially needed at this time in order to counter Jericho's idolatrous disbelief in God. In addition, the shofar blast reminded Israel that only trust in God's beneficence would save them in their spiritual conflict with the mighty Jericho.*

◆§ The Campaign against Jericho

1. וִירִיחוֹ — *Jericho.*

Malbim understands this verse as part of the prophetic vision that the angel inspired. [Thus, in his view, this verse should be included in the previous chapter. In fact, *Meam Loez* does include this verse in his commentary to Chapter 5. See *Commentary* to 3:6.]

סֹגֶרֶת וּמְסֻגֶּרֶת — *Had closed its gates and was barred* [lit. *closed and impenetrable*].

וּמְסֻגֶּרֶת מִפְּנֵי בְּנֵי יִשְׂרָאֵל אֵין יוֹצֵא וְאֵין
בָּא: ב וַיֹּאמֶר יהוה אֶל־יְהוֹשֻׁעַ
רְאֵה נָתַתִּי בְיָדְךָ אֶת־יְרִיחוֹ וְאֶת־מַלְכָּהּ
ג גִּבּוֹרֵי הֶחָיִל: וְסַבֹּתֶם אֶת־הָעִיר כֹּל אַנְשֵׁי
הַמִּלְחָמָה הַקֵּיף אֶת־הָעִיר פַּעַם אֶחָת
ד כֹּה תַעֲשֶׂה שֵׁשֶׁת יָמִים: וְשִׁבְעָה כֹהֲנִים
יִשְׂאוּ שִׁבְעָה שׁוֹפְרוֹת הַיּוֹבְלִים לִפְנֵי
הָאָרוֹן וּבַיּוֹם הַשְּׁבִיעִי תָּסֹבּוּ אֶת־הָעִיר

This verse should be understood according to *Targum's* interpretation: closed with iron gates and reinforced with copper bolts.

This repetitive phraseology is explained by the end of this verse *no one could leave or enter:* סֹגֶרֶת thus means *closed*, i.e., no one could leave the city, and מְסֻגֶּרֶת means *impenetrable*, i.e., no one could enter the city *(Radak).* Since Jericho was impenetrable, conventional warfare was precluded. God therefore promised Joshua that the Israelites would gain victory through a miracle *(Abarbanel).*

Metzudos comments that Jericho's gate was always carefully locked (סֹגֶרֶת); however, when the inhabitants heard of Israel's proximity, they reinforced the city gate so that no one could even leave (מְסֻגֶּרֶת).

מִפְּנֵי בְּנֵי יִשְׂרָאֵל — *Because of the Children of Israel.*

This phrase means 'because of their great fear of the Children of Israel' *(Lev Aharon). Meam Loez* explains that when the inhabitants of Jericho heard that the Israelites conquered the highly fortified city of Cheshbon *(Numbers* 21:30), they attributed Israel's victory to the fact that the inhabitants of Cheshbon had fought outside their city wall in order to defend the city. Consequently, the inhabitants of Jericho fortified the walls of their city and remained within.

אֵין יוֹצֵא וְאֵין בָּא — *No one could leave or enter.*

Targum interpolates: No one left to wage war and no one entered to ask for peace.

Forty years before the destruction of the *Beis HaMikdash,* the Temple gates opened miraculously *(Yoma* 39b) to warn the Jews that the Temple would be destroyed *(Rashi). Mekor Chaim* comments that had Jericho's inhabitants been similarly forewarned that their fortifications would be of no avail, they might have escaped from the Israelites. Thus, Scripture adds the seemingly superfluous clause *no one could leave or enter* in order to convey that God did not want to give Jericho's inhabitants opportunity to flee, for He wanted them to be annihilated *(Chida).* [See *footnote* to 11:20.]

☙ God's Instructions

2. וַיֹּאמֶר ה׳ — *And* HASHEM said.

Until this point, Joshua's prophetic vision had been inspired by the angel; now, however, God addressed him directly *(Malbim).*

Others understand that God did not speak directly to Joshua, but communicated with him through the angel *(Radak).* [See *Commentary* to 5:13, s.v. 'and saw.']

רְאֵה — *See.*

This verse indicates that God elevates the humble who 'lower themselves' by modest behavior. In his humility, Joshua accepted the agency of the angel and did not feel that he deserved the direct guidance which God had granted

*because of the Children of Israel; no one could leave
or enter.*
*2 And HASHEM said to Joshua, 'See, I have given
you Jericho and its king and the mighty warriors.
3 And you shall go around the city, all the men of war
— encircle the city once. Thus shall you do six days.
4 And seven Kohanim shall carry seven shofars of
rams' horn before the Ark. On the seventh day you*

to Moses. Therefore, God told him, *'See,* I personally, as opposed to an intermediary, will deliver Jericho to you. You will need no battering rams, for when you encircle the city, it will miraculously fall' *(Poras Yosef).*

נָתַתִּי בְיָדְךָ — *I have given you* [lit. *I have put into your hand*].

[See 8:1 and *Commentary* to 10:8.]

According to *Abarbanel,* God was consoling Joshua who feared that he might not be able to vanquish this impenetrable city.

גִּבּוֹרֵי הֶחָיִל — *And the mighty warriors.*

R' Yishaye interpolates the word *and* before *mighty warriors.*

Even though they are men of strength, I will put the king and inhabitants of Jericho in your hands *(Radak).*

3. וְסַבֹּתֶם אֶת־הָעִיר — *And you shall go around the city.*

The men of battle were to march around Jericho so that they would recognize the impossibility of conquering Jericho through normal means *(Michtav M'Eliyahu).*

Malbim distinguishes between the roots סָבַב and הַקֵּף. סָבַב means *go around,* but does not necessarily imply a complete encirclement. הַקֵּף, on the other hand, denotes a full circuit.

Abarbanel explains that the Israelites were required to perform this curious ritual so that the inhabitants of Jericho would realize that their defeat was a direct result of God's Hand. Alternatively, he suggests that the Jews' march around Jericho demonstrated to the inhabitants that the Israelites were not refraining from attack because of cowardice.

כֹּל אַנְשֵׁי הַמִּלְחָמָה — *All the men of war.*

Michtav M'Eliyahu suggests that this lesson of trust in God was most appropriate for the *men of war* who would be risking their lives in the future battles against the Canaanites.

[See *Commentary to* 5:4.]

כֹּה תַעֲשֶׂה שֵׁשֶׁת יָמִים — *Thus shall you do six days.*

According to *Radak,* we cannot delve into why God commanded that there be seven priests, seven shofars, seven encirclings of the city, seven days, etc., for their significance is known only to Him.

Abarbanel, however, explains that the number seven is reminiscent of the seven days of Creation. In fact, the Canaanites were to understand that the miraculous conquest of Jericho was a miracle on the order of the creation of the universe.

4. שׁוֹפְרוֹת הַיּוֹבְלִים — *Shofars of rams' horn.*

The translation follows *Rashi.*

Abarbanel, however, suggests that this phrase alludes to the shofars that had been designated to be blown at the beginning of the jubilee (יוֹבֵל) year (see *Leviticus* 25:9).

In any event, Joshua did not use the two silver trumpets of which the Torah says, *And if you go to war in your land against the enemy that oppresses you, then you shall blow an alarm with the [silver] trumpets (Numbers* 10:9).

ו
ה־ז

שֶׁבַע פְּעָמִים וְהַכֹּהֲנִים יִתְקְעוּ בַּשּׁוֹפָרוֹת:
ה וְהָיָה בִּמְשֹׁךְ | בְּקֶרֶן הַיּוֹבֵל °בשמעכם (°כְּשָׁמְעֲכֶם ק׳)
אֶת־קוֹל הַשּׁוֹפָר יָרִיעוּ כָל־הָעָם תְּרוּעָה
גְדוֹלָה וְנָפְלָה חוֹמַת הָעִיר תַּחְתֶּיהָ וְעָלוּ
ו הָעָם אִישׁ נֶגְדּוֹ: וַיִּקְרָא יְהוֹשֻׁעַ בִּן־נוּן
אֶל־הַכֹּהֲנִים וַיֹּאמֶר אֲלֵהֶם שְׂאוּ אֶת־
אֲרוֹן הַבְּרִית וְשִׁבְעָה כֹהֲנִים יִשְׂאוּ
שִׁבְעָה שׁוֹפְרוֹת יוֹבְלִים לִפְנֵי אֲרוֹן יהוה:
ז °ויאמרו אֶל־הָעָם עִבְרוּ וְסֹבּוּ אֶת־הָעִיר (°וַיֹּאמֶר ק׳)

Midrash Rabbah (Behaaloscha 15:15) explains that these trumpets were only to be used by Moses when he went to war; while he was still alive, the trumpets were hidden so that no one else could use them. [Cf., however, *Avnei Nezer* (Responsa on *Orach Chaim,* Vol. II, 425).]

יִתְקְעוּ — *Shall blow.*

From the word יִתְקְעוּ rather than יָרִעוּ [which has the same meaning] *Malbim* deduces that this blasting of the shofar served to express joy and victory, rather than to alarm Jericho's inhabitants.

The Torah *(Numbers* 10:9) refers to the trumpet blast preceding a war with the verb וַהֲרֵעֹתֶם, *blast an alarm.* When referring to the trumpet sounded on the rejoicing of a holiday however, it uses the term וּתְקַעְתֶּם *(Numbers* 10:10).

יִתְקְעוּ בַּשּׁוֹפָרוֹת — *Shall blow (with) the shofars.*

They were to blast the shofar each day as they encircled the city *(Metzudos).*

5. בִּמְשֹׁךְ — *Upon an extended blast.*

The last shofar blast was to be extended *(Rashi).*

כְּשָׁמְעֲכֶם — *When you hear.*

Immediately with the last long shofar blast, the people were to shout until the two sounds combined and the wall sank *(Malbim).*

יָרִיעוּ כָל־הָעָם — *Shall cry out.*

'Crying' refers to prayer, as in *Exodus* 2:23, *and* [the Israelites] *cried, and their cry rose up to God (Harchev Davar* to *Exodus* 14:15).

The people were not worthy of the miracle until they demonstrated their recognition through prayer that they did not attribute their success to their own efforts *(Michtav M'Eliyahu).*

Abarbanel explains that the people were to refrain from shouting until the last day because their outcry was to be a symbol of victory.

וְנָפְלָה חוֹמַת הָעִיר — *And the wall of the city will sink* [lit. *fall*].

Anyone who wishes to deny the reality of a miracle can always find other explanations — no matter how far-fetched — to account for the miraculous event. In this case, one might conjecture that the reverberations from the high-pitched shofar blasts made the wall quiver and fall. However, the Jews realized that God's Will was the true cause of the phenomenon *(Michtav M'Eliyahu).*

תַּחְתֶּיהָ — *Into its place.*

The wall did not topple, but rather sank into the ground *(Targum).* The *Talmud (Berachos* 54b) explains that since the width of the wall was equal to its height, the Jews would still have been unable to enter the city if the wall had merely fallen. Part of the wall remained above ground as a memorial to the

6
5-7

shall go around the city seven times, and the Kohanim
shall blow the shofars. 5 *And it shall be upon an*
extended blast with the ram's horn — when you hear
the sound of the shofar — all the people shall cry out
with a great scream, and the wall of the city will sink
into its place, and the people shall invade.'

6 *Joshua son of Nun summoned the Kohanim and*
said to them, 'Bear the Ark of the Covenant and have
seven Kohanim carry seven shofars of rams' horn
before the Ark of HASHEM.'

7 *He said to the people, 'Advance and go around*

miracle. Indeed, according to *Shulchan Aruch (Orach Chaim* 218:1), one who sees the site of the walls of Jericho is required to recite the blessing 'who performed miracles for our fathers in this place.'

Radak comments that only the wall across from Israel's encampment fell. The other walls remained standing. Thus, Rachav's house, which was located in one of these other walls (2:15), was spared. [Cf. *Vilna Gaon* 2:15.] *Alshich* (verse 20), however, claims that all the walls sank into the ground, thereby enabling the Israelites to enter Jericho from all sides. He contends that *and the people invaded the city — each man straight ahead* (verse 20) means that the Jews could enter the city from any point along its periphery.

וְעָלוּ הָעָם אִישׁ נֶגְדּוֹ — *And the people shall invade* [lit. *go up towards it*].

Since the wall would sink into the ground (verse 20), the men could go directly into the city, without having to scale the rubble *(Metzudos).*

6. שְׂאוּ אֶת־אֲרוֹן הַבְּרִית — *Bear the Ark of the Covenant.*

[The command given to Joshua in verse 4 did not mention that the Kohanim were to transport the Ark.] *Malbim* comments that it was appropriate for the Kohanim to bear the Ark at this point, since the miraculous entry into Jericho would come about through their efforts.

Although God had mentioned the men of war before the Kohanim (verse 3), Joshua issued orders to the Kohanim first because they bore the Ark which was the resting place of the Divine Presence. God, on the other hand, mentioned the Israelites first as a sign of respect for the congregation *(Meam Loez).*

7. וַיֹּאמֶר — *He said.*

The verb is written in the plural, *they said,* but is to be read in the singular, *he said.*

The plural verb implies that Joshua and the Kohanim spoke to the people; the singular verb implies that Joshua *alone* spoke to the people *(Radak). Alshich* argues that it would have been impossible for Joshua to address the entire nation personally, for the congregation covered an area of 12 *mil* square. He suggests that the plural verb refers to the messengers who transmitted Joshua's message to the people.

עִבְרוּ — *Advance.*

During Israel's conquests, the Ark normally traveled before the men of war who traveled before the people. During the conquest of Jericho, however, this order was reversed: the people marched before the men of war, and the Ark followed in the procession. Thus, Joshua commanded the people 'pass

ו
ח־יא

ח וְהֶחָלוּץ יַעֲבֹר לִפְנֵי אֲרוֹן יהוה: וַיְהִי כֶּאֱמֹר
יְהוֹשֻׁעַ אֶל־הָעָם וְשִׁבְעָה הַכֹּהֲנִים נֹשְׂאִים
שִׁבְעָה שׁוֹפְרוֹת הַיּוֹבְלִים לִפְנֵי יהוה עָבְרוּ
וְתָקְעוּ בַּשּׁוֹפָרוֹת וַאֲרוֹן בְּרִית יהוה הֹלֵךְ
ט אַחֲרֵיהֶם: וְהֶחָלוּץ הֹלֵךְ לִפְנֵי הַכֹּהֲנִים
°תקעו הַשּׁוֹפָרוֹת וְהַמְאַסֵּף הֹלֵךְ אַחֲרֵי
י הָאָרוֹן הָלוֹךְ וְתָקוֹעַ בַּשּׁוֹפָרוֹת: וְאֶת־
הָעָם צִוָּה יְהוֹשֻׁעַ לֵאמֹר לֹא תָרִיעוּ וְלֹא־
תַשְׁמִיעוּ אֶת־קוֹלְכֶם וְלֹא־יֵצֵא מִפִּיכֶם
דָּבָר עַד יוֹם אָמְרִי אֲלֵיכֶם הָרִיעוּ
יא וַהֲרֵיעֹתֶם: וַיַּסֵּב אֲרוֹן־יהוה אֶת־הָעִיר
הַקֵּף פַּעַם אֶחָת וַיָּבֹאוּ הַמַּחֲנֶה וַיָּלִינוּ

°תִּקְעֵי ק׳

before the men of war.' Similarly, the verse says *and let the advance troop pass before the Ark of HASHEM.*

Malbim explains that with the Ark in the rear of the procession, it would be more apparent that it was the source of Israel's victory.

וְהֶחָלוּץ — *(And) ... the advance troop.*

These were the tribes of Reuben and Gad who pledged to take the lead in the Israelites' battles in return for the Trans-Jordan *(Rashi* to *Numbers* 32:17).

☙ Encircling the City

8. וַיְהִי ... וְתָקְעוּ בַּשּׁוֹפָרוֹת — *While ... and blew the shofars*

This verse informs us that the seven priests sounded the shofar while Joshua was commanding the people to file before the men of war (verse 7); their shofar blasts continued while the entire procession formed and prepared to circle the city *(Malbim).*

לִפְנֵי ה׳ — *Before* [*the Ark of*] *HASHEM.*

The interpolation follows *Targum.*

9. תִּקְעֵי הַשּׁוֹפָרוֹת — [*The Kohanim*] *who blew the shofars.*

Only the seven Kohanim bearing shofars marched near the Ark. The remainder of the priests joined the Levites and the rest of the people at the head of the procession *(Malbim).*

וְהַמְאַסֵּף הֹלֵךְ אַחֲרֵי הָאָרוֹן — *And the rear guard traveled after the Ark.*

Targum identifies this group as the tribe of Dan, whom the Torah calls *the rearward of all the camps* [tribes] *(Numbers* 10:25).

הָלוֹךְ וְתָקוֹעַ בַּשּׁוֹפָרוֹת — *While proceeding and blowing the shofars.*

Targum interprets that the Kohanim (priests), rather than the rear guard mentioned immediately before, are the subject of this clause.

Malbim notes that the Kohanim continued to sound the shofars as they marched in the procession.

Others disagree, maintaining that the Kohanim blew the shofar two separate times to signal two specific events. According to this view, the first blast informed the people that the priests had filed before the Ark so that the people would begin their march. The second blast (mentioned in this verse) fulfilled the commandment to blow the shofar while the people were encircling the

the city; let the advance troop pass before the Ark of
HASHEM.'
8 *While Joshua spoke to the people, the seven*
Kohanim bearing seven shofars of rams' horns
passed before the [Ark of] HASHEM and blew the
shofars; the Ark of the Covenant of HASHEM
followed them. 9 *And the advance troop went before*
the Kohanim who blew the shofars, and the rear
guard traveled after the Ark — while proceeding and
blowing the shofars. 10 *And Joshua commanded the*
people, saying, 'You shall not shout nor let your
voice be heard nor shall any word issue from your
mouth until the day I order you to shout, and then
you shall shout.' 11 *And he caused the Ark of*
HASHEM to go around the city, encircling one time.
Then they returned to the camp and lodged in the
camp.

city. This blast did not occur until the last group, the tribe of Dan, had joined the march *(Meam Loez).*

10. וְאֶת־הָעָם צִוָּה יְהוֹשֻׁעַ — *And Joshua commanded the people.*

Logically, this verse should have appeared after verse 7, when Joshua gave his orders to the people. However, the Kohanim were so alacritous in fulfilling Joshua's command, and the advance troop was so quick to rush before the Ark that Joshua's charge to the people was interrupted; he therefore completed his instructions to the people after the procession was organized *(Abarbanel).*

Poras Yosef, however, argues that since Scripture inverted this verse by placing the object first, it should be understood as *Joshua had already commanded the people.* In his view, the very fact that the people did not shout when the shofars were first blown (verse 9) indicates that they had already been instructed to remain silent; thus, this verse is out of chronological order. [See *Commentary* to 1:12.]

עַד יוֹם — *Until the day.*

This refers to the seventh day *(Radak).*

11. וַיַּסֵּב — *And he caused* [*the Ark*] *to go around.*

Since the verb is in the *hiphal* (causative) conjugation, the verse means, 'Joshua *caused* the Ark to go around' *(Radak).*

הַקֵּף פַּעַם אֶחָת — *Encircling one time.*

This verse relates the activity on Sunday, the first day of the siege *(Radak).*

וַיָּבֹאוּ הַמַּחֲנֶה — *Then they returned* [lit. *came*] *to the camp.*

They *returned* to their encampment in Gilgal *(Malbim).* [Cf. *Commentary* to verse 14.]

12-14. Verses 12 to 14 explain the procedure the Israelites followed the first six days in the siege against Jericho. While this seems to be a mere repetition of verses 6 to 11, *Malbim* suggests that Scripture relates the details a second time to indicate that from the second

יב בַּמַּחֲנֶה׃ וַיַּשְׁכֵּם יְהוֹשֻׁעַ בַּבֹּקֶר
יג וַיִּשְׂאוּ הַכֹּהֲנִים אֶת־אֲרוֹן יהוה׃ וְשִׁבְעָה
הַכֹּהֲנִים נֹשְׂאִים שִׁבְעָה שׁוֹפְרוֹת הַיֹּבְלִים
לִפְנֵי אֲרוֹן יהוה הֹלְכִים הָלוֹךְ וְתָקְעוּ
בַּשּׁוֹפָרוֹת וְהֶחָלוּץ הֹלֵךְ לִפְנֵיהֶם
°הָלוֹךְ ק׳ וְהַמְאַסֵּף הֹלֵךְ אַחֲרֵי אֲרוֹן יהוה °הוֹלֵךְ
יד וְתָקוֹעַ בַּשּׁוֹפָרוֹת׃ וַיָּסֹבּוּ אֶת־הָעִיר בַּיּוֹם
הַשֵּׁנִי פַּעַם אַחַת וַיָּשֻׁבוּ הַמַּחֲנֶה כֹּה עָשׂוּ
טו שֵׁשֶׁת יָמִים׃ וַיְהִי ׀ בַּיּוֹם הַשְּׁבִיעִי וַיַּשְׁכִּמוּ
כַּעֲלוֹת הַשַּׁחַר וַיָּסֹבּוּ אֶת־הָעִיר כַּמִּשְׁפָּט
הַזֶּה שֶׁבַע פְּעָמִים רַק בַּיּוֹם הַהוּא סָבְבוּ

day on, the procession started from the Jews' encampment at Gilgal, whereas on the first day it did not start until the Ark came to Jericho.

The Kohanim, who carried the Ark and blew the shofars on the first day, were the same ones who carried the Ark and blew the shofars on the six successive days *(Meam Loez).*

12. וַיַּשְׁכֵּם — [*Joshua*] *arose early.*

This verse refers to the second day of the siege *(Metzudos).*

13. הָלוֹךְ וְתָקְעוּ בַּשּׁוֹפָרוֹת ... הָלוֹךְ וְתָקוֹעַ בַּשּׁוֹפָרוֹת — *Proceeded and blew the shofars ... proceeding and blowing the shofars.*

This phrase is repeated to indicate that the Kohanim continuously blew the shofars *(Metzudos).*

14. וַיָּשֻׁבוּ — *And (they) returned.*

The language of Scripture would seem to indicate that the Israelites were not encamped in Gilgal at this time. Verse 11 states וַיָּבֹאוּ [lit. *they came*] *to their camp* while here Scripture writes וַיָּשֻׁבוּ [lit. *they returned*]. If they camped in Gilgal the entire time, Scripture should have used an expression denoting 'return' in both instances *(Poras Yosef).* [Thus, they must have camped outside Jericho instead of returning to Gilgal.]

15. בַּיּוֹם הַשְּׁבִיעִי — *On the seventh day.*

The *Midrash (Bereishis Rabbah* 14) interprets this phrase to mean that the invasion of Jericho took place on the Sabbath, the seventh day of the week.

The verse, *Ephraim is the strength of my head (Psalms* 60:9) refers to Joshua who descended from the tribe of Ephraim and who waged war on the Sabbath, as the verse states, *It was on the seventh day.* It can be determined that this was the Sabbath because seven days do not pass without a Sabbath. [Since they 'fought' for seven consecutive days, they must have fought on the Sabbath. Thus, if Scripture uses the term *the seventh day* it is reasonable to assume that it means the seventh day of the week.] Since Jericho was conquered on the Sabbath, Joshua declared all the booty holy.

During the invasion, the Jews killed and started fires, both of which violate the laws of the Sabbath. On this occasion, however, God instructed Joshua that the Sabbath laws were temporarily suspended; hence, both activities were permitted *(Radak,* verse 11).

כַּעֲלוֹת הַשַּׁחַר — *At dawn.*

[In *halachah,* this term refers to a

[12] Joshua arose early in the morning, and the
Kohanim carried the Ark of HASHEM. [13] And the
seven Kohanim bearing the seven shofars of rams'
horns before the Ark of HASHEM proceeded and blew
the shofars — the advance troop went before them
and the rear guard traveled after the Ark of HASHEM
— while proceeding and blowing the shofars. [14] And
they went around the city one time on the second day
and returned to the camp. So they did six days. [15] It
was on the seventh day that they arose at dawn, and
they went around the city in this manner seven times;
only on that day they went around the city seven
times.

point in time which is commonly accepted as seventy-two minutes before sunrise.]

This refers to the time when the first rays of the morning sun can be seen bending over the horizon *(Metzudos).*

Metzudos suggests that they rose early on the seventh day so that they would have enough daylight hours to encircle the large city seven times.

כַּמִּשְׁפָּט הַזֶּה שֶׁבַע פְּעָמִים — *In this manner seven times.*

They encircled the city once on the seventh day *(in the* [same] *manner* which they performed the circuit on the first six days) which made a total of *seven times.* Then they circled the city six more times which made a total of seven orbits on the seventh day[1] *(Radak).* Others suggest that they

1. According to tradition, it was on the seventh day of the siege of Jericho that Joshua composed the prayer עָלֵינוּ לְשַׁבֵּחַ, *It is our duty to praise,* which is recited at the conclusion of the three daily services in the synagogue *(Kol Bo,* 16). The paragraph beginning עַל כֵּן נְקַוֶּה, *Therefore, we hope,* was composed by Achan [the first three words form an acrostic of his name עכ״נ] after he repented of his misdeeds (see 7:20) *(Seder HaYom).*

Like many other hymns, the Aleinu prayer is an acrostic which includes the author's name. However, the self-effacing Joshua reversed the letters of his name; in addition he used his former name, הוֹשֵׁעַ, Hoshea (see *Numbers* 13:16). This indicates that although Joshua had replaced Moses as leader of Israel, he humbly considered himself to be the same as he had been before he rose to power.

עָלֵינוּ לְשַׁבֵּחַ לַאֲדוֹן הַכֹּל, — לָתֵת גְּדֻלָּה לְיוֹצֵר בְּרֵאשִׁית,
שֶׁלֹּא עָשָׂנוּ כְּגוֹיֵי הָאֲרָצוֹת, — וְלֹא שָׂמָנוּ כְּמִשְׁפְּחוֹת הָאֲדָמָה.
שֶׁלֹּא שָׂם חֶלְקֵנוּ כָּהֶם, — וְגוֹרָלֵנוּ כְּכָל הֲמוֹנָם.
שֶׁהֵם מִשְׁתַּחֲוִים לְהֶבֶל וָרִיק, — וּמִתְפַּלְלִים אֶל אֵל לֹא יוֹשִׁיעַ.
וַאֲנַחְנוּ כּוֹרְעִים וּמִשְׁתַּחֲוִים וּמוֹדִים — לִפְנֵי מֶלֶךְ מַלְכֵי הַמְּלָכִים הַקָּדוֹשׁ בָּרוּךְ הוּא.
שֶׁהוּא נוֹטֶה שָׁמַיִם וְיוֹסֵד אָרֶץ, וּמוֹשַׁב יְקָרוֹ בַּשָּׁמַיִם מִמַּעַל, — וּשְׁכִינַת עֻזּוֹ בְּגָבְהֵי מְרוֹמִים.
הוּא אֱלֹהֵינוּ, אֵין עוֹד — אֱמֶת מַלְכֵּנוּ, אֶפֶס זוּלָתוֹ, כַּכָּתוּב בְּתוֹרָתוֹ:
וְיָדַעְתָּ הַיּוֹם וַהֲשֵׁבֹתָ אֶל לְבָבֶךָ, כִּי יהוה הוּא הָאֱלֹהִים בַּשָּׁמַיִם מִמַּעַל וְעַל הָאָרֶץ מִתָּחַת, אֵין עוֹד.

Because this prayer has mystical connotations, Joshua recited it forwards and backwards during each circling of Jericho *(Seder HaYom* כוונת עלינו לשבח).

Iyun HaTefillah suggests that the second paragraph is recited at the conclusion of the service to emphasize that we are actually praying that evil *behavior* — not evil people — will be destroyed. Since all men are the creatures of God, we hope that those who do not follow His ways will repent rather than perish [see *Berachos* 10a.].

ו
טז־יז

טז אֶת־הָעִיר שֶׁבַע פְּעָמִים: וַיְהִי בַּפַּעַם
הַשְּׁבִיעִית תָּקְעוּ הַכֹּהֲנִים בַּשּׁוֹפָרוֹת
וַיֹּאמֶר יְהוֹשֻׁעַ אֶל־הָעָם הָרִיעוּ כִּי־נָתַן
יז יהוה לָכֶם אֶת־הָעִיר: וְהָיְתָה הָעִיר חֵרֶם
הִיא וְכָל־אֲשֶׁר־בָּהּ לַיהוה רַק רָחָב
הַזּוֹנָה תִּחְיֶה הִיא וְכָל־אֲשֶׁר אִתָּהּ בַּבַּיִת
כִּי הֶחְבְּאַתָה אֶת־הַמַּלְאָכִים אֲשֶׁר

encircled the city *seven* more times thereby completing eight circuits on the seventh day *(Meam Loez).*

☙ Joshua's Instructions

16-19. Verses 16 to 19 contain Joshua's instructions to the people concerning how they should conduct themselves after the wall of Jericho falls. *Malbim* explains that verse 16 serves as a preface to the instructions which Joshua was about to issue. Joshua was not directing the Kohanim to sound the extended shofar blast and the people to shout (as outlined in verse 5) *at the moment,* for this was to take place shortly afterwards (as explained in verse 20).

16. תָּקְעוּ הַכֹּהֲנִים בַּשּׁוֹפָרוֹת — *While the Kohanim were still blowing the shofars.*

This does not refer to the final long shofar blast mentioned in verse 20 as explained in the previous note. Rather, the Kohanim were still blowing their shofaros when Joshua began to instruct the people *(Malbim).*

הָרִיעוּ — *Shout.*

Joshua did not command them to shout *then;* rather he told them that the time was approaching for them to shout, because *HASHEM has given you the city (Malbim).*

17. חֵרֶם — *Shall be destroyed.*

[This word appears in Scripture with several connotations:

(a) something which an individual sets aside for use in the Holy Temple and which consequently becomes holy (see *Leviticus* 27:28);

(b) destruction (see *Isaiah* 34:2);

(c) something abominable (i.e. idolatry; see Deuteronomy 7:26).

Scripture does not mention that God commanded Joshua to prohibit benefit from the booty of Jericho. Several interpretations have been offered as to whether or not Joshua initiated this prohibition.]

Radak suggests that God did command Joshua not to benefit from the spoils, although Scripture does not record this command. Scripture includes such instances in which Divine commands are not explicitly stated. *Abarbanel,* however, advances that Joshua received this Divine command from the angel which appeared to him (5:13-15). When the angel told Joshua that the land was holy, he understood that he should ban Jericho's booty, since the word ban (חֵרֶם) also means *holy.*

According to the *Midrash,* Joshua declared the spoils holy on his own accord. The nation was later punished for violating Joshua's ban (Chapter 7), and the Sages identified this as one of the instances in which Scripture indicates that the Heavenly Court was merely sustaining the decree which had been issued by a human court. The *Midrash (Yalkut Shimoni* 15:6) offers three reasons why Joshua declared the spoils holy:

☐ Since the invasion of Jericho took place on the Sabbath, Joshua declared the spoils holy so that no one would derive benefit from the desecration of the Sabbath.

6
16-18 [16] *It was on the seventh time, while the Kohanim were still blowing the shofars, that Joshua said to the people, 'Shout, for HASHEM has given you the city. [17] The city shall be destroyed — it and all inside it — for the sake of HASHEM. Only Rachav the innkeeper shall live — she and all that is with her in the house — because she concealed the messengers we sent. [18] O*

□ Just as one is required to separate a fraction of dough *(challah)* and declare this portion holy before he bakes, so Joshua declared the first of his spoils in the conquest of the land holy.

□ Jericho was given the status of a city of idol worship from which no one is permitted to benefit *(Deuteronomy* 13:17).

Ralbag suggests a fourth reason for declaring the spoils holy: Joshua was concerned that if the people were allowed to use the booty of Jericho, they might attribute their future successes to the pagan articles they acquired from there.

Abarbanel contends that it was appropriate that the spoils of Jericho should be holy since they had been obtained by God's miraculous intervention and not by the Israelites' own militaristic effort. [It is inadvisable to benefit from the results of an open miracle. See *Rashi* to *Ta'anis* 24a, ד״ה אלא כאחד מעזיי ישראל.]

הִיא — *It.*

[The city of Jericho itself was declared holy, and the sanctity it assumed was similar to that of Jerusalem.]

Raavad, in his comment to *Tamid* (3:8), relates that ten acts of service performed in the Holy Temple in Jerusalem were miraculously audible in Jericho (about fifteen miles away), but in no other city. This miracle occurred because God wanted to publicize that the sanctity Jericho had assumed was similar to that of Jerusalem, since Joshua had declared it holy.

Radak explains that Jericho itself became *cherem* in the sense that it was prohibited to ever rebuild it (see *Commentary* to verse 26).

לַה' — *For the sake of HASHEM.*

The translation follows *Metzudos.*

HaRav Gifter notes that a similar usage appears in *Deuteronomy* 13:17 in the passage describing the laws of a city condemned for idol worship. The phrase כָּלִיל לַה' is understood by *Rashi (Deuteronomy* 13:17) as 'destroy for His sake.'

הַזּוֹנָה — *The innkeeper* [lit. *harlot*].

[According to the *Midrash* cited in the *Commentary* to 2:11, Rachav had completely repented from her immoral ways the night the messengers hid in her house. It is puzzling, therefore, why Joshua continued to refer to her by the derogatory appellation זוֹנָה which literally means *harlot.*

According to *Targum* and *Rashi* cited in the *Commentary* to 2:1, זוֹנָה can mean innkeeper, but according to *Radak,* זוֹנָה has a negative connotation, also.]

כִּי הֶחְבְּאַתָה אֶת־הַמַּלְאָכִים — *Because she concealed the messengers.*

Because Rachav saved the messengers, Joshua declared that she and her possessions, should be spared. Thus, her possessions although property of Jericho, were not included in Joshua's ban. Joshua cited the fact that Rachav saved the messengers to save her and her property, rather than the oath which the messengers had taken (verse 2:14). *Malbim* explains that the oath was only binding on the messengers; the rest of the Israelites who had not taken the oath were not bound. Although they could not have harmed Rachav since she had converted to Judaism (see *Commentary* to 2:15), her possessions would have been

ו
יח־כא

יח שָׁלָחְנוּ׃ וְרַק־אַתֶּם שִׁמְרוּ מִן־הַחֵרֶם פֶּן־
תַּחֲרִימוּ וּלְקַחְתֶּם מִן־הַחֵרֶם וְשַׂמְתֶּם
אֶת־מַחֲנֵה יִשְׂרָאֵל לְחֵרֶם וַעֲכַרְתֶּם
יט אוֹתוֹ׃ וְכֹל ׀ כֶּסֶף וְזָהָב וּכְלֵי נְחֹשֶׁת וּבַרְזֶל
כ קֹדֶשׁ הוּא לַיהוָה אוֹצַר יהוה יָבוֹא׃ וַיָּרַע
הָעָם וַיִּתְקְעוּ בַּשּׁוֹפָרוֹת וַיְהִי כִשְׁמֹעַ הָעָם
אֶת־קוֹל הַשּׁוֹפָר וַיָּרִיעוּ הָעָם תְּרוּעָה
גְדוֹלָה וַתִּפֹּל הַחוֹמָה תַּחְתֶּיהָ וַיַּעַל הָעָם
הָעִירָה אִישׁ נֶגְדּוֹ וַיִּלְכְּדוּ אֶת־הָעִיר׃
כא וַיַּחֲרִימוּ אֶת־כָּל־אֲשֶׁר בָּעִיר מֵאִישׁ וְעַד־
אִשָּׁה מִנַּעַר וְעַד־זָקֵן וְעַד שׁוֹר וָשֶׂה

subject to Joshua's ban on Jericho's property had he not exempted them.

18. וְרַק — *O that.*

[See *Commentary* to 1:17.] *Alshich* remarks that Joshua explained to the people that his ban on the spoils of Jericho carried severe penalties; therefore he warned the people to guard themselves lest they transgress by taking from the booty.

Malbim comments that Joshua warned the people about taking from the booty lest they mistakenly conclude that because the possessions of Rachav and her family were excluded from the ban, other property was also permitted.

שִׁמְרוּ מִן־הַחֵרֶם — *Guard yourselves from the holy things.*

Guard yourselves and guard your neighbors to insure that no one takes from the booty. Since Joshua held everyone responsible for each other, the entire nation was later held accountable when Achan took from the spoils *(Radak).*

וְשַׂמְתֶּם אֶת־מַחֲנֵה יִשְׂרָאֵל לְחֵרֶם — *And make the camp of Israel accursed.*

Joshua was emphatic in his admonition because he knew that one person's weakness could potentially affect the entire nation *(Abarbanel).*

וַעֲכַרְתֶּם — *Besmirch.*

Rashi explains that the root of this verb, עָכַר, is similar to the expression for 'cloudy water' (מַיִם עֲכוּרִים), and hence we have translated it as *besmirch.*

19. וְכֹל כֶּסֶף ... — *And all the silver ...*

These materials were specified because they were appropriate for the treasury *(Metzudos).* [Cf. *Abarbanel* to verse 24.]

The remainder of the booty (i.e., that which was not fit for the treasury) was destroyed *(Malbim).*

[See *Commentary* to 6:24.]

אוֹצַר ה׳ — *Treasury of HASHEM.*

This *treasury* was located in the Sanctuary, where Moses had stored the gold donated by Israel's leaders from the booty of the battle with Midian [see *Numbers* 31:48-54] *(Radak).*

יָבוֹא — *They shall come to.*

The translation follows *Targum.* Although the verb is written in the singular, it should be understood in the plural. This is one of fourteen instances in Scripture where this verb appears in the singular but should be understood in the plural *(Minchas Shai).*

☙ Jericho's Walls Go Down

20. וַיָּרַע ... וַיִּתְקְעוּ — [The people] *shouted ... blew.*

that you guard yourselves from the holy things, lest
you cause yourselves to be destroyed by taking from
the holy things and make the camp of Israel accursed
and besmirch it. 19 *And all the silver and gold and*
vessels of copper and iron are consecrated to
HASHEM; they shall come to the treasury of
HASHEM.'
20 *The people shouted, and the Kohanim blew the*
shofars. And it was when the people heard the sound
of the shofar, the people cried out with a great
scream, and the wall sank into its place, and the
people invaded the city — each man straight ahead —
and they conquered the city. 21 *And they destroyed*
everything in the city — man and woman, young and

It appears from the order of events described in this verse that the people shouted *before* they heard the extended shofar blast, in direct contradiction to the order expressed in verse 5.

Malbim suggests that the shofar blast actually occurred first. In his view, the second half of this verse is an explanation of the shout and trumpet blast mentioned in the first half of the verse.

Abarbanel, however, argues that the shofar blast and shouting related in the first half of the verse do *not* refer to the actions that the people were ordered to perform. Rather, they were an expression of the deep joy sparked by Joshua's statement that God had given them the city (verse 16). This spontaneous celebration is described in the first half of the verse; the second half of the verse[1] relates that the extended shofar blast was then sounded and the people shouted as they had been ordered (in verse 5).

וַתִּפֹּל הַחוֹמָה תַּחְתֶּיהָ — *And the wall sank into its place.*

The wall sank into the ground in an instant *(Meam Loez).* See *Commentary* to verse 5, s.v. 'into its place.'

According to the agreement that Rachav and the messengers had made, she was required to display the countersign of the scarlet cord from her window in the wall of the city upon the messengers' return (see 2:21). Since the messengers knew in advance that the wall of the city would disappear, they looked for the countersign in Rachav's window when they encircled the city and remembered its location after the wall sank into the earth *(Lev Aharon).*

1. R' Yehoshua ben Karchah said: 'The shofar was created solely for Israel's benefit.' The shofar accompanied the transmission of the Torah to Israel. *Exodus* 19:19 states: *And then the voice of the shofar sounded louder and louder.* And on account of the shofar, the wall of Jericho fell, as it states: *And it was when the people heard the sound of the shofar, the people cried out with a great scream, and the wall sank into its place.* In the future, God will blast the shofar at the time when He will reveal the Messiah from the House of David, as *Zechariah* 9:14 states: *HASHEM/ELOHIM shall blow the shofar.* God will also sound the shofar when the Jews are assembled from the Diaspora as *Isaiah* 27:13 states: *And it shall come to pass on that day that a great shofar shall be blown, and they shall come who were lost in the land of Assyria and the outcasts in the land of Egypt and shall worship HASHEM in the holy mountain at Jerusalem (Eliyahu Zuta* 22).

כב וַחֲמוֹר לְפִי־חָרֶב׃ וְלִשְׁנַיִם הָאֲנָשִׁים
הַמְרַגְּלִים אֶת־הָאָרֶץ אָמַר יְהוֹשֻׁעַ בֹּאוּ
בֵּית־הָאִשָּׁה הַזּוֹנָה וְהוֹצִיאוּ מִשָּׁם אֶת־
הָאִשָּׁה וְאֶת־כָּל־אֲשֶׁר־לָהּ כַּאֲשֶׁר
כג נִשְׁבַּעְתֶּם לָהּ׃ וַיָּבֹאוּ הַנְּעָרִים הַמְרַגְּלִים
וַיֹּצִיאוּ אֶת־רָחָב וְאֶת־אָבִיהָ וְאֶת־אִמָּהּ
וְאֶת־אַחֶיהָ וְאֶת־כָּל־אֲשֶׁר לָהּ וְאֵת כָּל־
מִשְׁפְּחוֹתֶיהָ הוֹצִיאוּ וַיַּנִּיחוּם מִחוּץ
כד לְמַחֲנֵה יִשְׂרָאֵל׃ וְהָעִיר שָׂרְפוּ בָאֵשׁ
וְכָל־אֲשֶׁר־בָּהּ רַק | הַכֶּסֶף וְהַזָּהָב וּכְלֵי
הַנְּחֹשֶׁת וְהַבַּרְזֶל נָתְנוּ אוֹצַר בֵּית־יְהוָה׃
כה וְאֶת־רָחָב הַזּוֹנָה וְאֶת־בֵּית אָבִיהָ וְאֶת־
כָּל־אֲשֶׁר־לָהּ הֶחֱיָה יְהוֹשֻׁעַ וַתֵּשֶׁב בְּקֶרֶב

21. לְפִי־חָרֶב — *By the edge of the sword.*

The translation follows *Metzudos.*

◆§ Rachav and Her Family are Spared

22. וְלִשְׁנַיִם הָאֲנָשִׁים — *And to the two men.*

[The *footnote* to 2:13 suggested that Joshua's messengers swore to Rachav that they would not kill her family immediately upon the conquest of Jericho; then, if Rachav's relatives chose to convert they would be spared. This view would explain why Joshua selected the messengers to retrieve Rachav's family, for the other Israelites, who were not obligated by oath to delay in killing Rachav's family, would have killed them immediately.]

כַּאֲשֶׁר נִשְׁבַּעְתֶּם לָהּ — *As you swore to her.*

See 2:14.

23. הַנְּעָרִים — *The attendants* [lit. *lads*].

Although this term connotes a youth, the term refers to servants of any age. For example, Joshua was called a נַעַר, *lad* (*Exodus* 33:11) when he served Moses, even though Joshua was already an adult (*Radak*). *Rashi* explains that נַעַר denotes an alacritous servant, because a young boy is quick to act; thus, this appellation implies approbation for the attendants.

Others suggest that *lad* in this context is used in a derogatory sense to signify 'naive lad.' According to this view, Scripture is intimating here that the messengers had been unwise to make an oath to save everyone in Rachav's house (2:19), because many Canaanites then married into Rachav's family in order to be spared (*Meam Loez*).

כָּל־מִשְׁפְּחוֹתֶיהָ — *All her families.*

According to the oath which the messengers had taken (2:13), they were only required to save Rachav's immediate family. However, since Joshua told them to rescue everything in the house, they complied and protected her extended family also (*Alshich*). [Here *Alshich's* comment is following his interpretation of the verse *we are absolved* (2:17). See *Commentary* there,

old, ox and sheep and ass — by the edge of the sword.
22 *And to the two men who had spied the country Joshua said, 'Go to the house of Rachav the innkeeper and bring out the woman and all that she has, as you swore to her.'*
23 *The attendants who were the spies entered and brought out Rachav, her father, her mother, her brother and all she possessed. They brought out all her families and situated them outside the camp of Israel.*
24 *And they burned the city and everything in it with fire. Only the silver, gold, and the vessels of copper and iron they gave to the treasury of the house of* HASHEM.
25 *And Rachav the innkeeper, and her father's household and all it contained, Joshua allowed to live. And she dwelled among the Israelites*

however, which cites other opinions that suggest that the messengers' oath *did* require them to save Rachav's family.]

See *Ramban, Genesis* 19:12.

מחוץ לְמַחֲנֵה יִשְׂרָאֵל — *Outside the camp of Israel.*

The Israelites placed Rachav's relatives *outside the camp* until they converted. After their conversion, they entered Israel's camp and remained among the Israelites forever *(Radak).*

24. ... הַכֶּסֶף — *The silver ...*

Abarbanel suggests that these metals were placed in the treasury because it would have been impossible to destroy them completely — even if they were filed into powder — in the fire which consumed the other property of Jericho. [Cf. *Metzudos* to verse 19.]

25. הֶחֱיָה יְהוֹשֻׁעַ — *Joshua allowed to live.*

[Since verse 23 states that the *attendants* saved Rachav and her family from destruction, in what sense did *Joshua* allow them to live?] Joshua indirectly saved Rachav and her family by ordering the attendants (verse 23) to uphold their oath to Rachav *(Radak).*

The messengers saved Rachav and her family from Jericho but made them stay outside Israel's camp (verse 23). It was Joshua who allowed them to dwell within Israel's camp *(Lev Aharon)* and provided them with food, money, and land *(Radak).*

According to the *Talmud (Megillah* 14b), Joshua married Rachav. *Radak* explains that by wedding Rachav, Joshua saved her family, for once they were married, the other leaders of Joshua's generation willingly associated with Rachav's relatives.

Joshua's marriage to Rachav raises a halachic question, for the Torah explicitly states, *'You may not marry them'* [Canaanites] *(Deuteronomy* 7:3). Some maintain that this prohibition only applies to the Seven Nations. Rachav, although she was a Canaanite, did not descend from the Seven Nations *(Tosafos, Megillah* 14b). According to *Rambam (Hil. Issurei Biah,* 12:1), this prohibition only applies to a non-Jewish Canaanite; thus, once Rachav converted to Judaism, the prohibition was no longer applicable. *Tosafos (Sotah* 35b) contends that Joshua married Rachav at God's

יִשְׂרָאֵל עַד הַיּוֹם הַזֶּה כִּי הֶחְבִּיאָה אֶת־
הַמַּלְאָכִים אֲשֶׁר־שָׁלַח יְהוֹשֻׁעַ לְרַגֵּל אֶת־
כו יְרִיחוֹ: וַיַּשְׁבַּע יְהוֹשֻׁעַ
בָּעֵת הַהִיא לֵאמֹר אָרוּר הָאִישׁ לִפְנֵי
יהוה אֲשֶׁר יָקוּם וּבָנָה אֶת־הָעִיר הַזֹּאת
אֶת־יְרִיחוֹ בִּבְכֹרוֹ יְיַסְּדֶנָּה וּבִצְעִירוֹ יַצִּיב
כז דְּלָתֶיהָ: וַיְהִי יהוה

command. According to *Koren Orah, Tosafos (Megillah* 14b) also advances the view that the prohibition to marry a Canaanite did not begin until fourteen years after the Israelites entered the land.

כִּי הֶחְבִּיאָה אֶת־הַמַּלְאָכִים — *Because she concealed the messengers.*

According to the messengers' oath, they were merely required to protect Rachav's family from harm; they were not obligated to bring them into the the Israelites' camp. However, out of a deep feeling of gratitude for her kindness, the Israelites welcomed her family to their ranks *(Poras Yosef).*

Abarbanel comments that Scripture mentions gratitude for Rachav's protection of the messengers as the reason for Joshua's concern for Rachav and her family, just as it had been the messengers' reason for pledging to save Rachav.

◆§ Joshua's Curse

26. וַיַּשְׁבַּע יְהוֹשֻׁעַ — *And Joshua adjured.*

Abarbanel contends that God — through the intermediary of the angel (Chapter 5) — commanded Joshua to make this oath. He maintains that Joshua would never have issued this prohibition on his own accord. When the angel came to Joshua and told him, *'the place upon which you stand is holy'* (5:15), Joshua inferred that no one should derive benefit from or dwell on that sacred location. [*Abarbanel's* view is substantiated by *I Kings* 16:34, which states that the curse was *according to the word of God which He spoke through Joshua son of Nun.*]

אָרוּר — *Cursed be.*

Whenever a Jewish Court *(beis din)* forbids a certain action,they can elect to include future generations in their prohibition *(Ramban, Mishpat HaCherem).*

אֲשֶׁר יָקוּם וּבָנָה — *Who rises up and builds.*

Rambam (Moreh Nevuchim 3:50) explains that Joshua forbade anyone to rebuild Jericho so that everyone would be able to view the sunken wall and recognize the magnitude of the miracle. [This reason, however, does not explain why it is prohibited to call another city by the same name (see next note).]

Others suggest that Joshua forbade the rebuilding of Jericho in order to prevent anyone from violating his ban on benefiting from Jericho and *all inside it* (verse 17), for even the soil of Jericho was included in Joshua's ban.

Aruch LaNer suggests that Joshua forbade anyone to rebuild Jericho so that Israel's role in destroying its wall, which occurred on the Sabbath, would never be construed as an act of destruction done for the purpose of rebuilding. According to the laws of the Sabbath, razing a wall without intent to rebuild something on its site is not forbidden by the Torah [but is forbidden by the Rabbis]. Therefore, by prohibiting the rebuilding of Jericho, Joshua insured that the Israelites' destruction of its wall would never retroactively be deemed a violation of the Sabbath.

אֶת־יְרִיחוֹ — *Jericho.*

This phrase appears redundant since Joshua had already cursed anyone who rebuilds *this city.* However, the Sages deduce from here that Joshua was

until this day because she concealed the messengers that Joshua dispatched to gather information about Jericho.

26 And Joshua adjured at that time, 'Cursed be the man before HASHEM who rises up and builds this city, Jericho. With his oldest son he will lay its foundation and with his youngest son he will set up its gates.'

27 And HASHEM was with Joshua, and his renown

actually issuing two prohibitions. First, he prohibited anyone from rebuilding a city on the ruins of Jericho, regardless of what the new city would be named. Second, he forbade them to build another city (anywhere) and to call it by the name *Jericho (Tosefta, Sanhedrin* 14).

Neither of these prohibitions is codified in the *Rambam's* all-inclusive *Mishneh Torah* which suggests that these decrees are no longer applicable today. *Meshech Chachmah (Parshas R'eh)* suggests that the prohibition only applied to the first person who attempted to rebuild Jericho. Once it was rebuilt, however, it was permissible to dwell in the city *(Radak, I Kings* 16:34). If the rebuilt city were to be razed, it would be permissible to rebuild it since Joshua only forbade the first reconstruction of Jericho. *Nachalas Shimon* suggests that when it is no longer forbidden to build Jericho, it is also no longer forbidden to call another city by its name. [Some conjecture that the modern Jericho is one and one-quarter miles southwest of the Biblical Jericho.]

בִּבְכֹרוֹ ... וּבִצְעִירוֹ — *With his oldest son ... and with his youngest son.*

Although the word בְּכוֹר literally means 'first born,' Scripture also employs this term to mean the *oldest son (Ramban, Genesis* 19:31).

His children will die in their order of birth, from the oldest to the youngest, from the time he first lays the foundation of the city until the time he completes the work on the gates *(Rashi).*[1]

Although no one is ever punished for the misdeed of another, because of the father's actions, God will not deal with his children with the Attribute of Mercy, but with the Attribute of Strict Judgment. Hence, God will not delay punishment for a sin in the hope that the child will repent, but will mete out judgment immediately. Thus, if the child deserves the death penalty, there will be no postponement *(Daas Sofrim).*

Why did Joshua choose this curse in particular for the one who rebuilds Jericho?

Joshua chose a punishment which would be 'measure for measure' for the violation. A person who builds a city typically becomes very famous, and he desires to transfer this fame to his children who will perpetuate the family legacy. Therefore, Joshua's curse insured that the individual who rebuilt Jericho would have no heirs to inherit his fame *(Meam Loez).*

Joshua chose a curse that would become fulfilled gradually so that the violator could see the evil of his ways and repent *(Meam Loez).*

27. וַיְהִי ה׳ אֶת־יְהוֹשֻׁעַ — *And HASHEM*

1. Jewish history substantiated the potency of this curse. Over 500 years later, Chiel of Beth El attempted to rebuild Jericho contrary to Joshua's decree. Scripture states, *With Abiram his first born he founded it, and with Segov his youngest he set up its gates* (*I Kings* 16:34).

According to the *Talmud* (*Sanhedrin* 113a), Chiel did not rebuild Jericho, but rather built another city which he called by the name Jericho.

ז אֶת־יְהוֹשֻׁעַ וַיְהִי שָׁמְעוֹ בְּכָל־הָאָרֶץ׃
א א וַיִּמְעֲלוּ בְנֵי־יִשְׂרָאֵל מַעַל בַּחֵרֶם וַיִּקַּח
עָכָן בֶּן־כַּרְמִי בֶן־זַבְדִּי בֶן־זֶרַח לְמַטֵּה

was with Joshua.

HASHEM was with Joshua in all his dealings with the Israelites *(Daas Sofrim).*[1]

VII

Collective responsibility is a cardinal precept in Jewish life. The extent to which each member of the community is held responsible for the actions of an individual forms the theme for the seventh chapter. In the previous chapter, Joshua prohibited the entire nation from deriving any benefit from the spoils of Jericho (6:17). Of the many thousands who participated in the invasion, only one man, Achan, overwhelmed by desire, erred by taking some gold and silver (7:21). For the misdeed of one man, the entire nation was blamed. The Children of Israel transgressed the ban concerning the forbidden property *(6:1). National punishment was meted out when Joshua suffered the only military defeat of his career: thirty-six men fell in the battle againt Ai (verse 5).*

The dictum of the Sages כָּל יִשְׂרָאֵל עֲרֵבִים זֶה לָזֶה*, 'all Israel is responsible for one another,' is more than a principle of legislation. It is a description of the cohesiveness of the Jewish people. When the* Talmud (Jerusalem, Nedarim *9:4) queried, 'How is it possible not to bear a grudge against another Jew?' the response was: 'If someone's hand slips while slicing meat, causing the knife to pierce his other hand, would he seek revenge against the hand that slipped and slash it in return? Obviously not, for they are attached to the same body.' Similarly, one Jew cannot bear a grudge against another because they are parts of a single body. All Jews must bear the consequences of the actions of an individual, just as the entire body suffers for the mistakes of the hand. It is for this reason that* Arizal *(see* Likutei Torah, Kedoshim) *enumerated transgressions he never committed in his confessions on Yom Kippur; although his personal behavior was guiltless, he felt accountable for the sins other Jews had committed.*

The derivation of collective responsibility comes from Israel's experience at Mount Sinai (Maharal). *The Decalogue was uttered in the singular, not the plural, because when God addressed Israel, the nation was a unified whole.* Sefer Chassidim *(chapter 233) even goes so far as to say that if but one Jew had refused to accept the Torah, it would not have been given. In* Rashi's *words, the Jewish people were 'as one man with one heart.' (See* Prefatory Remarks *to Chapter 3.) At this time each person agreed to accept the consequences of his fellow Jew's mistakes. However, the agreement at Mount Sinai only applied to overt, public transgressions committed by a member of the community. Transgressions which an individual committed covertly or privately were not at that time considered the responsibility of the nation as a whole.*

---

1. The *Midrash* relates that four Jews minted coins: Abraham, Joshua, David and Mordechai. On one side of Joshua's coin was a picture of an ox and on the other, a picture of a ram. *Mussar HaNeviim* explains the significance of these images according to *Sifri:* an ox possesses great strength, but its horns are not attractive; a ram is not as strong, but its horns are pleasant looking. Joshua possessed a rare combination of strengths. He was a mighty warrior who showed great strength in battle, but at the same time, he was full of compassion. Charitably, he married Rachav so that her family would find favor in the eyes of the Israelites (see *Commentary* to verse 24), and he expressed this gratitude to her by providing her with food and land. Indeed, he had the strength of an ox and the beauty of a ram.

7 *traversed the land.*
1 1 *The Children of Israel transgressed the ban*
concerning the forbidden property when Achan, the
son of Carmi, the son of Zavdi, the son of Zerach, of

There is no place on earth where the Jewish people can be more close-knit than in Eretz Yisrael. *In praise of Israel, David prayed,* Who is like Israel one nation in the land (II Samuel *7:23)* [*Be'er Moshe*]. *Since Israel achieves its greatest sense of fellowship in* Eretz Yisrael, *the Jews acquire greater responsibility there for one another's actions. Therefore, according to R' Yehudah* (Sanhedrin *43b), it was not until Israel crossed the Jordan that each individual became accountable even for the misdeeds which his neighbor perpetrated in privacy.*

Rashi (Sanhedrin *43b) explains that the Jews became responsible for these private transgressions when they heard the blessings and curses on Mount Gerezim and Mount Eval (8:34 and* Commentary *to 8:30). It may seem unreasonable to hold the community responsible for the individual's private acts. However, if the community at large abides by exacting standards and safeguards against sin, then no one will err. Since Joshua's generation was remiss in this regard,* the anger of HASHEM was kindled against the Children of Israel *(verse 1). The entire nation was held responsible for it was their failure which led to Achan's sin (see* Sefer Chassidim, *chapter 93). Because of this principle,* Meiri (Sanhedrin *43b) rules that the leaders of every community must attempt to be aware of the actions of each individual and to correct any failings so that punishment will not be levied against the entire community.*

◆§ Sin Causes Israel's Defeat

1. וַיִּמְעֲלוּ בְנֵי־יִשְׂרָאֵל — *The Children of Israel transgressed.*

Because each Jew was not mindful of his neighbor's actions, Scripture considers the entire nation to be at fault *(Metzudos).* [See *Prefatory Remarks* to this chapter.]

וַיִּקַּח עָכָן — *Achan ... took.*

Although only one person actually transgressed Joshua's ban concerning the booty of Jericho, thirty-six others perished. *Malbim* explains that God exacts punishment in two ways. When God punishes sinners directly, He only punishes those who have personally transgressed. However, when He punishes sinners indirectly by withdrawing His Divine protection, others who did not actually commit the misdeed may also suffer. God withdrew His Divine protection during the battle of Ai because of Achan's sin. In the absence of Divine intervention, thirty-six Israelites fell in battle. Those who did not take part in the battle, however, were unharmed.

עָכָן — *Achan.*

In *I Chronicles* 2:7, Achan's name is spelled differently: עָכָר, *Achar, the troubler of Israel, who transgressed the ban. Rashi (ibid.)* explains that Scripture changed Achan's name as a sign of deprecation. Similarly, in verse 26, the location where Achan was buried was called *the Valley of Achor.*

עָכָן בֶּן־כַּרְמִי ... — *Achan, the son of Carmi ...*

When writing this account, Joshua carefully traced Achan's genealogy in order to show that Achan came from an honorable family. This intensifies the grievousness of his wrongdoing *(Daas Sofrim).* [See *Commentary* to verse 18.]

Others suggest that Scripture exhaustively traces Achan's genealogy back to Judah to indicate the source of his sin. He descended from the house of Judah, the line from which the monarchy in Israel was destined to

ז
ב־ה

יְהוּדָה מִן־הַחֵרֶם וַיִּחַר־אַף יְהוָה בִּבְנֵי
ב יִשְׂרָאֵל: וַיִּשְׁלַח יְהוֹשֻׁעַ
אֲנָשִׁים מִירִיחוֹ הָעַי אֲשֶׁר עִם־בֵּית אָוֶן
מִקֶּדֶם לְבֵית־אֵל וַיֹּאמֶר אֲלֵיהֶם לֵאמֹר
עֲלוּ וְרַגְּלוּ אֶת־הָאָרֶץ וַיַּעֲלוּ הָאֲנָשִׁים
ג וַיְרַגְּלוּ אֶת־הָעָי: וַיָּשֻׁבוּ אֶל־יְהוֹשֻׁעַ
וַיֹּאמְרוּ אֵלָיו אַל־יַעַל כָּל־הָעָם כְּאַלְפַּיִם
אִישׁ אוֹ כִּשְׁלֹשֶׁת אֲלָפִים אִישׁ יַעֲלוּ וְיַכּוּ
אֶת־הָעָי אַל־תְּיַגַּע שָׁמָּה אֶת־כָּל־הָעָם כִּי
ד מְעַט הֵמָּה: וַיַּעֲלוּ מִן־הָעָם שָׁמָּה
כִּשְׁלֹשֶׁת אֲלָפִים אִישׁ וַיָּנֻסוּ לִפְנֵי אַנְשֵׁי
ה הָעָי: וַיַּכּוּ מֵהֶם אַנְשֵׁי הָעַי כִּשְׁלֹשִׁים

come. This knowledge affected him with a haughty pride which led to his audacious act of taking some of the banned spoils of Jericho. He felt confident that his family would protect him from punishment if he were apprehended *(Meam Loez).*

וַיִּחַר־אַף ה׳ — *The anger of HASHEM was kindled.*

Malbim states that this expression denotes the withdrawal of God's Divine Protection.

Daas Sofrim explains that God normally deals with Israel with the Attribute of אֶרֶךְ אַפַּיִם, *prolonged patience.* Even though the community commits transgressions, God delays punishment in the hope that the Jews will repent. However, when God's anger is finally kindled, this Attribute is suspended. At such times God may also punish the Jewish people for past transgressions. This reasoning explains how the sin of one individual could bring punishment to the entire community.

◆§ The Battle against Ai

2. וַיִּשְׁלַח — *[Joshua] dispatched.*

The remainder of the chapter concerns the punishment Israel incurred for Achan's sin *(Malbim). Lev Aharon* suggests that the fact that Joshua needed to dispatch spies was itself a punishment for it indicated that Joshua had not received a prophetic vision and consequently was required to fight the battle against Ai in a normal military manner. Joshua did not realize at this point that the lack of spectacular Divine intervention was a punishment, because he thought that the remainder of the conquest was to be fought militarily.

הָעַי — *To Ai.*

Radak explains that the letter ה functions here as the definite article 'the' and is used to distinguish this city from a smaller city of the same name. Scripture also distinguishes this Ai from its namesake by giving its precise geographical position. According to *R' Hirsch (Genesis 12:8),* the ה prefix indicates that it was a place rich in ruins even in Abraham's time.

Mateh Binyamin, however, believes that the letter ה, is not a prefix but an integral part of the name of this city, *Ha'ai.*

עִם — *Near* [lit. *with*].

The translation follows *Rashi.*

7
2-5

the tribe of Judah took of the forbidden property.
The anger of HASHEM was kindled against the
Children of Israel.
[2] *Joshua dispatched men from Jericho to Ai which*
is near Beis Aven, east of Beth El, and spoke to them,
saying, 'Go up and scout the land.' The men went up
and scouted Ai. [3] *They returned to Joshua and said to*
him, 'The entire nation need not invade. About two
or three thousand men can invade and vanquish Ai.
Do not weary the entire nation by bringing them
there, because they are few.'
[4] *Three thousand men from the nation invaded,*
but they fled before the men of Ai. [5] *And the men of*

מִקֶּדֶם — *East* [lit. *before* or *in front of*]. The translation follows *Rashi.*

וְרַגְּלוּ אֶת־הָאָרֶץ — *And scout the land.* Joshua asked the spies to search the outskirts of Ai as well as the city itself to determine if there were other Canaanites near the city who might oppose the Jews in their campaign against Ai. However, the spies did not fulfill their mission properly — they observed the city but not its outskirts. Thus, Scripture states *they scouted Ai,* but they failed to scout *the land* as Joshua had requested. Consequently, the scouts estimated that only two to three thousand troops need invade *(Malbim).*

Meam Loez, however, suggests the contrary. The scouts not only explored the *land* but *they* [even] *scouted Ai,* which was not included in Joshua's request. Although they were aware that Ai was a small city, they investigated it to determine whether Ai was harboring any foreign troops who could assist the inhabitants of Ai in battle.

3. אַל־יַעַל — *Need not invade.* The translation follows *Metzudos.*

כִּי מְעַט הֵמָּה — *Because they are few.* From this statement it appears that the spies misjudged Ai's strength, because in Chapter 8 we find that Ai was actually very strong. According to *Malbim* (cited in previous note), they misjudged Ai's strength because they did not completely fulfill their reconnaissance mission by reconnoitering the land around Ai. Troops from the nearby cities of Beth El and Beis Aven later came to Ai's defense (8:17).

4. וַיַּעֲלוּ ... וַיָּנֻסוּ — *Invaded ... but they fled.*

The invasion of the three thousand Israelites was repulsed immediately. They could not even engage the Canaanites in battle *(Malbim).*

Meam Loez suggests that because of Achan's sin, fear entered the Israelites' hearts, which caused them to retreat immediately.

וַיָּנֻסוּ לִפְנֵי — *They fled before.*

Metzudos interpolates: They fled [from] before their enemies.

Poras Yosef perceives in this phrase the fulfillment of the curse in *Deuteronomy* 28:25, *You will flee* [*before your enemies*] *in seven ways. Kli Chemdah* interprets this curse to mean 'even though you will flee, you will not be saved, because you will always be *before* your enemies.' Thus, even though the three thousand men retreated from Ai, they still suffered thirty-six casualties.

ז ו וְשִׁשָּׁה אִישׁ וַיִּרְדְּפוּם לִפְנֵי הַשַּׁעַר עַד־
הַשְּׁבָרִים וַיַּכּוּם בַּמּוֹרָד וַיִּמַּס לְבַב־הָעָם
ו וַיְהִי לְמָיִם׃ וַיִּקְרַע יְהוֹשֻׁעַ שִׂמְלֹתָיו וַיִּפֹּל°
עַל־פָּנָיו אַרְצָה לִפְנֵי אֲרוֹן יהוה עַד־
הָעֶרֶב הוּא וְזִקְנֵי יִשְׂרָאֵל וַיַּעֲלוּ עָפָר עַל־

◆§ Israelites Suffer Losses

5. כִּשְׁלֹשִׁים וְשִׁשָּׁה אִישׁ — *Thirty-six ... men.*

The Sages tell us that more than thirty-six souls[1] should have perished; however, because of the merit of Abraham who built an altar near Ai (*Genesis* 12:8) most of the Israelites went unscathed (*Radak*). Abraham had prophetic knowledge of a future sin that would occur in this area and prayed at Ai for his descendants, thereby protecting most of them from death (*Rashi* to *Genesis* 12:8).

On a less literal level, the *Talmud* (*Sanhedrin* 44b) explains that only one person — Yair son of Menashe — actually perished. According to this interpretation the letter כ means 'as,' for the loss of this individual was the equivalent to the death of thirty-six men. The pious Yair son of Menashe was as valuable as the thirty-six judges who constitute the majority of the Great Sanhedrin (High Court) (which comprised 71 judges).

עַד־הַשְּׁבָרִים — *To Shevarim.*

Targum renders: until they broke them, i.e., until they broke their bodies and their spirits (*Daas Sofrim*).

Radak, however, suggests that *Shevarim* is the name of the place where the warriors of Ai 'broke' the Israelites.

בַּמּוֹרָד — *On the slope.*

[The root of this word literally means 'to lower.'] The Israelites were defeated on the slope going down from Ai (*Radak*) which was situated on a mountain (*Metzudos*).

1. Divine Providence (*Hashgachah*) operates on many levels. Although the loss of thirty-six men was viewed as a national catastrophe, it also set into motion the fulfillment of a blessing.

Concerning the inheritance of *Eretz Yisrael,* the Torah promised the Jews *great and good cities which you* [*will not have*] *to build, houses full of good things which* [*you will not have to*] *fill ... vineyards and olive trees* (*Deuteronomy* 6:10-11). The implications of this blessing are staggering. When the Israelites would march into *Eretz Yisrael,* they would inherit developed cities, planted fields, and fully furnished houses. The only way this promise could have been fulfilled was the way in which it was fulfilled — all the Canaanite kings united to jointly battle the Israelites (11:5). After they were defeated, their cities were defenseless and Israel could plunder their houses and fields without opposition.

— Had the inhabitants of the Land left on their own volition, they certainly would have transported all their possessions with them.

— Had Israel made peace with them, they would have retained their cities.

— Had Israel fought each kingdom in succession, the remaining ones would have given up hope and out of spite burned their cities and fled.

With hindsight we can often perceive the subtle and extraordinary elements of God's Providence. Ai's initial success in warding off Israel's attack and mortally wounding some of its soldiers produced a concatenation of events which led to the defeat of the thirty-one Canaanite kings and to the fulfillment of the Torah's blessing. Since Israel had fled from their first encounter, the inhabitants of Ai never suspected the ambush from the rear (8:9) which precipitated their downfall. After Ai was defeated the Gibeonites sought admission to Israel, and this ultimately resulted in the formation of a confederacy of kings in the south and north. Thus, Israel was able to vanquish the Land with few battles and take possession of the cities and houses, as they were promised (*Niflaos MiToras Hashem*).

7 *Ai killed thirty-six of their men; they pursued them*
6 *from the front of the gate to Shevarim and killed*
them on the slope. The hearts of the people melted
and became water. [6] *Joshua rent his garments and fell*
to the ground on his face before the Ark of HASHEM
until evening, he and the elders of Israel. And they
placed dirt upon their heads.

וַיִּמַּס לְבַב־הָעָם — *The hearts of the people melted.*

Normally, Israel's morale would not have been so greatly affected by a relatively minor loss. However, the Jews understood that this loss meant a cancellation of the Divine promise of protection, and without Divine aid they would surely be doomed in their efforts to conquer the seven mighty nations which controlled the Land *(Meam Loez).*

6. וַיִּקְרַע יְהוֹשֻׁעַ — *Joshua rent.*

He tore his garment as a sign of mourning for the slain Israelites *(Malbim).*

[Since Jewish law forbids one to rend his garments unless he is required to mourn for the deceased *(Pischei Teshuvah* to *Yoreh Deah* 340:1), Joshua needed some justification to rend his garment for these victims, since he presumably was not related to them. According to the opinion that only Yair son of Menashe was killed (see *Commentary* to verse 5), Joshua was required to rend his garment because Yair son of Menashe was such an accomplished Torah scholar (see *Yoreh Deah* 340:7 and commentaries). According to the opinion that thirty-six individuals were slain, Joshua, being a Torah Sage himself, would not have been required to rend his garment unless at least one of the slain was also a Torah scholar (according to *Yoreh Deah* 340:6; cf., however, *Shach's* commentary).]

Joshua was the first to recognize that the loss of these men was not a matter of happenstance[1]. If God's Presence had been among the Israelites, this tragedy would not have happened *(Daas Sofrim).*

וַיִּפֹּל עַל־פָּנָיו — *And* [*he*] *fell* [*to the ground*] *on his face.*

Joshua prostrated himself in prayer. He pleaded to find out why Divine protection had been withdrawn from the Israelites and how Israel could become worthy of its restoration *(Daas Sofrim).*

לִפְנֵי אֲרוֹן ה׳ — *Before the Ark of HASHEM.*

The custom to lower one's head in the presence of a Torah scroll during the *Tachanun* prayer is derived from Joshua's prostration before the Ark which contained the Torah *(Rokeach* 324). Only an individual of Joshua's piety is permitted to actually prostrate himself *(Megillah* 22b).

וַיַּעֲלוּ עָפָר — *And they placed dirt.*

By putting dirt on their heads Joshua and the elders were symbolically

1. According to *Rambam (Hil. Taanis* 1:1-3), it is a positive commandment of the Torah for every individual to cry out and search his ways at times of national calamity, for God visits calamities upon Israel to inspire each Jew to repent for his misdeeds. If someone fails to recognize that tragedies occur through an act of God rather through happenstance, he is considered cruel, because he will not be motivated to improve his behavior. As a result, God will beset Israel with more troubles, until all are motivated to change their ways.

It is interesting to note that *Rambam* includes in this positive commandment the requirement to blow trumpets, as an additional call for repentance. According to *Igros Moshe (Orach Chaim* 169), only the trumpets used in the Holy Temple were acceptable for this purpose. Presumably, these could have been obtained from the Tabernacle in Gilgal, although this passage does not mention that Joshua blew these trumpets.

ז רֹאשָֽׁם׃ וַיֹּ֣אמֶר יְהוֹשֻׁ֗עַ אֲהָ֣הּ ׀ אֲדֹנָ֣י יֱהוִ֔ה
לָ֩מָּה֩ הֵעֲבַ֨רְתָּ הַעֲבִ֜יר אֶת־הָעָ֤ם הַזֶּה֙ אֶת־
הַיַּרְדֵּ֔ן לָתֵ֥ת אֹתָ֛נוּ בְּיַ֥ד הָאֱמֹרִ֖י
לְהַאֲבִידֵ֑נוּ וְל֚וּ הוֹאַ֔לְנוּ וַנֵּ֖שֶׁב בְּעֵ֥בֶר
ח הַיַּרְדֵּֽן׃ בִּ֖י אֲדֹנָ֑י מָ֣ה אֹמַ֔ר אַ֠חֲרֵי אֲשֶׁ֨ר
ט הָפַ֧ךְ יִשְׂרָאֵ֛ל עֹ֖רֶף לִפְנֵ֥י אֹיְבָֽיו׃ וְיִשְׁמְע֣וּ

likening themselves to dust *(Malbim)*.[1]

Alshich interprets this act as a symbolic interment: After hearing of the tragedy that befell Israel, Joshua and the elders considered themselves as dead.

Daas Sofrim suggests that the dirt was a sign of mourning, not for the thirty-six men who died, but for the withdrawal of the Divine Presence from Israel.

◆§ Joshua's Prayer

7-9. These verses relate the prayer with which Joshua besought God to restore His protection over Israel. The arguments he offered in his prayer are reminiscent of those marshaled by Moses[2], for Moses had said that if God did *not* save the Jews, His Name would become profaned among the Gentiles (see *Exodus* 32:12).

7. וַיֹּאמֶר יְהוֹשֻׁעַ — *And Joshua said.*

Scripture does not introduce Joshua's prayer with the phrase, 'Joshua prayed,' but rather with *Joshua said.* The former would have connoted a petition that God forgive Israel's sins, but Joshua was not praying on behalf of Israel, for he was not yet aware that a sin had been committed. Rather, he was raising objections against the way God was dealing with the Israelites, because he felt that such conduct would lead to the profanation of God's name *(Lev Aharon).*

אֲהָהּ — *Alas.*

1. The *Midrash* relates that R' Eliezer taught: They [Joshua and the Elders] began by mentioning the merit of Abraham who said, *I am but dust and ashes (Genesis* 18:27). They said, 'Did not Abraham build the altar in Ai so that his children would not fall there in battle?'

By mentioning Abraham's humility, Joshua and the Elders sought to rectify the sin which they thought Israel had committed — haughty behavior. In our evening prayer *(Ma'ariv)* we ask, 'Remove the Satan from before us and from behind us.' Before an individual performs a mitzvah, Satan attempts to dissuade him by minimizing its importance. However, after he performs it, Satan exaggerates its importance so that the person will become proud and haughty, thereby diminishing the merit which he derived from the mitzvah.

After the Israelites vanquished Jericho and restrained themselves from benefiting from the spoils, Joshua was afraid that a trace of pride could be found among the people. This, he felt, caused the Divine Presence to depart from Israel, for as the Sages commented *(Sotah* 5a): To whomever is haughty, God says, 'Both of us cannot live in the same world.' In his plea for mercy, Joshua mentioned Abraham's humility in order to cause the Divine Presence to return to the Jewish people *(Mussar HaNeviim).*

2. The *Talmud (Sanhedrin* 44a) explains the difference between the tone of Moses' and Joshua's prayers with the verse in *Proverbs* (18:23): *The poor man uses entreaties* — this refers to Moses; *but the rich man answers with impudence* — this refers to Joshua who said, *if only we had been content to dwell on the other side of the Jordan!* (verse 7). Joshua's statement appears mildly insolent, because he seems to imply that it would have been better had the Jews not listened to God's command to cross the Jordan.

Although it is clear that Moses was on a higher spiritual level than Joshua, Moses is referred to as 'poor' because he was not able to enter *Eretz Yisrael.* Since Joshua was granted this privilege, he is called 'rich' *(Ohel Ya'akov).*

[7] And Joshua said, 'Alas, my Lord, HASHEM / ELOHIM. Why have You brought this people over the Jordan to deliver us into the hand of the Emorites to cause us to perish? If only we had been content to dwell on the other side of the Jordan! [8] In prayer, my Lord, what shall I say after Israel has turned its back before its enemies? [9] The Canaanites and all the

Targum paraphrases: *accept my prayer.*

Joshua was motivated to pray because he knew that no Jews were supposed to die in a war which God had commanded the Jews to fight *(Ramban, Deuteronomy* 20:4).

לָמָּה הֶעֱבַרְתָּ ... אֶת־הַיַּרְדֵּן — *Why have You brought ... the Jordan.*

If Your intention was to withdraw Your Divine Presence from us, why did You lead us across the Jordan with such miracles? *(Abarbanel).*

לָתֵת אֹתָנוּ בְּיַד הָאֱמֹרִי — *To deliver us into the hand of the Emorites.*

Abarbanel continues: Your miracles will be for nought if You forsake us and allow us to be destroyed by the Emorites.

הָאֱמֹרִי — *Emorites.*

[*Emorites* is the generic name for all of the inhabiting nations of *Eretz Yisrael.* Although the Emorites were actually one specific nation, Scripture often uses the name to refer to all seven nations (see *Genesis* 15:16 and *Joshua* 24:18).]

Joshua saw that the defeat of the Jews by Ai represented a threat to Israel's campaign against all the nations in *Eretz Yisrael (Daas Sofrim).*

[However, in this context it appears that the inhabitants of Ai were from the Emorite nation and that this verse refers specifically to them. This can be inferred from Joshua's reference to all the Canaanites collectively in verse 9, for there he uses the word 'Canaanites' (הַכְּנַעֲנִי).]

וְלוּ הוֹאַלְנוּ וַנֵּשֶׁב בְּעֵבֶר הַיַּרְדֵּן — *If only we had been content to dwell* [lit. *and dwelled*] *on the other side of the Jordan!*

Joshua's plea implies that if Israel had not crossed the Jordan, they would not have suffered defeat. But certainly they could have lost battles on the eastern side of the Jordan as well! However, Joshua was referring to the collective responsibility they assumed when they crossed the Jordan, for only then did the entire community become responsible for an individual's sins (see *Prefatory Remarks* to this chapter). Had they remained on the east bank of the Jordan no one would have perished for Achan's hidden sin *(Margolios HaYam).*

Rashi interprets: If only we had decided to dwell on the east bank of the Jordan in the territory of Sichon and Og, which we have already conquered.

8. בִּי — *In prayer.*

The translation follows *Targum.* It is a term of entreaty *(Metzudos).*

מָה אֹמַר — *What shall I say?*

Joshua realized that the first words of his prayer had been disrespectful (see *footnote* to 7:7). Apologetically, he explained that he had spoken in this way only because the Israelites had been so utterly devastated by their defeat *(Metzudos).*

אַחֲרֵי אֲשֶׁר הָפַךְ יִשְׂרָאֵל עֹרֶף לִפְנֵי אֹיְבָיו — *After Israel has turned its back before its enemies.*

Joshua was concerned for the physical well-being of the nation when he witnessed the reversal of God's promise to the Israelites, for the Torah states, *'I [God] will make all your enemies turn their backs to you' (Exodus* 23:27). [I.e., the Canaanites will flee in fear.] Joshua feared that when the other nations realized that

ז
י־יב

הַכְּנַעֲנִי וְכֹל יֹשְׁבֵי הָאָרֶץ וְנָסַבּוּ עָלֵינוּ
וְהִכְרִיתוּ אֶת־שְׁמֵנוּ מִן־הָאָרֶץ וּמַה־
י תַּעֲשֵׂה לְשִׁמְךָ הַגָּדוֹל: וַיֹּאמֶר
יהוה אֶל־יְהוֹשֻׁעַ קֻם לָךְ לָמָּה זֶּה אַתָּה
יא נֹפֵל עַל־פָּנֶיךָ: חָטָא יִשְׂרָאֵל וְגַם עָבְרוּ
אֶת־בְּרִיתִי אֲשֶׁר צִוִּיתִי אוֹתָם וְגַם לָקְחוּ
מִן־הַחֵרֶם וְגַם גָּנְבוּ וְגַם כִּחֲשׁוּ וְגַם שָׂמוּ
יב בִכְלֵיהֶם: וְלֹא יֻכְלוּ בְּנֵי יִשְׂרָאֵל לָקוּם

God's promise was no longer in effect, they would attack the Israelites mercilessly and eliminate them from the face of the earth. As a result, God's name would become profaned, for He had promised the Patriarchs that their children would inherit the Land *(Meam Loez).*

9. וְיִשְׁמְעוּ — *[They] will hear.*

They will hear that our enemies routed us *(Metzudos).*

וּמַה־תַּעֲשֶׂה לְשִׁמְךָ הַגָּדוֹל — *What will You do for Your great Name?*

What will become of Your mighty reputation? The Gentiles will begin to say that you have become weak *(Rashi).* Consequently, Your Name will become diminished[1] *(Radak).*

◆§ God's Answer

10. קֻם לָךְ — *Arise.*

[This expression literally means *stand up.* Since Joshua was prostrated in prayer, God ordered him to rise.]

Rashi offers several interpretations from the *Midrash:*

☐ Your prayer has been accepted by Me (i.e., it has achieved 'a stand').

☐ You remained. Because you stayed in the camp and did not accompany your men, you brought this tragedy upon yourself, for I guaranteed your success only on the condition that you obey My command [given through Moses], *He [Joshua] shall go before this people [to war], and he shall cause them to inherit the Land (Deuteronomy* 3:28).

Although the Israelite's defeat was directly attributable to Achan's sin (as the next verse reveals), God chastised Joshua for not participating in the battle against Ai, thereby implying that even if Achan had not sinned, the Israelites would not have been successful. It is also possible that if Joshua had accompanied the Israelites to battle against Ai, his merit would have counterbalanced Achan's sin, and Israel would have been victorious *(Meam Loez).*

☐ 'This has occurred because of you (לָךְ), for I did not tell you to ban the spoils of Jericho.' [See 6:17-18 and *Commentary.*]

לָמָּה זֶּה אַתָּה נֹפֵל עַל־פָּנֶיךָ — *Why do you lie prostrate* [lit. *fall on your face*]?

Radak comments: You need not be occupied with supplications. Revoke the ban you made on Jericho's property, and I will forgive you.

Malbim suggests: Why do you

1. The *Midrash (Jerusalem Ta'anis* 4:6) beautifully expresses the relationship between God and Israel with a parable. There was once a king who had a small key which opened the lock to a jewelry box. He attached a chain to the key so that if he ever lost it, it would be easier to find. So said the Holy One, Blessed is He: 'If I leave Israel by itself, it will be swallowed up by the other nations. Therefore, I will attach My great Name to them so they will live forever, as Scripture states, *What will You do for Your Great Name?* The last two letters of Israel יִשְׂרָאֵל spell God's name.

7
10-12 *inhabitants of the Land will hear and surround us*
and cut off our name from the earth. What will You
do for Your great Name?'
10 *And HASHEM said to Joshua, 'Arise, why do you*
lie prostrate? 11 *Israel has sinned, and they have also*
broken My Covenant which I commanded them.
They have also taken banned property and have also
stolen and have also denied, and they have also put
into their vessels. 12 *The Children of Israel will not be*

entreat Me? There was a reason why I removed my Divine Presence. Do not pray, but rectify the problem!

11. חָטָא יִשְׂרָאֵל – *Israel has sinned.*

For one man's misdeed, the entire nation of Israel was blamed *(Metzudos).*

You need not entreat me so, for *you* did not sin; rather, *Israel has sinned (Alshich).*

Even though the Jews sinned, they are called by their noble title, *Israel (Sanhedrin* 44a).

וְגַם עָבְרוּ אֶת־בְּרִיתִי – *And they have also broken My Covenant.*

In the Covenant at Mount Sinai, you agreed to do all that I commanded. One mitzvah which I gave you was, *you shall heed [the prophet's words] (Deuteronomy* 18:16). Since Joshua, who is a prophet, banned all the spoils of Jericho, transgressing his ban is tantamount to violating the Covenant *(Radak).*

Malbim suggests that this is a reference to the Sabbath, which is also called *covenant.* Achan also sinned in that he violated the Sabbath by carrying the spoils from a public thoroughfare to a private domain on the Sabbath. [The conquest of Jericho took place on the Sabbath. (See *Commentary* to 6:15.)]

וְגַם גָּנְבוּ – *And have also stolen.*

If the perpetrator had stolen the spoils publicly, it would not have been so egregious. By stealing furtively, however, he created the impression that he thought he could conceal his sin from his Creator *(Radak)* [i.e., the thief displayed fear of detection by his fellow man, yet showed no fear of God].

Joshua issued two decrees concerning Jericho: that the gold and silver go to the Treasury (6:19), and that the rest of the city be burned (6:24). By taking the Babylonian garment from Jericho (7:21), Achan took something which was supposed to be burned; thus, the garment was legally ownerless and taking it constituted a sin, but not, strictly speaking, a theft. Therefore, God said in regard to this garment, *they [Israel] have also taken banned property.* The gold and silver, however, were earmarked for the treasury. By taking them, Achan *did* commit a theft. Thus, God said, *They, [Israel] have also stolen (Lev Aharon).*

וְגַם כִּחֲשׁוּ – *And have also denied.*

This clause is perplexing because Scripture does not relate that Achan denied his action. *Radak* offers two possible interpretations:

☐ Perhaps someone saw Achan take from the booty and accused him, but he denied it.

☐ Since Achan did not admit his sin until he was confronted by Joshua, it was as if he had been denying it until that point.

The word *also* appears five times in this verse. The *Talmud (Sanhedrin* 44a) comments that this repetition teaches that Achan had transgressed the Five Books of Moses. According to *Yad Ramah,* Achan had violated a commandment which he traces to each book of the Pentateuch. *Sefer Chasidim* (106), however, contends that whoever violates a ban is considered to have violated

ז
יג־טו

לִפְנֵי אֹיְבֵיהֶם עֹרֶף יִפְנוּ לִפְנֵי אֹיְבֵיהֶם כִּי
הָיוּ לְחֵרֶם לֹא אוֹסִיף לִהְיוֹת עִמָּכֶם אִם־
יג לֹא תַשְׁמִידוּ הַחֵרֶם מִקִּרְבְּכֶם: קֻם קַדֵּשׁ
אֶת־הָעָם וְאָמַרְתָּ הִתְקַדְּשׁוּ לְמָחָר כִּי כֹה
אָמַר יהוה אֱלֹהֵי יִשְׂרָאֵל חֵרֶם בְּקִרְבְּךָ
יִשְׂרָאֵל לֹא תוּכַל לָקוּם לִפְנֵי אֹיְבֶיךָ עַד־
יד הֲסִירְכֶם הַחֵרֶם מִקִּרְבְּכֶם: וְנִקְרַבְתֶּם
בַּבֹּקֶר לְשִׁבְטֵיכֶם וְהָיָה הַשֵּׁבֶט אֲשֶׁר־
יִלְכְּדֶנּוּ יהוה יִקְרַב לַמִּשְׁפָּחוֹת
וְהַמִּשְׁפָּחָה אֲשֶׁר־יִלְכְּדֶנָּה יהוה תִּקְרַב
לַבָּתִּים וְהַבַּיִת אֲשֶׁר יִלְכְּדֶנּוּ יהוה יִקְרַב
טו לַגְּבָרִים: וְהָיָה הַנִּלְכָּד בַּחֵרֶם יִשָּׂרֵף בָּאֵשׁ

the entire Torah, for the numerical equivalent (248) of the first and last letter of the final word found in each Book [במצרים, מסעיהם, סיני, ירחו, ישראל] is identical to the numerical equivalent of חֵרֶם, *ban*.

12. [In this verse we find a classic example of one of a prophet's functions — to identify sources of sin within Israel. Joshua and the rest of the people were perplexed, for they could not understand why the Divine Protection had been removed from them. News analysts and historians can describe the concatenation of events, but can only make hypotheses concerning their true causes. The Prophet, however, through Divine revelation, was permitted to see the underlying causes of Israel's troubles so that he could inform the people and lead them to correct their ways.]

וְלֹא יֻכְלוּ ... לָקוּם — *Will not be able to stand.*

In effect, God is agreeing with Joshua's statement (verse 9) that if He does not protect Israel, the Jews will be overwhelmed by their enemies *(Daas Sofrim).*

לֹא אוֹסִיף לִהְיוֹת עִמָּכֶם...מִקִּרְבְּכֶם — *I will not continue to be with you ... from your midst.*

In order to restore the Divine Protection to Israel, not only does the banned property have to be destroyed, but also the transgressor must be punished *(Malbim).* Here this word means *the one who violated the ban (Metzudos).*

13. קַדֵּשׁ — *Prepare* [lit. *sanctify*].

The translation follows *Targum.*

This means that any witnesses should *prepare* to come forward or that the evildoer should search his ways and *prepare* to admit his guilt *(Daas Sofrim).*

לְמָחָר — *For tomorrow.*

Joshua did not mention the method that would be used to determine the guilty individual, for he feared that if the guilty party had advance knowledge [of the lottery], he might plan a way to undercut its effectiveness *(Abarbanel).*

הֲסִירְכֶם הַחֵרֶם — *You remove the abominator* [lit. *the banned property*].

The translation follows *Metzudos* and *Malbim.*

This verse does not mention that the transgressor will be killed, because had the nation been so informed, the guilty

able to stand before their enemies; they will turn the
backs of their necks before their enemies because
they have become loathesome. I will not continue to
be with you if you do not extirpate the abominator
from your midst. 13 *Arise, prepare the people and*
say, "Prepare yourselves for tomorrow, for thus says
HASHEM, God of Israel: There is an abomination in
your midst, Israel. You will not be able to stand
before your enemies until you remove the
abominator from your midst. 14 *In the morning you*
shall approach according to your tribes. It will be that
the tribe which HASHEM entraps shall approach by
family; the family which HASHEM entraps shall
approach by households; the household which
HASHEM entraps shall approach by man. 15 *It will be*
that the one entrapped with banned property will be

person would not have admitted his crime *(Malbim).*

⁂ The Lottery to Identify the Offender

14-18. God did not immediately identify the man who had violated Joshua's ban on the spoils of Jericho; rather He commanded Joshua to conduct a lottery which would gradually disclose his identity by identifying his tribe, then his family, his house, and, finally, the name of the man himself.

Only by witnessing this lottery guided by Divine Providence would the people be certain that the offender was correctly identified. Had Joshua immediately revealed his identity, some people would have maintained that Joshua had accused Achan because of some personal grievance, rather than because he was truly the guilty individual *(Meam Loez).*

14. וְנִקְרַבְתֶּם – *You shall approach.*

They gathered near the Ark *(Metzudos).*

לְמִשְׁפְּחוֹת – *By family.*

One family comprises many households *(Rashi).*

אֲשֶׁר יִלְכְּדֶנּוּ ה' – *Which HASHEM entraps.*

Targum paraphrases: chooses.

Radak cites two opinions concerning the method used to select the guilty individual:

☐ Joshua made all the people pass before the Ark, and the person who was guilty became trapped and temporarily unable to move.

☐ In order to determine the tribe of the guilty person, Joshua consulted the *urim v'tumim,* the Priestly breastplace, which had twelve stones, each of which represented a particular tribe. When the stone of the tribe containing the guilty party dimmed, that tribe — Judah — was further scrutinized by lots to determine the guilty family, household, and individual. [*Pirkei De R' Eliezer,* Chapter 38 explains that if a tribe was free of sin, its stone in the breastplate glowed; if a tribe was not free of sin, its stone did not glow.]

אֹתוֹ וְאֶת־כָּל־אֲשֶׁר־ל֑וֹ כִּ֤י עָבַר֙ אֶת־
בְּרִ֣ית יהוה וְכִֽי־עָשָׂ֥ה נְבָלָ֖ה בְּיִשְׂרָאֵֽל׃
טז וַיַּשְׁכֵּ֤ם יְהוֹשֻׁ֙עַ֙ בַּבֹּ֔קֶר וַיַּקְרֵ֥ב אֶת־יִשְׂרָאֵ֖ל
יז לִשְׁבָטָ֑יו וַיִּלָּכֵ֖ד שֵׁ֥בֶט יְהוּדָֽה׃ וַיַּקְרֵב֙ אֶת־
מִשְׁפַּ֣חַת יְהוּדָ֔ה וַיִּלְכֹּ֕ד אֵ֖ת מִשְׁפַּ֣חַת
הַזַּרְחִ֑י וַיַּקְרֵ֞ב אֶת־מִשְׁפַּ֤חַת הַזַּרְחִי֙
יח לַגְּבָרִ֔ים וַיִּלָּכֵ֖ד זַבְדִּֽי׃ וַיַּקְרֵ֥ב אֶת־בֵּית֖וֹ
לַגְּבָרִ֑ים וַיִּלָּכֵ֗ד עָכָ֞ן בֶּן־כַּרְמִ֧י בֶן־זַבְדִּ֛י בֶּן־
יט זֶ֛רַח לְמַטֵּ֥ה יְהוּדָֽה׃ וַיֹּ֨אמֶר יְהוֹשֻׁ֜עַ אֶל־
עָכָ֗ן בְּנִי֙ שִֽׂים־נָ֣א כָב֞וֹד לַיהוָ֨ה אֱלֹהֵ֤י
יִשְׂרָאֵל֙ וְתֶן־ל֣וֹ תוֹדָ֔ה וְהַגֶּד־נָ֣א לִי֙ מֶ֣ה

15. וְהָיָה ... אֲשֶׁר לוֹ — *It will be ... he has.*

There is disagreement between the commentators regarding the meaning of the first half of this verse.

Abarbanel understands the phrase *he and all he has* as an explanation of those things which will be burned. He explains that it was appropriate to immolate the perpetrator and his belongings because the spoils of Jericho were supposed to be burned.

Rashi, however, claims that this is an elliptical verse [מִקְרָא קָצָר] which does not mention the penalty to be levied against *he* (the sinner) *and all he has.* Verse 25 mentions that Achan was stoned to death, rather than burned; only his immovable possessions were burned. In *Rashi's* view, the beginning of this verse — which mentions burning — only refers to the perpetrator's tent and movable objects.

כִּי עָבַר ... וְכִי־עָשָׂה נְבָלָה — *Because he has violated ... because he has committed an abomination.*

Achan committed two types of offenses: he sinned against God *(because he has violated the covenant of HASHEM)* and against the nation Israel *(because he has committed an abomination in Israel)* [*Malbim*].

17. וַיַּקְרֵב אֶת־מִשְׁפַּחַת יְהוּדָה — *And he had the family of Judah approach.*

One leader from each tribe came forth during the process of identifying the guilty individual. When the leader of Judah was selected, that tribe was further scrutinized. Next, a leader from each family came forth, followed by a leader representing each household *(Rashi).*

Judah was actually the name of one of the tribes, not families. However, Scripture uses the expression, *family of Judah. Metzudos* explains that the words 'family' and 'tribe' are interchangeable.

זַבְדִּי — *Zavdi.*

In I *Chronicles* 2:6, he is called Zimri *(Radak).*

◆§ Achan Found Guilty

18. עָכָן בֶּן־כַּרְמִי — *Achan, the son of Carmi.*

Margolios HaYam makes an interesting observation. Achan's genealogy is identified in verse 1 and verse 18 by four people — Judah, Zerach, Zeved, and Carmi. However, in the selection process mentioned in verses 17 and 18, only three selections were made — Judah, Zerach, and Zeved; Carmi was not mentioned. He suggests on the basis of this problem and other evidence that the name

7
16-19 *burned with fire, he and all he has, because he has violated the covenant of HASHEM, because he has committed an abomination in Israel".'*

16 *Joshua arose early in the morning and had Israel approach by tribes; the tribe of Judah was chosen.*
17 *And he had the family of Judah approach, and he chose the family of Zarchi. He summoned the family of Zarchi to approach by man, and Zavdi was chosen.*
18 *And he had his household approached by man, and Achan, the son of Carmi, the son of Zavdi, the son of Zerach of the tribe of Judah was chosen.*

19 *Then Joshua said to Achan, 'My son, give, I pray you, honor to HASHEM, God of Israel, and confess to Him. Tell me, I pray you, what you have*

son of Carmi was actually a part of Achan's name, rather than an identification of Achan's father. This view also helps to clarify *I Chronicles* 2:7.

19. בְּנִי — *My son.*

Even though he sinned, he was still considered a *son* of Israel *(Daas Sofrim).*

שִׂים־נָא כָבוֹד — *Give, I pray you, honor.*

When the lottery pointed to Achan, he argued, 'You wish to judge me with a lottery — if I were to make a lottery between two righteous leaders such as you and Elazar, one of you would be found guilty' [i.e., the lottery must identify someone, even if no one is guilty].

To this Joshua replied, *'Give, I pray you, honor ...'* Joshua asked him to confess, thereby admitting the validity of the lottery, which would also be used to divide the Land[1] *(Rashi).*

Malbim suggests that Achan's criticism about the method of casting lots was diminishing God's honor because He controlled the outcome of the lottery. Through his confession, Achan would be restoring the honor due God.

Radak adds that Joshua sought Achan's confession so that Achan would achieve an atonement for his sin upon his death. In fact, the *Talmud (Sanhedrin* 43b) derives from this verse that all people sentenced to the death penalty should be told to confess their sins, so that they will receive their rightful share in the World to Come.

וְתֶן־לוֹ תוֹדָה...מֶה עָשִׂיתָ — *Confess to Him* [lit. *give Him confession*] ... *what you have done.*

1. In 1802, when the city of Pressburg began its search for a new Rav, the names R' Akiva Eiger, R' Boruch Frankel, and R' Sholom Ullman were discussed. Five years later, still without a Rav, they added R' Moshe Sofer's name to the list and informed him that they would cast lots to determine the new replacement. R' Moshe replied in a letter that in all humility he felt unqualified for the position, and in addition, he opposed the decision to cast lots for, 'How can chance prove who is the greater man — the wiser man?' That night, R' Moshe had a dream in which his mentor R' Nosson Adler appeared and uttered the curious words, 'The Lots of Joshua.' When he arose, R' Moshe attempted to fathom the import of his dream, and he remembered that the *Talmud* states, 'Do not ridicule a lottery, for *Eretz Yisrael* was divided by Joshua through a lottery.' A few days later R' Moshe Sofer received a letter from the Pressburg community informing him that the lottery had chosen his name and offering him the appointment. Within the year he had assumed his new post *(R' Shubert Spero)* [see Responsa, *Chavos Yair* 61].

ז
כ־כג

כ עָשִׂיתָ אַל־תְּכַחֵד מִמֶּנִּי: וַיַּעַן עָכָן אֶת־
יְהוֹשֻׁעַ וַיֹּאמַר אָמְנָה אָנֹכִי חָטָאתִי
לַיהוה אֱלֹהֵי יִשְׂרָאֵל וְכָזֹאת וְכָזֹאת
°וָאֵרֶא ק׳ כא עָשִׂיתִי: °וארא בַשָּׁלָל אַדֶּרֶת שִׁנְעָר
אַחַת טוֹבָה וּמָאתַיִם שְׁקָלִים כֶּסֶף וּלְשׁוֹן
זָהָב אֶחָד חֲמִשִּׁים שְׁקָלִים מִשְׁקָלוֹ
וָאֶחְמְדֵם וָאֶקָּחֵם וְהִנָּם טְמֻנִים בָּאָרֶץ
כב בְּתוֹךְ הָאָהֳלִי וְהַכֶּסֶף תַּחְתֶּיהָ: וַיִּשְׁלַח
יְהוֹשֻׁעַ מַלְאָכִים וַיָּרֻצוּ הָאֹהֱלָה וְהִנֵּה
כג טְמוּנָה בְּאָהֳלוֹ וְהַכֶּסֶף תַּחְתֶּיהָ: וַיִּקָּחוּם

The commentators suggest different interpretations for the two directives that Joshua gave Achan:

□ *Confess to Him* the other sins you have committed and *tell me what you have done* in regard to the banned property of Jericho, so that the credibility of casting lots can be vindicated *(Malbim).*

□ *Confess to Him* that you actually stole the banned property, and *tell me what you have done,* i.e., what articles you have taken *(Metzudos).*

20. וַיַּעַן עָכָן — *And Achan answered.*

When Achan saw that people from his tribe of Judah were disturbed at the outcome of the casting of lots and were prepared to wage a civil war [to defend him], he said, 'It is better that I alone die, so that many thousands of Israelites will be saved' *(Rashi).*

Perhaps the tribe of Judah was disturbed at the outcome of the lot, since the monarchy of Israel was to descend from them. Scripture records many instances in which the tribe of Ephraim attempted to usurp the throne from Judah. In fact, later in Jewish history, the Land of Israel divided into two kingdoms, one ruled by Ephraim and one by Judah. In this incident with Achan, the tribe of Judah suspected that Joshua, who descended from Ephraim, was acting with ulterior motives. They thought Joshua purposely sought to discredit Judah by showing that at the time when Israel was occupied in the conquest of the Land, certain members of the tribe of Judah were not trustworthy *(Mussar HaNeviim).*

וְכָזֹאת וְכָזֹאת עָשִׂיתִי — *Thus and thus have I done.*

As the *Commentary* to verse 11 explains, Joshua issued two decrees: he banned the spoils of Jericho, and he declared that the silver and gold would be donated to the Treasury. When Achan uttered, *Thus and thus have I done,* he was referring to his violation of both decrees *(Meam Loez).*

The *Talmud (Sanhedrin* 43b) interprets Achan's statement as a confession not only that he had taken from the banned property of Jericho, but also that he had taken property banned by Moses in the Wilderness. Israel was not punished for the thefts Achan committed during Moses' time because communal reponsibility for covert individual transgressions did not begin until the Jews crossed the Jordan [see *Prefatory Remarks* to this chapter].

HaRav Gifter remarks that from Achan's statement it is apparent that if one wishes to fulfill the mitzvah of 'confessing sin,' he need only mention the actual transgressions. Although the mitzvah of repentance also requires the sinner to regret his transgression and to vow never to repeat it, these obligations are not considered part of the

7
20-23
done. Do not hide anything from me.'
20 *And Achan answered Joshua and said, 'In truth,*
I have sinned against HASHEM, God of Israel. Thus
and thus have I done. 21 *I saw among the spoils a*
lovely Babylonian garment, two hundred shekels of silver, and a bar of gold fifty shekels in weight, and I desired them and took them, and behold, they are concealed in the ground in my tent and the silver underneath it.'
22 *Joshua sent messengers, and they ran to the tent*
and behold it was hidden in his tent, and the silver
was underneath it. 23 *And they took them from the*

confession. The words of *Rambam (Hil. Teshuvah* 2:8) support this interpretation.

21. אַדֶּרֶת שִׁנְעָר — *A Babylonian garment.*

[שִׁנְעָר is identified as Babylon in *Genesis* 14:1.]

The *Talmud (Sanhedrin* 44a) records a dispute regarding the nature of this garment. One opinion is that it was a white woolen mantle; the other that it was an alum dyed garment (see *Margolios HaYam, ibid.).*

Rashi explains that the kings of countries outside of the Holy Land desired to have a palace in *Eretz Yisrael,* also. The king of Babylon owned a palace in Jericho; when he lodged there, he wore this garment. *Malbim* comments that Achan felt justified in taking the garment because its owner was not from Jericho. He thought that Joshua had banned the property of the inhabitants of Jericho, but not the property of foreigners who happened to be living in Jericho.

טוֹבָה — *Lovely* [lit. *goodly*].

The translation follows *Targum.*

Because it was so *lovely,* Achan desired the garment very much *(Malbim).*

וּלְשׁוֹן — *And a bar* [lit. *tongue*].

The *bar* of gold was in the shape of a tongue *(Abarbanel).*

וְהִנָּם טְמֻנִים בָּאָרֶץ — *And behold, they are concealed in the ground.*

Achan buried the items he stole so that they would not become damaged and so that he would not be able to derive benefit from them. One is not liable for stealing from *hekdesh,* 'sanctified articles,' unless he had damaged them or benefited from them *(Rambam, Hil. M'eilah,* Ch. 6). Achan thought that the laws of stealing from sanctified articles applied to the booty of Jericho, but was mistaken *(Malbim).*

בְּתוֹךְ הָאָהֳלִי — *In my tent.*

Achan had two tents, and thus he identified the one that contained the stolen goods as *my tent,* i.e., not the tent of the rest of his family *(Malbim).*

תַּחְתֶּיהָ — *Underneath it.*

The silver was underneath the garment *(Radak).*

22. וַיָּרֻצוּ — *And they ran.*

Joshua's messengers quickly went to the tent so that the tribe of Judah would not get there first and try to destroy the evidence in order to discredit the lottery *(Rashi).*

Radak, however, suggests that the messengers ran out of excitement and joy that the perpetrator had been found and that Israel as a whole was guiltless.

מִתּוֹךְ הָאֹהֶל וַיְבִאוּם אֶל־יְהוֹשֻׁעַ וְאֶל
כד כָּל־בְּנֵי יִשְׂרָאֵל וַיַּצִּקֻם לִפְנֵי יהוָה: וַיִּקַּח
יְהוֹשֻׁעַ אֶת־עָכָן בֶּן־זֶרַח וְאֶת־הַכֶּסֶף
וְאֶת־הָאַדֶּרֶת וְאֶת־לְשׁוֹן הַזָּהָב וְאֶת־בָּנָיו
וְאֶת־בְּנֹתָיו וְאֶת־שׁוֹרוֹ וְאֶת־חֲמֹרוֹ וְאֶת־
צֹאנוֹ וְאֶת־אָהֳלוֹ וְאֶת־כָּל־אֲשֶׁר־לוֹ וְכָל־
יִשְׂרָאֵל עִמּוֹ וַיַּעֲלוּ אֹתָם עֵמֶק עָכוֹר:
כה וַיֹּאמֶר יְהוֹשֻׁעַ מֶה עֲכַרְתָּנוּ יַעְכָּרְךָ יהוָה
בַּיּוֹם הַזֶּה וַיִּרְגְּמוּ אֹתוֹ כָל־יִשְׂרָאֵל אֶבֶן
וַיִּשְׂרְפוּ אֹתָם בָּאֵשׁ וַיִּסְקְלוּ אֹתָם

23. וַיַּצִּקֻם — *And* [*they*] *spread them out.*

The translation follows *Radak* who remarks that Joshua spread the booty out before God so that all Israel could witness the source of their troubles. *Metzudos* comments that Joshua put the articles on public view to show Israel that the lottery had been accurate.

As the Sages *(Bamidbar Rabbah* 23:6) understand this expression, Joshua threw the booty confiscated from Achan's tent on the ground and exclaimed, 'God, on account of these things, Your anger burned against Your children. Here they are.'

Targum renders 'they melted.'

24. עָכָן בֶּן־זֶרַח — *Achan the son of Zerach.*

Scripture identifies Achan by the name of his great grandfather, Zerach, because Zerach was the patriarch of the entire family *(Radak).* [According to *Margolios HaYam* cited in the *Commentary* to verse 18, Zerach was Achan's grandfather, rather than his great grandfather.]

וְאֶת־בָּנָיו וְאֶת־בְּנֹתָיו — *His sons and daughters.*

The *Talmud (Sanhedrin* 44a) explains that Achan's children were not executed, but they were brought to witness their father's execution in order to impress upon them the importance of not following in their father's evil ways. [Cf. *Pirkei D'Rabbi Eliezer* 32.]

...וְאֶת שׁוֹרוֹ וְאֶת חֲמֹרוֹ — *His ox, his ass.*

The burning of Achan's property was in keeping with Joshua's statement in verse 15 *(Rashi).*

וְכָל־יִשְׂרָאֵל — *And all of Israel.*

Joshua brought the entire nation to witness Achan's punishment so that they would be deterred from emulating his sinful behavior *(Rashi).*

וַיַּעֲלוּ — *And they brought* [*them*] *up.*

It would seem that Scripture should have said 'they descended' into the valley. However, it appears that there was a mountain between the camp and the valley so Scripture used the term 'ascended' *(Radak).*

Margolios HaYam suggests that the expression *they brought* [*them*] *up* refers to the place in the valley where Achan was executed. According to Jewish law, the penalty of stoning requires that the offender ascend a hill twice his height. He is pushed off and a large stone is placed on top of him. Thus, he was taken up to the platform of execution in the valley.

עֵמֶק עָכוֹר — *Emek Achor.*

T'vuos HaAretz conjectures that this is the valley which extends from the

7
24-26

tent and brought them to Joshua and to all the
Children of Israel and spread them out before
HASHEM.
[24] *And Joshua took Achan the son of Zerach and*
the silver, the garment, the bar of gold, his sons and
daughters, his ox, his ass, his sheep, his tent, all his
belongings and all of Israel with him, and they
brought them up to the Valley of Achor. [25] *Joshua*
said, 'Why have you troubled us? HASHEM should
trouble you this day.'
And all of Israel pelted him with stones, burned
them with fire, and stoned them with stones. [26] *And*

village Elaezria, which was located southeast of the Mount of Olives, to the Jordan River valley (Aravah).

25. בַּיּוֹם הַזֶּה — *This day.*

This implies *HASHEM will trouble you* this *day,* but not after your death, for since you admitted your guilt, your death will be atonement *(Sanhedrin* 43b).

וַיִּרְגְּמוּ אֹתוֹ — *And [all of Israel] pelted him with stones.*

On the basis of the *Talmud (Sanhedrin* 44a), *Rashi* understands that Achan was only stoned [but not burned]. *Radak,* however, cites his father's interpretation that as Achan was led to be burned, the onlookers stoned him out of anger. When they were in the valley of Achor, Achan and all his belongings were burned. Afterwards, they piled stones on his ashes to serve as a sign.

☙ For What Offense was Achan Guilty?

The commentators disagree in their identification of the offense for which Achan received the death penalty.

☐ *Rashi* maintains that Achan was stoned because he had violated the Sabbath [see *Commentary* to 7:11].

☐ Normally, the death penalty can only be meted out in a case in which two witnesses informed the transgressor of the severity of the sin which he intended to commit and then witnessed the transgression itself. However, *Rambam (Hil. Sanhedrin* 18:6) explains that Achan's case involved a *hora'as sha'ah* (הוֹרָאַת שָׁעָה), a temporary suspension of Torah law which is permitted in rare emergencies, such as to deter others from sin.

☐ On the basis of *Leviticus* 27:29, *Ramban* asserts that when Israel's king or Sanhedrin (Supreme Court) bans property, a transgressor is liable to the death penalty.

☐ *Emek Sha'alah* (142) advances that Achan was put to death in accordance with God's directive to Joshua (verse 15).

☐ Others say that since Achan rebelled against the king (Joshua), he was subject to the death penalty (see *Chasam Sofer, Orach Chaim,* 208).

וַיִּשְׂרְפוּ אֹתָם — *(And they) burned them with fire.*

His tent and movable belongings were *burned (Rashi).*

וַיִּסְקְלוּ אֹתָם — *And (they) stoned them.*

The oxen and other animals were *stoned (Rashi).*

ז
כו
כו בָּאֲבָנִים: וַיָּקִימוּ עָלָיו גַּל־אֲבָנִים גָּדוֹל עַד
הַיּוֹם הַזֶּה וַיָּשָׁב יהוה מֵחֲרוֹן אַפּוֹ עַל־כֵּן
קָרָא שֵׁם הַמָּקוֹם הַהוּא עֵמֶק עָכוֹר עַד
הַיּוֹם הַזֶּה:

ח
א־ב
א וַיֹּאמֶר יהוה אֶל־יְהוֹשֻׁעַ אַל־תִּירָא וְאַל־
תֵּחָת קַח עִמְּךָ אֵת כָּל־עַם הַמִּלְחָמָה
וְקוּם עֲלֵה הָעָי רְאֵה | נָתַתִּי בְיָדְךָ אֶת־
מֶלֶךְ הָעַי וְאֶת־עַמּוֹ וְאֶת־עִירוֹ וְאֶת־
ב אַרְצוֹ: וְעָשִׂיתָ לָעַי וּלְמַלְכָּהּ כַּאֲשֶׁר
עָשִׂיתָ לִירִיחוֹ וּלְמַלְכָּהּ רַק־שְׁלָלָהּ
וּבְהֶמְתָּהּ תָּבֹזּוּ לָכֶם שִׂים־לְךָ אֹרֵב לָעִיר

26. עָלָיו — *On him.*

They placed the stones on Achan's gravesite *(Metzudos).*

עַד הַיּוֹם הַזֶּה — *Until this day.*

According to the *Talmud (Sanhedrin* 46a), a person executed by the court is eventually buried in his own familial burial plot. Achan apparently forever remained buried under this pile of stones. However, according to *Rosh (Ohalos* 15:7), these stones served only as a temporary marker until Achan was buried.

VIII

◆§ The Second Attempt to Conquer Ai

1. וַיֹּאמֶר ה׳ אֶל־יְהוֹשֻׁעַ — *HASHEM said to Joshua.*

After Joshua carried out the judgment against Achan and the nation was cleansed from sin, the Divine Presence returned, and Joshua had a prophetic vision *(Meam Loez).*

אַל־תִּירָא וְאַל־תֵּחָת — *Do not fear and do not lose resolve.*

[For translation, see *Commentary* to 1:9.]

Do not interpret the fact that I am directing you to use military strategy in your conquest of Ai as a sign that I am diminishing My miraculous Providence over Israel *(Chida).*

[See *Commentary* to 10:8.]

Typically, an individual fears the place where something tragic has happened. Therefore, God comforted Joshua and told him not to fear, even though the Israelites had suffered their first defeat there *(Abarbanel).*

Lev Aharon suggests that Joshua feared that God would withdraw His special Providence. He interprets this phrase, *Do not fear ...,* as God's consolation to Joshua. Although God would partially withhold some measure of His special Providence until the nation had fully rectified its spiritual failure in the episode with Achan, some special Providence would still be operative. It was this partial withdrawal of Providence which necessitated the use of military strategems.

כָּל־עַם — *All the people.*

Israel used 60,000 warriors to conquer *Eretz Yisrael (Shir HaShirim Rabbah* 4).

Metzudos explains that God commanded Joshua to employ military strategems and to deploy the entire Jewish nation in the battle against Ai so

7 *they piled a great heap of stones on him until this*
26 *day, and HASHEM withdrew from his kindled anger.*
Therefore, the name of that place was called, 'The
Valley of Achor,' until this day.

8 [1] *HASHEM said to Joshua, 'Do not fear and do not*
1-2 *lose resolve. Take all the people of war with*
you and arise and invade Ai. See, I have given into
your hand the king of Ai, his people, city, and
country. [2] *And you shall do to Ai and its king as you*
did to Jericho and its king. Only, its spoils and its
animals you may take as booty for yourselves.
Ambush the city from its rear.'

that the Canaanites would not attribute the Jews' victory to Divine intervention. For only if the Canaanite nations believed that Israel's victory was the result of superior numbers and military tactics would they collaborate in an attempt to outnumber the Jews. If the Canaanites united, Israel would be saved the difficulty of fighting individual battles [see *footnote* to 7:5].

Ralbag, however, asserts that God commanded Israel to use normal military techniques because such strategems would be sufficient against Ai, thus avoiding the need for miraculous Divine intervention. After having routed the Jews once, the men of Ai would readily pursue them a second time, thereby enabling the Jews to surround and conquer them. Because God does not perform unneeded miracles, he directed Israel to use the ruse described in this chapter.

Others suggest that it was because the spoils of Ai were permitted to the people that the entire nation was told to participate, for those left behind would have envied those who amassed booty after the conquest *(Ayalah Shluchah).*

אֶת־מֶלֶךְ הָעַי וְאֶת־עַמּוֹ ... – *The king of Ai, his people ...*

Lev Aharon continues: Some measure of Divine intervention could be noticeable in Israel's conquest of Ai. Normally, an attacking nation first breaks the defending city's walls, and then proceeds to vanquish the inhabitants, and finally the king. However, in the case of Ai, the contrary would be true — first the king would fall into the Israelites' hands, then the inhabitants, and finally the city. This reversal indicated God's guidance of the events.

2. כַּאֲשֶׁר עָשִׂיתָ לִירִיחוֹ – *As you did to Jericho.*

Just as you killed the people of Jericho by sword, so should you kill the people of Ai *(Radak).*

תָּבֹזּוּ לָכֶם – *You may take as booty for yourselves.*

In Ai, unlike in Jericho, you may benefit from the spoils of war *(Radak).* In the future, do not ban the spoils of war *(Rashi).*

שִׂים־לְךָ אֹרֵב – *Ambush* [lit. *place yourself in ambush*].

The commentators perceive several reasons for this ambush strategy:

☐ The scouts originally underestimated Ai's strength when they reported *they are few* (7:3). In fact Ai was a highly fortified city with mighty warriors. Thus, God suggested that the Israelites employ an ambush strategy to simplify the conquest *(Abarbanel).*

☐ It was precisely because Israel

ח
ג־ט

ג מֵאַחֲרֶיהָ: וַיָּקָם יְהוֹשֻׁעַ וְכָל־עַם
הַמִּלְחָמָה לַעֲלוֹת הָעָי וַיִּבְחַר יְהוֹשֻׁעַ
שְׁלֹשִׁים אֶלֶף אִישׁ גִּבּוֹרֵי הַחַיִל וַיִּשְׁלָחֵם
ד לָיְלָה: וַיְצַו אֹתָם לֵאמֹר רְאוּ אַתֶּם
אֹרְבִים לָעִיר מֵאַחֲרֵי הָעִיר אַל־תַּרְחִיקוּ
מִן־הָעִיר מְאֹד וִהְיִיתֶם כֻּלְּכֶם נְכֹנִים:
ה וַאֲנִי וְכָל־הָעָם אֲשֶׁר אִתִּי נִקְרַב אֶל־
הָעִיר וְהָיָה כִּי־יֵצְאוּ לִקְרָאתֵנוּ כַּאֲשֶׁר
ו בָּרִאשֹׁנָה וְנַסְנוּ לִפְנֵיהֶם: וְיָצְאוּ אַחֲרֵינוּ
עַד הַתִּיקֵנוּ אוֹתָם מִן־הָעִיר כִּי יֹאמְרוּ
נָסִים לְפָנֵינוּ כַּאֲשֶׁר בָּרִאשֹׁנָה וְנַסְנוּ
ז לִפְנֵיהֶם: וְאַתֶּם תָּקֻמוּ מֵהָאוֹרֵב
וְהוֹרַשְׁתֶּם אֶת־הָעִיר וּנְתָנָהּ יְהוָה
ח אֱלֹהֵיכֶם בְּיֶדְכֶם: וְהָיָה כְּתָפְשְׂכֶם אֶת־
הָעִיר תַּצִּיתוּ אֶת־הָעִיר בָּאֵשׁ כִּדְבַר
ט יְהוָה תַּעֲשׂוּ רְאוּ צִוִּיתִי אֶתְכֶם: וַיִּשְׁלָחֵם

employed a strategy of ambush against Ai that the spoils were permitted. This strategy allowed Israel the opportunity to participate in Ai's defeat. In Jericho, however, where their victory was solely attributable to miraculous Divine intervention, the spoils of war were not permitted *(Malbim).*

☐ Since Ai was a small city, God wanted the Israelites to be actively engaged in its defeat so that the Canaanites would not think that the Israelites' army was so weak that they needed a miracle to conquer even a small city *(Meam Loez).*

☐ The ambush of Ai was planned to lull the Canaanites into thinking that God withdrew His Providence from the Israelites and that they needed to rely on their own strategies in the future. This resulted in the Canaanites uniting to overpower the Jews, at which time God performed a miracle that conveniently allowed Israel to defeat the Canaanites of the north in one battle *(Lev Aharon).*

3. וַיִּשְׁלָחֵם לָיְלָה — *And dispatched them at night.*

This took place two days before the conquest of Ai *(Malbim).* [Verses 9 and 13 recount that there were two intervening nights between the dispatching of these troops and the battle against Ai.]

They were sent at night so they would not be seen *(Daas Sofrim).*

◆§ The Ambush Strategy

4. אֹרְבִים לָעִיר — *Ambush the city.*

Malbim explains that they were to *ambush the city* itself, rather than the warriors of Ai, for Ai's soldiers would be pursuing the Israelites who were attacking them from the front. Therefore, the ambush force was stationed right behind the city. Thus, this ambush differed from others

3 And Joshua and the people of war prepared to invade Ai. Joshua chose thirty thousand mighty men of war and dispatched them at night. 4 He commanded them saying, 'Behold, you shall ambush the city from the city's rear. Do not distance yourselves too far from the city, and all of you be on alert. 5 And I and all the people that are with me will approach the city. It will be when they go out to oppose us as they previously did, we will flee before them. 6 They will go out after us until we have drawn them from the city, for they will say, "They flee before us, as they previously did." We will flee before them. 7 And you shall rise up from the ambush and drive out the city. HASHEM will deliver it into your hand. 8 It will be when you seize the city that you shall set the city on fire, according to the word of HASHEM you shall do. See, I have commanded you.'

described in Scripture (cf. *Judges* 9; 25; 43).

5. וַאֲנִי — *And I.*

[The fact that Joshua explicitly stated that he would accompany Israel's forces tends to support the interpretation (see *Commentary* to 7:10) that the Jews were not victorious in their first encounter with Ai because Joshua did not accompany Israel's forces.]

כַּאֲשֶׁר בָּרִאשֹׁנָה — *As they previously did.*

After having repulsed the Jews' first attempt to take Ai, Ai's warriors will be so confident of success that they will certainly leave the safety of their city to attack the Israelites *(Malbim).*

וְנַסְנוּ — *We will flee.*

We will pretend to flee in order to deceive them *(Metzudos).*

6. הַתִּיקֵנוּ — *We have drawn them.*

The translation follows *Radak.*

כַּאֲשֶׁר בָּרִאשֹׁנָה — *As they previously did.*

They will not suspect an ambush because of their previous success in routing our forces *(Malbim).* [See *footnote* to 7:5.]

וְנַסְנוּ — *We will flee.*

We will flee even further in order to increase the distance between the inhabitants of Ai and their city *(Metzudos).*

7. וְאַתֶּם תָּקֻמוּ — *And you shall rise up.*

You shall rise up and attack from the rear when you receive the signal *(Malbim).*

וְהוֹרַשְׁתֶּם אֶת־הָעִיר — *And* (you shall) *drive out* [*those who remain in*] *the city.*

You shall drive out and destroy the [remaining] inhabitants of the city *(Radak)* [for Ai's warriors will have already left the city to chase the Jews as they feign retreat].

8. כִּדְבַר ה׳ — *According to the word of HASHEM.*

Verse 2 states, *You shall do to Ai ... as you did to Jericho.* Thus, just as Jericho was burned (6:24), so shall Ai be burned *(Radak).*

ח
י־יב

יְהוֹשֻׁעַ וַיֵּלְכוּ אֶל־הַמַּאְרָב וַיֵּשְׁבוּ בֵּין
בֵּית־אֵל וּבֵין הָעַי מִיָּם לָעָי וַיָּלֶן יְהוֹשֻׁעַ
י בַּלַּיְלָה הַהוּא בְּתוֹךְ הָעָם׃ וַיַּשְׁכֵּם יְהוֹשֻׁעַ
בַּבֹּקֶר וַיִּפְקֹד אֶת־הָעָם וַיַּעַל הוּא וְזִקְנֵי
יא יִשְׂרָאֵל לִפְנֵי הָעָם הָעָי׃ וְכָל־הָעָם
הַמִּלְחָמָה אֲשֶׁר אִתּוֹ עָלוּ וַיִּגְּשׁוּ וַיָּבֹאוּ
נֶגֶד הָעִיר וַיַּחֲנוּ מִצְּפוֹן לָעַי וְהַגַּי בֵּינָו
יב וּבֵין הָעָי׃ וַיִּקַּח כַּחֲמֵשֶׁת אֲלָפִים אִישׁ
וַיָּשֶׂם אוֹתָם אוֹרֵב בֵּין בֵּית־אֵל וּבֵין הָעָי

רְאוּ צִוִּיתִי אֶתְכֶם — *See, I have commanded you.*

I have commanded you to be alacritous in fulfilling My instructions *(Radak).*

I have commanded you through prophecy to burn Ai, and thus you need not be concerned that the good spoils will not be available for your procurement *(Meam Loez).*

The Battle of Ai

(according to Malbim)

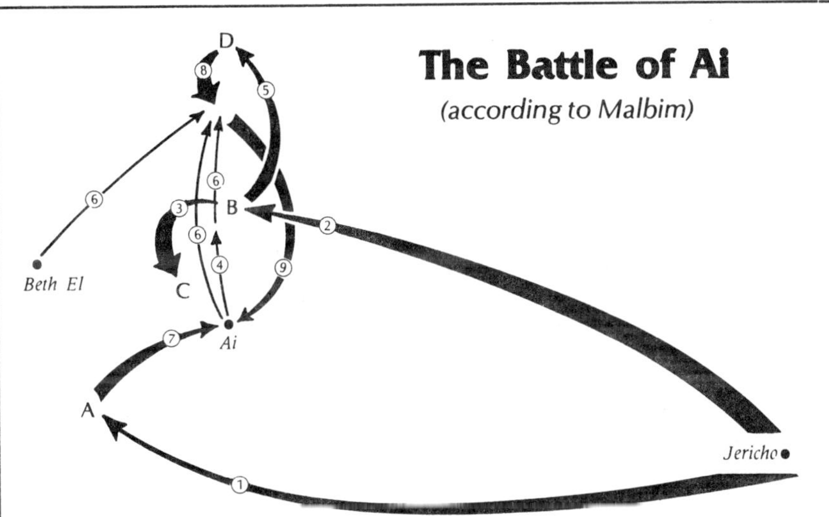

1. Joshua dispatches ambush party two days before the battle (A).

2. The Israelites' main army positions itself (B).

3. Joshua dispatches 5,000 troops to create a second flank (C).

4. The warriors of Ai launch attack against Israelites.

5. Joshua feigns retreat (D).

6. Aware of Joshua's retreat, all of Ai's warriors rush outside of the city, joining the initial thrust of Ai's army. Beth El also joins in this pursuit.

7. Ambush party raids defenseless Ai and sets it ablaze.

8. Joshua sees Ai burn, reverses his field, and vanquishes Ai's warriors.

9. Israelites return to Ai and kill its inhabitants.

⁹ *Joshua dispatched them, and they went to the
place of ambush and situated themselves between
Beth El and Ai, to the west of Ai. Joshua lodged that
night among the people.* ¹⁰ *Joshua arose early in the
morning and inspected the people; he and the elders
of Israel ascended before the people to Ai.* ¹¹ *All the
people of war who were with him ascended,
approached, and came before the city. They
encamped to the north of Ai, and the valley was
between them and Ai.* ¹² *He took five thousand men
and set them to lie in ambush between Beth El and Ai,*

I have commanded you personally and not through an agent so that you fulfill My orders fully *(Meam Loez).*

9. מִיָּם לָעָי — *To the west of Ai.*

Ai was east of Beth El and Beth El was west of Ai *(Rashi).*

Malbim explains that we can be sure that the ambush party did not lie in wait directly west of Ai for two reasons: (a) since Joshua's attacking party attacked from the north of Ai (verse 11), the ambush party, which was behind the city (verse 14), must have been situated to the south of Ai; (b) if the ambush party had lain in wait directly between Ai and Beth El, the men of Beth El would have seen them when they came to aid Ai (verse 17). Therefore, *Malbim* concludes that the ambush party hid southwest of Ai. [See diagram.]

בְּתוֹךְ הָעָם — *Among the people.*

Joshua lodged in the middle of Israel's encampment that night in order to encourage the people to arise early in the morning to prepare for war *(Radak).*

10. וַיִּפְקֹד אֶת־הָעָם — *And inspected the people.*

The translation follows *Radak. Targum* renders: *'He* counted the people.' *Meam Loez* suggests that this count was needed to determine the number of remaining troops after those eligible for battle deferments had left the ranks. (Those individuals eligible for deferments are explained in *Deuteronomy* 20:5-8.)

וַיַּעַל הוּא — *He [and the elders] ascended.*

The people would be successful only if Joshua led them in battle *(Rashi),* for *Numbers* 27:17 states, [*Joshua*] *will go out* [*to war*] *before them, and he will return before them.* With Joshua in the lead, the troops were more courageous *(Abarbanel).*

11. וַיַּחֲנוּ מִצְּפוֹן לָעָי — *They encamped to the north of Ai.*

Since the city gate was on the northern part of Ai, Joshua stationed his men to the north of the city *(Malbim).* [See diagram.]

וְהַגַּי בֵּינָו וּבֵין הָעָי — *And the valley was between them and Ai.*

Since the warriors of Ai would need to cross the valley in their pursuit of the Israelites, the Jews would have additional time to carry out their ploy of feigning retreat while the ambush party stationed to the north unobtrusively moved behind the advancing warriors of Ai and attacked from the rear *(Meam Loez).* [This comment assumes that the five thousand troop division was truly an ambush party. Cf., however, *Commentary* to verse 12.]

12. אוֹרֵב — *To lie in ambush.*

This was a second ambush party which was closer to Ai than the first group *(Rashi). Malbim* explains that this ambush party was located northwest of Ai and could be seen by the people there, whereas the first party, which was located in the southwest,

ח °לָעַי ק׳ יג מִיָּם °לעִיר: וַיָּשִׂימוּ הָעָם אֶת־כָּל־
יג־טז הַמַּחֲנֶה אֲשֶׁר מִצְּפוֹן לָעִיר וְאֶת־עֲקֵבוֹ
מִיָּם לָעִיר וַיֵּלֶךְ יְהוֹשֻׁעַ בַּלַּיְלָה הַהוּא
יד בְּתוֹךְ הָעֵמֶק: וַיְהִי כִּרְאוֹת מֶלֶךְ־הָעַי
וַיְמַהֲרוּ וַיַּשְׁכִּימוּ וַיֵּצְאוּ אַנְשֵׁי־הָעִיר
לִקְרַאת־יִשְׂרָאֵל לַמִּלְחָמָה הוּא וְכָל־עַמּוֹ
לַמּוֹעֵד לִפְנֵי הָעֲרָבָה וְהוּא לֹא יָדַע כִּי־
טו אֹרֵב לוֹ מֵאַחֲרֵי הָעִיר: וַיִּנָּגְעוּ יְהוֹשֻׁעַ
וְכָל־יִשְׂרָאֵל לִפְנֵיהֶם וַיָּנֻסוּ דֶּרֶךְ
°בָּעַי ק׳ טז הַמִּדְבָּר: וַיִּזָּעֲקוּ כָּל־הָעָם אֲשֶׁר °בעִיר
לִרְדֹּף אַחֲרֵיהֶם וַיִּרְדְּפוּ אַחֲרֵי יְהוֹשֻׁעַ

could not be seen. [See diagram.] He further comments that the brigade mentioned in this verse was not truly an ambush party since it was visible to the inhabitants of Ai. Rather, it was a second flank which would serve to surround the enemy from two sides. It is for this reason that Scripture later (verse 13) calls this brigade עֲקֵבוֹ, literally *its heel,* to denote that it was a subordinate flank to Joshua's main brigade.

Other commentators offer different reasons for this smaller contingent. According to *Abarbanel,* it served as an early warning system to alert the larger camp when the warriors of Ai left their city. *Kli Yakar* suggests that this division was to ambush the warriors of Ai from the rear when they charged after the thirty-thousand troop division. *Meam Loez* advances that this division was to serve as a visible ambush party to deceive the inhabitants of Ai into thinking that this was the only deception the Israelites were employing when, in fact, another ambush party lay in wait behind the city.

13. וַיָּשִׂימוּ הָעָם — *The people readied* [lit. *put*].

They *readied* themselves for war by approaching the city wall *(Radak).*

The people readied themselves without Joshua's prompting. Scripture recounts this event in order to praise their courage *(Abarbanel).*

וְאֶת־עֲקֵבוֹ — *And the ambush party.*

Translation follows *Targum. Rashi* notes that the root עָקֵב (lit. *heel)* can also mean deception as in *Genesis* 27:36.

וַיֵּלֶךְ יְהוֹשֻׁעַ — *Joshua went.*

Joshua and the elders went before the rest of the people and traveled into the most dangerous area — the valley — in order to reassure the Israelites that another tragedy similar to the first battle of Ai would not recur *(Ralbag).*

בְּתוֹךְ הָעֵמֶק — *Into the valley.*

Joshua traveled through the valley to make sure that the camp guards were awake, because he feared that the camp could be attacked on a moment's notice *(Radak).*

According to the *Talmud (Megillah* 3a), Joshua spent the entire night immersed in the study of Torah [see *Commentary* to 5:13]. *Into the valley,* [הָעֵמֶק] is interpreted figuratively as the profundity [עָמְקוֹ] of the law, *halachah.*

14. לִקְרַאת־יִשְׂרָאֵל לַמִּלְחָמָה — *To oppose Israel in war.*

The men of Ai did not wait until Israel approached the city's gates.

to the west of Ai. 13 *The people readied the entire*
camp which was to the north of the city and the
ambush party to the west. That night Joshua went
into the valley.

14 *It was when the king of Ai saw, the men of Ai*
hastened, rose early, and went out to oppose Israel in
war — he and all his people — at the appointed time
before the plain. He did not know that an ambush
party awaited him behind the city. 15 *Joshua and all*
Israel were beaten before them, and they fled toward
the grazing lands. 16 *They assembled all the people*
who remained in the city to pursue them. They
chased Joshua and were drawn from the city. 17 *No*

Instead, Ai's soldiers advanced to attack the Israelites in the valley, for they had been successful in defeating the Jews there in their first encounter *(Malbim).*

הוּא — *He.*

When the king of Ai saw that Joshua had gone out to battle to direct his men in war, he decided to accompany the soldiers of Ai *(Meam Loez).*

In addition, the king of Ai saw that Joshua was in a very vulnerable position in the valley so he became very eager to engage him in battle *(Meam Loez).*

לַמּוֹעֵד — *At the appointed time.*

Rashi renders: at the time which they [i.e., their soothsayers] had determined would be auspicious the previous day. *Radak,* however, based on the *Targum,* interprets: at the time the king commanded.

לִפְנֵי הָעֲרָבָה — *Before the plain.*

Because Israel's visible forces were stationed to the north and northwest of the city, the men of Ai proceeded to the plain in the east so that they would not be surrounded on two sides *(Malbim).* [See diagram.]

וְהוּא לֹא יָדַע כִּי־אוֹרֵב לוֹ מֵאַחֲרֵי הָעִיר — *He did not know that an ambush party awaited him behind the city.*

The men of Ai detected the ambush party to the north of the city and compensated by stationing themselves to the east of the city, but they did not realize that there was a second ambush party behind the city *(Malbim).*

Even though the king of Ai was a proficient soothsayer, he was not able to determine that the Israelites were lying in ambush because God had prevented him from obtaining that knowledge so that the Israelites would be victorious *(Meam Loez).*

15. וַיִּנָּגְעוּ — *Were beaten.*

Targum renders: were broken. *Rashi* adds that by retreating, the Israelites *gave the appearance* that they were beaten.

הַמִּדְבָּר — *The grazing lands.*

Radak renders: a place where animals graze.

Israel retreated to the grazing lands of Beis Aven, mentioned in 18:12. Beis Aven was located between Jericho and Beth El, to the north of Ai *(Malbim).*

They fled to the grazing lands because it was unpopulated *(Meam Loez).*

16. וַיִּזָּעֲקוּ — *They assembled* [lit. *they screamed*].

They banded forces to chase after the Israelites. The term 'scream' is used

ח
יז־כב

יז וַיִּנָּתְקוּ מִן־הָעִיר׃ וְלֹא־נִשְׁאַר אִישׁ בָּעַי
וּבֵית אֵל אֲשֶׁר לֹא־יָצְאוּ אַחֲרֵי יִשְׂרָאֵל
וַיַּעַזְבוּ אֶת־הָעִיר פְּתוּחָה וַיִּרְדְּפוּ אַחֲרֵי
יח יִשְׂרָאֵל׃ וַיֹּאמֶר יהוה אֶל־יְהוֹשֻׁעַ
נְטֵה בַּכִּידוֹן אֲשֶׁר־בְּיָדְךָ אֶל־הָעַי כִּי בְיָדְךָ
אֶתְּנֶנָּה וַיֵּט יְהוֹשֻׁעַ בַּכִּידוֹן אֲשֶׁר־בְּיָדוֹ
יט אֶל־הָעִיר׃ וְהָאוֹרֵב קָם מְהֵרָה מִמְּקוֹמוֹ
וַיָּרוּצוּ כִּנְטוֹת יָדוֹ וַיָּבֹאוּ הָעִיר וַיִּלְכְּדוּהָ
כ וַיְמַהֲרוּ וַיַּצִּיתוּ אֶת־הָעִיר בָּאֵשׁ׃ וַיִּפְנוּ
אַנְשֵׁי הָעַי אַחֲרֵיהֶם וַיִּרְאוּ וְהִנֵּה עָלָה
עֲשַׁן הָעִיר הַשָּׁמַיְמָה וְלֹא־הָיָה בָהֶם
יָדַיִם לָנוּס הֵנָּה וָהֵנָּה וְהָעָם הַנָּס הַמִּדְבָּר
כא נֶהְפַּךְ אֶל־הָרוֹדֵף׃ וִיהוֹשֻׁעַ וְכָל־יִשְׂרָאֵל
רָאוּ כִּי־לָכַד הָאֹרֵב אֶת־הָעִיר וְכִי עָלָה
עֲשַׁן הָעִיר וַיָּשֻׁבוּ וַיַּכּוּ אֶת־אַנְשֵׁי הָעָי׃
כב וְאֵלֶּה יָצְאוּ מִן־הָעִיר לִקְרָאתָם וַיִּהְיוּ
לְיִשְׂרָאֵל בַּתָּוֶךְ אֵלֶּה מִזֶּה וְאֵלֶּה מִזֶּה

because a [war] cry served as the signal when to muster their troops *(Radak).* Their war cry was heard as far as Beis Aven *(Meam Loez).*

Malbim comments that even the guards who were left behind to guard the city left to chase the Israelites.

18. נְטֵה בַּכִּידוֹן — *Extend the spear.*

This was a signal that the ambush party behind the city should attack *(Malbim).*

HaRav Gifter comments that it is not reasonable to assume that the ambush party on the other side of Ai was able to see the extension of Joshua's spear. He explains the efficacy of Joshua's act according to the principle laid down by *Ramban (Genesis* 12:6): when a Heavenly decree is given symbolic expression it cannot be revoked. For example, Jeremiah commanded his disciple Baruch, *'And it will be, when you have finished reading this book that you shall tie a a stone to it and throw it into the Euphrates and you shall say, "Thus shall Babylon sink"' (Jeremiah* 51:63-4). By extending his spear, Joshua performed a symbolic act of victory which assured Israel's success.

בַּכִּידוֹן — *Spear.*

The translation follows *Targum.*

◆§ Joshua Leads the Israelites to Victory

19. וְהָאוֹרֵב ... וַיָּרוּצוּ — *The ambush party ... they ran.*

Although the beginning of the verse is in the *singular* [קָם ... מִמְּקוֹמוֹ, lit. *he* stood ... in *his* place] the verse continues in the plural *They* ran ... *they* arrived ... *they* hastened, *they* set afire.

man remained in Ai and Beth El who did not go out
after Israel; they left the city open and pursued Israel.
18 *And HASHEM said to Joshua, 'Extend the spear in*
your hand toward Ai, for in your hand will I give it.'
And Joshua extended the spear in his hand toward
the city. 19 *The ambush party quickly rose from its*
place, and they ran when he stretched out his hand
and arrived at the city and conquered it. They
hastened and set the city afire. 20 *The men of Ai*
looked behind them and saw and behold, smoke of
the city ascended toward heaven, and they did not
have the strength to flee this way or that way. The
people who had retreated to the grazing lands turned
back upon the pursuer.
21 *And Joshua and all Israel saw that the ambush*
party had taken the city and that the smoke of the
city ascended. They returned and slew the men of Ai.
22 *And these left the city to oppose them, and it was*
that they were in the midst of Israel, some on this side

Abarbanel comments that by so doing, Scripture intends to communicate by the first half of the verse that each ambush party left its respective place. The second half of the verse indicates that they jointly acted to burn the city.

וַיַּצִּיתוּ אֶת־הָעִיר בָּאֵשׁ — *And* [they] *set the city afire.*

Joshua decreed that the city should be burned to remind the Israelites of their ignominious defeat because they had sinned and of their glorious victory immediately after they repented, thus underscoring the importance of faithful observance of the Torah (*Abarbanel* to verse 26).

See *Commentary* to verse 28.

20. יָדַיִם — *Strength* [lit. *hands*].

The translation follows *Targum. Radak* renders: room or space.

When Joshua extended his spear, his contingent stopped retreating, turned, and faced the enemy. The men of Ai were astonished to see smoke rising from their city and froze. When Joshua estimated that enough time had elapsed for the ambush party to leave Ai and join in battle, he led the Israelites in combat against the men of Ai *(Malbim).*

וְהָעָם הַנָּס — *The people who had retreated.*

This refers to Joshua's troops who had retreated to the grazing lands *(Rashi; Radak).*

22. וְאֵלֶּה יָצְאוּ מִן־הָעִיר — *And these left the city.*

These refers to the ambush party which had just set Ai on fire *(Rashi).*

וַיִּהְיוּ לְיִשְׂרָאֵל בַּתָּוֶךְ — *And it was that they were in the midst of Israel.*

The Israelites surrounded the enemy on four sides: Joshua's contingent was stationed to the north and his ambush party to the west; the ambush party which was leaving Ai attacked from the

ח
כג־כט

וַיַּכּוּ אוֹתָם עַד־בִּלְתִּי הִשְׁאִיר־לוֹ שָׂרִיד
כג וּפָלִיט׃ וְאֶת־מֶלֶךְ הָעַי תָּפְשׂוּ חָי וַיַּקְרִבוּ
כד אֹתוֹ אֶל־יְהוֹשֻׁעַ׃ וַיְהִי כְּכַלּוֹת יִשְׂרָאֵל
לַהֲרֹג אֶת־כָּל־יֹשְׁבֵי הָעַי בַּשָּׂדֶה בַּמִּדְבָּר
אֲשֶׁר רְדָפוּם בּוֹ וַיִּפְּלוּ כֻלָּם לְפִי־חֶרֶב
עַד־תֻּמָּם וַיָּשֻׁבוּ כָל־יִשְׂרָאֵל
כה הָעַי וַיַּכּוּ אֹתָהּ לְפִי־חָרֶב׃ וַיְהִי כָל־
הַנֹּפְלִים בַּיּוֹם הַהוּא מֵאִישׁ וְעַד־אִשָּׁה
כו שְׁנֵים עָשָׂר אָלֶף כֹּל אַנְשֵׁי הָעָי׃ וִיהוֹשֻׁעַ
לֹא־הֵשִׁיב יָדוֹ אֲשֶׁר נָטָה בַּכִּידוֹן עַד
כז אֲשֶׁר הֶחֱרִים אֵת כָּל־יֹשְׁבֵי הָעָי׃ רַק
הַבְּהֵמָה וּשְׁלַל הָעִיר הַהִיא בָּזְזוּ לָהֶם
יִשְׂרָאֵל כִּדְבַר יהוה אֲשֶׁר צִוָּה אֶת־
כח יְהוֹשֻׁעַ׃ וַיִּשְׂרֹף יְהוֹשֻׁעַ אֶת־הָעָי וַיְשִׂימֶהָ
כט תֵּל־עוֹלָם שְׁמָמָה עַד הַיּוֹם הַזֶּה׃ וְאֶת־
מֶלֶךְ הָעַי תָּלָה עַל־הָעֵץ עַד־עֵת הָעָרֶב
וּכְבוֹא הַשֶּׁמֶשׁ צִוָּה יְהוֹשֻׁעַ וַיּוֹרִידוּ אֶת־
נִבְלָתוֹ מִן־הָעֵץ וַיַּשְׁלִיכוּ אוֹתָהּ אֶל־פֶּתַח

south, and to the east stood Jericho, which was already under Israel's control *(Malbim).*

שָׂרִיד וּפָלִיט — [*No one who*] *remained or escaped.*

The translation follows *Targum.*

23. תָּפְשׂוּ חָי — *They captured* [*the king*] *alive.*

Typically, the king was the fiercest and most relentless of all combatants, so it was truly a miracle that the king of Ai was captured alive *(Meam Loez).*

24. וַיָּשֻׁבוּ — [*They*] *returned.*

According to the Mesorah (traditional reading of the text) this is an 'interrupted verse.' See Commentary to 4:1, s.v., 'HASHEM said.'

וַיַּכּוּ אֹתָהּ — *And (they) slaughtered it.*

They returned to slay the women and children *(Metzudos)* who were not consumed by the fire *(Abarbanel).*

26. לֹא־הֵשִׁיב יָדוֹ — [*Joshua*] *did not retract his hand.*

Joshua's extension of the spear during the entire battle is reminiscent of Moses' raising his hand during the battle against Amalek described in *Exodus* 17:12 *(Daas Sofrim).*

The *Talmud (Rosh HaShanah* 29a) cites *Exodus* 17:12 and explains that Moses' hands were certainly not the source of the Jews' victory. Scripture is not attributing any supernatural power to Moses' hands. Rather, Moses pointed his hands heavenward as a symbolic reminder that the Israelites should look to God for deliverance, for the Jews would only be victorious as long as they consecrated their hearts to their Father

8
23-29

and some on that. They slew them until no one who
remained or escaped was left to him. 23 *They captured*
the king of Ai alive and brought him to Joshua.
24 *When Israel finished slaying all the inhabitants of*
Ai in the field — in the grazing land where they
pursued them — and they had all fallen by the edge of
the sword until their annihilation.

All the Israelites returned to Ai and slaughtered it by the edge of the sword.

25 *All that fell that day including men and women*
totaled twelve thousand — all the people of Ai.
26 *Joshua did not retract his hand which he had*
extended with the spear until he had destroyed all the
inhabitants of Ai. 27 *Only the animals and booty of*
that city Israel took as spoils, according to the word
of HASHEM which He had commanded to Joshua.
28 *Joshua burned Ai and made it a mound forever, a*
wasteland until this day. 29 *He hanged the king of Ai*
on a gallows until evening. When the sun went
down, Joshua issued an order, and they lowered his
dead body from the gallows and threw it at the

in heaven.

Abarbanel, however, interprets this expression figuratively to mean that Joshua personally participated in all the battling.

27. בָּזְזוּ לָהֶם יִשְׂרָאֵל — *Israel took as spoils.*

Joshua did not ban the booty of Ai as he did with Jericho so that another episode similar to that with Achan would not reoccur *(Abarbanel).* [Cf. *Abarbanel* cited in *Commentary* to 6:17.]

כִּדְבַר ה׳ — *According to the word of HASHEM.*

Israel only took from the spoils of Ai in order to fulfill the command of God, not out of any motivations of aggrandizement *(Meam Loez).*

28. וַיִּשְׂרֹף ... וַיְשִׂימֶהָ — [*Joshua*] *burned ... made it.*

Joshua burned Ai so that people could not say that this was the place where Israel had faltered when Achan sinned *(Poras Yosef).*

In verse 19, Scripture records that the ambush party set fire to Ai, not Joshua, as this verse mentions. *Meam Loez* suggests that the ambush party started the fires, but the whole city did not burn. Joshua completed the destruction and Scripture attributes the entire act to him because he completed the mitzvah [see *Commentary* to 24:32].

29. עַל־הָעֵץ — *On a gallows* [lit. *tree*].

The translation follows *Targum* (see *Sanhedrin* 46a).

וַיּוֹרִידוּ אֶת־נִבְלָתוֹ — *And they lowered his dead body.*

They lowered his body in accordance with the Biblical injunction, *his body shall not remain all night upon the tree*

שַׁעַר הָעִיר וַיָּקִימוּ עָלָיו גַּל־אֲבָנִים גָּדוֹל
עַד הַיּוֹם הַזֶּה׃
ל אָז יִבְנֶה יְהוֹשֻׁעַ מִזְבֵּחַ לַיהוָה אֱלֹהֵי
לא יִשְׂרָאֵל בְּהַר עֵיבָל׃ כַּאֲשֶׁר צִוָּה מֹשֶׁה

(*Deuteronomy* 21:23), which applies to both Jewish and Gentile corpses[1] (*Radak*).

וַיָּקִימוּ עָלָיו גַּל־אֲבָנִים גָּדוֹל — *And piled a great heap of stones on it.*

He did this in order to publicize his victory so that the other Canaanite kings would be afraid to wage war against Israel (*Ralbag*).

◆§ The Altar on Mount Eval

30-35. In the *Prefatory Remarks* to Chapter 4, two views were expressed concerning the exact chronological sequence of the events described in the next six verses. *Rashi* (4:3 and 8:30) contends that the building of the altar on Mount Eval did not occur immediately after the victory at Ai, but rather took place earlier on the same day that the Jews crossed the Jordan,[2] the tenth of Nissan. *Lev Aharon* explains that this passage was not recounted in its true chronological sequence because Scripture wished to relate the events according to *where* they occurred not *when* they occurred. By so doing

1. *Rashi (Deuteronomy* 21:23) explains the reason for the prohibition of allowing one who was executed to remain on the gallows for the entire evening: 'It is a degradation of the King, for man is made in His image and the Israelites are His children. It may be compared to identical twins: one became the king, the other a robber who was executed by hanging. A person passing the gallows would think that it was the king who was hanged.' Thus, it would appear that *Rashi* is of the opinion that this prohibition applies only to Jews who were executed, since it was Adam and Jacob who 'resembled' God, and the Jews were their descendants (*Maharsha, Sanhedrin* 46a).

Ramban (ibid.), however, contends that this prohibition also applies to non-Jews who are executed and substantiates his view from the fact that Joshua was careful to bury the Canaanite kings the day they were executed (see Chapter 10).

Maharsha (ibid.) explains *Rashi's* view by noting that the verse in *Deuteronomy* actually gives two reasons why the executed victim must be buried before the next day: (a) *for he that is hanged is a degradation to God;* and (b) *that the land not be defiled. Maharsha* argues that while a Gentile, according to *Rashi's* view, does not 'resemble' God, and therefore would not fall under the purview of this prohibition, his body, however, still causes a defilement in the Land (see *Chavos Yair* 139). Thus, Joshua ordered that the body of the king of Ai be lowered from the gallows in order to prevent defilement of the land as *Radak* explains in his comment to 10:27.

Meshech Chachmah (Deuteronomy 21:23) notes that there would be a difference in *halachah* between the views of *Rashi* and *Ramban* in a case where a Gentile was hanged outside the Land of Israel. According to *Rashi's* view, the body would not have to be lowered before morning since there is no concern of defiling the Land outside of *Eretz Yisrael*, but according to *Ramban*, the body would have to be lowered since both the Jew and Gentile 'resemble' God: the hanging body would be a degradation to the Creator.

2. The directive to erect the stone monument on Mount Eval anticipated a grim era in Jewish history. *Deuteronomy* 27:4 states: *And it shall be when you have crossed the Jordan that you shall set up these stones ... on Mount Eval.* It is puzzling that the Torah commands the Jews to travel the great distance to Shechem (the location of Mount Eval) to erect the stone monument instead of allowing them to erect it in Gilgal where they crossed. Furthermore, why did the Torah decree that the monument be placed on Mount Eval, the mountain where the curses were uttered (*Deuteronomy* 27:13), and not on Mount Gerizim where the blessings were recited?

Niflaos M'Toras HaShem explains that the monument was erected and the curses uttered on

8
30-31

entrance to the gates of the city and piled a great heap of stones on it until this day.

30 *Then Joshua built an altar to HASHEM the God of Israel on Mount Eval,* 31 *as Moses, the servant of*

Scripture makes clear that these mountains were not located near the Jordan, but rather near Ai *(Meam Loez).*

Haamek Davar and *Malbim,* however, disagree; they assert that the Jews made two stone memorials, one in Gilgal (as recorded in Chapter 4) and one at Mount Eval (recorded here) after the battle of Ai. *Abarbanel* explains that after the victory of Ai and the rectification of the sin of Achan, Joshua requested that the curses be recited on Mount Eval to remind the nation of the severity of relaxing their Torah observance.

30. אָז יִבְנֶה יְהוֹשֻׁעַ – *Then Joshua built* [lit. *will build*].

Only a prophet can authorize the construction of an altar. After this altar was erected, it became permissible to build altars outside the Tabernacle until the Sanctuary was established at Shiloh and the tribes occupied their territories *(Radak).* [Then such construction was forbidden.]

[See *Commentary* to 10:12 for an explanation of the difficulty posed by the then-future (אָז יִבְנֶה) constructions. The commentators suggest several possible reasons for this problematic usage. According to *Ibn Ezra,* the Hebrew language often uses verbs in the future tense to refer to past events. Thus, although יִבְנֶה literally means 'will build,' in this instance, it means 'had built.'

Rashi (Exodus 15:1), however, is of the view that the י prefix of verbs following the word אָז, *then,* connotes *intention.* In this case, an apt rendering would be: אָז, *Then* after conquering the city of Ai, יִבְנֶה, Joshua *decided to build* the altar.

Perhaps the two views regarding the chronological sequence of this passage (see *Prefatory Remarks* to Chapter 4) are dependent upon the two exegeses of the אָז יִבְנֶה construction. According to *Ibn Ezra's* view that the Hebrew language sometimes uses the future tense for past events, this passage does not necessarily refer to events which took place after those of the previous passage, concerning the battle of Ai. Thus the building of the altar could have taken place immediately after the crossing of the Jordan. However, it could be argued that according to *Rashi's* view in *Exodus,* this passage chronologically follows the previous passage, for Joshua thought to build this altar *after* the victory over Ai. (According to this explanation, however, *Rashi's* comment to this verse which explains that this passage is indeed not in chronological sequence is inconsistent with the application we have made of *Rashi's* comment to *Exodus* 15:1 and is thus an issue which requires further elucidation.) Here this verse has been rendered in the past tense, in accordance with *Ibn Ezra* and *Rashi's* comments.]

בְּהַר עֵיבָל – *On Mount Eval.*

The Sages disagree as to the location

Mount Eval as a warning in anticipation of a future event which forever scarred the Jewish nation. Shechem was in the territory of Ephraim, which bordered the Ten Tribes to the north and Judah and Benjamin to the south. It was in Shechem that the Ten Tribes later seceded through the influence of Yeravam ben Nevat *(I Kings* 12:17). Yeravam added two likenesses of golden calves in his temples at Beth El and Dan *(I Kings* 12:29), an act which led to the eventual dispersion of the Ten Tribes. It was precisely on Mount Eval – which is north of Shechem and hence in the boundary of the Ten Tribes – that the oath forbidding the construction of graven images was made: *Cursed be the man who makes any carved or molten idol (Deuteronomy* 27:16). Thus, the Torah anticipated Yeravam's sin and attempted to prevent it by decreeing that the stone monument upon which this curse was etched be erected on Mount Eval. Because the Ten Tribes disregarded this curse, however, their secession at Shechem led to their dispersion and eventual extinction.

עֶבֶד־יהוה אֶת־בְּנֵי יִשְׂרָאֵל כַּכָּתוּב
בְּסֵפֶר תּוֹרַת מֹשֶׁה מִזְבַּח אֲבָנִים שְׁלֵמוֹת
אֲשֶׁר לֹא־הֵנִיף עֲלֵיהֶן בַּרְזֶל וַיַּעֲלוּ עָלָיו
לב עֹלוֹת לַיהוה וַיִּזְבְּחוּ שְׁלָמִים׃ וַיִּכְתָּב־שָׁם
עַל־הָאֲבָנִים אֵת מִשְׁנֵה תּוֹרַת מֹשֶׁה
לג אֲשֶׁר כָּתַב לִפְנֵי בְּנֵי יִשְׂרָאֵל׃ וְכָל־
יִשְׂרָאֵל וּזְקֵנָיו וְשֹׁטְרִים ׀ וְשֹׁפְטָיו עֹמְדִים
מִזֶּה ׀ וּמִזֶּה ׀ לָאָרוֹן נֶגֶד הַכֹּהֲנִים הַלְוִיִּם
נֹשְׂאֵי ׀ אֲרוֹן בְּרִית־יהוה כַּגֵּר כָּאֶזְרָח
חֶצְיוֹ אֶל־מוּל הַר־גְּרִזִים וְהַחֶצְיוֹ אֶל־

of Mount Eval and Mount Gerizim. Some say that they were located in the region of the Cuthites [between Upper Beis Choron and Shechem and slightly east *(T'vuos HaAretz)*], and some say they were located near Gilgal and were not truly mountains, but were hills manufactured for this occasion *(Tosafos, Sotah* 33b). [Note that this second opinion is expressed in the *Jerusalem* Talmud, not the *Babylonian.* The view mentioned in the *Prefatory Remarks* to 8:30 does not follow this second opinion.]

31. אֲבָנִים שְׁלֵמוֹת אֲשֶׁר לֹא־הֵנִיף עֲלֵיהֶן בַּרְזֶל — *An altar of whole stones upon which no [man] has lifted up iron.*

[This requirement for the altar stones is stated in *Exodus* 20:22.]

According to *Ibn Ezra (Exodus* 20:22), the Torah forbade the use of broken stones in building the altar so that the unused fragments could not be used for the altars of idolatry. He also suggests that it would not have been proper to have part of the stone used for holy purposes and the remainder discarded. *Rambam (Moreh Nevuchim* 3:45) contends that the Torah banned the use of iron instruments as a safeguard to prevent images from being etched into the altar stones, which was the prevalent custom of idol worshipers.

Ramban (Exodus 20:2) argues that the prohibition of iron instruments coming in contact with the altar stones is characteristic of a more general prohibition of the use of iron anywhere in the Tabernacle or Temple. Although iron would have provided a stronger base foundation for the Tabernacle, the Torah only permitted copper to be used, because iron is a metal typically used for destructive purposes [and would thus be inappropriate in an edifice designed to promote peace and atonement].

וַיַּעֲלוּ עָלָיו עֹלוֹת לַה׳ וַיִּזְבְּחוּ שְׁלָמִים — *And they sacrificed burnt offerings to HASHEM, and they offered peace offerings.*

Just as the Jews offered sacrifices on Mount Sinai in order to seal the covenant they were making with the Almighty *(Exodus* 24:5), so did they offer sacrifices on Mount Eval. *Haamek Davar (Deuteronomy* 27:5) explains that on Mount Eval the Jews reaffirmed as a community that which Abraham had affirmed as an individual — to eschew idol worship and believe only in God.

32. אֵת מִשְׁנֵה תּוֹרַת מֹשֶׁה — *A repetition of the Torah of Moses.*

There is a difference of opinion among the commentators concerning the explanation of this phrase:

HASHEM, commanded the Children of Israel, as it is written in the Book of the Torah of Moses — an altar of whole stones upon which no [man] has lifted up iron. And they sacrificed burnt offerings to HASHEM, and they offered peace offerings. 32 *He inscribed on the stones a repetition of the Torah of Moses, which he wrote before the Children of Israel.*
33 *And all Israel and their elders, officers and their judges stood on both sides of the Ark opposite the Kohanim — Levites, bearers of the Ark of the Covenant of HASHEM, the convert like the natural born Jew, half of them on the slope of Mount Gerizim and half of them on the slope of Mount Eval,*

□ *R' Saadiah Gaon* maintains that only a summary of each of the 613 commandments of the Torah was written on the stones. *Radak* commends this interpretation, emphasizing that it would be unreasonable to assume that the entire Pentateuch was inscribed.

□ *Ramban (Deuteronomy* 27:3) argues that the Israelites were required to inscribe every verse of the Pentateuch on these stones (even including the crownlets on top of the letters, as in a Torah scroll). He suggests that either the stones were very large or that a miracle provided enough space for all the writing.

□ *Metzudos* suggests that only the *Book of Deuteronomy* was written, for this book is often referred to as מִשְׁנֵה תּוֹרָה, the repetition of the Torah.

תּוֹרַת מֹשֶׁה — *Torah of Moses.*

Normally, this expression denotes both the Written and Oral Torah which Moses received. Therefore, the verse continues *'which he wrote'* to indicate that this verse refers only to the Written Torah *(Haamek Davar, Deuteronomy* 24:16, note).

◆§ The Blessings and the Curses

33. מוּל — *Opposite.*

They were situated on the slope of the mountain *(Radak).*

כָּאֶזְרָח — *Natural born Jew* [lit. *citizen*].

This expression refers to a Jew who was born to a Jewish mother [as opposed to a proselyte] *(Metzudos).*

חֶצְיוֹ — *Half of them.*

Six tribes ascended Mount Gerizim (Simeon, Levi, Judah, Yisachar, Joseph and Benjamin) and six tribes ascended Mount Eval (Reuben, Gad, Asher, Zevulun, Dan and Naftoli). The older Kohanim and Levites gathered around the Ark, which was situated between the two mountains. The Kohanim were close to the Ark, the Levites surrounded them, and the Israelites stood on the mountains on both sides.

The Levites first turned their heads towards Mount Gerizim and recited the blessing, 'Blessed is the man who does not make a graven image.'

And all twelve tribes responded, 'Amen.'

Then the Levites turned their heads to Mount Eval and recited, *'Cursed is the man who makes a graven image ...'*

Then all twelve tribes responded, *'Amen.'*

They continued in this manner until they recited all the curses in *Deuteron-*

ח
לד־לה

מוּל הַר־עֵיבָל כַּאֲשֶׁר צִוָּה מֹשֶׁה עֶבֶד־
יהוה לְבָרֵךְ אֶת־הָעָם יִשְׂרָאֵל בָּרִאשֹׁנָה׃
לד וְאַחֲרֵי־כֵן קָרָא אֶת־כָּל־דִּבְרֵי הַתּוֹרָה
הַבְּרָכָה וְהַקְּלָלָה כְּכָל־הַכָּתוּב בְּסֵפֶר
לה הַתּוֹרָה׃ לֹא־הָיָה דָבָר מִכֹּל אֲשֶׁר־צִוָּה
מֹשֶׁה אֲשֶׁר לֹא־קָרָא יְהוֹשֻׁעַ נֶגֶד כָּל־
ט קְהַל יִשְׂרָאֵל וְהַנָּשִׁים וְהַטַּף וְהַגֵּר
א א הַהֹלֵךְ בְּקִרְבָּם׃ וַיְהִי

omy 27:15*ff*, first stating the curse in the form of a blessing and then reciting the curse *(Radak)*.[1]

The *Talmud (Sotah* 37a) explains how the Levites could be located both on Mount Gerizim and in the valley. According to R' Eliezer ben Yaakov, the older Levites and Kohanim were in the valley and the others were on Mount Gerizim. According to R' Oshiah, the Levites who were of the age to perform the service in the Tabernacle were in the valley and the others were on Mount Gerizim. According to Rebi, the word עַל does not mean 'on' in this instance, but rather 'near.' Thus all the Levites were in the valley, some near the Ark and some near Mount Gerizim.

מוּל — *On the slope of* [lit. *opposite*].

The translation follows *Radak*.

כַּאֲשֶׁר צִוָּה — *As* [Moses] *had commanded.*

Moses had commanded them to recite the blessings before the curses *(Sotah* 32a; *Rashi)*.

בָּרִאשֹׁנָה — *First.*

[*First* the blessings should be recited, then the curses.]

34. קָרָא — *He read.*

Joshua read these passages, as the following verse explains *(Metzudos)*.

אֶת־כָּל־דִּבְרֵי הַתּוֹרָה — *All the words of the Torah.*

This refers to the blessings and curses previously mentioned or to the passages in *Deuteronomy* 28:1*ff* starting, *'And if you listen ...,'* and, *'If you do not listen ... ' (Radak).*

35. לֹא־הָיָה דָבָר — *There was not a word.*

The commentators differ in the interpretation of this expression. *Radak* suggests that upon completion of the

1. *Sforno (Deuteronomy* 27:15) explains the true significance of a curse. When the Jews crossed the Jordan, they became responsible for each other's transgressions, including sins committed in absolute secrecy (see *Prefatory Remarks* to Chapter 7). When the people answered, 'Amen' to the curses, they were in effect agreeing to banishment by the community if they were guilty of violating the commandments subsumed in these curses. Consequently, the evildoers would no longer be considered a part of the nation Israel, and the community would not incur punishments because of their actions. Thus, the curses absolved the righteous of their collective responsibility for the transgressors. Conversely, the blessings reaffirmed the ties between the righteous and the Jewish community.

Perhaps, it is for this reason that the passage dealing with the recitation of the blessings and curses is not written in its proper place, which, according to *Rashi* (see *Commentary* to verse 30), would have been in Chapter 4. From Achan's sin and its bitter consequences an entirely different understanding of the curses emerges. After Achan was removed from the community, Israel was no longer besmirched on his account and handily conquered Ai. What became clear through the sharp relief between the initial defeat and final victory against Ai was the importance of a guiltless community. Thus, the curses uttered on Mount Eval which segregated the evildoers from the community were in truth the greatest blessings to the Jewish people (see *Mussar HaNeviim).*

8
34-35 *as Moses the servant of HASHEM had commanded, to*
bless the people of Israel first. 34 *Afterwards, he read*
all the words of the Torah, the blessings and the curses, according to all that is written in the Book of the Torah.
35 *There was not a word of all that Moses commanded that Joshua did not read to the entire community of Israel — the women, the children, and the converts that traveled among them.*

recitation of the blessings and curses, Joshua read to the people every positive and negative commandment in the Torah. *Metzudos,* however, understands this expression to refer to the aforementioned blessings and curses: there was not one that Joshua omitted.

הַהֹלֵךְ — *That traveled.*

Scripture uses the expression *traveled* to connote that these Gentiles decided to travel with the Jews and convert to Judaism after hearing of the wonders which God wrought for the Jews *(Radak).*

IX

The Torah forbids waging war against another people without first giving the opposition the opportunity to capitulate. This prohibition applies even in a case where the Torah requires that the Jews wage war, as in the conquest of Eretz Yisrael (Rambam, Hil. Melachim 6:1).

Thus, the Talmud (Jerusalem Shivi'is *6:1) teaches that Joshua sent three written proclamations to the Seven Nations inhabiting* Eretz Yisrael *before the Israelites crossed the Jordan. Although the exact wording of these proclamations is not recorded, they undoubtedly reiterated a fact which was known to all — that it was Israel's destiny according to Divine sanction to take possession of the land which God had promised to their patriarch Abraham. The first proclamation, according to the* Talmud, *stated that any Canaanite who wished to be spared from the Torah's decree,* you shall not allow any [Canaanite] soul to live (Deuteronomy *20:16), should leave the Land of Israel. The second proclamation stated that any Canaanite who wished to remain unharmed in the Land must accept three conditions: (a) to abide by the seven Noachide laws, (b) to accept no jobs of leadership, and (c) to be willing to assist the king both through his labor and contributions* (Rambam, Hil. Melachim *6:10). These three conditions must be met in order for the Israelites to make a covenant of peace with their opposition. The third proclamation stated that non-compliance with the first two proclamations would bring a declaration of war against the Canaanites.*

In response, the Girgashites fled to Africa and the thirty-one Canaanite kings (listed in Chapter 12) decided to militarily confront the Israelites. The Gibeonites discussed in this chapter, however, reacted in a third manner. They attempted to conceal from the Jews that they were from the Hivvites (one of the Seven Nations) and disguised themselves as emissaries from a distant nation, claiming to have been inspired by all the miracles which God had wrought for the Jews in Egypt and requesting that a covenant of peace be established between them and the Israelites.

Since the Gibeonites could have capitulated at any time by agreeing to the three

ט כִשְׁמֹעַ כָּל־הַמְּלָכִים אֲשֶׁר בְּעֵבֶר הַיַּרְדֵּן
א בָּהָר וּבַשְּׁפֵלָה וּבְכֹל חוֹף הַיָּם הַגָּדוֹל
אֶל־מוּל הַלְּבָנוֹן הַחִתִּי וְהָאֱמֹרִי הַכְּנַעֲנִי

conditions for living in Eretz Yisrael, *why then did they choose to perpetrate a deception?*[1]

Rambam (ibid.) *explains that the Gibeonites did not realize that after they had rejected Joshua's initial proposals they could reverse their decision and capitulate.* Radak *(verse 7) suggests that the Gibeonites were fearful that the Israelites would not abide by their word and leave them unharmed, for they had thought that Jericho and Ai had capitulated but were vanquished nevertheless.* Ramban (Deuteronomy *20:11) speculates that the Gibeonites had not yet received Joshua's proclamations. (According to this view, Joshua did not send these proclamations before the Israelites crossed the Jordan, as the* Jerusalem Talmud *cited above states, but rather after. This view, however, has its source in* Midrash Rabbah [Shoftim 5:14]). *As a result, they had not known that Joshua would give them the opportunity to surrender conditionally and* were very afraid for [their] lives *(verse 24) and thus adopted this scheme.* Ramban (ibid.) *also advances that the Gibeonites had originally rejected Joshua's proposals, but then feared the consequences of their decision. Since they preferred becoming full-fledged Jews instead of accepting Joshua's second proposal and becoming servants, they pretended they were from a distant nation.*

When the Israelites discovered that the Gibeonites were indeed not from a distant nation, but one of the seven indigenous nations of Eretz Yisrael, *they exercised great restraint by not killing them (verse 16).* Ramban (Gittin *46a) asserts that had it not been for the oath*[2] *that the princes swore to allow the Gibeonites to live, the Israelites would have been justified in killing the Gibeonites because they had not met the criteria of Joshua's second proclamation. Instead of becoming servants they became of equal status with the Israelites. However, since they forswore idol worship, the Jews were not required to kill them. They were, however, permitted, since the Gibeonites duped them into making an oath and covenant (see also* Lechem Mishneh *to* Rambam ibid., *and* Ramban *to* Deuteronomy *20:11).*

According to Jewish law, an individual must meticulously abide by any oath which he has made; however, if it was made under mistaken assumptions it is not binding. Therefore, the oath made to the Gibeonites was not valid, since the Israelites would never have made an oath to them knowing that they descended from the Seven Nations. It is perplexing, then, that Scripture states that the Israelites refrained from killing the Gibeonites, because the leaders of the

1. According to *Rashi* and *Tosafos (Sotah* 35b), however, the Israelites were not required to provide an opportunity for the Canaanites to capitulate *after* they crossed the Jordan, and thus Joshua issued these three proclamations *before* the Israelites crossed (cf. *Kesef Mishnah* to *Rambam, ibid.* 6:5). According to this view, the Gibeonites, therefore, had no alternative to planning a deception after they had rejected Joshua's initial proposals and the Jews had crossed the Jordan.

2. According to *Rashi (Sotah* 35b), the Israelites' justification for killing the Gibeonites would have been the commandment of Canaanite extermination which, in his view, applies even if the Canaanites wished to convert to Judaism. *Rambam,* however, is of the opinion that the commandment of Canaanite extermination does not apply to those who wished to convert to Judaism. Thus, he argues that the Israelites' justification for wanting to kill the Gibeonites was the violation of making a covenant.

9
1 ¹ *When all the kings west of the Jordan heard — in*
the mountains and in the valleys and on the shore of
the Mediterranean opposite the Lebanon — the Hit-
tite, Emorite, Canaanite, Perizzite, Hivvite, and

congregation had sworn to them by HASHEM, God of Israel *(verse 18). According to R' Yehudah* (Gittin *46a), an oath taken in public is forever binding even if taken under mistaken assumptions. The Sages, however, disagree and hold that the oath is void* ab initio *since it was mistakenly taken. In their view the Israelites refrained from killing the Gibeonites to avoid desecration of God's name, for the non-Jews, not knowing that such an oath was invalid, might have thought that the Israelites do not honor their oaths.*

Joshua allowed the Gibeonites to remain among the Israelites, but relegated them to servitude as water drawers and wood choppers. By so doing, Joshua dealt with them most appropriately for the Gibeonites wanted to avoid the servitude required by Joshua's second proclamation and therefore deceived the Israelites. After their ruse was discovered, Joshua imposed the same restrictions upon them as they would have had had they capitulated (Ramban *to* Deuteronomy *20:11).*

1. **וַיְהִי כִשְׁמֹעַ כָּל־הַמְּלָכִים** — *When all the kings ... heard.*

The kings heard two things regarding the methodology of the Israelites: (a) that they did not offer to make peace before their battles against Jericho and Ai and (b) that they needed to employ military strategy in order to conquer Ai. The kings interpreted this as a sign that the Jews could not count on miraculous Divine aid [as they had received at Jericho], but must depend on their own military strength. Therefore, the Canaanites grouped their vast forces together in order to secure a military advantage by greatly outnumbering the Jews, since the Israelites were not willing to make peace *(Malbim).*

Ralbag contends that these kings formed an alliance so that each individual kingdom would not have to face the Israelites unassisted, as did the cities of Jericho and Ai.

Abarbanel, however, suggests that the kings heard that the Israelites had built an altar and inscribed the Torah upon it, which they interpreted as a marker of conquest of *Eretz Yisrael* (see *Prefatory Remarks* to Chapter 4). They, therefore, formed an alliance to ward off the invasion.

Even though the confederacy of all these kings is described *before* the Gibeonites' ruse, *Radak* asserts that this confederacy *was a result* of the Gibeonites' deception and, thus it is described in detail following this episode [in Chapter 10]. [Unlike the other commentators who identify some previously mentioned event which these kings *heard, Radak* is of the opinion that they *heard* the account which Scripture is about to describe.]

בְּעֵבֶר הַיַּרְדֵּן בָּהָר וּבַשְּׁפֵלָה — *West of* [lit. *across*] *the Jordan ... in the mountains and in the valleys ...*

Meam Loez suggests that these geographical areas were mentioned because they were the sites of the events about which the kings had heard. *West of the Jordan* refers to the splitting of the Jordan when the Israelites crossed. *In the mountains* refers to the victory at Ai which was located in the mountains. *In the valleys* refers to the conquest of Jericho which was located in the valley.

הַחִתִּי וְהָאֱמֹרִי — *The Hittite, Emorite ...*

The Girgashites, who were one of the seven indigenous Canaanite nations, are not mentioned in this enumeration because they fled from the Land when they heard that the Israelites were approaching *(Jerusalem Talmud, Sheviis* 6:1).

ב הַפְּרִזִּי הַחִוִּי וְהַיְבוּסִי: וַיִּתְקַבְּצוּ יַחְדָּו
לְהִלָּחֵם עִם־יְהוֹשֻׁעַ וְעִם־יִשְׂרָאֵל פֶּה
ג אֶחָד: וְיֹשְׁבֵי גִבְעוֹן שָׁמְעוּ אֵת
ד אֲשֶׁר עָשָׂה יְהוֹשֻׁעַ לִירִיחוֹ וְלָעָי: וַיַּעֲשׂוּ
גַם־הֵמָּה בְעָרְמָה וַיֵּלְכוּ וַיִּצְטַיָּרוּ וַיִּקְחוּ
שַׂקִּים בָּלִים לַחֲמוֹרֵיהֶם וְנֹאדוֹת יַיִן
ה בָּלִים וּמְבֻקָּעִים וּמְצֹרָרִים: וּנְעָלוֹת בָּלוֹת
וּמְטֻלָּאוֹת בְּרַגְלֵיהֶם וּשְׂלָמוֹת בָּלוֹת
עֲלֵיהֶם וְכֹל לֶחֶם צֵידָם יָבֵשׁ הָיָה נִקֻּדִים:

2. וַיִּתְקַבְּצוּ יַחְדָּו — *They gathered together.*

[Unlike *Malbim* cited in *Commentary* to verse 1,] *Lev Aharon* contends that the kings' assembly was merely to decide an appropriate response to the Israelites' invasion, not to join forces and fight together. Scripture recounts further on that they ultimately decided to band together against the Israelites.

פֶּה אֶחָד — *With a signal accord* [lit. *one mouth*].

They all decided to wage war against the Israelites. Their other option of perpetrating a deception against the Jews was rejected because it was deemed lowly and dishonorable. The Gibeonites, however, disagreed with these kings and decided not to fight the Israelites, because they sensed that it was not the Jews' military might which brought them the victory of Ai, but Divine aid. Therefore, they reasoned that their only hope of salvation was to plan a deception *(Lev Aharon).*

◆§ The Gibeonites' Ruse

3. וְיֹשְׁבֵי גִבְעוֹן — *The inhabitants of Gibeon.*

It can be assumed that the Gibeonites designed this scheme without the knowledge of their king, since he had planned to fight the Israelites by joining the confederacy mentioned in verse 1 (he was a Hivvite king) and since Scripture never mentions his participation in the ruse *(Abarbanel).*

לִירִיחוֹ וְלָעָי — *To Jericho and Ai.*

They saw that Israel employed a different method against each of these cities: Jericho was conquered through a miracle, whereas Ai was defeated through military strategy. The Gibeonites concluded that the Jews' strategy against Ai was only a ruse to deceive the other Canaanites *(Metzudos).*

The Gibeonites needed to devise their ruse because they acted *after* they heard what had happened to Jericho and Ai. Had they decided to make peace before these battles — before Joshua had crossed the Jordan — they would have been able to escape the decree of Canaanite extermination. Now, however, the only way they could avoid the decree would be to deceive their invaders *(Alshich).* [See *Prefatory Remarks.*]

4. גַם־הֵמָּה — *They also.*

Also implies that the Gibeonites behaved similarly to another group of people. The commentators note several groups of people whose behavior resembled that of the Gibeonites:

□ The *Israelites* acted deceitfully to Shechem the Hivvite who abducted Jacob's daughter Dinah *(Genesis* 34:2), by requesting that he and his countrymen circumcise themselves in order to marry Jewish daughters. While they

9
2-5

Jebusite, [2] *they gathered together to wage war with*
Joshua and Israel, with a single accord.
[3] *The inhabitants of Gibeon heard what Joshua*
had done to Jericho and Ai. [4] *They also acted with*
guile and went and disguised themselves. They took
worn sacks for their donkeys and wine bottles which
were worn, cracked, and mended, [5] *worn, patched*
shoes on their feet and worn garments on themselves.
All the bread of their provisions was dry and toasted.

were recuperating from their circumcision, Simeon and Levi slaughtered them. In return, the Gibeonites, who were also Hivvites, therefore felt justified to deceive the Israelites *(Rashi).*

□ The *Midrash (Tanchuma)* explains that the Gibeonites had come to Moses in the Wilderness asking to be admitted to Israel. Thus, Scripture states that the Gibeonites now *also* attempted to be admitted (cf. *Rashi* to *Deuteronomy* 29:10).

□ The men of Jericho and Ai took action to protect themselves against the Jews; Jericho locked its gates and Ai launched an attack on the Israelites. The Gibeonites *also* responded. Their tactic, however, was a deceptive one done in order to make peace *(Radak).*

□ *Kli Yakar* suggests an entirely different interpretation. Not only did the Gibeonites perpetrate their deception through old clothes and the like, but *they themselves,* appeared to be traveling a long time, for their faces appeared parched and browned from the sun.

וַיִּצְטַיָּרוּ – *And disguised themselves.*

They sought to appear as messengers who had come from a distant land. This word is similar to the expression וְצִיר בַּגּוֹיִם שֻׁלָּח *and an ambassador is sent among the nations (Obadiah* 1:1; *Rashi).*

They brought an epistle from a distant king with them, which testified to their being his messengers, for such was the custom of messengers in those times *(Meam Loez).*

Targum, however, understands this expression as deriving from צֵדָה provisions [as if the word were spelled וַיִּצְטַיָּדוּ] and would thus render 'they provided themselves with provisions.' *Radak* does not understand how *Targum* could interpret this verb as if it contained a ד when it is spelled with a ר.

שַׂקִּים בָּלִים – *Worn sacks.*

These worn sacks which they placed on their donkeys were also intended to give the appearance of having just arrived after a long journey *(Rashi).*

וּמְצֹרָרִים – *And mended.*

Rashi understands this word as a synonym for the previous word *split. Metzudos,* however, renders *bound* or *tied.*

5. וּמְטֻלָּאוֹת – *Patched.*

The translation follows *Targum. Metzudos* understands this word to mean *discolored.*

From the fact that they wore patched shoes and worn clothes there was not undeniable evidence that they were traveling for a long time, because they could have been a very poor people who normally dressed in this fashion. However, since they were messengers of a king it was unthinkable that they should be so poorly dressed if not for the fact that they were traveling from a great distance *(Meam Loez).*

נִקֻּדִים – *Toasted.*

The translation follows *Rashi. Ralbag* suggests *dry and crumbling,* and *Radak* renders *spotted* with mold.

ט
ו־י

ו וַיֵּלְכוּ אֶל־יְהוֹשֻׁעַ אֶל־הַמַּחֲנֶה הַגִּלְגָּל
וַיֹּאמְרוּ אֵלָיו וְאֶל־אִישׁ יִשְׂרָאֵל מֵאֶרֶץ
רְחוֹקָה בָּאנוּ וְעַתָּה כִּרְתוּ־לָנוּ בְרִית:
ז °ויאמרו אִישׁ־יִשְׂרָאֵל אֶל־הַחִוִּי אוּלַי
בְּקִרְבִּי אַתָּה יוֹשֵׁב וְאֵיךְ °אכרות־לְךָ
ח בְרִית: וַיֹּאמְרוּ אֶל־יְהוֹשֻׁעַ עֲבָדֶיךָ אֲנָחְנוּ
וַיֹּאמֶר אֲלֵיהֶם יְהוֹשֻׁעַ מִי אַתֶּם וּמֵאַיִן
ט תָּבֹאוּ: וַיֹּאמְרוּ אֵלָיו מֵאֶרֶץ רְחוֹקָה מְאֹד
בָּאוּ עֲבָדֶיךָ לְשֵׁם יְהוָה אֱלֹהֶיךָ כִּי־
שָׁמַעְנוּ שָׁמְעוֹ וְאֵת כָּל־אֲשֶׁר עָשָׂה
י בְּמִצְרָיִם: וְאֵת | כָּל־אֲשֶׁר עָשָׂה לִשְׁנֵי

°וַיֹּאמֶר ק׳
°אֶכְרָת־ ק׳

6. הַגִּלְגָּל — *In Gilgal.*

The Israelites maintained their camp in Gilgal even after the battles of Jericho and Ai. Only the soldiers had gone to these cities to fight, but by now they had returned to Gilgal *(Daas Sofrim).*

וְאֶל־אִישׁ יִשְׂרָאֵל — *And to the men of Israel.*

The men of Israel were the common people, not the leaders *(Abarbanel).*

Alshich however maintains that the phrase *Children of Israel,* would have been employed if Scripture meant the common people. Therefore, he interprets this phrase to mean the princes of the congregation.

מֵאֶרֶץ רְחוֹקָה — *From a distant land.*

Since we are not from the land of Canaan, we are not included in your law concerning the extermination of the Canaanites [*Deuteronomy* 20:16], and you are therefore permitted to make a covenant with us *(Metzudos).*

וְעַתָּה כִּרְתוּ־לָנוּ בְרִית — *Now, make a covenant with us.*

The Gibeonites presented their epistle from a foreign king to Joshua and the Elders, which 'validated' that they were his emissaries. They requested that the Israelites make a covenant with them without delay so that they could report back to their countrymen as soon as possible. In truth, however, they wanted to leave as soon as possible so that Joshua would not detect their deception *(Kli Yakar).*

7. וַיֹּאמֶר אִישׁ־יִשְׂרָאֵל — *Each man of Israel said.*

Joshua delayed in responding to the Gibeonites because he was suspicious of them. Therefore the princes retorted *(Alshich).*

The singular אִישׁ, *man,* is used because all the men [whether prince or commoner (see *Commentary* to previous verse)] were unanimous in their response *(Alshich).*

אוּלַי בְּקִרְבִּי אַתָּה יוֹשֵׁב — *Perhaps you live in my midst.*

Perhaps you are indeed Canaanites *(Rashi),* in which case we would be forbidden to make a covenant with you *(Radak).*

8. וַיֹּאמְרוּ אֶל־יְהוֹשֻׁעַ — *They said to Joshua.*

In verse 6, Scripture relates that the Gibeonites spoke with both Joshua and the people; here they spoke only to Joshua, for when they saw that the common people were suspicious they directed their remarks away from them and spoke only to Joshua (*Abarbanel*).

*6 They went to Joshua at his camp in Gilgal and said
to him and to the men of Israel, 'We have come from
a distant land. Now, make a covenant with us.'*
*7 Each man of Israel said to the Hivvites, 'Perhaps
you live in my midst. How can I make a covenant
with you?'*
8 They said to Joshua, 'We are your servants.'
*Joshua responded, 'Who are you and from where
do you come?'*
*9 They said to him, 'Your servants have come from
a very distant land for the sake of HASHEM, your
God. We have heard of His fame and all that He did
in Egypt 10 and all that He did to the two kings of*

עֲבָדֶיךָ אֲנָחְנוּ — *We are your servants.*
Alshich comments that the Gibeonites interpreted Joshua's silence as disapproval that they sought to make themselves servants to both the princes and Joshua, instead of Joshua alone.

We do not intend to be servants to the entire Jewish people, but only to you, and you surely know that we are not Canaanites *(Metzudos).*

According to *Kli Yakar,* the Gibeonites made this statement to further deceive the Israelites. They figured that the Israelites would think that had they truly been Canaanites, they would have capitulated earlier by becoming servants (see *Prefatory Remarks* to this chapter). By their offering to make themselves servants at this time, they further implied that they were from a distant nation.

מִי אַתֶּם — *Who are you?*
From what nation do you come? *(Metzudos).*

Joshua also became suspicious of the Gibeonites' motives because it is unlike nations who are outside military range to be so interested in making a treaty and also in making it so quickly *(Alshich).*

וּמֵאַיִן תָּבֹאוּ — *And from where do you come?*
From what province do you come? *(Metzudos).*

Joshua thought that even if they were from the Seven Nations, perhaps they were from outside the Land of Israel. In such a case, it would be permitted to make a treaty with them *(Meam Loez).*

9. רְחוֹקָה מְאֹד — *Very distant.*
We are from a land so distant that we are certain that you have not heard of the name of our country or of our province *(Metzudos).*

לְשֵׁם ה׳ אֱלֹהֶיךָ — *For the sake of HASHEM, your God.*
The Gibeonites understood that their motives for coming such a great distance to become Joshua's servants were suspect so they explained that they came *for the sake of HASHEM (Alshich).*

We want to subscribe to your faith and beliefs, for we realize from the miracles which He performed in Egypt that your God is the Creator, sustainer, and guide of the world *(Malbim).*

בְּמִצְרָיִם — *In Egypt.*
They did not mention the more recent miracle at the Jordan, for they realized that if they betrayed their familiarity with such recent local events, the Jews would see through their pretense of having just arrived from a distant land *(Radak).*

מַלְכֵי הָאֱמֹרִי אֲשֶׁר בְּעֵבֶר הַיַּרְדֵּן לְסִיחוֹן
מֶלֶךְ חֶשְׁבּוֹן וּלְעוֹג מֶלֶךְ־הַבָּשָׁן אֲשֶׁר
יא בְּעַשְׁתָּרוֹת: וַיֹּאמְרוּ אֵלֵינוּ זְקֵנֵינוּ וְכָל־
יֹשְׁבֵי אַרְצֵנוּ לֵאמֹר קְחוּ בְיֶדְכֶם צֵידָה
לַדֶּרֶךְ וּלְכוּ לִקְרָאתָם וַאֲמַרְתֶּם אֲלֵיהֶם
עַבְדֵיכֶם אֲנַחְנוּ וְעַתָּה כִּרְתוּ־לָנוּ בְרִית:
יב זֶה | לַחְמֵנוּ חָם הִצְטַיַּדְנוּ אֹתוֹ מִבָּתֵּינוּ
בְּיוֹם צֵאתֵנוּ לָלֶכֶת אֲלֵיכֶם וְעַתָּה הִנֵּה
יג יָבֵשׁ וְהָיָה נִקֻּדִים: וְאֵלֶּה נֹאדוֹת הַיַּיִן
אֲשֶׁר מִלֵּאנוּ חֲדָשִׁים וְהִנֵּה הִתְבַּקָּעוּ
וְאֵלֶּה שַׂלְמוֹתֵינוּ וּנְעָלֵינוּ בָּלוּ מֵרֹב
יד הַדֶּרֶךְ מְאֹד: וַיִּקְחוּ הָאֲנָשִׁים מִצֵּידָם
טו וְאֶת־פִּי יְהֹוָה לֹא שָׁאָלוּ: וַיַּעַשׂ לָהֶם
יְהוֹשֻׁעַ שָׁלוֹם וַיִּכְרֹת לָהֶם בְּרִית לְחַיּוֹתָם
טז וַיִּשָּׁבְעוּ לָהֶם נְשִׂיאֵי הָעֵדָה: וַיְהִי מִקְצֵה

11. וַיֹּאמְרוּ אֵלֵינוּ — *[They] spoke to us.*

You should not be suspicious of us for not first mentioning that we have come for the sake of heaven. We were only fulfilling the orders our elders had given us, namely, that we should say to you, *'We are your servants. Now make a covenant with us.'* They felt that submitting ourselves to you as servants would be more efficacious than mentioning our true motivations of coming to you for the sake of heaven *(Alshich).*

עַבְדֵיכֶם אֲנַחְנוּ — *We are your servants.*

You may collect taxes from us *(Metzudos).*

12. זֶה לַחְמֵנוּ — *This is our bread.*

This bread which you see in our hands ... *(Metzudos).*

14. וַיִּקְחוּ הָאֲנָשִׁים מִצֵּידָם — *The men accepted their deception* [lit. *their provisions* or *their trap*].

The translation follows *Targum. Rashi* explains: The men accepted their words which they had set as a trap in their mouths.

Radak cites some commentators who understand וַיִּקְחוּ [lit. *they took*] as *they learned,* i.e., the men learned from their provisions which were dry that they were telling the truth.

Radak offers an alternative interpretation: the men accepted ['took'] their provisions and ate with them to establish a covenant.

וְאֶת־פִּי ה׳ לֹא שָׁאָלוּ — *And did not seek the counsel of HASHEM.*

They could have sought *the counsel of HASHEM* from Joshua who was a prophet or from Elazar the Kohen Gadol who wore the *urim v'tumim,* which communicated God's messages *(Ralbag).*

The Israelites judged the truth of the Gibeonites' words from the articles they offered as evidence. Even though they could have asked God if the Gibeonites

the Emorites that were on the eastern side of the
Jordan, to Sichon, king of Chesbon, and to Og, king
of Bashan, who was in Ashtaros. [11] *Our elders and all*
the inhabitants of our country spoke to us, saying,
"Take provisions for the journey and go meet them
and say to them: We are your servants. Now make a
covenant with us." [12] *This is our bread. While it was*
still hot we packed it for our provisions from our
houses on the day we left to travel to you. Now it is
dry and toasted. [13] *These wine flasks which we filled*
were new, and now they have cracked. These are our
clothes and shoes which are worn from the very long
journey.'

[14] *The men accepted their deception and did not*
seek the counsel of HASHEM. [15] *And Joshua made*
peace with them and made a covenant with them to
let them live; the leaders of the congregation swore to
them.

should be accepted, they did not *(Malbim).*

The Israelites erred by not seeking the truth from God. For when the Jews accepted the Gibeonites' provisions, it should have been apparent to them that although the bread was dry, their other provisions were *fresh.* This fact should have aroused the Jews' suspicions concerning the veracity of the Gibeonites' claim and prompted them to seek Divine guidance before establishing a covenant with the Gibeonites *(Alshich).*

[This interpretation also explains why the Israelites, and not Joshua, were required to seek God's counsel. Only they discovered the anomaly in the Gibeonites' story.]

☙§ A Covenant is Mistakenly made with the Gibeonites

15. וַיַּעַשׂ לָהֶם ... שָׁלוֹם – *And [Joshua] made peace.*

Some say that the verb 'made' indicates that Joshua prepared a written peace treaty *(Chida).*

בְּרִית לְחַיּוֹתָם – *Covenant ... to let them live.*

The Israelites erred by not imposing conditions in the covenant, for as mentioned in the *Prefatory Remarks* to this chapter, Jewish law stipulates that a covenant can only be established upon three conditions. Thus, the force of this expression is: Joshua made with them a *covenant to let them live,* and not a covenant which would have obligated the Gibeonites to servitude *(Malbim).*

וַיִּשָּׁבְעוּ לָהֶם נְשִׂיאֵי הָעֵדָה – *The leaders of the congregation swore to them.*

The leaders of the congregation swore to uphold the covenant without Joshua's knowledge *(Abarbanel).* Joshua himself did not want to take an oath so that in the event that the Gibeonites were lying, he could renege *(Meam Loez).*

The oath was binding on all the Israelites, even though only the leaders swore. The leaders acted as guardians

שְׁלֹ֣שֶׁת יָמִ֔ים אַחֲרֵ֕י אֲשֶׁר־כָּרְת֥וּ לָהֶ֖ם
בְּרִ֑ית וַֽיִּשְׁמְע֗וּ כִּֽי־קְרֹבִ֥ים הֵם֙ אֵלָ֔יו
יז וּבְקִרְבּ֖וֹ הֵ֥ם יֹשְׁבִֽים׃ וַיִּסְע֣וּ בְנֵֽי־יִשְׂרָאֵ֗ל
וַיָּבֹ֛אוּ אֶל־עָרֵיהֶ֖ם בַּיּ֣וֹם הַשְּׁלִישִׁ֑י
וְעָֽרֵיהֶם֙ גִּבְע֣וֹן וְהַכְּפִירָ֔ה וּבְאֵר֖וֹת וְקִרְיַ֥ת
יח יְעָרִֽים׃ וְלֹ֤א הִכּוּם֙ בְּנֵ֣י יִשְׂרָאֵ֔ל כִּֽי־נִשְׁבְּע֤וּ
לָהֶם֙ נְשִׂיאֵ֣י הָעֵדָ֔ה בַּֽיהוָ֖ה אֱלֹהֵ֣י יִשְׂרָאֵ֑ל
יט וַיִּלֹּ֥נוּ כָל־הָעֵדָ֖ה עַל־הַנְּשִׂיאִֽים׃ וַיֹּאמְר֨וּ
כָל־הַנְּשִׂיאִים֙ אֶל־כָּל־הָ֣עֵדָ֔ה אֲנַ֙חְנוּ֙
נִשְׁבַּ֣עְנוּ לָהֶ֔ם בַּֽיהוָ֖ה אֱלֹהֵ֣י יִשְׂרָאֵ֑ל
כ וְעַתָּ֕ה לֹ֥א נוּכַ֖ל לִנְגֹּ֥עַ בָּהֶֽם׃ זֹ֚את נַעֲשֶׂ֣ה
לָהֶ֔ם וְהַחֲיֵ֖ה אוֹתָ֑ם וְלֹֽא־יִהְיֶ֤ה עָלֵ֙ינוּ֙ קֶ֔צֶף
עַל־הַשְּׁבוּעָ֖ה אֲשֶׁר־נִשְׁבַּ֥עְנוּ לָהֶֽם׃

and agents for the entire nation and, as such, any oath which they took was binding on all the Israelites (*Terumas HaDeshen*, Vol. 2, Ch. 254). [Cf. *Katzos HaChoshen*, Ch. 123, par. 4.] [Perhaps only the leaders, and not Joshua, were considered guardians and agents for the entire nation since they represented the people. If this is so, then it is understandable why the leaders, rather than Joshua, made the oath.]

This oath was binding on all future generations as well, since it had the legal status of a חֵרֶם, *decree* (*Noda B'Yehudah, II Yoreh Deah,* Ch. 146).

The Gibeonites' Deception is Uncovered

16. כִּי־קְרֹבִים הֵם אֵלָיו — *That they were their neighbors.*

The Israelites then discovered that these people were indeed members of one of the Seven Canaanite Nations (*Poras Yosef*).

וּבְקִרְבּוֹ הֵם יֹשְׁבִים — *And that they dwelled among them.*

Since the Gibeonites whose lives were protected by the covenant lived among the Israelites, they posed a potential threat to the spiritual development of the Jewish children (*Poras Yosef*).

17. וַיִּסְעוּ בְנֵי־יִשְׂרָאֵל — *(And) the Children of Israel traveled.*

The Israelites went to the Gibeonites' camps in order to annihilate them, for they knew that the covenant and oath were void *ab initio*, since they were made on a false assumption. Thus, the Gibeonites fell under the decree of Canaanite extermination (*Abarbanel*).

18. כִּי־נִשְׁבְּעוּ לָהֶם נְשִׂיאֵי הָעֵדָה — *Because the leaders of the congregation had sworn to them.*

Although the Israelites went to the Gibeonites' cities with the intent to annihilate them, they decided to the contrary, as this verse explains (*Abarbanel*).

The congregation refrained from slaying the Gibeonites because the princes had sworn to let them live. According to one view mentioned in the *Prefatory Remarks* to this chapter, the oath made by the leaders was not halachically binding, since it had been based on a false premise, namely, that

16 *It was the end of three days after they had made
a covenant with them when they heard that they were
their neighbors and that they dwelled among them.*
17 *The Children of Israel traveled and came to their
cities on the third day; their cities were Gibeon,
Kefirah, B'eros, and Kiryas Yarim.* 18 *The Children of
Israel did not slay them because the leaders of the
congregation had sworn to them by HASHEM, God of
Israel; the entire congregation complained against the
leaders.* 19 *All the leaders said to the entire
congregation,'We have sworn to them by HASHEM,
God of Israel; now we may not touch them.* 20 *This
we will do to them — let them live; there will be no
wrath upon us because of the oath which we have
sworn to them.'* 21 *And the leaders said to them, 'Let*

these people were not from the Seven Nations. Nevertheless, the leaders did not annul their oath, lest the non-Jews who were ignorant of the Gibeonites' deception might conclude that the Israelites failed to keep their sworn promises. If God's people were deemed faithless and unreliable, it would cause desecration of the Divine Name *(Gittin* 46a). According to the second view, the Israelites were halachically bound to keep their oath, even though it was taken on a false premise. Whenever an oath is made in public, there is no way to annul it *(Gittin* 46a).

וַיִּלֹּנוּ כָל־הָעֵדָה עַל־הַנְּשִׂיאִים — *The entire congregation complained against the leaders.*

The congregation was not upset with the leaders because they had made an oath, but because they had restrained the congregation from slaying the Gibeonites. Thus, the congregation's discontent was only directed toward the leaders, and not Joshua, for only they had restrained the congregation *(Abarbanel).*

19. בַּה׳ אֱלֹהֵי יִשְׂרָאֵל — *By HASHEM, God of Israel.*

The fact that the leaders took this oath with the most solemn names of God indicates how seriously they viewed their promise to the Gibeonites and how completely they had been deceived by them *(Daas Sofrim).*

לֹא נוּכַל לִנְגֹּעַ בָּהֶם — *Now we may not touch them.*

We were obligated to restrain you from killing the Gibeonites because the oath *we* [the leaders] made also obligates you to preserve their lives *(Abarbanel).*

20. זֹאת נַעֲשֶׂה — *This we will do.*

We can uphold our oath by making the Gibeonites into servants, since we merely promised to allow them to live, but not to spare them from servitude. By making them our servants, we will not be violating the injunction of Canaanite destruction by allowing them to live (as *Malbim* explains in the following verse).

וְלֹא־יִהְיֶה עָלֵינוּ קֶצֶף — *There will be no wrath upon us.*

Radak (verse 7) comments that the leaders were referring to the Divine *wrath* which would have descended upon them for their failure to fulfill the oath they had made.

ט
כא־כד

כא וַיֹּאמְרוּ אֲלֵיהֶם הַנְּשִׂיאִים יִחְיוּ וַיִּהְיוּ
חֹטְבֵי עֵצִים וְשֹׁאֲבֵי־מַיִם לְכָל־הָעֵדָה
כב כַּאֲשֶׁר דִּבְּרוּ לָהֶם הַנְּשִׂיאִים׃ וַיִּקְרָא
לָהֶם יְהוֹשֻׁעַ וַיְדַבֵּר אֲלֵיהֶם לֵאמֹר לָמָּה
רִמִּיתֶם אֹתָנוּ לֵאמֹר רְחוֹקִים אֲנַחְנוּ
כג מִכֶּם מְאֹד וְאַתֶּם בְּקִרְבֵּנוּ יֹשְׁבִים׃ וְעַתָּה
אֲרוּרִים אַתֶּם וְלֹא־יִכָּרֵת מִכֶּם עֶבֶד
וְחֹטְבֵי עֵצִים וְשֹׁאֲבֵי מַיִם לְבֵית אֱלֹהָי׃
כד וַיַּעֲנוּ אֶת־יְהוֹשֻׁעַ וַיֹּאמְרוּ כִּי הֻגֵּד הֻגַּד
לַעֲבָדֶיךָ אֵת אֲשֶׁר צִוָּה יְהוָה אֱלֹהֶיךָ

◆ The Gibeonites are Spared and Relegated to Lowly Positions

21. וַיִּהְיוּ חֹטְבֵי עֵצִים — *So they became wood choppers.*

The translation follows *Radak* (see next note) who interprets this half of the verse as a third person account of what happened to the Gibeonites. *Abarbanel,* however, contends that this half of the verse is a continuation of the conversation which the leaders had with the congregation. The Israelites were angered that the Gibeonites' ruse would succeed in exempting them from all retaliation, but the leaders assured them that it would be more difficult for the Gibeonites now than if they had originally capitulated, for now they will be *wood choppers and water drawers.*

Radak explains that the use of the conversive prefix וַ changes the tense of the future word יִהְיוּ, *they will become,* to the past, *they became.* Therefore the new clause is not part of the leaders' words, but an account of what actually occurred.

Minchas Shai reports that some editions of Scripture erroneously substitute the conjunctive prefix וְ, *and.* Perhaps *Abarbanel* had such a reading and consequently views the clause as a continuation of the leaders' statement.

Since the Israelites swore only to allow the Gibeonites to live, they were within their rights to declare them servants. This cannot be construed as a violation of the covenant they made with the Gibeonites, because the Israelites had stated explicitly (verse 7), *Perhaps you live in my midst. How can I make a covenant with you?* By this they meant that if these people were indeed neighboring Canaanites the covenant was null and void. The Gibeonites were relegated to being wood choppers, a form of tax and slavery, and were thus allowed to remain in Israel, even though they were from the Seven Nations *(Malbim).* [See *Prefatory Remarks* to this Chapter where it is explained that Joshua's second proclamation exempted the Canaanites from the Biblical injunction of Canaanite destruction if they were to accept three conditions of conduct.]

The Gibeonites were relegated to being wood choppers and water drawers because in these jobs they would have the least deleterious influence on the Israelites *(Daas Sofrim).* Others explain that the Gibeonites were assigned to work for the Sanctuary, because working closely with the Kohanim who were known for their piety would have a beneficial spiritual effect on them *(Rabbi A. Miller).* [See *Ramban* cited at the conclusion of the *Prefatory Remarks* to this Chapter.]

לְכָל־הָעֵדָה — *For the entire congregation.*

In verse 23, Joshua declares that the

them live.' So they became wood choppers and water drawers for the entire congregation, as the leaders had told them.

22 *And Joshua called them and spoke to them saying, 'Why have you deceived us, saying, "We are very distant from you," when you dwell among us?*
23 *Now you are cursed, and there shall never cease to be slaves, wood choppers, and water drawers from you for the House of my God.'*

24 *And they answered Joshua and said, 'Because it was told to your servants that HASHEM, your God,*

Gibeonites would be wood choppers and water drawers for the Sanctuary, whereas here it says that they served *the entire congregation. Radak* explains that before the Land was divided, the Gibeonites were to be servants *for the entire congregation* of Israel. After the division, however, they were to be servants for the Sanctuary.

כַּאֲשֶׁר דִּבְּרוּ לָהֶם הַנְּשִׂיאִים — *As the leaders had told them.*

Although Scripture never mentions that the leaders had advised this, we can derive from here that they had suggested this course of action *(Radak).*

According to *Abarbanel* (mentioned above) who interprets the entire verse except for this clause as part of the conversation between the leaders and the congregation, this clause is difficult to understand for it implies that the earlier portion of this verse is in the third person and is not second person conversation. Thus *Abarbanel* suggests that this clause should be understood as the beginning of the following verse. *As the leaders had spoken to them* [*the Israelites*], and Joshua saw that they (the Israelites) agreed with the leaders, he immediately called the Gibeonites to speak to them.

22. לָמָּה רִמִּיתֶם אֹתָנוּ — *Why have you deceived us?*

By saying this, Joshua intended to inform the Gibeonites that the covenant he had made with them was void *ab initio,* for it was predicated on a false assumption *(Malbim).*

23. אֲרוּרִים אַתֶּם — *You are cursed.*

This curse had the halachic status of banishment (נִדּוּי). When a group of people is banished, Jews may not come within four *amos* (approximately seven feet) of the group members, nor may they have any business dealings with them. This banishment would have the desired effect of distancing the Gibeonites from the Israelites so that they would not have a deleterious influence on the Jewish nation *(Meam Loez).*

In addition to the servitude imposed upon the Gibeonites, *Rashi (Kesubos* 29a) maintains that a Rabbinical decree was issued forbidding Jews to marry them (cf. *R' Tam, ibid.).* The *Talmud (Yevamos* 79a) states that Joshua imposed slavery on the Gibeonites only for the time that the Temple was still standing. King David, however, extended their servitude and barred their entry into the nation of Israel for all time.

24. וַיַּעֲנוּ אֶת־יְהוֹשֻׁעַ — *And they answered Joshua.*

We did not perpetrate this deception in order to avoid slavery and taxes. We were merely trying to save our lives, because we thought that there was no other way to avoid the decree that we be annihilated *(Malbim).*

אֶת־מֹשֶׁה עַבְדּוֹ לָתֵת לָכֶם אֶת־כָּל־
הָאָרֶץ וּלְהַשְׁמִיד אֶת־כָּל־יֹשְׁבֵי הָאָרֶץ
מִפְּנֵיכֶם וַנִּירָא מְאֹד לְנַפְשֹׁתֵינוּ מִפְּנֵיכֶם
כה וַנַּעֲשֵׂה אֶת־הַדָּבָר הַזֶּה: וְעַתָּה הִנְנוּ
בְיָדֶךָ כַּטּוֹב וְכַיָּשָׁר בְּעֵינֶיךָ לַעֲשׂוֹת לָנוּ
כו עֲשֵׂה: וַיַּעַשׂ לָהֶם כֵּן וַיַּצֵּל אוֹתָם מִיַּד
כז בְּנֵי־יִשְׂרָאֵל וְלֹא הֲרָגוּם: וַיִּתְּנֵם יְהוֹשֻׁעַ
בַּיּוֹם הַהוּא חֹטְבֵי עֵצִים וְשֹׁאֲבֵי מַיִם
לָעֵדָה וּלְמִזְבַּח יהוה עַד־הַיּוֹם הַזֶּה אֶל־
י א הַמָּקוֹם אֲשֶׁר יִבְחָר: וַיְהִי
א כִשְׁמֹעַ אֲדֹנִי־צֶדֶק מֶלֶךְ יְרוּשָׁלַםִ כִּי־לָכַד

25. וְעַתָּה — *And now.*

We are prepared to do that which you feel is just *(Malbim).*

כַּטּוֹב וְכַיָּשָׁר — *According to what seems good and right.*

The Gibeonites requested that Joshua deal with them with clemency and kindness [*according to what seems good*] as well as strict justice [*and right*] *(Abarbanel).* [See next note.]

26. וַיַּעַשׂ לָהֶם כֵּן — *And so he did to them.*

Abarbanel continues: Joshua heeded the Gibeonites' request. He acted with clemency by not allowing the Gibeonites to be killed, as this verse relates. He also acted with justice by relegating them to positions of servitude, for had they originally capitulated, they would have had inferior positions in the community.

וַיַּצֵּל אוֹתָם — *(And) he saved them.*

Had they not accepted the servitude and taxes, the Israelites would have killed them, for they felt that the oath of the princes was null and void *(Malbim).*

27. לָעֵדָה וּלְמִזְבַּח ה׳ — *For the congregation and for the altar of HASHEM.*

[See *Commentary* to verse 21.]

They were to be servants for the Sanctuary in all its future locations as well: Shiloh, Nov, Givon, and Jerusalem *(Radak).*

X

Although Joshua was not able to conquer all of Eretz Yisrael, *as we read in the beginning of Chapter 13, he did succeed in subjugating most areas of the country. This chapter relates details of Joshua's conquest of the south of* Eretz Yisrael.

Divine Providence simplified the Israelites' task by causing the Canaanites of the south to unite against Gibeon (see footnote *to 7:5). As a result, the Jews were able to defeat the confederacy of five kings in a single battle and to subsequently vanquish their cities. After these initial victories, the Jews carried their campaign further south of Devir (see map). Some commentators maintain that Joshua extended the southwestern border of* Eretz Yisrael *to the Nile River in Egypt (see* Commentary *to 10:41).*

The Israelites' southern conquest was spearheaded by Gabriel, the angel Joshua had encountered prior to the defeat of Jericho (see Commentary *to 5:14). Each angel*

9
25-27 *commanded Moses His servant to give you all the*
land and to exterminate all the inhabitants of the land
from before you, we were very afraid for our lives
because of you. Therefore, we have done this thing.
[25] And now, we are in your hand. According to what
seems good and right in your eyes to do with us, do.'
[26] And so he did to them; he saved them from the
hand of the Children of Israel, and they did not kill
them. [27] And Joshua made them wood choppers and
water drawers that day for the congregation and for
the altar of HASHEM until this day in the place where
10
He would choose.
1
[1] When Adoni Tzedek, king of Jerusalem, heard

specializes in a certain kind of mission and Gabriel was assigned to perform missions of unusual destruction. It was he, for example, who carried out the destruction of the city of Sodom (Genesis *9:1). Moses had prayed that the Israelites not be under the aegis of any angel during their wanderings in the Wilderness. In effect, Moses himself filled Gabriel's role during the battles of Sichon and Og by leading the Jews into battle* (R' Bachya *to* Exodus *23:20).*

Moses' prayer, however, was fulfilled only during his lifetime. Gabriel returned when Joshua led the Jews outside Jericho, as described at the conclusion of Chapter 5. R' Bachya *explains that it was due to Gabriel that the Canaanites were defeated in bizarre and destructive ways. For example, giant hailstones descended from heaven (verse 10 below) during the battle against the five kings, although nothing so extraordinary had occurred during the battles of Moses' time* [*cf.* Commentary *to v. 13 below*]. *In addition, we find that Scripture repeats six times,* and he put them to death by the edge of the sword and all the souls within it, *although Scripture does not state that the souls of the enemy were destroyed in the battles led by Moses. Thus, Scripture indicates that Gabriel's participation enabled Joshua to eliminate the Canaanites both physically (i.e., from this world) and spiritually (i.e., from the world to come).*

In the next several chapters, the names of many kings are mentioned. Ramban (Numbers *20:14) comments that Scripture cites the mightiest and most renowned kings in order to underscore the magnitude of the miracle that led to their defeat.*

◆§ The Southern Conquest

1. אֲדֹנִי־צֶדֶק — *Adoni Tzedek.*

All the kings of Jerusalem were then called either Malchi Tzedek or Adoni Tzedek. The word *tzedek* (righteousness) was appropriately used in reference to Jerusalem, which was the center of righteousness *(Radak). Daas Sofrim* explains that Jerusalem housed the *beis medrash,* (house of study) of Noah's son Shem and his great-grandson Ever, from which emanated righteous judgments. [See also *Isaiah* 1:21: *righteousness lodged in her,* i.e., in Jerusalem.]

יְרוּשָׁלַם — *Jerusalem.*

This verse contains the first reference to Jerusalem in all of Scripture. As in all verses in Scripture (with the exception of five [*Minchas Shai*]), Jerusalem is

יְהוֹשֻׁעַ אֶת־הָעַי֮ וַיַּחֲרִימָהּ֒ כַּאֲשֶׁר עָשָׂה
לִירִיחוֹ֙ וּלְמַלְכָּהּ כֵּן־עָשָׂה לָעַי וּלְמַלְכָּהּ
וְכִי הִשְׁלִימוּ יֹשְׁבֵי גִבְעוֹן֙ אֶת־יִשְׂרָאֵל
ב וַיִּהְיוּ בְּקִרְבָּם׃ וַיִּירְאוּ מְאֹד כִּי עִיר
גְּדוֹלָה גִּבְעוֹן כְּאַחַת עָרֵי הַמַּמְלָכָה וְכִי
הִיא גְדוֹלָה֙ מִן־הָעַי וְכָל־אֲנָשֶׁיהָ גִּבֹּרִים׃
ג וַיִּשְׁלַח אֲדֹנִי־צֶדֶק מֶלֶךְ יְרוּשָׁלַםִ אֶל־
הוֹהָם מֶלֶךְ־חֶבְרוֹן וְאֶל־פִּרְאָם מֶלֶךְ־
יַרְמוּת וְאֶל־יָפִיעַ מֶלֶךְ־לָכִישׁ וְאֶל־דְּבִיר
ד מֶלֶךְ־עֶגְלוֹן לֵאמֹר׃ עֲלוּ־אֵלַי וְעִזְרֻנִי
וְנַכֶּה אֶת־גִּבְעוֹן כִּי־הִשְׁלִימָה אֶת־
ה יְהוֹשֻׁעַ וְאֶת־בְּנֵי יִשְׂרָאֵל׃ וַיֵּאָסְפוּ וַיַּעֲלוּ

written without the second י which appears in its modern spelling יְרוּשָׁלַיִם.

The *Midrash (Bereishis Rabbah* 56) states that Abraham called Jerusalem, יִרְאֶה, *Yireh;* as *Genesis* 22:14 states, *Abraham called that place HASHEM Yireh.* Malchi Tzedek called Jerusalem, שָׁלֵם, *Shaleim,* as *Genesis* 14:18 states, *Malchi Tzedek King of Shaleim.* God said, 'I will combine these two names,' and He called the city 'Yerushaliyim.'

Chida points out that the numerical value of יִרְאֶה (216) is equivalent to that of יְרוּ, thus permitting the combination יְרוּשָׁלַיִם.

Tosafos (Ta'anis 16a) explains that Scripture refrains from including the second י since the original name for Jerusalem, שָׁלֵם, *Shaleim,* was not spelled with a י.

אֶת־הָעַי וַיַּחֲרִימָהּ — [*Had defeated*] *Ai and had ravaged it.*

[The verse mentions the events involving Ai, Jericho and Gibeon out of chronological sequence as a reflection of Adoni Tzedek's thoughts.] Adoni Tzedek became terribly frightened that Joshua might totally vanquish the remainder of the Land when he heard that Ai, which was conquered through ostensibly natural means, was completely destroyed. It was understood that Jericho was destroyed so that no individual would benefit from the miracle. However, Adoni Tzedek reasoned that if Ai were completely destroyed, it would not be benefiting from a miracle which motivated Joshua's conduct, but rather a systematic plan to destroy the enemy. Thus, Scripture mentions the battle of Ai first, even though it occurred after the battle of Jericho because it was the battle of Ai which clearly indicated Joshua's plan for dealing with his opposition *(Meam Loez).*

וְכִי הִשְׁלִימוּ יֹשְׁבֵי גִבְעוֹן — *And that the inhabitants of Gibeon had made peace.*

The fact that the mighty Gibeonites made peace with Israel put fear into the hearts of the other Canaanites, for they said, 'If even Gibeon was afraid to fight against the Israelites, how could *we* possibly survive?' *(Malbim).*

וַיִּהְיוּ בְּקִרְבָּם — *And were among them.*

The Gibeonites intermingled with the Israelites *(Metzudos).*

2. וַיִּירְאוּ מְאֹד — *They greatly feared.*

[Although the apparent subject of the verb is Adoni Tzedek, it is nevertheless written in the plural form.]

Not only Adoni Tzedek, but all the

10
2-4

that Joshua had defeated Ai and had ravaged it — as
he had done to Jericho and its king so he had done to
Ai and its king — and that the inhabitants of Gibeon
had made peace with Israel and were among them,
2 *they greatly feared because Gibeon was a great city,*
as one of the royal cities, and because it was greater
than Ai and all its men were mighty. 3 *So Adoni*
Tzedek, king of Jerusalem, sent to Hoham, king of
Hebron, and to Piram, king of Yarmus, and to Yafia,
king of Lachish, and to Devir, king of Eglon, saying,
4 *'Come up to me and help me, and we will attack*
Gibeon, for it has made peace with Joshua and with
the Children of Israel.'

kings became very frightened *(Poras Yosef).*

Their fear was based on the fact that although Gibeon was superior to Ai, which the Jews had defeated (Chapter 8), the Gibeonites nevertheless surrendered to the Israelites. The verse now specifies the three respects in which Gibeon was superior to Ai: *Because Gibeon was a great city, i.e.,* Gibeon's reputation surpassed that of Ai, and the conduct of her citizens was superior; *as one of the royal cities,* for Gibeon was larger than Ai; *and all its men were mighty, i.e.,* Gibeon's warriors were mightier than Ai's *(Malbim).*

◆§ Five Emorite Kings Unite against Gibeon

3. וַיִּשְׁלַח אֲדֹנִי־צֶדֶק – *So Adoni Tzedek sent.*

Adoni Tzedek enlisted the support of other Canaanites because he knew that the Israelites would come to the support of the Gibeonites *(Meam Loez).*

חֶבְרוֹן ... יַרְמוּת ... לָכִישׁ ... עֶגְלוֹן – *Hebron ... Yarmus ... Lachish ... Eglon.*

These cities are located in the South of *Eretz Yisrael.* Yarmus is the closest to Jerusalem and Lachish is furthest away *(T'vuos HaAretz).*

4. וְנַכֶּה אֶת־גִּבְעוֹן – *We will attack Gibeon.*

The Gibeonites not only violated the kings' mutual decision to war against Israel, but they also joined the Israelites' forces and aided them. Therefore, they provoked Adoni Tzedek's wrath *(Malbim).*

Daas Sofrim contends that the Gibeonites were attacked because, by capitulating to the Israelites, they gave Israel the geographical means to surround Jerusalem and to divide the north from the south of the country.

Abarbanel comments that Adoni Tzedek also intended to conquer Gibeon in order to deprive the Israelites of their cities which could be used as a military stronghold.

כִּי־הִשְׁלִימָה – *For it has made peace.*

Gibeon's making peace with Israel struck fear in the hearts of all the Canaanites. By attacking Gibeon, Adoni Tzedek intended to deter any other Canaanite nation from capitulating with the Israelites *(Abarbanel).*

אֶת־יְהוֹשֻׁעַ וְאֶת־בְּנֵי יִשְׂרָאֵל – *With Joshua and with the Children of Israel.*

Adoni Tzedek mentioned Joshua separately because his name inspired particular fear in the Canaanites *(Daas Sofrim).*

חֲמֵשֶׁת ׀ מַלְכֵי הָאֱמֹרִי מֶלֶךְ יְרוּשָׁלִַם
מֶלֶךְ־חֶבְרוֹן מֶלֶךְ־יַרְמוּת מֶלֶךְ־לָכִישׁ
מֶלֶךְ־עֶגְלוֹן הֵם וְכָל־מַחֲנֵיהֶם וַיַּחֲנוּ עַל־
גִּבְעוֹן וַיִּלָּחֲמוּ עָלֶיהָ׃ וַיִּשְׁלְחוּ אַנְשֵׁי ו
גִבְעוֹן אֶל־יְהוֹשֻׁעַ אֶל־הַמַּחֲנֶה הַגִּלְגָּלָה
לֵאמֹר אַל־תֶּרֶף יָדֶיךָ מֵעֲבָדֶיךָ עֲלֵה
אֵלֵינוּ מְהֵרָה וְהוֹשִׁיעָה לָּנוּ וְעָזְרֵנוּ כִּי
נִקְבְּצוּ אֵלֵינוּ כָּל־מַלְכֵי הָאֱמֹרִי יֹשְׁבֵי
הָהָר׃ וַיַּעַל יְהוֹשֻׁעַ מִן־הַגִּלְגָּל הוּא ז
וְכָל־עַם הַמִּלְחָמָה עִמּוֹ וְכֹל גִּבּוֹרֵי
הֶחָיִל׃ וַיֹּאמֶר יְהוָה אֶל־ ח
יְהוֹשֻׁעַ אַל־תִּירָא מֵהֶם כִּי בְיָדְךָ נְתַתִּים

6. אַל־תֶּרֶף יָדֶיךָ — *Do not forsake* [lit. *do not withdraw your hands*].

Even though we have deceived you, *do not forsake* us *(Meam Loez).*

מֵעֲבָדֶיךָ — *(From) your servants.*

The Gibeonites used this expression because it is proper for a master to defend his servants *(Ralbag),* for an attack on a servant is an affront to his master *(Meam Loez).*

וְהוֹשִׁיעָה לָּנוּ וְעָזְרֵנוּ — *And save us or help us.*

Malbim explains that הוֹשִׁיעָה denotes salvation or total deliverance, whereas עָזַר merely denotes partial assistance. Thus, although the Gibeonites preferred that Joshua take complete responsibility for saving them from the Emorites' attack, they were willing to accept even limited aid.

כִּי נִקְבְּצוּ אֵלֵינוּ — *For* [*they*] *have rallied against us.*

If you do not come to our defense, they will eventually attack you. Therefore, protecting us is truly in your best interest *(Meam Loez).*

כָּל־מַלְכֵי הָאֱמֹרִי יֹשְׁבֵי הָהָר — *All the Emorite kings who dwell in the mountains.*

[This was an exaggeration, for only five of the Emorite kings had banded against them, and of those five, only two dwelled in the mountains.]

◆§ Joshua Comes to the Aid of Gibeon

7. וַיַּעַל יְהוֹשֻׁעַ מִן־הַגִּלְגָּל — *Joshua ascended from Gilgal.*

Joshua first asked God to determine whether he should go *(Ralbag).*

Poras Yosef [who apparently does not assume *Ralbag's* interpretation] points out that this verse illustrates Israel's love for these converts, for even though they had deceived the Israelites, Joshua nevertheless rushed to their rescue.

8. אַל־תִּירָא מֵהֶם — *Do not fear them.*

[This verse prompts two questions. Joshua was given assurance of victory before the battles of Jericho (6:2) and Ai (8:1). Before this battle against the Gibeonites and before the battle against Ai, God told Joshua, *Do not fear;* before the battle of Jericho, however, Scripture does not state that God told Joshua not to fear. What is the reason for this omission? A second and more fundamental question concerns why Joshua had *any* fears after God promised the

10
5-8

[5] *And the five kings of the Emorites joined
together and ascended — the king of Jerusalem, the
king of Hebron, the king of Yarmus, the king of
Lachish, the king of Eglon — they and all their camps,
and encamped at Gibeon and waged war against it.*
[6] *The men of Gibeon sent to Joshua, to the camp of
Gilgal, saying, 'Do not forsake your servants; come
up to us quickly and save us or help us, for all the
Emorite kings who dwell in the mountains have
rallied against us.'*
[7] *Joshua ascended from Gilgal, he and all the
people of war with him, and all the mighty warriors.*
[8] *And* HASHEM *said to Joshua, 'Do not fear them,*

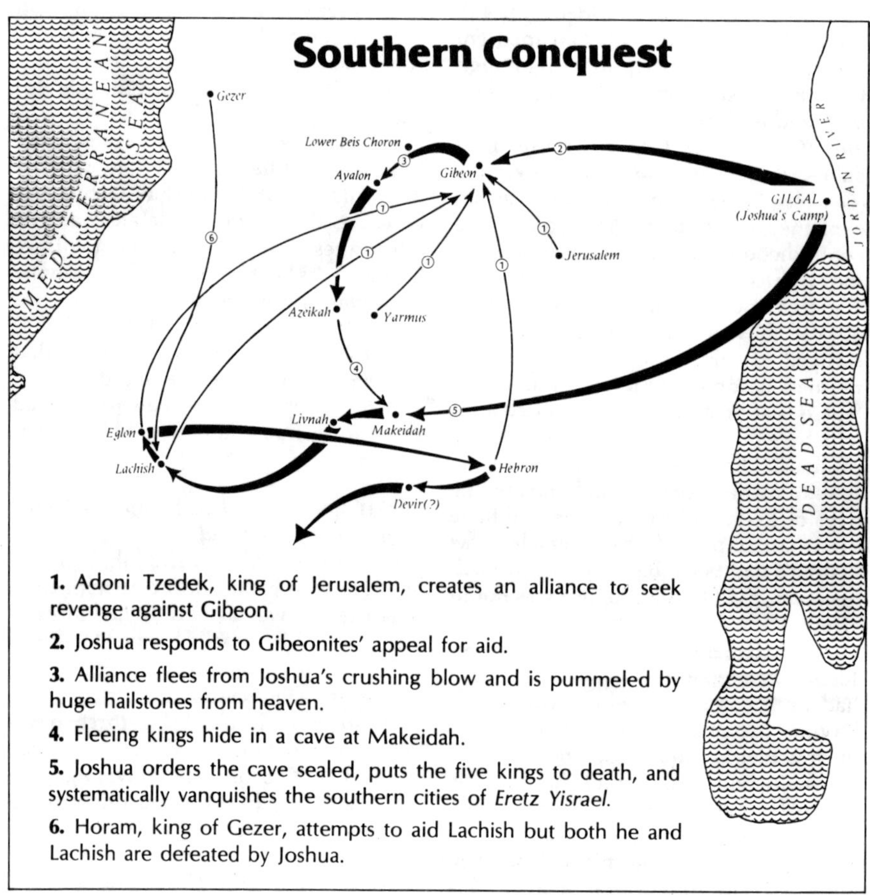

1. Adoni Tzedek, king of Jerusalem, creates an alliance to seek revenge against Gibeon.

2. Joshua responds to Gibeonites' appeal for aid.

3. Alliance flees from Joshua's crushing blow and is pummeled by huge hailstones from heaven.

4. Fleeing kings hide in a cave at Makeidah.

5. Joshua orders the cave sealed, puts the five kings to death, and systematically vanquishes the southern cities of *Eretz Yisrael*.

6. Horam, king of Gezer, attempts to aid Lachish but both he and Lachish are defeated by Joshua.

י
ט־יא

ט לֹא־יַעֲמֹד אִישׁ מֵהֶם בְּפָנֶיךָ: וַיָּבֹא
אֲלֵיהֶם יְהוֹשֻׁעַ פִּתְאֹם כָּל־הַלַּיְלָה עָלָה
י מִן־הַגִּלְגָּל: וַיְהֻמֵּם יהוה לִפְנֵי יִשְׂרָאֵל
וַיַּכֵּם מַכָּה־גְדוֹלָה בְּגִבְעוֹן וַיִּרְדְּפֵם
דֶּרֶךְ מַעֲלֵה בֵית־חוֹרֹן וַיַּכֵּם עַד־עֲזֵקָה
יא וְעַד־מַקֵּדָה: וַיְהִי בְּנֻסָם | מִפְּנֵי יִשְׂרָאֵל
הֵם בְּמוֹרַד בֵּית־חוֹרֹן וַיהוה הִשְׁלִיךְ
עֲלֵיהֶם אֲבָנִים גְּדֹלוֹת מִן־הַשָּׁמַיִם

Jews that they would be successful in their conquest of the Land.

The answers to both questions can be gleaned from the *Talmud (Berachos* 4a). Rabbi Yaakov bar Idi noted an apparent contradiction in Scripture: [although God promised Jacob] *'Behold I am with you, and will protect you wherever you go' (Genesis* 28:15), Scripture later states, *And Jacob feared* [*Esau*] *greatly (Genesis* 32:8). Rabbi Yaakov bar Idi explained that there is actually no contradiction, for Divine promises to the righteous are not unconditional: The righteous man must remain worthy of the Divine aid which has been pledged to him, otherwise, the Divine promise becomes annulled. Thus, Jacob feared that he may have committed a sin which would invalidate the Divine promise. The Sages said that when the Jews returned to the Land during the days of Ezra, their re-entry should have been accompanied by miracles, as Joshua's had been. Because they sinned, however, the Divine promise was not in effect.

After Israel's initial defeat at Ai, Joshua had reason to believe that a sin had been committed which voided the Divine promise to protect the Jews during their conquest of *Eretz Yisrael.* Thus Joshua was afraid because he realized that without Divine help, Israel's army would certainly be defeated by the Canaanites. God then appeared to him and allayed his anxieties, indicating that the Divine promise had not been abrogated. Before the battle of Jericho, however, Joshua had no reason to think that any sin had been committed. Therefore he was not concerned that Israel might meet with defeat. Thus, 6:2 does not state *'Do not fear.'*

Concerning the battle against the Emorites, Joshua was uncertain whether he would receive Divine aid. Joshua was entering the battle in defense of the Gibeonites whom he should not have accepted as converts without Divine approval. Because the Jews *did not seeks the counsel of HASHEM* (9:14) about the Gibeonites, Joshua feared that this sin might cause the withdrawal of Divine support. Consequently, God came to Joshua and reassured him. (See *Commentary* to 11:6.)]

כִּי בְיָדְךָ נְתַתִּים — *For I have delivered them into your hand.*

God explained to Joshua that since it was He who arranged the attack of the Emorites, it was as if they had *already* been placed in Israel's hands *(Malbim).*

9. פִּתְאֹם — *Suddenly.*

Even though it was a three day's journey from Gilgal to Gibeon, the Jews arrived in Gibeon after traveling only one night. God performed this miracle so that the Gibeonites' attackers would not overpower them before the Israelites arrived to aid them *(Meam Loez).*

for I have delivered them into your hand. None of
their men shall withstand you.'
9 Joshua came to them suddenly. He had ascended
from Gilgal all night. 10 HASHEM confounded them
before Israel and smote them with a mighty blow at
Gibeon. They pursued them on the way that goes up
to Beis Choron and smote them to Azeikah and
Makeidah. 11 It was when they fled before Israel and
were on the slope of Beis Choron, that HASHEM cast
down huge stones from heaven upon them until

כָּל־הַלַּיְלָה עָלָה מִן־הַגִּלְגָּל — *He had ascended from Gilgal all night.*

The Jews traveled all through the night so that their departure from Gilgal would go undetected *(Metzudos).*

10. וַיְהֻמֵּם — [*HASHEM*] *confounded them.*

Daas Sofrim explains that God often protects Israel by causing its attackers to become greatly confused (see *Exodus* 14:24, *Exodus* 23:27, and *Deuteronomy* 7:23).

וַיִּרְדְּפֵם דֶּרֶךְ מַעֲלֵה בֵית־חורן — *They pursued them on the way that goes up to Beis Choron.*

Even though the Israelites' attackers were stationed at higher elevation, the Jews nevertheless pursued them. This action was contrary to common military procedure, which dictates that the army of higher elevation is offensive, not defensive; it indicates the extent of Divine protection which the Jews enjoyed *(Meam Loez).*

בֵית־חורן — *Beis Choron.*

There are two cities by the name of Beis Choron. The one called Upper Beis Choron (16:5) was north of Lower Beis Choron (16:3). This verse refers to Lower Beis Choron *(T'vuos HaAretz).*

עֲזֵקָה — *Azeikah.*

See *Commentary* to 15:35 for its location.

מַקֵּדָה — *Makeidah.*

See *Commentary* to 15:41 for its location.

◆§ Hailstones Pummel Israel's Enemies

11. וַה׳ הִשְׁלִיךְ — *That HASHEM cast down.*

The fact that hailstones descended from heaven and killed people could be construed as a natural event. In this case, however, it was clearly miraculous, because the hailstones killed only Emorites, not the Israelites who were following in close pursuit *(Malbim).*

אֲבָנִים גְּדלות — *Huge stones.*

Further in this verse these *huge stones* are described as אַבְנֵי הַבָּרָד, *the hailstones. Maharsha (Berachos* 54b) explains that the use of the definite article 'the' implies that Scripture is referring to specific hailstones, which the *Midrash (Tanchuma, Va'Eira)* identifies as the hailstones which had fallen on Egypt during the Ten Plagues. When Moses prayed *(Exodus* 9:33) for the cessation of the hailstorm, the hail that was in the process of falling became suspended in mid-air, and the hail remaining in the clouds did not fall. It was these suspended hailstones which grew larger and fell, killing the Emorites. The remainder will fall during the pre-Messianic war of Gog and Magog.

י עַד־עֲזֵקָה וַיָּמֻתוּ רַבִּים אֲשֶׁר־מֵתוּ
יב בְּאַבְנֵי הַבָּרָד מֵאֲשֶׁר הָרְגוּ בְּנֵי יִשְׂרָאֵל
בֶּחָרֶב׃ יב אָז יְדַבֵּר יְהוֹשֻׁעַ לַיהוה
בְּיוֹם תֵּת יהוה אֶת־הָאֱמֹרִי לִפְנֵי בְּנֵי
יִשְׂרָאֵל וַיֹּאמֶר | לְעֵינֵי יִשְׂרָאֵל שֶׁמֶשׁ

☙ The Halting of the Sun

12. Joshua's causing the sun to stop in its orbit is one of the most famous miracles in the Bible. Indeed, this event is even chronicled in the contemporary literatures of other cultures (see *Torah Nation* by Rabbi A. Miller).

This miracle was another instance in which God fulfilled the promise He had made to Joshua (1:4): *As I was with Moshe, so will I be with you (Poras Yosef).* The *Talmud (Ta'anis* 20a) informs us that just as the sun stood still for Joshua, it also stood still for Moses.

A closer analysis of the context of this miracle shows that the battle with which Joshua was occupied was for the sake of the Gibeonites, who were not even Jews of full status (see 9:27 and *Commentary* to 9:23). The oath he publicly made when accepting the Gibeonites was not binding, for it had been based on a false assumption. However, Joshua was concerned that if he broke his promise, the Name of God might be diminished; therefore, he refrained from executing them (see *Prefatory Remarks* to Chapter 9).

Just as the Gibeonites had provided an occasion for the sanctification of God's Name, the battle which Joshua fought on their behalf resulted in a further sanctification of His Name. Thus the verse reads, *Then Joshua thought that he should speak* לַה׳, 'for the sake of HASHEM,' for his sole aim was the sanctification of God's name. The verse, *There was no day like that before or after it,* implies that the similar miracle which occurred in the times of Moses was performed for the sake of Israel, whereas this miracle was performed to fulfill Joshua's request that the desecration of the Divine Name should not occur through him. The fulfillment of a request of this nature by the performance of a miracle of this magnitude was something the world had never seen before and never will in the future *(Be'er Moshe).*

אָז — *Then.*

Then means 'upon seeing the miracle of the hailstones' *(Rashi, Exodus* 15:1).

Lev Aharon interprets *then* to refer to a point in time, namely *that* day, which was Friday. Since the Israelites did not want to wage war on the Sabbath, Joshua saw it necessary to request the sun stop on Friday. (See further, *Commentary* to *'Sun, stand still upon Gibeon.')*

יְדַבֵּר — [*Joshua*] *decided to speak* [lit. *will speak*].

Although this verb is in the future tense, *Rashi (Exodus* 15:1) notes that a literal translation 'will speak' is untenable, for then the construction אָז יְדַבֵּר would be a contradiction in terms (see *Sifsei Chachamim, Exodus* 15:1), since אָז, *then,* refers to the past, whereas יְדַבֵּר, *will speak,* refers to the future. On the basis of other Scriptural passages, *Rashi* concludes that the י prefix here connotes *intention;* therefore he renders יְדַבֵּר as *he decided to speak.* According to *Rashi,* Joshua acted on this intention in the second half of this verse: *and he said in the sight of Israel.*

Ibn Ezra (Exodus 5:1), however, disagrees with *Rashi;* he contends that in Hebrew the future tense is sometimes used idiomatically to refer to a past event. He substantiates his point of view by finding analogous construc-

10 *[they reached] Azeikah and died. More died through*
12 *the hailstones than whom the Children of Israel*
killed with the sword.
12 Then Joshua decided to speak to HASHEM
on the day when HASHEM delivered up the Emorites
in front of the Children of Israel, and he
said in the sight of Israel, 'Sun, stand still upon

tions in Arabic. Thus, in his view, יְדַבֵּר should be rendered in the past: *Then Joshua spoke.*

[This 'then-future' construction is found in two other passages in *Joshua.* See verses 8:30 and 22:1 and the *Commentary.*]

אָז יְדַבֵּר יְהוֹשֻׁעַ לַה' — *Then Joshua decided to speak to HASHEM.*

Rashi, following *Targum,* understands this phrase as an introduction to the song which Joshua was about to sing, for since he wanted the sun to halt its movement, he would have to provide a substitute for the song of praise which the sun 'sings' while in motion. [See *Overview* to ArtScroll *Song of Songs,* Part III for an explanation of the songs which inanimate objects 'sing' to God.] The song continues until the words, *that HASHEM fought for Israel (Meam Loez).*

Radak suggests two interpretations of Joshua's song. First, he advances that this verse is Joshua's prayer[1] that the sun stand still and that his actual song is not mentioned in Scripture. *(Meam Loez* reports the lengthy song without citing a source.) Second, he suggests that Joshua's song appears in verse 13, and that his prayer begins in the middle of this verse: *And he said in the sight of Israel, 'Sun stand still upon Gibeon.' Radak* also cites a *Midrash* in support of *Rashi's* interpretation that this phrase introduces a song, for the *Midrash* identifies this verse as one of the ten instances in Scripture in which a song was sung (see *Yalkut Shimoni* for a listing of the nine other instances).

יְהוֹשֻׁעַ לַה' — *Joshua ... to HASHEM.*

Joshua requested that God perform a miracle. This was highly unusual, as verse 14 states: *There was no day like that ... that HASHEM heeded the voice of a man,* for normally God informs man that a miracle will be performed, but man does not request it *(Daas Sofrim).*

Joshua first prayed to God before ordering the sun to stand still, for he felt it would have been inappropriate for him to try to interrupt God's plan for the celestial bodies without first requesting from God that He decree it *(Meam Loez).*

לְעֵינֵי יִשְׂרָאֵל — *In the sight of Israel.*

Radak offers two interpretations of this phrase. *In the sight of Israel* may refer to *'Sun, stand still upon Gibeon,'*

1. *Ramban (Deuteronomy* 34:10) resolves a difficulty inherent in his interpretation that Moses was distinguished from all other prophets by the fact that no other prophet was able to perform miracles as great as those performed by Moses. He interprets the verse, *There will be no other prophet like Moses (Deuteronomy* 34:10), to mean both that no other prophet will be granted the same level of prophetic vision as Moses attained and that no other prophet will perform miracles as great as those performed by Moses. Although several passages in Scripture seem to indicate that Elijah, Elisha, and Joshua performed miracles which surpassed those of Moses in that their miracles were viewed by a wider public, *Ramban* explains that these prophets prayed to God for miraculous intervention, whereas Moses was granted the power to perform miracles without request. (Cf. *Sha'arei Orah,* 'The power of prayer' and *Brisker Rav* to *Exodus* 3:11.)

י יג בְּגִבְעוֹן דּוֹם וְיָרֵחַ בְּעֵמֶק אַיָּלוֹן׃ וַיִּדֹּם
יג הַשֶּׁמֶשׁ וְיָרֵחַ עָמָד עַד־יִקֹּם גּוֹי אֹיְבָיו
הֲלֹא־הִיא כְתוּבָה עַל־סֵפֶר הַיָּשָׁר וַיַּעֲמֹד

indicating that the miracle should be visible to all the Jews. Or, this phrase may refer to *'he said,'* indicating all Israel could hear Joshua's prayer for this miracle. [*Ramban,* cited in the *footnote* to this verse, apparently understands this phrase according to *Radak's* second interpretation.] *Daas Sofrim* explains that if the people had not heard Joshua request the miracle, they might have dismissed the anomaly of the sun standing still as a mere oddity of nature.

Rambam (Moreh Nevuchim 2:35) contends that Moses was distinguished from all other prophets in that his miracles were performed before great multitudes, whereas the miracles of the other prophets were merely performed before individuals. *Ramban (Deuteronomy* 34:10) rejects *Rambam's* view on the basis that the splitting of the Jordan River and the halting of the sun by Joshua were known by all the Jews as our verse states, *In the sight of* [*all*] *Israel,* and indeed to all other peoples as well.

Ritva (Sefer HaZikaron) in defense of *Rambam's* position suggests that a careful analysis of *Rambam's* words reveals that he intended to distinguish between Moses' powers and those of other prophets in a different manner. Only in the case of Moses were the miracles performed publicly in the sight of those who both challenged and supported him. In the case of the splitting of the Jordan, Israel's enemies were not present as they were at the splitting of the Red Sea. The halting of the sun for Joshua was not even performed before all the Israelites [unlike *Ramban's* view], for our verse states that Joshua ordered the sun to halt *in the sight of Israel,* but not in the sight of *all* Israel as Scripture states in regard to Moses *(Deuteronomy* 34:12). Even though verse 43 states that *Joshua and all Israel with him returned to the encampment at Gilgal,* all Israel was not with him. Verse 7 indicates that Joshua only took warriors with him to fight the Emorite kings. Hence, *all Israel* in verse 43 must mean all the Israelite warriors who returned with Joshua, not all the Israelites.

שֶׁמֶשׁ בְּגִבְעוֹן דּוֹם — *Sun, stand still upon Gibeon.*

Even though the sun, by standing still in Gibeon, would necessarily stand still over the entire world, Joshua mentioned the city of Gibeon, because it was there that he needed the miracle to take place *(Alshich).*

After Joshua prayed for the sun and moon to stop in their place, he took the *Book of Deuteronomy* and displayed it to the sun and moon and declared, '[Because] I have never ceased from studying this book, you should cease from your movement [at my request].' Immediately, *The sun's movement ceased and the moon stood still* (verse 13) *(Bereishis Rabbah* 19).

◆§ Why did Joshua order the sun to stand still?

□ *Metzudos* comments that Joshua was concerned that after the sun set, the Emorites would escape into the darkness.

□ The *Midrash* explains that the sun stood still for 36 hours. (There are other opinions in the *Midrash* which maintain that the miracle lasted 24 or 48 hours.) The battle against the Emorites took place on Friday and Joshua was concerned lest Israel desecrate the Sabbath if the battle extend into the night. He therefore opened his hands to heaven and asked that the sun stand still.

Be'er Moshe points out that although waging war on the Sabbath was permissible during the conquest of the Land, this did not allow the Jews to do battle on the Sabbath to protect the Gibeonites for since they had

10 *Gibeon, and Moon, in the Valley of Ayalon ...'*
13 *[13] And the sun's movement ceased, and the moon*
stood still '... until the people take retribution against
their enemies. Is not this written in the Book of
Yashar?' So the sun stood still in the midst of the

converted through deception, they did not have the status of full-fledged Jews.

□ Others suggest that Joshua sought to instill in the Jews a deeper belief in God as they entered *Eretz Yisrael.* He wanted to demonstrate that not only is God master of earthly affairs (as evidenced by the seige of Jericho) but also He is the master of the entire universe, able to control the orbits of the celestial bodies *(Meam Loez).*

□ *Abarbanel* advances that Joshua was concerned for the safety of the Israelites who would be pursuing the enemy at night. He therefore requested that the sun stand still to alleviate the perils of darkness.

□ *Alshich* comments that Joshua wanted the entire world to know unequivocally that it was God who wrought the defeat of the Emorites. So that no one could attribute the Emorite defeat and the Israelite victory to the vagaries of the zodiac, Joshua ordered the sun and moon to stand still so that all mankind could witness that the position of the celestial bodies was the same before and after the battle, and hence it was not a change in their positions which brought the Israelites' victory. Similarly, we find that the positions of the zodiac did not change during the Flood of Noah's time so that those who came later could not explain the Flood on the basis of astrology.

וְיָרֵחַ בְּעֵמֶק אַיָּלוֹן – *And Moon, in the Valley of Ayalon.*

When the sun stood still over Gibeon, the moon was a great distance away in Ayalon. [We know that Gibeon and Ayalon were some distance apart because Gibeon was in Benjamin's territory, and Ayalon was in Dan's.] *(Rashi)*

Although a city named Ayalon existed in Dan's territory (see 21:23), *T'vuos HaAretz* disagrees with *Rashi* that Scripture here is referring to that one. He claims that this Ayalon was located two and one-half miles west of Gibeon.

Radak explains that Joshua also appealed to the moon to stand still. It was mid-day in Gibeon when Joshua prayed that the sun should stand still (as verse 13 relates, *The sun stood still in the midst of the heaven).* The sun stood still for a full day, during which time the Israelites pursued the Emorites into the Valley of Ayalon. By the time they approached the valley, the sun had set, and the moon was visible. Joshua then prayed that the moon should stand still and provide sufficient light for him to finally overpower the enemy.

Metzudos suggests that Joshua prayed that the moon should maintain its position because he was afraid that the moon might pass in front of the sun and eclipse it, thus nullifying the miracle of the sun standing still.

13. **וַיִּדֹּם הַשֶּׁמֶשׁ וְיָרֵחַ עָמָד** – *And the sun's movement ceased and the moon stood still.*

Malbim understands that this phrase was interjected by Joshua when he authored the *Book of Joshua.* Even before he finished saying, *'Sun, stand still upon Gibeon, and Moon, in the Valley of Ayalon until the people take retribution against their enemies,'* the sun stopped. This is noted with the interposition, *And the sun's movement ceased and the moon stood still.*

עַל־סֵפֶר הַיָּשָׁר – *Book of Yashar* [*lit. Book of Rectitude*].

Most commentators suggest that the *Book of Yashar* is the Pentateuch. *Rashi* identifies *Genesis* 48:19 as the reference made in this verse, for it is in that

י הַשֶּׁמֶשׁ בַּחֲצִי הַשָּׁמַיִם וְלֹא־אָץ לָבוֹא
יד־טז יד כְּיוֹם תָּמִים׃ וְלֹא הָיָה כַּיּוֹם הַהוּא לְפָנָיו
וְאַחֲרָיו לִשְׁמֹעַ יהוה בְּקוֹל אִישׁ כִּי יהוה
טו נִלְחָם לְיִשְׂרָאֵל׃ וַיָּשָׁב יְהוֹשֻׁעַ וְכָל־
טז יִשְׂרָאֵל עִמּוֹ אֶל־הַמַּחֲנֶה הַגִּלְגָּלָה׃ וַיָּנֻסוּ

passage that Jacob justified his decision to accord Ephraim greater status than his older brother Menashe. When Jacob said, '[*Ephraim's*] *offspring will fill the nations,*' he was referring to the day on which the sun would stand still on account of Joshua the Ephraimite, for when Joshua would make the sun stand still, the whole world would become aware of his name (cf. *Rashi* to *Avodah Zarah* 25a, s.v., *Sefer Avraham).*

Niflaos M'Toras HaShem identifies a different verse in *Genesis* to which this statement refers. Joseph had a dream in which he saw eleven stars, the sun, and the moon bow down to him *(Genesis* 37:9). The words 'bow down' do not mean a physical prostration, but rather a subjugation. The sun and the moon, Joseph saw, will subjugate their motion to the will of Joseph's descendant Joshua, when he requests that they stop their motion.

Others identify a different verse in the Pentateuch to which this verse refers. In Chapter 34, God promises Moses that spectacular events will occur when the Jews drive out the Emorites from the Land *(Exodus* 34:10-11). In *Exodus* 34:27, God specifically tells Moses to record this promise, and this transcription constituted the *Sefer HaYashar (Malbim).*

The *Book of Yashar* is interpreted by other commentators to be the *Book of Deuteronomy.* It is referred to by this name ['Rectitude'] because this book contains inspirational ethics, admonitions, and entreaties to be righteous, [see *Introduction*] as the verse states, *Do the righteous* [הַיָּשָׁר] *and the good (Deuteronomy* 6:18). Specifically, the reference made in our verse is to the battles of Moses against Sichon and Og. Through tradition we know that the sun stood still for Moses during this battle. Thus, the force of our verse is: do not be unduly surprised by this miracle of the sun stopping, for it has happened before and is alluded to in the *Book of Yashar* [*Deuteronomy*]. This miracle was explicitly stated in our verse because it was of an entirely different nature than Moses' miracle. Whereas for Moses God performed this miracle without his requesting it in order to magnify his name, for Joshua God performed this miracle at his request in consonance with the dictum, 'A tzaddik (righteous man) decrees and God fulfills his requests' *(Meam Loez).*

Ralbag, however, contends that the *Book of Yashar* refers to a chronicle of miracles which God had wrought for the Israelites, but which has been lost.

כְּיוֹם תָּמִים — *For a whole day.*

According to the most literal meaning of the text, the sun stopped for twenty four hours. Even though it was not militarily necessary for the sun's movement to be halted for this length of time, a briefer cessation would have disrupted the precise relationship which must be maintained between the sun's orbit and the periodic revolutions of the other celestial bodies *(Malbim).*

There are other interpretations as to the duration of the sun's cessation (*Avodah Zarah* 25a):

☐ Some suggest that the sun stopped for a total of six hours. At noon, Joshua requested that the sun stand still, and it stopped for two hours. Everyone became aware of this miracle, for the noon-time shadows had not grown longer. When the sun began to move again, it set in the west at such an

heaven and did not hasten to set for a whole day.
14 *There was no day like that before or after it, that*
HASHEM heeded the voice of a man, that HASHEM
fought for Israel.
15 *And Joshua and all Israel with him returned to*
the camp at Gilgal. 16 *These five kings fled and hid in*

unusually slow pace that it took twelve hours for it to set, including the time that it remained stationary. This event is referred to in the second part of the verse, *did not hasten to set for a whole day. A whole day* in this context refers to the daylight part of the day, i.e., twelve hours. These two changes in the sun's movement demonstrated that Joshua had the power both to decelerate and stop the course of the sun *(Meam Loez).*

□ Others suggest that the sun stopped for twelve hours — six at noon and six towards sunset. Therefore, the day was light for twenty-four hours, *a whole day.*

□Some explain that the sun stopped for twenty-four hours — twelve at noon and twelve towards sunset. Therefore, the extra daylight which was added equaled a twenty-four hour day.

□ R' Shmuel Bar Nachmani holds that the sun stopped for a total of thirty-six hours — twelve at noon and twenty-four towards sunset. Therefore, the second half of the day when [*the sun*] *did not hasten to set* contained a *whole day* (twenty-four hours) that the sun did not set.

14. וְלֹא הָיָה כַּיּוֹם הַהוּא לְפָנָיו וְאַחֲרָיו — *There was no day like that before or after it.*

Even though a similar miracle of the halting of the sun was performed for Moses and for Nakdimon ben Gurion [see *Taanis* 19b], the miracle performed for Joshua was different in two ways: (a) the sun stood still for a longer period of time, and (b) the miracle was accompanied by hailstones *(Avodah Zarah* 25a). *Meam Loez* adds that this day was also unique in that Joshua conquered the five Emorite kings who were the most formidable of all the thirty-one Canaanite kings.

R' Bachya (Exodus 10:14) and *Radak* explain another unique feature of this day. It was initiated by request, rather than by unilateral Divine intervention.

בְּקוֹל אִישׁ — *The voice of a man.*

Targum paraphrases: The prayer of a man.

כִּי ה׳ נִלְחָם לְיִשְׂרָאֵל — *That HASHEM fought for Israel.*

Malbim comments that this event was unusual in that the entire miracle was wrought for the sole purpose of publicizing the fact that *HASHEM fought for Israel.*

Militarily, Joshua did not need the sun to stop, since he was already near victory *(Meam Loez).*

15. וַיָּשָׁב יְהוֹשֻׁעַ — *And Joshua ... returned.*

This verse indicates that Joshua returned to Gilgal, yet verse 21 implies that he returned to Makeidah and made camp there. *Malbim* explains that Joshua originally considered returning to Gilgal (as this verse relates) in order to rest before the next battle. He reasoned that since the bodies of the kings were not found on the battlefields, they must have returned to their camps to regroup their forces for a second attack. However, when Joshua received word that the kings had been discovered hiding, he realized that Divine Providence had prevented them from returning home. Therefore, he changed his plans and camped in Makeidah.

הַגִּלְגָּלָה — *At Gilgal.*

Abarbanel cites a comment attributed

חֲמֵשֶׁת הַמְּלָכִים הָאֵלֶּה וַיֵּחָבְאוּ בַמְּעָרָה
יז בְּמַקֵּדָה: וַיֻּגַּד לִיהוֹשֻׁעַ לֵאמֹר נִמְצְאוּ
חֲמֵשֶׁת הַמְּלָכִים נֶחְבְּאִים בַּמְּעָרָה
יח בְּמַקֵּדָה: וַיֹּאמֶר יְהוֹשֻׁעַ גֹּלּוּ אֲבָנִים
גְּדֹלוֹת אֶל־פִּי הַמְּעָרָה וְהַפְקִידוּ עָלֶיהָ
יט אֲנָשִׁים לְשָׁמְרָם: וְאַתֶּם אַל־תַּעֲמֹדוּ
רִדְפוּ אַחֲרֵי אֹיְבֵיכֶם וְזִנַּבְתֶּם אוֹתָם אַל־
תִּתְּנוּם לָבוֹא אֶל־עָרֵיהֶם כִּי נְתָנָם יְהוָה
כ אֱלֹהֵיכֶם בְּיֶדְכֶם: וַיְהִי כְּכַלּוֹת יְהוֹשֻׁעַ
וּבְנֵי יִשְׂרָאֵל לְהַכֹּתָם מַכָּה גְדוֹלָה־מְאֹד
עַד־תֻּמָּם וְהַשְּׂרִידִים שָׂרְדוּ מֵהֶם וַיָּבֹאוּ
כא אֶל־עָרֵי הַמִּבְצָר: וַיָּשֻׁבוּ כָל־הָעָם אֶל־
הַמַּחֲנֶה אֶל־יְהוֹשֻׁעַ מַקֵּדָה בְּשָׁלוֹם לֹא־
חָרַץ לִבְנֵי יִשְׂרָאֵל לְאִישׁ אֶת־לְשֹׁנוֹ:
כב וַיֹּאמֶר יְהוֹשֻׁעַ פִּתְחוּ אֶת־פִּי הַמְּעָרָה
וְהוֹצִיאוּ אֵלַי אֶת־חֲמֵשֶׁת הַמְּלָכִים
כג הָאֵלֶּה מִן־הַמְּעָרָה: וַיַּעֲשׂוּ כֵן וַיֹּצִיאוּ
אֵלָיו אֶת־חֲמֵשֶׁת הַמְּלָכִים הָאֵלֶּה מִן־

to *Radak* that Joshua *first* returned to Gilgal and was *then* informed that the five kings were in hiding. He then issued the order for the stones to be rolled to the opening of the cave and dispatched troops.

Abarbanel disagrees, claiming that it is unreasonable to assume that after the sun stopped for Joshua he returned to Gilgal without waging war against the Emorites. He therefore suggests that verse 15 is a general statement which describes the final event of that day on which the sun stood still. Verses 16 to 43 flashback to that day and describe the specific events which occurred when the sun stopped.

Meam Loez suggests that Joshua returned to Gilgal to anticipate a surprise attack that might be made by the five Emorite kings on the defenseless Israelite women and children who remained in Gilgal. [This view apparently does not follow the comment of *Abarbanel.*]

18. גֹּלּוּ אֲבָנִים גְּדֹלוֹת — *Roll huge stones.*

Joshua ordered that the mouth of the cave be blocked off so that the kings could not make a quick escape *(Metzudos).*

19. וְזִנַּבְתֶּם — *And kill their stragglers.*

This verb is derived from זָנָב, *tail.* Joshua ordered the men to kill the rear of the enemy's camp *(Radak). Meam Loez* interprets this to mean that Joshua not only commanded the Israelites to kill the leaders of the enemy's ranks

10
17-23

a cave at Makeidah. 17 *Joshua was told, saying, 'The*
five kings have been found hiding in a cave at
Makeidah.'

18 *Joshua said, 'Roll huge stones to the opening of*
the cave and designate men to guard them. 19 *You, do*
not stay. Pursue your enemies and kill their
stragglers. Do not let them reach their cities, because
HASHEM, your God, has delivered them into your
hand.'

20 *It was when Joshua and the Children of Israel*
finished striking them a massive blow until they were
completely routed, that those who managed to
survive returned to the fortressed cities. 21 *Then the*
entire nation [of Israel] returned safely to the camp,
to Joshua at Makeidah. None whetted his tongue
against any of the Children of Israel.

22 *Joshua said, 'Open the mouth of the cave and*
deliver those five kings to me from the cave.' 23 *And*
they did so. They delivered those five kings to him

who were stationed in the front, but even the non-commissioned troops who were in the rear.

20. וַיְהִי כְּכַלּוֹת יְהוֹשֻׁעַ — *It was when Joshua ... finished.*

[This verse cannot be describing the pursuit Joshua ordered in the previous verse, for verse 21 relates that the people who pursued the enemy returned to Joshua in Makeidah, thereby indicating that Joshua did not participate in that pursuit. Therefore, this verse must be a description of another routing of the Emorites; it is included here to inform us that there were survivors among the Emorites who did succeed in reaching the fortified cities, despite Joshua's exhortation (verse 19) to prevent them from entering their fortresses.]

Meam Loez, however, suggests that even though he did not participate in the pursuit, Joshua was mentioned in this verse because the Israelites' victory was a result of Joshua's merit.

לְהַכֹּתָם מַכָּה גְדוֹלָה־מְאֹד עַד־תֻּמָּם — *Striking them a massive blow until they were completely routed.*

Since the number of survivors mentioned in the second half of the verse was negligible, Scripture states that the enemy was *completely* routed *(Metzudos).*

21. לֹא־חָרַץ לִבְנֵי יִשְׂרָאֵל לְאִישׁ אֶת־לְשֹׁנוֹ — *None whetted his tongue against any of the Children of Israel.*

The translation follows *Targum.*

Meam Loez suggests an interpretation which is closer to the literal meaning of the verse. The custom of warfare in those days was that the enemy hurled insults and execrations at their opposition. [Cf. *I Samuel* 1:17*ff.*]

Besides the miracle that not one Jew was even injured in battle, not one suffered a verbal insult *(Rashi),* because

הַמְּעָרָה אֵת | מֶלֶךְ יְרוּשָׁלַםִ אֶת־מֶלֶךְ
חֶבְרוֹן אֶת־מֶלֶךְ יַרְמוּת אֶת־מֶלֶךְ לָכִישׁ
כד אֶת־מֶלֶךְ עֶגְלוֹן: וַיְהִי כְּהוֹצִיאָם אֶת־
הַמְּלָכִים הָאֵלֶּה אֶל־יְהוֹשֻׁעַ וַיִּקְרָא
יְהוֹשֻׁעַ אֶל־כָּל־אִישׁ יִשְׂרָאֵל וַיֹּאמֶר אֶל־
קְצִינֵי אַנְשֵׁי הַמִּלְחָמָה הֶהָלְכוּא אִתּוֹ
קִרְבוּ שִׂימוּ אֶת־רַגְלֵיכֶם עַל־צַוְּארֵי
הַמְּלָכִים הָאֵלֶּה וַיִּקְרְבוּ וַיָּשִׂימוּ אֶת־
כה רַגְלֵיהֶם עַל־צַוְּארֵיהֶם: וַיֹּאמֶר אֲלֵיהֶם
יְהוֹשֻׁעַ אַל־תִּירְאוּ וְאַל־תֵּחָתּוּ חִזְקוּ
וְאִמְצוּ כִּי כָכָה יַעֲשֶׂה יהוה לְכָל־אֹיְבֵיכֶם
כו אֲשֶׁר אַתֶּם נִלְחָמִים אוֹתָם: וַיַּכֵּם יְהוֹשֻׁעַ
אַחֲרֵי־כֵן וַיְמִיתֵם וַיִּתְלֵם עַל חֲמִשָּׁה
עֵצִים וַיִּהְיוּ תְּלוּיִם עַל־הָעֵצִים עַד־
כז הָעָרֶב: וַיְהִי לְעֵת | בּוֹא הַשֶּׁמֶשׁ צִוָּה
יְהוֹשֻׁעַ וַיֹּרִידוּם מֵעַל הָעֵצִים וַיַּשְׁלִכֻם
אֶל־הַמְּעָרָה אֲשֶׁר נֶחְבְּאוּ־שָׁם וַיָּשִׂמוּ
אֲבָנִים גְּדֹלוֹת עַל־פִּי הַמְּעָרָה עַד־עֶצֶם
כח הַיּוֹם הַזֶּה: וְאֶת־מַקֵּדָה
לָכַד יְהוֹשֻׁעַ בַּיּוֹם הַהוּא וַיַּכֶּהָ לְפִי־
חֶרֶב וְאֶת־מַלְכָּהּ הֶחֱרִם אוֹתָם וְאֶת־

the Emorites were overwrought with fear *(Metzudos).*

◈ Joshua Kills the Five Kings

24. שִׂימוּ אֶת־רַגְלֵיכֶם — *Place your feet.*

The verse describes the fulfillment of Moses' prediction *(Deuteronomy* 33:29), *'Your enemies shall submit to you and you shall tread upon their high places' (Sifri),* for high places refers to the rulers of Israel's enemies.

This was a symbolic gesture signifying that all the remaining Canaanites would be trampled by the Israelites. [Joshua ordered that this act take place in the presence of *all the men of Israel* to inspire them in their conquest of the Canaanites.] *(Malbim).*

[See *Commentary* to 8:18. Perhaps this incident can be viewed as another illustration of *Ramban's* principle concerning the efficacy of symbolic acts.]

Ralbag maintains that this act was calculated to instill fear in the remaining Canaanites in order to deter them from waging war against Israel. To increase the effect of the deterrent, Joshua

from the cave — the king of Jerusalem, the king of
Hebron, the king of Yarmus, the king of Lachish, the
king of Eglon. 24 *It was when they brought out those*
kings to Joshua that Joshua summoned all the men of
Israel and said to the officers of the men of war who
had accompanied him, 'Approach — place your feet
on the necks of these kings.' They approached and
placed their feet on their necks. 25 *Joshua said to*
them, 'Fear not, nor be dismayed; be strong and
resolute, for this is what HASHEM will do to all your
enemies with whom you battle.' 26 *Afterwards Joshua*
struck them and killed them and hanged them on five
gallows, and they remained hanging on the gallows
until evening. 27 *It was at sunset that Joshua ordered*
that they be lowered from the gallows and that they
be thrown into the cave in which they had hidden.
They placed large stones at the opening of the cave —
to this very day.
28 *On that day Joshua captured Makeidah and put*
it to death by the edge of the sword with its king. He
utterly vanquished them and all the souls within it.

ordered that their bodies be hanged on gallows and cast into the cave. The placing of the large stones in front of the opening was designed to serve as a remembrance for the Israelites of this miraculous battle.

26. וַיִּתְלֵם עַל חֲמִשָּׁה עֵצִים — *And* [*he*] *hanged them on five gallows.*

Joshua hanged the kings on five different gallows to demonstrate to the world that their unity was of no avail. In the end they were each hanged separately *(Meam Loez).*

27. וַיְהִי לְעֵת בּוֹא הַשֶּׁמֶשׁ — *It was at sunset.*

Joshua ordered that the corpses be buried at nightfall, for a corpse left unburied overnight defiles the Holy Land *(Radak).* [See *Commentary* and *footnote* to 8:29. Apparently *Radak* follows *Rashi's* view that non-Jews are buried in *Eretz Yisrael* to prevent defilement of the Land, not because their non-burial would be a desecration to the Divine image in which they were created.]

◆§ The City by City Conquest of the South

28. וְאֶת־מַקֵּדָה — *Makeidah.*

Malbim comments that Joshua had not waged war against Makeidah earlier because he was concerned that the kings who had been trapped there might rally forces and attack the Israelites from behind as they invaded the city. (The cave was located outside the city.) When the kings had been put to death, however, Joshua felt secure in attacking Makeidah.

הֶחֱרִם אוֹתָם — *He utterly vanquished* [lit. *finished*] *them.*

The translation follows *Targum.*

כָּל־הַנֶּפֶשׁ אֲשֶׁר־בָּהּ לֹא הִשְׁאִיר שָׂרִיד
וַיַּעַשׂ לְמֶלֶךְ מַקֵּדָה כַּאֲשֶׁר עָשָׂה לְמֶלֶךְ
כט יְרִיחוֹ: וַיַּעֲבֹר יְהוֹשֻׁעַ
וְכָל־יִשְׂרָאֵל עִמּוֹ מִמַּקֵּדָה לִבְנָה וַיִּלָּחֶם
ל עִם־לִבְנָה: וַיִּתֵּן יהוה גַּם־אוֹתָהּ בְּיַד
יִשְׂרָאֵל וְאֶת־מַלְכָּהּ וַיַּכֶּהָ לְפִי־חֶרֶב
וְאֶת־כָּל־הַנֶּפֶשׁ אֲשֶׁר־בָּהּ לֹא־הִשְׁאִיר
בָּהּ שָׂרִיד וַיַּעַשׂ לְמַלְכָּהּ כַּאֲשֶׁר עָשָׂה
לא לְמֶלֶךְ יְרִיחוֹ: וַיַּעֲבֹר
יְהוֹשֻׁעַ וְכָל־יִשְׂרָאֵל עִמּוֹ מִלִּבְנָה לָכִישָׁה
לב וַיִּחַן עָלֶיהָ וַיִּלָּחֶם בָּהּ: וַיִּתֵּן יהוה אֶת־
לָכִישׁ בְּיַד יִשְׂרָאֵל וַיִּלְכְּדָהּ בַּיּוֹם הַשֵּׁנִי
וַיַּכֶּהָ לְפִי־חֶרֶב וְאֶת־כָּל־הַנֶּפֶשׁ אֲשֶׁר־בָּהּ
לג כְּכֹל אֲשֶׁר־עָשָׂה לְלִבְנָה: אָז עָלָה
הֹרָם מֶלֶךְ גֶּזֶר לַעְזֹר אֶת־לָכִישׁ וַיַּכֵּהוּ
יְהוֹשֻׁעַ וְאֶת־עַמּוֹ עַד־בִּלְתִּי הִשְׁאִיר־לוֹ
לד שָׂרִיד: וַיַּעֲבֹר יְהוֹשֻׁעַ וְכָל־
יִשְׂרָאֵל עִמּוֹ מִלָּכִישׁ עֶגְלֹנָה וַיַּחֲנוּ עָלֶיהָ

The commentators do not discuss why Scripture uses the plural object *them* when the antecedent *its king* is singular. *Minchas Shai* notes that some printed versions of Joshua contain the word אוֹתָהּ, *it*, which is in agreement with the singular antecedent. *Targum* apparently also had the plural object.

וְאֶת־כָּל־הַנֶּפֶשׁ — *And all the souls.*
See *Prefatory Remarks* to this chapter.

כַּאֲשֶׁר עָשָׂה לְמֶלֶךְ יְרִיחוֹ — *As he had done to the king of Jericho.*
This informs us that the Israelites did not individually execute this king as they had done to the king of Ai and to the five Emorite kings; rather, they killed him in the course of combat together with the other troops *(Radak).*

29. לִבְנָה — *Livnah.*
See *Commentary* to 12:15 for its location.

31. לָכִישָׁה — *To Lachish.*
T'vuos HaAretz cites sources which locate this city seven miles east and south of Beis Guvrin. However, *T'vuos HaAretz* disagrees and places Lachish about twelve and one half miles west of Beis Guvrin.

וַיִּחַן עָלֶיהָ — *He encamped there.*
They did not immediately wage war against Lachish [as the next verse indicates, for it states that they conquered Lachish on the second day]. First they rested for a day *(Poras Yosef).*

He let none remain, and he did to its king as he had
done to the king of Jericho.
29 *Joshua and all Israel with him proceeded from*
Makeidah to Livnah, and he waged war against
Livnah. 30 *HASHEM had also delivered it and its king*
into the hands of Israel; he put it to death by the edge
of the sword and all the souls within it. He left no
survivor, and he did to its king as he had done to the
king of Jericho.
31 *Joshua and all Israel with him proceeded from*
Livnah to Lachish; he encamped there and waged war
against it. 32 *HASHEM had delivered Lachish in the*
hand of Israel, and he captured it on the second day.
They put it to death by the edge of the sword and all
the souls within it, just as they had done to Livnah.
33 *Then Horam, the king of Gezer, ascended to*
help Lachish. Joshua vanquished him and his people
until none survived.
34 *Joshua and all Israel with him proceeded from*
Lachish to Eglon; they encamped there and waged

According to *Abarbanel* (cited in *Commentary* to verse 15), all the battles recorded in the previous verses occurred on the same day that the sun stood still. When the Israelites arrived at Lachish, the sun was about to set so they camped there. According to tradition, the sun stopped on Friday, and thus the Israelites made camp for the Sabbath. When verse 32 states that they waged war against Lachish *on the second day,* it refers to the second day of the Israelites' encampment, Sunday. Thus they avoided having to battle on the Sabbath day *(Meam Loez).* [See *Commentary* to verse 32.]

32. אֶת־לָכִישׁ — *Lachish.*

Since Scripture mentions that the kings of Makeidah and Livnah were put to death, but does not mention that the king of Lachish was delivered into the hands of Israel, evidently Lachish had not yet appointed a new monarch to replace the king killed by Joshua [verse 26] *(Poras Yosef).*

בַּיּוֹם הַשֵּׁנִי — *On the second day.*

This refers to the second day of Israel's encampment *(Radak).* [See *Poras Yosef* to verse 31.]

Kli Yakar suggests that *the second day* refers to Monday, the second day of the week. On Friday, the day on which the sun stopped, the Jews battled Makeidah and Livnah. On Sunday they traveled to Lachish and camped, and on Monday they conquered the city.

33. מֶלֶךְ גֶּזֶר — *The king of Gezer.*

For the location of Gezer see *Commentary* to 16:3.

34. עֶגְלוֹנָה — *To Eglon.*

T'vuos HaAretz cites sources which locate Eglon ten miles from Beis Guvrin in the direction of Azah. He himself

לה וַיִּלָּחֲמוּ עָלֶיהָ׃ וַיִּלְכְּדוּהָ בַּיּוֹם הַהוּא
וַיַּכּוּהָ לְפִי־חֶרֶב וְאֵת כָּל־הַנֶּפֶשׁ אֲשֶׁר־
בָּהּ בַּיּוֹם הַהוּא הֶחֱרִים כְּכֹל אֲשֶׁר־עָשָׂה
לו לְלָכִישׁ׃ וַיַּעַל יְהוֹשֻׁעַ וְכָל־
יִשְׂרָאֵל עִמּוֹ מֵעֶגְלוֹנָה חֶבְרוֹנָה וַיִּלָּחֲמוּ
לז עָלֶיהָ׃ וַיִּלְכְּדוּהָ וַיַּכּוּהָ־לְפִי־חֶרֶב וְאֶת־
מַלְכָּהּ וְאֶת־כָּל־עָרֶיהָ וְאֶת־כָּל־הַנֶּפֶשׁ
אֲשֶׁר־בָּהּ לֹא־הִשְׁאִיר שָׂרִיד כְּכֹל אֲשֶׁר־
עָשָׂה לְעֶגְלוֹן וַיַּחֲרֵם אוֹתָהּ וְאֶת־כָּל־
לח הַנֶּפֶשׁ אֲשֶׁר־בָּהּ׃ וַיָּשָׁב יְהוֹשֻׁעַ
וְכָל־יִשְׂרָאֵל עִמּוֹ דְּבִרָה וַיִּלָּחֶם עָלֶיהָ׃
לט וַיִּלְכְּדָהּ וְאֶת־מַלְכָּהּ וְאֶת־כָּל־עָרֶיהָ
וַיַּכּוּם לְפִי־חֶרֶב וַיַּחֲרִימוּ אֶת־כָּל־נֶפֶשׁ

claims that it was located about two miles east of Lachish.

36. חֶבְרוֹנָה — *Hebron.*

Hebron was located in the Mountains of Judah (11:21) and was the first piece of land that was acquired in *Eretz Yisrael,* for Abraham bought the Cave of Machpelah in Hebron as a burial place for his wife Sarah *(Genesis* 23:16). Scripture also refers to Hebron by the name Kiryas Arba (see *footnote* to 14:15). It was located in the vicinity of the modern day city of Hebron.

ויעל — [*They;* lit. he] ascended.

In regard to the conquest of all previous city-states, Scripture states, [*they*] *proceeded,* yet here Scripture employs the expression, [*they*] *ascended. Kli Yakar* explains that Hebron was of a much higher elevation than Eglon, and thus it was necessary to make an ascent to conquer it.

37-39. *Malbim* notes that verses 37 to 39 speak of Joshua's conquest of the cities of Hebron and Devir, whereas *Joshua* 15:14 relates that Calev conquered Hebron, and 15:17 and *Judges* 1:13 state that Asniel ben Kenaz conquered Devir. The commentators offer several ways to reconcile this apparent contradiction:

□ *Rashi* comments that 15:14 which recounts Calev's conquest of Hebron refers to an event which did not take place until after Joshua's death, for only then did Calev conquer Hebron as *Judges* 1:20 states. Scripture mentions this even in *Joshua* 15:14 because it was pertinent to the division of the Land which is discussed in that chapter. [*Rashi* leaves unresolved the apparent contradiction between our verse and 15:14.]

□ *Radak* (11:21) suggests that although Calev conquered Hebron, Scripture (here and in 11:21) credits the victory to Joshua, because it was he who issued the command to eliminate the Anakim.

□ *Radak* offers a second interpretation: Joshua fought the battle against the Anakim, but Scripture attributes the victories to Calev and Asniel ben Kenaz because they expended tremendous effort in these battles. They had a

war against it. 35 *On that day they captured it and put*
it to death by the edge of the sword and all the souls
within it he completely destroyed that day, just as he
had done to Lachish.

36 *Joshua and all Israel with him ascended from*
Eglon to Hebron and waged war against it. 37 *They*
captured it and put it to death by the edge of the
sword — its king and its villages and all the souls
within it; he let no survivor remain just as he did to
Eglon. He utterly vanquished it and all the souls
within it.

38 *Joshua and all Israel with him returned to Devir*
and waged war against it.

39 *And he captured it, its king, and its villages and*
put them to death by the edge of the sword and
utterly vanquished all the souls within it; they let no

special interest in conquering these two cities, since Joshua had allocated the territory in which the cities were located to their tribe, Judah.

☐ *Ralbag (Judges* 1:11) asserts that the city Devir mentioned here is not the same city Devir which was conquered by Asniel ben Kenaz that Scripture relates in *Judges* 1:11.

☐ *Malbim* maintains that Joshua conquered Hebron itself, while Calev conquered the suburbs of the city. Similarly, Joshua conquered Devir, and Asniel ben Kenaz conquered its outskirts.

37. וְאֶת־מַלְכָּהּ — *Its king.*

Verse 26 relates that Joshua had killed the king of Hebron, so which king of Hebron is referred to in this verse?

Radak suggests that the people of Hebron had appointed another king after their former monarch and his four allies were killed.

Although the king of Hebron headed a powerful monarchy as evidenced by the fact that Adoni Tzedek requested Hebron's former king Hoham to participate in his alliance against Gibeon (verse 3), this second king of Hebron is not listed in Chapter 12 among the thirty-one powerful kings which Joshua conquered. *Kli Yakar* explains that Hoham's replacement was not powerful, and thus the conquest of Hebron did not compare to the conquest of the other city-states mentioned in Chapter 12.

Malbim alternatively suggests that Hebron had two kings.

עָרֶיהָ —*Its villages* [*lit. cities*].

The translation follows *Targum.*

All the cities and their inhabitants which were within the district lines of Hebron were referred to by Hebron's name. Hence, the possessive adjective *its (Radak).*

38. וַיָּשָׁב — [*They;* lit. *he*] *returned.*

Radak suggests that although Joshua had passed Devir while *en route* to Hebron, he did not wage war against it until he had vanquished Hebron. Hebron contained the burial site of the Patriarchs, and Joshua was very eager to acquire it *(Meam Loez).*

דְּבִרָה — *To Devir.*

See *Commentary* to 12:13.

י אֲשֶׁר־בָּהּ לֹא הִשְׁאִיר שָׂרִיד כַּאֲשֶׁר עָשָׂה
מ־מג לְחֶבְרוֹן כֵּן־עָשָׂה לִדְבִרָה וּלְמַלְכָּהּ
מ וְכַאֲשֶׁר עָשָׂה לְלִבְנָה וּלְמַלְכָּהּ: וַיַּכֶּה
יְהוֹשֻׁעַ אֶת־כָּל־הָאָרֶץ הָהָר וְהַנֶּגֶב
וְהַשְּׁפֵלָה וְהָאֲשֵׁדוֹת וְאֵת כָּל־מַלְכֵיהֶם
לֹא הִשְׁאִיר שָׂרִיד וְאֵת כָּל־הַנְּשָׁמָה
הֶחֱרִים כַּאֲשֶׁר צִוָּה יְהֹוָה אֱלֹהֵי יִשְׂרָאֵל:
מא וַיַּכֵּם יְהוֹשֻׁעַ מִקָּדֵשׁ בַּרְנֵעַ וְעַד־עַזָּה וְאֵת
מב כָּל־אֶרֶץ גֹּשֶׁן וְעַד־גִּבְעוֹן: וְאֵת כָּל־
הַמְּלָכִים הָאֵלֶּה וְאֶת־אַרְצָם לָכַד יְהוֹשֻׁעַ
פַּעַם אֶחָת כִּי יְהֹוָה אֱלֹהֵי יִשְׂרָאֵל נִלְחָם
יא מג לְיִשְׂרָאֵל: וַיָּשָׁב יְהוֹשֻׁעַ וְכָל־יִשְׂרָאֵל עִמּוֹ
א א אֶל־הַמַּחֲנֶה הַגִּלְגָּלָה: וַיְהִי

39. וְכַאֲשֶׁר עָשָׂה לְלִבְנָה וּלְמַלְכָּהּ — *And as he did to Livnah and its king.*

Just as the king of Livnah was killed in battle, so was the king of Devir (*Malbim*).

⤛§ The Remainder of the Southern Conquest

40-43.

Chapter 10 concludes with a general account of the remainder of Joshua's southern conquest. It should be noted that although the kings of Jerusalem and Yarmus were among the five kings who plotted against Gibeon in the beginning of this chapter and were subsequently killed, Scripture here does not state that the cities of Jerusalem and Yarmus were among the cities which Joshua conquered.

It is explained in 15:63 that Joshua did not conquer the city of Jerusalem (see *Commentary* there), but no mention is made that the city of Yarmus was never conquered.

40. אֶת־כָּל־הָאָרֶץ — *The entire country.*

This refers to the entire southern part of *Eretz Yisrael* (*Malbim*).

הָהָר — *The mountains.*

This refers to the mountains of Hebron (*Daas Sofrim*).

וְהַנֶּגֶב — *The Negev.*

Targum renders 'the South.' Joshua vanquished the cities south of Devir, such as Tziklag and Arad (*Daas Sofrim*).

Others, however, understand this as a reference to a desert or 'dry region' (*Metzudos*).

Malbim notes that the four regions mentioned in this verse are in two pairs, each member of the pair is the opposite of the other — mountains and valleys, dry regions and wet regions.

וְהַשְּׁפֵלָה — *The valley.*

This valley region is located where the valley of the Philistines meets the valley of Sharon, which is south of Jaffa, Ramaleh, and Yavneh. It is a very fertile region and extends in the south to Azah and in the west to Wadi El Arish (*T'vuos HaAretz*).

וְהָאֲשֵׁדוֹת — *And the land of the falls.*

Rashi understands this word as *waterfalls,* while *Radak* renders

survivor remain. As he did to Hebron so did he do to
Devir and its king and as he did to Livnah and its
king. 40 *Joshua put to death the entire country — the*
mountains, the Negev, the valley, and the land of the
falls and all their kings. He let no survivor remain.
He utterly vanquished every soul as HASHEM, the
God of Israel, had commanded. 41 *Joshua put them to*
death from Kadesh Barnea to Azah and the entire
land of Goshen to Gibeon. 42 *And all those kings and*
their land Joshua captured in one sweep because
HASHEM, the God of Israel fought for Israel.
43 *Joshua and all Israel with him returned to the*
encampment at Gilgal.

'mountain slopes.'

כַּאֲשֶׁר צִוָּה ה׳ אֱלֹהֵי יִשְׂרָאֵל — *As HASHEM, the God of Israel, had commanded.*

Joshua did not vanquish these cities out of malice, but out of obedience to the Divine decree that these cities and their inhabitants be destroyed *(Daas Sofrim).*

41. מִקָּדֵשׁ בַּרְנֵעַ וְעַד־עַזָּה — *From Kadesh Barnea to Azah.*

This forms a part of the southern border of *Eretz Yisrael* from east to west *(Rashi).* For more detail, see *Commentary* to 13:3.

אֶרֶץ גֹּשֶׁן — *Land of Goshen.*

In the Pentateuch, Eretz Goshen is located in Egypt, but here Scripture refers to a part of *Eretz Yisrael* with the same name (Radak). It was located in Judah's territory *(Malbim).*

Others claim, however, that Joshua actually conquered sections of Egypt[1] bordering the Nile River and that this territory is thus a portion of *Eretz Yisrael* (see *Radak* to 11:16 and *R' S. Sirilio* to *Jerusalem Talmud, Sheviis* 6:1).

42. פַּעַם אֶחָת — *One sweep* [lit. *one time*].

This indicates that these kings were conquered one after another, without interruptions or lengthy battles *(Radak).*

Since the battle of Ai took two confrontations, Scripture explains that the following victories were accomplished in a single encounter *(Metzudos).*

This is in contradistinction to the battles mentioned in the next chapter, which were not won in a single stroke *(Malbim).*

כִּי ה׳ אֱלֹהֵי יִשְׂרָאֵל נִלְחָם — *Because HASHEM, the God of Israel, fought.*

Without this extraordinary Divine assistance, the southern conquest would not have proceeded so rapidly *(Daas Sofrim).*

43. וַיָּשָׁב — [*They;* lit. *he*] *returned.*

See *Commentary* to verse 15.

1. The tribe of Judah merited the land of Goshen because Judah fulfilled his father Jacob's request of preparing his descent to Goshen (by establishing yeshivos [*Rashi*]) so that he could meet his long-mourned-for son Joseph. (*And he sent Judah before him to Joseph to show the way to Goshen* [*Genesis* 46:28].) The Egyptians did not contest the allocation of Goshen to Judah because Pharaoh had given it to Sarah many years before *(Daas Zekanim to Genesis* 46:29).

יא כִּשְׁמֹעַ יָבִין מֶלֶךְ־חָצוֹר וַיִּשְׁלַח אֶל־יוֹבָב
ב מֶלֶךְ מָדוֹן וְאֶל־מֶלֶךְ שִׁמְרוֹן וְאֶל־מֶלֶךְ
ב אַכְשָׁף׃ וְאֶל־הַמְּלָכִים אֲשֶׁר מִצְּפוֹן בָּהָר
וּבָעֲרָבָה נֶגֶב כִּנֲרוֹת וּבַשְּׁפֵלָה וּבְנָפוֹת

XI

After the Israelites' success in their campaign against the Canaanites to the south, they turned their attention to the final stage of their conquest — the northern Canaanite kingdoms. The Israelites' mission continued to be simplified by Divine Providence (see footnote *to 7:5). Yavin, the king of Chatzor, formed a confederacy of the most powerful northern kingdoms in an attempt to stem the tide of the Israelites' successes. Without warning, Joshua struck the unsuspecting confederacy while they were planning their attack against the Israelites. From this overwhelming victory Joshua marched through the north of* Eretz Yisrael *and concluded the conquest by seizing the cities whose kings joined Yavin's confederacy. In the concluding portion of this chapter, which summarizes the Israelites' victories in general terms, Scripture succinctly adds that* it was HASHEM's doing *(verse 20).*

1-15. The Northern Conquest

◆§ The Northern Confederacy

1. וַיְהִי כִּשְׁמֹעַ — *It was when* [*he*] *heard.*

The text does not explain what Yavin heard. *Chida* suggests that Yavin heard two frightening reports: (a) that the Israelites were merciless in their campaign to eradicate the Canaanites and (b) that the Israelites subjected the five kings to great embarrassment when they stepped on the kings' necks before executing them.

[Apparently, Yavin figured that his only chance of salvation would be a unified attack by all the northern kings against the Israelites.]

Lev Aharon, however, suggests that Yavin heard that the Israelites returned to their camp at Gilgal (10:43). Yavin interpreted this return as the conclusion of the Israelites' strikes and thought that they would be vulnerable to attack.

חָצוֹר — *Chatzor.*

This city was located north of the Sea of Merom, to the west of Banias. Perhaps it is this city which King Solomon later rebuilt *(I Kings* 9:15).

וַיִּשְׁלַח — *He sent.*

Yavin saw that the other kings were defeated one by one, because they did not make a unified effort against the Israelites. He therefore attempted to involve the other northern kings in his reprisal against the Jews *(Ralbag).*

מָדוֹן — *Madon.*

This city was located about five miles north of Tzipori.

שִׁמְרוֹן — *Shimron.*

This city was called Simoni *(Jerusalem Talmud, Megillah* 1:1) and was located about five miles southwest of Tzipori. It was later given to Naftali (19:15).

אַכְשָׁף — *Achshaf.*

Although the *Septuagint* identifies Achshaf as the present day Haifa, *T'vuos HaAretz* disagrees and places it north of Akko. It was later given to Asher (19:25).

2. וְאֶל־הַמְּלָכִים — *And to the kings.*

[According to *Ramban* (cited in the *Prefatory Remarks* to Chapter 10), the fact that Scripture did not mention these kings by name indicates that they were not the Israelites' most formidable foes.]

מִצְּפוֹן — *From the north.*

Yavin had to look to the north for support since the kings to the south had already been eliminated *(Malbim).*

11
1-2 [1] *It was when Yavin the king of Chatzor heard, he
sent to Yovav the king of Madon and to the king of
Shimron and to the king of Achshaf* [2] *and to the
kings from the north of the mountains, from the
plains south of Kinros, and from the plains and in*

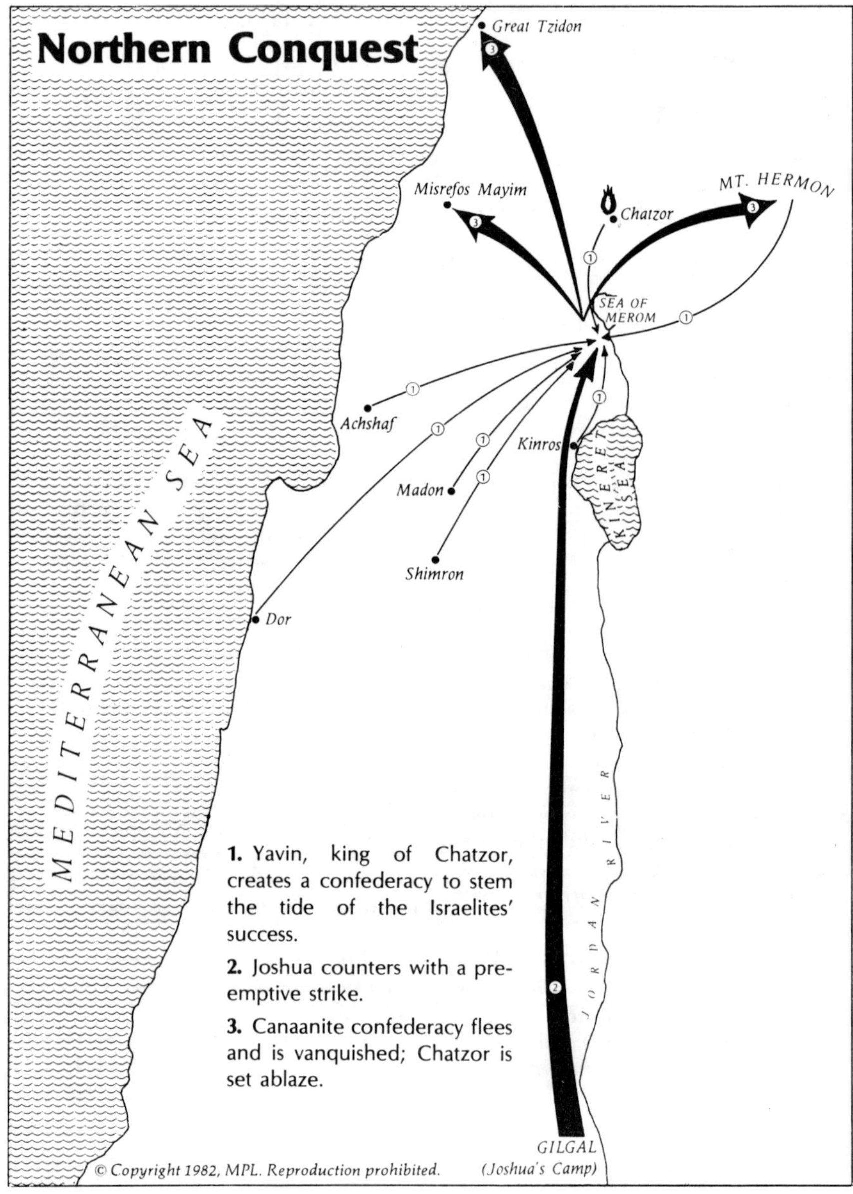

יא
ג־ו

ג דּוֹר מִיָּם: הַכְּנַעֲנִי מִמִּזְרָח וּמִיָּם וְהָאֱמֹרִי
וְהַחִתִּי וְהַפְּרִזִּי וְהַיְבוּסִי בָּהָר וְהַחִוִּי
ד תַּחַת חֶרְמוֹן בְּאֶרֶץ הַמִּצְפָּה: וַיֵּצְאוּ הֵם
וְכָל־מַחֲנֵיהֶם עִמָּם עַם־רָב כַּחוֹל אֲשֶׁר
עַל־שְׂפַת־הַיָּם לָרֹב וְסוּס וָרֶכֶב רַב
ה מְאֹד: וַיִּוָּעֲדוּ כֹּל הַמְּלָכִים הָאֵלֶּה וַיָּבֹאוּ
וַיַּחֲנוּ יַחְדָּו אֶל־מֵי מֵרוֹם לְהִלָּחֵם עִם־
ו יִשְׂרָאֵל: וַיֹּאמֶר יהוה
אֶל־יְהוֹשֻׁעַ אַל־תִּירָא מִפְּנֵיהֶם כִּי מָחָר
כָּעֵת הַזֹּאת אָנֹכִי נֹתֵן אֶת־כֻּלָּם חֲלָלִים
לִפְנֵי יִשְׂרָאֵל אֶת־סוּסֵיהֶם תְּעַקֵּר

מִצָּפוֹן בָּהָר — *From the north of the mountains.*

This verse could be rendered in either one of two ways. '[And to the kings] of the north, in the mountains and in the plains ...' *or* '[And to the kings] north of the mountains and the plains ...'*(Radak).*

כִּנְרוֹת — *Kinros.*

Targum identifies this as the city of Ginosar, noted for its bountiful fruits *(Radak)* which were very sweet *(Aruch).*

It is located approximately two and one-half miles north of Tiberias on the western shore of the Kineret Sea.

The *Midrash (Bereishis Rabbah* 98:17) interprets Ginosar as a compound word: *gan* (garden) and *sar* (prince). The area around the Kineret Sea was very fertile, and the land produced all types of fruits — i.e., it was splendid with fruits as a prince is with finery.

וּבְנָפוֹת דּוֹר — *And in the districts of Dor.*

Targum renders נָפוֹת, *districts.* The city of Dor was located on the Mediterranean, about five miles north of Caesarea. [See *Commentary* to 12:23.]

3. הַכְּנַעֲנִי ... וְהַיְבוּסִי — *The Canaanites ... and the Jebusites.*

Even after the many wars in the south, members from all six Canaanite nations remained since the population of each nation was distributed throughout the entire land *(Daas Sofrim).*

[Although there were *seven* tribes of Canaanites, only six are mentioned because the seventh, the Girgashites, fled to Africa when they heard that the Israelites were entering the Land.]

תַּחַת חֶרְמוֹן — *At the foothills* [lit. *under*] *of Mount Hermon.*

The translation follows *Radak's* interpretation. [See *Commentary* to 12:1.]

בְּאֶרֶץ הַמִּצְפָּה — *In the land of Mitzpah.*

Radak conjectures that Joshua built an altar in the Mitzpah region commemorating the enormous salvation that the Israelites experienced in their encounter with the northern kings (verse 8), and that it is this location which is referred to in *Judges* 11:11, in *I Samuel* 7:5, and 10:17, as a place of assembly.

Alternatively, *Radak* suggests that this expression refers to Mount Hermon i.e., it was located *in the land of Mitzpah.*

T'vuos HaAretz identifies this place of assembly not as the Mitzpah in

the districts of Dor to the west. 3 *The Canaanites in*
the east and in the west; the Emorites, Hittites, and
the Perizzites and the Jebusites in the mountains. The
Hivvites were at the foothills of Mount Hermon in
the land of Mitzpah. 4 *They went out along with all*
their camps, many people — as numerous as the sand
on the seashore — and a great multitude of horses and
chariots. 5 *And all these kings gathered together;*
they came and encamped together at the Sea of
Merom to wage war with Israel.
6 *HASHEM said to Joshua, 'Do not fear them, for*
tomorrow at this time, I will deliver them slain before
Israel. You shall hamstring their horses and burn

Gilead (east of the Jordan), but rather as another city of the same name which was located about twelve miles northwest of Jerusalem.

4. וַיֵּצְאוּ — *They went out.*

These kings instituted two changes which Israel's previous opponents had not tried: (a) they took to the battlefield as a single unit, and (b) they used horses and chariots for combat *(Malbim).*

5. מֵי מֵרוֹם — *Sea of Merom* [lit. *waters of Merom*].

The Sea of Merom is located north of the Kineret Sea *(T'vuos HaAretz).*

6. אַל תִּירָא — *Do not fear.*

Malbim cites the verse *(Deuteronomy* 20:1): *When you see the horses and chariots, do not fear.*

[In the *Commentary* to 10:8, it was suggested that 'fear' in this context referred to fear of the consequences of sin, rather than to fear of a physical threat. Had Joshua committed a sin, the Divine promise of extraordinary Providence might have been rescinded, in which case Israel would then have been forced to oppose the mighty northern confederacy without Divine aid. *Poras Yosef* suggests that Joshua may have been unsure whether he acted correctly in ordering his soldiers to step on the necks of the five kings, for as *Rashi (Amos* 2:1) explains, it is an egregious error to show disrespect to even a non-Jewish king. Joshua's action was vindicated at this time, for God told him not to worry; since he had ordered this action to raise the Israelites' *esprit de corps* rather than to humiliate the kings, it was not considered a sin.]

תְּעַקֵּר — *You shall hamstring.*

Although most codifiers rule that causing pain to an animal is a prohibition of Torah law (see *Rosh* to *Bava Metzia* 32b and *SeferHaChinuch* 451), Joshua was permitted to inflict pain on these horses because he received a direct decree from God to do so *(Tosafos* to *Avodah Zarah* 13a).

Ralbag explains that this Divine injunction to hamstring the horses was issued to prevent the Israelites from taking the horses and chariots as spoils and using them in other battles against the Canaanites. With such powerful instruments of war at their disposal, the Israelites might have lost sight of the fact that God alone was responsible for their victories.

Malbim adds that since a king is enjoined from possessing too many horses (see *Deuteronomy* 17:16), this decree was a preventive measure lest Joshua take horses in violation of this prohibition. *Daas Sofrim* takes excep-

ז וְאֶת־מַרְכְּבֹתֵיהֶם תִּשְׂרֹף בָּאֵשׁ׃ וַיָּבֹא
יְהוֹשֻׁעַ וְכָל־עַם הַמִּלְחָמָה עִמּוֹ עֲלֵיהֶם
עַל־מֵי מֵרוֹם פִּתְאֹם וַיִּפְּלוּ בָּהֶם׃
ח וַיִּתְּנֵם יְהוָה בְּיַד־יִשְׂרָאֵל וַיַּכּוּם
וַיִּרְדְּפוּם עַד־צִידוֹן רַבָּה וְעַד מִשְׂרְפוֹת
מַיִם וְעַד־בִּקְעַת מִצְפֶּה מִזְרָחָה וַיַּכֻּם עַד־
ט בִּלְתִּי הִשְׁאִיר־לָהֶם שָׂרִיד׃ וַיַּעַשׂ לָהֶם
יְהוֹשֻׁעַ כַּאֲשֶׁר אָמַר־לוֹ יְהוָה אֶת־
סוּסֵיהֶם עִקֵּר וְאֶת־מַרְכְּבֹתֵיהֶם שָׂרַף
י בָּאֵשׁ׃ וַיָּשָׁב יְהוֹשֻׁעַ בָּעֵת הַהִיא
וַיִּלְכֹּד אֶת־חָצוֹר וְאֶת־מַלְכָּהּ הִכָּה בֶחָרֶב
כִּי־חָצוֹר לְפָנִים הִיא רֹאשׁ כָּל־
יא הַמַּמְלָכוֹת הָאֵלֶּה׃ וַיַּכּוּ אֶת־כָּל־הַנֶּפֶשׁ
אֲשֶׁר־בָּהּ לְפִי־חֶרֶב הַחֲרֵם לֹא נוֹתַר כָּל־

tion to *Malbim's* interpretation, arguing that this prohibition exists during times of peace, but not in times of war. [See *Rambam, Hil. Melachim* 3:3 that horses may be amassed for military purposes.]

Radak comments that the hamstringing process did not kill the animals, but just hindered their ability to walk.

וְאֶת־מַרְכְּבֹתֵיהֶם תִּשְׂרֹף בָּאֵשׁ — *And burn their chariots with fire.*

Although most codifiers seem to agree that the destruction of property is forbidden by Torah law (see *Minchas Chinuch* 529), if this destruction is done for a purpose, it is permissible *(Radak)*. The benefit given by *Ralbag* in the previous note regarding the horses would apply in this case as well.

✎ Joshua's Pre-emptive Strike

7. פִּתְאֹם — *Suddenly.*

The word *suddenly* could be understood both from the point of view of the Canaanites and from the point of view of the Israelites.

Daas Sofrim explains that the Canaanite kings did not expect to be confronted because they had such a large camp and because the Israelites had been such a great distance away. [From Gilgal to the Sea of Merom is some sixty-five miles.]

Meam Loez suggests that the word *suddenly* is used to show how alacritous Joshua was in fulfilling the command he received in the prophetic vision (verse 6).

8. צִידוֹן רַבָּה — *Great Tzidon.*

It was located on the Mediterranean, northwest of the Sea of Merom [the city of Sidar in Lebanon (see *Commentary* to 19:28)].

There was a smaller city which was also named Tzidon; therefore Scripture specifies that the Israelites chased their enemies to *Great Tzidon (Radak).*

This city was most likely named for Tzidon who was the first born of Canaan (*Genesis* 10:15) and formed the most northern point of the Canaanite possessions *(ibid.,* 19).

מִשְׂרְפוֹת מַיִם — *Misrefos Mayim* [lit. *burning places of water*].

their chariots with fire.'
7 *Joshua with all his men of war suddenly came*
upon them at the waters of Merom and pounced
upon them. 8 *And HASHEM delivered them into*
Israel's hand, and they killed them and pursued them
all the way to Great Tzidon and Misrefos Mayim and
to the Valley of Mitzpeh eastward. They killed them
until none remained. 9 *And Joshua dealt with them as*
HASHEM had ordered; he hamstrung their horses and
burned their chariots with fire.
10 *Joshua returned at that time and captured*
Chatzor and put its king to death with the sword
because Chatzor was formerly the leader of all those
kingdoms. 11 *They killed every soul that was there —*
by the edge of the sword were they utterly
vanquished — not one soul remained. He burned

T'vuos HaAretz does not identify its location.

Targum translates this as *ditches of the sea.*

The inhabitants would dig ditches in which the salt water would accumulate. When the water would evaporate ['burn'], they would collect the salt *(Rashi).* [See *Rashi* to *Shabbos* 72b, s.v. דכניף and *Har Tzvi* (Responsa), *Orach Chaim* I:213.]

בִּקְעַת מִצְפֶּה — *Valley of Mitzpeh.*

[Since verse 3 located Mount Hermon in the region of Mitzpah, this was therefore located east of the Sea of Merom.]

10. וְאֶת־מַלְכָּהּ — *Its king.*

Presumably, this refers to Yavin, the King of Chatzor (verse 1). Verse 8, however, relates that all the members of the northern confederacy were killed. What happened to Yavin?

Lev Aharon suggests that Yavin did not participate in the battle against Joshua. Since he was the confederacy's leader, they did not want to expose him to the risks of combat.

Kli Yakar advances that Yavin did indeed die in combat. This verse refers to the death of the regent Yavin established before his departure to battle to keep order while he was away. It is for this reason that Scripture does not mention his name.

[According to the *Midrash* cited in the *Commentary* to 12:9, the *king* referred to in this verse could be the second in command of the kingdom.]

כִּי־חָצוֹר לְפָנִים הִיא — *Because Chatzor was formerly.*

Because Chatzor had been the leader of the surrounding kingdoms, Joshua smote it first *(Metzudos).*

Joshua felt compelled to attack the very large city of Chatzor, because he was concerned that many soldiers would seek haven there when they heard that Joshua had defeated the northern confederacy *(Kli Yakar).*

11. לֹא נוֹתַר — *Not [one soul] remained.*

No one was overlooked. *Malbim* distinguishes between לֹא נִשְׁאַר (cognates of which are used in verse 8) which means 'none were intentionally allowed to live' and לֹא נוֹתַר which means 'none were even accidentally overlooked.' In the battles mentioned in

יא
יב־טו

יב נְשָׁמָה וְאֶת־חָצוֹר שָׂרַף בָּאֵשׁ: וְאֶת־כָּל־
עָרֵי הַמְּלָכִים־הָאֵלֶּה וְאֶת־כָּל־מַלְכֵיהֶם
לָכַד יְהוֹשֻׁעַ וַיַּכֵּם לְפִי־חֶרֶב הֶחֱרִים
יג אוֹתָם כַּאֲשֶׁר צִוָּה מֹשֶׁה עֶבֶד יְהוָה: רַק
כָּל־הֶעָרִים הָעֹמְדוֹת עַל־תִּלָּם לֹא־
שְׂרָפָם יִשְׂרָאֵל זוּלָתִי אֶת־חָצוֹר לְבַדָּהּ
יד שָׂרַף יְהוֹשֻׁעַ: וְכֹל שְׁלַל הֶעָרִים הָאֵלֶּה
וְהַבְּהֵמָה בָּזְזוּ לָהֶם בְּנֵי יִשְׂרָאֵל רַק אֶת־
כָּל הָאָדָם הִכּוּ לְפִי־חֶרֶב עַד־הִשְׁמִדָם
טו אוֹתָם לֹא הִשְׁאִירוּ כָּל־נְשָׁמָה: כַּאֲשֶׁר
צִוָּה יהוה אֶת־מֹשֶׁה עַבְדּוֹ כֵּן־צִוָּה מֹשֶׁה
אֶת־יְהוֹשֻׁעַ וְכֵן עָשָׂה יְהוֹשֻׁעַ לֹא־הֵסִיר
דָּבָר מִכֹּל אֲשֶׁר־צִוָּה יְהוָה אֶת־מֹשֶׁה:
טז וַיִּקַּח יְהוֹשֻׁעַ אֶת־כָּל־הָאָרֶץ הַזֹּאת הָהָר
וְאֶת־כָּל־הַנֶּגֶב וְאֵת כָּל־אֶרֶץ הַגֹּשֶׁן וְאֶת־
הַשְּׁפֵלָה וְאֶת־הָעֲרָבָה וְאֶת־הַר יִשְׂרָאֵל

verses 8 and 14, some Canaanites managed to escape, but in this campaign none survived.

12. וְאֶת־כָּל־עָרֵי הַמְּלָכִים — *And all the cities of these kings.*

These battles did not take place at this time, but later, during the seven years of conquest, as explained in verse 18 *(Malbim).*

13. הָעֹמְדוֹת עַל־תִּלָּם — *That were standing in their strength.*

Targum renders תִּלָּם as *strength,* i.e., their walls were still erect.

Their walls were not razed during the conquest, as were Jericho's and Ai's *(Rashi).*

זוּלָתִי אֶת־חָצוֹר לְבַדָּהּ — *Only Chatzor* [lit. *except Chatzor by itself*].

Rashi cites the *Midrash (Bereishis Rabbah* 81:4) which states that Joshua burned Chatzor because of a Divine command which Moses had transmitted to him.

Abarbanel explains that Chatzor was burned to serve as a deterrent to any king who might want to make a coalition against the Israelites in the future.

Alternatively, *Chida* suggests that Chatzor was burned because it served as a haven for many Canaanites.

שָׂרַף יְהוֹשֻׁעַ — *Did Joshua burn.*

Although Scripture has already mentioned in verse 11 that Chatzor was burned, perhaps Scripture repeats it here after the phrase in verse 12, *as Moses the servant of HASHEM had commanded,* to indicate that Joshua burned Chatzor because of a tradition he had received from Moses [see *Midrash* cited in previous note] *(Chida).*

15. כַּאֲשֶׁר צִוָּה ה׳ ... כֵּן צִוָּה מֹשֶׁה — *As HASHEM commanded ... so did Moses charge.*

This refers to the tradition Moses received from God to burn Chatzor,

Chatzor with fire. [12] *And all the cities of these kings and all their kings Joshua captured and put to death by the edge of the sword and utterly vanquished them, as Moses the servant of HASHEM had commanded.* [13] *However, all the cities that were standing in their strength, Israel did not burn. Only Chatzor did Joshua burn.* [14] *All the spoils of these cities and the animals the Children of Israel took for themselves as booty; every man they put to death by the edge of the sword until they exterminated them. They did not spare a soul.* [15] *As HASHEM commanded Moses his servant so did Moses charge Joshua; and so Joshua did. He was not remiss in anything which HASHEM commanded Moses.*

[16] *And Joshua conquered this entire country: the mountains, all the Negev, all the land of Goshen, the valley, the Aravah, and the Mountain of Israel and its*

which he transmitted to Joshua (*Rashash* to *Midrash* cited above).

לֹא־הֵסִיר דָּבָר מִכֹּל ... — *He was not remiss in anything* [*lit. He did not violate one thing from all*].

[According to *Rashash* (cited in previous note), this clause would presumably refer to other commands, not the tradition to burn Chatzor.]

The *Talmud* (*Jerusalem, Peah* 2:1) notes that Scripture does not state 'as Moses commanded him [Joshua],' but rather, '*As HASHEM commanded Moses.*' From here the *Midrash* deduces that Joshua was able to intuitively reconstruct those commands which God had told Moses even though he had not heard them from him. [See *Ali Shor* pages 75-76.]

◆§ Summary of the Israelites' Victories

16. הָהָר — *The mountains.*
See *Commentary* to 10:40.

אֶרֶץ הַגֹּשֶׁן — *The land of Goshen.*
See *Commentary* to 10:41. *Radak*, following the view that this refers to the region east of the Nile, adds that the Jews merited this land because Judah obeyed his father Jacob by establishing a Torah academy in Goshen before his other brothers descended to Egypt (*Genesis* 46:28, *Rashi*).

Meam Loez explains that the prefix ה (the demonstrative adjective 'the') preceding Goshen indicates that the Goshen mentioned was well known, and hence, Scripture is referring to the land of Goshen where Jacob and his sons resided.

וְאֶת־הַשְּׁפֵלָה — *The valley.*
See *Commentary* to 10:40.

וְאֶת־הָעֲרָבָה — *The Aravah* [lit. *plains*].
This region refers to the Jordan River valley which extends between the Dead Sea and the Kineret Sea. It is the lowest region in *Eretz Yisrael* and measures about five miles wide in the north near Beis Shean and about seven and one half miles wide in the south near Jericho.

וְאֶת־הַר יִשְׂרָאֵל — *The Mountain of Israel.*
Radak explains that this mountain

יז וּשְׁפֵלָתֹה: מִן־הָהָר הֶחָלָק הָעוֹלֶה שֵׂעִיר
וְעַד־בַּעַל גָּד בְּבִקְעַת הַלְּבָנוֹן תַּחַת הַר־
חֶרְמוֹן וְאֵת כָּל־מַלְכֵיהֶם לָכַד וַיַּכֵּם
יח וַיְמִיתֵם: יָמִים רַבִּים עָשָׂה יְהוֹשֻׁעַ אֶת־
יט כָּל־הַמְּלָכִים הָאֵלֶּה מִלְחָמָה: לֹא־הָיְתָה
עִיר אֲשֶׁר הִשְׁלִימָה אֶל־בְּנֵי יִשְׂרָאֵל
בִּלְתִּי הַחִוִּי יֹשְׁבֵי גִבְעוֹן אֶת־הַכֹּל לָקְחוּ
כ בַמִּלְחָמָה: כִּי־מֵאֵת יְהוָה | הָיְתָה לְחַזֵּק
אֶת־לִבָּם לִקְרַאת הַמִּלְחָמָה אֶת־יִשְׂרָאֵל
לְמַעַן הַחֲרִימָם לְבִלְתִּי הֱיוֹת לָהֶם תְּחִנָּה
כִּי לְמַעַן הַשְׁמִידָם כַּאֲשֶׁר צִוָּה יְהוָה אֶת־
כא מֹשֶׁה: וַיָּבֹא יְהוֹשֻׁעַ בָּעֵת הַהִיא

was named for Jacob who had lived there, for he was also called Israel. (See *Genesis* 32:29.)

T'vuos HaAretz conjectures that this was located in the mountains of Ephraim and included Mount Gerizim and Mount Eval.

17. הָהָר הֶחָלָק — *Mount Chalak.*

T'vuos HaAretz does not locate this mountain, but others suggest that it formed the southeastern boundary of Joshua's conquest.

Metzudos (based on *Targum*) comments that because the mountain was divided in two, it was called *chalak,* which means 'divided.' *Rashi,* however, understands *chalak* to be a cognate of the adjective 'smooth' and states that it was a smooth mountain, i.e., without trees *(Radak).*

בַּעַל גָּד — *Ba'al Gad.*

Targum renders *'plains of Gad.'* This formed part of the northern border. *T'vuos HaAretz* identifies it as the city of Banias located west of Mount Hermon in the Anti-Lebanon mountain range and north of the Sea of Merom. It represented the most northern point in Joshua's conquest *(Rashi).* [The Anti-Lebanon range parallels the Lebanon range in the northern part of the Land. These ranges extend from southwest to northeast.]

18. יָמִים רַבִּים — *For a long time.*

The previous chapter (10:42), which states that Joshua captured all the kings in a sudden, stunning victory, refers to the battles which Joshua fought before he returned to Gilgal. When he left Gilgal, he fought the remaining kings. It is to these protracted battles that this verse refers *(Radak).*

Joshua had received God's guarantee that he would be the one to allocate the land to all the tribes (1:6). According to the *Midrash (Bamidbar Rabbah* 22:6), this verse criticizes Joshua for intentionally delaying the conquest in order to extend his life, for the sooner the conquest was completed the sooner the land would be divided. Joshua was originally supposed to live as long as Moses (120 years) [see *Commentary* to 1:6], but ten years were deducted from his life in punishment for his dalliance. *Maharzu (ibid.)* explains Joshua's motivation for extending his life. He knew that for as long as he lived, the

valley. 17 *From Mount Chalak which ascends to Seir,*
to Ba'al Gad in the valley of the Lebanon at the
foothills of Mount Hermon; and he captured all their
kings, smote them, and executed them.
18 *For a long time did Joshua wage war with all*
these kings. 19 *There was not one city which made*
peace with the Children of Israel with the exception
of the Hivvites who dwelled in Gibeon; they took
them all in battle. 20 *For it was HASHEM's doing to*
harden their hearts to battle Israel so that they would
be completely destroyed — since they would not be
pitied — and so that they would be annihilated, as
HASHEM had commanded Moses.
21 *At that time Joshua went and destroyed the*

Israelites would not sin as 24:31 states, *And Israel served HASHEM all the days of Joshua.* Thus, he attempted to extend his life for the good of the nation. The *Midrash (ibid.),* however, concludes that *Many are the thoughts in a man's heart, but the plan of HASHEM endures* (*Proverbs* 19:21).

19. לֹא־הָיְתָה — *There was not.*

Verse 20 explains why no city chose to make peace with the Israelites *(For it was HASHEM's doing to harden their hearts).* This verse reveals how God's plan came about. Since the wars were carried out over an extended period of time, the Canaanites' hearts became hardened, and they opted to fight against the Israelites instead of submitting to them. Had the Israelites waged wars against each individual city immediately after their initial successes, these cities would have requested a truce, which the Israelites would have had to accept [see *Prefatory Remarks* to Chapter 9] *(Malbim).*

20. כִּי־מֵאֵת ה׳ הָיְתָה לְחַזֵּק אֶת־לִבָּם — *For it was HASHEM's doing to harden their hearts.*

God hardened the Canaanites' hearts for two reasons: (a) to punish them for their misdeeds[1] and (b) to ensure that they would be eliminated in order that they would not be able to exert a negative influence on the Jews *(Radak).*

[See *Introduction.*]

21. בָּעֵת הַהִיא — *At that time.*

After Joshua fought against Eglon, he waged war against the Anakim in Hebron and Devir (10:36-39) *(Radak).*

1. *Rambam (Hil. Teshuvah* 6:1-3) explains that it is not unjust for God to harden an individual's heart. In brief, man can receive punishment for his sins in this world, the next world, or in both. However, punishment is only meted out if the individual does not repent. If a person commits a terrible sin or many sins, God sometimes punishes him by denying him the opportunity to repent, thus causing him to die with sins to his discredit. Such was the case with Pharaoh. After he decided to kill all the newborn Jewish males, God withdrew Pharaoh's ability to repent by 'hardening his heart' *(Exodus* 7:13). Moses' repeated warnings to Pharaoh were designed to show all men that when God eliminates the paths to repentance, there is no hope of return. Similarly, *Rambam* writes, the Canaanites were guilty of egregious abominations, and God therefore 'hardened their hearts' and did not permit them the opportunity to repent.

יא כב־כג

וַיַּכְרֵת אֶת־הָעֲנָקִים מִן־הָהָר מִן־חֶבְרוֹן
מִן־דְּבִר מִן־עֲנָב וּמִכֹּל הַר יְהוּדָה וּמִכֹּל
הַר יִשְׂרָאֵל עִם־עָרֵיהֶם הֶחֱרִימָם יְהוֹשֻׁעַ׃
כב לֹא־נוֹתַר עֲנָקִים בְּאֶרֶץ בְּנֵי יִשְׂרָאֵל רַק
כג בְּעַזָּה בְּגַת וּבְאַשְׁדּוֹד נִשְׁאָרוּ׃ וַיִּקַּח
יְהוֹשֻׁעַ אֶת־כָּל־הָאָרֶץ כְּכֹל אֲשֶׁר דִּבֶּר
יְהוָה אֶל־מֹשֶׁה וַיִּתְּנָהּ יְהוֹשֻׁעַ לְנַחֲלָה
לְיִשְׂרָאֵל כְּמַחְלְקֹתָם לְשִׁבְטֵיהֶם וְהָאָרֶץ
יב א שָׁקְטָה מִמִּלְחָמָה׃ וְאֵלֶּה | מַלְכֵי

וַיַּכְרֵת אֶת־הָעֲנָקִים — *And destroyed the Anakim.*

[See *Prefatory Remarks* to 10:37-39 for a discussion of the conqueror of the Anakim.]

The translation *destroyed,* follows *Targum.*

הָעֲנָקִים — *The Anakim.*

All the dwellings of the Anakim were located in the Negev *(Daas Sofrim).*

[The members of the reconnaissance mission dispatched by Moses described the huge men they saw, who were the Anakim *(Numbers* 13:33). Their frightening report concerning those giants made the Israelites afraid to enter *Eretz Yisrael.*]

דְּבִר — *Devir.*

See *Commentary* to 12:13.

עֲנָב — *Anav.*

T'vuos HaAretz conjectures that this is the city mentioned in Judah's territory (15:50). See *Commentary* to 15:50.

הַר יְהוּדָה — *Mountains of Judah.*

These were the mountains which were located in what would become Judah's territory *(Radak).* Included in this range is Mount Zion, the Mount of Olives, and Mount Moriah.

22. רַק בְּעַזָּה ... — *However, in Azah.*

Some commentators assert that many Anakim remained in these cities, and others claim that only two remained. According to the latter view, one Anak ruled the cities of Azah and Gas and the other ruled Ashdod. It is for this reason that Scripture omitted the ו, *and,* before בְּגַת, which would have implied that Anakim resided in all three cities *(Meam Loez).*

These three cities are mentioned in Chapter 13 as cities of the Philistines.

The city of *Azah* is known in Arabic as 'Gaza.' It was located near the Mediterranean south of Ashkelon.

בְּגַת — *(In) Gas.*

According to *Kaftor V'Ferach,* it was the city of Ramelah, located just southwest of Lud. *T'vuos HaAretz* is certain, however, that it was located about four miles south of Jaffa on the coast of the Mediterranean.

It was the choicest of all the lands of the Philistines (see *Amos* 6:2, *Mahari Kra, ibid.).*

וּבְאַשְׁדּוֹד — *And Ashdod.*

This city was located about five miles southwest of Yavneh and two miles from the Mediterranean.

23. כָּל־הָאָרֶץ — *The entire Land.*

Even though there were many parts of the Land which were not yet conquered, *Meam Loez* explains that the kings mentioned above were the most important; therefore, it was as if Joshua had conquered the entire Land.

11 22-23 *Anakim from the mountains, from Hebron, Devir,*
and Anav and from all the Mountains of Judah, and
from all the Mountains of Israel; Joshua utterly
vanquished them and their cities. 22 *No Anakim were*
left in the land of the Children of Israel; however, in
Azah, Gas, and Ashdod some remained. 23 *Thus,*
Joshua conquered the entire Land, according to all
that HASHEM *said to Moses. Joshua gave it to Israel*
as an inheritance according to their tribal divisions.
And the Land rested from war.

בְּמַחְלְקֹתָם — *According to their [tribal] divisions.*

These *divisions* are set forth in the following chapters *(Metzudos).*

וְהָאָרֶץ שָׁקְטָה מִמִּלְחָמָה — *And the Land rested from war.*

The Canaanites no longer tried to rally against Israel, and the Israelites did not attempt to conquer more territory [during Joshua's time] *(Radak).*

Daas Sofrim explains that the Jews conquered the land gradually, in keeping with the Biblical verse: *You may not consume them* [the Canaanites] *at once (Deuteronomy* 7:22).

XII

The last verse in the previous chapter 'and the Land rested from war' *(11:23) marked the conclusion of the battles which Joshua fought, the close of the seven years of conquest and the beginning of the seven years of division. Before each tribe was to receive its allocation of land, Chapter 12 records all the territories which the Israelites had conquered until this time, both under the lead of Moses and of Joshua. Verses 1 through 6, as* Rashi *notes, refer to the lands of Sichon and Og which were conquered during Moses' lifetime on the eastern bank of the Jordan. Although these victories are clearly mentioned in the Pentateuch* (Numbers *21:21-35), they are repeated here to indicate that this land was also worthy of being divided among the tribes and that the tribes of Reuben, Gad and part of Menashe received these territories as an inheritance from Moses. (Whether this area in the Trans-Jordan has the same status as the land to the west of the Jordan is discussed in the* footnote *to 22:19.) Therefore, in the upcoming division of the land, only nine and one-half tribes remained to receive their inheritance* (Lev Aharon). *The Levites did not receive a specific territory, but rather forty-eight cities scattered throughout the land, as described in Chapter 21.*

The remainder of this chapter discusses the territory acquired during Joshua's lifetime. The thirty-one kings he defeated are described in verses 9 through 24 in a poetic passage which is considered one of the songs in Tanach. This passage has the same visual appearance (see footnote *to verse 9) as the passage in the* Book of Esther *which describes the hanging of Haman's ten sons* (Esther *9:7).* Or HaChaim (Exodus *15:1) notes that mentioning the downfall of the wicked is itself a praise to God for, as Scripture states,* When the wicked perish, there is jubilation (Proverbs *11:10). These Canaanite kingdoms were the source of idolatry in the world* (Rambam, Sefer HaMitzvos, Aseh *187); thus the downfall of each monarchy was a great cause for rejoicing, since it brought mankind one step closer to* that day when God will be [*known to all as*] One and His name One (*Zechariah 14:9*).

יב הָאָרֶץ אֲשֶׁר הִכּוּ בְנֵי־יִשְׂרָאֵל וַיִּרְשׁוּ אֶת־
ב אַרְצָם בְּעֵבֶר הַיַּרְדֵּן מִזְרְחָה הַשָּׁמֶשׁ
מִנַּחַל אַרְנוֹן עַד־הַר חֶרְמוֹן וְכָל־הָעֲרָבָה
מִזְרָחָה: ב סִיחוֹן מֶלֶךְ הָאֱמֹרִי הַיּוֹשֵׁב
בְּחֶשְׁבּוֹן מֹשֵׁל מֵעֲרוֹעֵר אֲשֶׁר עַל־שְׂפַת־
נַחַל אַרְנוֹן וְתוֹךְ הַנַּחַל וַחֲצִי הַגִּלְעָד וְעַד

Moses' victory over Sichon and Og was a greater accomplishment than Joshua's victory over the thirty-one Canaanite kings, for Sichon and Og ruled stronger and more powerful kingdoms, which exercised political control over the thirty-one kings of Canaan. It is for this reason that David mentioned only Sichon and Og in Psalm *136, which lists the many reasons why an individual should thank God:* To Him who smote great ... and mighty kings ... Sichon, King of Emori ... and Og, King of Bashan: for His steadfast love endures forever (Psalms *136, 16-20)* (Meam Loez).

◆§ Moses' Conquest.

1-6. These verses give the extent of the kingdoms of Sichon and Og, whom Moses defeated; their land extended from the Arnon River in the south to Mount Hermon in the north *(Rashi).*

אֲשֶׁר הִכּוּ בְנֵי־יִשְׂרָאֵל — *Whom the Children of Israel defeated.*

According to *Rashi* (mentioned in the *Prefatory Remarks* to this chapter), this verse refers to the kings whom Moses defeated. *Abarbanel* puzzles why Scripture failed to mention Moses' name. According to *Rashi,* the verse should have stated 'whom *Moses* and the Children of Israel defeated,' just as Scripture stated in regard to the territory which Joshua conquered, *These are the kings whom Joshua and the Children of Israel defeated* (verse 7).

Abarbanel suggests that Scripture omitted Moses' name out of respect for him, for it would appear that he did not accomplish as much as Joshua, since he only conquered two kingdoms, while Joshua defeated thirty-one. Therefore, when the *Book* of *Joshua* mentions Moses' conquest (in this verse) his name is omitted. [Later, when his conquest is summarized (in verse 6), Scripture does mention Moses' name to establish the fact that Moses was indeed responsible for the defeat of these two kingdoms.]

Kli Yakar suggests that Moses' name was omitted because he did not accompany the Israelites in their campaign against Sichon. Since this verse introduces the victory against Sichon mentioned in verse 2, Moses' name is not mentioned. In the campaign against Og, however, Moses did participate, because Og was a more formidable enemy than his brother Sichon. Thus, verse 6 mentions Moses, because of his participation in the victory against Og.

Ralbag comments that Moses' name was omitted in the beginning of this passage to indicate that Israel's victories against Sichon and Og were due to the promise that God had given the Israelites, not because of Moses' merit.

Abarbanel also suggests a second interpretation of this verse [unlike *Rashi's*]. According to this approach, the first half of this verse, *These are the kings of the Land whom the Children of Israel defeated and whose land ... they inherited,* is a general statement which refers to both the acquisitions of Moses and Joshua, and the second half of the verse through verse six details Moses' conquest, *on the other side of the Jordan ... from the Arnon River ...*

מִזְרְחָה הַשָּׁמֶשׁ — *The eastern side* [lit. *toward the rising of the sun*].

1 These are the kings of the Land whom the
Children of Israel defeated and whose land on the
other side of the Jordan — the eastern side — they
inherited, from the Arnon River to Mount Hermon
and all the Aravah to the east: 2 Sichon, the king of
the Emorites, who lived in Cheshbon and who ruled
from Aroer, which was located on the edge of the
Arnon River and in the river, to part of the Gilead as

[Scripture is about to recount the Israelites' victories on the eastern side of the Jordan.]

מִנַּחַל אַרְנוֹן — *Arnon River.*

This river formed the southern boundary of the land acquired east of the Jordan. It flows into the center of the Dead Sea, due east of Hebron on the other side of the Jordan and formed the boundary between the Moabites to the south and the Emorites to the north (*Numbers* 21:13).

הַר חֶרְמוֹן — *Mount Hermon.*

T'vuos HaAretz comments that this verse refers to Mount Hermon in the Anti-Lebanon range (which is east of the Jordan River), not to the Mount Hermon in the Lebanon (which is west of the Jordan). The *Jerusalem Targum* (see *Deuteronomy* 3:9 and *Rashi*) refers to Mount Hermon as the mountain of snow. This range stretches as far east as Damascus and then gradually decreases in elevation. In the north it goes as far as the plains of Chamas and in the south to the village of Dan or Lish. It formed the northern boundary of the land acquired east of the Jordan.

וְכָל־הָעֲרָבָה מִזְרָחָה — *And all the Aravah to the east.*

These are the plains which stretched along the entire length of the edge of the Jordan (*Daas Sofrim*).

◈ Sichon's Territory.

2. סִיחוֹן מֶלֶךְ הָאֱמֹרִי — *Sichon, the king of the Emorites.*

Sichon was the first king conquered by Moses (see *Numbers* 21:2-31 and *Deuteronomy* 2:31-37). He had conquered the territories of Ammon and Moab which had originally been reserved for the Children of Lot, and God prohibited the Jews from annexing them (*Deuteronomy* 2:9, 19). However, since they later fell into the possession of Sichon, whose territories the Israelites *were* permitted to conquer, the territories of Ammon and Moab also became permitted to the Jews (*Chullin* 60b).

בְּחֶשְׁבּוֹן — *In Cheshbon.*

It was located about twelve and one-half miles east of the northern tip of the Dead Sea and is presently called Chesban.

Scripture intends to emphasize the miracle which allowed the Israelites to defeat Sichon: not only was he a very powerful king, but he also dwelled in the highly fortified city of Cheshbon. Nevertheless, the Israelites prevailed (*Meam Loez*).

T'vuos HaAretz reports that there is a region in Cheshbon which has many pools of water, just as Scripture states, *Your eyes are like the pools in Cheshbon* (*Song of Songs* 7:5).

◈ From South to North.

מֵעֲרֹעֵר — *From Aroer.*

This city was located east of Hebron on the eastern side of the Jordan.

וְתוֹךְ הַנַּחַל — *And in the river.*

Meam Loez suggests that the city of Aroer was located on an island within the Arnon River as well as on the shore of the river.

וַחֲצִי הַגִּלְעָד — *To part of the Gilead.*

Gilead is a general term which refers

ג יַבֹּק הַנַּחַל גְּבוּל בְּנֵי עַמּוֹן: וְהָעֲרָבָה עַד־
יָם כִּנְרוֹת מִזְרָחָה וְעַד יָם הָעֲרָבָה יָם־
הַמֶּלַח מִזְרָחָה דֶּרֶךְ בֵּית הַיְשִׁמוֹת
ד וּמִתֵּימָן תַּחַת אַשְׁדּוֹת הַפִּסְגָּה: וּגְבוּל
עוֹג מֶלֶךְ הַבָּשָׁן מִיֶּתֶר הָרְפָאִים הַיּוֹשֵׁב
ה בְּעַשְׁתָּרוֹת וּבְאֶדְרֶעִי: וּמֹשֵׁל בְּהַר חֶרְמוֹן
וּבְסַלְכָה וּבְכָל־הַבָּשָׁן עַד־גְּבוּל הַגְּשׁוּרִי
וְהַמַּעֲכָתִי וַחֲצִי הַגִּלְעָד גְּבוּל סִיחוֹן
ו מֶלֶךְ־חֶשְׁבּוֹן: מֹשֶׁה עֶבֶד־יְהוָה וּבְנֵי

to the entire region east of the Jordan.

יַבֹּק הַנַּחַל — *The Yabok River.*

This river is due east of Shechem on the eastern side of the Jordan and is located approximately equidistant from the Dead Sea and the Kineret.

It formed the southern border of Ammon *(Rashi).*

This is the river Jacob crossed with his wives *(Genesis* 32:23) when fleeing from Esau. It was in this area that Jacob wrestled with Esau's angel and was injured in the leg.

◆§ The Aravah

Sichon's territory also included the plains region which stretched from the Kineret Sea in the north to the Dead Sea in the south.

3. וְהָעֲרָבָה — *And the Aravah.*

[These plains are bounded on the east by mountains as they stretch north to the Kineret Sea. According to modern contour maps of the region, these plains vary between three and ten miles in width.]

יָם כִּנְּרוֹת מִזְרָחָה — *[From] the Kineret Sea in the east.*

The nature of this sea is diametrically opposite that of the Dead Sea. It is composed of sweet water, all varieties of fish and is surrounded by very fertile land. It is also known as the Sea of Galilee.

יָם־הַמֶּלַח — *Dead Sea* [lit. *Sea of Salt*].

On the eastern and western shores of this sea are mountains and high rocks. No animal or vegetable life can be found in its immediate vicinity. The southeastern shore, however, is a fertile area. Its water has a sulfuric odor and is so saltly that it is almost impossible to keep in one's mouth. If salt is placed in a sample of its water, it will not dissolve. Its water boils at 105° c. [whereas pure water boils at 100° c.].

The *Talmud (Shabbos* 108b) reports that no one ever drowned in the Dead Sea because the high salt concentration creates buoyancy *(Rashi).*

בֵּית הַיְשִׁמוֹת — *Beis Hayeshimos.*

This was an area located on the northern border of the Dead Sea. It was one of the encampment areas of the Israelites when they were in the Wilderness *(Numbers* 33:49).

וּמִתֵּימָן — *And from Teiman.*

See *Commentary* to 15.1.

◆§ Og's Territory

4. וּגְבוּל עוֹג — *And the boundary of Og.*

Og is the second of the kings alluded to in verse 1 *(Metzudos).*

הָרְפָאִים — *The giants.*

Metzudos notes that this word derives from the Hebrew רָפֶה which means *weak,* for anyone who saw these giants became weak from fear. [See *Commentary* to 13:12.]

12
3-6

far as the Yabok River, the border of the Children of
Ammon. 3 *And the Aravah: from the Kineret Sea in*
the east until the Sea of Aravah, the Dead Sea, in the
east, the way to Beis Hayeshimos and from Teiman,
under the falls of Pisgah. 4 *And the boundary of Og,*
king of Bashan, one of the last of the giants, who
lived in Ashtaros and Edrei. 5 *And who reigned in*
Mount Hermon and Salchah, and in all of Bashan up
to the border of the Geshurites and Ma'achasites and
part of the Gilead until the border of Sichon, king of
Cheshbon. 6 *Moses, servant of* HASHEM, *and the*

בְּעַשְׁתָּרוֹת — *Ashtaros.*

According to *R' Saadiah Gaon,* this is the city of Altznamin, which today is called Tzanamein and is located southwest of Damascus. *T'vuos HaAretz,* however, identifies it as the city of Mitzrib (El Muzerib).

וּבְאֶדְרֶעִי — *And (in) Edrei.*

This city is the present day city of Der'a [in Syria].

Edrei was located between mountains and surrounded by large rocks, but Divine assistance enabled the Israelites to prevail over these natural fortifications *(Meam Loez).*

5. וּבְסַלְכָה — *And Salchah.*

It is located at the foot of the Choran mountains and is called Tzulchat. [It appears to be in the southeast of Og's territory.]

Kaftor V'Ferach identifies this city as Salchad [which is presently on the southern border of Syria].

הַגְּשׁוּרִי — *Geshurites.*

This nation was located to the east of the Kineret Sea *(Daas Sofrim* to 13:1).

וַחֲצִי הַגִּלְעָד — *And part of the Gilead.*

Part of Gilead belonged to Sichon and part belonged to Og *(Rashi).*

6. ... מֹשֶׁה — *Moses.*

Even though in general it was not permissible to conquer land outside of *Eretz Yisrael* until the land proper had been conquered (see *footnote* to 1:3),

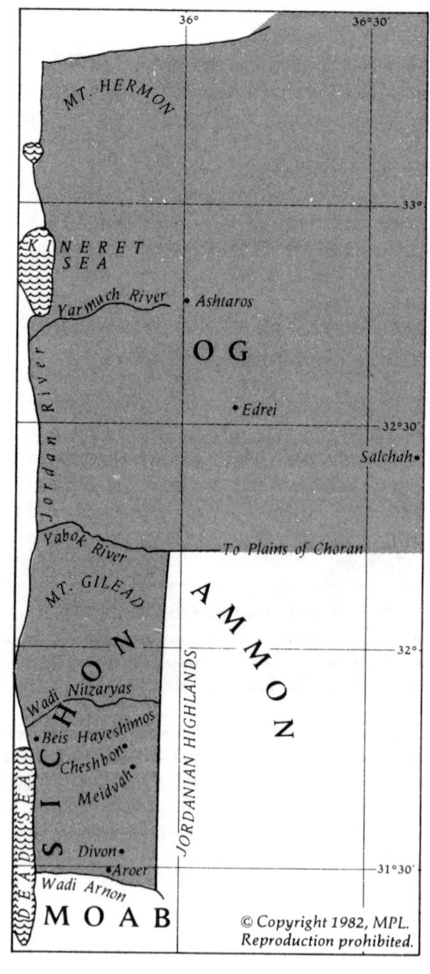

יִשְׂרָאֵל הִכּוּם וַיִּתְּנָהּ מֹשֶׁה עֶבֶד־יְהוָה
יְרֻשָּׁה לָרְאוּבֵנִי וְלַגָּדִי וְלַחֲצִי שֵׁבֶט
ז הַמְנַשֶּׁה: וְאֵלֶּה מַלְכֵי הָאָרֶץ
אֲשֶׁר הִכָּה יְהוֹשֻׁעַ וּבְנֵי יִשְׂרָאֵל בְּעֵבֶר
הַיַּרְדֵּן יָמָּה מִבַּעַל גָּד בְּבִקְעַת הַלְּבָנוֹן
וְעַד־הָהָר הֶחָלָק הָעֹלֶה שֵׂעִירָה וַיִּתְּנָהּ
יְהוֹשֻׁעַ לְשִׁבְטֵי יִשְׂרָאֵל יְרֻשָּׁה
ח כְּמַחְלְקֹתָם: בָּהָר וּבַשְּׁפֵלָה וּבָעֲרָבָה
וּבָאֲשֵׁדוֹת וּבַמִּדְבָּר וּבַנֶּגֶב הַחִתִּי הָאֱמֹרִי
וְהַכְּנַעֲנִי הַפְּרִזִּי הַחִוִּי וְהַיְבוּסִי:

Moses had been commanded by God to conquer these territories first *(Malbim).*

[See *Otzar HaSifri* who argues that the land of Sichon and Og did not come under this prohibition, because these kings attacked the Israelites. The prohibition only forbade the Israelites to strike first. (See *Deuteronomy* 2:32.)]

לָרְאוּבֵנִי ... — *To Reuben ...*
See *Prefatory Remarks* to 1:13.

⁂ Joshua's Conquest

7. אֲשֶׁר הִכָּה — *Whom [Joshua] defeated.*

Much land was left unconquered upon Joshua's death (see 13:1). Here Scripture only recounts the lands that were conquered during Joshua's lifetime *(Malbim).*

מִבַּעַל גָּד — *From Ba'al Gad.*
This was located in the north of *Eretz Yisrael.* See *Commentary* to 11:17.

הָהָר הֶחָלָק — *Mount Chalak.*
This was located in the south of *Eretz Yisrael.*
See *Commentary* to 11:17.

⁂ The Thirty-one Canaanite Kings[1]

9-24. Of the thirty-one kings listed, only seventeen are explicitly mentioned in the preceding chapters. According to *Malbim* the remaining fourteen are included in the general statement *and all their kings Joshua captured and put to death* (11:12). [The kings appear to be listed in the order in which they were

1. According to tradition *(Shabbos* 103b), songs in copies of Scripture written by a scribe are visually distinguishable from narrative portions, because they are periodically interrupted by long blank spaces between phrases in a stich. The song in verses 9 through 24 is written in the style which the *Talmud (Megillah* 16b) calls 'half-brick on top of half-brick and whole brick on top of whole brick.' *Rashi* explains that a 'half-brick' refers to a phrase of written words and that a 'whole brick' refers to the blank space between phrases. (The blank spaces are twice as long as the written phrases.) Thus, the written phrases in each line are vertically stacked above the written phrases in the line below it, and the blank spaces are similarly stacked.

The *Talmud* explains that this passage and the passage in the *Book* of *Esther* which mentions the ten sons of Haman who were hanged *(Esther* 9:7) are written in this style so that 'these evildoers will never rise again from their downfall.' Had the half and whole bricks been stacked in an overlapping fashion, as in bricklaying, the base of this brick pattern could be widened by adding bricks to the left and right. But since this passage was not constructed in an overlapping manner, the 'base' (which in this case represents their evil) can never spread *(Rashi).* [Cf. *R' Tam* cited by *Ran (Megillah* 16b) and *Mikra'ei Kodesh,* Purim p.140.]

*Children of Israel defeated them; and Moses, servant
of HASHEM, gave it as an inheritance to Reuben, Gad
and part of the tribe of Menashe.*
*7 These are the kings of the Land whom Joshua
and the Children of Israel defeated on the western
side of the Jordan from Ba'al Gad in the Lebanon
valley to Mount Chalak which ascends to Seir;
Joshua gave it as an inheritance according to the
tribal divisions of Israel: 8 In the mountains and in
the valley, in the Aravah and the falls in the
wilderness and in the Negev — the Hittites, Emorites,
Canaanites, Perizzites, Hivvites, and Jebusites.*

defeated.] *Vilna Gaon,* however, traces all thirty-one kings to battles and geographical references made in the preceding chapters.

1-Jericho (Ch. 6, and 10:1); 2-Ai (8:29); 3-Jerusalem (10:26); 4-Hebron (10:26); 5-Yarmus (10:26); 6-Lachish (10:26); 7-Eglon (10:26); 8-Makeidah (10:28); 9-Livnah (10:30); 10-Devir (10:39); 11-Horam, King of Gezer (10:33); 12-Har (10:40); 13-Negev (10:40); 14-Shefeilah (10:40); 15-Asheidos (10:40); 16-Chatzor (11:10); 17-Madon (11:12); 18-Shimron (11:12); 19-Achshaf (11:12); 20-Northern Har (11:17); 21-Aravah (11:17); 22-Negev Kineret (11:17); 23-Shefeilah (11:17); 24-Nofes Dor (11:2); 25-Eastern Canaanites (11:3); 26-Western Canaanites (11:3); 27-Emorites (11:3); 28-Hittites (11:3); 29-Perizzites (11:3); 30-Jebusites (11:3); 31-Hivvites (11:3).

Radak notes that these kings were not only rulers of the cities mentioned, but also of the outlying smaller cities and rural areas.

The *Midrash (Bereishis Rabbah* 53:10) comments that all thirty-one kings attended the banquet which Abraham made when Isaac was weaned *(Genesis* 21:8). They were granted long life so that they could witness the fulfillment of the Divine promise that Isaac's seed would be numerous. As a result, these kings lived to see more than six hundred thousand Israelites conquer the Land *(Meam Loez).*

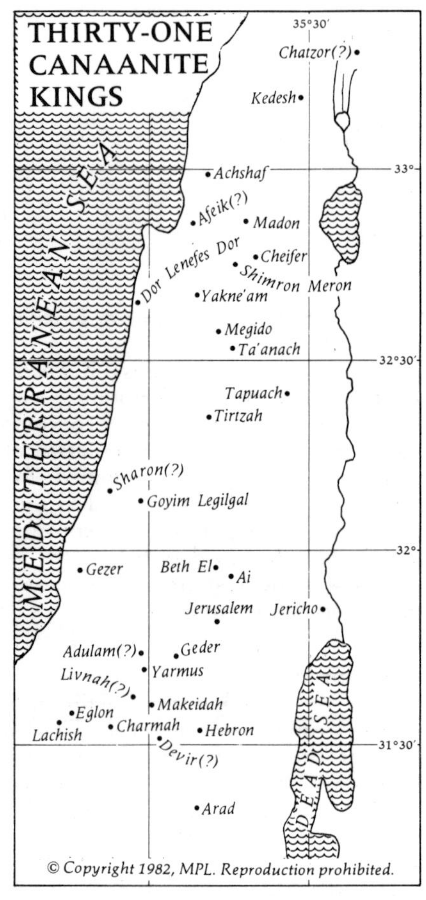

ט מֶלֶךְ יְרִיחוֹ אֶחָד
מֶלֶךְ הָעַי אֲשֶׁר־מִצַּד בֵּית־אֵל אֶחָד:
י מֶלֶךְ יְרוּשָׁלַםִ אֶחָד
מֶלֶךְ חֶבְרוֹן אֶחָד:
יא מֶלֶךְ יַרְמוּת אֶחָד
מֶלֶךְ לָכִישׁ אֶחָד:
יב מֶלֶךְ עֶגְלוֹן אֶחָד
מֶלֶךְ גֶּזֶר אֶחָד:
יג מֶלֶךְ דְּבִר אֶחָד
מֶלֶךְ גֶּדֶר אֶחָד:
יד מֶלֶךְ חָרְמָה אֶחָד
מֶלֶךְ עֲרָד אֶחָד:
טו מֶלֶךְ לִבְנָה אֶחָד
מֶלֶךְ עֲדֻלָּם אֶחָד:
טז מֶלֶךְ מַקֵּדָה אֶחָד
מֶלֶךְ בֵּית־אֵל אֶחָד:

9. מֶלֶךְ יְרִיחוֹ אֶחָד — *The King of Jericho one.*

The *Midrash (Bereishis Rabbah* 53:10) comments that Scripture need not count each king as *one*, for the reader could do that himself. It therefore suggests that *one* is mentioned to include the second in command to the king, in which case there were sixty-two rulers whom Joshua defeated.

This was the first city the Israelites conquered (see Chapter 6).

הָעַי אֲשֶׁר־מִצַּד בֵּית־אֵל — *Ai, which was near Beth El.*

Ai is the only kingdom in this list whose location is mentioned. *T'vuos HaAretz* suggests that there was more than one city named Ai. Josephus implies that there was a city named Ai near Jericho. Therefore, Scripture avoids confusion by specifying that the Ai discussed here *was near Beth El.*

10. יְרוּשָׁלַםִ — *Jerusalem.*

The King of Jerusalem was killed, but the city of Jerusalem was not conquered. See 15:63 and *Commentary, ibid.*

חֶבְרוֹן — *Hebron.*

See *Commentary* to 10:36.

11. יַרְמוּת — *Yarmus.*

This city was located about seven and one half miles north and slightly east of Beis Guvrin.

לָכִישׁ — *Lachish.*

See *Commentary* to 10:31 for its location.

12. עֶגְלוֹן — *Eglon.*

See *Commentary* to 10:34 for its location.

גֶּזֶר — *Gezer.*

See *Commentary* to 16:3 for its location.

13. דְּבִר — *Devir.*

[9] The King of Jericho one;
The King of Ai, which was near Beth El one.
[10] The King of Jerusalem one;
The King of Hebron one.
[11] The King of Yarmus one;
The King of Lachish one.
[12] The King of Eglon one;
The King of Gezer one.
[13] The King of Devir one;
The King of Geder one.
[14] The King of Charmah one;
The King of Arad one.
[15] The King of Livnah one;
The King of Adulam one.
[16] The King of Makeidah one;
The King of Beth El one.

Its exact location is not known, but there is a valley southwest of the mountains of Hebron named Wadi Debir. It is likely that Devir was located in this valley.

גֶּדֶר — *Geder.*

This is a city located either ten miles north-northwest of Hebron or two and one-half miles east of Mount Modiim.

14. חָרְמָה — *Charmah* [lit. *total destruction*].

T'vuos HaAretz locates Charmah about four miles south of Beis Guvrin.

The details of its conquest are mentioned in *Judges* 1:17.

עֲרָד — *Arad.*

Arad is located south of Hebron and is called Tel Arad.

According to *Ramban (Numbers* 21:1), this is not the city of the king who attacked the Israelites, for that Arad was located *west* of the Jordan River, while the one mentioned in this verse was located to the *east* of the Jordan River. In *Ramban's* second interpretation, he explains that there were two kings of Arad, one killed by Moses, and his successor by Joshua after he crossed the Jordan. Joshua totally vanquished these Canaanite settlements in fulfillment of the vow the Israelites took when threatened by the Canaanites' attack *(Numbers* 21:2). Hence one of the cities was called *Charmah* which means *total destruction.* (See *Gilyon HaShas* to *Rashi, Eruvin* 64b.)

15. לִבְנָה — *Livnah.*

T'vuos HaAretz claims that its location is unknown, but cites another source which asserts it is the city of Beis Guvrin.

This city was conquered during Joshua's southern conquest (10:29).

עֲדֻלָּם — *Adulam.*

This city is located ten miles northeast of Beis Guvrin near the city of Timnah.

Perhaps this is the city where Judah found his wife Shua *(Genesis* 38:1).

16. מַקֵּדָה — *Makeidah.*

T'vuos HaAretz cites a source which locates this city approximately eight miles east of Beis Guvrin.

בֵּית אֵל — *Beth El.*

See *Commentary* to 16:2.

יז מֶלֶךְ תַּפּוּחַ אֶחָד
מֶלֶךְ חֵפֶר אֶחָד:
יח מֶלֶךְ אֲפֵק אֶחָד
מֶלֶךְ לַשָּׁרוֹן אֶחָד:
יט מֶלֶךְ מָדוֹן אֶחָד
מֶלֶךְ חָצוֹר אֶחָד:
כ מֶלֶךְ שִׁמְרוֹן מְראוֹן אֶחָד
מֶלֶךְ אַכְשָׁף אֶחָד:
כא מֶלֶךְ תַּעְנַךְ אֶחָד
מֶלֶךְ מְגִדּוֹ אֶחָד:
כב מֶלֶךְ קֶדֶשׁ אֶחָד
מֶלֶךְ־יָקְנְעָם לַכַּרְמֶל אֶחָד:
כג מֶלֶךְ דּוֹר לְנָפַת דּוֹר אֶחָד
מֶלֶךְ־גּוֹיִם לְגִלְגָּל אֶחָד:

17. תַּפּוּחַ — *Tapuach.*

This later became a border city between the tribes of Ephraim and Menashe (16:8) and was located northeast of Shechem near the Jordan River.

חֵפֶר — *Cheifer.*

It is also known as Git Cheifer and was located southeast of Tzipori. See *Commentary* to 19:13.

18. אֲפֵק — *Afeik.*

T'vuos HaAretz found five cities named Afeik which were located in different parts of *Eretz Yisrael.* He deduces from the order of the kings mentioned that the reference in this verse was to the Afeik in the Valley of Yizrael located in Yissachar's territory. Later in Jewish history, King Saul fought the Philistines in Afeik *(I Samuel* 29:1).

לַשָּׁרוֹן — *(To) Sharon.*

The Valley of Sharon runs along the border of the Mediterranean near the city of Caesarea. Midway between Caesarea and Yafo is the city Saran, which was the site of this kingdom.

19. מָדוֹן — *Madon.*

It was located about five miles north of Tzipori.

חָצוֹר — *Chatzor.*

It was located north of the Sea of Merom to the west of Banias.

The cities of Madon (11:12) and Chatzor (11:10) were conquered during Joshua's northern conquest.

20. שִׁמְרוֹן מְראוֹן — *Shimron Meron.*

On the basis of the *Jerusalem Talmud* (*Megillah* 1:1), *T'vuos HaAretz* deduces that Shimron was the city Simoni which was located about two miles southwest of Tzipori. *Kaftor V'Ferach,* however, states that Dor Meroan was one of the thirty-one kings, and it was distant from the city of Simoni. *T'vuos HaAretz* reconciles these two sources by suggesting that this kingdom contained both the cities of Shimron and Meron.

Meron is one of forty-eight words in Scripture that contain an *aleph* in the middle

12
17-23

17 *The King of Tapuach* *one;*
The King of Cheifer *one.*
18 *The King of Afeik* *one;*
The King of Sharon *one.*
19 *The King of Madon* *one;*
The King of Chatzor *one.*
20 *The King of Shimron Meron* *one;*
The King of Achshaf *one.*
21 *The King of Ta'anach* *one;*
The King of Megido *one.*
22 *The King of Kedesh* *one;*
The King of Yakne'am in the Carmel *one.*
23 *The King of Dor to the districts of Dor* *one;*
The King of Goyim Legilgal *one.*

of the word which does not affect the pronunciation *(Minchas Shai).*

אַכְשָׁף — *Achshaf.*

Although the *Septuagint* identifies Achshaf as the present day Haifa, *T'vuos HaAretz* disagrees and locates it northeast of Akko.

The conquest of this city is mentioned in 11:12 in Joshua's northern conquest.

21. תַּעְנָךְ — *Ta'anach.*

It was located in the valley of Yizre'el and is identical with the Levite city Aner, which is mentioned in I *Chronicles* 6:55.

מְגִדּוֹ — *Megido.*

This city is located slightly northeast of *Ta'anach.*

Perhaps this is one of the cities which King Solomon rebuilt *(I Kings* 9:19.)

22. קֶדֶשׁ — *Kedesh.*

It is located in the mountains of Naftali about fifteen miles north of Tzfas.

It was later designated as a city of refuge (20:7).

יָקְנְעָם — *Yakne'am.*

A precise determination of its location is unknown. *T'vuos HaAretz* conjectures that it was located seven and one half miles north of Megido. [There is a city Yakne'am located six miles northwest of Megido today. This city has been shown on the map with a question mark.]

It was later given to the tribe of Zevulun (19:11).

לַכַּרְמֶל — *In the* [lit. *to*] *Carmel.*

This mountain range was located west of the Valley of Yizre'el, not far from the Mediterranean coast.

23. דּוֹר לְנָפַת דּוֹר — *Dor to the districts of Dor.*

The translation follows *Targum* and implies that this word was not the name of the city.

T'vuos HaAretz, however, found a city two and one-half miles southeast of Dor by the name 'Nafasa'; therefore, he believes that לְנָפַת is the name of a city. He locates Dor on the Mediterranean about five miles north of Caesarea.

גּוֹיִם לְגִלְגָּל — *Goyim Legilgal.*

It is located northeast of Yafa [and should not be confused with the city Gilgal near Jericho].

יב כד כד מֶלֶךְ תִּרְצָה אֶחָד
כד כָּל־מְלָכִים שְׁלֹשִׁים וְאֶחָד׃
יג א וִיהוֹשֻׁעַ זָקֵן בָּא בַּיָּמִים וַיֹּאמֶר יְהוָה אֵלָיו
א־ג אַתָּה זָקַנְתָּה בָּאתָ בַיָּמִים וְהָאָרֶץ
ב נִשְׁאֲרָה הַרְבֵּה־מְאֹד לְרִשְׁתָּהּ׃ זֹאת
הָאָרֶץ הַנִּשְׁאָרֶת כָּל־גְּלִילוֹת הַפְּלִשְׁתִּים
ג וְכָל־הַגְּשׁוּרִי׃ מִן־הַשִּׁיחוֹר אֲשֶׁר | עַל־פְּנֵי

24. תִּרְצָה — *Tirtzah.*

This city was located in Menashe's territory, several miles north of Shechem. Tirtzah was one of Tzelofchad's daughters (17:3) who inherited land in Menashe's territory. Some suggest that this city was named after her.

XIII

This chapter is divided into two parts, the latter setting the stage for the next several chapters. Verses 1 through 14 delineate those places in Eretz Yisrael *which the Jews were not able to conquer during the seven years of conquest. Beginning with verse 15 and continuing through Chapter 19, Scripture systematically outlines the borders of the territories that the tribes were to inherit. In the concluding segment of this chapter, the territories on the eastern side of the Jordan River (which Moses parceled out before his death) are recounted.*

Rashi (Sotah *7b) teaches that the tribe of Reuben was rewarded by receiving the first inheritance in* Eretz Yisrael, *although the Pentateuch implied that the tribe of Gad would be given this honor* (Numbers *32:33)* [see Ohel David]. *By what merit did the tribe of Reuben take precedence over the tribe of Gad, which evidently also deserved to receive the first inheritance in* Eretz Yisrael?

The Talmud (Sotah *7b) relates that in order to encourage a woman who was suspected of being unfaithful to her husband to confess her sin, it was customary to read her the passage in* Genesis *which describes Reuben's sin with his father's bed* (Genesis *35:22). The woman would then be asked, 'Do you know how Reuben was rewarded in this world for confessing his sin?' She would be told that as compensation, his grandchildren received the first portion of land when* Eretz Yisrael *was divided* (Rashi, Sotah *7b).*

Public admission of guilt is one of the most difficult tests of human character. From Rashi's *comment to* Genesis *38:24-5, we see that it is really a test of an individual's ability to humble himself before God. When Tamar was accused of immorality, she hoped that Judah, the father of her unborn children, would come forward on his own accord when she said,* 'Recognize to whom these belong: the signet ring, the wrap, and the staff' (Genesis *38:24-5).*

Rashi *explains that when Tamar said 'Recognize,' she was telling Judah to recognize his Creator, the owner and possessor of all things, and to admit his paternity.* Rashi, *in his illuminating comment, implies that the mere identification of these articles would not have enabled Judah to make this humiliating public confession. This admission was possible only because Judah humbled himself before God.*

As Chida *explains* (Commentary *to 5:12), the Pentateuch and Early Prophets refer to* Eretz Yisrael *as Eretz Canaan because the word 'Canaan' derives from the*

12
24

12 [24] *The King of Tirtzah one;*
24 *All the kings, thirty-one.*

13 [1] *Joshua was old, advanced in years, and HASHEM*
1-3 *said to him, 'You have grown old, advanced in*
years, and a great deal of the Land still remains to be
possessed. [2] *This is the land which still remains: all*
the districts of the Philistines and all the Geshurites.
[3] *From the Shichor which is before Egypt to the*

Hebrew הַכְּנָעָה *which means 'humility.' The Land of Israel was given to those who would humble themselves before God and subordinate themselves to His Torah.*

It was indeed appropriate then that Reuben, who displayed such admirable humility, was rewarded by having his progeny receive the first inheritance of Eretz Canaan. [The Trans-Jordan was also considered a part of Eretz Canaan (see footnote *to 22:19).] Judah was similarly rewarded by having his progeny receive the first inheritance of the land to the west of the Jordan. Thus, their exemplary humility became etched into the border of* Eretz Yisrael *for all to remember in successive generations.*

1. זָקֵן בָּא בַּיָּמִים — *Old, advanced in years.*

Metzudos understands this phrase to mean that Joshua had not aged prematurely; he was truly old. According to *Ibn Ezra (Exodus* 33:11), he was 103 at this time.

Meam Loez interprets this phrase as praise to Joshua. He reached his lofty spiritual level in gradual stages. His activity in the conquest of the Land allowed him to attain the level he was on at this point in time, and now God wants him to increase his level by performing the mitzvah of dividing the Land.

וְהָאָרֶץ נִשְׁאֲרָה הַרְבֵּה־מְאֹד לְרִשְׁתָּהּ — *And a great deal of the Land still remains to be possessed.*

Of the land which I promised to Abraham,[1] much remains unconquered *(Rashi),* and it is not possible that you will possess it during your lifetime since you are so old *(Ralbag).* As noted in the *Commentary* to 11:10, the *Midrash* interprets נִשְׁאֲרָה as *purposely left over* and rebukes Joshua for not having shown more alacrity in conquering the Land.

Chida detects a source in this verse for the *Midrash's* interpretation. The final letters of the first four words of the verse ויהושע זָקֵן בָּא בַּיָּמִים can be arranged to form the word אֶמְנַע, which means *I will refrain* [from conquering the Land quickly].

◆§ The Unconquered Territory

2. גְּלִילוֹת — *Districts.*

Radak offers two translations: *borders* (following *Targum* and *Rashi)* or *districts* (as in *Isaiah* 8:23).

הַפְּלִשְׁתִּים ... הַגְּשׁוּרִי — *Philistines ... Geshurites.*

[There is evidence in Scripture that

1. Joshua did not conquer all the land of *Eretz Yisrael* as the verse mentions. But what are the Land's boundaries and what precisely had Joshua left unconquered?

There are two types of descriptions given in the Pentateuch concerning the borders of *Eretz Yisrael* — general and specific. In each instance where the Torah gives a general description of the boundaries, an additional element of the Land's extent is added. The first description of the Land occurred in the Covenant Between the Parts when God promised Abraham, *To your seed*

the Geshurites were located in diametrically opposite ends of *Eretz Yisrael* — in the northeast (see verse 11 and *II Samuel* 15:8) and in the southwest (see *I Samuel* 27:7-8 which places the Geshurites *in the fields of the Philistines*). Given their geographical separation, however, it is unclear whether these are the same tribes. Most probably, the Geshurites mentioned in this verse were the ones referred to in *I Samuel* 27:7-8 in the southwest portion of *Eretz Yisrael.*]

A question arises in regard to Israel's legal claim to the land of the Philistines. Since the Philistines were descendants of Canaan's brother Mitzrayim rather than of Canaan, their land was not included in God's gift of the Land to Abraham (see *Genesis* 15:19). *Ramban* to *Genesis* 10:15 explains that the Philistines conquered part of the land of the Canaanites, and it was that territory of the Philistines (the five cities mentioned in verse 3) which the Jews were to possess.

◆§ In the Southwest

3-4. Verse 3 recounts the southern border [of the unconquered territory] from east to west, and verse 4 indicates the width of that area from north to south (*Rashi*, verse 4).

3. מִן־הַשִּׁיחוֹר — *From the Shichor.*

[This river was the southernmost boundary of the unconquered territory.]

Rashi identifies the river Shichor as the southwest border of *Eretz Yisrael.* The only part of the southwestern border which Joshua conquered during his lifetime was the stretch from Mount

have I given the Land, from the **River of Egypt** [Wadi El Arish] *to the* **great river** [Euphrates] (*Genesis* 15:18). The borders were further defined in *Exodus* 23:31, *And I will set your borders from the* **Sea of Reeds** [in the South] *to the* **Sea of the Philistines** [Mediterranean], *from* **the desert** [in the east] *to the* **river** [Euphrates] (see *Ha'amek Davar, ibid.*). Another element of the boundary of the Land is introduced in *Deuteronomy* 11:24 and repeated in *Joshua* 1:4 — the Lebanon — *from the desert* [in the east] *to the* **Lebanon,** *from the Euphrates to the Mediterranean.*

From all of Scripture's descriptions of the extent of *Eretz Yisrael,* it is evident that the northeastern boundary of the Land was to be the Euphrates (*Ramban* to *Gittin* 8a). Surprisingly, however, when Scripture delineates in specific terms the boundaries of the Land in *Numbers* 34:2*ff.*, no mention is made of the Euphrates River (35° 50′ N.). In fact, according to *T'vuos HaAretz,* the point furthest north is Tzedad (34° 15′ N.), some 117 miles south of the Euphrates!

T'vuos HaAretz resolves this difficulty by suggesting that the verses which place *Eretz Yisrael* as far north as the Euphrates refer to the time when the Israelites would be so numerous that they would require additional land for expansion. However, when the Jews entered the Land, they were given land commensurate with their needs at that time, and thus the Torah limited the area of their conquest to the detailed borders stated in *Numbers* 34. The Israelites were charged with eliminating all the Canaanites within these borders, and it was within *these* borders that Joshua was unable to fully extirpate these Seven Nations. However, during the times of King David and King Solomon, the Israelites acquired all the land within the borders specified in *Numbers* 34 as it states, *And at that time Solomon and all Israel held a feast, a great congregation from Lavo Chamas to the River of Egypt* (*I Kings* 8:65) (*Kaftor V'Ferach*). [See *HaAretz LeGevuloschah,* p. 17.]

In the North, Joshua was unable to conquer even the land which extended to the northern border mentioned in *Numbers* 34. His conquests only went as far north as Ba'al Gad (see 11:17, *Commentary*) and Tzidon Rabbah (19:28). The land north of these cities to Har HaHar went unconquered.

Support for this assertion may be found in Chapter 12 where the thirty-one kings which Joshua conquered are enumerated. No kingdom north of Kedesh and Chatzor is listed. In addition, when King David dispatched Yoav to take a census of the Israelites, he traveled only as far north as Dan and Tzidon (*II Samuel* 24:6), which also suggests that the Jews had not yet settled to the northern border described in *Numbers* 34.

According to *T'vuos HaAretz,* Joshua did not divide any of the Land north of Tzidon Rabbah and Ba'al Gad since he did not conquer this territory. Thus, we find that all the cities mentioned in the territories of Naftali and Asher did not stretch further north than these two cities.

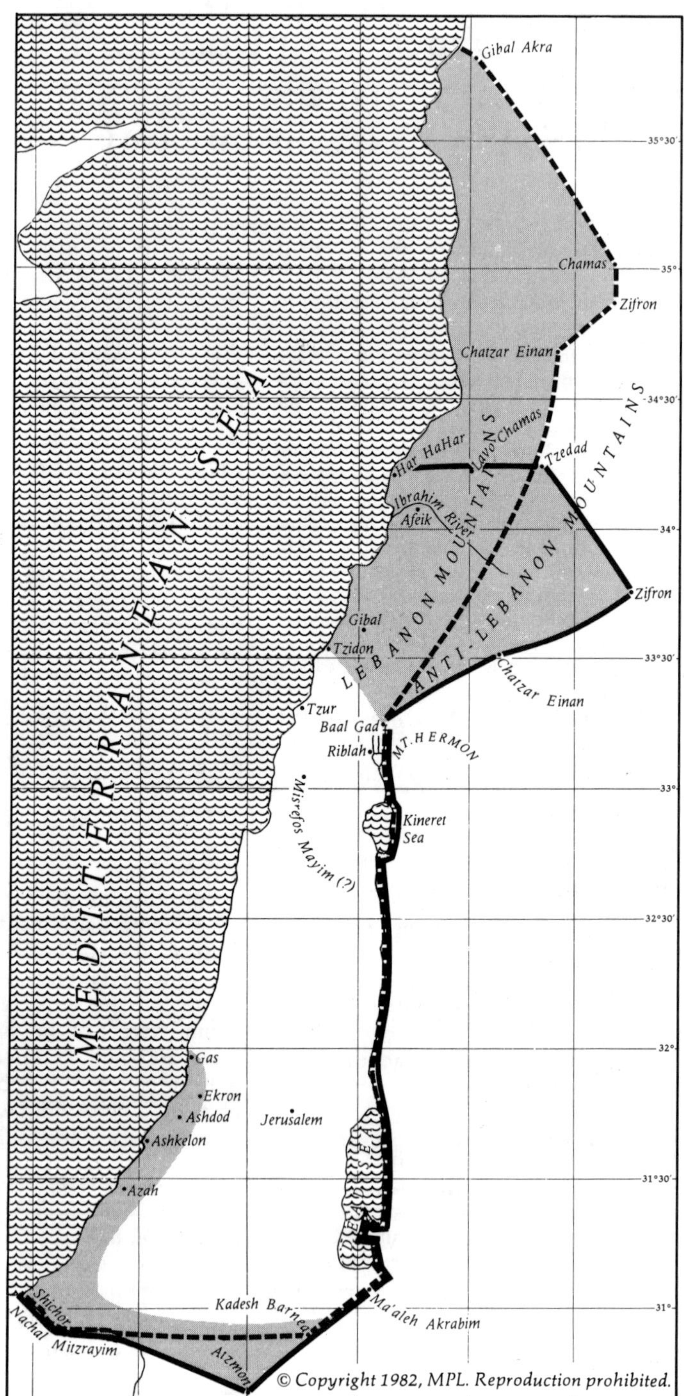

'. . . a great deal of the Land still remains to be possessed.'

This map illustrates the borders of *Eretz Yisrael* as given in *Numbers* 34, according to the views of *Kaftor V'Ferach* (broken line) and *T'vuos HaAretz* (solid line). Grey areas indicate unconquered portions of *Eretz Yisrael.*

יג מִצְרַ֫יִם וְעַ֫ד גְּב֣וּל עֶקְר֤וֹן צָפ֔וֹנָה לַֽכְּנַעֲנִ֖י
ד תֵּחָשֵׁ֑ב חֲמֵ֣שֶׁת ׀ סַרְנֵ֣י פְלִשְׁתִּ֗ים הָֽעַזָּתִ֤י
וְהָֽאַשְׁדּוֹדִ֙י הָֽאֶשְׁקְלוֹנִ֔י הַגִּתִּ֖י וְהָֽעֶקְרוֹנִ֑י
ד וְהָֽעַוִּֽים׃ מִתֵּימָ֞ן כָּל־אֶ֣רֶץ הַֽכְּנַעֲנִ֗י וּמְעָרָ֛ה

Chalak, which was surrounded by the Wilderness of Tzin, to the river of Shichor near the city of Azah. 10:42, *from Azah to Kadesh Barneya,* refers to this region.

[*Rashi* identifies this river as נִילוּס, which several commentators have interpreted as the Nile River in Egypt. Although the *Commentary* to 10:41 includes several opinions which hold that the western border of *Eretz Yisrael* stretched to the Nile, here *Rashi* does not seem to be alluding to that, since at the end of his comment he explains that Shichor formed the boundary of the city of Azah. Therefore, we have conjectured that Shichor, according to *Rashi,* is either the Egyptian River or the Azah River. *R' Saadiah Gaon* states in his translation of the Torah *(Numbers* 34) that he possesses a tradition that Wadi El Arish is the western border of *Eretz Yisrael.* On our map, this has been labeled Egyptian River. (See also *Commentary* to 15:4.)

Further clarification of *Rashi's* view is needed. Compare *Rashi* to 10:41 with *Rashi's* comment here. See also *Otzar HaNechmad* to *Kuzari* II, 14 and *Radvaz* (Responsa) V, 2206.]

גְּבוּל עֶקְרוֹן צָפוֹנָה — [*To the*] *border of Ekron northward.*

The Ekronites dwelled along the Mediterranean and spread further north than the other Philistine nations *(Rashi).*

This city was located about seven miles northwest of Timnah near the Zarai River *(T'vuos HaAretz).*

[According to the view of *T'vuos HaAretz,* the city of Gas is further north than Ekron (see map). Therefore, *northward* in this verse must refer to the northernmost part of the city of Ekron, not the northernmost boundary of the Philistines as *Rashi* explains. One difficulty with the view of *T'vuos HaAretz* is why Scripture mentioned Ekron in this verse when the city of Gas was in reality the northern boundary of the Philistines. Perhaps, Ekron was mentioned because it was the northwest boundary. Further elucidation is required.]

The city of Ekron formed the border between the territories of Dan and Judah (see 15:11 and 19:43). Although the tribe of Judah was able to subdue this city *(Judges* 1:18) as well as Azah and Ashkelon, Ekron later was a border city between Judah and the Philistines *(II Samuel* 17:52).

לַכְּנַעֲנִי תֵּחָשֵׁב — *Is considered to be the Canaanite.*

In *Genesis* 15:21, God promised Abraham that his offspring would receive the territories of the ten nations occupying *Eretz Yisrael,* one of which was the Canaanites. The corridor of land described by the beginning of this verse was the site of these Canaanites *(Rashi).* Therefore, the Jews were required to conquer it *(Daas Sofrim).*

חֲמֵשֶׁת סַרְנֵי פְלִשְׁתִּים — *Five princes of the Philistines.*

These princes ruled over the land described in the beginning of this verse *(Meam Loez).*

Scripture numbers the princes as five, yet six names are mentioned.

Rashi (based on *Chullin* 60b) offers two interpretations: (a) Scripture only numbered the important princes. The Avim were not important, and were therefore not counted; (b) Scripture only intended to number the *Philistine* princes. The Avim, who did not descend from the Philistines, were consequently not counted.

Tosafos (Chullin 60b) suggests the phrase *and the Avim* has no connection to the Philistine princes named, but refers to the beginning of the following verse. Thus verse 4 should be understood: *From the South, the Avim and all the Canaanite country ... (Vilna Gaon).* [See *Commentary to* 13:8, *Vilna Gaon.*]

13
4

border of Ekron northward is considered to be the Canaanite: the five princes of the Philistines: the Azasites, Ashdodites, Eshkelonites, Gittites, Ekronites, and the Avim. [4] *In the south: all the Canaanite country, M'arah which belongs to the*

הָעַזָּתִי — *The Azasites.*

They lived in the city of Gaza (Arabic) which was located north of Ashkelon on the Mediterranean.

וְהָאַשְׁדּוֹדִי — *(And the) Ashdodites.*

They lived in the city of Ashdod which was located southwest of Yavne.

הָאֶשְׁקְלוֹנִי — *(The) Eshkelonites.*

This people resided in Ashkelon, located on the Mediterranean north of Gaza.

The tribe of Judah conquered this area *(Judges* 1:18), but later in history it became a Philistine stronghold *(II Samuel* 1:2).

הַגִּתִּי — *(The) Gittites.*

For the location of the city of Gas, see *Commentary* to 11:22.

[According to *Rashi,* these five cities mentioned were enumerated from east to west in order to describe the east-west dimension of the unconquered land. This is contrary to the view of *T'vuos HaAretz.*]

וְהָעַוִּים — *And the Avim.*

This nation's land stretched west from Kadesh Barnea to the Mediterranean in the southernmost portion of the Philistine province.

There is a difference of opinion among the commentators in regard to the origins of this people:

☐ *Rashi (Deuteronomy* 2:23) identifies this people as a part of the Philistine nation. Because of the oath that Abraham swore to Avimelech, King of the Philistines *(Genesis* 21:23), the Jews were not permitted to evict these Philistines from their land. Later, however, the Kaftorim conquered the Avim *(Deuteronomy* 2:23). Thus, their land was no longer guaranteed by Abraham's oath, and the Israelites were permitted to conquer it.

☐ *Ramban (Deuteronomy* 2:23), however, argues that the Avim were, in fact, Canaanites. He conjectures that they were the Hivvites (חִוִּי). *Ramban* supports this thesis by demonstrating that the letter ע is often interchanged with the letter ח; thus חִוִּי and עַוִּי could actually be the same word. The Kaftorim conquered the Avim and seized this land, which had been reserved for Esau's children. Once the land passed from the hands of the Avim, the Jews were allowed to take ownership of it. [See *Commentary* to 12:2 for a similar concept.]

4. מִתֵּימָן — *In the south* [lit. *from the south*].

This translation follows *Radak* who understands the phrase *In the south: all the Canaanite country* to be a summary of the unconquered territory in the south. [Beginning with the word *M'arah* is a description of the unconquered territories in the north.]

This translation has been chosen to conform to the view of *T'vuos HaAretz* who places Tzidonia in the north of *Eretz Yisrael.*

Rashi, however, understands that the land of Tzidonia was located in the southwest of *Eretz Yisrael.* מִתֵּימָן, according to *Rashi,* is translated *from the south* and refers to the city of Azah which was the southernmost city of the unconquered land in the southwest. Afeikah and the border of the Emorites form the northernmost boundary of the unconquered southwest territory. *Rashi* does not mention the precise location of these places.

◆§ In the North

וּמְעָרָה — *(And) M'arah.*

T'vuos HaAretz does not mention where in the land of Tzidonia this was located.

יג
ה־ח

אֲשֶׁר לַצִּידֹנִים עַד־אֲפֵקָה עַד גְּבוּל
ה הָאֱמֹרִי: וְהָאָרֶץ הַגִּבְלִי וְכָל־הַלְּבָנוֹן
מִזְרַח הַשֶּׁמֶשׁ מִבַּעַל גָּד תַּחַת הַר־חֶרְמוֹן
ו עַד לְבוֹא חֲמָת: כָּל־יֹשְׁבֵי הָהָר מִן־
הַלְּבָנוֹן עַד־מִשְׂרְפֹת מַיִם כָּל־צִידֹנִים
אָנֹכִי אוֹרִישֵׁם מִפְּנֵי בְּנֵי יִשְׂרָאֵל רַק
הַפִּלֶהָ לְיִשְׂרָאֵל בְּנַחֲלָה כַּאֲשֶׁר צִוִּיתִךָ:
ז וְעַתָּה חַלֵּק אֶת־הָאָרֶץ הַזֹּאת בְּנַחֲלָה
לְתִשְׁעַת הַשְּׁבָטִים וַחֲצִי הַשֵּׁבֶט הַמְנַשֶּׁה:
ח עִמּוֹ הָרְאוּבֵנִי וְהַגָּדִי לָקְחוּ נַחֲלָתָם אֲשֶׁר
נָתַן לָהֶם מֹשֶׁה בְּעֵבֶר הַיַּרְדֵּן מִזְרָחָה
כַּאֲשֶׁר נָתַן לָהֶם מֹשֶׁה עֶבֶד יְהוָה:

לַצִּידֹנִים — [*Which belongs*] *to the Tzidonians.*

This people occupied a region of land that extended from the city of Tzur to Trablos (Tripoli in Northern Lebanon).

אֲפֵקָה — *Afeikah.*

This city is located on the river called Ibrahim (formerly known as Adanis) east of the city of Gibal. [It is therefore not identical with Afeik mentioned in 12:18.]

עַד גְּבוּל הָאֱמֹרִי — *To the border of the Emorites.*

[Presumably the Emorites owned land in the north of *Eretz Yisrael.* The commentators do not precisely locate the reference made in this verse.]

5. וְהָאָרֶץ הַגִּבְלִי — *And the land of the Givalites.*

This nation's land was located around the city of Gibal which was known by the Greeks as Biblos. It was located on the Mediterranean Sea, north of the river Ibrahim. [The ancient city of Biblos is located today in Syria at 35° 30'.]

The people of Gival assisted in hewing the foundation stones of the First Temple (*I Kings* 5:32).

וְכָל־הַלְּבָנוֹן — *And all the Lebanon.*

T'vuos HaAretz maintains that this is a reference to the mountain range east of the Jordan known today as the Anti-Lebanon. It is not the Lebanon mountain range west of the Jordan.

מִזְרַח הַשֶּׁמֶשׁ — *Eastern* [lit. *toward the rising of the sun*].

מִבַּעַל גָּד — *From Ba'al Gad.*

This city was south of Lavo Chamas. *T'vuos HaAretz* identifies it as the city of Banias, located west of the Mount Hermon and north of the Sea of Merom. [See *Commentary* to 11:17.]

לְבוֹא חֲמָת — *Lavo Chamas* [lit. *entrance to Chamas*].

This district was located in the northern part of the valley between the Lebanon and Anti-Lebanon mountains (Coelesyria), north of the city of Baalbek and south of Chamas. It formed part of the northern border of *Eretz Yisrael* as related in *Numbers* 34:8.

Jerusalem Targum (Numbers 34:8) identifies Lavo Chamas as Antucia.

According to *Rashi,* only verse 5 records the unconquered northern territory (see *Commentary* to verse 4, s.v. 'In the south'). It extended from Ba'al Gad in the south to the northern border of *Eretz Yisrael* and on the

Tzidonians to Afeikah all the way to the border of the
Emorites; 5 *and the land of the Givalites and all the*
eastern Lebanon — from Ba'al Gad at the foot of
Mount Hermon to Lavo Chamas; 6 *all the inhabitants*
of the mountains — from the Lebanon to Misrefos-
Mayim. All the Tzidonians I will drive out for the
Children of Israel. You have only to divide it by
lottery for the Israelites as an inheritance, as I have
commanded you. 7 *And now, divide this land for an*
inheritance for the nine tribes and part of the tribe of
Menashe.'
8 *With him, the Reubenites and Gadites took their*
inheritance which Moses had given them on the
eastern side of the Jordan, just as Moses, servant of

northern border from Ba'al Gad in the east to Lavo Chamas in the west.

6. מִשְׂרְפֹת מַיִם — *Misrefos Mayim.*
See *Commentary* to 11:8.

אָנֹכִי אוֹרִישֵׁם — *I will drive out.*
God will drive them out after Joshua's death *(Rashi).*

◆§ The Division of the Land

הַפִּלֶהָ לְיִשְׂרָאֵל בְּנַחֲלָה — *Divide it by lottery for the Israelites as an inheritance.*

All these unconquered areas were mentioned so that Joshua would include them in the division of the Land *(Meam Loez).*

In the future, each tribe should conquer those Canaanites which remain in its territory *(Rashi).* [See *Rambam (Hil. Terumos* 1:2).]

Malbim makes a distinction between two Hebrew words — יְרוּשָּׁה and נַחֲלָה — which mean inheritance. נַחֲלָה refers to the bequeathing of property to children, while יְרוּשָּׁה refers to the transfer of property from one owner to another. Since our verse refers to the bequeathing of territory which has not yet been conquered, and thus the transfer of ownership from the Canaanites to the Israelites had not yet been effected, Scripture employs the expression נַחֲלָה. However, in 12:7, Scripture uses the word יְרוּשָּׁה since that verse speaks of land which the Jews had conquered and was about to be transferred from the Canaanites to the tribes of Israel.

כַּאֲשֶׁר צִוִּיתִיךָ — *As I have commanded you.*

This command is found in *Deuteronomy* 3:28: *Command Joshua ... and he will cause them to inherit the Land (Metzudos).* [See also *Joshua* 1:6.] Thus Joshua was required to divide the Land, even though all the Canaanites were not yet displaced *(Malbim).*

7. חַלֵּק אֶת־הָאָרֶץ הַזֹּאת — *Divide this land.*

First divide the Land into nine and one-half parts and then draw lots to decide which tribe receives each plot of land *(Metzudos).*

◆§ Each Tribe's Inheritance

8. Joshua begins by recounting the inheritances of Reuben, Gad, and Menashe on the eastern bank of the Jordan which were given not by him, but by Moses.

Lev Aharon explains that although Moses had already assigned these territories to these tribes, they did not actually acquire ownership of their inheritances until the time *Eretz Yisrael* was conquered, as the verse in *Numbers* 32:29 implies, *If the Children of Gad and the Children of Reuben will cross*

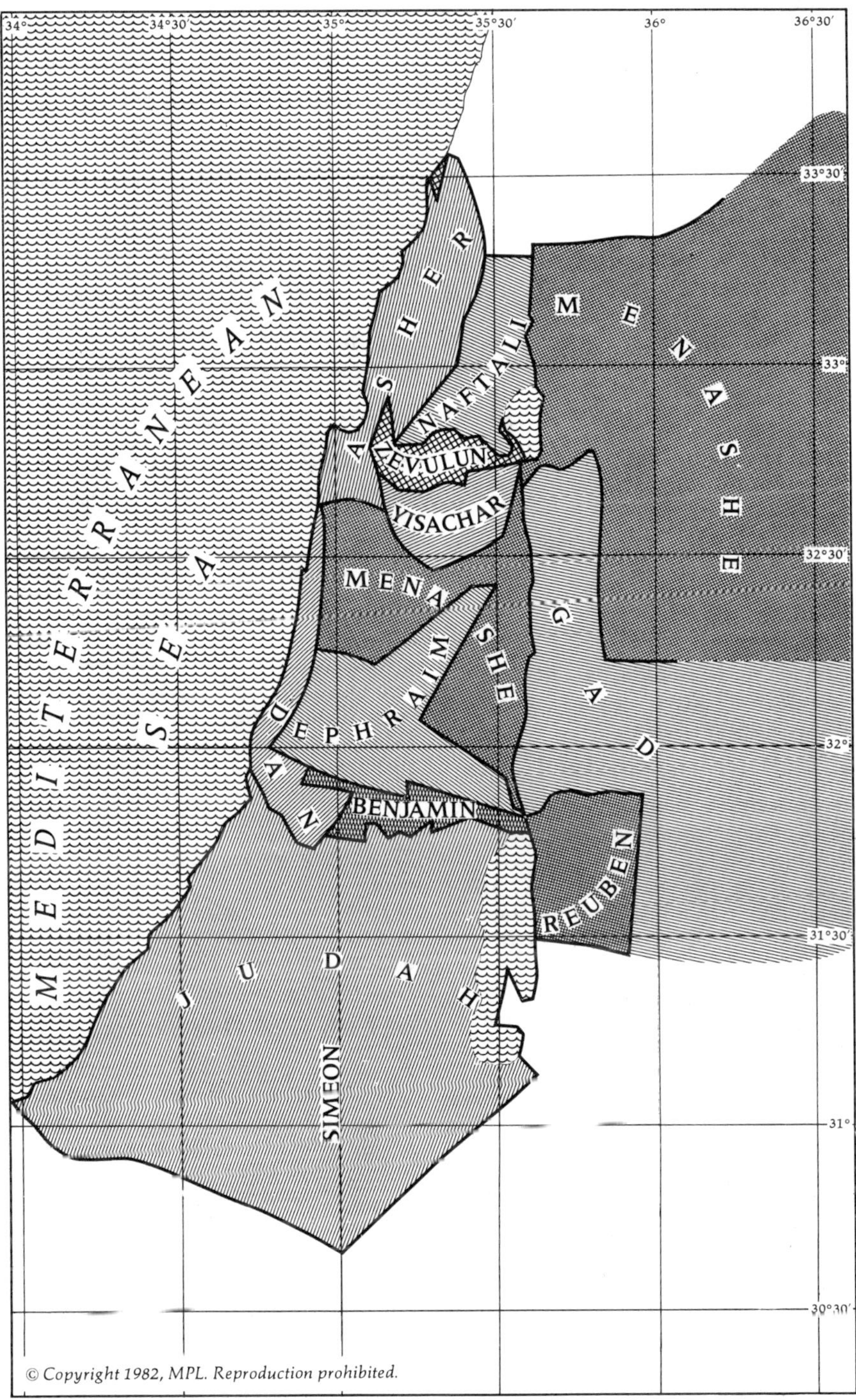
34°
34°30′
35°
35°30′
36°
36°30′
33°30′
33°
32°30′
32°
31°30′
31°
30°30′
MEDITERRANEAN SEA
ASHER
NAFTALI
ZEVULUN
YISACHAR
MENASHE
MENASHE
MENASHE
EPHRAIM
DAN
BENJAMIN
GAD
REUBEN
JUDAH
SIMEON

On the opposite page is a map illustrating the territory of land allocated to each tribe in *Eretz Yisrael* based on the deductions of *T'vuos HaAretz*. It cannot be overemphasized that these borders, as well as geographical identifications displayed on all the other maps, are merely reasonable approximations and are in many cases based on conjecture. (See *Preface* for a discussion of the problems relating to a precise geography of the Land.)

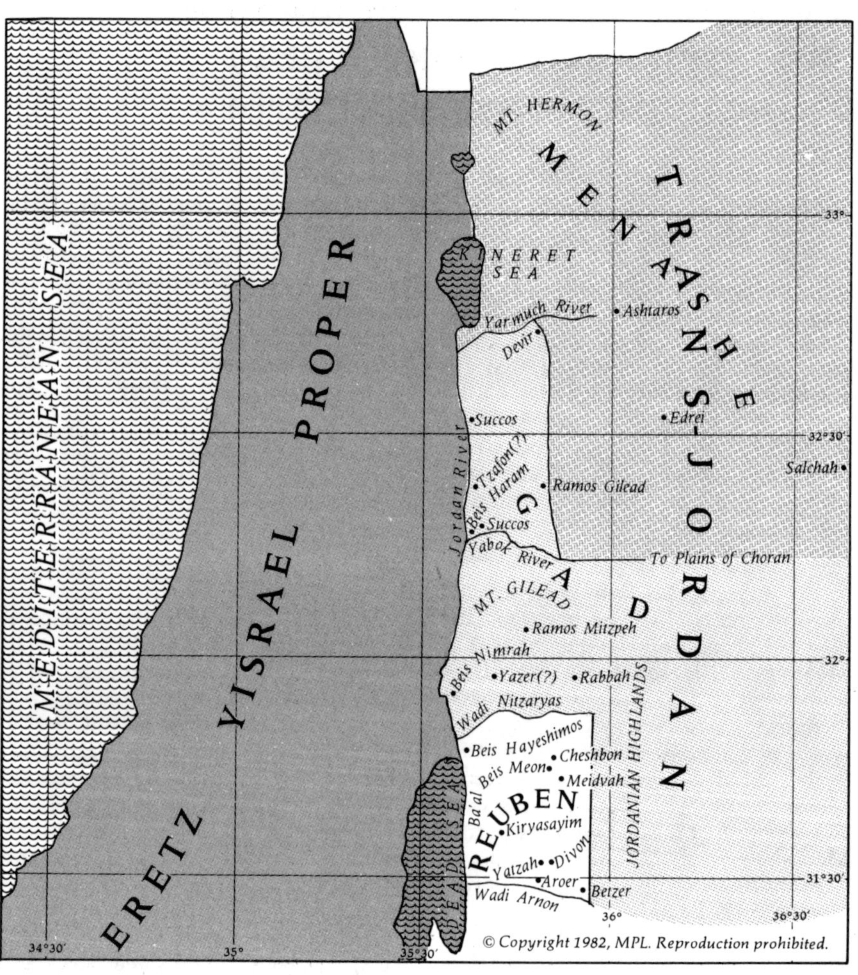

יג
ט־יד

ט מֵעֲרוֹעֵר אֲשֶׁר עַל־שְׂפַת־נַחַל אַרְנוֹן
וְהָעִיר אֲשֶׁר בְּתוֹךְ־הַנַּחַל וְכָל־הַמִּישֹׁר
י מֵידְבָא עַד־דִּיבוֹן׃ וְכֹל עָרֵי סִיחוֹן מֶלֶךְ
הָאֱמֹרִי אֲשֶׁר מָלַךְ בְּחֶשְׁבּוֹן עַד־גְּבוּל
יא בְּנֵי־עַמּוֹן׃ וְהַגִּלְעָד וּגְבוּל הַגְּשׁוּרִי
וְהַמַּעֲכָתִי וְכֹל הַר חֶרְמוֹן וְכָל־הַבָּשָׁן
יב עַד־סַלְכָה׃ כָּל־מַמְלְכוּת עוֹג בַּבָּשָׁן
אֲשֶׁר־מָלַךְ בְּעַשְׁתָּרוֹת וּבְאֶדְרֶעִי הוּא
נִשְׁאַר מִיֶּתֶר הָרְפָאִים וַיַּכֵּם מֹשֶׁה
יג וַיֹּרִשֵׁם׃ וְלֹא הוֹרִישׁוּ בְּנֵי יִשְׂרָאֵל אֶת־
הַגְּשׁוּרִי וְאֶת־הַמַּעֲכָתִי וַיֵּשֶׁב גְּשׁוּר
יד וּמַעֲכָת בְּקֶרֶב יִשְׂרָאֵל עַד הַיּוֹם הַזֶּה׃ רַק

over the Jordan with you ... and the Land shall be subdued before you, **then** *you shall give them the land of Gilead for a possession.* Even though there was still much unconquered land, God commanded Joshua, *And now divide the Land* (verse 7). This command was an implicit promise by God that He would drive out the remainder of the Land's inhabitants. Thus, the time had arrived that the Land was considered *subdued* and Reuben, Gad, and Menashe could take legal ownership of their land.

עִמּוֹ — *With him.*

The tribe of Menashe was divided into two parts. Verse 7 mentions the directive to apportion land to the part of Menashe which would inherit territory to the west of the Jordan, and this verse mentions the other part of Menashe which had already received its territory to the east of the Jordan in the times of Moses, along with Reuben and Gad. Thus, *with him* means: with the part of Menashe east of the Jordan *(Rashi).*

According to *Vilna Gaon,* the phrase 'part of the tribe of Menashe' should be inserted in the beginning of this verse. This explanation follows the principle of exegesis that sometimes the concluding phrase of one verse could be considered as having been written twice; the repeated phase is then inserted in the beginning of the following verse.

This is the eleventh principle stated in the thirty-two principles of exegesis formulated by R' Yosi HaGalili (סדר שנחלק). For other cases, see *Vilna Gaon* to *I Chronicles* 1:36. Cf. *Ramban* to *Genesis* 36:12 who apparently has a different understanding of this principle. See also *Nesivos Olam* for a more extensive treatment.

כַּאֲשֶׁר נָתַן לָהֶם מֹשֶׁה — *Just as Moses ... had given them.*

This clause describes the manner in which Reuben and Gad *took their inheritance.* They were pleased with their inheritance *just as Moses had given it,* and thus they did not need to be given any land in *Eretz Yisrael* proper *(Metzudos).*

[See *Prefatory Remarks* to 1:13.]

Moses assigned each tribe its territory on the eastern bank of the Jordan and did not utilize a lottery system as Joshua did for the tribes' acquisition of the land on the western side. *Sforno (Numbers* 34:2) explains that since the land

HASHEM, had given them. 9 *From Aroer which is on*
the edge of the Arnon River and the city which is in
the middle of the river — the entire plain from
Meidva to Divon; 10 *and all the cities of Sichon, the*
Emorite king, who ruled from Cheshbon to the
border of the Ammonites; 11 *and Gilead, the border*
of the Geshurites and the Ma'achausites, all Mount
Chermon, and all Bashan to Salchah; 12 *the entire*
kingdom of Og in Bashan who ruled from Ashtaros
and Edrei and who was of the surviving Rephaim —
these Moses defeated and drove out. 13 *But the*
Children of Israel did not drive out the Geshurites or
the Ma'achasites, and the Geshurites and
Ma'achasites live among the Israelites until this day.

outside *Eretz Yisrael* does not have the same sanctity as the Land of Israel proper (see *footnote* to 22:19), it would not have been appropriate to use the Divinely controlled lottery to assign the Trans-Jordan territory.

The Boundaries of the Trans-Jordan

9. ... מֵעֲרוֹעֵר — *From Aroer.*

See *Commentary* to 12:2.

The boundaries of the land on the eastern bank of the Jordan are identical with those of Sichon and Og mentioned in 12:2-5. In this chapter additional detail is given, in order to prevent the possibility of border disputes *(Daas Sofrim).*

נַחַל אַרְנוֹן — *Arnon River.*

[See *Commentary* to 12:1.] This formed the southern border of Sichon's kingdom.

מֵידְבָא עַד־דִּיבוֹן — *[From] Meidva to Divon.*

These cities were not mentioned in Chapter 12. Meidva was located about five miles southeast of Cheshbon, and Divon was located about two and a half miles northeast of Aroer.

10. אֲשֶׁר מָלַךְ בְּחֶשְׁבּוֹן — *Who ruled from Cheshbon.*

Sichon ruled from Cheshbon because Cheshbon was the first Moabite city he conquered. Sichon destroyed Cheshbon and then rebuilt it as his capital. There he planned his strategy for the conquest of the southern portion of the Moabites' territory *(Ramban, Numbers* 21:26).

עַד־גְּבוּל בְּנֵי־עַמּוֹן — *To the border of the Ammonites.*

Sichon conquered Ammon's territory which was located between the Arnon River and the Yabok River. See 12:2.

12. הָרְפָאִים — *Rephaim.*

The Rephaim were the giants who lived in the northern part of *Eretz Yisrael. Genesis* 14:4-13 describes an attack launched by Chedorlaomer and his accompanying kings against these giants. Of the Rephaim, only Og escaped from this battle *(Deuteronomy* 3:11).

13. ... וְלֹא הוֹרִישׁוּ — *Did not drive out.*

Moses did not conquer these nations in his campaign against Sichon and Og. *Abarbanel* identifies this as a similarity between Moses and Joshua: they both divided the land of their conquests

לְשֵׁבֶט הַלֵּוִי לֹא נָתַן נַחֲלָה אִשֵּׁי
יְהוָה אֱלֹהֵי יִשְׂרָאֵל הוּא נַחֲלָתוֹ כַּאֲשֶׁר
טו דִּבֶּר־לוֹ: וַיִּתֵּן מֹשֶׁה לְמַטֵּה
טז בְנֵי־רְאוּבֵן לְמִשְׁפְּחֹתָם: וַיְהִי לָהֶם הַגְּבוּל
מֵעֲרוֹעֵר אֲשֶׁר עַל־שְׂפַת־נַחַל אַרְנוֹן
וְהָעִיר אֲשֶׁר בְּתוֹךְ־הַנַּחַל וְכָל־הַמִּישֹׁר
יז עַל־מֵידְבָא: חֶשְׁבּוֹן וְכָל־עָרֶיהָ אֲשֶׁר
בַּמִּישֹׁור דִּיבוֹן וּבָמוֹת בַּעַל וּבֵית בַּעַל
יח־יט מְעוֹן: וְיַהְצָה וּקְדֵמֹת וּמֵפָעַת: וְקִרְיָתַיִם

before all the indigenous nations were driven out.

14. לְשֵׁבֶט הַלֵּוִי — *To the tribe of Levi.*

The Kohanim (priests) were also a part of the tribe of Levi.

לֹא נָתַן נַחֲלָה — *He gave no inheritance.*

Rambam (Hil. Shmittah V'Yovel 13:10) rules that it is prohibited to give the tribe of Levi a portion in the Land of Israel. He explains *(ibid.,* 13:12) that the Levites were forbidden to acquire land in *Eretz Yisrael* or to take a portion in the spoils of war, because the Levites were separated from the other tribes in order to devote themselves exclusively to Divine service. Specifically, they were to perform the service in the Holy Temple and to teach the other tribes about the Torah's guidelines for living. Thus, they were forbidden to engage in agriculture or war.

Although the Levites did not receive a portion of the Land, the other tribes were commanded to give them some of their cities in which to dwell *(Numbers* 35:2-3). These cities are mentioned in Chapter 21.

אִשֵּׁי ה׳ אֱלֹהֵי יִשְׂרָאֵל הוּא נַחֲלָתוֹ — *The offerings to HASHEM, the God of Israel, are* [lit. *it is*] *his inheritance.*

The Levites were in charge of bequeathing the spiritual (but not the physical) achievements of the Israelites to their children. *R' Hirsch (Numbers* 18:20) explains that *his inheritance* refers to spiritual matters.

אִשֵּׁי ה׳ — *The offerings to Hashem.*

The word אִשֵּׁי derives from the word אֵשׁ, *fire. Metzudos* explains that this expression refers to those parts which are given to the Kohanim after the altar portions have been put into the fire.

כַּאֲשֶׁר דִּבֶּר־לוֹ — *As He said to him.*

God said to Aaron in *Numbers* 18:20, *'You will have no inheritance in the Land, nor will you have any part among them: I am your portion and your inheritance ...'*

◆§ The Boundaries of Reuben's Territory

15-23. Reuben's territory was bordered on the north by the Nitzaryas River which empties into the Dead Sea near the site where the Jordan meets the Dead Sea. The Arnon River formed its southern border and the Dead Sea its western border. The mountain range which was located east of the plains of Moab and stretched in a north-south direction formed its eastern border *(T'vuos HaAretz).*

[We have conjectured that *T'vuos HaAretz* was referring to Wadi Nitzaryas from his description of the area, although he does not mention the name of this river. Because of the ambiguities in his description it is also possible that he was referring to Wadi Uzimi.]

According to *Ramban (Numbers* 32:38), the names of the cities in Reuben's territory are the names that

[14] *But, to the tribe of Levi, he gave no inheritance; the*
offerings to HASHEM, the God of Israel, are his
inheritance, as He said to him.
[15] *Moses gave to the tribe of the Children of*
Reuben according to their families. [16] *And their*
border was from Aroer which is on the edge of the
Arnon River and the city that is in the middle of the
river and all the plain to Meidva; [17] *Cheshbon and all*
its cities in the plain — Divon, Bamos Ba'al, and Beis
Ba'al Meon; [18] *and Yatzah, Kedeimos, and Meifa'as;*

the Moabites had originally assigned them. When the Emorites conquered these cities they changed their names; the Israelites, however, changed their names back to the Moabite version either to embarrass the Moabites or to avoid using the Emorite names which were derived from the names of the Emorite idolatry.

15. לְמִשְׁפְּחֹתָם — *According to their families.*

Moses did not assign the entire territory of the tribe of Reuben and allow them to subdivide it; rather he himself divided the land and assigned a section to each family *(Metzudos).*

The families of Reuben are listed in *Numbers* 26:5-10.

As mentioned in the *Prefatory Remarks* to this chapter, Reuben was granted the first portion of land. *Ramban (Deuteronomy* 33:6) remarks that the tribe of Reuben received the first blessing from Moses shortly before his death precisely because this tribe received the first portion in the Land.

16. מֵעֲרוֹעֵר — *From Aroer.*

See *Commentary* to 12:2 for its location.

וְהָעִיר אֲשֶׁר בְּתוֹךְ־הַנַּחַל — *And the city that is in the middle of the river.*

See *Commentary* to 12:2.

17. ... וּבָמוֹת בַּעַל — *Bamos Ba'al ...*

T'vuos HaAretz does not identify its location.

Ibn Ezra to *Numbers* 22:41 identifies this place with בַּעֲלֵי בָּמוֹת אַרְנֹן of *Numbers* 21:28. *Targum,* in each case, renders *the hills* [or *high places*] where the idols [*Ba'al*] are worshiped.

וּבֵית בַּעַל מְעוֹן — *Beis Ba'al Meon.*

This city was located about 2 miles south of Cheshbon.

18. וְיַהְצָה — *Yatzah.*

This city was located west and slightly south of Divon. When the prophet Isaiah had a vision that Sancheriv would destroy Moab, he predicted that the howls of the inhabitants of Cheshbon would be heard as far as Yatzah *(Radak* to *Isaiah* 15:4).

וּקְדֵמֹת — *Kedeimos.*

T'vuos HaAretz is not certain of its location.

וּמֵפָעַת — *Meifa'as.*

T'vuos HaAretz does not identify its location.

I Chronicles 6:63-64 states that Reuben gave these three cities to the Levites; in *Jeremiah* 48:24, we read that Moab repossessed Meifa'as.

19. וְקִרְיָתַיִם — *And Kiryasayim.*

This city was located south of Mount Atara and was located between Meidva and Divon.

This is one of the cities that the Reubenites built when they were guaranteed the land east of the Jordan *(Numbers* 32:37). It was later repossessed by Masha, the King of Moab *(Jeremiah* 48:1).

כ וְשִׂבְמָה וְצֶרֶת הַשַּׁחַר בְּהַר הָעֵמֶק׃ וּבֵית
פְּעוֹר וְאַשְׁדּוֹת הַפִּסְגָּה וּבֵית הַיְשִׁמוֹת׃
כא וְכֹל עָרֵי הַמִּישֹׁר וְכָל־מַמְלְכוּת סִיחוֹן
מֶלֶךְ הָאֱמֹרִי אֲשֶׁר מָלַךְ בְּחֶשְׁבּוֹן אֲשֶׁר
הִכָּה מֹשֶׁה אֹתוֹ | וְאֶת־נְשִׂיאֵי מִדְיָן
אֶת־אֱוִי וְאֶת־רֶקֶם וְאֶת־צוּר וְאֶת־חוּר
וְאֶת־רֶבַע נְסִיכֵי סִיחוֹן יֹשְׁבֵי הָאָרֶץ׃
כב וְאֶת בִּלְעָם בֶּן־בְּעוֹר הַקּוֹסֵם הָרְגוּ
כג בְנֵי־יִשְׂרָאֵל בַּחֶרֶב אֶל־חַלְלֵיהֶם׃ וַיְהִי
גְּבוּל בְּנֵי רְאוּבֵן הַיַּרְדֵּן וּגְבוּל זֹאת
נַחֲלַת בְּנֵי־רְאוּבֵן לְמִשְׁפְּחוֹתָם הֶעָרִים
כד וְחַצְרֵיהֶן׃ וַיִּתֵּן מֹשֶׁה לְמַטֵּה

וְשִׂבְמָה — *Sivmah.*

Kaftor V'Ferach locates this city northeast of Yazer, but *T'vuos HaAretz* argues that this is untenable because Yazer was situated in Gad's territory. This was another city built by the Reubenites.

From *Isaiah* 16:9, it appears that Sivmah was an area known for its vineyards.

וְצֶרֶת הַשַּׁחַר — *Tzeres HaShachar.*

Its location is unknown.

20. וּבֵית פְּעוֹר וְאַשְׁדּוֹת הַפִּסְגָּה — *And Beis Pe'or and Ashdos HaPisgah.*

T'vuos HaAretz does not identify these locations.

According to *Tosafos* (*Sotah* 14a) Beis Pe'or was located across from Mount Nevo, the burial place of Moses. Mount Nevo was located on the eastern side of the Jordan River, across from Jericho. See *Commentary* to 22:17.

וּבֵית הַיְשִׁמוֹת — *And Beis Hayeshimos.*

This city was located opposite Jericho on the eastern side of the Jordan.

21. וְאֶת־נְשִׂיאֵי מִדְיָן — *With the Midianite princes.*

These were the princes of Midian before Sichon conquered them. He allowed them to continue their rule as his vassals (*Ramban, Numbers* 22:4).

The Jews conquered the Midianites' land when it was under the control of Sichon (*Radak*).

וְאֶת־רֶקֶם — *(And) Rekem.*

This was the city of Sela and is the Rekem referred to in *Gittin* 2a (cf. ArtScroll *Bereishis* to *Genesis* 16:14).

The other cities of this verse are not identified by *T'vuos HaAretz.*

יֹשְׁבֵי הָאָרֶץ — *Inhabitants of the land.*

These princes dwelled in the land of Sichon (*Metzudos*).

22. בִּלְעָם בֶּן־בְּעוֹר — *Bilaam ben Be'or.*

[Bilaam was the evil Midianite soothsayer who had been commissioned to curse the Jews by Balak, the king of Moab. To rebuke the wicked seer, God granted Bilaam's donkey the power of speech, and He bade Bilaam to bless the Israelites (*Numbers* 22-24).]

Scripture implies that Bilaam remained in Midian. However, *Numbers* 24:25 states that he left Midian to return to Pesor, his home. *Radak* comments

[19] *and Kiryasayim, Sivmah, and Tzeres HaShachar*
on Mount HaEmek; [20] *and Beis Pe'or, and Ashdos*
HaPisgah, and Beis Hayeshimos; [21] *and all the cities*
of the plain; and all the kingdom of Sichon, the
Emorite King who ruled in Cheshbon, whom Moses
defeated with the Midianite princes — Evi, Rekem,
Tzur, Chur, Reva — dukes of Sichon, inhabitants of
the land. [22] *And Bilaam ben Be'or, the sorcerer, the*
Children of Israel slayed with the sword along with
their slain. [23] *And the border of the Children of*
Reuben was the Jordan and its border. This was the
inheritance of the Children of Reuben, according to
their families — the cities and their villages.

that Bilaam returned to Midian to receive his reward for the advice he had given Moab and Midian in regard to ensnaring the Israelites through harlotry (*Numbers* 25), but he was originally from the city of Pesor (*Radak*).

הַקּוֹסֵם — *The sorcerer.*
From *Rashi* (*Sanhedrin* 106a) it would appear that Bilaam was originally a prophet, but when he decided to curse the Israelites, prophecy was withdrawn from him and he became a mere sorcerer.

According to *Ramban* (*Deuteronomy* 18:9), however, Bilaam was not a real prophet. God granted him prophecy only on that night, not because he merited it, but because God wanted to honor Israel. Having received this prophecy, Bilaam was able to see the angel (*Numbers* 22:31) and talk to him, but when he returned home from Moab, he reverted to his previous status as a mere sorcerer; it was this title with which he died.

הָרְגוּ בְנֵי־יִשְׂרָאֵל בַּחֶרֶב — *The Children of Israel slayed with the sword.*
See *Rashi* to *Numbers* 31:8.

אֶל־חַלְלֵיהֶם — *Along with* [lit. *to*] *their slain.*

The translation follows *Radak*.

Targum, however, renders *on those who were slain by them.* This translation follows the *Midrash* which relates that when Bilaam saw the Israelites wreaking havoc on the Midianites, he attempted to escape through use of his sorcery by lifting himself up in the air. Pinchas showed him the holy mitre worn on the head of the *Kohen Gadol*, which has the name of God engraved on it, and Bilaam fell to the ground *on* top of the slain Midianites.

Abarbanel suggests that the phrase *those who were slain by them* does not refer to the Midianites whom the Israelites killed, but rather to the Israelites who were killed by the nefarious plan devised by Bilaam and executed by the Midianites (*Numbers* 25).

23. וּגְבוּל — *And its border.*
This refers to the cities on the Jordan (*Rashi*, verse 27).

The word *its* is interpolated by *Targum*.

וְחַצְרֵיהֶן — *And their villages.*
This refers to open, unwalled cities which surround a walled city (*Metzudos*).

כה גָּד לִבְנֵי גָד לְמִשְׁפְּחֹתָם: וַיְהִי לָהֶם
הַגְּבוּל יַעְזֵר וְכָל־עָרֵי הַגִּלְעָד וַחֲצִי אֶרֶץ
בְּנֵי עַמּוֹן עַד־עֲרוֹעֵר אֲשֶׁר עַל־פְּנֵי רַבָּה:
כו וּמֵחֶשְׁבּוֹן עַד־רָמַת הַמִּצְפֶּה וּבְטֹנִים
כז וּמִמַּחֲנַיִם עַד־גְּבוּל לִדְבִר: וּבָעֵמֶק בֵּית
הָרָם וּבֵית נִמְרָה וְסֻכּוֹת וְצָפוֹן יֶתֶר
מַמְלְכוּת סִיחוֹן מֶלֶךְ חֶשְׁבּוֹן הַיַּרְדֵּן וּגְבֻל
עַד־קְצֵה יָם־כִּנֶּרֶת עֵבֶר הַיַּרְדֵּן מִזְרָחָה:
כח זֹאת נַחֲלַת בְּנֵי־גָד לְמִשְׁפְּחֹתָם הֶעָרִים

◆§ The Boundaries of Gad's Territory

24-28. The Yarmuch River formed the northern border of Gad's territory; the Jordan, its western border. In the south it stretched as far as Reuben's territory (Wadi Nitzaryas) and in the east it extended to the plains of Choran.[1]

24. לְמִשְׁפְּחֹתָם — *According to their families.*
See *Commentary* to verse 15.

25. יַעְזֵר — *Yazer.*
It was located where Ein Chatzir meets the Nimrin River.
This was one of the cities that the tribe of Gad had already built for their sheep *(Numbers* 32:35). Later they gave this city to the Levites (see 21:37).

וַחֲצִי אֶרֶץ בְּנֵי עַמּוֹן — *And half the land of the Children of Ammon.*
The Israelites were forbidden to wage war against the nation of Ammon, as it says, *Do not harass them* [*Ammon*] *and do not contend with them (Deuteronomy* 2:19). Scripture here refers to the territory of Ammon which was conquered by Sichon. After Sichon acquired ownership of this land it was no longer prohibited to the Israelites (*Chullin* 60b).

עֲרוֹעֵר — *Aroer.*
It was located near Amman [not to be confused with Aroer in Reuben's territory].

רַבָּה — *Rabbah.*
This is the city of Amman [Jordan].

26. וּמֵחֶשְׁבּוֹן — *And from Cheshbon.*
This city was on the northern border of Reuben (verse 17) and the southern border of Gad. It was later given to the Levites (see 21:37).

רָמַת הַמִּצְפֶּה — *Ramas HaMitzpeh.*
This city is also known as Mitzpeh Gilead and is the present day city of Salt. It should not be confused with the city of refuge Ramas Gilead which was located north of this city.
It is mentioned in *Judges* 11:29 as one of the cities from which Yiftach[2] launched his attack against the Ammonites.

1. Before his death Moses blessed the tribe of Gad with the following words: *Blessed is he that enlarges Gad, he dwells like a lion (Deuteronomy* 33:20). *Sifri* explains *enlarging Gad* to mean that Gad's territory extended far to the east [much further than Reuben's] and *dwelling like a lion* to mean that his territory formed one of the borders of the Land [and thus had to be strong enough to defend it like a lion. See *Sifsei Chachamim, ibid.*].

2. From the Torah *(Numbers* 32:39-40) it would appear that Machir son of Menashe received the city of Gilead from Moses, and he was from the tribe of Menashe, not Gad! *Maharatz*

13
24-28

24 And Moses gave to the tribe of Gad, to the
Children of Gad, according to their families. 25 Their
border was Yazer, all the cities of Gilead, and half the
land of the Children of Ammon, to Aroer which was
before Rabbah; 26 and from Cheshbon to Ramas
HaMitzpeh and Betonim; and from Machanayim to
the border of Devir; 27 and in the valley: Beis Haram,
Beis Nimrah, Succos, and Tzafon — the rest of the
kingdom of Sichon, King of Cheshbon — the Jordan
and its border, to the shore of the Kineret Sea on the
eastern side of the Jordan. 28 This is the inheritance of
the Children of Gad according to their families — the
cities and their villages.

וּבְטֹנִים — *And Betonim.*
Its location is unknown.

וּמִמַּחֲנַיִם — *And from Machanayim.*
It was located east of Beis Shean, but its precise location is not known. It formed the border between the tribe of Menashe in the north (verse 30) and the tribe of Gad.

We read in *Genesis* 32:2 that Jacob gave this city its name. This was this city to which David fled from Abshalom *(II Samuel* 17:24). It was later given to the Levites (see 21:36).

גְּבוּל לִדְבִר — *The border of Devir.*
Devir was located six and a half miles east of Tzafin and south of the Yarmuch River and is the city of Ibdir. [This should not be confused with the city Devir mentioned in 12:9 which was in Judah's territory.]

27. בֵּית הָרָם — *Beis Haram.*
It was located where the Yabok River intersects the Jordan River. Others say it was located further south, about two and a half miles north of Beis Nimrah. This was one of the cities which the tribe of Gad built before crossing the Jordan *(Numbers* 32:36).

וּבֵית נִמְרָה — *(And) Beis Nimrah.*
This city was located on the Nimrin River, not far from the Jordan.

This was also one of the cities Gad built before their entry into *Eretz Yisrael (Numbers* 32:36).

וְסֻכּוֹת — *Succos.*
This city was located southeast of Beis Shean near the Jordan on the eastern side. It should not be confused with the city on the western side of the Jordan which is also called Succos.

וְצָפוֹן — *And Tzafon.*
Its precise location is unknown, but it was located somewhere near the Jordan not far from Ramas Gilead. [The Jordan River is in a valley.]

עַד־קְצֵה יָם־כִּנֶּרֶת — *To the shore of the Kineret Sea.*
After locating the cities in this passage and other cities referred to as being in Gad's territory, *T'vuos*

Chayes (Ta'anis 3a), however, suggests that only the capital city Gilead was given to Machir; the smaller surrounding cities in that region were given to the tribe of Gad. It is to these cities which our verse refers. This distinction would also explain why the *Midrash* identifies Yiftach of Gilead (see *Judges* 11:1) as a member of the tribe of Menashe, for he came from the capital city of Gilead. Elijah the Prophet, however, the *Midrash* identifies as a member of the tribe of Gad, since he came from one of the smaller cities of the region.

יג כט וְחַצְרֵיהֶֽם׃ וַיִּתֵּ֣ן מֹשֶׁ֔ה לַחֲצִ֖י
כח-לג שֵׁ֣בֶט מְנַשֶּׁ֑ה וַיְהִ֗י לַחֲצִ֛י מַטֵּ֥ה בְנֵֽי־מְנַשֶּׁ֖ה
ל לְמִשְׁפְּחוֹתָֽם׃ וַיְהִ֣י גְבוּלָ֗ם מִֽמַּחֲנַ֙יִם֙ כָּל־
הַבָּשָׁ֔ן כָּל־מַמְלְכ֣וּת ׀ ע֣וֹג מֶֽלֶךְ־הַבָּשָׁ֔ן
וְכָל־חַוֺּ֥ת יָאִ֖יר אֲשֶׁ֣ר בַּבָּשָׁ֑ן שִׁשִּׁ֖ים עִֽיר׃
לא וַחֲצִ֨י הַגִּלְעָ֜ד וְעַשְׁתָּר֣וֹת וְאֶדְרֶ֗עִי עָרֵ֛י
מַמְלְכ֥וּת ע֖וֹג בַּבָּשָׁ֑ן לִבְנֵ֞י מָכִ֣יר בֶּן־מְנַשֶּׁ֗ה
לב לַחֲצִ֛י בְנֵֽי־מָכִ֖יר לְמִשְׁפְּחוֹתָֽם׃ אֵ֕לֶּה
אֲשֶׁר־נִחַ֥ל מֹשֶׁ֖ה בְּעַרְב֣וֹת מוֹאָ֑ב מֵעֵ֛בֶר
לג לְיַרְדֵּ֥ן יְרִיח֖וֹ מִזְרָֽחָה׃ וּלְשֵׁ֙בֶט֙ הַלֵּוִ֔י לֹֽא־
יד נָתַ֥ן מֹשֶׁ֖ה נַחֲלָ֑ה יהוה אֱלֹהֵ֤י יִשְׂרָאֵל֙ ה֣וּא
א א נַחֲלָתָ֔ם כַּאֲשֶׁ֖ר דִּבֶּ֥ר לָהֶֽם׃ וְאֵ֛לֶּה אֲשֶׁר־

HaAretz concludes that the tribe of Gad did not extend to the shores of the Kineret Sea. He, therefore, concludes that the Yarmuch River was the northern border of Gad, [and presumably it is to this that the phrase *to the shore of the Kineret Sea* refers. *To* in this context appears to mean 'towards.']

◆§ The Boundaries of Menashe's Territory

29-32. As verse 30 mentions, Menashe's territory was composed of Og's territory which was described in 12:4-5. Og's territory stretched from the Yabok River in the south to Mount Hermon in the north. In the east it extended as far as the plains of Choran, and in the west it was bordered by the Jordan River.

30. כָּל־מַמְלְכוּת עוֹג — *All the kingdom of Og.*

Sichon's territory was divided between Reuben and Gad, but part of the tribe of Menashe received all of Og's territory. *Daas Sofrim* suggests two reasons for this apparent inequity: (a) Menashe was larger in number than the other tribes [and therefore needed more land], and (b) by receiving this larger area, Menashe was compensated for the two shortcomings of Og's territory — it was not centrally located in regard to the other tribes, and it had little contact with the Jordan River.

חַוֺּת יָאִיר — *Chavos Yair.*

These cities were called *Chavos Yair* after Yair son of Menashe who conquered them *(Numbers* 32:41). *Chavos* means villages *(Targum).*

He named them after himself as a remembrance, because he did not have any children *(Rashi, ibid.). Ibn Ezra (ibid.)* explains that Yair son of Menashe was not from the tribe of Menashe, but from Judah. His ancestry is traceable to the tribe of Menashe through his grandmother (Cf., however, *Radak* and *Malbim* to *I Chronicles* 2:22).

Ibn Ezra also explains how someone from the tribe of Judah could inherit land in the Trans-Jordan.

אֲשֶׁר בַּבָּשָׁן — *In Bashan.*

[This qualifier is needed because Yair son of Menashe conquered all the villages in Gilead. Only those in Og's

[29] *And Moses gave to part of the tribe of Menashe;
and it was for part of the tribe of the Children of
Menashe according to their families.* [30] *Their bound-
ary was from Machanayim, all the Bashan, all the
kingdom of Og, king of Bashan, and all of Chavos
Yair in Bashan — sixty cities.* [31] *Part of the Gilead,
Ashtaros and Edrei — the royal cities of Og in Bashan
— were given to the sons of Machir son of Menashe,
to part of the sons of Machir, according to their
families.* [32] *These are the tribes to whom Moses
allocated territory in Arvos Moav, on the eastern side
of the Jordan across from Jericho.*

[33] *And to the tribe of Levi, Moses gave no
inheritance; HASHEM, the God of Israel, was their
inheritance, as He said to them.*

territory, however, became a part of Menashe's inheritance.]

31. וַחֲצִי הַגִּלְעָד — *Part of the Gilead.*

This refers to the northern part of Gilead.

לִבְנֵי מָכִיר בֶּן־מְנַשֶּׁה — *To the sons of Machir son of Menashe.*

[Machir was Menashe's only son, and he himself had only one son, Gilead (*Numbers* 26:29). Hence, *to part of the* **sons** *of Machir* must refer to Machir's grandsons. See *Numbers* 26:29 where the plural 'sons' is also mentioned. In that passage the grandchildren are also listed, which would support this thesis.]

32. אֵלֶּה — *These [are the tribes].*

These are the tribes to whom Moses gave an inheritance (*Metzudos*).

33. וּלְשֵׁבֶט הַלֵּוִי — *And to the tribe of Levi.*

This verse, almost identical with verse 14, informs us that the Levites did not receive their cities on the eastern side of the Jordan even though Moses had completely parceled out that territory. Only after all the tribes received their territory did the Levites receive their cities (*Malbim*).

Meam Loez suggests that verse 14, which speaks of *the offerings to HASHEM,* refers to the Kohanim, who are entitled to eat the sacrifices, and this verse speaks of the Levites.

XIV

Before any of the territories in Eretz Yisrael *were allocated to the tribes, Calev asked Joshua for the city of Hebron. In order to understand Calev's request, it is essential to recount the events to which he alludes in his plea.*

As mentioned in the Prefatory Remarks *to Chapter 2, Moses dispatched a reconnaissance mission composed of Joshua, Calev, and ten other princes to survey* Eretz Yisrael *before the entire nation was about to enter* (Numbers *13). During their mission, the scouts traveled the length and width of the Land as a group. When they neared the city of Hebron, however, only Calev entered.* Abarbanel *explains that the*

נָֽחֲלוּ בְנֵי־יִשְׂרָאֵל בְּאֶרֶץ כְּנָעַן אֲשֶׁר נִֽחֲלוּ
אוֹתָם אֶלְעָזָר הַכֹּהֵן וִיהוֹשֻׁעַ בִּן־נוּן
וְרָאשֵׁי אֲבוֹת הַמַּטּוֹת לִבְנֵי יִשְׂרָאֵל׃
ב בְּגוֹרַל נַחֲלָתָם כַּאֲשֶׁר צִוָּה יהוה בְּיַד־
ג מֹשֶׁה לְתִשְׁעַת הַמַּטּוֹת וַחֲצִי הַמַּטֶּה׃ כִּי־

other spies were afraid to enter Hebron because it was inhabited by fierce giants. The Talmud (Sotah *34b) comments that Calev intended to prostrate himself on the gravesite of the Patriarchs in order to strengthen his determination not to be influenced by the ten evil princes in his mission.*

When the group returned, ten members publicly indicted the Land, saying that the land eats its inhabitants and is populated by invincible giants (Numbers *13:32). Joshua and Calev denounced their accusations and reported that the Land was as good as God had promised. The Jews, however, were frightened by the false report and cried that they were being led to their deaths. They would have preferred, they said, to have remained in Egypt than to fall in battle for* Eretz Yisrael.

God was deeply angered by the Jews' lack of trust in Him, especially since they had witnessed all the miracles which He performed on their behalf. In His first communication to Moses, God vowed that generation would never see the Land of Israel. Only Calev, who had not yielded, would be allowed to enter and take possession of the Land (Numbers *14:11-25).*

In his second communication to Moses (Numbers *14:26-30), God condemned that generation with the words,* Your carcasses will fall in the wilderness (Numbers 14:29). *Joshua and Calev were excluded from this decree, since they had decried the evil report.* Malbim *notes that Calev alone was mentioned in the first communication even though Joshua also had not yielded to the other ten spies. He explains that Calev understood from this curious omission that he would be rewarded with that part of* Eretz Yisrael *which he alone had visited, the city of Hebron.*

Nevertheless, Scripture does not explicitly mention that Calev was to receive Hebron (see Commentary *to verse 9).* Daas Sofrim *suggests that Calev asked Joshua for Hebron in order to demonstrate to the Israelites that his words concerning the land were sincere and that he truly believed in God's protection, for Hebron was the home of the land's most terrifying giants, Achiman, Sheishai and Talmai, and they could not be overcome without Divine aid.*

In another sense, Calev's inheritance of Hebron could be viewed as a reward for employing prayer as his defense against the strong challenge posed by his mission. Since Calev used the gravesite of the Patriarchs to fortify himself against the evil plot of the reconnaissance mission, God rewarded him with this land in order to allow him the opportunity to pray at the Patriarchs' Tomb during future challenges. This is in accordance with the principle laid down by the Mishnah (Avos *4:2), 'The reward for performing a mitzvah is [the opportunity to perform another] mitzvah' (See* Biuri HaGra, *loc. cit.).*

1. וְאֵלֶּה — *And these are* [*the cities*].

These are the cities which the Children of Israel inherited. They are enumerated in Chapter 15 and in successive chapters *(Metzudos).*

אֲשֶׁר נִחֲלוּ אוֹתָם ... — *Which were assigned* [lit. *caused to be inherited*].

In regard to the division of the land the Torah states *(Numbers* 34:16-18), *And HASHEM spoke to Moses saying,*

[1] *And these are what the Children of Israel*
inherited in the land of Canaan, which were assigned
by Elazar the Kohen and Joshua son of Nun and the
family heads of the tribes of the Children of Israel
[2] *with the lottery of their inheritance, as* HASHEM *had*
commanded through Moses, for the nine tribes and
for part of the tribe, [3] *because Moses gave an*

'These are the names of the men who shall divide the land for an inheritance: Elazar the Kohen and Joshua son of Nun. And you shall take one prince of every tribe to divide the land as an inheritance.'

אֶלְעָזָר הַכֹּהֵן וִיהוֹשֻׁעַ בִּן־נוּן – *Elazar the Kohen and Joshua son of Nun.*

Elazar the Kohen (priest) is mentioned first because Joshua consulted him before allocating the Land *(R' Bachya* to *Numbers* 34:17). Since Elazar was the *Kohen Gadol* (High Priest), he wore the breastplate [*Exodus* 28:30] which communicated God's Will concerning making war and dividing the Land.

Abarbanel suggests that Elazar was mentioned first out of respect for the priesthood.

2. בְּגוֹרַל נַחֲלָתָם – *With the lottery of their inheritance.*

Scripture never mentions the details of the lottery procedure. However, the *Talmud (Bava Basra* 122a) explains that Elazar wore the breastplate[1] which contained the *urim v'tumim,* while Joshua and the people stood before him. In addition, there were two containers, each holding a set of cards. One set bore the names of the tribes who were to receive a portion of land in *Eretz Yisrael,* and the other set listed the borders of the available plots. The *urim v'tumim* was consulted and predicted that Zevulun would receive the land near Akko. Immediately following, the prince *(Rashi, Parshas Pinchas)* from the tribe of Zevulun mixed up the container of cards listing the tribes and chose a card at random, and it said 'Zevulun.' He then mixed up the cards in the container of plots and chose a card at random, and it said 'the land near Akko.' This procedure was repeated for all the tribes in order to demonstrate to all the Jews that each tribe was receiving its fair share, according to the Divine plan *(Rashbam).*

The translation follows the traditional reading of the text, in which the word בְּגוֹרַל is in the construct state with a *pasach* below the *reish* (בְּגוֹרַל). *Targum,* however, treats the word as if it were spelled with a *kametz* (בְּגוֹרָל) and renders: with a lottery were their inheritances apportioned to them.

כַּאֲשֶׁר צִוָּה – *As [HASHEM] had commanded.*

The command was given in *Numbers* 33:54, *And you should divide the Land ... by a lottery.* Through the oral

1. [If Elazar's breastplate which contained the *urim v'tumim* was essential for the division of the Land, why is it that Scripture itself does not mention that it was used?

The *Talmud (Eruvin* 63a) explains that Elazar was punished by God for a grievous error that he committed. He violated a long-standing tradition in Israel that a student may not render a decision regarding the *halachah* (law) in a particular case when in the vicinity of his teacher (see *Tosafos, Eruvin* 62b, s.v. רב), by informing the Israelites of the laws of making cooking utensils kosher *(Numbers* 31:21). Although Moses had temporarily forgotten these laws because he was in a state of anger *(Rashi),* Elazar should have waited until his teacher had regained his composure *(Maharsha).* The *Talmud* continues that while Moses had promised Elazar that he would aid Joshua by using the *urim v'tumim (Numbers* 27:19), 'we never find that Joshua needed his help' *(Eruvin* 63a, *Rashi).*

As mentioned in the *Commentary,* the *Talmud* in *Bava Basra* (122a) clearly states that it was

יד
ד־ו

נָתַן מֹשֶׁה נַחֲלַת שְׁנֵי הַמַּטּוֹת וַחֲצִי
הַמַּטֶּה מֵעֵבֶר לַיַּרְדֵּן וְלַלְוִיִּם לֹא־נָתַן
ד נַחֲלָה בְּתוֹכָם׃ כִּי־הָיוּ בְנֵי־יוֹסֵף שְׁנֵי
מַטּוֹת מְנַשֶּׁה וְאֶפְרָיִם וְלֹא־נָתְנוּ חֵלֶק
לַלְוִיִּם בָּאָרֶץ כִּי אִם־עָרִים לָשֶׁבֶת
ה וּמִגְרְשֵׁיהֶם לְמִקְנֵיהֶם וּלְקִנְיָנָם׃ כַּאֲשֶׁר
צִוָּה יהוה אֶת־מֹשֶׁה כֵּן עָשׂוּ בְּנֵי יִשְׂרָאֵל
ו וַיַּחְלְקוּ אֶת־הָאָרֶץ׃ וַיִּגְּשׁוּ
בְנֵי־יְהוּדָה אֶל־יְהוֹשֻׁעַ בַּגִּלְגָּל וַיֹּאמֶר
אֵלָיו כָּלֵב בֶּן־יְפֻנֶּה הַקְּנִזִּי אַתָּה יָדַעְתָּ
אֶת־הַדָּבָר אֲשֶׁר־דִּבֶּר יהוה אֶל־מֹשֶׁה
אִישׁ־הָאֱלֹהִים עַל אֹדוֹתַי וְעַל אֹדוֹתֶיךָ

tradition, it was known that the *urim v'tumim* should also be consulted *(Bava Basra* 122a).

3-4. The next two verses explain why only nine and one-half tribes received land, although there were twelve tribes.

3. שְׁנֵי הַמַּטּוֹת וַחֲצִי ... וְלַלְוִיִּם לֹא־נָתַן נַחֲלָה בְּתוֹכָם — *Two and a half tribes ... (but) to the Levites he gave no inheritance among them.*

Since two and one half tribes had been given their land, it would appear that nine and one-half of the twelve tribes remained without land. But since the Levites received no inheritance *among them* [i.e., their fellow Jews] only eight and one-half tribes actually remained without land. [This apparent contradiction to verse 2 is resolved by the following verse.]

4. שְׁנֵי מַטּוֹת — *Two tribes.*

The verse explains that Joseph's two sons were reckoned as separate tribes. As a result, there was an additional tribe awaiting its inheritance, bringing the total to nine and one-half tribes, despite the exclusion of the tribe of Levi.

In accordance with Jacob's blessing *(Genesis* 48:5), the sons of Joseph were considered as individual tribes, on the same status as their uncles. This was unique to Joseph's sons. The sons of Reuben, for instance, divided their father's territory among themselves, whereas Joseph's sons each received a separate inheritance *(Rashi, ibid.).*

לָשֶׁבֶת — *To live in.*

The Levites had rights to merely *dwell* in these cities. They did not completely own them *(Metzudos).*

וּמִגְרְשֵׁיהֶם — *And open land.*

See *Commentary* to 21:2 for an explanation of this open land.

לְמִקְנֵיהֶם וּלְקִנְיָנָם — *For their cattle and their flocks.*

The translation follows *Targum* as understood by *Radak.*

indeed Elazar who officiated with Joshua in the division of the Land by using the *urim v'tumim.* However, this perhaps is what the passage in *Eruvin* 63a means, 'we never find that Joshua needed his help.' The punishment Elazar received was not that he never had the opportunity to help Joshua with the *urim v'tumim.* The punishment, rather, was that Scripture never explicitly mentioned it. (Cf., however, *Tosafos, Sanhedrin* 16a, s.v. מה.)]

inheritance to two and a half tribes across the Jordan; to the Levites he gave no inheritance among them,
4 *but the Children of Joseph were two tribes, Menashe and Ephraim. They gave no share to the Levites in the Land, only cities to live in and open land about them for their cattle and their flocks.*
5 *As HASHEM had commanded Moses, so the Children of Israel did, and they divided the land.*
6 *The Children of Judah approached Joshua in Gilgal, and Calev son of Yefuneh the Kenizzi said to him, 'You are aware of that which HASHEM told Moses, the man of God, concerning me and*

5. כַּאֲשֶׁר צִוָּה ה׳ — *As HASHEM had commanded.*

He commanded Moses not to give the Levites a plot of land *(Metzudos).*

וַיַּחְלְקוּ אֶת־הָאָרֶץ — *And they divided the land.*

They divided the land among themselves *(Metzudos).*

6. וַיִּגְּשׁוּ בְנֵי־יְהוּדָה — *The Children of Judah approached.*

Abarbanel suggests that the tribe of Judah accompanied Calev out of respect, because he was their prince. *Meam Loez* suggests that Calev came with an entourage to greet Joshua, their leader, and display their respect for him.

בַּגִּלְגָּל — *In Gilgal.*

Gilgal was the site of the Tabernacle, and hence Joshua was encamped there *(Ralbag).*

כָּלֵב בֶּן־יְפֻנֶּה הַקְּנִזִּי — *Calev the son of Yefuneh the Kenizzi.*

If Calev's father was Yefuneh, why is he called *Kenizzi* which implies that he was the son of Kenaz? The *Talmud (Sotah* 11) explains that after Calev's father Yefuneh died, his mother remarried to Kenaz. Thus, the appellation Kenizzi was added to his name because Kenaz was his step-father.

אֲשֶׁר־דִּבֶּר ה׳ אֶל־מֹשֶׁה — *That which HASHEM told Moses.*

See *Numbers* 14:24,30.

אִישׁ־הָאֱלֹהִים — *The man of God.*

[Inasmuch as this appellation for Moses is employed only once in the Pentateuch *(Deuteronomy* 33:1), it is especially significant that Calev used it here. (Compare for example, *Joshua* 1:13, where Joshua called Moses, *'servant of HASHEM.')*

Ramban explains that the title *man of God,* indicates that Moses' prophecy was directly from God and represented His Will (see *R' Chavel, Ramban* to *Deuteronomy* 33:1). Thus, Calev was strengthening his claim to Hebron by reminding Joshua that Moses, who was the faithful conduit of God's Will, had promised him this city.]

עַל אֹדוֹתַי וְעַל־אֹדוֹתֶיךָ — *Concerning me and concerning you.*

[Since Calev did not combine these phrases by simply saying 'what Hashem said about *us,*' it would appear that God had made two distinct statements, one concerning Calev and one concerning Joshua. According to *Malbim* (cited in the *Prefatory Remarks* to this chapter), Calev understood that Hashem had promised him alone the city of Hebron in God's first communication to Moses after the spies' evil report *(Numbers* 14:11-25). It is this promise to which Calev refers with the phrase *concerning me.* The phrase *concerning you* is meant to emphasize the fact that Joshua was not mentioned in that promise and

יד
ז־י

ז בְּקָדֵשׁ בַּרְנֵעַ: בֶּן־אַרְבָּעִים שָׁנָה אָנֹכִי
בִּשְׁלֹחַ מֹשֶׁה עֶבֶד־יְהוָה אֹתִי מִקָּדֵשׁ
בַּרְנֵעַ לְרַגֵּל אֶת־הָאָרֶץ וָאָשֵׁב אוֹתוֹ דָּבָר
ח כַּאֲשֶׁר עִם־לְבָבִי: וְאַחַי אֲשֶׁר עָלוּ עִמִּי
הִמְסִיו אֶת־לֵב הָעָם וְאָנֹכִי מִלֵּאתִי אַחֲרֵי
ט יְהוָה אֱלֹהָי: וַיִּשָּׁבַע מֹשֶׁה בַּיּוֹם הַהוּא
לֵאמֹר אִם־לֹא הָאָרֶץ אֲשֶׁר דָּרְכָה רַגְלְךָ
בָּהּ לְךָ תִהְיֶה לְנַחֲלָה וּלְבָנֶיךָ עַד־עוֹלָם
י כִּי מִלֵּאתָ אַחֲרֵי יְהוָה אֱלֹהָי: וְעַתָּה הִנֵּה
הֶחֱיָה יְהוָה | אוֹתִי כַּאֲשֶׁר דִּבֵּר זֶה
אַרְבָּעִים וְחָמֵשׁ שָׁנָה מֵאָז דִּבֶּר יְהוָה

hence does not have any claim on Hebron.]

With this phrase, Calev was alluding to the fact that he and Joshua were not decreed to die in the Wilderness along with the other spies. He left his language vague because he did not want to mention their great sin which turned into a national calamity *(Meam Loez)*.

בְּקָדֵשׁ בַּרְנֵעַ — *Kadesh Barnea.*

This was the location from which the reconnaissance mission was dispatched *(Numbers* 32:8) and to which it returned *(Numbers* 13:26).

7. בֶּן־אַרְבָּעִים שָׁנָה — *I was forty years old.*

As explained in the *Prefatory Remarks* to this chapter, God punished the Jews — who placed their faith in the spies' false report, rather than in God's own promise of Divine protection — by condemning the men aged twenty to sixty to death in the Wilderness *(Numbers* 14:11-25), for they were unworthy of *Eretz Yisrael.*

Calev mentions that he was forty years old at the time of this Divine decree in order to emphasize that although men of his age were sentenced to die, he was excluded from the decree [because of his devotion to God *(Numbers* 14:24)] *(Abarbanel).*

כַּאֲשֶׁר עִם־לְבָבִי — *As it was in my heart.*

During the entire reconnaissance mission, Calev appeared to be in complicity with the spies' evil plan, because he feared that if he did not agree, they would murder him. Only when he returned to Moses did Calev express his true convictions about the Land, for then he felt free to speak 'his heart' *(Rashi; Radak).*

According to *Abarbanel,* Calev agreed with the other spies that there were giants in the Land and that its cities were well fortified. He did not make this publicly known, however. Only to Moses did he speak what was *in his heart,* for he knew that this frank report would not dishearten him. When addressing the nation as a whole, however, Calev merely expressed his unshakeable faith in God's promise to install the Jews in *Eretz Yisrael,* [for he recognized that the people would not share this faith if they were told about the obstacles to their conquest of the Land].

8. וְאַחַי — *My brothers.*

Calev is referring to the ten evil members of the reconnaissance mission *(Metzudos).*

הִמְסִיו — *Shattered.*

The translation follows *Targum.*

14
7-10

concerning you in Kadesh Barnea. 7 I was forty years
old when Moses, the servant of HASHEM sent me
from Kadesh Barnea to survey the Land, and I
brought him back a report as it was in my heart. 8 My
brothers who went up with me shattered the heart of
the people, but I fulfilled the will of HASHEM, my
God. 9 And Moses swore on that day saying, "Surely
the land on which your foot trod will be your
inheritance and your children's forever, because you
fulfilled the word of HASHEM my God." 10 And now,
behold, HASHEM has kept me alive as he said — these
forty-five years — from the time HASHEM spoke this

Others suggest *melted (Metzudos; Minchas Shai).*

9. וַיִּשָּׁבַע מֹשֶׁה — *And Moses swore.*

[Calev seems to be referring to Moses' statement in *Deuteronomy* 1:36, which parallels this verse very closely. However, Moses was not making a personal promise to Calev in that verse; he was only communicating to him the words of God.] *Radak*, therefore, maintains that Calev is alluding to another promise which Moses made him, but which Scripture did not record. Support for this interpretation, *Radak* argues, can be found from Joshua's compliance with Calev's request and from the verse in *Judges* 1:20, *And they gave Calev Hebron, as Moses said.*

אִם־לֹא — *Surely* [lit. *if not*].

This is an expression which introduces an oath. It is as if Moses said, 'If not, I should be punished by such and such' *(Metzudos).*

אֲשֶׁר דָּרְכָה רַגְלְךָ בָּהּ — *On which your foot trod.*

This refers to Hebron, since it was the only part of *Eretz Yisrael* which Calev surveyed alone, unaccompanied by the other spies. Joshua did not accompany Calev on his trip to the gravesite of the Patriarchs, even though he was not afraid of the giants there, because Moses had prayed on his behalf that he should not become influenced by the other spies' evil motives *(Sotah* 34b, *Rashi).* [See *Commentary* to 1:1, s.v. 'Joshua'.]

Lev Aharon suggests that included in Calev's demand for the city of Hebron was a request for permission to conquer it by himself. His belief that God would help him in his mission was so strong that he shunned the help of his fellow Israelites.

כִּי מִלֵּאתָ אַחֲרֵי ה׳ — *Because you fulfilled the word of HASHEM* [lit. *because you fully filled after HASHEM*].

10. הֶחֱיָה ה׳ אוֹתִי — *HASHEM has kept me alive.*

Because Calev was faithful to God, he merited two things: life and an inheritance in the Land. Calev now claims that since he has received long life by being exempt from the decree of death on all the Israelites in the Wilderness, there remains only one more promise to be fulfilled. He, therefore, requests his territory *(Abarbanel).*

זֶה אַרְבָּעִים וְחָמֵשׁ שָׁנָה — *These forty-five years.*

From Calev's statement, we can deduce that the conquest of *Eretz Yisrael* lasted seven years. Moses dispatched the reconnaissance mission during the second year of Israel's

אֶת־הַדָּבָר הַזֶּה אֶל־מֹשֶׁה אֲשֶׁר־הָלַךְ
יִשְׂרָאֵל בַּמִּדְבָּר וְעַתָּה הִנֵּה אָנֹכִי הַיּוֹם
יא בֶּן־חָמֵשׁ וּשְׁמֹנִים שָׁנָה: עוֹדֶנִּי הַיּוֹם חָזָק
כַּאֲשֶׁר בְּיוֹם שְׁלֹחַ אוֹתִי מֹשֶׁה כְּכֹחִי אָז
וּכְכֹחִי עָתָּה לַמִּלְחָמָה וְלָצֵאת וְלָבוֹא:
יב וְעַתָּה תְּנָה־לִּי אֶת־הָהָר הַזֶּה אֲשֶׁר־
דִּבֶּר יהוה בַּיּוֹם הַהוּא כִּי־אַתָּה שָׁמַעְתָּ
בַּיּוֹם הַהוּא כִּי־עֲנָקִים שָׁם וְעָרִים
גְּדֹלוֹת בְּצֻרוֹת אוּלַי יהוה אוֹתִי
יג וְהוֹרַשְׁתִּים כַּאֲשֶׁר דִּבֶּר יהוה: וַיְבָרְכֵהוּ

journey through the Wilderness. When the spies incited the people to lose faith in God and in the Land, God decreed that the Jews would wander in the Wilderness for a total of forty years prior to entering *Eretz Yisrael (Numbers* 14:33-34). [Each year of wandering in the Wilderness served as punishment for one of the forty days in which the spies surveyed the Land.] Thus, the Jews remained in the Wilderness for thirty-eight more years. Since Calev says that forty-five years had elapsed since the reconnaissance mission, we see that the conquest of *Eretz Yisrael* took seven years *(Rashi).* The division of the Land lasted for another seven years *(Radak; Arachin* 12b).

מֵאָז דִּבֶּר ה׳ — *From the time* [lit. *from then*] *HASHEM spoke this word.*

According to *Radak,* Moses had told Calev in the name of God that he would receive Hebron. (See *Prefatory Remarks* and *Commentary* to *v.* 9.)

11. עוֹדֶנִּי הַיּוֹם חָזָק — *I am still as strong today.*

Calev made this statement about his strength to dispel any doubt Joshua might have had concerning Calev's capability to conquer the fierce inhabitants of Hebron in his old age *(Metzudos).*

כְּכֹחִי אָז וּכְכֹחִי עָתָּה — *As my strength was then, so is my strength now.*

Radak explains that this expression (כְּ...כְּ) implies a reciprocal comparison; Calev was as strong at eighty-five as he was at forty and as strong as forty as he was at eighty-five.

Malbim remarks that according to Hebrew syntax it seems that Calev's comparison should have been in the reverse order, since the present is always compared to another time. Thus in our case it should have read, 'I am as strong at eighty-five [now] as I was at forty [then].' However, Calev had been unaware of the extent of his strength when he was forty; his awareness came later when he fought the Canaanites during the Jews' conquest of the Land. He therefore estimated that his strength at forty had been no less than it was at the present.

Alternatively, *Be'er Moshe* suggests a figurative interpretation in which strength does not refer to physical power, but rather to the ability to withstand temptation. An elderly man typically has little passion and is thus 'strong' in the face of physical temptation. Calev claims that his moral fortitude had been as great in his youth as it was now in his old age. According to this view, *war* mentioned at the conclusion of the verse refers to the internal war between the good and evil inclinations within each individual. [See

14
11-13

*word to Moses when Israel journeyed through the
wilderness, and now I am eighty-five years old today.
11 I am still as strong today as I was on the day that
Moses dispatched me. As my strength was then, so is
my strength now, for war — to go out and to come in.
12 And now, give me this mountain to which
HASHEM spoke on that day, because you heard on
that day that the Anakim were there and that the
cities were large and strong. Perhaps HASHEM will be
with me, and I will drive them out as HASHEM had
said.'*
13 And Joshua blessed him and gave Hebron to

Commentary to 2:1; where the tradition is cited that Calev was one of the two spies sent to Rachav's house. It could be his ability to refrain from temptation in that incident to which Calev refers here.]

In some printed versions of the text, the initial כ of the word כְּכֹחִי is written in print considerably larger than the other print in the text. *Minchas Shai* reports that he has not found this large כ in the older printed and hand written versions of *Joshua* [which seems to cast doubt on the authenticity of the large כ].

12. וְעַתָּה תְּנָה־לִּי אֶת־הָהָר הַזֶּה — *And now, give me this mountain.*

God allowed me to live and granted me strength *(Malbim)* so that I could drive out the inhabitants of Hebron. Therefore, *give me this mountain.*

הָהָר הַזֶּה — *This mountain.*

This refers to Hebron *(Metzudos).* Calev used the pejorative term *mountain* instead of city to indicate that his desire for Hebron was motivated only by God's decree that he should inherit it, rather than by the city's intrinsic worth. Indeed, this is one of four locations in *Eretz Yisrael* about which the Sages speak disparagingly *(Poras Yosef).*

כִּי־אַתָּה שָׁמַעְתָּ — *Because you heard.*

If *you* receive a portion of land without going through the process of the lottery, *I* certainly should for you, Joshua, only *heard* that there were giants in Hebron, but I *saw* them with my own eyes and still did not fear *(Lev Aharon).*

אוּלַי ה׳ אוֹתִי — *Perhaps HASHEM will be with me.*

And if you ask, 'Who could possibly battle these giants?,' then I respond, *'Perhaps HASHEM will be with me' (Metzudos).*

Calev was not doubting God's promise that Hebron would be vanquished when he used the word *perhaps.* Rather, it is the manner of righteous people not to rely on their merits for God's protection because they are always concerned that they may have committed a sin which would revoke His promise *(Meam Loez).* [See *Commentary* to 10:8.]

13. וַיְבָרְכֵהוּ — *And Joshua blessed him.*

Joshua blessed Calev that he should be victorious in battle against the giants who inhabited Hebron *(Metzudos).*

[How Calev actually fared in battle is described in 15:13-15.]

When Joshua heard that Calev was as strong now as he was at forty, he blessed him so that he would not become subject to the *ein hara,* misfortune *(Alshich).*

Meam Loez cites *Zohar* which states that whenever an individual compliments another person's children or possessions, he is

יד
יד־טו

יְהוֹשֻׁעַ וַיִּתֵּן אֶת־חֶבְרוֹן לְכָלֵב בֶּן־יְפֻנֶּה
יד לְנַחֲלָה: עַל־כֵּן הָיְתָה־חֶבְרוֹן לְכָלֵב בֶּן־
יְפֻנֶּה הַקְּנִזִּי לְנַחֲלָה עַד הַיּוֹם הַזֶּה יַעַן
אֲשֶׁר מִלֵּא אַחֲרֵי יהוה אֱלֹהֵי יִשְׂרָאֵל:
טו וְשֵׁם חֶבְרוֹן לְפָנִים קִרְיַת אַרְבַּע הָאָדָם
טו הַגָּדוֹל בָּעֲנָקִים הוּא וְהָאָרֶץ שָׁקְטָה
א א מִמִּלְחָמָה: וַיְהִי הַגּוֹרָל לְמַטֵּה

required to bless him that God should grant him many more. This principle is derived from Moses when he addressed all Israel and remarked how large they had become by saying, *you are this day like the stars of heaven for multitude.* Immediately, he said to them that, *HASHEM should make you a thousand times so many more as you are* (*Deuteronomy* 1:10-11). The custom has thus developed when someone hears of the number of another individual's children or fortune he says וְכֵן יִרְבּוּ, *so they should multiply* based on the verse, *the more they multiplied, and the more they grew (Exodus* 1:12).

וַיִּתֵּן אֶת־חֶבְרוֹן לְכָלֵב — *And* [*he*] *gave Hebron to Calev.*

The city proper was not given to Calev, since 21:11 indicates that it was given to the Kohanim. Only the surrounding villages and city's outlying fields were given to Calev *(Radak).* [See 21:11-13.]

14. עַל־כֵּן — *Therefore.*

Calev was granted the city of Hebron only because he *fulfilled the will of HASHEM, the God of Israel (Metzudos).*

יַעַן אֲשֶׁר... — *Because...*

Poras Yosef explains that the verse explicitly states, *because he fulfilled the will of HASHEM,* so that no one would imagine that Calev received Hebron as a result of Joshua's blessing.

15. קִרְיַת אַרְבַּע — *Kiryas Arba.*

The city was named for the man Arba who lived there or for the Hebrew word meaning 'four'[1] in reference to the four notorious men who lived there: Arba and his sons, Achiman, Sheishai and Talmai *(Rashi).*

הָאָדָם הַגָּדוֹל בָּעֲנָקִים — *Who was the largest man among the Anakim.*

Arba[2] was the tallest of the Anakim,

1. The city of Kiryas Arba had seven distinctions:
(a) It was the city of the three righteous men Aner, Eshcol, and Mamre who dwelled there because of the sanctity of the area. They were later joined by Abraham. Calev, also, chose the city because of its sanctity.
(b) It was the city where Abraham had his circumcision.
(c) It was the burial site of four righteous men — Adam, Abraham, Isaac, and Jacob.
(d) It was the burial site of four righteous women — Eve, Sarah, Rebecca, and Leah.
(e) It was the dwelling place of giants, which indicated that the air of the city was salubrious. This was another reason why Calev wanted to live there — he would have better health and strength to carry out his service to God.
(f) It was the city from which Abraham departed to fight the battle against the Four Kings to save his nephew Lot. Because his victory against them was through a miracle, it was appropriate to call the city 'the city of four.'
(g) This city was allocated four times: first, to the tribe of Judah in the general lottery; second, to Calev upon his request; third, to the Levites when they were given cities by the different tribes; and fourth, to the sons of Aaron the Kohen, who had greater sanctity than the other Levites *(Meam Loez).*

2. The *Midrash* notes that although the Canaanites were as morally degenerate as the Egyptians, they were destroyed forty-seven years after the Egyptians. [*Numbers* 13:22 states

14
14-15 *Calev the son of Yefuneh as an inheritance.*
[14] *Therefore, Hebron became the inheritance of Calev the son of Yefuneh the Kenizzi to this day because he fulfilled the will of HASHEM, God of Israel.*
[15] *The former name of Hebron was Kiryas Arbah, who was the largest man among the Anakim. And the Land had rest from war.*

who themselves were giants *(Metzudos).*

וְהָאָרֶץ שָׁקְטָה מִמִּלְחָמָה — *And the Land had rest from war.*

This expression refers to the end of Chapter 11, which concludes the account of the seven years of conquest. When the Emorites were humbled and ceased to make war against Israel, the Jews began to divide the Land *(Rashi).*

Radak, however, understands this is a derogatory statement: The Land rested from war because the Israelites delayed their conquest of the remaining unconquered territories. [See *Commentary* to 11:18.]

XV

This chapter discusses the fourteen borders and the one hundred twelve cities that formed the territory of Judah. Its thoroughness and minute details are representative of approximately one third of the Book *of* Joshua. *The* Talmud (Nedarim *22b) states that had the Israelites not sinned, only six books would have been included in Scripture — the* Five Books *of* Moses *and the* Book *of* Joshua. Joshua *would have been included, the* Talmud *says, because it details the inheritances of each tribe* (Rashi). Lev Aharon *explains that Scripture incorporated these territorial descriptions in the text in order to prevent future border disputes among the tribes. He also suggests that Scripture included this geographical detail in order to delineate the exact borders of* Eretz Yisrael, *for since there are certain mitzvos which can only be performed in the Land, the determination of its boundaries is of utmost importance.*

Chapters 16 and 17 describe the territories of Ephraim and Menashe, with the tribe of Ephraim receiving the first portion. Thus, the tribes of Judah and Ephraim were the first to receive their inheritances in Eretz Yisrael *proper. This is illustrative of their trend to be in the vanguard of the Jewish people. During Israel's encampments in the Wilderness, the tribes of Judah and Ephraim were the leaders of their respective camps (see* Numbers *2:1-34). The first kings of Israel were from these tribes. In the final redemption, the two Messiahs will also come from Judah and Ephraim* (Vilna Gaon). *(See the* Prefatory Remarks *to Chapter 13 for another reason why Judah was the first to inherit land to the west of the Jordan.)*

In the following chapters, the names of many cities are mentioned. Daas Sofrim

---

that Hebron was built seven years before Tzoan Mitzrayim (Egypt); thus Hebron was spared those seven years in addition to the forty years which transpired after the Jews left Egypt and entered *Eretz Yisrael.*] R' Yosi Hagalili declared that the Canaanites were temporarily spared in merit of their referring to Abraham as *a prince of God in our midst (Genesis* 23:6). Rabban Shimon ben Gamliel added that the verse *who was the largest man among the Anakim (Joshua* 14:15) refers to Abraham. This explains the juxtaposition of *and the Land had rest from war (ibid.).* The Canaanites were spared destruction for those forty-seven years because of the merit derived from the largest man among them — Abraham *(Yalkut* from *Toras Kohanim).*

בְּנֵי יְהוּדָה לְמִשְׁפְּחֹתָם אֶל־גְּבוּל אֱדוֹם
ב מִדְבַּר־צִן נֶגְבָּה מִקְצֵה תֵימָן: וַיְהִי לָהֶם
גְּבוּל נֶגֶב מִקְצֵה יָם הַמֶּלַח מִן־הַלָּשֹׁן
ג הַפֹּנֶה נֶגְבָּה: וְיָצָא אֶל־מִנֶּגֶב לְמַעֲלֵה

remarks that in listing these cities, Scripture is underscoring the fulfillment of the promise which God made in Deuteronomy *6:10:* And it shall be when HASHEM your God will bring you to the land He swore to your fathers, to Abraham, to Isaac and to Jacob to give you great and goodly cities which you did not build ... *The* Book *of* Joshua *indicates clearly that the Jews inherited a land which had been settled by its Canaanite caretakers, thus sparing the Jews the difficulties of groundbreaking and building.*

◆§ The Southern Border of Judah

1-4. The southern border of Judah formed the southern border of *Eretz Yisrael (Katzvei Eretz).*

1. וַיְהִי הַגּוֹרָל לְמַטֵּה בְּנֵי יְהוּדָה — *The outcome of the lottery for the tribe of the Children of Judah.*

The tribe of Judah received a portion of land which comprised the entire southern border of *Eretz Yisrael.* It is for this reason that the *Talmud* refers to the south of *Eretz Yisrael* with Judah's name. The tribes of Menashe and Ephraim were located in the Galilee, and their territory was referred to as the 'north' of *Eretz Yisrael* as 18:5 states: *Judah will occupy his territory to the south and the House of Joseph* [Menashe and Ephraim] *will occupy their territory to the north (Vilna Gaon).* [Although other tribes were located north of Ephraim and Menashe, the 'northern part' of *Eretz Yisrael* began at their territory.]

לְמִשְׁפְּחוֹתָם — *According to their families.*

Each family of the tribe received its own portion of land so that it would retain its individual identity, without intermingling *(Metzudos).*

אֶל־גְּבוּל אֱדוֹם — *To the border of Edom.*

The northwestern boundary of Edom met the southeastern boundary of *Eretz Yisrael.* This point of intersection formed the beginning of the southern border of Judah, which extended to the Mediterranean Sea *(Vilna Gaon).*

מִדְבַּר־צִן — *Wilderness of Tzin.*

This was located south of Edom near the southern border of *Eretz Yisrael (Vilna Gaon).*

נֶגְבָּה — *In the south.*

Negbah, usually translated as *south,* is derived from נֶגֶב, which means *to dry,* because the southern part of *Eretz Yisrael* is parched by the sun both in the summer and in the winter *(Vilna Gaon).*

מִקְצֵה תֵימָן — *The Teiman section.*

The entire wilderness of Tzin did not form the southern border of *Eretz Yisrael;* the boundary followed only the part from the border of Teiman *(Metzudos).*

Edom was inhabited by the offspring of Esau. The oldest of these was Teiman, whose border intersected the southern border of *Eretz Yisrael.* Thus, the south of *Eretz Yisrael* is called *Teiman (Vilna Gaon).*

According to *Targum,* however, *teiman* is the compass point 'south,' not a section of land. [The Teiman referred to in this verse is not the modern day country of Yemen located on the Arabian peninsula, which is sometimes called Teiman.]

2. מִקְצֵה יָם הַמֶּלַח — *From the edge of the Dead Sea* [lit. *Sea of Salt*].

This formed the southeastern extremity of *Eretz Yisrael (Rashi).*

See *Commentary* to 12:3.

הַלָּשֹׁן הַפֹּנֶה נֶגְבָּה — *From the southern tip.*

15
1-3

¹ *The outcome of the lottery for the tribe of the*
Children of Judah — according to their families —
was: in the south, to the border of Edom and the
Teiman section of the Wilderness of Tzin. ² *Their*
southern border began from the edge of the Dead
Sea, from the southern tip. ³ *It broadened to the*

The commentators understand this expression to refer to the southern tip of the Dead Sea. They interpret the unusual expression לָשׁוֹן [lit. *tongue*] as a description of the southern portion of the Dead Sea, which narrows in the shape of a tongue *(Vilna Gaon; Metzudos).*

Targum, however, interprets this expression to mean 'rock.' [Presumably there was a rock at the southern end of the Dead Sea that was used as a marker.]

3. וְיָצָא — *It broadened.*

Malbim comments that Scripture is now tracing a diagonal from the Dead Sea to Ma'aleh Akrabim which was located south and to the west of the Dead Sea.

There are six terms used by Scripture in this chapter to delineate borders. In this verse, we find four expressions: וְיָצָא, וְעָבַר, וְעָלָה, וְנָסַב. In verses 9 and 10, two more expressions are introduced: וְתָאַר, וְיָרַד. *Rashi* does not differentiate between the terms וְיָצָא,

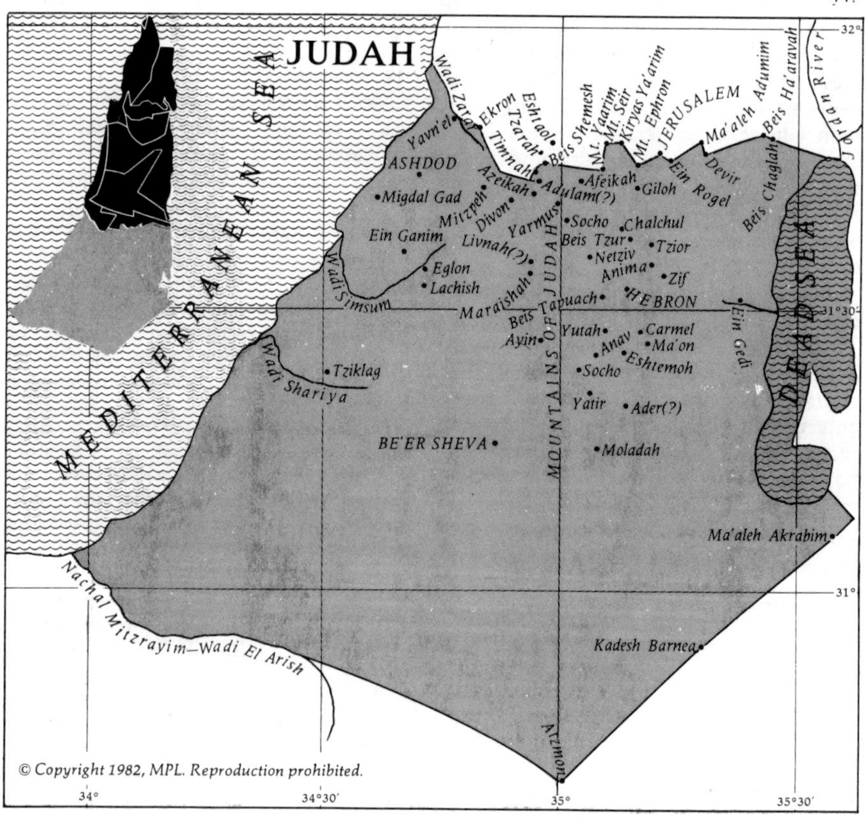

טו
ד־ה

עַקְרַבִּים וְעָבַר צִנָה וְעָלָה מִנֶּגֶב לְקָדֵשׁ
בַּרְנֵעַ וְעָבַר חֶצְרוֹן וְעָלָה אַדָּרָה וְנָסַב
ד הַקַּרְקָעָה: וְעָבַר עַצְמוֹנָה וְיָצָא נַחַל
°וְהָיוּ ק׳ מִצְרַיִם °והיה תֹּצְאוֹת הַגְּבוּל יָמָּה זֶה־
ה יִהְיֶה לָכֶם גְּבוּל נֶגֶב: וּגְבוּל קֵדְמָה יָם
הַמֶּלַח עַד־קְצֵה הַיַּרְדֵּן וּגְבוּל לִפְאַת

וְנָסַב ,וְתָאַר; they all indicate that Scripture is tracing a border which does not follow a straight line, but rather becomes convex or concave. Based on the *Talmud (Zevachim* 54b) *Rashi* distinguishes between וְעָלָה (lit. *and it ascended)* and וְיָרַד (lit. *and it descended).* Whenever Scripture traces a border from east to west, if the longitude of Jerusalem has not been crossed, Scripture terms the path of travel an 'ascent.' If, however, the longitude of Jerusalem has been crossed, Scripture terms the path of travel a 'descent.' Thus, the Rabbis have deduced that Jerusalem is the highest point in *Eretz Yisrael. Vilna Gaon* clarifies: the expression וְעָלָה indicates that the border being traced rises in elevation. Conversely, the term וְיָרַד indicates that the border being traced decreases in elevation.

Vilna Gaon, however, ascribes different meanings to some of these terms. The expression וְיָצָא is employed when Scripture wishes to indicate that the territory is widening (and thus enlargening) in the transition between two geographical points. The expression וְעָבַר is used to indicate that the border being traced passes through a city. The expression וְנָסַב is used to signal that the border being traced circles around the site mentioned and then continues in a straight fashion. The term וְתָאַר is used to indicate that the border follows a straight line.

Rashbam (Numbers 34:4) explains that both the terms וְעָבַר and וְיָצָא indicate that the border Scripture traces is a straight line.

מִנֶּגֶב לְמַעֲלֵה עַקְרַבִּים — *To the south of Ma'aleh Akrabim.*

Since the border skirted the south side of Ma'aleh Akrabim, it can be assumed that this city lies within *Eretz Yisrael (Rashi).*

Literally, *Ma'aleh Akrabim* means 'the ascent of the scorpions,' i.e., a dangerous hill. *T'vuos HaAretz* reports that not far from the Kurehy River west of the village Chansir is a fearfully high acclivity which is extremely dangerous to pass. He conjectures that this is Ma'aleh Akrabim.

צִנָה — *Tzin.*

Rashi claims that the name of the city was *Tzin* and that the final ה is equivalent to a ל preceeding a noun which in English is the preposition 'to.' *Vilna Gaon,* however, contends that the city's true name was *Tzinah.*

[There is, however, ambiguity in *Vilna Gaon's* words, for he calls the city *Tzinah,* but concludes that the Wilderness of Tzin was named for this city — 'the Wilderness of the city *Tzin.*' He thus implies that the city was truly called *Tzin.* Further elucidation is required.]

Targum Yonasson (Numbers 34:3) renders Tzin as צִינֵי טוּר פַּרְזְלָא, *palms of the iron mountain. T'vuos HaAretz* notes that the *Mishnah (Succah* 3:1) uses this term for an uncommonly strong and hard species of palms. He therefore understands this verse to mean that the border passed through territory in which these hard palms grew.

It is mentioned as one of the border cities in the south of *Eretz Yisrael* in *Numbers* 34:4.

וְעָלָה מִנֶּגֶב לְקָדֵשׁ בַּרְנֵעַ — *(And) ascended to the south of Kadesh Barnea.*

Since the border went south of Kadesh Barnea, it can be deduced that

15
4-5 *south of Ma'aleh Akrabim, passed through Tzin,*
ascended to the south of Kadesh Barnea, passed
through Chetzron, ascended toward Adar, and
circled around Karka'ah. 4 *It passed through Atzmon*
and broadened to the Egyptian River; the border's
enlargement proceeded to the Sea. This shall be your
southern border. 5 *The eastern border stretched from*
the Dead Sea to the end of the Jordan River. The

Kadesh Barnea was within Judah's territory *(Rashi).*

Katzvei Eretz asks: Why if Kadesh Barnea was inside the boundary of *Eretz Yisrael,* did the Jews need to ask the king of Edom (*Numbers* 20:14) permission to travel through his land when they were stationed in Kadesh? They should have proceeded north from their encampment in Kadesh instead of proceeding circuitously through Edom which was located south of *Eretz Yisrael.* Perhaps, Moses chose not to bring the entire nation through the mountainous region of Kadesh, but rather wished to travel less directly through Edom. This approach to the verse is consistent with the *Vilna Gaon's* rule that the term וְעָלָה, implies rising elevation. (Cf., however, *Ibn Ezra* to *Numbers* 20:14 and *Da'as Zakeinim* to *Numbers* 34:4.)

It is mentioned as one of the border cities in the south of *Eretz Yisrael* in *Numbers* 34:4.

חֶצְרוֹן ... אַדָּרָה ... הַקַּרְקָעָה — *Chetzron ... toward Adar ... Karka'ah.*

Although the exact location of these cities is unknown, they must have been between Kadesh Barnea and Atzmon.

Numbers 34:4 lists Chetzron and Adar as one place, but our verse indicates that they were actually two different cities. *T'vuos HaAretz* identifies the Chetzron of this verse with the city Chatzar Gadah mentioned in verse 27.

4. עַצְמוֹנָה — *Atzmon.*

This is the city of Atzmon mentioned in *Numbers* 34:4-5 as one of the border cities of *Eretz Yisrael.*

T'vuos HaAretz locates Atzmon twenty-two miles southeast of the junction of the Bierin and Kiseimi Rivers. [*Targum Yonasson ben Uziel* to *Numbers ibid.* identifies this city as Keisam.]

נַחַל מִצְרַיִם — *The Egyptian River.*

Two main opinions have been advanced regarding the precise identification of this river. Some suggest that it is an eastern tributary of the Nile River [see map, *Encyclopedia Talmudis,* s.v. ארץ ישראל] *(Targum Yonasson* to *Numbers* 34:5 and *Targum Yerushalmi; ibid.; Radak* to *Joshua* 13:3; and *Vilna Gaon* to *Joshua* 15:4). Others suggest that the Egyptian River is Wadi El Arish, approximately one hundred miles east of the Nile *(R' Saadiah Gaon* to *Numbers* 34:5). [See also *Commentary* to 13:3.]

לָכֶם — *Your.*

Since this entire section is a third person account of the boundaries, it would seem that Scripture should have used the word לָהֶם, *to them,* rather than the second person לָכֶם, *to you. Radak* suggests that Scripture here parallels *Numbers* 34:6, in which God uses the second person to trace the borders of *Eretz Yisrael,* even though the second person is inconsistent with the grammar of this passage.

◈ The Eastern Border of Judah

5. וּגְבוּל קֵדְמָה — *The eastern border.*

This border is traced from south to north *(Metzudos).*

יָם הַמֶּלַח — *Dead Sea.*

Katzvei Eretz is of the opinion that the Dead Sea itself was not considered a part of Judah's territory.

T'vuos HaAretz (according to *R' Nissan Tucazinsky)* maintains that the

ו צָפוֹנָה מִלְּשׁוֹן הַיָּם מִקְצֵה הַיַּרְדֵּן׃ וְעָלָה
הַגְּבוּל בֵּית חָגְלָה וְעָבַר מִצְּפוֹן לְבֵית
הָעֲרָבָה וְעָלָה הַגְּבוּל אֶבֶן בֹּהַן בֶּן־
ז רְאוּבֵן׃ וְעָלָה הַגְּבוּל | דְּבִרָה מֵעֵמֶק עָכוֹר
וְצָפוֹנָה פֹּנֶה אֶל־הַגִּלְגָּל אֲשֶׁר־נֹכַח
לְמַעֲלֵה אֲדֻמִּים אֲשֶׁר מִנֶּגֶב לַנָּחַל וְעָבַר
הַגְּבוּל אֶל־מֵי עֵין־שֶׁמֶשׁ וְהָיוּ תֹצְאֹתָיו
ח אֶל־עֵין רֹגֵל׃ וְעָלָה הַגְּבוּל גֵּי בֶן־הִנֹּם

Dead Sea was included in *Eretz Yisrael* proper, and hence in Judah's territory.

עַד־קְצֵה הַיַּרְדֵּן — *To the end of the Jordan River.*

Judah's territory stretched northward to the point where the Jordan River empties into the Dead Sea *(Rashi).*

◆§ The Northern Border of Judah

וּגְבוּל לִפְאַת צָפוֹנָה — *The border on the northern side.*

Scripture is delineating the northern border, proceeding in a westerly direction *(Rashi).*

מִלְּשׁוֹן הַיָּם — *From the tip* [lit. *the tongue*] *of the Dead Sea.*

Here, 'the tongue of the sea' refers to the northern tip of the Dead Sea *(Metzudos).*

6. בֵּית חָגְלָה — *Beis Chaglah.*

This city is located about four miles northwest of the northern tip of the Dead Sea. [It lies in the territory of Benjamin as related in 18:21.]

וְעָבַר מִצְּפוֹן לְבֵית הָעֲרָבָה — *And passed through the northern section of Beis Ha'aravah.*

The translation follows *Vilna Gaon.*

Further (18:22) we find that Beis Ha'aravah is a part of Benjamin's territory. *Metzudos* avoids this problem by suggesting that there were two cities by this name, one in each territory.

However, according to the general rule proposed by *Vilna Gaon* (see *Commentary* verse 3), the word עָבַר means that the boundary actually *passed through* the city. Thus, the meaning of our verse is that the boundary of Judah *passed through the northern section of* the city of *Beis HaAravah;* consequently the northern section belonged to Benjamin while the southern and central sections belonged to Judah.

T'vuos HaAretz locates this city somewhere west of Beis Chaglah.

אֶבֶן בֹּהַן בֶּן־רְאוּבֵן — *Even of Bohan son of Reuben.*

The ruler of this district was Bohan, the son of Reuben. The word *Even,* (lit. *stone)* was the name of the district. Perhaps there was a large stone there which served as a landmark *(Radak).*

Metzudos suggests that the city's name was Even Bohan which was ruled by a man named Reuben. The word בֶּן, *son,* in this context means *city.*

Other commentators suggest that *Even Bohan* was the ruler's name *(Katzvei Eretz).*

T'vuos HaAretz found several unusually large rocks on the mountain which runs west of the valley of the Jordan, but was unable to make a conclusive determination that those rocks are the ones referred to in this verse.

[Since Judah's northern border was identical with Benjamin's southern border, this city could very well be the city of Even mentioned in 18:17 on Benjamin's southern border.]

7. דְּבִרָה — *Toward Devir.*

This is not the city of Devir

15
6-7

border on the northern side stretched from the tip of
the Dead Sea at the end of the Jordan River. 6 *The*
border ascended to Beis Chaglah and passed through
the northern section of Beis HaAravah; the border
ascended to Even of Bohan son of Reuben. 7 *The*
border ascended toward Devir from the Valley of
Achor and turned north to Gilgal which faced
Ma'aleh Adumim which is south of the valley. And
the border passed through to the waters of Ein
Shemesh and its enlargement proceeded to Ein Rogel.

mentioned in 10:39 *(Daas Sofrim).*

On the mountains adjacent to the valley of the Jordan, *T'vuos HaAretz* found a large area which the Arabs call Tugrit al Dibi. He identifies this as Devir.

מֵעֵמֶק עָכוֹר — *From the Valley of Achor.*

The Valley of Achor was a city located between Even of Bohan and Devir *(Rashi).*

This valley was named after Achan, who was stoned there after disobeying Joshua's directive (see 7:25). Since this incident took place outside of Jericho, which is in the north of Benjamin's territory, it is clear that this valley ran from north to south, through Benjamin's territory to Judah's *(Vilna Gaon).*

The valley extended through the mountains to the valley of the Jordan opposite Jericho *(T'vuos HaAretz).*

וְצָפוֹנָה פֹּנֶה אֶל־הַגִּלְגָּל — *And turned north to Gilgal.*

When the border approached Gilgal, the territory widened sharply, and the border proceeded north to Gilgal, which is across from the hill known as Ma'aleh Adumim *(Rashi).*

The Gilgal mentioned in this verse is not identical with the Gilgal mentioned in previous chapters, which served as the national center. That Gilgal was located near Jericho, in the north of Benjamin's territory *(Katzvei Eretz). Radak* identifies this city as Gelilos mentioned in 18:17.

לְמַעֲלֵה אֲדֻמִּים — *Ma'aleh Adumim.*

This hill was located about one mile northwest of Devir and six miles east northeast of Jerusalem.

מִנֶּגֶב לַנָּחַל — *Which is south of the valley.*

This was a valley without water *(Rashi).* [Normally, נַחַל means *river.* See *Mahartz Chayes* to *Niddah* 8b.]

מֵי עֵין־שֶׁמֶשׁ — *Waters of Ein Shemesh.*

This is the spring Ein al Chot located in the valley which the Arabs call Wadi Chot.

וְהָיוּ תֹצְאֹתָיו ... — *And its enlargement proceeded.*

The territory's maximum width continued until Ein Rogel; from there it narrowed *(Metzudos).* [According to *T'vuos HaAretz,* however, the territory did become enlarged after Ein Rogel. See map.]

עֵין רֹגֵל — *Ein Rogel.*

Rashi analyzes the components of this name, עַיִן, *spring,* and רֶגֶל, *foot,* and comments that the spring received this name because people used to do their laundry there by treading on the clothing with their feet. It was located at the end of Emek Kadron and is known as the well of Job.

Yonasson and Achima'atz received a message in Ein Rogel to relay to King David during Abshalom's rebellion *(II Samuel* 17:17).

I Kings 1:9 mentions that there was a stone called Even HaZocheles near Ein

טו אֶל־כֶּתֶף הַיְבוּסִי מִנֶּגֶב הִיא יְרוּשָׁלָ͏ִם
ט־י וְעָלָה הַגְּבוּל אֶל־רֹאשׁ הָהָר אֲשֶׁר עַל־
פְּנֵי גֵי־הִנֹּם יָמָּה אֲשֶׁר בִּקְצֵה עֵמֶק־
רְפָאִים צָפוֹנָה׃ וְתָאַר הַגְּבוּל מֵרֹאשׁ ט
הָהָר אֶל־מַעְיַן מֵי נֶפְתּוֹחַ וְיָצָא אֶל־עָרֵי
הַר־עֶפְרוֹן וְתָאַר הַגְּבוּל בַּעֲלָה הִיא
קִרְיַת יְעָרִים׃ וְנָסַב הַגְּבוּל מִבַּעֲלָה יָמָּה י
אֶל־הַר שֵׂעִיר וְעָבַר אֶל־כֶּתֶף הַר־יְעָרִים
מִצָּפוֹנָה הִיא כְסָלוֹן וְיָרַד בֵּית־שֶׁמֶשׁ

Rogel where Adoniyah slaughtered sheep and oxen during his attempt to dethrone King David.

8. גֵּי בֶן־הִנֹּם — *Gei Ben Hinom.*

It was located between Emek Kadron and Emek Rephaim and separates the mount upon which the Holy Temple stood and Mount Zion (which was north of Emek Rephaim).

The *Talmud (Eruvin* 19a) relates that there are two date palms in Gei Ben Hinom and smoke rises from the ground between them, for there lies the door to Gehinnom (purgatory). *Maharsha* explains that the *Talmud* intends to teach that one begins (door) to decline spiritually (Gehinnom) when he is drawn after the sweet pleasures (date honey) of this world.

אֶל־כֶּתֶף הַיְבוּסִי מִנֶּגֶב — *To the south side of the Jebusites.*

Therefore, Jerusalem was outside Judah's border and hence in Benjamin's territory *(Rashi).*

עֵמֶק־רְפָאִים — *Valley of Rephaim.*

This valley was named after the רְפָאִים, *giants,* who once lived there *(Radak).* It was located on the southern side of Jerusalem during the period of King Solomon *(R' Tucazinsky).*

The soil in this valley was not fertile, and consequently little grain grew there. Thus Isaiah prophesied that those few who managed to escape the exile forced by the King of Assyria would be captured, as one who plucks the few standing grain in the Valley of Rephaim — one by one (see *Isaiah* 17:5; *Radak* and *Metzudos).*

When the Philistines heard that David was anointed as king, they pursued him and stationed themselves in the Valley of Rephaim *(II Samuel* 5:17).

9. וְתָאַר — *Proceeded directly.*

According to *Rashi* (see *Commentary* to *verse* 3), this expression indicates that the border took a circuitous route. However, *Vilna Gaon* interprets this expression to mean that the border proceeded in a straight line.

מֵי נֶפְתּוֹחַ — *Mei Neftoach.*

The Rabbis of the *Talmud* refer to this place as Ein Itim *(Radak).* Its elevation is slightly higher than Jerusalem's *(Rashi)* and was the source of water for the *mikveh* used by the Kohen Gadol on Yom Kippur *(Yoma* 31a; *Rashi).*

The city of Itim was located about seven and one half miles south of Jerusalem. Water flowed underground from a large, fresh spring there by way of Beis Lechem to the south of Jerusalem. The conduit proceeded westerly to the south of Mount Zion and then proceeded east and north and entered Jerusalem near the Sha'ar HaAshpah.

T'vuos HaAretz conjectures that

*[8] And the border ascended from Gei Ben Hinom to
the south side of the Jebusites, which is Jerusalem.
The border then ascended to the top of the mountain
which flanks Gei Hinom on the west, which is at the
northern end of the Valley of Rephaim. [9] The border
proceeded directly from the top of the mountain to
the spring of Mei Neftoach and broadened to the
cities of Mount Ephron. And the border proceeded
directly toward Ba'alah, which is Kiryas Y'arim.
[10] The border circled around from Ba'alah westward
to Mount Seir and passed through to the north side
of Mount Y'arim, which is Chesalon. It descended to
Beis Shemesh and passed through Timnah. [11] The*

open pipes were placed on the western side of Mount Zion to catch the water and bring it into the city. The word for 'open,' פָּתוּחַ, is similar to נֶפְתּוֹחַ.

וְיָצָא אֶל־עָרֵי הַר־עֶפְרוֹן — *And broadened to the cities of Mount Ephron.*

The border proceeded diagonally north *(Katzvei Eretz)*, and the territory widened until the cities of Mount Ephron *(Rashi)*.

Between the two deep valleys located west of Jerusalem, there is a high plain. In relation to these valleys, the plain appears as a mountain. *T'vuos HaAretz* conjectures that this plain is Mount Ephron.

וְתָאַר הַגְּבוּל בַּעֲלָה — *The border proceeded directly toward Ba'alah.*

The border is proceeding in a northerly direction at this point, not westward *(Rashi)*.

Rashi (II Samuel 6:2) explains that the word *Ba'alah* means 'plains.'

This city was located about seven miles northwest of Jerusalem. It is also referred to as Ba'alei Yehudah *(II Samuel* 6:2) and Kiryas Y'arim *(I Chronicles* 13:5) from which King David brought the Holy Ark to the home of Oved Edom *(Rashi, ibid.)*.

קִרְיַת יְעָרִים — *Kiryas Y'arim.*

Judges 18:12 recounts that this city's name was changed to Machaneh Dan.

10. וְנָסַב הַגְּבוּל מִבַּעֲלָה — *The border circled around from Ba'alah.*

Scripture now returns to recounting the cities in an east-west direction *(Rashi)*.

הַר שֵׂעִיר — *Mount Seir.*

[This is not the Mount Seir which was the home of Esau, to the east of the Dead Sea.] This Mount Seir was so named because it was covered with a growth of small reeds as a man's head is covered with hair. שֵׂעִיר, *Seir* derives from the root שֵׂעָר, *hair (Vilna Gaon)*.

It was located two and one-half miles west of Kiryas Y'arim and formed the highest point between Jerusalem and Ramlah.

הַר־יְעָרִים — *Mount Y'arim.*

T'vuos HaAretz conjectures that Mount Y'arim is Mount Midian, which was located two and one-half miles south of Saide.

מִצְּפוֹנָה — *North.*

Thus, Mount Y'arim is within Judah's territory *(Rashi)*.

בֵּית־שֶׁמֶשׁ — *Beis Shemesh.*

There was a second Beis Shemesh in Yisachar's territory (19:22) and a third

יא וְעָבַר תִּמְנָה: וְיָצָא הַגְּבוּל אֶל־כֶּתֶף
עֶקְרוֹן צָפוֹנָה וְתָאַר הַגְּבוּל שִׁכְּרוֹנָה
וְעָבַר הַר־הַבַּעֲלָה וְיָצָא יַבְנְאֵל וְהָיוּ
יב תֹּצְאוֹת הַגְּבוּל יָמָּה: וּגְבוּל יָם הַיָּמָּה
הַגָּדוֹל וּגְבוּל זֶה גְּבוּל בְּנֵי־יְהוּדָה סָבִיב
יג לְמִשְׁפְּחֹתָם: וּלְכָלֵב בֶּן־יְפֻנֶּה נָתַן חֵלֶק
בְּתוֹךְ בְּנֵי־יְהוּדָה אֶל־פִּי יהוה לִיהוֹשֻׁעַ
אֶת־קִרְיַת אַרְבַּע אֲבִי הָעֲנָק הִיא חֶבְרוֹן:
יד וַיֹּרֶשׁ מִשָּׁם כָּלֵב אֶת־שְׁלוֹשָׁה בְּנֵי הָעֲנָק
אֶת־שֵׁשַׁי וְאֶת־אֲחִימָן וְאֶת־תַּלְמַי יְלִידֵי

in Naftali's territory (19:38) *(Malbim).*

This is the modern village of Ein Sems.

תִּמְנָה — *Timnah.*

Timnah was situated about one mile west of Beis Shemesh.

[If this is the same Timnah mentioned in *Judges* 14:1, then it was invaded and conquered by the Philistines after the Israelites' conquest.]

11. עֶקְרוֹן — *Ekron.*

Ekron was situated seven and one-half miles northwest of Timnah; it lies northeast of Wadi Zarar.

[From this verse and *Judges* 1:18, it would appear that Ekron was contained within Judah's border. However, *Joshua* 19:43 places it within Dan's inheritance. Perhaps, the city proper was located in Judah's territory, but the outskirts to the north, which also carried the same name as the city, were contained within Dan's boundary.]

שִׁכְּרוֹנָה ... הַר־הַבַּעֲלָה — *Shikron ... Mount Ba'alah*

T'vuos HaAretz could not locate these places.

יַבְנְאֵל — *Yavn'el.*

This city was located on Wadi Zarar.

It has been suggested that this is the city of Yavneh mentioned in *II Chronicles* 26:6 and many times by the *Talmud* (see glosses to *T'vuos HaAretz).*

וְהָיוּ תֹּצְאוֹת הַגְּבוּל יָמָּה — *(And) the border's enlargement proceeded to the Sea.*

The border followed the course of Wadi Zarar to the Mediterranean Sea.

◆§ The Western border of Judah

12. וּגְבוּל — *And its border.*

This expression refers to the islands in the Mediterranean which were considered a part of Judah's territory *(Metzudos).* [See *Commentary* to 1:4, s.v. 'The Mediterranean Sea westward.']

זֶה גְּבוּל בְּנֵי־יְהוּדָה — *This is the border of the Children of Judah.*

In regard to each of the other tribes Scripture states, 'This is the inheritance of ...,' but in regard to Judah, Scripture uses the expression, *This is the border. Malbim* (18:20) explains that here Scripture is delineating the perimeter of Judah's territory, but not *everything* within these borders belongs to Judah; for, as Chapter 19 states, Simeon received his inheritance within Judah's borders. No other tribe was completely contained within another's border.

סָבִיב לְמִשְׁפְּחֹתָם — *Surrounding their families.*

This boundary encircles the inheritance of all the families of the tribe of Judah *(Metzudos).*

border broadened to the north side of Ekron; the
border proceeded directly toward Shikron, passed
through Mount Ba'alah, and broadened to Yavn'el;
the border's enlargement proceeded to the Sea.
12 *The western border was the Mediterranean Sea and*
its border. This is the border of the Children of Judah
surrounding their families.

13 *And to Calev the son of Yefuneh he gave a por-*
tion among the Children of Judah in accordance with
HASHEM's directive to Joshua — Kiryas Arba, the
father of the giants, which is Hebron. 14 *Calev routed*
the three sons of the Anak from there — Sheishai,
Achiman, and Talmai, the children of the Anak. 15 *He*

◈§ Calev's Inheritance

13. וּלְכָלֵב — *And to Calev.*

All the families of Judah received their portions of land through the lottery, except for Calev who received Hebron directly [as God had promised him through Moses] *(Daas Sofrim).* [See 14:6-15 and *Commentary.*]

אֶל־פִּי ה׳ — *In accordance with HASHEM's directive.*

Typically, the phrase used is עַל־פִּי ה׳. *Malbim* comments that this unusual form is used three times in Scripture and all occur in *Joshua:* 17:4, 21:3, and here. In each case Scripture is repeating a Divine command, rather than stating a new one.

Abarbanel explains that after God promised Calev the city of Hebron, the Divinely ordained lottery determined that the tribe of Judah would receive the very plot of land which contained Hebron. In this manner, Divine Providence ensured that Calev, the leader of the tribe of Judah, would not be separated from his people *(Meam Loez).*

אֲבִי הָעֲנָק — *The father of the giants.*

Arba was *the father* of the Anakim, i.e., he was the largest of these giants *(Metzudos).*

14. וַיֹּרֶשׁ מִשָּׁם כָּלֵב — *Calev routed ... from there.*

Rashi comments that this verse refers to an event which did not take place until after Joshua's death, for only then did Calev vanquish Hebron, as stated in *Judges* 1:20. However, Scripture mentions the fact here because it is relevant to the division of the land.

Malbim, however, maintains that Calev's conquest of Hebron did occur during Joshua's lifetime. (For a fuller explanation, see *Commentary* to 10:37-39.)

שְׁלוֹשָׁה בְּנֵי הָעֲנָק — *The three sons of Anak.*

Why does Scripture relate the number of Calev's adversaries before naming them? *Poras Yosef* suggests that Scripture counts these tribes to indicate that although these giants *united* against Calev, he was victorious.

אֶת־שֵׁשַׁי וְאֶת־אֲחִימַן וְאֶת־תַּלְמַי — *Sheishai, Achiman and Talmai.*

Numbers 13:22 lists these giants in a different order: Achiman, Sheishai and Talmai. *Meam Loez* suggests that in this passage they are listed in order of their birth, while in *Numbers* they are listed in order of their strength. Alternatively, he suggests that the order was changed to indicate that they were all of equal strength. [See *Commentary* to 17:3.]

יְלִידֵי הָעֲנָק — *The children of the Anak.*

In the beginning of this verse the

טו הָעֲנָק׃ וַיַּעַל מִשָּׁם אֶל־יֹשְׁבֵי דְּבִר וְשֵׁם־
טז דְּבִר לְפָנִים קִרְיַת־סֵפֶר׃ וַיֹּאמֶר כָּלֵב
אֲשֶׁר־יַכֶּה אֶת־קִרְיַת־סֵפֶר וּלְכָדָהּ וְנָתַתִּי
יז לוֹ אֶת־עַכְסָה בִתִּי לְאִשָּׁה׃ וַיִּלְכְּדָהּ
עָתְנִיאֵל בֶּן־קְנַז אֲחִי כָלֵב וַיִּתֶּן־לוֹ אֶת־
יח עַכְסָה בִתּוֹ לְאִשָּׁה׃ וַיְהִי בְּבוֹאָהּ

giants are referred to as *sons of the Anak,* while here they are called *children of the Anak.* These *children of the Anak* were the formidable giants seen by the reconnaissance mission which Moses dispatched over forty years ago *(Numbers* 13:22). Although these giants had undoubtedly grown even larger in the interim, Calev vanquished them as though they were little *children (Meam Loez).*

15. אֶל־יֹשְׁבֵי דְּבִר — *To the inhabitants of Devir.*

Although 10:39 clearly states that Joshua did not leave any live inhabitants of Devir after his conquest, perhaps in the time between Joshua's battle and Calev's, some people attempted to resettle this city *(R' Avie Gold).*

After vanquishing the giants in Hebron, Joshua levied a pre-emptive strike against *the inhabitants* of Devir to prevent them from attacking the Israelites *(Meam Loez).*

וְשֵׁם־דְּבִר לְפָנִים קִרְיַת־סֵפֶר — *The former name of Devir was Kiryas Sefer* [lit. *book*].

For what purpose does Scripture relate that Devir had formerly been known as Kiryas Sefer? In fact, it was known by two other names as well — Danah and Kiryas Saneh (verse 49). This multiplicity of names tells us that four different monarchs ruled over this city, each calling it a different name. If for a relatively unimportant city as Devir four kings vied, how much the more so for the choicer cities in *Eretz Yisrael (Yalkut* 1:743).

The *Talmud* reports that *devir* is the Persian[1] word for ספרא, a word which might mean 'book' [סִפְרָא] or 'scribe' [סָפְרָא] *(Avodah Zarah* 24b). [In modern Judeo-Persian *dabir* means 'teacher.']

According to the *Talmud (Temurah* 16a), the city *Kiryas Sefer* refers to the three hundred Jewish laws which had been forgotten during the thirty day mourning period for Moses and which were reestablished through the brilliant deductive reasoning of Asniel ben Kenaz[2]

The air in every part of *Eretz Yisrael* makes a person wise (see *footnote* to 22:19), yet the air in Kiryas Sefer had

1. *Shalah (Torah SheB'ul Peh* 15) explains that the Torah never employs words which are not of Hebrew origin. If at times it appears that the Torah 'borrowed' a word from another language, it is only because we are shortsighted in our understanding of the origin of languages in general. When God created the world, the only language extant was Hebrew. It was during the generation of the Separation (after the Tower of Babel) when God confounded man's speech and many languages developed. Some words of Hebrew filtered into these new languages. *Malbim* adds that many words in the Hebrew language were lost but were regained when the Rabbis of the *Talmud,* who were very sensitive to the sublime nature of Hebrew, studied other languages and identified the words of Hebrew origin. The definition of the word in the foreign language revealed the true meaning of the lost Hebrew term (see *Margolios HaYam* to *Sanhedrin* 4b).

2. Two questions could be raised here. First, why does the *Talmud (Temurah* 16a) depart from the simple meaning of the text and call the city of Kiryas Sefer 'three hundred Jewish laws'? Second, why did Calev, who had already conquered the awesome giants of Hebron find it

15
16-17 ascended from there to the inhabitants of Devir; the
former name of Devir was Kiryas Sefer. [16] Calev said,
'He who attacks Kiryas Sefer and captures it, to him
will I give my daughter Achsah for a wife.'
[17] Asniel ben Kenaz, the brother of Calev,
captured it, and he gave him his daughter Achsah for

the greatest effect. It is called Kiryas Sefer because the city's rarefied atmosphere enabled its inhabitants to become extremely learned. Calev chose to live in this city because of the greater wisdom attainable there *(Meam Loez).*

16. וְנָתַתִּי־לוֹ — *To him will I give.*

[At first glance it is difficult to understand why Calev was willing to take a warrior for his son-in-law, when the Torah obviously values piety and scholarship above physical prowess. However, according to the *footnote* to verse 15, Calev clearly recognized that the key to the conquest of Devir lay in Torah scholarship. Thus, he knew that the man who could capture Devir would be a pious Torah scholar, the ideal mate for his daughter (cf., *Yalkut* II,25). [See *Rashi* to *Ta'anis* 4a, s.v. באגדה.]

עַכְסָה — *Achsah.*

The name Achsah is derived from כַּעַס, *anger,* for Calev's daughter was so beautiful that anyone who saw her became angry at his own wife for not being equally beautiful (*Temurah* 16a, *Rashi). Lev Aharon* explains that Achsah's beauty lay in her piety and good deeds, rather than in her physical attributes.

See *Pri Chadash* to *Even HaEzer* 119:1 for the halachic implications of the jealousy Achsah inspired.

17. אֲחִי — *Brother of.*

Rashi comments that Calev and Asniel were half-brothers through their mother, for Asniel was the son of Kenaz, and Calev was the son of Yefuneh *(Radak).*

Calev is thus called 'the Kenizi' and not 'the son of Kenaz,' because he was not the son of Kenaz, but rather was raised in Kenaz's house *(Sotah* 12a, *Rashi).*

Radak suggests another interpretation according to which Calev and Asniel were full brothers: their father was called Yefuneh the Kenizi after his ancestor Kenaz. In regard to Calev, Scripture states his father's full name, but in regard to Asniel,[1] only the last part of the name is mentioned.

necessary to offer his daughter in marriage to anyone who could conquer Devir? Why did not Calev simply conquer the city himself?

Arvei Nachal (Parshas Shelach) explains that the Torah constitutes the blueprint of the world; when God created the world, he 'consulted' the Torah. In this manner the metaphysical laws of the Torah were given physical representation on earth, with each part of the world 'representing' and being governed by specific Torah laws. *Eretz Yisrael,* more than any other land, is intimately bound to the laws of the Torah which govern it and which it 'represents.' Thus, when the Jews accepted the Torah on Mount Sinai, they naturally became the rightful heirs to *Eretz Yisrael.* It was this metaphysical claim which enabled the Jews to gain possession of the Land so effortlessly.

However, Calev was powerless to conquer Devir because that city represented and was governed by the three hundred laws of the Torah which the Jews had forgotten during the mourning period for Moses. Metaphysically, Kiryas Sefer actually *was* these three hundred laws, as the *Talmud* states. Thus, only after Asniel ben Kenaz 'recaptured' (לכד) the city's lost laws through his brilliant, deductive reasoning could the Jews inherit Devir.

1. The deeds and wisdom of a righteous man *(tzaddik)* are compared to the light of the sun. *Ecclesiastes* 1:5 states, *The sun rises, the sun sets.* The *Midrash* notes that Scripture would not mention this obvious fact except to teach us that before God takes the life of one righteous

וַתְּסִיתֵהוּ לִשְׁאוֹל מֵאֵת־אָבִיהָ שָׂדֶה
וַתִּצְנַח מֵעַל הַחֲמוֹר וַיֹּאמֶר־לָהּ כָּלֵב
יט מַה־לָּךְ: וַתֹּאמֶר תְּנָה־לִּי בְרָכָה כִּי
אֶרֶץ הַנֶּגֶב נְתַתָּנִי וְנָתַתָּה לִי גֻּלֹּת מָיִם
וַיִּתֶּן־לָהּ אֵת גֻּלֹּת עִלִּיּוֹת וְאֵת גֻּלֹּת
כ תַּחְתִּיּוֹת: זֹאת נַחֲלַת מַטֵּה
כא בְנֵי־יְהוּדָה לְמִשְׁפְּחֹתָם: וַיִּהְיוּ הֶעָרִים
מִקְצֵה לְמַטֵּה בְנֵי־יְהוּדָה אֶל־גְּבוּל אֱדוֹם
כב בַּנֶּגְבָּה קַבְצְאֵל וָעֵדֶר וְיָגוּר: וְקִינָה

18. וַיְהִי בְּבוֹאָה — *(And it was) when she entered.*

Radak interprets: as she entered her husband's house.

וַתְּסִיתֵהוּ — *She coaxed him.*

Achsah tried to convince her husband to ask her father for a field, but he refused. Therefore, she took matters into her own hands, as the conclusion of the verse indicates *(Radak)*.

According to *Metzudos*, Achsah asked her husband's permission to allow her to request a field from her father.

שָׂדֶה — *Field.*

Be'er Moshe explains that Achsah did not seek this field for her own benefit, but for higher motives. Since Asniel ben Kenaz was to replace Joshua as Israel's national leader (see *footnote* to verse 17), Achsah felt it important that he have a dependable source of income, lest financial burdens interfere with his communal responsibilities. The *Midrash (Terumah* 16a), however, criticizes Achsah for not relying on God's providence, for, as Scripture states, *I have never seen a righteous person forsaken, nor his children in need of bread (Psalms* 37:25).

וַתִּצְנַח — *(And) she threw herself off.*

Rashi interprets: she caused herself to fall to Calev's feet. *Metzudos* suggests that she caused herself to fall to the ground.

Either Achsah intended to kiss her father's feet as a sign of entreaty or she wanted to show her father that she was so troubled that she could not concentrate on keeping her balance on the donkey. When her father saw her distress, he asked her what the matter was *(Poras Yosef)*.

מַה־לָּךְ — *What is the matter* [lit. *what to you*].

You have [obviously] come to ask for something. What is it that you are lacking? *(Metzudos)*.

19. תְּנָה־לִּי בְרָכָה — *Give me a source of livelihood.*

Rashi interprets: give me a source of livelihood. *Targum* renders *property.*

Radak, however, understands Achsah's demand more literally: Give me a blessing; increase your gift to me, because you gave me arid land, as stated later in the verse. ['Blessing' signifies 'increase.']

She requested that Calev give them an additional field that contained water so that the land they received could be watered.

Alternatively, *Radak* suggests that the word בְּרָכָה (lit. *blessing)* could be read as בְּרֵכָה which means *pool.*

leader, he kindles the light of his successor. Before Moses died, Joshua was prepared to take his place, and before Joshua died Asniel ben Kenaz was prepared to take his place *(Bereishis Rabbah* 58:2). [He became the first of the Judges.]

a wife. [18] *When she entered, she coaxed him to ask*
her father for a field. She threw herself off the
donkey, and Calev asked her, 'What is the matter?'
[19] *And she said, 'Give me a source of livelihood,*
for you have given me an arid land — give me springs
of water.' And he gave her the upper springs and the
lower springs.
[20] *This is the inheritance of the tribe of the*
Children of Judah according to their families. [21] *The*
cities at the extremity of the tribe of the Children of
Judah on the border of Edom in the Negev were
Kav'tz'el, Eider, and Yagur; [22] *and Kinah, Dimonah,*

אֶרֶץ הַנֶּגֶב — *And an arid land.*[1]
The translation follows *Rashi. Targum* renders 'land in the south.'

גֻּלֹּת מָיִם — *Springs.*
The translation follows *Rashi. Radak* suggests 'pools,' and *Targum* renders 'irrigated soil.'

☙§ The Cities in the South of Judah

20-32. The enumeration of these cities proceeds from east to west.

21. וַיִּהְיוּ הֶעָרִים מִקְצֵה ... — *The cities at the extremity.*
The Sages have noted that Joshua mentioned only those cities which were located on the borders *(Rashi). Meam Loez* comments that the Sages' statement reflects credit on the tribe of Judah, for even though many of their cities were in close proximity to the bellicose Edom to the south, they did not fear, because they trusted that God would protect them.

קַבְצְאֵל — *Kav'tz'el.*
Its exact location is unknown, but it was the birth place of B'nayahu son of Yehoyadah *(II Samuel* 23:20).

וְעֶדֶר — *Eider.*
This may be the city of Arad mentioned in 12:14 [for if the ד and ר are interchanged, the spelling changes from עֶדֶר, *Eider,* to עֲרָד, *Arad;* this is a common interchange].

וְיָגוּר — *Yagur.*
This city's location is not known.

22. וְקִינָה — *Kinah.*
T'vuos HaAretz conjectures that this is the city of Tzinah in the Wilderness of Tzin.

1. The *Talmud (Temurah* 16a) interprets the dialogue between Achsah and her father on a symbolic level:
□ וַתִּצְנַח מֵעַל הַחֲמוֹר — [lit. *she threw herself off the donkey*] — 'She brayed like a donkey.' Just as a donkey brays as soon as the feedbag is empty, so does a woman complain as soon as the grain supply in the house is depleted.
□ אֶרֶץ הַנֶּגֶב נְתַתָּנִי — [lit. *you have given me an arid land*] — 'You have given me a house which is dry of all [material] good.'
□ וְנָתַתָּה לִי גֻּלֹּת מָיִם — [lit. *give me springs of water*] — 'You have given me a man who only possesses Torah [but no resources with which to feed us]' (Torah is oftentimes compared to water).
□ אֵת גֻּלֹּת עִלִּיּוֹת וְאֵת גֻּלֹּת תַּחְתִּיּוֹת — [lit. *upper springs and lower springs*] — [Calev replied to Achsah] 'For him who is privy to all the secrets of the upper and lower spheres, must one request a livelihood?'

כג וְדִימוֹנָה וְעַדְעָדָה׃ וְקֶדֶשׁ וְחָצוֹר וְיִתְנָן׃
כד־כה זִיף וָטֶלֶם וּבְעָלוֹת׃ וְחָצוֹר | חֲדַתָּה
כו וּקְרִיּוֹת חֶצְרוֹן הִיא חָצוֹר׃ אֲמָם וּשְׁמַע
כז וּמוֹלָדָה׃ וַחֲצַר גַּדָּה וְחֶשְׁמוֹן וּבֵית פָּלֶט׃
כח־כט וַחֲצַר שׁוּעָל וּבְאֵר שָׁבַע וּבִזְיוֹתְיָה׃ בַּעֲלָה
ל וְעִיִּים וָעָצֶם׃ וְאֶלְתּוֹלַד וּכְסִיל וְחָרְמָה׃
לא־לב וְצִקְלַג וּמַדְמַנָּה וְסַנְסַנָּה׃ וּלְבָאוֹת
וְשִׁלְחִים וְעַיִן וְרִמּוֹן כָּל־עָרִים עֶשְׂרִים
לג וָתֵשַׁע וְחַצְרֵיהֶן׃ בַּשְּׁפֵלָה

וְדִימוֹנָה וְעַדְעָדָה — *Dimonah and Adadah.*
Their exact locations are unknown.[1]

23. וְקֶדֶשׁ — *Kedesh.*
This is the city of Kadesh Barnea (verse 3).

וְחָצוֹר — *Chatzor.*
This passage mentions three cities with this name: (a) the city mentioned in this verse; (b) Chatzor mentioned in the beginning of verse 25; and (c) Chatzor mentioned at the end of verse 25 (*Metzudos* to verse 25).

וְיִתְנָן — *Yisnan.*
Its location is unknown.

24. זִיף — *Zif.*
This city was located north of Mount Madora.

וָטֶלֶם — *Telem.*
This is identical with the city of Telaim (טְלָאִים) mentioned in *I Samuel* 15:4. It was there that Saul battled Amalek [see *Yoma* 22b.]

וּבְעָלוֹת — *B'alos.*
This is identical with the modern city of Kubit Alba'ul (קוביט אלבאעול).

25. חֲדַתָּה — *Chadatah.*
According to the cantillation (reading accents), *Chadatah* is a noun, rather than an adjective describing the previous word, Chatzor. In Aramaic, *chadatah* means 'new,' but here it is the name of a city.
According to *Metzudos*, Chadatah is one of four cities mentioned in this verse. The other three are: Chatzor, Keriyos, and Chetzron.

26. וּמוֹלָדָה — *Moladah.*
It is located approximately four miles southwest of Tel Arar.
As 19:2 relates, this city was later given to the tribe of Simeon (see *Malbim* 19:2). However, in the time of Nechemiah, some members of the tribe of Judah resettled in Moladah (see *Nechemiah* 11:26).

27. וַחֲצַר גַּדָּה — *Chatzar Gadah.*
T'vuos HaAretz places this city near Ein Gedi.

28. וַחֲצַר שׁוּעָל — *Chatzar Shu'al.*
This city was later given to the tribe of Simeon (19:3).

וּבְאֵר שָׁבַע — *Be'er Sheva.*

1. Because the name of each of the three cities in this verse ends with a ה, which is seemingly superfluous *(Maharsha)*, the *Talmud (Gittin* 7a) expounds on this verse by use of a word play. Scripture intends to teach: that one who is angry *(kinah* [*Rashi*]) at his fellow and remains silent *(domeim)*, the One who lives forever *(adei ad)* will judge him accordingly. Similarly, the *Talmud* expounds on the cities mentioned in verse 31: that one who unfairly competes against his fellow in business *(tzakas legima)* and is silent *(domeim)*, the One who appeared in a bush *(seneh)* [the Burning Bush in *Exodus* 3:2] will judge him accordingly.

15
23-32

and Adadah; 23 and Kedesh, Chatzor, and Yisnan;
24 Zif, Telem, and B'alos; 25 and Chatzor, Chadatah,
Keriyos; Chetzron is Chatzor; 26 Amam, Shema, and
Moladah; 27 and Chatzar, Gadah, Cheshmon, and
Palet; 28 and Chatzar Shu'al, Be'er Sheva, and
Bizyosya; 29 Ba'aleh, I'yim, and Etzem; 30 and Eltolad,
Kesil, and Charmah; 31 Tziklag, Madmanah, and
Sansanah; 32 Levos, Shilchim, Ayin, and Rimon; all
the cities total twenty-nine and their villages.

In Arabic this city is called Bir Siba (ביר סיבא); it is located approximately 30 miles southwest of Hebron.

Be'er Sheva had been known since the time of the Patriarchs. It was later given to the tribe of Simeon (19:2). Archeological digs revealed ancient ruins approximately three miles east of the modern day city of Be'er Sheva.

29. וְעָצֶם — *Etzem.*

This is the city of Atzmon, found on Wadi Kisimi (ואדי קיסיימי). Ba'alah and Atzem were later given to the tribe of Simeon (19:3).

30. וְאֶלְתּוֹלַד — *Eltolad.*

This was later given to the tribe of Simeon (19:3).

וּכְסִיל — *Kesil.*

T'vuos HaAretz identifies this city as Besul (בתול), later mentioned in 19:4 as belonging to the tribe of Simeon. Kesil was also called Beth El. *I Samuel* 30:27 mentions that this city received booty from David's conquests.

וְחָרְמָה — *Charmah.*

This is probably the city mentioned in *Judges* 1:17 which Judah and Simeon conquered together.

Joshua 12:14 lists it among the thirty-one kingdoms which Joshua conquered. See *Commentary* to 12:14 for its location.

31. וְצִקְלַג — *Tziklag.*

Its exact location is not known, but it is located between Wadi Shariya and Wadi Simsum. It was later given to the tribe of Simeon (19:15).

This is the city that Achish, king of Gas, gave to King David *(I Samuel* 27:6). *Radak (ibid.)* explains that either the Israelites conquered this city during the Conquest and the Philistines wrestled it back, or it was not taken during the Conquest, but was listed here because in the future it would belong to Judah.

וּמַדְמַנָּה — *Madmanah.*

This is the city of Mondo (מנדא).

וְסַנְסַנָּה — *Sansanah.*

Some identify this as the city of Sumsum (סומסום) located to the northeast of Azah.

32. וְעַיִן וְרִמּוֹן — *Ayin and Rimon.*

These cities were later given to the tribe of Simeon (19:7).

כָּל־עָרִים עֶשְׂרִים וָתֵשַׁע — *All the cities total twenty-nine.*

Actually, Scripture enumerates thirty-eight cities, not twenty-nine. However, Scripture here counts only those cities which would be retained by the tribe of Judah. Nine cities were later given to the tribe of Simeon, leaving twenty-nine. The cities given to the tribe of Simeon are: Be'er Sheva, Moladah, Chatzar, Shu'al, Etzem, Eltolad, Charmah, Tziklag, Ayin and Rimon *(Rashi).*

Malbim, however, finds this interpretation untenable, since the total of thirty-eight cities assumes that four cities are mentioned in verse 25. The

טו
לד־מג

לד אֶשְׁתָּאוֹל וְצָרְעָה וְאַשְׁנָה: וְזָנוֹחַ וְעֵין
לה גַּנִּים תַּפּוּחַ וְהָעֵינָם: יַרְמוּת וַעֲדֻלָּם
לו שׂוֹכֹה וַעֲזֵקָה: וְשַׁעֲרַיִם וַעֲדִיתַיִם
וְהַגְּדֵרָה וּגְדֵרֹתָיִם עָרִים אַרְבַּע־עֶשְׂרֵה
לז וְחַצְרֵיהֶן: צְנָן וַחֲדָשָׁה וּמִגְדַּל־
לח-לט גָּד: וְדִלְעָן וְהַמִּצְפֶּה וְיָקְתְאֵל: לָכִישׁ
מ וּבָצְקַת וְעֶגְלוֹן: וְכַבּוֹן וְלַחְמָס וְכִתְלִישׁ:
מא וּגְדֵרוֹת בֵּית־דָּגוֹן וְנַעֲמָה וּמַקֵּדָה עָרִים
מב שֵׁשׁ־עֶשְׂרֵה וְחַצְרֵיהֶן: לִבְנָה
מג וָעֶתֶר וְעָשָׁן: וְיִפְתָּח וְאַשְׁנָה וּנְצִיב:

verse itself indicates that there are actually only three *different* cities, because Chatzor is identical with Chetzron. Similarly, there are other cities mentioned above which have more than one name. Twenty-nine is the total of *different* cities. Thus, *Malbim* contends that Scripture has in fact listed only twenty-nine *different* cities [despite the thirty-eight *names*].

וְחַצְרֵיהֶן — *And their villages.*
This phrase means: besides their villages.

⊷§ The Cities in the Lowlands of Judah

33-44. *T'vuos HaAretz* reports that the entire Valley of the Jordan as well as the Mediterranean Sea can be seen from the mountains which are to the west of Jerusalem and to the east of the city of Ein Koram.

⊷§ The Northern Lowlands

33. אֶשְׁתָּאוֹל וְצָרְעָה — *Eshta'ol, Tzarah.*
These cities are located to the west of Mount Modi'im. They are the present-day cities of צארא and שטואל.

These two cities are mentioned in 19:41 as belonging to Dan. However, *I Chronicles* 2:53 enumerates them as Judah's cities. *Rashi (ibid.)* explains that the cities proper belonged to Judah but the outskirts belonged to Dan.

34. וְזָנוֹחַ — *Zanoach.*
This is the city Zamea, located southeast of Zarea.

וְעֵין גַּנִּים — *Ein Ganim.*
This is situated southeast of Ashkalon and is identical with the city G'inin (ג׳ינין).

תַּפּוּחַ — *Tapuach.*
It was located about five miles northwest of Beis Guvrin.

וְהָעֵינָם — *Einam.*
This is identical with the city of Beis Ani (בית עני) which was located two and one-half miles from Zo'afin.

According to one opinion in the Talmud *(Sotah* 10a), this was the city where Tamar stationed herself in order to entice Judah *(Genesis* 34:14).

According to *Rashi* (verse 36), Einam was not a separate city, but rather the springs of Tapuach.

35. יַרְמוּת — *Yarmus.*
See *Commentary* to 12:11.

וַעֲדֻלָּם — *Adulam.*
See *Commentary* to 12:15.

שׂוֹכֹה — *Socho.*
This is the present-day city of So'avica (סואווייכע) located to the north of Beis Guvrin.

וַעֲזֵקָה — *Azeikah.*
T'vuos HaAretz identifies this as the city of Tel Azakria (תל עזאקריא). He

33 In the lowlands: Eshta'ol, Tzarah, and Ashnah;
34 and Zanoach, Ein Ganim, Tapuach, and Anam;
35 Yarmus, Adulam, Socho, and Azeikah;
36 Sha'arayim, Adisayim, Hagdeirah, and
Gedeirosayim; fourteen cities and their villages.
37 Tzenan, Chadashah, and Migdal Gad; 38 Dilan,
Mitzpeh, and Yaks'el; 39 Lachish, Batzkas, and
Eglon; 40 and Chabon, Lachmas, and Chislish;
41 Gedeiros, Beis Dagon, Na'amah, and Makeidah;
sixteen cities and their villages.
42 Livnah, Eser, and Ashan; 43 Yiftach, Ashnah,

takes exception to *Kaftor V' Ferach's* claim that Azeikah is located between Azah and El Arish. This was the city upon which the hailstones descended as described in 10:10.

36. וְשַׁעֲרַיִם — *Sha'arayim.*
This city is mentioned in *I Samuel* 17:52 as the city where the Israelites killed many Philistines; it is near the cities of Gas and Ekron, in the land of the Philistines. Both *Admos Kodesh* and *T'vuos HaAretz* identify this city as Tre'in (תרעין).

עָרִים אַרְבַּע־עֶשְׂרֵה — *Fourteen cities.*
If the above cities are counted, the total will yield fifteen, not fourteen. *Rashi* suggests that the cities Tapuach and Einam (verse 34) were identical — Einam being the springs of Tapuach — while *Radak* suggests that the cities Hagdeirah and Gedeirosayim (verse 36) were identical. *T'vuos HaAretz* favors *Radak's* interpretation.

◆§ The Southern Lowlands

37. צְנָן — *Tzenan.*
Perhaps this is the city of Tzon Evra (צאן עברא).
This city is mentioned by the prophet Michah. When the inhabitants of the city of Shafir, who were the first to go into exile, passed by the city of Tzenan, the inhabitants of Tzenan did not offer any comfort, for they knew that they also would be condemned to exile in the future *(Radak* to *Michah* 1:11).

וַחֲדָשָׁה — *Chadashah.*
In the opinion of *T'vuos HaAretz,* this is the city G'ara Di Elchadosh located between the cities of Migdal and Ashkalon.
It is mentioned in the Mishnah *(Eruvin* 59a) as being a small city in the times of the *Talmud* (50 inhabitants) [*Rashi* to *Kiddushin* 76a, s.v. אף מי].

וּמִגְדַּל־גָּד — *Migdal Gad.*
This is the present city of Migdal.

38. וְדִלְעָן וְהַמִּצְפֶּה — *Dilan, Mitzpeh.*
Both are located near the village Tel Tzofi (תל צאפי).

39. לָכִישׁ — *Lachish.*
See *Commentary* to 10:31.

וְעֶגְלוֹן — *Eglon.*
See *Commentary* to 10:34.

41. וּגְדֵרוֹת — *Gedeiros.*
This is the present-day ruins of Gador (גאדאר) located on the Wadi of Tzar.
The invasion of this city by the Philistines prompted Achaz to enlist the kings of Assyria to aid the Israelites *(II Chronicles* 28:18).

וּמַקֵּדָה — *Makeidah.*
See *Commentary* to 12:16.

◆§ The Eastern Lowlands

42. לִבְנָה — *Livnah.*
See *Commentary* to 12:15.

וְעָשָׁן — *And Ashan.*
This is identical with the city of Cor

טו
מד־נה

מד וּקְעִילָה וְאַכְזִיב וּמָרֵאשָׁה עָרִים תֵּשַׁע
מה וְחַצְרֵיהֶן׃ עֶקְרוֹן וּבְנֹתֶיהָ
מו וַחֲצֵרֶיהָ׃ מֵעֶקְרוֹן וָיָמָּה כֹּל אֲשֶׁר־עַל־יַד
מז אַשְׁדּוֹד וְחַצְרֵיהֶן׃ אַשְׁדּוֹד
בְּנוֹתֶיהָ וַחֲצֵרֶיהָ עַזָּה בְּנוֹתֶיהָ וַחֲצֵרֶיהָ
°הַגָּדוֹל ק׳ עַד־נַחַל מִצְרָיִם וְהַיָּם °הגְּבוּל וּגְבוּל׃
מח־מט וּבָהָר שָׁמִיר וְיַתִּיר וְשׂוֹכֹה׃ וְדַנָּה וְקִרְיַת־
נ סַנָּה הִיא דְבִר׃ וַעֲנָב וְאֶשְׁתְּמֹה וְעָנִים׃
נא וְגֹשֶׁן וְחֹלֹן וְגִלֹה עָרִים אַחַת־עֶשְׂרֵה
נב וְחַצְרֵיהֶן׃ אֲרַב וְדוּמָה וְאֶשְׁעָן׃
°וְיָנוּם ק׳ נג־נד °וינִים וּבֵית־תַּפּוּחַ וַאֲפֵקָה׃ וְחֻמְטָה
וְקִרְיַת אַרְבַּע הִיא חֶבְרוֹן וְצִיעֹר עָרִים
נה תֵּשַׁע וְחַצְרֵיהֶן׃ מָעוֹן

Ashan (כור עשן) mentioned in *I Samuel* 30:30, which received some of the spoils of war from King David's victories. It is located 15 miles west of Jerusalem.

Ashan and Eser were later given to the tribe of Simeon (19:7).

43. וּנְצִיב — *And Netziv.*

Netziv is located to the east of Beis Guvrim, where the city Beis Notzib (בית נוציב) is found.

44. וּקְעִילָה — *And K'ilah.*

It is located between Beis Guvrin and Hebron.

[Perhaps this is the city mentioned in *I Samuel* 23:6 where King Saul thought David was trapped and where he thought he could have him assassinated.]

וְאַכְזִיב — *Achziv.*

It was located just north of Adulam (see *Commentary* to 12:15) and was also called Keziv, mentioned in *Genesis* 38:5 as the location of Judah when his son Sheilah was born from Shua *(Radak* to *Michah* 1:14).

וּמָרֵאשָׁה — *And Mareishah.*

This city was located just south of Beis Guvrin.

☙ The Southwestern Shore Region

45-47. In these verses the boundaries of the southwestern shore region are delineated, but the cities contained within these boundaries are not enumerated. It has been suggested that Scripture does not record any specific cities here because this region was not conquered during Joshua's lifetime (see 11:22). This view is consistent with the fact that the region around Jerusalem was also not conquered until later, and its cities also remained unmentioned (see verse 63).

In *Judges* (1:19) this region is referred to as *The Valley.*

45. עֶקְרוֹן — *Ekron.*

See *Commentary* to 13:3 for its location.

46. אַשְׁדּוֹד — *Ashdod.*

See *Commentary* to 11:22.

47. עַזָּה — *Azah.*

In Turkish, this city is called Gaza (גאזא). When Napoleon marched to *Eretz Yisrael* from Egypt, he stormed Gaza, and all the Jews living there fled to Jerusalem and Hebron.

See *Commentary* to 10:41.

15
44-54 *and Netziv; 44 and K'ilah, Achziv, and Mareishah;
nine cities and their villages.*

*45 Ekron, with its hamlets and villages; 46 from
Ekron to the Sea, all that lay near Ashdod and their
villages.*

*47 Ashdod with its hamlets and villages, Azah with
its hamlets and villages to the Egyptian River and the
Mediterranean Sea, and its border; 48 In the mountain
region: Shamir, Yatir, and Socho; 49 and Danah, and
Kiryas Sanah, which is Devir; 50 and Anav,
Eshtemoh, and Anim; 51 Goshen, Cholon, and Giloh;
eleven cities and their villages.*

*52 Arav, Dumah, and Eshan; 53 Yanum, Beis
Tapuach, and Afeikah; 54 Chumtah, Kiryas Arba,
which is Hebron, and Tzior; nine cities and their
villages.*

◆§ The Mountain Region

48-60. The mountain range discussed here is Mount Judah, located south of Jerusalem. It is not a prominent range, for its highest point (near the valley of Hebron) is only 2664 feet above sea level.

48. וְיַתִּיר — *Yatir.*
This is the village of Yatir (יאתיר) located south of Hebron about three-quarters of the way between Hebron and Moladah. Yatir was later given to the Kohanim (21:14).

וְשׁוֹכֹה — *Socho.*
It was located about two miles north of Yatir and about three miles west of Soavica (Arabic).

49. וְקִרְיַת־סַנָּה — *And Kiryas Sanah.*
See *Commentary* to verse 15.

50. וַעֲנָב — *Anav.*
This is the city Anab (אנאב) which is perhaps identical with the city mentioned in 11:21. It is located slightly more than a mile north of Socho.

וְאֶשְׁתְּמֹה — *Eshtemoh.*
T'vuos HaAretz identifies this as the city Samua (סאמוּא). It was later given to the Kohanim (21:14).

וְעָנִים — *And Anim.*
Located to the east of Hebron and slightly to the north, it is the city Bin Anim (בין ענים).

51. וְגֹשֶׁן — *Goshen.*
[This is not the same as the Goshen mentioned in Chapters 11 and 12.]

וְחֹלֹן — *Cholon.*
This was later given to the Levites (see 21:15).

וְגִלֹה — *And Giloh.*
This is the large village Beis G'olo (בית ג׳אלא).

52. וְדוּמָה — *Dumah.*
Its location cannot be ascertained.

53. וּבֵית־תַּפּוּחַ — *Beis Tapuach.*
This is the city Tapuach (תאפוח).

וַאֲפֵקָה — *And Afeikah.*
T'vuos HaAretz identifies this city as Abiq (אביק).

54. חֶבְרוֹן — *Hebron.*
See *Commentary* to 10:36.

טו
נו־סג

נו כַּרְמֶל וָזִיף וְיוּטָּה׃ וְיִזְרְעֶאל וְיָקְדְעָם
נז וְזָנוֹחַ׃ הַקַּיִן גִּבְעָה וְתִמְנָה עָרִים עֶשֶׂר
נח וְחַצְרֵיהֶן׃ חַלְחוּל בֵּית־צוּר
נט וּגְדוֹר׃ וּמַעֲרָת וּבֵית־עֲנוֹת וְאֶלְתְּקֹן
ס עָרִים שֵׁשׁ וְחַצְרֵיהֶן׃ קִרְיַת־
בַּעַל הִיא קִרְיַת יְעָרִים וְהָרַבָּה עָרִים
סא שְׁתַּיִם וְחַצְרֵיהֶן׃ בַּמִּדְבָּר
סב בֵּית הָעֲרָבָה מִדִּין וּסְכָכָה׃ וְהַנִּבְשָׁן
וְעִיר־הַמֶּלַח וְעֵין גֶּדִי עָרִים שֵׁשׁ
סג וְחַצְרֵיהֶן׃ וְאֶת־הַיְבוּסִי
°יָכְלוּ ק׳ יוֹשְׁבֵי יְרוּשָׁלַם לֹא־°יוכלו בְנֵי־יְהוּדָה
טז לְהוֹרִישָׁם וַיֵּשֶׁב הַיְבוּסִי אֶת־בְּנֵי יְהוּדָה
א בִּירוּשָׁלַם עַד הַיּוֹם הַזֶּה׃ וַיֵּצֵא

וְצִיעֹר — *And Tzior.*
Tzior is located northeast of Hebron; it is identical with the village Z'tzior (זציעור).

55. מָעוֹן — *Ma'on.*
This is the city Ma'on (מאעון) located south of Hebron.

כַּרְמֶל — *Carmel.*
Carmel is north of Ma'on and is the city Alkormol (אלקורמול). The Dead Sea can be seen from here.

וָזִיף — *Zif.*
This city is located midway between Hebron (to the northeast) and Carmel (to the south).

וְיוּטָּה — *And Yutah.*
This is the city Yata (יאטא) situated south of Hebron.

56. וְיִזְרְעֶאל — *Yizr'el.*
[Perhaps this is city from which Achinoam, one of King David's wives, came *(I Samuel* 25:43).]
T'vuos HaAretz does not locate this city.

וְיָקְדְעָם — *Yakde'am.*
T'vuos HaAretz does not describe this city.

וְזָנוֹחַ — *And Zanoach.*
It was located about four miles southwest of Samoh. [It is not identical with the city by the same name mentioned in verse 34.]

57. וְתִמְנָה — *And Timnah.*
T'vuos HaAretz cites a source which places Timnah ten miles east of Beis Guvrin.

58. חַלְחוּל — *Chalchul.*
It is situated about five miles north of Hebron. The grave of the prophet Gad lies here.

בֵּית־צוּר — *Beis Tzur.*
This city is located approximately fifteen miles southwest of Jerusalem in the Wadi of Tzor. Calev's sons later occupied this area as reported in *I Chronicles* 2:42 *(Rashi, ibid.).*

59. וּמַעֲרָת — *And Ma'aras.*
This city is identical with M'ror (מראר).

וְאֶלְתְּקֹן — *Eltekon.*
See *Commentary* to 19:44 for its location.

60. קִרְיַת־בַּעַל — *Kiryas Ba'al.*
This is the village Kiria (קיריע).

15
55-63

55 Ma'on, Carmel, Zif, and Yutah; 56 Yizr'el,
Yakde'am, and Zanoach; 57 Kayin, Givah, and
Timnah; ten cities and their villages.
58 Chalchul, Beis Tzur, and Gador; 59 and Ma'aras,
Beis Anos, and Eltekon; six cities and their villages.
60 Kiryas Ba'al, which is Kiryas Y'arim, and
Harabah; two cities and their villages.
61 In the wilderness: Beis HaAravah, Midin, and
Sechachah; 62 and Nivshan, Ir HaMelach, and Ein
Gedi; six cities and their villages.
63 But the Jebusites who lived in Jerusalem, the
Children of Judah were not able to drive out. And the
Jebusites live in the land of the Children of Judah in
Jerusalem until this day.

◆§ The Boundary of the Wilderness of Judah

61-62. The Wilderness of Judah is located on the Western shore of the Dead Sea.

61. בֵּית הָעֲרָבָה — *Beis HaAravah.*
See *Commentary* to verse 6.

מִדִּין — *Midin.*
Perhaps this is the city mentioned in Deborah's song *(Judges* 5:10) [*Radak, ibid.*].

62. וְעֵין גֶּדִי — *And Ein Gedi.*
Although *T'vuos HaAretz* states that this is located southeast of Jericho, he evidently means southeast of *Hebron* on the shore of the Dead Sea.

He advances that there were two cities by this name, one on the northwest shore of the Dead Sea and one on the shore of the Dead Sea north of Tzoar, and is uncertain to which this verse refers. At one time, dates grew in abundance in Ein Gedi, and thus it was also called Chatzatzon Tamar (lit. *the cutting place of the dates).* It is mentioned in *Genesis* 14:7 as the habitation of the Emorites who were killed by the Four Kings.

According to the *Midrash (Shir HaShirim* [Greenhot]), the vineyards in Ein Gedi would produce fruit four or five times a year. The ritually pure wine which was used for the libations in the Holy Temple was produced here.

63. הַיְבוּסִי — *The Jebusites.*
This tribe was not one of the Seven Nations which the Jews were commanded to exterminate, even though its name is identical to one of the Seven Nations. Rather, the tribe descended from a Philistine named Jebus, who was a descendant of Avimelech *(Radak).*

לֹא־יָכְלוּ בְנֵי־יְהוּדָה לְהוֹרִישָׁם — *The children of Judah were not able to drive out.*
Rashi cites *Sifri* which states that the Jews were actually capable of defeating the Jebusites, but refrained from doing so because of the oath which Abraham had made with Avimelech (see *Genesis* 21:23-4).

Malbim points out that *Judges* 1:8 seems to imply the contrary of this verse, for it states that *the Children of Judah battled in Jerusalem and defeated it. Malbim* explains that Jerusalem was composed of two parts: the city and the fortress, known as Metzudas Zion. After Joshua's death, the sons of Judah were able to overtake the city, but they were not able to conquer the fortress until the days of King David (see II *Samuel* 5:7-8).

טז הַגּוֹרָל לִבְנֵי יוֹסֵף מִיַּרְדֵּן יְרִיחוֹ לְמֵי
א יְרִיחוֹ מִזְרָחָה הַמִּדְבָּר עֹלֶה מִירִיחוֹ בָּהָר

עַד הַיּוֹם הַזֶּה — *Until this day.*

Until this day refers to the era of the author, Joshua, for Jerusalem was not conquered during his lifetime *(Radak).*

XVI

The beginning of this chapter (verses 1-3) details the common southern border of the tribes which descended from Joseph's sons, Ephraim and Menashe (Genesis *41:51-2). The remaining verses of this chapter describe the other borders of Ephraim's territory. In addition to the consolidated territory which Ephraim received, the tribe was granted a number of discrete cities within the borders of Menashe's territory. These were known as the 'separated cities' and will be explained further in the introduction to verse 8. The remaining borders of Menashe's territory are described in Chapter 17.*

Because the details of the geography affect the interpretation of several verses in this chapter, a single approach has been presented in the Commentary *based on the conclusions of* T'vuos HaAretz. *His comments are given as the primary interpretation of each verse; however,* Malbim *and* Katzvei Eretz *are also cited (in smaller print) when they disagree with* T'vuos HaAretz.

The western border of Ephraim is not mentioned in this chapter. According to T'vuos HaAretz, *whose opinion is followed in regard to the map, the western border of Ephraim was the eastern border of neighboring Dan (see 19:40-48).* Malbim, *however, argues that the western border was formed by the line connecting Upper Beis Choron in the north and Ataros Adar in the south.*

☙ The Southern Border of Ephraim and Menashe

1. וַיֵּצֵא הַגּוֹרָל לִבְנֵי יוֹסֵף — *The outcome of the lottery for the Children of Joseph was.*

Joseph's sons inherited the northernmost region of *Eretz Yisrael* which was conquered during Joshua's lifetime, as *Joshua* 18:5 states, *and the House of Joseph, will occupy their territory to the north.* There was a large plot of land which lay between the tribes of Judah and Joseph. Most of this area was occupied by the tribe of Benjamin *(Rashi);* some was allocated to the tribe of Dan. [Note that *Rashi's* comment differs from *T'vuos HaAretz* cited in the *footnote* to 13:1. In his view, Asher and Naftali were in the northermost region of *Eretz Yisrael* which was conquered during Joshua's lifetime. The maps reflect the view of *T'vuos HaAretz.*]

Scripture is about to delineate the southern border of the territory of Joseph's sons, which is identical with the northern border of Benjamin's territory *(Malbim).*

לִבְנֵי יוֹסֵף — *For the Children of Joseph.*

Joseph's sons were Menashe and Ephraim, each of whom received a separate share in the Land, as did each of Jacob's sons. Their inheritance stretched across the entire width of the country, as did Judah's *(Metzudos).*

Scripture delineates the two tribes' inheritance together at this point because the southern border about to be described is common to both. When, however, the remaining borders of each territory are given (starting in verse 4), Scripture states the borders of each tribe's territory separately.

מִיַּרְדֵּן יְרִיחוֹ לְמֵי יְרִיחוֹ — *From the Jordan opposite Jericho to the Waters of Jericho.*

The border is outlined from the east *(Rashi).* It began from the Jordan River at the point across from Jericho and continued to the Waters of Jericho. The

16 *¹ The outcome of the lottery for the Children of*
1 *Joseph was: In the east — from the Jordan opposite*
Jericho to the Waters of Jericho to the wilderness
which ascends from Jericho via the mountain to Beth

city of Jericho, however, was not contained within Joseph's boundary, but within Benjamin's [see 18:2] *(Malbim).*

T'vuos HaAretz identifies *the Waters of Jericho* as Ein Sultan, which begins as a spring and then runs as a brook. Ein Sultan is located northwest of Jericho.

According to the *Talmud (Jerusalem, Berachos* 5:1), the spring of waters into which Elisha threw a flask of salt in order to prevent miscarriages *(II Kings* 2:21) was called the Waters of Jericho.

מִזְרָחָה — *In the east* [*lit. toward the east*].

This expression refers to the direction from which the border is about to be described *(Rashi).* According to *Vilna Gaon, in the east* may refer to the Waters of Jericho indicating that they were located to the east of Jericho. [*Vilna Gaon's* comment differs from *T'vuos HaAretz* who places the Waters of Jericho (Ein Sultan) to the *west* of Jericho.]

הַמִּדְבָּר עֹלֶה מִירִיחוֹ — *To the wilderness which ascends from Jericho.*

According to *Targum,* it was the Wilderness which ascended and approached the western side of Beth El.

Rashi, however, understands that *ascends* refers to the *border* which continued through the Wilderness outside Jericho and ascended and approached the western side of Beth El *(Rashi).*

[Modern contour maps of *Eretz Yisrael* display the region of Ein Sultan as one hundred meters higher in elevation than the city of modern-day Jericho.]

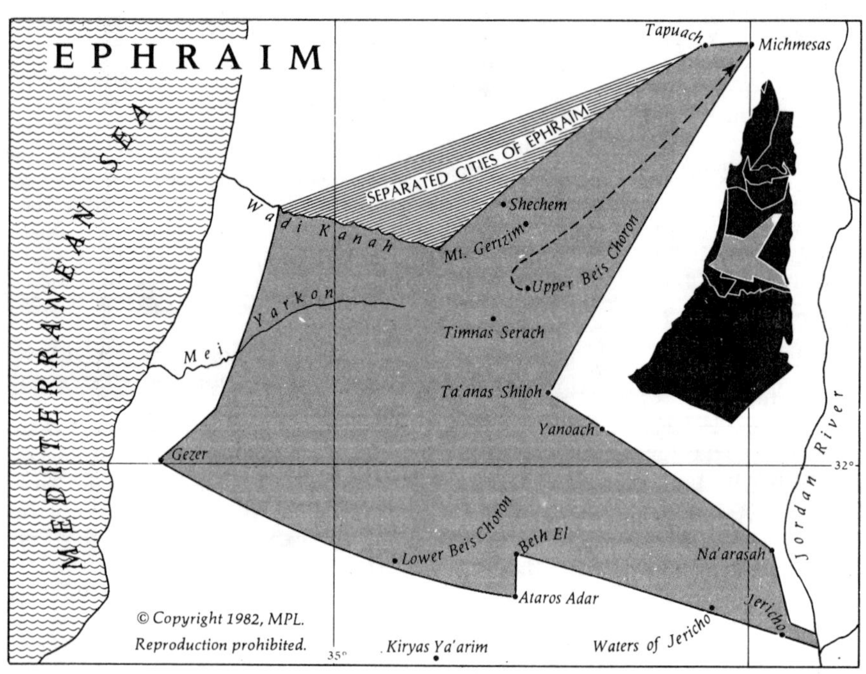

טז
ב־ו

ב בֵּית־אֵל: וְיָצָא מִבֵּית־אֵל לוּזָה וְעָבַר אֶל־
ג גְּבוּל הָאַרְכִּי עֲטָרוֹת: וְיָרַד יָמָּה אֶל־גְּבוּל
הַיַּפְלֵטִי עַד־גְּבוּל בֵּית־חֹרוֹן תַּחְתּוֹן וְעַד־
ד גָּזֶר וְהָיוּ תֹצְאֹתָו יָמָּה: וַיִּנְחֲלוּ בְנֵי־יוֹסֵף
ה מְנַשֶּׁה וְאֶפְרָיִם: וַיְהִי גְּבוּל בְּנֵי־אֶפְרַיִם
לְמִשְׁפְּחֹתָם וַיְהִי גְּבוּל נַחֲלָתָם מִזְרָחָה
ו עַטְרוֹת אַדָּר עַד־בֵּית חֹרוֹן עֶלְיוֹן: וְיָצָא

2. וְיָצָא — *It broadened.*

[The boundary line being traced took a diagonal course.]

מִבֵּית־אֵל לוּזָה — *From Beth El to Luz.*

Radak contends that the city Beth El mentioned in this verse is not the city which Jacob named Beth El in *Genesis* 28:9, since there it states that the city's name had originally been Luz, which is also mentioned in this verse. *Daas Sofrim,* however, suggests that Jacob was not in Luz proper at the time he changed its name, but some distance from it. Thus Beth El was the name he gave to the place where he lodged, outside of Luz. According to this view, this verse teaches that the border extended from the place where Jacob lodged (Beth El) to Luz.

Luz was contained within Joseph's border *(Malbim). Rashi* (18:13) shares *Radak's* view that there were two cities named Beth El; he states that the Beth El mentioned in this verse was in Benjamin's territory.

אֶל־גְּבוּל הָאַרְכִּי — *To the border of (the) Arki.*

The translation follows *Targum.*

According to *Malbim,* this expression means: *on the long border* [from אֹרֶךְ, *length*], which is the northern boundary of Benjamin.

עֲטָרוֹת — *Ataros.*

This is the city Atros Adar, which is mentioned further in 18:13 *(Malbim).*

T'vuos HaAretz conjectures that Ataros is located directly south of Beth El and east of the village Biria (Be'eros).

The palm tree under which the prophetess Deborah rendered judgments for Israel was located in Ataros *(Targum, Judges* 4:5).

3. בֵּית־חֹרוֹן תַּחְתּוֹן — *Lower Beis Choron.*

This is the city Beis Ur. The border went to the south of this city *(Metzudos).*

According to *I Chronicles* 7:24, it was She'era who built this city and Upper Beis Choron.

גָּזֶר — *Gezer.*

T'vuos HaAretz conjectures that Gezer is located between the city of Ramalah and Jaffa and was located where the village of Gazor stood.

וְהָיוּ תֹצְאֹתָו יָמָּה — *Its enlargement proceeded westward.*

The border went slightly westward from Gezer but did not reach the Mediterranean because the territory of Dan flanked Ephraim on the west *(T'vuos HaAretz).* Thus, Ephraim's territory was landlocked.

4. מְנַשֶּׁה וְאֶפְרָיִם — *Menashe and Ephraim.*

Although Scripture mentions Menashe and Ephraim together in this verse, the inheritance of each tribe was determined by a separate draw of the lottery *(Malbim).* [Cf., however, *Ramban* cited in *Commentary* to 17:14.]

Menashe is mentioned before Ephraim because he was Joseph's firstborn son (see verse 17:1). *Meam Loez* suggests that Joshua mentioned Ephraim last out of humility, because Joshua himself was from the tribe of Ephraim.

El. [2] *It broadened from Beth El to Luz and passed to*
the border of Arki to Ataros. [3] *It descended westerly*
to the border of Yafleiti to the border of Lower Beis
Choron and to Gezer; its enlargement proceeded
westward. [4] *The Children of Joseph received their*
inheritance — Menashe and Ephraim. [5] *The border of*
the Children of Ephraim according to their families
was: the border of their inheritance in the east was
Atros Adar to Upper Beis Choron. [6] *The border*

◈§ Ephraim's Territory

5-10. According to *T'vuos HaAretz,* Ephraim's territory was bordered by Benjamin in the south, Dan in the west, and Menashe in the north and east.

5. וַיְהִי גְּבוּל בְּנֵי־אֶפְרַיִם — *The border of the Children of Ephraim.*

Even though Menashe was Joseph's first-born (see previous note), Ephraim's territory is mentioned first. *Be'er Moshe* explains that since Jacob blessed Ephraim before Menashe *(Genesis* 48:20), Scripture almost always accords Ephraim precedence. For example, the standard of Ephraim was mentioned before Menashe's and the princes of Ephraim preceded those of Menashe in offering their gift at the dedication ceremony for the Tabernacle. Thus, Scripture mentions Ephraim's inheritance first.

In a broad sense, the border of Ephraim's territory stretched across the entire width of *Eretz Yisrael. Malbim* maintains that Ephraim acquired a consolidated territory in the eastern part of the country (see further) and received cities dispersed through Menashe's territory in the western part of the country. [These cities are described in verses 8 and 9 according to *Malbim* or verse 9 according to *T'vuos HaAretz.* See introduction to verse 8 for further explanation.] *Malbim* explains the twice-repeated phrase in this verse *the border.* The first mention of this phrase is Scripture's introduction to verses 5-9 which describe Ephraim's entire territory — both the consolidated territory in the east and the separated cities in the west; the second mention of this phrase is the introduction to the description of only the consolidated territory in the east.

[According to the map, which follows the opinion of *T'vuos HaAretz,* Ephraim's consolidated territory appears primarily in the *west* of the country, rather than in the east, as *Malbim* asserts.]

מִזְרָחָה — *In the east.*

Ephraim's land was on the eastern side of *Eretz Yisrael (Malbim).* [See note in previous comment.]

[According to *T'vuos HaAretz,* who maintains that most of Ephraim's territory was located in the western part of *Eretz Yisrael, in the east* would presumably mean that Scripture at this point intends to describe that small portion of land that Ephraim owned in the eastern part of *Eretz Yisrael.*]

עַטְרוֹת אַדָּר עַד־בֵּית חוֹרוֹן עֶלְיוֹן — *Atros Adar to Upper Beis Choron.*

T'vuos HaAretz identifies Upper Beis Choron as the city Beis Ur Fuk or Choara, which is south of Shechem.

There is a difference of opinion as to why these two cities in particular are cited. According to *Malbim,* they represent the north-south dimension of Ephraim's territory, Upper Beis Choron in the north and Atros Adar in the south.

According to *T'vuos HaAretz,* an imaginary north-south line should be drawn between these two cities. East of this imaginary line, Ephraim possessed

טז הַגְּבוּל הַיָּמָּה הַמִּכְמְתָת מִצָּפוֹן וְנָסַב
ו הַגְּבוּל מִזְרָחָה תַּאֲנַת שִׁלֹה וְעָבַר אוֹתוֹ

no cities within Benjamin's territory, which was south of Ephraim's border. [As will be explained *(Commentary* to 19:19), a tribe's territory was not necessarily contained within the borders mentioned by Scripture. In some cases, tribes also owned cities in a neighboring tribe's territory.]

From this comment of *T'vuos HaAretz* (p. 179), it would appear that to the west of this imaginary line the tribe of Ephraim did possess territory within the borders of Benjamin, although *T'vuos HaAretz* does not identify the extent of this territory. *T'vuos HaAretz* (p. 150) cited in the *Commentary* to 18:14 mentions that Benjamin owned cities to the west of Kiryas Y'arim and some, such as Lod, appear to have been in Ephraim's territory.[1]

◆§ The Eastern Border

6-7. According to *T'vuos HaAretz,* these verses describe the eastern border of Ephraim's territory from Michmesas in the north to Jericho in the south. The northern border is described in verse 8.

Malbim, however, refers to the description given in these verses as the northern border. Although the border traced in these verses proceeds in a north-south direction (except for the line which connects Upper Beis Choron and Michmesas), it may be termed the northern border because from Upper Beis Choron to Jericho it is always proceeding in an easterly direction as well. No eastern border is given, in his view, because the northern border converges with the southern border (verse 7).

The difference between these two opinions is not merely a matter of semantics, but depends upon where each commentator locates the city of Michmesas. According to *T'vuos HaAretz,* the city is northeast of Upper Beis Choron and thus the border described from Michmesas to Jericho and the Jordan is essentially a north-south border, thus defining the eastern border of Ephraim. *Malbim,* however, locates Michmesas to the west of Upper Beis Choron, and thus the description of the border from Upper Beis Choron to Jericho and the Jordan is essentially a diagonal one which *Malbim* interprets as the northern border converging with the southern border.

The placement of the city of Michmesas also affects the meaning of verse 8. Since *T'vuos HaAretz* locates Michmesas in the east of *Eretz Yisrael,* according to his view, Scripture has never defined a northern border. He therefore concludes that verse 8 must describe the northern border. *Malbim,* however, places Michmesas to the west of

1. It is very unclear whether Judah and Ephraim had a common border. *Katzvei Eretz* maintains that the tribe of Benjamin separated Judah and Ephraim in the east of *Eretz Yisrael,* but not in the west. Therefore, the two tribes would share a border somewhere west of Kiryas Y'arim, which defined the western border of Benjamin (see *Commentary* to 18:14). However, from Scripture's description of the northern border of Judah west of Kiryas Y'arim (15:10), it becomes evident that Judah's northern border is *not* coincident with Ephraim's border west of Kiryas Y'arim (which is described in 16:3). It is thus very difficult to understand this approach.

T'vuos HaAretz does not mention whether Judah and Ephraim shared a common border. Even if it is assumed that they did not, it is still very unclear which tribe owned the territory to the west of Benjamin. *T'vuos HaAretz* defines the western border of Benjamin as the line connecting Lower Beis Choron and Kiryas Y'arim; he hypothesizes that the border also 'bulged' further in a westward direction to include other cities. Which tribe owned the land west of Kiryas Y'arim not included in the 'bulge' is indeterminate, since this undefined land is north of Judah's northern border (15:10), south of Ephraim's southern border (16:3), and west of Benjamin's western border (18:14). While it is possible that this undefined land could be included in Dan's territory to the west, it is not likely, according to the description of Dan's territory given by *T'vuos HaAretz* on pages 166-67.

On the map we have assigned this undefined land to Benjamin's territory, assuming that it is the 'bulge' *T'vuos HaAretz* mentions on page 150. In addition, a connecting line between Lower Beis Choron and Kiryas Y'arim has been included since he defines this area as the western border of Benjamin.

16
6 *broadened westward to the north of Michmesas, and it circled to the east of Ta'anas Shiloh, and it passed*

Upper Beis Choron and interprets the line connecting Upper Beis Choron and Michmesas as an extension of the northern border. Verse 8, *Malbim* concludes, must be the definition of the separated cities mentioned in verse 9.

וְיָצָא הַגְּבוּל הַיָּמָּה — *The border broadened westward.*

[The border being traced is in the north of Ephraim's territory.]

Ephraim's border stretched westward from Upper Beis Choron to the north of Michmesas, which belonged to the tribe of Menashe *(Metzudos)*. [This view follows *Katzvei Eretz* and *Malbim* mentioned in *Commentary* to 16:6.]

T'vuos HaAretz, however, describes the border's enlargement in a different manner. He maintains that the border ran in a westerly direction for a short distance from Upper Beis Choron and then continued northeasterly until it approached Michmesas. From there, it went south to the east of Ta'anas Shiloh; then it continued in a southeasterly direction to the Jordan.

Thus, the border described here was not the western extreme of the northern border, for that is given in verse 8 [according to the view of *T'vuos HaAretz.* See introduction to verse 8.] *Westward,* here, means slightly west of Upper Beis Choron. [Cf., however, the view of *Katzvei Eretz* mentioned in the following note.]

הַמִּכְמְתָת — *Michmesas.*

According to *T'vuos HaAretz,* this city was located fifteen miles from Shechem and six miles from Beis Shean, which means that it was located to the *northeast* of Upper Beis Choron. [Thus, at this point, the border traveled in a northeasterly direction from the area west of Upper Beis Choron to Michmesas.]

Katzvei Eretz and *Malbim,* however, place Michmesas *west-southwest* of Upper Beis Choron and explain that at this point the northern border took a westerly direction, north of Michmesas. According to their view, Michmesas is the furthest west of any location mentioned on the northern border (according to *Y'sod V'Shoresh HaAvodah).*

The map follows the view of *T'vuos HaAretz* that Michmesas is northeast of Upper Beis Choron.

וְנָסַב הַגְּבוּל מִזְרָחָה — *It circled to the east of [Ta'anas Shiloh].*

According to *T'vuos HaAretz,* the border went in a southerly direction from Michmesas to Ta'anas Shiloh.

Malbim, (see previous note) places Michmesas west of Upper Beis Choron; he interprets the verb וְנָסַב to mean that the border being traced reversed directions. While previously it went in a westerly direction from Upper Beis Choron to Michmesas, here it begins to trace in an easterly direction from Upper Beis Choron to Ta'anas Shiloh.

תַּאֲנַת שִׁלֹה — *Ta'anas Shiloh.*

According to *Vilna Gaon,* this city was located near Jericho.

T'vuos HaAretz, however, cites the *Talmud (Jerusalem, Megillah* 1:14) which identifies Ta'anas Shiloh as the city of Shiloh, which was some distance from Jericho.

According to the *Talmud (Zevachim* 118b), Ta'anas Shiloh was the site of the Tabernacle (see *Prefatory Remarks* to Chapter 18). Although Scripture always refers to this city as Shiloh *(Meam Loez),* here Scripture adds the word *Ta'anas,* which derives from the Hebrew word for 'mourning,' אֲנִיָּה. The site of the Tabernacle, while in Benjamin's territory, legally belonged to the tribe of Ephraim, because a narrow corridor of land extended from Ephraim's territory to the city of Shiloh located in Benjamin's territory. Because Benjamin was deprived of the ownership of this holy site, he mourned.

T'vuos HaAretz finds several difficulties with this Talmudic passage. Consequently, he suggests that a scribal error caused a reversal of the words 'Ephraim' and 'Benjamin' in the Talmudic text. Shiloh, which is identical with Ta'anas Shiloh

טז
ז־י

ז מִמִּזְרַח יָנוֹחָה: וְיָרַד מִיָּנוֹחָה עֲטָרוֹת
וְנַעֲרָתָה וּפָגַע בִּירִיחוֹ וְיָצָא הַיַּרְדֵּן:
ח מִתַּפּוּחַ יֵלֵךְ הַגְּבוּל יָמָּה נַחַל קָנָה וְהָיוּ
תֹצְאֹתָיו הַיָּמָּה זֹאת נַחֲלַת מַטֵּה בְנֵי־
ט אֶפְרַיִם לְמִשְׁפְּחֹתָם: וְהֶעָרִים הַמִּבְדָּלוֹת
לִבְנֵי אֶפְרַיִם בְּתוֹךְ נַחֲלַת בְּנֵי־מְנַשֶּׁה כָּל־
י הֶעָרִים וְחַצְרֵיהֶן: וְלֹא הוֹרִישׁוּ אֶת־

mentioned in this verse, was located, he argues, within *Ephraim's* territory, not Benjamin's. Thus the narrow corridor of land mentioned by the *Talmud* extended from *Benjamin's* territory north to Shiloh, and it was *Ephraim,* not Benjamin, who mourned because the site of the Tabernacle did not belong to him. (The *Talmud* is not explicit concerning who mourned.) He further substantiates his emendation of this passage with a parallel version of this text which is cited by *Radak* in *I Samuel* 7:5.

Another interpretation given by the *Talmud (Zevachim* 118b) for the word תַּאֲנַת, *mourning,* which precedes Shiloh is that a certain advantage was lost when the Tabernacle moved from Shiloh. Sacrifices which would later have to be eaten within the confines of the walls of Jerusalem when the Temple was located there (e.g., the Pesach offering) did not have to be eaten within the walls of Shiloh. Any place from which Shiloh could be seen without obstruction, even if it was many miles outside the city limits, was fit for eating these sacrifices. When the *Beis HaMikdash* was built, the loss of this advantage was mourned by the Jews.

וְעָבַר אוֹתוֹ מִמִּזְרַח יָנוֹחָה — *And passed through it to the east of Yanoach.*

Yanoach was south of Ta'anas Shiloh *(Malbim)* [and thus the border being traced went in a southerly direction].

The border passed through Ta'anas Shiloh and continued past the eastern side of Yanoach *(Rashi).*

T'vuos HaAretz cites a source which places Yanoach twelve miles east [and apparently south] of Shechem.

7. עֲטָרוֹת — *Ataros.*

[The border went in a southwesterly direction from Yanoach to Ataros.]

T'vuos HaAretz does not locate this city. [It is not the Ataros mentioned in verse 2.]

וְנַעֲרָתָה — *Na'arasah.*

[The border followed a southeasterly course from Ataros to Na'arasah.

This is the city called Nama located about five miles north of Jericho.

According to *Katzvei Eretz,* the cities Ta'anas Shiloh, Yanoach, Ataros, and Na'arasah were all located to the west of Upper Beis Choron (according to *Yesod V'Shoresh HaAvodah).*

וּפָגַע — *Converged.*

According to *T'vuos HaAretz* this verse represents the intersection between the eastern border and the southern one (see introduction to verses 6-7).

The term *converged* is used because the northern border described in verses 6 and 7 intersected the southern border described in verses 1 through 3 *(Malbim).*

בִּירִיחוֹ — *At Jericho.*

The border approached Ein Sultan (see *Commentary* to 16:1) and continued until it reached the Jordan River *(Metzudos).* Thus, there was only a very narrow corridor of Ephraim's territory from Ein Sultan to the Jordan *(Malbim).*

וְיָצָא הַיַּרְדֵּן — *And broadened to the Jordan.*

The border went east from Jericho until it met the Jordan *(Malbim).*

through it to the east of Yanoach. [7] *It descended from*
Yanoach to Ataros and Na'arasah, converged at
Jericho, and broadened to the Jordan. [8] *The border*
stretched westward from Tapuach to the Kanah
River and its enlargement proceeded to the Sea. This
is the inheritance of the Children of Ephraim
according to their families. [9] *And the separated cities*
that belonged to the Children of Ephraim within the
inheritance of the Children of Menashe, all the cities
and their villages. [10] *And they did not drive out the*

◆§ The Northern Border

8. מִתַּפּוּחַ — *From Tapuach.*

After the most southern portion of Ephraim's eastern border (Jericho) was described, Scripture moves north to Tapuach in order to describe Ephraim's northern border.

Tapuach was situated near the Jordan River in the territory of Menashe, but it belonged to Ephraim *(Metzudos).* It was located northeast of Shechem and was the city the Arabs called 'Balad Tupah.' The northern border went from Michmesas through Tapuach to the Kanah River.

As was mentioned in the introduction to verses 6-7, *Malbim* and *Katzvei Eretz* maintain that this verse does not intend to describe the northern border of Ephraim, but rather indicates the area in which the 'separated cities' appear. These were cities which belonged to the tribe of Ephraim but were located in Menashe's territory. *Malbim* is of the opinion that Ephraim's western boundary ended at Upper Beis Choron, except for the corridor that proceeded toward Michmesas (see *Commentary* to verse 6). The land to the west of Upper Beis Choron belonged to Menashe, except for the cities which lay between Tapuach (which *Malbim* apparently locates in the south of Menashe's territory to the west of Atros Adar [unlike *T'vuos HaAretz*]) in the south and the Kanah River in the north. These cities were distant from the main territory of Ephraim and were thus known as 'separated cities.'

Katzvei Eretz locates Tapuach in the east of *Eretz Yisrael* and claims that the 'separated cities' were defined by an imaginary line stretching in an east-west direction, from Tapuach to the Kanah River. In a north-south direction, the cities went from the Kanah River to Michmesas (which *Katzvei Eretz* locates to the west of Upper Beis Choron [see *Commentary* to 16:6]).

נַחַל קָנָה — *Kanah River.*

The *Kanah River* was located to the west of Shechem and flowed into the Mediterranean Sea.

זֹאת — *This.*

This refers to the boundaries of Ephraim described in verses 1 through 8 *(Metzudos).*

9. וְהֶעָרִים הַמִּבְדָּלוֹת — *And the separated cities.*

Because the previous verse concluded, *this is the inheritance of the Children of Ephraim,* Scripture here intends to include the separated cities that belonged to Ephraim but were located within the borders of Menashe *(Radak).* [See 17:9.]

According to the view of *T'vuos HaAretz* mentioned in the previous verse, these separated cities were not yet mentioned. After Scripture concluded its description of the consolidated territory of Ephraim in the first eight verses, it then adds that Ephraim possessed additional territory in the form of 'separated cities.' According to *Malbim,* however, verse 8 defined the location of these 'separated' cities, and thus this verse, together with the last half of the previous verse, is a recapitulation of the territories Ephraim received.

יז הַכְּנַעֲנִי הַיּוֹשֵׁב בְּגָזֶר וַיֵּשֶׁב הַכְּנַעֲנִי
א־ב בְּקֶרֶב אֶפְרַיִם עַד־הַיּוֹם הַזֶּה וַיְהִי לְמַס־
א עֹבֵד׃ וַיְהִי הַגּוֹרָל לְמַטֵּה
מְנַשֶּׁה כִּי־הוּא בְּכוֹר יוֹסֵף לְמָכִיר בְּכוֹר
מְנַשֶּׁה אֲבִי הַגִּלְעָד כִּי הוּא הָיָה אִישׁ
ב מִלְחָמָה וַיְהִי־לוֹ הַגִּלְעָד וְהַבָּשָׁן׃ וַיְהִי

10. בְּגָזֶר — *In Gezer.*

They were not able to drive the Canaanites from Gezer because it was one of the separated cities lying in Menashe's territory *(Malbim).* [According to *T'vuos HaAretz,* Gezer belonged to Ephraim.]

עַד־הַיּוֹם הַזֶּה — *Until this day.*

This day refers to the time when Joshua wrote this book *(Daas Sofrim).*

וַיְהִי לְמַס־עֹבֵד — *And they paid tribute with service.*

This does not refers to a tax, but to physical servitude *(Metzudos).* [See *Commentary* to verse 9:4 where the conditions which exempt a Canaanite from the commandment of extermination are stated.]

XVII

☙ Menashe's Inheritance

1. כִּי־הוּא בְּכוֹר יוֹסֵף — *Even though he was Joseph's first-born.*

In this context, the word כִּי does not mean *because,* but *even though. Even though* Menashe was the older of Joseph's sons and consequently should have received his portion of land before Ephraim, he received his inheritance second, because Jacob had blessed Ephraim first [see *Genesis* 48:20] *(Metzudos).* [See *Commentary* to 16:5.]

Malbim, however, does understand כִּי in its usual sense of *because.* Menashe received territory both east and west of the Jordan, because as Joseph's first-born, he was entitled to a double portion of land. He cites a *Midrash* which states that Menashe's inheritance was torn in two because his father Joseph caused his brothers to tear their garments (see *Genesis* 44:13). Although Ephraim was also a descendant of Joseph, his territory was not affected. Menashe's was divided *because he was the first-born.*

According to *Vilna Gaon,* [even though the land about to be described includes Ephraim's territory as well,] it was called Menashe's *because* he was Joseph's first-born.

לְמָכִיר בְּכוֹר מְנַשֶּׁה — *For Machir the first-born of Menashe.*

Since Machir was the first-born, he was the first of his tribe to be assigned land [i.e., the lands of Gilead and the Bashan] on the eastern side of the Jordan River. He was granted this inheritance by Moses [*Numbers* 32:40] *(Rashi).*

אֲבִי הַגִּלְעָד — *The father of Gilead.*

Machir may have been called *the father of Gilead* for either of two reasons: (a) he had a *son* named Gilead, or (b) he became the ruling prince over the *territory* of Gilead *(Metzudos).*

הָיָה אִישׁ מִלְחָמָה — *He was a man of war.*

Since Machir and his father were both first-born sons, Machir was endowed with great strength. Consequently, he inherited the land east of the Jordan River, which was occupied by fierce inhabitants. Reuben and Gad asked for the land east of the Jordan because it was rich in the grazing land needed for their large flocks, but Menashe sought that territory because he had the ability to protect himself from its inhabitants. Moses presaged this strength in his blessing to Menashe, *The first-born bull, grandeur is his, his*

17
1-2
Canaanites that dwelled in Gezer, but rather the Canaanites lived among Ephraim until this day, and they paid tribute with service.

1 *The outcome of the lottery for the tribe of Menashe, even though he was Joseph's first-born: for Machir the first-born of Menashe, the father of Gilead — because he was a man of war — the land of Gilead and the Bashan.* 2 *There was a portion for the*

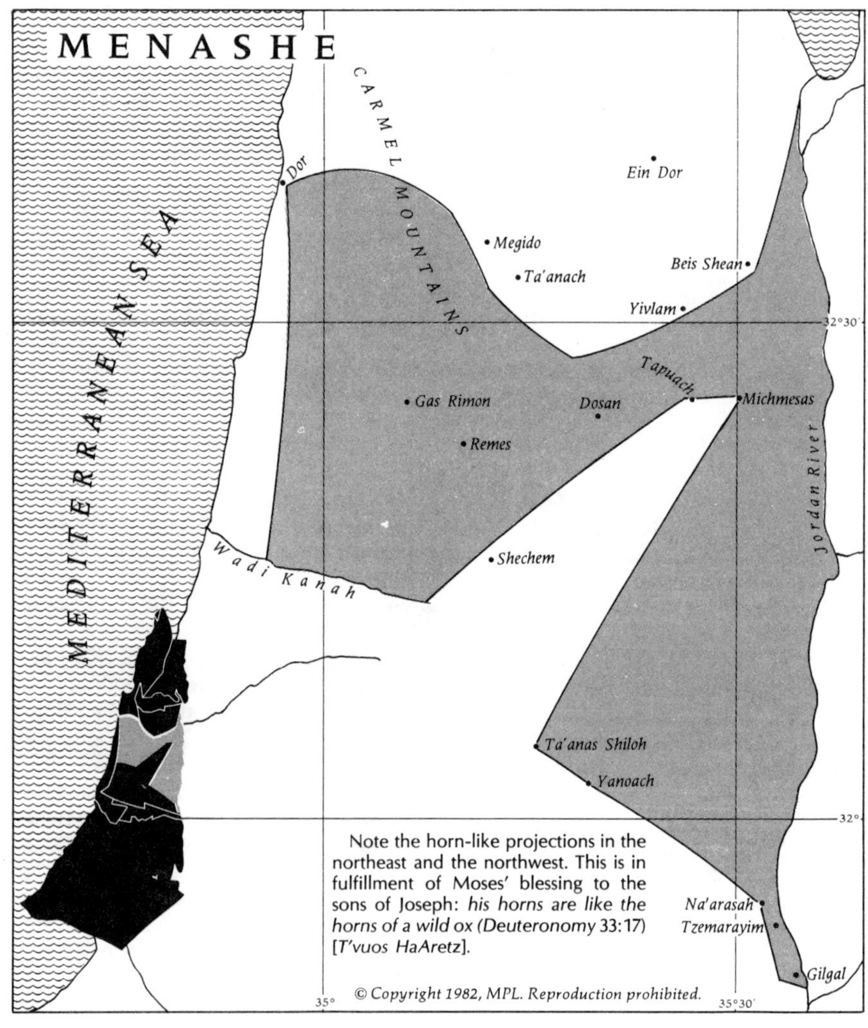

יז לִבְנֵי מְנַשֶּׁה הַנּוֹתָרִים לְמִשְׁפְּחֹתָם לִבְנֵי
ג־ד אֲבִיעֶזֶר וְלִבְנֵי־חֵלֶק וְלִבְנֵי אַשְׂרִיאֵל
וְלִבְנֵי־שֶׁכֶם וְלִבְנֵי־חֵפֶר וְלִבְנֵי שְׁמִידָע
אֵלֶּה בְּנֵי מְנַשֶּׁה בֶּן־יוֹסֵף הַזְּכָרִים
ג לְמִשְׁפְּחֹתָם: וְלִצְלָפְחָד בֶּן־חֵפֶר בֶּן־גִּלְעָד
בֶּן־מָכִיר בֶּן־מְנַשֶּׁה לֹא־הָיוּ לוֹ בָּנִים כִּי
אִם־בָּנוֹת וְאֵלֶּה שְׁמוֹת בְּנֹתָיו מַחְלָה
ד וְנֹעָה חָגְלָה מִלְכָּה וְתִרְצָה: וַתִּקְרַבְנָה

horns are like the horns of a wild ox: with them he shall push the peoples ... to the end of the earth (Deuteronomy 33:17) *(Radak).*

2. ...וַיְהִי — *There was a portion* [lit. *and it was*].

After Machir received his inheritance, the lottery was drawn for the remaining sons of Menashe *(Metzudos).*

הַזְּכָרִים — *The male children.*

Because the daughters of Tzlofchad also received a portion of the Land, Scripture stipulates that this verse refers to the portion given to the males *(Vilna Gaon).*

✤§ Tzlofchad's Daughters

3-4. After God charged Moses with the details of the division of the Land *(Numbers* 26:52), the daughters of Tzlofchad, a member of the tribe of Menashe, became distressed. They feared that the portion of land which their deceased father would have received would be lost because he had no male heirs. Therefore, they approached Moses and argued, *'Why should the name of our father be eliminated from among his family?' (Numbers* 27:4). The *Talmud (Bava Basra* 119b) explains that they presented Moses with the very compelling legal argument: either they should receive their father's portion or their uncle (father's brother) should receive it, depending upon whether female offspring are considered 'seed' of their father. If female offspring are considered 'seed,' then Tzlofchad's daughters could claim to be their father's rightful heirs. If, however, female offspring are not considered 'seed,' then their uncle would be required to marry their mother according to the laws of Levirate marriage *(Deuteronomy* 25:5-10) and could then receive ownership of his deceased brother's estate, which would include his portion of the land in *Eretz Yisrael.*

Moses then consulted God for a ruling. In response, God informed Moses of the laws of inheritance. Although Moses should not have needed an incident such as this to prompt him to learn these laws, since the daughters of Tzlofchad were so meritorious, God rewarded them by promulgating these laws of inheritance in response to their request *(Rashi* to *Numbers* 27:4; cf. *Rashi's* alternative interpretation).

The laws of inheritance *(Numbers* 27:6-14) dictate that daughters do inherit their father's estate if their father had no sons. Thus, the daughters of Tzlofchad deserved to inherit their father's portion in *Eretz Yisrael.*

In our passage we find that when Menashe's territory was about to be assigned, Tzlofchad's daughters approached Joshua for their rightful share of land. Although the men of their generation had perished in the Wilderness, as punishment for believing the spies' slanderous report concerning

remaining sons of Menashe according to their
families: to the children of Aviezer, to the children of
Chalek, to the children of Asriel, to the children of
Shechem, to the children of Cheifer, and to the
children of Shemida. These are the male children of
Menashe son of Joseph according to their families.
[3] But Tzlofchad, son of Cheifer, son of Gilead, son of
Machir, son of Menashe, had no sons, only
daughters. And these are the names of his daughters:
Machlah, Noah, Chaglah, Milcah, and Tirzah. [4] And

Eretz Yisrael, this decree did not apply to the women, for their great love for the Land prevented them from believing the spies' report. Thus, the daughters of Tzlofchad survived the journey through the Wilderness *(Kli Yakar* to *Numbers* 27:1).

3. וְלִצְלָפְחָד בֶּן־חֵפֶר — *But Tzlofchad, son of Cheifer.*

Scripture recounts Tzlofchad's genealogy to indicate that he was a righteous man *(tzaddik)* whose father was also a righteous man *(Vilna Gaon).* [See *Megillah* 15a.]

In *Numbers* 27:3, Tzlofchad's daughters told Moses that their father *died because of his own sin.* The *Talmud (Shabbos* 96b) cites a difference of opinion regarding the nature of this sin. According to one opinion, Tzlofchad was the unnamed individual who violated the Sabbath by gathering wood *(Numbers* 15:32). According to the other opinion, he was one of the rebellious group who ascended the mountain during the battle with Amalek and the Canaanites *(Numbers* 14:44) in defiance of Moses' command. The *Midrash* (see *Tosafos, Bava Basra* 119b) comments that Tzlofchad had the purest intentions and was acting 'for the sake of heaven' when he violated the Sabbath. Either he intended to demonstrate to the other Jews that although they were sentenced to die in the Wilderness as punishment for having believed the evil report about *Eretz Yisrael* given by the reconnaissance mission, they were still obligated to observe the laws of the Torah *(Tosafos, Bava Basra* 119b), or he wanted to teach them that the penalty for violating the Sabbath was death by stoning *(Maharsha, ibid.).*

[Perhaps *Vilna Gaon's* comment that Tzlofchad was a righteous person is predicated upon the view that Tzlofchad was the Sabbath violator, for as *Maharsha* explains, Tzlofchad would not have been culpable for this act if his intention was not to desecrate the Sabbath, but rather to teach others. In this case, gathering sticks would have had the legal status of *melachah she'einah tzrichah l'gufah* which does not constitute a Biblical Sabbath violation (according to Rebi Shimon; it is, however, forbidden by Rabbinic law). According to the second opinion (that Tzlofchad participated in a rebellion), however, it would appear that Tzlofchad was *not* totally righteous, unless, of course, he repented.]

מַחְלָה וְנֹעָה ... וְתִרְצָה — *Machlah, Noah, ... and Tirtzah.*

The five daughters are listed in this order in *Numbers* 27:1, but in *Numbers* 36:11 they are presented in a different order: Machlah, Tirtzah, Chaglah, Milcah, and Noah. *Rashi (Numbers* 27:1) comments that the change in order indicates that they were all of equal worth. *Rashbam (Bava Basra* 120a), however, interprets the *Talmud* to mean that the passage in *Numbers* 27 lists the daughters in order of their wisdom, whereas the passage in *Numbers* 36 lists them in order of their age. (Cf. *Or HaChaim* to *Numbers* 27:1.)

4. וַתִּקְרַבְנָה — *And they came.*

Or HaChaim (Numbers 27:1) explains that תִּקְרַבְנָה implies that Tzlofchad's daughters consulted with each other before they talked to Joshua,

יז
ה־ז

לִפְנֵי אֶלְעָזָר הַכֹּהֵן וְלִפְנֵי | יְהוֹשֻׁעַ בִּן־נוּן
וְלִפְנֵי הַנְּשִׂיאִים לֵאמֹר יהוה צִוָּה אֶת־
מֹשֶׁה לָתֶת־לָנוּ נַחֲלָה בְּתוֹךְ אַחֵינוּ וַיִּתֵּן
לָהֶם אֶל־פִּי יהוה נַחֲלָה בְּתוֹךְ אֲחֵי
אֲבִיהֶן: וַיִּפְּלוּ חַבְלֵי־מְנַשֶּׁה עֲשָׂרָה לְבַד ה
מֵאֶרֶץ הַגִּלְעָד וְהַבָּשָׁן אֲשֶׁר מֵעֵבֶר
לַיַּרְדֵּן: כִּי בְּנוֹת מְנַשֶּׁה נָחֲלוּ נַחֲלָה בְּתוֹךְ ו
בָּנָיו וְאֶרֶץ הַגִּלְעָד הָיְתָה לִבְנֵי־מְנַשֶּׁה
הַנּוֹתָרִים: וַיְהִי גְבוּל־מְנַשֶּׁה מֵאָשֵׁר ז
הַמִּכְמְתָת אֲשֶׁר עַל־פְּנֵי שְׁכֶם וְהָלַךְ

Elazar, and the princes. *Meam Loez* suggests that they repeated the argument which they had presented to Moses before Joshua.

לִפְנֵי אֶלְעָזָר הַכֹּהֵן וְלִפְנֵי יְהוֹשֻׁעַ — *Before Elazar the Kohen, before Joshua.*

Joshua, who authored this book, placed Elazar's name before his own name out of modesty *(Meam Loez).*

אֲחֵי אֲבִיהֶן — *The brothers of their father.*

[The daughters of Tzlofchad received an inheritance from two sources. All men who left Egypt including Tzlofchad received a portion of land in *Eretz Yisrael.* Tzlofchad's portion was inherited by his daughters (see *Numbers* 27:1-11). However, the daughters also received an inheritance from Tzlofchad's father, Cheifer. Since Cheifer was also among those men who left Egypt, he too was deserving of a portion of land in *Eretz Yisrael.* After Cheifer died in the Wilderness, his portion in *Eretz Yisrael* was divided among his sons, one of whom was Tzlofchad. However, since Tzlofchad also died in the Wilderness, his inheritance from his father also passed to his daughters.]

It is this second source of inheritance which is referred to by the phrase *among the brothers of their father,* for Tzlofchad's daughters were to share Cheifer's land with their uncles *(Malbim).*

5. עֲשָׂרָה — *Ten.*

There were ten sections of land given to the offspring of Menashe in *Eretz Yisrael (Metzudos).* Of these, six portions went to the brothers mentioned above in verse 2. The remaining four portions went to Tzlofchad's daughters: they received one portion from their father, who was one of the people of the exodus (see previous comment); in addition, they received two portions of Cheifer's property, because their father Tzlofchad was a first-born son; finally, they received a portion from their uncle, who died childless in the Wilderness *(Rashi).*

The ten portions were as follows: (a) from Michmesas to Ein Tapuach (verse 7); (b) Eretz Tapuach until the Kanah River (verses 8-9); (c) from the northern part of Nachal Kanah until the Mediterranean Sea (verse 9); (d) Beis Shean and its villages (verse 11); (e) Yivlam and its villages (verse 11); (f) Dor and its villages (verse 11); (g) Ein Dor and its villages (verse 11); (h) Ta'anach and its villages (verse 11); (i) Megido and its villages (verse 11); and (j) Shloshes HaNefes (verse 11) *(Malbim).*

6. בְּתוֹךְ בָּנָיו — *Among his sons.*

they came before Elazar the Kohen, before Joshua
son of Nun, and before the leaders saying, 'HASHEM
commanded Moses to give us an inheritance among
our brethren.'
And he gave them an inheritance among the
brothers of their father according to the word of
HASHEM. [5] *Ten portions were allotted to Menashe —*
besides the land of Gilead and the Bashan which are
on the other side of the Jordan — [6] *because the*
daughters of Menashe received an inheritance among
his sons. The land of Gilead went to Menashe's
remaining sons.
[7] *And the border of Menashe proceeded from*
Asher to Michmesas which is east of Shechem, and

This verse indicates the great love that the daughters of Tzlofchad had for *Eretz Yisrael*, for they were only willing to take land in *Eretz Yisrael* proper, but not in the Trans-Jordan, where other members of their tribe settled *(Meam Loez)*. [For the difference between *Eretz Yisrael* and the Trans-Jordan, see *footnote* to 22:19.]

◆§ Menashe's Territory

7-13. Menashe's northern border adjoined the territories of Asher (in the west) and Yisachar (in the east). In the south, Menashe's inheritance was bordered by Ephraim's territory; in the east, the Jordan River formed a natural boundary. Menashe's western border adjoined the territory of Dan.

T'vuos HaAretz states (p. 184) that Menashe's northern border went from the Carmel mountains to the northeast of Megido, and then proceeded southeast to Ein Ganim. From there it traveled to the northwest of Beis Shean and continued to the Jordan, just south of the Kineret sea. However, he writes (p. 207) that Yisachar's southern border went as far south as Ramah (Remes) which is clearly within Menashe's territory, according to his description of Menashe's northern border! Perhaps there is no contradiction, for the borders between tribes need not have run in straight lines, as do the border between modern states. It is possible that the tribal boundaries were disjointed and fragmented. Since no author provides more specific information, we have rendered the tribal borders as straight lines to clarify the distinctions between territories. It must be kept in mind, however, that these lines are only first-order approximations.

◆§ Southern Border

7-9. According to *T'vuos HaAretz*, verses 7 through 9 trace Menashe's southern border. Other commentators disagree, as the *Commentary* explains.

7. מֵאָשֵׁר הַמִּכְמְתָת — *From Asher to Michmesas.*

Targum understands מֵאָשֵׁר as a reference to the tribe of Asher. According to this view, since Asher's territory was located to the northwest of Menashe, Scripture is tracing the northern border of Menashe *(Katzvei Eretz)*. Michmesas (as mentioned in the *Commentary* to 16:6-7) was located in the west of *Eretz Yisrael* according to

הַגְּבוּל אֶל־הַיָּמִין אֶל־יֹשְׁבֵי עֵין תַּפּוּחַ:
ח לִמְנַשֶּׁה הָיְתָה אֶרֶץ תַּפּוּחַ וְתַפּוּחַ אֶל־
ט גְּבוּל מְנַשֶּׁה לִבְנֵי אֶפְרָיִם: וְיָרַד הַגְּבוּל
נַחַל קָנָה נֶגְבָּה לַנַּחַל עָרִים הָאֵלֶּה
לְאֶפְרַיִם בְּתוֹךְ עָרֵי מְנַשֶּׁה וּגְבוּל מְנַשֶּׁה
י מִצְּפוֹן לַנַּחַל וַיְהִי תֹצְאֹתָיו הַיָּמָּה: נֶגְבָּה
לְאֶפְרַיִם וְצָפוֹנָה לִמְנַשֶּׁה וַיְהִי הַיָּם גְּבוּלוֹ
וּבְאָשֵׁר יִפְגְּעוּן מִצָּפוֹן וּבְיִשָּׂשכָר
יא מִמִּזְרָח: וַיְהִי לִמְנַשֶּׁה בְּיִשָּׂשכָר וּבְאָשֵׁר
בֵּית־שְׁאָן וּבְנוֹתֶיהָ וְיִבְלְעָם וּבְנוֹתֶיהָ
וְאֶת־יֹשְׁבֵי דֹאר וּבְנוֹתֶיהָ וְיֹשְׁבֵי עֵין־
דֹּר וּבְנוֹתֶיהָ וְיֹשְׁבֵי תַעְנַךְ וּבְנֹתֶיהָ

many commentators. *Targum* appears to be the author of this view.

עַל־פְּנֵי — *East of* [lit. before].
The translation follows *T'vuos HaAretz.*

שְׁכֶם — *Shechem.*
Shechem was a part of Ephraim's territory *(Katzvei Eretz).*

In Abraham's journey to the Land of Canaan, the first city in the Land mentioned as his resting place was Shechem *(Genesis* 12:6). Both Jacob and Abraham built altars in this city.

אֶל־יֹשְׁבֵי עֵין תַּפּוּחַ — *To the inhabitants of Ein Tapuach.*
[Scripture is proceeding in an east-west direction.]

8. אֶרֶץ תַּפּוּחַ — *The land of Tapuach.*
The villages and outlying areas of Tapuach belonged to Menashe, but the city proper belonged to Ephraim *(Rashi).*

◈§ Ephraim's Separated Cities

9. נֶגְבָּה לַנַּחַל — *South of the river.*
This additional phrase is not mentioned in 16:8 which describes these 'separated cities' according to *Malbim.* The phrase implies, and *Katzvei Eretz* maintains, that Menashe's territory actually went south of the Kanah River. The map, however, places the border at the Kanah River proper, in accordance with *T'vuos HaAretz,* who does not comment on this additional phrase.

[See *Commentary* to 16:8-9.]

עָרִים הָאֵלֶּה — *These are the cities.*
These are the 'separated cities' mentioned in 16:9. [See *Commentary* to 16:8 and map.]

Ephraim received the cities within Menashe's territory from Tapuach to the Kanah River *(Rashi).*

Daas Sofrim suggests that these cities were given to Ephraim because Ephraim's territory contained so few cities, while Menashe's had many.

10. נֶגְבָּה לְאֶפְרַיִם — *To the south it was Ephraim's.*
Ephraim was given the southern part of Joseph's inheritance, and Menashe was granted the northern part *(Metzudos).*

Vilna Gaon interprets *to the south* to mean 'to the south of the Kanah River.' [The map does not follow this view as explained in the *Commentary* to 16:6-7.]

the border went to the south to the inhabitants of
Ein Tapuach. 8 *To Menashe belonged the land of*
Tapuach, but Tapuach on the border of Menashe
belonged to the Children of Ephraim. 9 *The border*
descended to the Kanah River — south of the river.
These are the cities of Ephraim among the cities of
Menashe. The border of Menashe was on the north
side of the river, and its enlargement proceeded to the
Sea. 10 *To the south it was Ephraim's and to the north*
it was Menashe's, and the Sea formed his border.
With Asher they met in the north and with Yisachar
in the east. 11 *And Menashe owned in Yisachar and in*
Asher: Beis Shean and its towns, Yivlam and its
towns, the inhabitants of Dor and its towns, the
inhabitants of Ein Dor and its towns, the inhabitants

גְּבוּלוֹ — *His border.*

This refers to Menashe's border *(Metzudos).*

◆§ Northern Border

וּבְאָשֵׁר יִפְגְּעוּן — *With Asher they met.*

This is Scripture's first indication of the northern border of Menashe. Menashe's territory extended northward to Asher's land *(Malbim).*

T'vuos HaAretz comments that Menashe's territory extended in the northwest to Mount Carmel, which belonged to Asher.

מִמִּזְרָח — *In the east.*

Yisachar's territory was located along the Jordan River to the east of Menashe's inheritance *(Metzudos).*

[According to *T'vuos HaAretz* (see map), Yisachar was in the east of *Eretz Yisrael* but not east of Menashe's territory.]

◆§ Menashe's Separated Cities

11. וַיְהִי — *And* [lit. *and it was*].

In addition to the territory mentioned above, Menashe possessed cities in Yisachar's and Asher's territories *(Malbim).*

בֵּית־שְׁאָן — *Beis Shean.*

In the *Talmud* this city was referred to as Bei-Shan. It was located ten miles south of Tiberias and two miles east of the Jordan.

Many natural springs surrounded the city of Beis Shean; Jacob may have been alluding to these in his blessing to Joseph, *blessings of the deep that couches beneath (Genesis* 49:25) [see *Bereishis Rabbah* 98].

Reish Lakish said that if the Garden of Eden is located in *Eretz Yisrael,* its entrance would be Beis Shean. *Rashi* explains that the sweetest fruits in *Eretz Yisrael* grow in this city *(Eruvin* 19a).

For the halachic status of Beis Shean, see *Mikra'ei Kodesh,* Purim, p. 116.

וְיִבְלְעָם — *Yivlam.*

This is probably the village known as Jabla, located southwest of Beis Shean and two miles south of the village Kafra.

דֹּאר — *Dor.*

This city is located on the Mediterranean Sea about ten miles north of Caesarea.

עֵין־דֹּר — *Ein Dor.*

This city was located about three miles northeast of Yizre'el.

יז
יב־יד

וְיֹשְׁבֵי מְגִדּוֹ וּבְנוֹתֶיהָ שְׁלֹשֶׁת הַנָּפֶת׃
יב וְלֹא יָֽכְלוּ בְּנֵי מְנַשֶּׁה לְהוֹרִישׁ אֶת־
הֶעָרִים הָאֵלֶּה וַיּוֹאֶל הַֽכְּנַעֲנִי לָשֶׁבֶת
יג בָּאָרֶץ הַזֹּאת׃ וַיְהִי כִּי חָֽזְקוּ בְּנֵי יִשְׂרָאֵל
וַיִּתְּנוּ אֶת־הַֽכְּנַעֲנִי לָמַס וְהוֹרֵשׁ לֹא
יד הוֹרִישֽׁוֹ׃ וַיְדַבְּרוּ בְּנֵי יוֹסֵף אֶת־

תַּעְנָךְ — *Ta'anach.*
This city was situated in the Valley of Yizre'el, two and one-half miles south of Megido on the Kishon River *(T'vuos HaAretz).*

מְגִדּוֹ — *Megido.*
This city was located on the Kishon River.

Both Ta'anach and Megido are mentioned in Deborah's song in *Judges* 5:19.

שְׁלֹשֶׁת הַנָּפֶת — *In all, three provinces.*
The translation follows *Metzudos.*

T'vuos HaAretz conjectures that this term refers to three places of the same name, all situated in the region of Dor. He asserts that they were located in Asher's territory (p. 242).

12. וְלֹא יָכְלוּ — *But were not able.*
The cities which Menashe was granted in the territories of Yisachar and Asher were not immediately inhabitable. In the future they would be inhabited by Menashe *(Malbim).*

וַיּוֹאֶל הַכְּנַעֲנִי — *And the Canaanites desired.*
Even though the Israelites inhabited the area surrounding these cities, *the Canaanites desired* to dwell in these cities *(Daas Sofrim).*

13. וְהוֹרֵשׁ לֹא הוֹרִישׁוֹ — *But they did not drive them out.*
Scripture gives no reason why the Israelites did not drive out the Canaanites. It is puzzling that the Jews did not fulfill God's command to exterminate the Canaanites *(HaRav Gifter).*

Daas Sofrim comments that it appears that the Jews were not militarily able to drive out the Canaanites. He also suggests that the Jews may not have sought to dislodge the Canaanites because they saw no immediate physical or spiritual danger in sparing them. [This approach, however, does not provide any justification for ignoring the commandment to exterminate the Canaanites.]

[According to *Rambam's* view mentioned in the Prefatory Remarks to Ch. 9, Canaanites may be spared from the Divine decree of extermination if they: (a) accept the seven Noachide laws, (b) pay taxes; and (c) become servants to the Jewish king. Perhaps the Canaanites in these cities did accept these conditions. In this case, the verse could be read as follows: 'When the Jews became strong (and it appeared as though they had enough strength to battle the Canaanites), the Jews intimidated them (through fear of death) into becoming servants (and accepting the other two conditions), and *therefore* they were not required to drive them out.']

This interpretation assumes that the Canaanites could have capitulated to the Israelites even after the Jews crossed the Jordan. This is in accordance with *Rambam's* view that the Canaanites were able to capitulate even after the Israelites crossed the Jordan (see

17 *of Ta'anach and its towns, and the inhabitants of*
12-14 *Megido and its towns; in all, three provinces.* [12] *But*
the Children of Menashe were not able to drive out
the inhabitants of these cities, and the Canaanites
desired to dwell in this land. [13] *It was when the*
Children of Israel became strong that they imposed
tribute on the Canaanites, but they did not drive
them out.
[14] *And the Children of Joseph reproached Joshua*

Prefatory Remarks to Chapter 9 and *footnote* 1).

◆§ Joseph's Demand

14-18. In the following passage, the sons of Joseph reproach Joshua for not giving them sufficient land for their many children. Joshua's reply seems to ignore their request for additional territory, for he merely gives the sons of Joseph his blessing to drive the Canaanites from the land which Joseph's sons had already been given in the lottery.

To understand this passage we must examine exactly how *Eretz Yisrael* was divided. *Numbers* 26:52-54 contains the Torah's directive concerning the division of the Land:

And HASHEM said to Moses saying, 'To these the Land shall be divided for an inheritance according to the number of names. To the more numerous you shall give more inheritance, and to the fewer you shall give less inheritance.'

It would appear from the statement *'To the more numerous you shall give more'* that the sons of Joseph had a strong argument against Joshua, for this verse implies that inheritances could be adjusted in accordance with each tribe's population.

According to *Rashi (Genesis* 48:5 and *Numbers* 26:54), the Torah's command means that each Israelite should receive an equal portion of land, except for a first-born son, who should receive a double portion. It would therefore not be possible, according to this view, for one Israelite to receive a smaller portion than another (except for first-borns) regardless of the size of the tribe to which he belonged. A larger tribe would consequently receive more territory to accommodate its many members.

Ramban (Numbers 26:54), however, maintains that *Eretz Yisrael* was divided into nine and one-half equal divisions [since Reuben, Gad, and part of Menashe received their territory on the eastern side of the Jordan] (see *Rashash* to *Bava Basra* 122a). Within these divisions, the land was further subdivided according to the number of families within each tribe. According to *Ramban,* the directive in *Numbers* 26:54 means merely that a family with more members should receive more land than a family *in the same tribe* with fewer members. However, an individual who belongs to a large tribe will generally not receive as much territory as an individual who belongs to a smaller one, since each tribe received an equal amount of land.

Abarbanel advances a third opinion. In his view the Land was divided so that a tribe with more people *would* receive a larger portion of land, but the increase would not be precisely commensurate with the number of people within the tribe (as *Rashi* maintains). Thus, an individual belonging to a large tribe would still probably receive less land than an individual belonging to a smaller tribe.

יז יְהוֹשֻׁעַ לֵאמֹר מַדּוּעַ נָתַתָּה לִּי נַחֲלָה
יד גּוֹרָל אֶחָד וְחֶבֶל אֶחָד וַאֲנִי עַם רָב עַד

Menashe's complaint *'Why have you given me an inheritance of one draw of the lottery and one portion, seeing that I am a numerous people?'* implies that he received a disproportionately small amount of land, given the large numbers of people in his tribe.[1] This complaint would be understood differently according to the views of *Rashi, Ramban,* and *Abarbanel.*

☐ According to *Ramban,* this disproportion did exist, since each tribe received an equal share of land, no matter how numerous it was. Thus, Menashe was complaining that it was too numerous for this standard plot of land, because the fierce Canaanites populated a significant portion of their territory as related in verses 12 and 13. Joshua replied that there was sufficient land for the tribe of Menashe, if they ascended the forested region and routed the indigenous Canaanites. Menashe more than any other tribe was in a position to do this because he would be able to enlist the aid of Ephraim who was also given land in the same area.

☐ According to *Abarbanel,* Menashe's argument is based on the fact that as a larger tribe, it did not have its living requirements fully met, despite the fact that it received a larger inheritance than did the tribes with fewer members. Joshua suggested that Menashe use Mount Ephraim as a military advantage and eliminate the Canaanites who were occupying part of their territory, thus providing a solution for Menashe's problem of overcrowding.

☐ According to *Rashi's* view that each Israelite received an equal portion of land, however, what was Menashe's complaint? Should each of Menashe's members have received *more* land than the other Israelites?

Mizrachi (Numbers 26:54) explains *Rashi's* view of Menashe's argument. The number of individual plots of land into which *Eretz Yisrael* was divided was based on the census of males between twenty and sixty years of age at the time of the Exodus from Egypt. Each of these males received a plot of land, but those who were younger received nothing (see *Bava Basra* 118a). Similarly, a child born in the Wilderness would not receive his own section of land in *Eretz Yisrael.* When the tribe of Menashe left Egypt it numbered 32,200 *(Numbers* 1:35) and was thus entitled to 32,200 plots of land in *Eretz Yisrael.* When the tribes were counted in Arvos Moav, however, Menashe numbered 52,700 *(Numbers* 26:34). Thus, there were already 20,500 members of the tribe who did not have their own plots of land in *Eretz Yisrael.* Since Menashe had more landless members than any other tribe, Menashe complained to Joshua concerning the overcrowded conditions within its territory.

According to *Rashi,* Joshua emphasized to the tribe of Menashe that since it was such a numerous tribe, it

1. Neither in the census that was taken in the Wilderness nor in the census that was taken in Arvos Moav do we find that the tribes of Menashe and Ephraim were more numerous than the other tribes. However, when they entered the Land, they complained to Joshua, *'Why have you given me an inheritance of one draw of the lottery and one portion, seeing that I am a numerous people whom HASHEM has blessed so greatly?'* (verse 14). Within the seven year span between the conquest and division of the Land, their ranks increased in an extraordinary fashion. This was in fulfillment of Jacob's blessing to them, *let them grow into a multitude in the midst of the Land* (אָרֶץ) [*Genesis* 48:16]. They were to achieve great numbers once they were *in the midst of the Land,* not before. Thus, the Rabbis *(Bava Basra* 118a) interpreted Joshua's reply to them, *If you are such a numerous people, ascend to the forest* (verse 15) to mean that they should remain aloof from the public eye so that the *ein hara* (misfortune) does not befall them *(Vilna Gaon).*

17 *saying, 'Why have you given me an inheritance of*
14 *one draw of the lottery and one portion, seeing that I*

had a great advantage in clearing and settling the forested region from the hands of the Canaanites who occupied it.

Malbim, expressing a minority view among the commentators, takes a different approach in this passage. What divides him from the other commentators is his understanding of how the lottery worked. Most commentators hold that Joshua was unable to alter the territorial borders which were set by God through the procedure of the lottery (see *Commentary* to 14:2). But *Malbim,* in the name of the great Talmudic commentator *Ravad,* contends that Joshua was given Divine sanction to adjust the borders according to the census of each tribe. According to this view, the lottery served only to identify that part of the country — the mountain region, the shore line, etc. — which each tribe would receive.

According to *Malbim,* the tribe of Menashe did succeed in its attempt to gain territory. Menashe was compensated by receiving cities in the territories of Yisachar and Asher (mentioned previously in verse 11). Thus, *Malbim* understands this passage as a flashback which explains why Menashe was granted these cities outside its borders.

14. וַיְדַבְּרוּ — *And [the Children of Joseph] reproached* [lit. *spoke*].

[This term connotes a harsh form of address. Since *the Children of Joseph* were angry, they spoke adamantly to Joshua (see *Sifri* to *Bahaloscha* 12:1).]

וַיְדַבְּרוּ בְּנֵי יוֹסֵף — *And the Children of Joseph reproached.*

It would appear from verse 16 that the term *Children of Joseph* here refers strictly to the tribe of Menashe and does not include the tribe of Ephraim, for in verse 16 they make reference to Beis Shean which was Menashe's city according to verse 11 *(Radak).*

In addition, since this passage records the complaint of *the Children of Joseph* concerning their lack of living space, it would be more reasonable to assume that this was a problem only for the tribe of Menashe, because Menashe's population increased by 20,500 in the Wilderness, while Ephraim's decreased by 8,000. In fact, Ephraim became the least numerous of all the tribes [see *Numbers* 26:37] *(Radak).* [See *Prefatory Remarks* to this passage.]

[In verse 17, however, Joshua responded to both Ephraim and Menashe, thereby implying that both tribes *had* addressed him in verse 14. In this case, *the Children of Joseph* would retain its literal meaning, but Ephraim's motive in complaining to Joshua would require explanation, since Ephraim was not a numerous tribe. Perhaps Ephraim merely joined Menashe's protest in order to support his brother's cause.]

According to *Vilna Gaon* cited in the *footnote,* Ephraim also grew to great numbers after the Israelites entered the Land. The increase was not reflected in the census in Arvos Moav because it occurred chronologically later. Thus, Ephraim also needed more land.

גּוֹרָל אֶחָד וְחֶבֶל אֶחָד — *One draw of the lottery and one portion.*

Ramban (Numbers 26:54) explains this part of Menashe's argument as follows: although the combined territories of Menashe and Ephraim contained the area of two tribes, they had only enough inhabitable land for one tribe. Half the land was useless to them because the Canaanites were so thoroughly entrenched there as verses 12 and 13 indicate. Thus, all this land was equivalent to one draw of the lottery. Consequently, it was only after the tribe of Menashe failed in its attempt to conquer its territory that Menashe approached Joshua for additional land.

Ramban interprets גּוֹרָל אֶחָד literally, as *one draw of the lottery.* He explains that the tribes of Menashe and Ephraim received a double portion of land in one draw the lottery as verse 16:1 indicates. Afterwards, a second draw of the lottery determined which tribe received each sub-division of land, as verses 16:5 and

יז
טו־יז

טו אֲשֶׁר־עַד־כֹּה בֵּרְכַנִי יהוה: וַיֹּאמֶר
אֲלֵיהֶם יְהוֹשֻׁעַ אִם־עַם־רַב אַתָּה עֲלֵה
לְךָ הַיַּעְרָה וּבֵרֵאתָ לְךָ שָׁם בְּאֶרֶץ הַפְּרִזִּי
וְהָרְפָאִים כִּי־אָץ לְךָ הַר־אֶפְרָיִם:
טז וַיֹּאמְרוּ בְּנֵי יוֹסֵף לֹא־יִמָּצֵא לָנוּ הָהָר
וְרֶכֶב בַּרְזֶל בְּכָל־הַכְּנַעֲנִי הַיֹּשֵׁב בְּאֶרֶץ־
הָעֵמֶק לַאֲשֶׁר בְּבֵית־שְׁאָן וּבְנוֹתֶיהָ
יז וְלַאֲשֶׁר בְּעֵמֶק יִזְרְעֶאל: וַיֹּאמֶר יְהוֹשֻׁעַ

17:1 imply. According to *Ramban*, Menashe complained to Joshua that since so many children were born to his tribe in the Wilderness (see *Prefatory Remarks* to this passage), Joshua should not have given him only half of the double portion drawn for the Children of Joseph. [Cf. *Brisker Rav* to *Deuteronomy* 33:17.]

Alternatively, *Ramban* suggests that Menashe may have been contending that it was inequitable to draw just one lot to determine the territory that would contain both Menashe and Ephraim. Instead, Menashe argued, two separate draws should have been made, which would probably have resulted in the two tribes' receiving different land, which might have been easier to vanquish. [Cf. *Malbim* cited in *Commentary* to 16:4. *Malbim* disagrees with *Ramban*, contending that Menashe and Ephraim did have independent draws in the lottery.]

עַם רָב — *A numerous people.*

Menashe increased by more than 20,000 members during the years in the Wilderness *(Rashi)*. (See *Prefatory Remarks* to this passage.)

עַד־כֹּה בֵּרְכַנִי ה׳ — *Whom HASHEM has blessed so greatly* [lit. *until this*].

The translation follows *Rashi.*

The *Midrash* views this statement as the fulfillment of the blessing which God gave to Abraham: *Gaze at the heavens and count the stars if you are able to do so. And He said to him* [*Abraham*], *'So will be the number of your children' (Genesis* 15:5). The word *so* in *Genesis* is כֹּה as in this verse. According to the *Midrash,* the many progeny promised to Abraham were granted through the tribe of Menashe, which increased more than any other tribe *(Rashi).*

Ba'al HaTurim (Numbers 26:28) notes that the word כה has the numerical equivalent of 20 and 5. He suggests that these numbers also hint to the increase in population of Menashe's ranks: 20 thousand and 5 hundred.

15. אִם־עַם־רַב אַתָּה — *If you are such a numerous people.*

If you are as numerous as you say, then you certainly have the manpower to remove the trees in the forested areas *(Rashi).*

According to *Ramban* (cited on the previous verse), Joshua's response means: Even though much of your land is inhabited by Canaanites, there are still areas which can be developed within your borders, *ascend to the forest country and clear an area.*

Malbim (who understands this passage differently than most commentators [see *Prefatory Remarks*]) interprets: I [Joshua] cannot give you territory in any other part of the land, because the lottery has determined that you occupy this area. However, you can extend your territory by ascending into the forested areas.

Joshua is suggesting to Menashe that

am a numerous people whom HASHEM has blessed so greatly?'

15 *Joshua said to them, 'If you are such a numerous people, ascend to the forest country and clear an area for yourselves there — in the land of the Perizzites and Rephaim — if Mount Ephraim is too confined for you.'*

16 *And the Children of Joseph replied, 'The mountain is insufficient for us, and all the Canaanites that inhabit the valley have iron chariots — those in Beis Shean and its villages and those in the Valley of Yizre'el.'*

he extend his borders into the territory of Ephraim *(Radak).*

וּבֵרֵאתָ לְךָ שָׁם — *And clear an area for yourselves there.*

Malbim continues: In the forests you can carve out a new land full of fields and vineyards.

According to *Abarbanel,* however, Joshua was not suggesting that Menashe should deforest Mount Ephraim, but that he should ascend the mountain to gain a military advantage over the Perizzites and Rephaim. Joshua was suggesting that by using the mountain as his base, Menashe should be able to rout the Perizzites and the Rephaim; then he should deforest this Canaanite territory.

כִּי־אָץ לְךָ הַר־אֶפְרָיִם — *If Mount Ephraim is too confined for you.*

The translation follows *Rashi.*

Radak explains that although the valley near this mountain belonged to Menashe, the mountain itself was in Ephraim's territory.

Abarbanel, however translates אָץ as *close by* [for the word אָץ can also mean *quickly* as in 10:13; something which is close by can be quickly obtained]. Thus: You [Menashe] should have no difficulty in vanquishing the Perizzites and Rephaim, since Mount Ephraim (which is your base of operations) is close by.

16. לֹא־יִמָּצֵא לָנוּ הָהָר — *The mountain is insufficient* [lit. *the mountain is not found for us*].

The mountain country is too confined, as you said *(Rashi).*

Abarbanel understands Menashe's comment more literally as a response to Joshua's offering him part of Ephraim's territory. (See *Radak,* verse 15.) Menashe's reply is taken to mean: Ephraim never gave us the mountain; the mountain is not ours.

וְרֶכֶב בַּרְזֶל — *Iron chariots.*

As for your suggestion that we rout the Perizzites and Rephaim, we cannot do this, for they are a mighty nation, with *iron chariots (Rashi).*

Abarbanel continues: And if you did not mean that we should snatch Ephraim's territory, but just use it as a military advantage, how could we fight the Perizzites and Rephaim? They have *iron chariots.*

According to *Malbim,* in this segment of the verse, the tribe of Menashe presents another reason why not to ascend Mount Ephraim: It would be better for us [Menashe] not to deforest the mountain. Let us keep it as a buffer between us and the Canaanites, since they are so mighty. [Presumably, *Malbim* means that if the forest were left standing, the Canaanites' chariots would be unable to attack Menashe.]

אֶל־בֵּית יוֹסֵף לְאֶפְרַיִם וְלִמְנַשֶּׁה לֵאמֹר יז
עַם־רַב אַתָּה וְכֹחַ גָּדוֹל לָךְ לֹא־יִהְיֶה לְךָ יח
גּוֹרָל אֶחָד׃ יח כִּי הַר יִהְיֶה־לָּךְ כִּי־יַעַר הוּא
וּבֵרֵאתוֹ וְהָיָה לְךָ תֹּצְאֹתָיו כִּי־תוֹרִישׁ
אֶת־הַכְּנַעֲנִי כִּי רֶכֶב בַּרְזֶל לוֹ כִּי חָזָק

17. וַיֹּאמֶר יְהוֹשֻׁעַ — *And Joshua responded.*

Malbim, who maintained that Joshua was authorized to give Menashe additional land (see *Prefatory Remarks* to verses 14-18), comments that Joshua became convinced that he needed to add land to Menashe's territory. Therefore, he now granted Menashe those cities within Yisachar's and Asher's territories which are mentioned in verse 17:11.

לְאֶפְרַיִם וְלִמְנַשֶּׁה — *To Ephraim and Menashe.*

[Here, as elsewhere in Scripture, Ephraim is accorded precedence over Menashe. (See *Commentary* to 16:4.)]

עַם־רַב אַתָּה — *You are indeed a numerous people.*

Since you constitute two tribes and are so numerous, you can aid each other in driving out the Canaanites. Thus, you have an advantage over all the other tribes in carrying out this mission *(Ramban).*

לֹא־יִהְיֶה לְךָ גּוֹרָל אֶחָד — *You will not have but one draw of the lottery.*

Since you have such great strength, you will be able to increase your inhabitable area so that you will not have such limited space which appears as *one draw of the lottery (Metzudos).*

Abarbanel continues: I [Joshua] did not mean that Menashe should usurp Ephraim's rights to Mount Ephraim and that you and Menashe will then, in effect, have but one draw of the lottery. Rather, I meant only that he should use Mount Ephraim as a stepping-stone to the territories of the Perizzites and Rephaim. I know that you (Menashe and Ephraim) did not jointly received *one draw of the lottery,* but two. (See *Abarbanel* to verse 16.)

18. The translation of this verse follows *Rashi;* other commentators have rendered it differently.

כִּי הַר יִהְיֶה־לָּךְ — *That mountain shall be yours.*

The verse is referring to that mountain which Joshua suggested they ascend, when he said (verse 15), *'Ascend to the forest country' (Rashi).*

According to *Abarbanel,* Joshua is addressing Ephraim to reassure him that Menashe will not take possession of his mountain. Thus, the verse means: the mountain will always remain yours, Ephraim.

כִּי־יַעַר הוּא — *Precisely because it is a forest.*

Rashi explains: Since it is a forest, it is appropriate that a numerous tribe, such as you, raze and clear it.

Metzudos interprets: Since it is a forest, it will be easy to conquer, because few of the Canaanites live there.

Abarbanel continues: You need not fear, Ephraim, that the mountain's inhabitants will repossess it, because it is an uninhabited forest.

וּבֵרֵאתוֹ — *You can cut it down.*

Rashi explicates: You will be able to cut it down, since you are so numerous.

Abarbanel continues: You, Ephraim, can derive benefit from the forest by cutting wood.

וְהָיָה לְךָ תֹּצְאֹתָיו — *And possess it to its farthest limits.*

Malbim [consistent with his general approach which is explained in the *Prefatory Remarks* to verses 14-18] maintains that Joshua gave Menashe land beyond the mountain, in the territories of Yisachar and Asher.

17
17-18 [17] *And Joshua responded to the House of Joseph, to Ephraim and Menashe, saying, 'You are indeed a numerous people and you possess great strength. You will not have but one draw of the lottery.* [18] *That mountain shall be yours precisely because it is a forest; you can cut it down and possess it to its farthest limits. You are the ones to drive out the Canaanites because they have iron chariots and are strong.'*

וְהָיָה לְךָ תֹּצְאֹתָיו כִּי־תוֹרִישׁ אֶת־הַכְּנַעֲנִי — *And possess it to its farthest limits. You are the ones to drive out the Canaanites.*

You will drive them out because you are so numerous *(Rashi).*

By occupying the mountain region first, you will easily drive out the Canaanites living in Beis Shean *(Metzudos).*

According to *Abarbanel,* Joshua here addresses Menashe: You (Menashe) will be able to drive out the Canaanites because you will establish your base of operations on the mountain. The mountain, however, will not be yours.

כִּי רֶכֶב בַּרְזֶל לוֹ — *Because they have* [lit. *iron*] *iron chariots.*

Since they have chariots of iron, no other tribe could wage war against them *(Rashi).*

Metzudos translates כִּי *in this context* as *although.* He renders: although they have chariots, you will be victorious, because you can use the altitude of the mountain to your military advantage. [See *ArtScroll* edition of *Yechezkel,* Vol. I, p. 93 for a definitive treatment of the word כִּי.]

כִּי חָזָק הוּא — *And are strong.*

You have the strength to succeed in driving them out *(Rashi).*

Since your *mountain* post is so strategically advantageous [it is *strong*], you will succeed in driving them out *(Abarbanel).*

XVIII

The Sanctuary, which had been located in Gilgal, was moved to the city of Shiloh, located in Ephraim's territory [see Commentary *to 16:6*]. *For 369 years, the Sanctuary at Shiloh was to serve as the national focal point of the Jews' service to God (see* Tosefta, Zevachim *13:6). According to* Seder Olam, *this Tabernacle stood from the year 2503 to 2872; Eli was the last Kohen Gadol to serve in it.*

The command to erect a Sanctuary is found in Exodus *25:8,* Make for Me a Sanctuary. *The Torah indicates that this mitzvah was to be fulfilled in several stages. During the Jews' wanderings in the Wilderness, the mitzvah was performed by erecting the portable Tabernacle in each new encampment.*

Two other phases of this mitzvah were specified by the following verses in Deuteronomy: When you cross the Jordan ... to the place where HASHEM will choose ... to dwell' *(11:31-12:5); and,* And they will cross the Jordan ... and when He will give you rest from all your enemies ... and you will dwell in safety; the place which HASHEM will choose ... there bring everything which I command you *(12:10-11).*

Though both passages refer to a Sanctuary, only the second one predicates its

א הוּא: וַיִּקָּהֲלוּ כָּל־עֲדַת בְּנֵי־
יִשְׂרָאֵל שִׁלֹה וַיַּשְׁכִּינוּ שָׁם אֶת־אֹהֶל
ב מוֹעֵד וְהָאָרֶץ נִכְבְּשָׁה לִפְנֵיהֶם: וַיִּוָּתְרוּ
בִּבְנֵי יִשְׂרָאֵל אֲשֶׁר לֹא־חָלְקוּ אֶת־
ג נַחֲלָתָם שִׁבְעָה שְׁבָטִים: וַיֹּאמֶר יְהוֹשֻׁעַ
אֶל־בְּנֵי יִשְׂרָאֵל עַד־אָנָה אַתֶּם מִתְרַפִּים
לָבוֹא לָרֶשֶׁת אֶת־הָאָרֶץ אֲשֶׁר נָתַן לָכֶם

construction on 'rest from enemies and safety.' This distinction implies that, in the first phase, a Sanctuary was to be erected after the Jews crossed the Jordan, but before they achieved rest from their enemies; in the second phase, a Sanctuary was to be built after the Jews were able to dwell in safety in the Land of Israel. The first phase of the command to erect a sanctuary was fulfilled when the Sanctuary was erected at Shiloh; and the second phase was fulfilled when the Beis Hamikdash *[Holy Temple] was erected in Jerusalem.*

Thus, the enumeration of Menashe's difficulties with the unconquered Canaanites within its territory [17:12-18] serves as the background for this chapter in which Scripture informs us that the Sanctuary was moved to Shiloh, thereby inaugurating the first phase of the erection of a Sanctuary in Eretz Yisrael (Daas Sofrim).

The Sanctuary's architecture indicates its semi-permanent status; whereas the portable Tabernacle in the Wilderness had been made of collapsible wooden walls and a roof of draperies, the Sanctuary at Shiloh was made of stone walls and a roof of draperies.

[See Megillah *9b for the halachic differences between the two Sanctuaries.]*

After Scripture's brief account of the establishment of the Sanctuary at Shiloh, Chapter 18 provides a detailed description of Benjamin's territory.

The seven tribes which had not yet received their inheritance are dealt with in the remainder of Chapter 18 and in Chapter 19.

☙ The Sanctuary Moves to Shiloh

1. וַיִּקָּהֲלוּ כָּל־עֲדַת בְּנֵי־יִשְׂרָאֵל — *And the entire community of the Children of Israel assembled.*

This event occurred fourteen years after the Jews entered *Eretz Yisrael,* after the seven years of conquest and the seven years of division of territory among the tribes. The Sanctuary remained in Shilo for 369 years, until the Philistines captured the Holy Ark. Before the Sanctuary stood, it was permissible to offer sacrifices on private altars; however, after it was erected this practice was forbidden *(Radak).*

The entire community of Israelites assembled, including those who were not eligible combatants, out of respect for the Sanctuary *(Chida).*

אֹהֶל מוֹעֵד — *Sanctuary* [lit. *Tent of Meeting*].

We find that this Sanctuary is referred to as a house *(and* [*Chana*] *brought him to the* **house** *of HASHEM in Shiloh* [*I Samuel* 1:24]) and we also find it is referred to as a tent *(He forsook the Sanctuary of Shilo; the* **tent** *where He made his dwelling among man* [*Psalms* 78:60]). The Rabbis *(Zevuchim* 118a) concluded that this Sanctuary had the properties of both a *house* and a *tent* — *stone walls and a roof made of material.*

וְהָאָרֶץ נִכְבְּשָׁה לִפְנֵיהֶם — *The Land had been conquered before them.*

1 *And the entire community of the Children of*
Israel assembled at Shiloh and erected the Sanctuary
there. The Land had been conquered before them.
2 *However, seven tribes remained among the*
Children of Israel who had not yet received their
inheritance. 3 *So Joshua said to the Children of Israel,*
'How long will you be lax in coming to possess the
Land which HASHEM, the God of your fathers, has

Rashi comments that from the time the Sanctuary was established, the land became easier to conquer.

Most of the land had been conquered, but not all. The remainder of the land was not conquered until after Joshua's death *(Vilna Gaon).*

Chida explains that it was the merit of the establishment of the Sanctuary which facilitated the final stage of the conquest.

Malbim, however, preserves the literal meaning of the verse and interpolates: [the southern part of] *Eretz Yisrael* (where Shiloh was located) had been conquered.

Chida comments that this clause explains why the Sanctuary had not been erected earlier. Now that *the Land had been conquered* a permanent location for the Holy Ark would be needed since the Ark would no longer be needed to accompany the Israelites to battle.

2. וַיִּוָּתְרוּ — *However,* [*seven tribes*] *remained.*

The remaining territories of land in *Eretz Yisrael* had not yet been conquered. Had each remaining tribe accepted its territory it would have had the burden of eliminating the Canaanites within their territorial borders. Therefore, the remaining seven tribes stalled the lottery process for the division of the Land so that they could enlist the assistance of the other tribes in the conquest of their territory *(Abarbanel).*

שִׁבְעָה שְׁבָטִים — *Seven tribes.*

The tribes of Reuben, Gad and part of Menashe had already received their inheritances on the eastern side of the Jordan during the days of Moses. In *Eretz Yisrael* proper, the tribes of Judah, Ephraim, and the remainder of Menashe had received their territories. Thus, five tribes had been settled and seven tribes remained *(Rashi).*

[The tribe of Levi is omitted because it received no land.]

3. עַד־אָנָה אַתֶּם מִתְרַפִּים ... לָרֶשֶׁת — *How long will you be lax in coming to possess.*

Joshua emphasized their laxity in *possessing* the Land, not in *dividing* it, for their unwillingness to divide it stemmed from the fact that the entire Land had not yet been conquered (see *Abarbanel* to verse 2).

According to *Malbim,* the Israelites were lax in possessing the Land *because* they were lax in dividing it. God had promised Joshua (13:6) that He would conquer the Land if Joshua divided it, and each tribe learned which territory it would receive. Thus, a delay in the Land's division meant a delay in the Divine conquest.

There is no longer any excuse to delay the further conquest of the Land now that the Sanctuary has been established, and its merit provides protection *(Meam Loez).*

אֲשֶׁר נָתַן לָכֶם ה׳ — *Which HASHEM ... has given you.*

Since the Land is a gift from God, you should be more zealous concerning its acquisition *(Daas Sofrim).*

ד יְהוָה אֱלֹהֵי אֲבוֹתֵיכֶם׃ הָבוּ לָכֶם שְׁלֹשָׁה
אֲנָשִׁים לַשָּׁבֶט וְאֶשְׁלָחֵם וְיָקֻמוּ וְיִתְהַלְּכוּ
בָאָרֶץ וְיִכְתְּבוּ אוֹתָהּ לְפִי נַחֲלָתָם וְיָבֹאוּ
ה אֵלָי׃ וְהִתְחַלְּקוּ אֹתָהּ לְשִׁבְעָה חֲלָקִים
יְהוּדָה יַעֲמֹד עַל־גְּבוּלוֹ מִנֶּגֶב וּבֵית יוֹסֵף
ו יַעַמְדוּ עַל־גְּבוּלָם מִצָּפוֹן׃ וְאַתֶּם תִּכְתְּבוּ
אֶת־הָאָרֶץ שִׁבְעָה חֲלָקִים וַהֲבֵאתֶם אֵלַי
הֵנָּה וְיָרִיתִי לָכֶם גּוֹרָל פֹּה לִפְנֵי יְהוָה
ז אֱלֹהֵינוּ׃ כִּי אֵין־חֵלֶק לַלְוִיִּם בְּקִרְבְּכֶם
כִּי־כְהֻנַּת יְהוָה נַחֲלָתוֹ וְגָד וּרְאוּבֵן וַחֲצִי
שֵׁבֶט הַמְנַשֶּׁה לָקְחוּ נַחֲלָתָם מֵעֵבֶר
לַיַּרְדֵּן מִזְרָחָה אֲשֶׁר נָתַן לָהֶם מֹשֶׁה עֶבֶד
ח יְהוָה׃ וַיָּקֻמוּ הָאֲנָשִׁים וַיֵּלֵכוּ וַיְצַו יְהוֹשֻׁעַ
אֶת־הַהֹלְכִים לִכְתֹּב אֶת־הָאָרֶץ לֵאמֹר

4. שְׁלֹשָׁה אֲנָשִׁים — *Three men.*

The men chosen had the judgment necessary to evaluate the different plots of land and divide them equally according to quality. Although normally one man would have been sufficient to represent the interests of each tribe, here Joshua requested three. *Meam Loez* comments that since the judgment rendered by these men would have financial consequences, the *halachah* requires a three man panel *(beis din)* to make such a decision when a single expert is not available.

לַשָּׁבֶט — *For each tribe.*

This means: for each one of the seven tribes *(Rashi)*.

וְיִכְתְּבוּ אוֹתָהּ לְפִי נַחֲלָתָם — *And describe it in writing according to their inheritance.*

The blessings of Jacob [*Genesis* 49:1-27] and Moses [*Deuteronomy* 33:6-25] formed the basis of a long-standing tradition identifying the location of each tribe's eventual inheritance. Knowing this, Joshua was confident that the tribal messengers would be granted the Divine inspiration to describe the borders of each tribe's land according to God's plan. Therefore he assigned them the task of determining the boundaries *(Malbim)*.

Abarbanel explains that the written description was ordered by Joshua: (a) so that he would learn the different cities and boundaries which were included in each territory or (b) so that the tribes of more numerous population would be given larger areas of land [see the *Prefatory Remarks* to 17:14 for a discussion of the division of the Land]. According to the second explanation, the lottery was employed merely as Divine confirmation of the human decisions made in dividing the Land *(Malbim)*.

וְיָבֹאוּ אֵלָי — *Then they shall return to me.*

Joshua promised them that they would definitely return from their mission *(Meam Loez)*.

5. וְהִתְחַלְּקוּ אֹתָהּ — *They shall divide it.*

This refers both to the land which

18
4-8

given you. 4 *Appoint for yourselves three men for*
each tribe. I will dispatch them, and they will arise
and traverse the Land and describe it in writing
according to their inheritance. Then they shall return
to me. 5 *They shall divide it into seven parts; Judah*
will occupy his territory to the south and the House
of Joseph will occupy their territory to the north.
6 *You shall make a written description of seven parts*
of the Land and bring it here to me. I will then draw
lots for you here before HASHEM our God. 7 *For the*
Levites have no share among you since the service of
HASHEM is their inheritance. Gad, Reuben and part
of Menashe have taken their inheritance on the
eastern side of the Jordan, which Moses the servant
of HASHEM gave them.'
8 *And the men arose and went. Joshua ordered the*
men that went to write a description of the Land,

had previously been conquered and to the land which would be conquered in the future *(Rashi).*

יַעֲמֹד עַל־גְּבוּלוֹ — *Will occupy his territory* [lit. *will stand on his border*].

מִצָּפוֹן — *To the north.*

Joseph's territory occupied the northern stretch of the land that had previously been conquered. There was, however, more land in the north which was still to be conquered *(Rashi).*

6. וְאַתֶּם תִּכְתְּבוּ — *You shall make a written description.*

Joshua now addresses the messengers *(Radak).* Previously he had been addressing the leaders of each tribe *(Meam Loez).*

Meam Loez suggests another interpretation to explain why the command to describe the borders in writing was made twice (once in verse 4 and a second time here). In his view, not all three men requested by Joshua were required to evaluate the Land, only two. The third man was to be the scribe who would write the results of the two surveyors. In verse 4, Joshua told the surveyors to analyze the land which the scribes will write down. Here, Joshua addresses the scribes and commands them to commit their results to writing. [See *Meam Loez* to verse 4.]

פֹּה — *Here.*

This refers to the Sanctuary of Shiloh *(Daas Sofrim).*

7. כִּי אֵין־חֵלֶק לַלְוִיִּם — *For the Levites have no share.*

Scripture explains why only seven portions of land are to be distributed. The Levites do not receive a portion and Judah, Reuben, Gad, Menashe and Ephraim had already received their portions *(Malbim).*

8. וַיָּקֻמוּ הָאֲנָשִׁים — *And the men arose.*

Meam Loez continues: The surveyors immediately left to fulfill Joshua's charge, but the scribes dallied. Joshua ordered them to execute their mission as the later half of this verse recounts.

לְכוּ וְהִתְהַלְּכוּ בָאָרֶץ וְכִתְבוּ אוֹתָהּ
וְשׁוּבוּ אֵלַי וּפֹה אַשְׁלִיךְ לָכֶם גּוֹרָל לִפְנֵי
ט יְהוָה בְּשִׁלֹה׃ וַיֵּלְכוּ הָאֲנָשִׁים וַיַּעַבְרוּ
בָאָרֶץ וַיִּכְתְּבוּהָ לֶעָרִים לְשִׁבְעָה חֲלָקִים
עַל־סֵפֶר וַיָּבֹאוּ אֶל־יְהוֹשֻׁעַ אֶל־הַמַּחֲנֶה
י שִׁלֹה׃ וַיַּשְׁלֵךְ לָהֶם יְהוֹשֻׁעַ גּוֹרָל בְּשִׁלֹה
לִפְנֵי יְהוָה וַיְחַלֶּק־שָׁם יְהוֹשֻׁעַ אֶת־הָאָרֶץ
יא לִבְנֵי יִשְׂרָאֵל כְּמַחְלְקֹתָם׃ וַיַּעַל
גּוֹרַל מַטֵּה בְנֵי־בִנְיָמִן לְמִשְׁפְּחֹתָם וַיֵּצֵא
גְּבוּל גּוֹרָלָם בֵּין בְּנֵי יְהוּדָה וּבֵין בְּנֵי
יב יוֹסֵף׃ וַיְהִי לָהֶם הַגְּבוּל לִפְאַת צָפוֹנָה

וְהִתְהַלְּכוּ ... וְכִתְבוּ — *Go ... describe it in writing.*

Joshua cautioned the scribes not to rely on the words of the surveyors, but to actually see the territories for themselves to insure that everything was reported accurately *(Meam Loez).*

9. לֶעָרִים — *The cities.*

When one tribe received a large city, another tribe would receive two small cities in compensation *(Metzudos).*

10. וַיַּשְׁלֵךְ לָהֶם יְהוֹשֻׁעַ גּוֹרָל — *And Joshua cast lots for them.*

It is surprising that Scripture does not mention that Elazar the Kohen also participated in the lottery as it does in 14:1 (see *Commentary* there). *Meam Loez* suggests that the tribal divisions had previously been made [and unreported by Scripture]. The division mentioned in this verse was the division of each individual tribal inheritance into smaller sub-divisions for each family.

Abarbanel (who disagrees with this interpretation as mentioned in the *Commentary* to verse 2) comments that the lottery mentioned in this verse was not made to determine *where* each of the seven tribes would receive its territory, but rather *how much* territory in each prearranged location each tribe would receive. [See *Commentary* to 17:14. *Abarbanel* here is consistent with his view mentioned there.]

כְּמַחְלְקֹתָם — *According to their divisions.*

That is: according to the divisions as expressed in the following verse *(Metzudos).*

◆§ Benjamin's Territory

11-28. Benjamin's territory was bordered by Ephraim in the north, Judah in the south, and the Jordan River in the east. Benjamin's western border, however, is much more difficult to describe. The problem of its description is discussed in the *footnote* to 16:5.

11. וַיַּעַל גּוֹרַל — *And the draw of the lottery.*

It appears that the lottery for the remaining tribes differed to some degree from that of the five tribes which had already been settled. In *Eretz Yisrael,* Judah, Ephraim, and Menashe had previously received their inheritance in the order of their importance. The lottery merely served to define the borders of the land they were to receive. For the other tribes, however, it appears that the lottery determined not only the borders but also the order in which the respective tribes received their

18
9-12

saying, 'Go, traverse the Land, describe it in writing,
and return to me. I will cast lots for you here before
HASHEM in Shiloh.'

9 And the men went and passed through the land;
they described it in writing, according to the cities of
the seven parts, in a book, and they returned to
Joshua tc the encampment at Shiloh. 10 And Joshua
cast lots for them in Shiloh before HASHEM; there
Joshua apportioned the Land for the Children of
Israel according to their divisions.

11 And the draw of the lottery for the tribe of the
Children of Benjamin came up, according to their
families; the boundary of their lot lay between the
children of Judah and the Children of Joseph.
12 Their border on the northern side was from the

inheritance. This premise is supported by Scripture's statement, *the draw of the lottery for Benjamin came up,* because the expression 'came up' is not used by Scripture concerning the inheritance of the first three tribes *(Daas Sofrim). (Cf. Bava Basra* 122a and *Commentary* to 14:2.)

בֵּין בְּנֵי יְהוּדָה — *Between the Children of Judah.*

Judah's northern border is described in 15:5-11.

וּבֵין בְּנֵי יוֹסֵף — *And between the Children of Joseph.*

Joseph's southern border is described in 16:1-3.

⸎ Benjamin's Northern Border.

[When describing the borders of the territories of Judah and Ephraim,

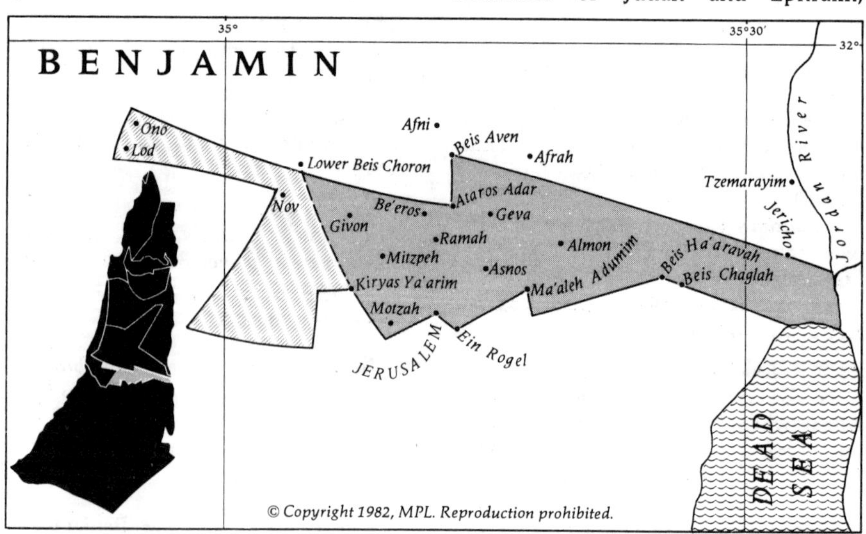

מִן־הַיַּרְדֵּן וְעָלָה הַגְּבוּל° אֶל־כֶּתֶף יְרִיחוֹ
°וְהָיוּ ק׳ מִצָּפוֹן וְעָלָה בָהָר יָמָּה °והיה תֹּצְאֹתָיו
יג מִדְבַּרָה בֵּית אָוֶן: וְעָבַר מִשָּׁם הַגְּבוּל
לוּזָה אֶל־כֶּתֶף לוּזָה נֶגְבָּה הִיא בֵּית־אֵל
וְיָרַד הַגְּבוּל עַטְרוֹת אַדָּר עַל־הָהָר אֲשֶׁר
יד מִנֶּגֶב לְבֵית־חֹרוֹן תַּחְתּוֹן: וְתָאַר הַגְּבוּל°
וְנָסַב לִפְאַת־יָם נֶגְבָּה מִן־הָהָר אֲשֶׁר עַל־
°וְהָיוּ ק׳ פְּנֵי בֵית־חֹרוֹן נֶגְבָּה °והיה תֹּצְאֹתָיו אֶל־
קִרְיַת־בַּעַל הִיא קִרְיַת יְעָרִים עִיר בְּנֵי
טו יְהוּדָה זֹאת פְּאַת־יָם: וּפְאַת־נֶגְבָּה מִקְצֵה
קִרְיַת יְעָרִים וְיָצָא הַגְּבוּל יָמָּה וְיָצָא אֶל־

Scripture commenced with the southern border. In the case of Benjamin, however, the northern border is first to be delineated. Perhaps, this departure from the norm may be explained by the fact that Benjamin, who shared a common border with both Judah in the south and Ephraim in the north, was more closely related to Ephraim, for Rachel was the mother of Benjamin and the grandmother of Ephraim. Benjamin and Judah were only related through their (grand)fathers.]

12. וַיְהִי לָהֶם הַגְּבוּל — *Their border ... was.*

The border commenced at the Jordan and passed to the south of Jericho. Thus, Jericho was in Benjamins' terriotory (*Rashi*).

Benjamin's northern border coincided with Ephraim's southern border (*Katzvei Eretz*).

Scripture is describing the border from east to west (*Malbim*).

יְרִיחוֹ — *Jericho.*

To the east of Jericho was the city of Gilgal where the Jews lodged the first night after crossing the Jordan (4:19). This Gilgal is not to be confused with the other city named Gilgal, which was in Judah's territory (*Katzvei Eretz*).

בָהָר — *To the mountain* [lit. *in the mountain*].

This is the mountain of Beth El (*Metzudos*).

13. בֵּית־אֵל — *Beth El.*

This is the city that Jacob named, not the city of the same name near Ai which was in Joseph's territory. This Beth El was located in Benjamin's territory as verse 22 indicates (*Rashi*).

לוּזָה נֶגְבָּה — *To the southern side of Luz.*

Thus, Luz was outside of Benjamin's border, in the territory of Ephraim (*Rashi*).

עַטְרוֹת אַדָּר — *Atros Adar.*

See *Commentary* to 16:2 for its location.

עַל־הָהָר — *To the mountain.*

The border only went to the mountain near Lower Beis Choron, for that city itself was part of Joseph's territory (16:3).

14. וְתָאַר הַגְּבוּל — *The border proceeded directly.*

Although this verse would seem to describe the western border of Benjamin's territory, this point is in dispute among the commentators.

Rashi understands that Benjamin's

18
13-15

*Jordan. It ascended to the northern side of Jericho
and ascended westward to the mountain; its
enlargement proceeded to the wilderness of Beis
Aven.* 13 *And from there the border passed through
Luz to the southern side of Luz which is Beth El. And
the border descended to Atros Adar to the mountain
on the southern side of Lower Beis Choron.* 14 *The
border proceeded directly and then circled around the
western side, southward from the mountain which
lies before the south side of Beis Choron. Its
enlargement proceeded to Kiryas Ba'al, which is
Kiryas Y'arim, a city of the Children of Judah. This
was the western boundary.* 15 *The southern
boundary: from the edge of Kiryas Y'arim. And the
border broadened toward the sea and broadened to*

northern border ended in Atros Adar and continued south from the mountain on the south side of Lower Beis Choron to Kiryas Y'arim. Thus, Benjamin occupied only the eastern half of the corridor between Ephraim and Judah.

T'vuos HaAretz, however, questions the validity of this interpretation because *Nechemiah* (11:31) and *I Chronicles* (8:12) state that the cities Nov, Chadid, Lod and On were in Benjamin's territory, even though they were fifteen to eighteen miles west of Kiryas Y'arim. He, therefore, asserts that verse 14 does not intend to define absolutely the western border [but only the point at which the northern and southern borders converged]. In reality, the border continued westward at this point and encompassed the areas of Ono, Lod, etc. From this extreme western point, it then returned eastward to Mei Neftoach.

קִרְיַת יְעָרִים — *Kiryas Y'arim.*

The city was located about seven and one half miles north of Jerusalem.

◆§ Benjamin's Southern Border

15-28. Many cities mentioned in the following verses are described in the *Commentary* to other verses. Refer to the *Geographical Index* for the address.

15. וּפְאַת נֶגְבָּה — *The southern boundary.*

Benjamin's southern border coincided with Judah's northern border. Scripture now describes the southern border from west to east *(Rashi).*

וְיָצָא הַגְּבוּל יָמָּה — *And the border broadened toward the sea.*

The interpretation of this phrase is dependent upon the interpretation of verse 14.

Rashi, who holds that Benjamin's western border ended at Atros Adar, understands this phrase to refer to Benjamin's southern border. Thus, the sea referred to here was not the Mediterranean. Because there were no inland seas in this area, however, *Rashi* comments that he does not know which sea Scripture means.

According to *T'vuos HaAretz,* this phrase does not refer to Benjamin's southern border, but to its western border. The boundary proceeded in a western direction, to include the cities mentioned later in the chapter, and then turned around toward Mei Neftoach on the southern border. According to this

יח
טז־כה

טז מַעְיַן מֵי נֶפְתּוֹחַ׃ וְיָרַד הַגְּבוּל אֶל־קְצֵה
הָהָר אֲשֶׁר עַל־פְּנֵי גֵּי בֶן־הִנֹּם אֲשֶׁר
בְּעֵמֶק רְפָאִים צָפוֹנָה וְיָרַד גֵּי הִנֹּם אֶל־
יז כֶּתֶף הַיְבוּסִי נֶגְבָּה וְיָרַד עֵין רֹגֵל׃ וְתָאַר
מִצָּפוֹן וְיָצָא עֵין שֶׁמֶשׁ וְיָצָא אֶל־גְּלִילוֹת
אֲשֶׁר־נֹכַח מַעֲלֵה אֲדֻמִּים וְיָרַד אֶבֶן בֹּהַן
יח בֶּן־רְאוּבֵן׃ וְעָבַר אֶל־כֶּתֶף מוּל־הָעֲרָבָה
יט צָפוֹנָה וְיָרַד הָעֲרָבָתָה׃ וְעָבַר הַגְּבוּל אֶל־
°וְהָיוּ ק׳ כֶּתֶף בֵּית־חָגְלָה צָפוֹנָה °והיה |
°תּוֹצְאוֹת ק׳ °תוצאותיו הַגְּבוּל אֶל־לְשׁוֹן יָם־הַמֶּלַח
צָפוֹנָה אֶל־קְצֵה הַיַּרְדֵּן נֶגְבָּה זֶה גְּבוּל
כ נֶגֶב׃ וְהַיַּרְדֵּן יִגְבֹּל־אֹתוֹ לִפְאַת־קֵדְמָה
זֹאת נַחֲלַת בְּנֵי בִנְיָמִן לִגְבוּלֹתֶיהָ סָבִיב
כא לְמִשְׁפְּחֹתָם׃ וְהָיוּ הֶעָרִים לְמַטֵּה בְּנֵי
בִנְיָמִן לְמִשְׁפְּחוֹתֵיהֶם יְרִיחוֹ וּבֵית־חָגְלָה
כב וְעֵמֶק קְצִיץ׃ וּבֵית הָעֲרָבָה וּצְמָרַיִם
כג־כד וּבֵית־אֵל׃ וְהָעַוִּים וְהַפָּרָה וְעָפְרָה׃ וּכְפַר
°הָעַמּוֹנָה ק׳ °העמוני וְהָעָפְנִי וָגָבַע עָרִים שְׁתֵּים־
כה עֶשְׂרֵה וְחַצְרֵיהֶן׃ גִּבְעוֹן וְהָרָמָה

view, the sea mentioned here is the Mediterranean.

17. גְּלִילוֹת — *Gelilos.*
Katzvei Eretz identifies this city as the Gilgal located in Judah's territory.

18. הָעֲרָבָתָה — *To Aravah.*
This is identical with Beis HaAravah mentioned in Judah's border *(Metzudos).*

19. אֶל־לְשׁוֹן יָם־הַמֶּלַח צָפוֹנָה — *To the northern tip of the Dead Sea.*
Thus, the Dead Sea was in Judah's territory *(Rashi).*

Benjamin's Eastern border

20. וְהַיַּרְדֵּן יִגְבֹּל־אֹתוֹ — *(And) the Jordan borders it.*
The Jordan River ran the entire length of the eastern side of Benjamin's territory *(Rashi).*

Benjamin's Cities

21. וְעֵמֶק קְצִיץ *Emek Ketzitz.*
It was located in Emek Achor but its precise location is unknown.

22. וּצְמָרַיִם — *Tzemarayim.*
It is located approximately four miles north of Jericho near the Jordan.

23. וְעָפְרָה — *And Afrah.*
T'vuos HaAretz cites a source which locates this city five miles east of Beth El.

18 *the spring of Mei Neftoach.* 16 *And the border*
16-25 *descended to the edge of the mountain that lies before*
Gei Ben Hinom at the northern end of the Valley of
Rephaim and descended to Gei Hinom along the
southern side of the Jebusites and descended to Ein
Rogel. 17 *It proceeded directly from the north and*
then broadened to Ein Shemesh. It then broadened to
Gelilos which was across from Ma'aleh Adumim. It
then descended toward Even of Bohan son of
Reuben. 18 *It passed through the northern part which*
lay across from Aravah, and it descended to Aravah.
19 *And the border passed through the northern side*
of Beis Chaglah; the border's enlargement proceeded
to the northern tip of the Dead Sea at the end of the
Jordan. This was the southern border. 20 *The Jordan*
borders it on the eastern side. This is the inheritance
of Benjamin according to its surrounding borders,
according to their families.

21 *These are the cities of the tribe of the Children of*
Benjamin according to their families: Jericho, Beis
Chaglah, and Emek Ketzitz; 22 *Beis HaAravah,*
Tzemarayim, and Beth El; 23 *Avim, Porah, and*
Afrah; 24 *Kefar Amonah, Afni, and Geva — twelve*
cities and their villages; 25 *Givon, Ramah, and Be'eros;*

24. וְהָעָפְנִי — *Afni.*

This city was located approximately two miles north and slightly west of Beth El. It is referred to in *Berachos* 44a as 'Gufnis,' since there is an ג־ע interchange.

וָגָבַע — *Geva.*

It was located about two and one half miles east of Ramah. This is the city where the dastardly incident took place as recounted in *Judges* 20:10.

25. גִּבְעוֹן — *Givon.*

It was located about one mile north and slightly east of Mitzpeh. This was the city where Yochanan ben Kereiach found Yishmael ben Nesanya after Yishmael had killed Gedaliah ben Achikam (*Jeremiah* 41:12).

This city was later given to the Levites by Benjamin (see 21:17).

וְהָרָמָה — *Ramah.*

This city was located about two and one half miles northeast of Mitzpeh.

וּבְאֵרוֹת — *Be'eros.*

This city was located about two and one half miles north and slightly west of *Ramah.*

יח כו וּבְאֵרוֹת: וְהַמִּצְפֶּה וְהַכְּפִירָה וְהַמֹּצָה:
כו־כח כז־כח וְרֶקֶם וְיִרְפְּאֵל וְתַרְאֲלָה: וְצֵלַע הָאֶלֶף
וְהַיְבוּסִי הִיא יְרוּשָׁלִַם גִּבְעַת קִרְיַת עָרִים
אַרְבַּע־עֶשְׂרֵה וְחַצְרֵיהֶן זֹאת נַחֲלַת בְּנֵי־
יט א בִנְיָמִן לְמִשְׁפְּחֹתָם: וַיֵּצֵא
א הַגּוֹרָל הַשֵּׁנִי לְשִׁמְעוֹן לְמַטֵּה בְנֵי־שִׁמְעוֹן

26. וְהַמִּצְפֶּה — *Mitzpeh.*
This town should not be confused with Mitzpeh-Gilead. Rather, it was the place where the prophet Samuel often assembled the people (see *I Samuel* 7:5). It was located north and slightly west of Jerusalem.

וְהַכְּפִירָה — *Kefirah.*
This city was located in the valley of On.

וְהַמֹּצָה — *Motzah.*
This city was located about four miles west and slightly north of Jerusalem and mentioned in the *Mishnah (Succah* 4:5) as the place where the willow branches were gathered for the special *aravah* ritual performed in the *Beis HaMikdash* on Succos.

27. וְתַרְאֲלָה — *Taralah.*
Perhaps this city was located in the vicinity of Lod.

28. וְצֵלַע — *Tzeila.*
This city was located very close to Jerusalem. Kish, the father of King Saul, was buried here *(II Samuel* 21:14).

הָאֶלֶף — *Elef.*
According to *Rashi,* there are five cities mentioned in this verse to make the total of fourteen. Thus, Elef must be a city. Its location is unknown.

Malbim disagrees with *Rashi* that Elef and Kiryas are two individual place names. Rather, he argues that they are a part of the names that precede them. Although the verse states that there were *fourteen cities,* only twelve are mentioned here. The two missing cities are Anasos and Alman which are recorded in 21:18 among the cities which Benjamin gave to the Levites.

וְהַיְבוּסִי הִיא יְרוּשָׁלִַם — *(And) Yevusi which is Jerusalem.*
Scripture also mentions that Judah was given Jerusalem (15:63) for Benjamin and Judah shared the city. There are various opinions concerning whether the altar of the Holy Temple was in Benjamin's territory or in Judah's. One opinion maintains that the altar spanned the territory of both tribes *(Radak).*

גִּבְעַת — *Givas.*
This city was located near Kiryas Y'arim. It was the birthplace of King Saul and was mentioned by the Prophet Samuel after he anointed Saul *(I Samuel* 10:5).

XIX

Chapter 19 contains the geographical delineations of the remaining six tribes: Simeon, Zevulun, Yisachar, Asher, Naftali, and Dan. As the order of inheritances is completed, the tribes of Simeon and Levi are striking in terms of the manner in which they received property in Eretz Yisrael. *Whereas all the tribes received discrete territories within the Land, Simeon and Levi were not allocated any territory* (Ramban, *see* Commentary *to 19:1), only cities.* Ramban (Genesis *49:7) explains that their inheritances differed from the other tribes' in fulfillment of Jacob's words to them before his death,* 'I will divide them in Jacob and scatter them in Israel' (Genesis *49:7).*

18 *26 Mitzpeh, Kefirah, and Motzah; 27 Rekem, Yirp'el,*
26-28 *and Taralah; 28 Tzeila, Elef, Yevusi which is*
Jerusalem, Givas, and Kiryas — fourteen cities and
their villages. This is the inheritance of the Children
of Benjamin according to their families.

19 *1 And the second draw of the lottery was for*
1 *Simeon, to the tribe of the Children of Simeon*

As evidenced from their ruthless scheme of revenge aginst Shechem who violated their sister, Simeon and Levi possessed an impetuous and choleric disposition. Under certain conditions this character trait could be valuable, but under others, it could create serious problems.

When explaining Jacob's words to Simeon and Levi, R' Hirsch (Genesis *49:7) analyzes four key words. The appellations Jacob and Israel are both applied to the Jewish people. Jacob* [יַעֲקֹב *from* עָקֵב, heel] *refers to the Jewish nation in the diaspora, trodden upon and adversely influenced by the other nations. Israel* [יִשְׂרָאֵל *from* שַׂר, prince], *however, is the term used to describe the Jewish people who are independent of the Gentile nations, firmly established in the Land of Israel and guided by Torah leadership. The terms 'divide' and 'scatter' are thematically related to these two terms for the Jewish people.*

When the Jews were settled in Eretz Yisrael *and their state was flourishing, Simeon and Levi needed to be scattered. 'Scatter' has the connotation of dividing something into the smallest possible parts so that it no longer remains intact. In this way their impetuousness would not jeopardize the public welfare, for they would not be able to assume any role of national leadership. Thus Jacob uttered,* 'I will scatter them in Israel', *implying that when the Jewish state is flourishing (Israel), Simeon and Levi's potential for leadership needs to be thwarted. Perhaps it was for this reason that Simeon's cities were scattered through the territory of Judah, for the Jewish monarchy was to descend from the tribe of Judah. As the designated leader of the Jewish people, Judah would be able to maintain firm control over Simeon with this tribe in their midst.*

When, however, the Jews were dispersed from the Land and their sense of Jewish self-esteem might have waned from the alien pressures levied against them, Jacob blessed the nation that Simeon's pluck and tenacity should be divided among all Jews to withstand the pressures of the diaspora. 'Divide,' R' Hirsch *explains, does not mean to break up a whole, but rather to apportion something valuable so that many people can gain a part. Their energy and courage were transmitted to the nation through education, for Simeon as well as Levi constituted the most important group of Jewish scholars and teachers. Thus Jacob said,* 'I will divide them in Jacob,' *for when they are subject to the harsh conditions of exile (Jacob), all will need the qualities of Simeon and Levi to survive.*

◆§ Simeon's Territory

1-8. Simeon's territory[1] stretched as far east as the city of Moladah and in the south to the city of Etzem. The westernmost city was Tziklag and the city furthest north was Ba'alos Be'er.

1. הַגּוֹרָל הַשֵּׁנִי — *The second draw of the lottery.*

1. In addition to the tribe of Simeon receiving cities within the border of Judah, there is evidence that this tribe dwelled among the other tribes as well. According to *Targum Yonason (Genesis 49:7), I will divide them in Jacob* refers to the division of the tribe of Simeon into two

לְמִשְׁפְּחוֹתָם וַיְהִי נַחֲלָתָם בְּתוֹךְ נַחֲלַת
ב בְּנֵי־יְהוּדָה: וַיְהִי לָהֶם בְּנַחֲלָתָם בְּאֵר־
ג שֶׁבַע וְשֶׁבַע וּמוֹלָדָה: וַחֲצַר שׁוּעָל וּבָלָה
ד־ה וָעָצֶם: וְאֶלְתּוֹלַד וּבְתוּל וְחָרְמָה: וְצִקְלַג
ו וּבֵית־הַמַּרְכָּבוֹת וַחֲצַר סוּסָה: וּבֵית

This is the second lottery of the seven remaining tribes mentioned in Chapter 18 *(Rashi).*

לְשִׁמְעוֹן לְמַטֵּה בְנֵי־שִׁמְעוֹן — *For Simeon, to the tribe of the Children of Simeon.*

Simeon is unique in regard to the way Scripture introduces the result of the lottery for its inheritance. The results for the other tribes are introduced either as *For Simeon* or *for the tribe of the Children of Simeon.* Here Scripture employs both expressions. *Poras Yosef* explains that the tribe of Simeon received two different types of inheritance. It received cities directly through the lottery like the other tribes, and thus Scripture uses the expression *to the tribe of the Children of Simeon.* In addition, this tribe received cities from the tribe of Judah. Scripture indicates this method of inheritance by the phrase, *For Simeon.*

בְּתוֹךְ נַחֲלַת בְּנֵי־יְהוּדָה — *Amid the inheritance of the Children of Judah.*

All the other tribes (with the exception of the Levites) received separate, independent portions of land, but Simeon received its inheritance among the tribe of Judah. *Ramban (Genesis* 49:7) explains that Simeon never received a continuous stretch of land; instead the tribe was given scattered cities. [This is why Scripture makes no mention of a border when describing Simeon's inheritance, only individual cities.] This curious form of inheritance was in fulfillment of Jacob's decree *(Genesis* 49:5), *'I will divide them in Jacob and scatter them in Israel.'* [See *Prefatory Remarks.*]

Poras Yosef understands Simeon's dispersion throughout the territory of Judah as retribution for the sin which the prince of Simeon (Zimri ben Salu) committed with the Midianite woman (see *Numbers* 25:6-15).

Some maintain that Scripture only describes the perimeter of Simeon's territory and that the land contained within these borders was also granted to Simeon *(T'vuos HaAretz).*

2. בְּאֵר־שֶׁבַע וְשֶׁבַע — *Be'er Sheva.*

This was one city *(Radak). Malbim,* however, contends they were two different cities.

Vilna Gaon identifies *Be'er Sheva* and *Sheva* as the Be'er Sheva and Bizyosya of Judah's territory, mentioned in 15:28.

parts. One part was distributed among the tribe of Judah and the remainder among the other tribes. This would explain how Yeravam [Jeroboam] ben Nevat ruled over ten tribes, leaving the tribes of Judah and Benjamin within the control of Rechavam ben Shlomo. Scripture makes no mention that the tribe of Simeon made a mass exodus to be ruled by Yeravam, although the tribe of Simeon was counted among the tribes that Yeravam ruled. Simply, Yeravam ruled over those members of Simeon who were dispersed among the other tribes, not the ones within the territory of Judah.

In explaining a particularly difficult *Midrash (Bereishis Rabbah* 98:5), *Netziv (Meishiv Davar* II,64 and *Emek Sha'alah* 30:23) suggests that the fraction of Simeon which dwelled outside the border of Judah lived in close proximity to the Levite cities. *Maharzu (ibid.),* however, advances that this fraction actually lived within all forty-eight Levite cities which were cities of refuge (see Chapters 20 and 21) because they were considered murderers [on account of the action they took against Shechem *(Genesis* 34)].

19
2-5

according to their families. Their inheritance was
situated amid the inheritance of the Children of
Judah. 2 *And they received for their inheritance:*
Be'er Sheva, Sheva, and Moladah; 3 *and Chatzar*
Shu'al, Balah, and Etzem; 4 *and Eltolad, Besul, and*
Charmah; 5 *and Tziklag, Beis Markavos, and Cha-*

וּמוֹלָדָה — *And Moladah.*
T'vuos HaAretz asserts that Simeon's border stretched north of Moladah (mentioned in 15:26) and passed outside Yatir (mentioned in 15:48) and Eshtemoh (mentioned in 15:50) so that these cities were included within Simeon's border.

3. וַחֲצַר שׁוּעָל — *Chatzar Shu'al.*
This city is mentioned in Judah's territory in 15:28.

וּבָלָה — *Balah.*
This is the city Ba'alah (בַּעֲלָה) mentioned in Judah's territory in 15:29 *(Vilna Gaon).* Etzem is also mentioned in 15:29 *(Malbim).*

4. וְאֶלְתּוֹלַד — *Eltolad.*
This city is mentioned in 15:30

וּבְתוּל — *Besul.*
This is the city Kesil mentioned in Judah's territory in 15:30 *(Vilna Gaon).* Charmah is also mentioned in 15:30 *(Malbim).*

5. וְצִקְלַג — *Tziklag.*
Tziklag remained in the possession of Simeon until the times of King David when it was given to the kings of Judah

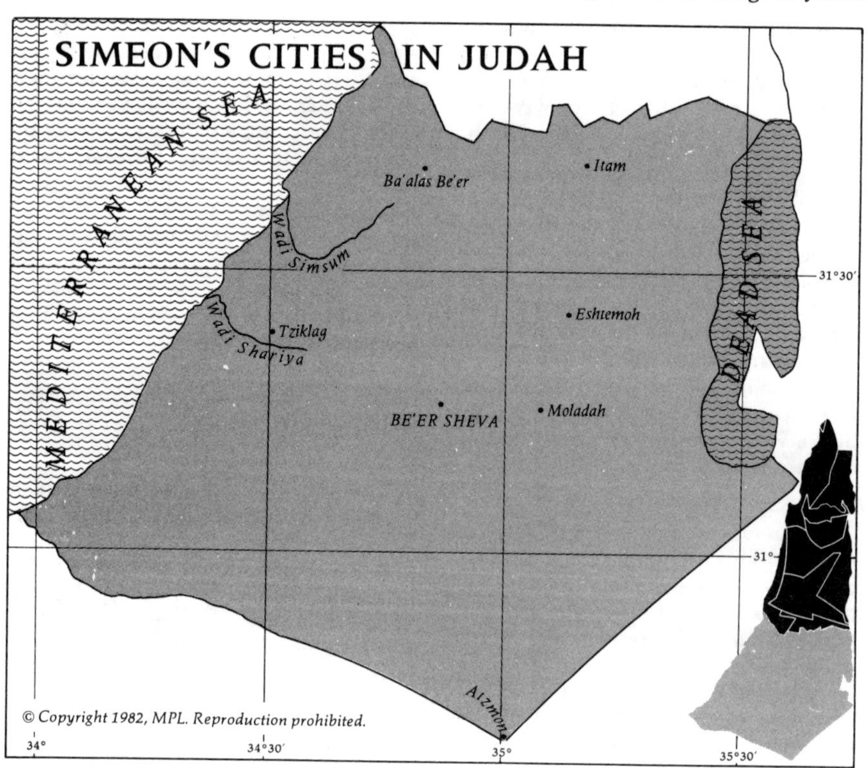

לְבָא֖וֹת וְשָׁרוּחֶ֑ן עָרִ֖ים שְׁלֹשׁ־עֶשְׂרֵ֖ה
ז וְחַצְרֵיהֶֽן׃ עַ֥יִן רִמּ֖וֹן וָעֶ֣תֶר וְעָשָׁ֑ן עָרִ֥ים
ח אַרְבַּ֖ע וְחַצְרֵיהֶֽן׃ וְכָל־הַחֲצֵרִ֗ים אֲשֶׁר֙
סְבִיבוֹת֙ הֶעָרִ֣ים הָאֵ֔לֶּה עַד־בַּעֲלַ֥ת בְּאֵ֖ר
רָאמַ֣ת נֶ֑גֶב זֹ֗את נַחֲלַ֛ת מַטֵּ֥ה בְנֵֽי־
ט שִׁמְע֖וֹן לְמִשְׁפְּחֹתָֽם׃ מֵחֶ֙בֶל֙ בְּנֵ֣י יְהוּדָ֔ה
נַחֲלַ֖ת בְּנֵ֣י שִׁמְע֑וֹן כִּֽי־הָיָ֞ה חֵ֤לֶק בְּנֵֽי־
יְהוּדָה֙ רַ֣ב מֵהֶ֔ם וַיִּנְחֲל֥וּ בְנֵֽי־שִׁמְע֖וֹן בְּת֥וֹךְ
י נַחֲלָתָֽם׃ וַיַּ֙עַל֙ הַגּוֹרָ֣ל
הַשְּׁלִישִׁ֔י לִבְנֵ֥י זְבוּלֻ֖ן לְמִשְׁפְּחֹתָ֑ם וַיְהִ֛י

as *I Samuel* 27:6 states it was mentioned in 15:31 *(Malbim).*

וּבֵית־הַמַּרְכָּבֹת וַחֲצַר סוּסָה — *Beis Markavos and Chatzar Susah.*

Vilna Gaon, followed by *T'vuos HaAretz,* conjectures that these were the cities of Madmanah and Sansanah mentioned in 15:31 as Judah's cities. *Malbim* argues that they were not mentioned previously in Judah's territory.

6. עָרִים שְׁלֹשׁ־עֶשְׂרֵה — *Thirteen cities.*

A count of the city names mentioned above yields fourteen, not *thirteen. Malbim* asserts that Beis Levaos and Sharuchen were the same city. *Sharuchen* refers to the infertile fields situated in front of the city Beis Levaos.

According to *Radak* mentioned in the *Commentary* to verse 2, Be'er Sheva and Sheva were the same city and the total of cities is *thirteen.*

7. עַיִן רִמּוֹן — *Ayin Rimon*

Metzudos maintains that these are two separate cities, but *T'vuos HaAretz* cites the Septuagint which translates these two words as the city of Talca, which *T'vuos HaAretz* locates fifteen miles south of Beis Guvrin. [If these were indeed one city, it is unclear how this verse yields a total of four cities as the latter half of the verse indicates.]

According to *Vilna Gaon* these were the cities of Ein and Rimon mentioned in 15:32.

וָעֶתֶר וְעָשָׁן — *Eser and Ashan.*

These cities were mentioned in 15:42.

עָרִים אַרְבַּע — *Four cities.*

[These cities were located in the south and in the lowlands of Judah's territory, and there is no obvious reason for their exclusion from the above list of thirteen cities. The commentators to *Joshua* do not address this point. However, *Rashi* to *I Chronicles* 4:32 understands that these cities were the villages of the thirteen cities mentioned above, and thus verse 7 is an explanation of the last word in verse 6 — *their villages Metzudos* to *Chronicles* comments that although these places are called cities, they were smaller than the previously mentioned cities and in comparison were called villages.]

8. עַד־בַּעֲלַת — *Until Ba'alas.*

The outskirts of the cities which extended to Ba'aleh were called B'er, Ramas, and Negev *(Malbim).*

According to *T'vuos HaAretz,* Ba'alas Be'er was the name of this city. It is the village Bilin located slightly less than one mile north of Barkus. This city is mentioned in verse 44 as belonging to the tribe of Dan.

9. רַב מֵהֶם — *Was too large for them.*

Judah's portion was larger than they

19
6-10

tzar Susah; [6] *and Beis Levaos and Sharuchen — thir-*
teen cities and their villages. [7] *Ayin, Rimon, Eser,*
and Ashan — four cities and their villages. [8] *And all*
the surrounding villages to these cities until Ba'alas
Be'er and Ramas Negev; this is the inheritance of the
tribe of the Children of Simeon according to their
families. [9] *From the portion of the Children of Judah*
came the inheritance of the Children of Simeon
because the lot of the Children of Judah was too large
for them. Therefore, the Children of Simeon received
their portion inside their inheritance.
[10] *And the third draw of the lottery was for the*
Children of Zevulun according to their families; the

needed, because they conquered much of their territory with the help of Simeon (see *Judges* 1:3,17) *(Radak).* Therefore, it was appropriate that the tribe of Simeon be granted their inheritance within Judah's territory.

☙ Zevulun's Territory[1]

10-16. *T'vuos HaAretz* reports that he exhaustively researched the early and later authorities as well as personally explored the Land and was not able to locate Sarid, Maralah, Dabeshes, Es Katzin, Nei'ah, Chanason, and Gei Yiftach El. It is, therefore, the most difficult of all the inheritances to demarcate. He speculates, based mainly on evidence from the *Talmud,* that Zevulun's eastern border was the Kineret Sea. From there, Zevulun's southern border extended towards Mount Tabor to Davras. From there it traveled slightly north of Shion (which was in Yisachar's territory; see verse 19) which was located between Davras and Yafia and then toward Mount Carmel. It then traveled a northern course from the Kishon River to Akko. In the northeast, Zevulun's territory began at Nachum and traveled westward to Tzipori. From there, a narrow corridor stretched north to Tzidon on the Mediterranean. The borders shown on the map are only reasonable approximations.

It is very important to note that almost every tribe has a portion of its inheritance within the borders of a neighboring tribe. For instance, although Akko was within Asher's boundary, the *Talmud* states that it belonged to Naftali. Although Tzidon Rabbah is within Asher's boundary, it belongs to Zevulun. The Kineret Sea is within Naftali's boundary, but Zevulun had many cities on its coast. Similarly, Menashe owned cities within the borders of Yissachar and Asher, as Scripture mentions (17:11).

10. הַגּוֹרָל הַשְּׁלִישִׁי — *The third draw of the lottery.*

This is the *third draw* of the seven remaining tribes.

1. The relationship between the tribes of Yisachar and Zevulun was novel and famous. Zevulun provided Yisachar with all his material needs so that Yisachar was freed from the burden of earning a livelihood to devote his entire day to the study of Torah. For his largesse, Zevulun was accorded first mention in the blessings of Jacob *(Genesis* 49:13-14) and Moses *(Deuteronomy* 33:18) *(Tanchuma* to *Genesis* 49:11). How appropriate, then, that Zevulun's inheritance in *Eretz Yisrael* is described before Yisachar's, as our passage relates, for it was

יט
יא־יג

יא גְּבוּל נַחֲלָתָם עַד־שָׂרִיד: וְעָלָה גְבוּלָם |
לַיָּמָּה וּמַרְעֲלָה וּפָגַע בְּדַבָּשֶׁת וּפָגַע אֶל־
יב הַנַּחַל אֲשֶׁר עַל־פְּנֵי יָקְנְעָם: וְשָׁב מִשָּׂרִיד
קֵדְמָה מִזְרַח הַשֶּׁמֶשׁ עַל־גְּבוּל כִּסְלֹת
תָּבֹר וְיָצָא אֶל־הַדָּבְרַת וְעָלָה יָפִיעַ:
יג וּמִשָּׁם עָבַר קֵדְמָה מִזְרָחָה גִּתָּה חֵפֶר

שָׂרִיד — *Sarid.*

Some commentators place this city in the northeastern part of *Eretz Yisrael (Katzvei Eretz)*, but others maintain that it is located in the northwestern part (*Metzudos* and *Malbim*).

☙ Zevulun's Western Border

11. וְעָלָה גְבוּלָם — *Their border ascended.*

Their border ascended from Sarid, located in the northwest and proceeded from north to south (*Metzudos*).

לַיָּמָּה — *Westward.*

The translation follows *Targum*. According to *Vilna Gaon*, however, this was the name of a city.

[*Malbim*, who locates Sarid in the northwest, understands this word like *Targum*. According to this view, the western border of Zevulun spread further west as it went south.]

הַנַּחַל — *The wadi.*

Some commentators identify this as the Kishon River, which formed the southwest border of Zevulun's territory (*Malbim*).

This river, also known as Mei Megido, is the area where Elijah the Prophet killed the leaders of the idol Ba'al. It runs south of Mount Tabor westward to the Valley of Yizre'el and empties into the Mediterranean Sea. Its waters are greenish and exist primarily during the rainy season. In the summer the river has very little water.

יָקְנְעָם — *Yakne'am.*

Perhaps this is the city Kaman located about seven and one half miles north of Megido. See *Commentary* to 12:22.

☙ Zevulun's Northern Border

12. וְשָׁב — *And it returned.*

Scripture now recounts the northern border, moving from west to east (*Metzudos* and *Malbim*).

According to the locations that *T'vuos HaAretz* assigns the following cities, it does not appear that Zevulun's northern border is being traced in this

from this land that he actually developed the wherewithal to accommodate Yisachar's uninterrupted Torah study.

According to *Rabenu Yeruchem*, one may stipulate before he studies Torah that his reward should be divided between himself and the individual who financially supports him. However, after he has studied Torah he may not transfer his reward to another. *Rama (Yoreh Deah* 246:1) concurs with *Rabenu Yeruchem*.

Rav Hai Gaon (cited by *Maharam Al Ashker*, Chapter 101) explains that one individual can never purchase the spiritual reward that another has obtained or will obtain from the performance of a mitzvah. By providing another with the means to perform a mitzvah (and especially the mitzvah of Torah study), however, he has done a very meritorious act which brings its own reward. The *Midrash (Vayikra Rabbah* 25:2) states that in the future God will cast a shadow and make a special canopy for benefactors near those in Gan Eiden who actually performed the mitzvos.

Imrei Binah (*Responsum* 13) suggests that *Rabenu Yeruchem* is in complete harmony with *Rav Hai Gaon*, for *Rabenu Yeruchem* only refers to the division of the reward which comes as a result of one who *caused* Torah to be studied. The spiritual reward which accrues for the *actual* study, however, is not subject to division.

border of their inheritance was to Sarid. 11 *Their*
border ascended westward toward Maralah and
reached to Dabeshes and reached to the river
alongside Yakne'am. 12 *And it returned from Sarid*
eastward to the border of Kislos Tavor, and it
broadened to Davras and ascended to Yafia. 13 *And*
from there it passed through the eastern side of Gas

passage, for these cities are located throughout Zevulun's territory.

In *Genesis* (49:13), Jacob blessed his son Zevulun, *'Zevulun shall dwell at the shore of the sea; and he shall be a haven for ships; and his border shall be at Tzidon.'* Thus, Zevulun's territory was to reach Tzidon, which was located considerably north of Zevulun's territory. *Vilna Gaon* followed by *T'vuos HaAretz* suggests that a narrow corridor of land stretched from Zevulun's northern border (around the city of Tzipori) to the city of Tzidon. This corridor cut through Asher's territory. When it approached Tzidon, the corridor widened and resembled a leg. [The word וְיַרְכָתוֹ, *and his border,* could derive from the word יֶרֶךְ, *leg.*]

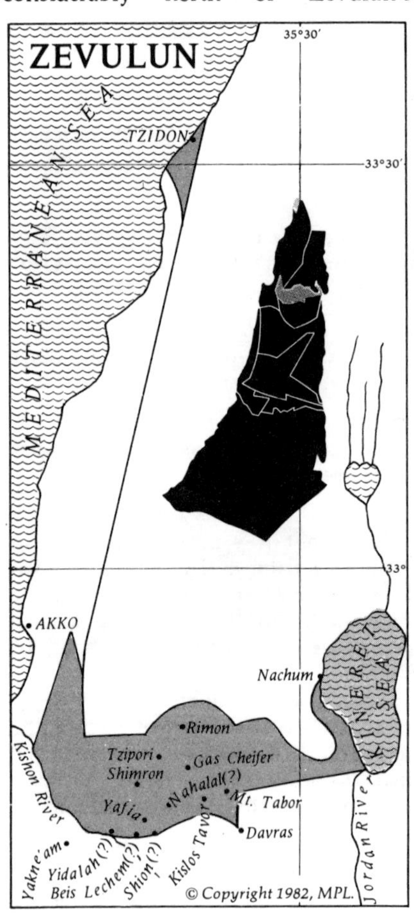

כִּסְלֹת תָּבֹר — *Kislos Tavor.*

It was located approximately two and one-half miles west of Mount Tabor.

Rashi argues that the word *Kislos* is derived from the Hebrew כֶּסֶל [*kesel*] which means the *flank* of an animal (see *Leviticus* 3:4). This city was located on the flank of Mount Tabor and is not identical with Aznos Tavor (cf. however, *Radak* to verse 34). [See *Commentary* to verse 18.]

According to the *Midrash (Bereishis Rabbah* 98:12), it was also known as the city Ichsali.

הַדָּבְרַת — *Davras.*

This city was located about one mile west of Mount Tabor. In Chapter 21, it is identified as a city which the tribe of Yisachar gave to the Levites (verse 28). It, therefore, must have been on the border between Zevulun and Yisachar.

יָפִיעַ — *Yafia.*

This city was located about two and one half miles west and north of Kislos Tavor.

13. וּמִשָּׁם — *And from there.*

From Yafia, the border went south to the east of Gas Cheifer. Thus Gas Cheifer was within Zevulun's border *(Metzudos).*

גִּתָּה חֵפֶר — *Of Gas Cheifer.*

יט
יד־כ

עִתָּה קָצִין וְיָצָא רִמּוֹן הַמְּתֹאָר הַנֵּעָה:
יד וְנָסַב אֹתוֹ הַגְּבוּל מִצְּפוֹן חַנָּתֹן וְהָיוּ
טו תֹּצְאֹתָיו גֵּי יִפְתַּח־אֵל: וְקַטָּת וְנַהֲלָל
וְשִׁמְרוֹן וְיִדְאֲלָה וּבֵית לָחֶם עָרִים
טז שְׁתֵּים־עֶשְׂרֵה וְחַצְרֵיהֶן: זֹאת נַחֲלַת בְּנֵי־
זְבוּלֻן לְמִשְׁפְּחוֹתָם הֶעָרִים הָאֵלֶּה
יז וְחַצְרֵיהֶן: לְיִשָּׂשכָר יָצָא
הַגּוֹרָל הָרְבִיעִי לִבְנֵי יִשָּׂשכָר
יח לְמִשְׁפְּחוֹתָם: וַיְהִי גְּבוּלָם יִזְרְעֶאלָה
יט וְהַכְּסֻלּוֹת וְשׁוּנֵם: וַחֲפָרַיִם וְשִׁיאֹן
כ וַאֲנָחֲרַת: וְהָרַבִּית וְקִשְׁיוֹן וָאָבֶץ:

This was located about two and one half miles southeast of Tzipori and was the burial place of the prophet Jonah *(T'vuos HaAretz).*

עִתָּה קָצִין — *To Es Katzin.*
According to *Rashi,* this was the name of one city.

רִמּוֹן — *Rimon.*
It is located about two miles northeast of Tzipori. Based on a comment of *Alshich, T'vuos HaAretz* identifies this city as Roni mentioned many times in Talmudic literature as the city of Antonious. [This is not the Rimon mentioned in verse 7.]

וְיָצָא רִמּוֹן הַמְּתֹאָר הַנֵּעָה — *And it broadened to Rimon where it curved to Nei'ah.*
The translation follows *Targum.*
Metzudos, however, suggests that the border curved around the city of Nei'ah.
Malbim offers an entirely different understanding. The border which was proceeding from west to east curved around Rimon on three sides and then continued in a westerly manner to the city of Nei'ah. Rimon was referred to as Rimon HaMesoar [lit. *Rimon which was surrounded*] because it was located at the tip of a horn-like projection from Zevulun's territory in the east.

◆§ Zevulun's Southern Border

14. וְנָסַב — *[The border] circled around.*
This is the southern border from east to west *(Malbim).*

15. וְקַטָּת — *And Katas.*
T'vuos HaAretz locates this city approximately three miles east of Tzipori.

וְנַהֲלָל — *Nahalal.*
It was located about two miles southeast of Shimron.

וְיִדְאֲלָה — *Yidalah.*
This city was located about six miles southwest of Shimron.

וּבֵית לָחֶם — *And Beis Lechem.*
This is not the same city mentioned in Judah's territory. In Scripture two different cities are often called by the same name *(Radak).* It was located about seven and one half miles south of Shimron.
According to *Sifri (Deuteronomy* 33:12), this city is not identical with the Beis Lechem [Bethlehem] where Rachel died *(Genesis* 35:19) since that Beis Lechem was located in Benjamin's territory.

עָרִים שְׁתֵּים־עֶשְׂרֵה — *Twelve cities.*
[There appear to be eighteen cities (or

*Cheifer to Es Katzin, and it broadened to Rimon
where it curved to Nei'ah.* 14 *The border circled
around to the north of Chanason, and its
enlargement proceeded to Gei Yiftach El.* 15 *And
Katas, Nahalal, Shimron, Yidalah, and Beis Lechem
— twelve cities and their villages.* 16 *This is the
inheritance of the Children of Zevulun according to
their families — these cities and their villages.*

17 *And the fourth draw of the lottery was for
Yisachar, to the Children of Yisachar according to
these families.* 18 *And their border was: Yizre'el,
Kesulos, and Shuneim;* 19 *and Chafarayim, Shion,
and Anacharas;* 20 *and Harabis, Kishyon, and Evetz;*

nineteen cities, depending upon whether Yamah in verse 11 is truly the name of a city — see *Commentary)* mentioned in the verses which describe Zevulun's territory.]

Metzudos computes the sum of twelve cities as follows: (a) the five cities mentioned in verse 15 and (b) seven cities from the cities mentioned as being on the borders of Zevulun's territory. The additional six border cities actually belonged to neighboring tribes.

Malbim, however, identifies the following as the twelve cities: (1) Sarid, (2) Maralah, (3) Yakne'am, (4) Yafia, (5) Gas Cheifer, (6) Es Katzin, (7) Rimon (Nei'ah), (8) Katas, (9) Nahalal, (10) Shimron, (11) Yidalah, and (12) Beis Lechem. The following cities are excluded: (a) Yamah (which *Malbim* does not identify as a city), (b) Dabashes (because the border only approached this city; it was not contained within Zevulun's border), (c) Davras (which belonged to Yisachar — see 21:28), (d) Chanason (which lay outside Zevulun's territory), and (e) Gei Yiftach El (which was a valley, not a city). [*Malbim* does not explain why Kislos Tavor and Nei'ah were excluded from the total of twelve cities.]

◆§ Yisachar's Territory

17-23. Scripture does not state any borders in regard to Yisachar's territory; only cities are mentioned. By joining these cities, however, Yisachar's border can be derived.

According to *Malbim,* Yizre'el and Kesulos were located on the southwestern border of Yisachar. From these cities the border proceeded northerly on the western flank of Yisachar's territory. The cities mentioned in verses 19, 20, 21 were on this border. From Beis Patzeitz, Yisachar's northern border headed east to the Jordan where it converged with the southern border.

Yisachar's territory reached the Jordan River in the east. It stretched as far north as Mount Tabor and from there the border went past Kesulos and Avetz until Mount Carmel. The entire valley of Yizrael belonged to Yisachar.

Yisachar's territory was surrounded by Menashe on three sides. Perhaps this was hinted at in Jacob's blessing *(Genesis* 49:14), *Yisachar is a strong donkey crouching down between the boundaries (T'vuos HaAretz).*

[Since the boundaries are unknown, the borders shown in the map are only reasonable approximations.]

17. הַגּוֹרָל הָרְבִיעִי — *The fourth draw* of the lottery.

This is the *fourth* draw of the seven remaining tribes.

18. יִזְרְעֶאלָה — *Yizre'el.*

It was located about three miles north

יט
כא־כה

כא וְרֶמֶת וְעֵין־גַּנִּים וְעֵין חַדָּה וּבֵית פַּצֵּץ:
כב וּפָגַע הַגְּבוּל בְּתָבוֹר °ושחצומה וּבֵית
שֶׁמֶשׁ וְהָיוּ תֹּצְאוֹת גְּבוּלָם הַיַּרְדֵּן
כג עָרִים שֵׁשׁ־עֶשְׂרֵה וְחַצְרֵיהֶן: זֹאת נַחֲלַת
מַטֵּה בְנֵי־יִשָּׂשכָר לְמִשְׁפְּחֹתָם הֶעָרִים
כד וְחַצְרֵיהֶן: וַיֵּצֵא הַגּוֹרָל
הַחֲמִישִׁי לְמַטֵּה בְנֵי־אָשֵׁר לְמִשְׁפְּחוֹתָם:
כה וַיְהִי גְּבוּלָם חֶלְקַת וַחֲלִי וָבֶטֶן וְאַכְשָׁף:

°וְשַׁחֲצִימָה ק׳

and slightly east of Ein Ganim.

וְהַכְּסֻלּוֹת — *Kesulos.*
It was located west of Mount Tabor. This is the city Kislos Tavor mentioned in verse 12.

וְשׁוּנֵם — *Shuneim.*
Shuneim was located just north of Yizre'el.

19. וַחֲפָרַיִם — *And Chafarayim.*
Some suggest that this is the city mentioned in the *Mishnah (Menachos* 8a) which supplied the fine flour for the offerings in the Temple *(T'vuos HaAretz).*

וְשִׁיאוֹן — *Shion.*
This city was located near Mount Tabor.

20. וְהָרַבִּית — *Harabis.*
Harabis was located about three miles west of Beis Shean.

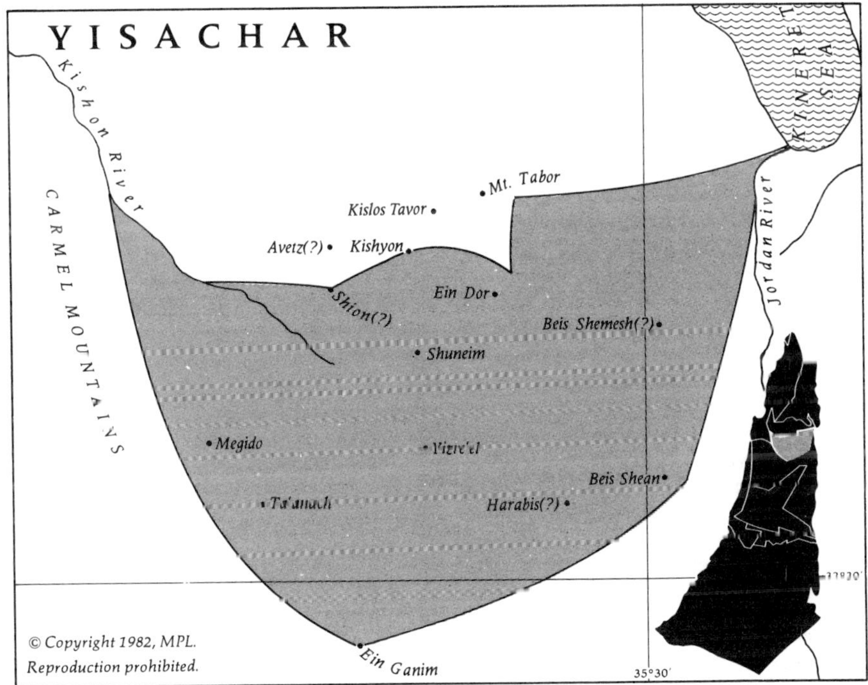

[21] *and Remes, Ein Ganim, Ein Chadah, and Beis*
Patzeitz; [22] *and the border reached Tavor, Shacha-*
tzimah, and Beis HaShemesh. Their border's
enlargement proceeded to the Jordan — sixteen cities
and their villages. [23] *This is the inheritance of the*
tribe of Children of Yisachar according to their
families — the cities and their villages.

[24] *And the fifth draw of the lottery was for the*
tribe of the Children of Asher according to their
families. [25] *And their border was: Chelkas, Chali,*
Beten, and Achshaf; [26] *and Alamelech, Amad, and*

וְקִשְׁיוֹן — *Kishyon.*

It was situated about two and one half miles south of Kesulos and was the source of the Kishon River.

וָאָבֶץ — *And Evetz.*

T'vuos HaAretz speculates that Evetz was located about three miles west of Kesulos and to the south.

21. וְרֶמֶת — *And Remes.*

According to *T'vuos HaAretz,* this city was located on Mount Ephraim. It was known by other names: Yarmus (21:29), Ramos *(I Chronicles* 6:58), Ramah *(I Samuel* 25:1), Ramasayim Tzofim *(I Samuel* 1:1). It was a city given to the Levites and was the place from which Elkanah came. The prophet Samuel was born in this city.

וְעֵין־גַּנִּים — *Ein Ganim.*

The valley of Yizre'el began at Ein Ganim which was located about three miles south of Yizre'el. In *I Chronicles* 6:58 it is referred to as Aneim.

22. בְּתָבוֹר — *Tavor.*

T'vuos HaAretz asserts that this city was located at the top of Mount Tabor.

וּבֵית שֶׁמֶשׁ — *Beis Shemesh.*

According to *T'vuos HaAretz,* Beis Shemesh was located slightly more than six miles southeast of Mount Tabor. This should not be confused with the Beis Shemesh mentioned in Naftali's (verse 38) or Judah's territory (15:10) *(Metzudos).*

◆§ Asher's Territory

24-31. Since precise boundaries are unknown, the borders shown on the map are only reasonable approximations based on the deductions of *T'vuos HaAretz.*

According to *Malbim,* Scripture first traces Asher's southern boundary from east to west, commencing with Chelkas in the southeast to Mishal in the southwest. The western border is then traced from Carmel to Shichor Livnas. Verse 27 begins with the border in the northwest of Asher's territory, traveling from west to east where it intersects Zevulun's territory. At the city of N'i'el the border turns north to the northernmost part of *Eretz Yisrael* — Kavul. In the very north of *Eretz Yisrael* the border travels from Evron to Tzidon Rabbah. The border then turns south and encloses the eastern side of Asher to Charmah and the fortress city of Tzor which is in the southeast of Asher's territory. From there the border traveled westward to Achziv and finally back to Chelkas. The cities mentioned in verse 30 were additional cities Asher was given.

24. הַגּוֹרָל הַחֲמִישִׁי — *The fifth draw of the lottery.*

This is the *fifth draw* of the seven remaining tribes.

25. חֶלְקַת — *Chelkas.*

Chelkas was located about two miles east of Achshaf. It was later given to the Levites (21:31).

וָבֶטֶן — *Beten.*

T'vuos HaAretz cites a source that

כו וְאַלַּמֶּלֶךְ וְעַמְעָד וּמִשְׁאָל וּפָגַע בְּכַרְמֶל
כז הַיָּמָּה וּבְשִׁיחוֹר לִבְנָת׃ וְשָׁב מִזְרַח
הַשֶּׁמֶשׁ בֵּית דָּגֹן וּפָגַע בִּזְבֻלוּן וּבְגֵי
יִפְתַּח־אֵל צָפוֹנָה בֵּית הָעֵמֶק וּנְעִיאֵל
כח וְיָצָא אֶל־כָּבוּל מִשְּׂמֹאל׃ וְעֶבְרֹן וּרְחֹב
כט וְחַמּוֹן וְקָנָה עַד צִידוֹן רַבָּה׃ וְשָׁב הַגְּבוּל
הָרָמָה וְעַד־עִיר מִבְצַר־צֹר וְשָׁב הַגְּבוּל
°וְהָיוּ ק׳ חֹסָה °ויהיו תֹּצְאֹתָיו הַיָּמָּה מֵחֶבֶל
ל אַכְזִיבָה׃ וְעֻמָה וַאֲפֵק וּרְחֹב עָרִים

Beten was situated eight miles east of Akko.

וְאַכְשָׁף — *And Achshaf.*
The Septuagint identifies Achshaf as Haifa, but *T'vuos HaAretz* disagrees and claims that it is located five miles northeast of Akko.

26. וְאַלַּמֶּלֶךְ — *And Alamelech.*
This city was located six miles east and slightly south of Haifa.

וְעַמְעָד — *Amad.*
This city was situated about two and one half miles north of Achshaf.

וּמִשְׁאָל — *And Mishal.*
See *Commentary* to 21:30.

וּבְשִׁיחוֹר לִבְנָת — *And Shichor Livnas.*
This is a river which was once called Belus. Its source is east of Akko and empties near Akko into the Mediterranean Sea. The sand from this area was used to make glass (see *Megillah* 6a).

27. בֵּית דָּגֹן — *Beis Dagon.*
This city was located about two and one half miles [east] of the valley of Bekei'ah.

וּבְגֵי יִפְתַּח־אֵל — *And Gei Yiftach El.*
This valley was mentioned earlier (verse 14) in the description of Zevulun's territory.

בֵּית הָעֵמֶק — *Bais HaEmek.*
This city was located about twelve and one half miles north of Tzfas, and slightly to the west.

כָּבוּל — *Kavul.*
T'vuos HaAretz reports that it is located about five miles northeast of Akko.

מִשְּׂמֹאל — *To the north* [lit. *to the left*].
The translation follows *Targum* to *Genesis* 13:9 that the direction 'left' refers to the compass point north. [Our convention is to place 'north' on the top of the page, but according to Scripture, the directions are given in terms of a person facing east; hence north is to the left and south is to the right. (See *Psalms* 89:13 צָפוֹן וְיָמִין, *north and south). Vilna Gaon's diagram of Eretz Yisrael* showing each tribe's territory places east at the top of the page.]

28. וְעֶבְרֹן — *And Evron.*
This city is identical to Avden which was one of the cities given to the Levites (21:30). It was located in the valley of Wadi Kasmia.

וְחַמּוֹן — *Chamon.*
T'vuos HaAretz conjectures that this city was located about one mile west of Kanah.

וְקָנָה — *And Kanah.*
This city was located about four miles southeast of Tzur.

צִידוֹן רַבָּה — *Tzidon Rabbah.*
This was the burial place of Zevulun,

19 *Mishal; and it reached Carmel westward and Shichor*
27-30 *Livnas.* [27] *And it turned eastward to Beis Dagon, and*
it reached Zevulun and Gei Yiftach El to the north of
Beis HaEmek and N'i'el. It then broadened to Kavul
on the left; [28] *and Evron, Rechov, Chamon, and*
Kanah until Tzidon Rabbah: [29] *And the border*
turned to Ramah and to the fortress city of Tzor; and
the border turned to Chosah, and its enlargement
proceeded to the Sea from the border of Achziv;
[30] *and Umah, Afeik, and Rechov— twenty-two cities*

the son of Jacob. Thus, Zevulun's territory extended to Tzidon, through

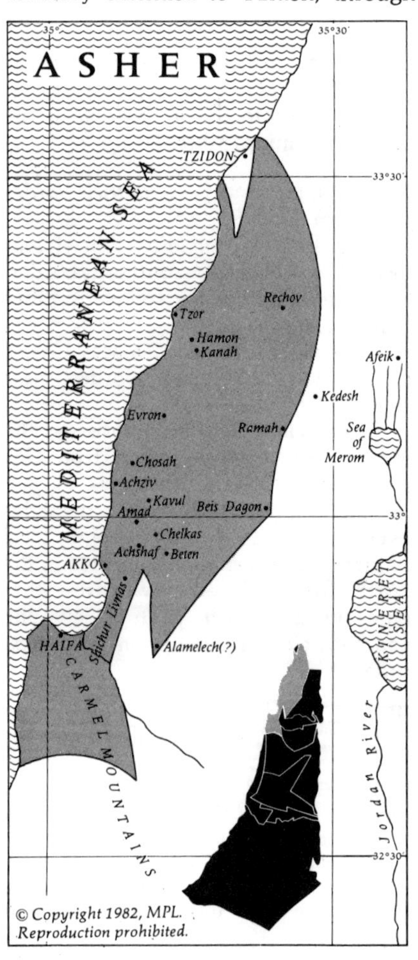

Asher's territory. [The earlier maps of *Eretz Yisrael* reputed to have been based on the view of *Vilna Gaon* show Zevulun's corridor passing through the middle of Asher's territory.]

29. הָרָמָה — *To Ramah.*

This city was located about five miles southwest of Dedesh.

מִבְצַר־צֹר — *The fortress city of Tzor.*

This city is located on the coast of the Mediterranean Sea and was known by the ancients as Tyre.

חֹסָה — *Chosah.*

T'vuos HaAretz conjectures that it was located about two and one half miles northeast of Achshaf.

מֵחֶבֶל אַכְזִיבָה — *From the border of Achziv.*

The boundary proceeded from Chosah to Achziv and from there it went to the sea *(Metzudos).*

Achziv was located about five miles north of Akko on the Mediterranean coast.

30. וַאֲפֵק — *Afeik.*

T'vuos HaAretz conjectures that it was situated about three miles southwest of Banias. Even though this would place it in Naftali's territory, Asher's territory may have stretched through a corridor to that location.

וּרְחֹב — *And Rechov.*

T'vuos HaAretz locates it on his map about ten miles east of Tzor.

לא עֶשְׂרִים וּשְׁתַּיִם וְחַצְרֵיהֶן: זֹאת נַחֲלַת
מַטֵּה בְנֵי־אָשֵׁר לְמִשְׁפְּחֹתָם הֶעָרִים
לב הָאֵלֶּה וְחַצְרֵיהֶן: לִבְנֵי
נַפְתָּלִי יָצָא הַגּוֹרָל הַשִּׁשִּׁי לִבְנֵי
לג נַפְתָּלִי לְמִשְׁפְּחֹתָם: וַיְהִי גְבוּלָם מֵחֵלֶף
מֵאֵלוֹן בְּצַעֲנַנִּים וַאֲדָמִי הַנֶּקֶב וְיַבְנְאֵל
לד עַד־לַקּוּם וַיְהִי תֹצְאֹתָיו הַיַּרְדֵּן: וְשָׁב
הַגְּבוּל יָמָּה אַזְנוֹת תָּבוֹר וְיָצָא מִשָּׁם
חוּקֹקָה וּפָגַע בִּזְבֻלוּן מִנֶּגֶב וּבְאָשֵׁר פָּגַע
מִיָּם וּבִיהוּדָה הַיַּרְדֵּן מִזְרַח הַשָּׁמֶשׁ:

עָרִים עֶשְׂרִים וּשְׁתַּיִם — *Twenty-two cities.*

The fortress city of Tzor was not counted in this total because it belonged to the tribe of Naftali *(Malbim).*

◆§ Naftali's Territory

32-39. The tribe of Naftali was given many cities on the coast of the Kineret Sea even though, according to the *Zohar,* the Kineret Sea itself belonged to Zevulun. Naftali's eastern border stretched along the Jordan River from the village of Tanchum north to the Sea of Merom and the city of Dan. It then traveled west and met Asher's eastern border. Naftali's western border remained east of Gush Chalav and continued south until Zevulun's territory near Shefaram. From there it traveled eastward and remained north of Rimon until it reached the village of Tanchum and the Kineret Sea.

Naftali's territory was blessed[1] with beautiful fruits which would be the earliest to ripen in *Eretz Yisrael (Genesis* 49:21, *Rashi).*

32. הַגּוֹרָל הַשִּׁשִּׁי — *The sixth draw of the lottery.*

This refers to the *sixth draw* of the seven remaining tribes.

33. וַיְהִי גְבוּלָם מֵחֵלֶף — *And their border was from Chelef.*

According to *Metzudos,* Chelef was located on Naftali's southern border. Scripture recounts the following cities from west to east.

Vilna Gaon, however, places *Chelef* on Naftali's northern border near Asher's territory.

T'vuos HaAretz does not discuss the location of this city, but from his placement of the other cities in this verse it is quite apparent that the cities listed are not in any geographical sequence. Betza'ananim is located in the north of Naftali's territory and the other cities in the south. In his view, the southern cities are not in any east-west order.

בְּצַעֲנַנִּים — *Betza'ananim.*

This city was located in the

1. In the blessing Moses bestowed upon Naftali, he said, *O Naftali, whose will is satisfied and is full with the blessing of HASHEM, inherit the west* (or *sea) and the south (Deuteronomy* 33:23). *Sifri* expounds: *whose will is satisfied* — this teaches that Naftali was satisfied with his portion of land, with the seas, fish, and dates; *and is full with the blessing of HASHEM* — this refers to the fields of Ginosar or the court of Tiberias; *west* (or *sea)* — this refers to the sea of Sufni (according to *T'vuos HaAretz,* the Sea of Merom); *south* — this refers to the Sea of Tiberias (Kineret Sea).

19
31-35
and their villages. 31 This is the inheritance of the
tribe of the Children of Asher according to their
families — these cities and their villages.
32 For the Children of Naftali was the sixth draw of
the lottery, the Children of Naftali according to their
families. 33 And their border was: From Chelef, from
Alon Betza'ananim, Adami, Nekev, and Yavn'el until
Lakum. Its enlargement proceeded to the Jordan.
34 The border turned westward to Aznos Tavor and
broadened from there to Chukok; it reached Zevulun
in the south, Asher in the west, and Judah at the
Jordan in the east. 35 And the fortress cities are:

mountains of Naftali, near the city of Kedesh on the coast of the Sea of Merom. According to the *Talmud* (*Jerusalem Megillah* 1:1), Alon and Betza'ananim were two different cities. Alon was Ayalon and Betza'ananim was Aganaya of Kedesh.

וְאֲדָמִי — *Adami.*
This city was located about three miles southwest of Tiberias.

הַנֶּקֶב — *Nekev.*
T'vuos HaAretz identifies this as the city of Tzaidasah located to the southwest of the Kineret Sea.

וְיַבְנְאֵל — *And Yavn'el.*
[The modern day city of Yavn'el is located about two miles southwest of Tzeidasah.]

34. אַזְנוֹת תָּבוֹר — *Aznos Tavor.*
Radak comments that this city is identical with Kislos Tavor mentioned in Zevulun's territory (verse 12; but cf. *Rashi* there). *T'vuos HaAretz* conjectures that it was located near Mount Tabor.

חוּקֹקָה — *Chukok.*
This was the burial place of the Prophet Chabakuk. It was located about ten miles northeast of Mount Tabor.

וּבִיהוּדָה הַיַּרְדֵּן — *And Judah at the Jordan.*
How could Naftali's territory in the north of *Eretz Yisrael* have approached Judah's territory which was located in the south?

Naftali's territory met Judah's at the

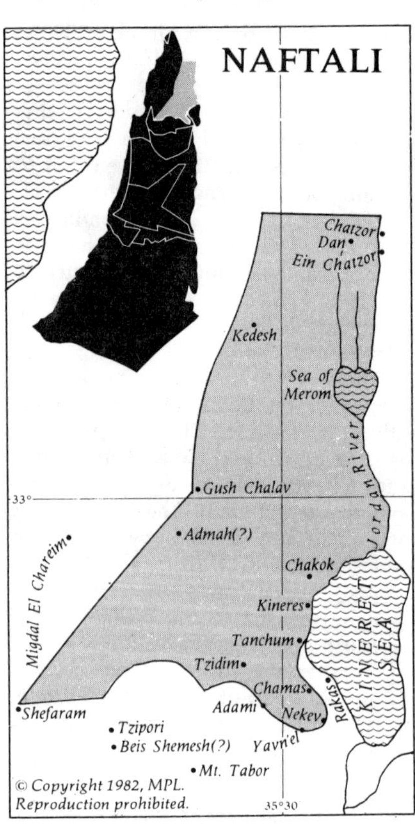

לה וְעָרֵי מִבְצָר הַצִּדִּים צֵר וְחַמַּת רַקַּת
לו-לז וְכִנָּרֶת: וַאֲדָמָה וְהָרָמָה וְחָצוֹר: וְקֶדֶשׁ
לח וְאֶדְרֶעִי וְעֵין חָצוֹר: וְיִרְאוֹן וּמִגְדַּל־
אֵל חֳרֵם וּבֵית־עֲנָת וּבֵית שָׁמֶשׁ עָרִים
לט תְּשַׁע־עֶשְׂרֵה וְחַצְרֵיהֶן: זֹאת נַחֲלַת מַטֵּה
בְנֵי־נַפְתָּלִי לְמִשְׁפְּחֹתָם הֶעָרִים
מ וְחַצְרֵיהֶן: לְמַטֵּה בְנֵי־דָן
מא לְמִשְׁפְּחֹתָם יָצָא הַגּוֹרָל הַשְּׁבִיעִי: וַיְהִי

Jordan, because Naftali inherited the entire river. Consequently, Naftali's territory adjoined that of all the tribes whose border was formed by the Jordan. However, Scripture chose to name Judah because his territory was the furthest south. From this we can deduce that all the other territories which bordered on the Jordan adjoined Naftali's inheritance *(Vilna Gaon; Metzudos).*

Malbim maintains, however, that Naftali inherited land all along the west bank of the Jordan River. The tribes of Ephraim, Benjamin, and Yisachar, in his view, did not receive land extending to the Jordan. Thus, a narrow north-south corridor remained and was allocated to Naftali. Accordingly, Naftali's inheritance in the north connected with Judah's in the south.

T'vuos HaAretz advances a very novel interpretation. The Jordan River within Naftali's territory approached the cities on the east bank of the Jordan called Chavos Yair. As explained in the *Commentary* to 13:30, these cities were conquered and owned by Yair ben Menashe who was from the tribe of Judah. Thus, Naftali's territory extended to Judah's across the Jordan, not in the south of *Eretz Yisrael.*

[Whether the Jordan River itself is considered a part of *Eretz Yisrael* proper is a controversy in the *Talmud (Bechoros* 55a).]

35. הַצִּדִּים — *Tzidim.*

This city was located about five miles west of Tiberias and slightly north.

וְחַמַּת — *Chamas.*

The *Talmud (Megillah* 6a) states that the city Chamas was identical with the city Chamsan. In another passage *(Megillah* 2b), the *Talmud* reports that the distance from Tiberias to Chamsan was one *mil* (approx. 7/10 mile).

רַקַּת — *Rakas.*

The *Talmud (Megillah* 6a) identifies Rakas the city of Tiberias.

וְכִנֶּרֶת — *And Kineres.*

This city was located about two and one half miles north of Tiberias on the shore of the Kineret Sea.

36. וַאֲדָמָה — *And Adamah.*

T'vuos HaAretz places this city five miles west and slightly north of Tzfas.

וְחָצוֹר — *And Chatzor.*

[See *Commentary* to 12:19.]

37. וְקֶדֶשׁ — *And Kedesh.*

This city was located about five miles northwest of the Sea of Merom. The graves of Deborah and Barak are found there *(T'vuos HaAretz).*

According to the *Talmud (Makkos* 10a), the city of Kedesh mentioned in this verse is not the Kedesh mentioned in 20:7 as a city of refuge, but rather a larger city next to it *(Rashi, ibid.).* [Cf., however, *Mishneh LeMelech, Hil. Rotzeach* 8:8 who understands that Kedesh in our verse was disqualified as a city of refuge because it had a wall around it. *Piskei Teshuvah III* explains

19
36-40 *Tzidim, Tzeir, Chamas, Rakas, and Kineres; [36] and*
Adamah, Haramah, and Chatzor; [37] and Kedesh,
Edrei, and Ein Chatzor; [38] and Yiron, Migdal El
Chareim, Beis Anas, and Beis Shemesh — nineteen
cities and their villages. [39] This is the inheritance of
the tribe of the Children of Naftali according to their
families — the cities and their villages.
[40] For the tribe of the Children of Dan according to
their families was the seventh draw of the lottery.

that a walled city, because of its sanctity, has the requirement that a *metzorah* [see *Leviticus* 13:46] must leave its walls. If the murderer, however, became a *metzorah* he would also be required to leave and would thereby violate the prohibition of leaving the city of refuge. See also *Ambuha D'Sifri (Parshas Massei).*]

וְעֵין חָצוֹר — *And Ein Chatzor.*

This city was located about two and one half miles south of Chatzor.

38. וּמִגְדַּל־אֵל חֳרֵם — *Migdal El Chareim.*

This city was situated about eight miles east of Akko.

וּבֵית־עֲנָת — *Beis Anas.*

T'vuos HaAretz conjectures that it was located about twelve and one half miles north of Tzipori.

וּבֵית שָׁמֶשׁ — *Beis Shemesh.*

It was located about two and one half miles south of Tzipori.

עָרִים תְּשַׁע־עֶשְׂרֵה — *Nineteen cities.*

A count will reveal that some twenty-four cities were mentioned. *Metzudos* suggests that Scripture counts the sixteen walled cities and only three of the border cities mentioned in verses 33 and 34. The remaining border cities belonged to neighboring tribes.

Malbim identifies fifteen walled cities in addition to Adomi, Nekev, Yavn'el, Lakum, and Chukok. Chelef and Alon were not names of cities, but places. [*T'vuos HaAretz* identifies Adami and Nekev as two different cities.]

◆§ Dan's Territory

40-48. Just as the camp of Dan followed all the other camps during their travels in the wilderness in Moses' time, so did the tribe of Dan follow all the other tribes in receiving their portion of land *(Daas Sofrim).*

In the southeast, Dan's border began at Ba'alas and continued westward to Ashdod and then to the Mediterranean Sea. *T'vuos HaAretz* cites an opinion that Dan's territory stretched as far north as the city of Dor on the coast of the Mediterranean. Its eastern border (from north to south) began at Ba'alas and traveled through Beis HaShemesh to Ayalon and from there proceeded northwest between Lod and Ramaleh. It then continued north past B'nei Brak to Dor.

The description *T'vuos HaAretz* gives for Dan's southern border could not be reconciled with the map, for his placement of Ba'alas and Ashdod is south of Judah's northern border, which would create the anomaly of Judah's border passing through Dan's territory. We have, therefore, used Judah's northern border as Dan's southern border.

40. הַגּוֹרָל הַשְּׁבִיעִי — *The seventh draw of the lottery.*

This refers to the *seventh draw* of the seven remaining tribes.

גְּבוּל נַחֲלָתָם צָרְעָה וְאֶשְׁתָּאוֹל וְעִיר
מב־מג שָׁמֶשׁ: וְשַׁעֲלַבִּין וְאַיָּלוֹן וְיִתְלָה: וְאֵילוֹן
מד וְתִמְנָתָה וְעֶקְרוֹן: וְאֶלְתְּקֵה וְגִבְּתוֹן
מה־מו וּבַעֲלָת: וִיהֻד וּבְנֵי־בְרַק וְגַת־רִמּוֹן: וּמֵי
הַיַּרְקוֹן וְהָרַקּוֹן עִם־הַגְּבוּל מוּל יָפוֹ:

41. צָרְעָה וְאֶשְׁתָּאוֹל — *Tzarah, Eshta'ol.*
These cities belonged to Judah. Dan's lot fell very close to them *(Rashi).* [See *Commentary* to 15:33 for their location.]

וְעִיר שָׁמֶשׁ — *Ir Shemesh.*
This is the city of Beis Shemesh [see *Commentary* to 15:10].

42. וְשַׁעֲלַבִּין — *Sha'alabin.*
T'vuos HaAretz cites a source which locates this city in the vicinity of Shomron.

וְאַיָּלוֹן — *Ayalon.*
This is the city mentioned in 10:12 where the moon stopped in its course. It is located about twelve miles northwest of Jerusalem.

43. וְאֵילוֹן — *And Aylon.*
Its precise location is unknown, but based on *I Kings* 4:9, it may be deduced that it was located in the vicinity of Sha'alabin and Beis Shemesh.

וְתִמְנָתָה — *Timnah.*
See *Commentary* to 15:10.

וְעֶקְרוֹן — *Ekron.*
See *Commentary* to 15:45.

44. וְאֶלְתְּקֵה — *Eltekei.*
This is the city Eltekon mentioned in Judah's territory (15:59). Perhaps it is the present day village Eltini near Bilin (Balah).

וְגִבְּתוֹן — *Gibson.*
This city was later given to the Levites (21:23). Although its precise location is not known, it was located between Eltekei and Bilin (Balah).
I Kings 15:27 mentions that it was in the city of Gibson that Basha killed Nadav ben Yaravam and usurped the monarchy of Israel.

וּבַעֲלָת — *Ba'alas.*
See *Commentary* to verse 8.

45. וִיהֻד — *And Yehud.*
This city was located about seven and one half miles east of Jaffa.

וּבְנֵי־בְרַק — *Bnei Brak.*
This was the location of Rabbi Akiva's yeshiva *(Sanhedrin* 32b).
It was located about four miles northeast of Jaffa.

וְגַת־רִמּוֹן — *And Gas Rimon.*
T'vuos HaAretz cites a source which locates this city twelve miles north northwest of Beis Guvrin. It was later given to the Levites (21:24).

46. וּמֵי הַיַּרְקוֹן — *And Mei Yarkon.*
T'vuos HaAretz identifies this as Wadi Avgo which flows from the mountains of Lod. Perhaps the city of Yarkon is located near the wadi.

יָפוֹ — *Jaffa* [*Yafo*].
Jaffa is the port city of Jerusalem and is located on the coast of the Mediterranean Sea about twelve miles northwest of Lod.

47. וַיֵּצֵא גְּבוּל בְּנֵי־דָן מֵהֶם — *And the boundary of the Children of Dan was not sufficient for them* [lit. *went out*].
The translation follows *Radak.*
Since the tribe of Dan did not receive a sufficient amount of land, they waged war against Leshem to acquire more property. This territory was not located in *Eretz Yisrael* proper, but rather in the northeast section,[1] across from the

1. Dan's receiving land in two separate parts of *Eretz Yisrael* was in fulfillment of Moses' blessing to Dan, *Dan is a lion's whelp that leaps from Bashan (Deuteronomy* 33:22). *Sifri*

19 41 The border of their inheritance was: Tzarah,
41-47 Eshta'ol, and Ir Shemesh; 42 and Sha'alabin, Ayalon,
and Yislah; 43 and Aylon, Timnas, and Ekron; 44 and
Eltekei, Gibson, and Ba'alas; 45 and Yehud, Bnei
Brak, and Gas Rimon; 46 and Mei Yarkon and
HaYarkon with the border opposite Jaffa. 47 And the

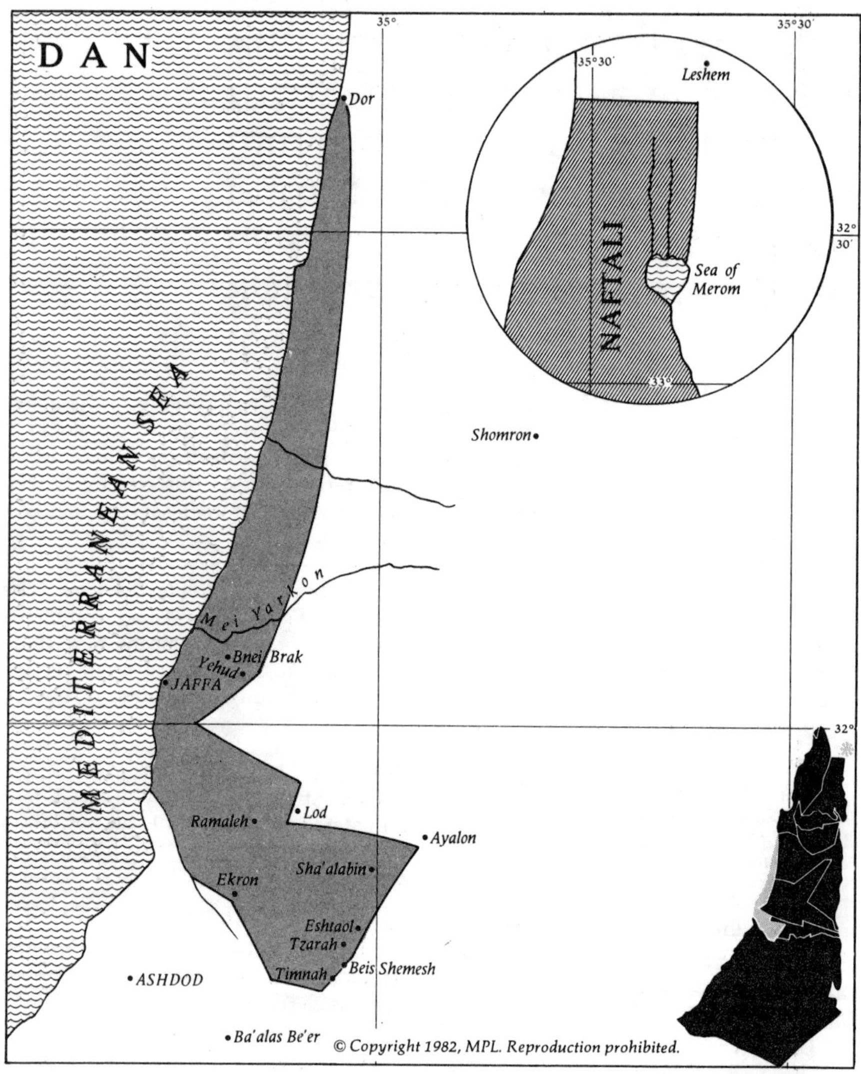

expounds: Just as the Jordan River originates from one source and divides into two [*R' Menachem Stern*] so the tribe of Dan will take his inheritance in two places. The tribe of Dan is compared to a lion because his inheritance [in the northeast] was on the border of the Land.

מז וַיֵּצֵ֥א גְב֥וּל בְּנֵי־דָ֖ן מֵהֶ֑ם וַיַּעֲל֣וּ בְנֵי־דָ֡ן
וַיִּלָּחֲמ֣וּ עִם־לֶ֠שֶׁם וַיִּלְכְּד֨וּ אוֹתָ֜הּ | וַיַּכּ֧וּ
אוֹתָ֣הּ לְפִי־חֶ֗רֶב וַיִּֽרְשׁ֤וּ אוֹתָהּ֙ וַיֵּ֣שְׁבוּ בָ֔הּ
מח וַיִּקְרְא֤וּ לְלֶ֙שֶׁם֙ דָּ֔ן כְּשֵׁ֖ם דָּ֥ן אֲבִיהֶֽם׃ זֹ֗את
נַחֲלַ֛ת מַטֵּ֥ה בְנֵי־דָ֖ן לְמִשְׁפְּחֹתָ֑ם הֶעָרִ֥ים
מט הָאֵ֖לֶּה וְחַצְרֵיהֶֽן׃ וַיְכַלּ֥וּ לִנְחֹ֛ל
אֶת־הָאָ֖רֶץ לִגְבוּלֹתֶ֑יהָ וַיִּתְּנ֨וּ בְנֵי־יִשְׂרָאֵ֧ל
נ נַחֲלָ֛ה לִיהוֹשֻׁ֥עַ בִּן־נ֖וּן בְּתוֹכָֽם׃ עַל־פִּ֨י
יְהוָ֜ה נָ֣תְנוּ ל֗וֹ אֶת־הָעִיר֙ אֲשֶׁ֣ר שָׁאָ֔ל אֶת־
תִּמְנַת־סֶ֖רַח בְּהַ֣ר אֶפְרָ֑יִם וַיִּבְנֶ֥ה אֶת־
נא הָעִ֖יר וַיֵּ֥שֶׁב בָּֽהּ׃ אֵ֣לֶּה הַנְּחָלֹ֡ת
אֲשֶׁר־נִחֲל֣וּ אֶלְעָזָ֣ר הַכֹּהֵ֣ן | וִיהוֹשֻׁ֣עַ בִּן־נ֡וּן
וְרָאשֵׁ֣י הָאָב֣וֹת לְמַטּ֣וֹת בְּנֵי־יִשְׂרָאֵ֣ל |

inheritance of Naftali. This is what the Rabbis meant when they said that the Jordan received its name because it originated in the territory of Dan *(Metzudos).* [See *Commentary* to 1:2.]

Some commentators suggest that Leshem had originally been given to the tribe of Dan, but they delayed in conquering it; others suggest that the territory of Leshem had never been a part of the division, but was annexed by Dan later in history *(Radak).*

וַיַּעֲלוּ בְנֵי־דָן — *The Children of Dan ascended.*

This battle took place after Joshua's death during the days of Asniel ben Kenaz *(Rashi)* [It is mentioned in *Judges* 18.]

לֶשֶׁם — *Leshem.*

This is the city of Layish mentioned in *Judges* 18:29 in the conquest of Dan.

48. זֹאת נַחֲלַת מַטֵּה בְנֵי־דָן — *This is the inheritance of the tribe of the Children of Dan.*

The commentators do not explain why Scripture does not list the number of cities Dan was given as it does with Benjamin and all the successive tribes.

50. עַל־פִּי ה׳ — *According to the directive of HASHEM.*

This phrase informs us that Joshua took possession of this city by Divine fiat, not out of self-serving motives *(Ralbag).*

Numbers (26:55) states, *But with a lottery you shall divide the land.* The *Talmud (Bava Basra* 122a) comments that the word *but* is meant to exclude Calev and Joshua, who did not receive their land through the lottery [but by gift].

נָתְנוּ לוֹ — *They gave him.*

Even though Joshua himself administered the lottery, he did not take a city until others gave it to him *(Meam Loez).*

אֲשֶׁר שָׁאָל — *Which he requested.*

They consulted the *urim v'tumim,* which confirmed Joshua's choice of Timnas Serach.

תִּמְנַת־סֶרַח — *Timnas Serach.*

This city was located five miles south and slightly west of Shechem. It is shown on the map of Ephraim's territory (Chapter 16). Joshua, his

19
48-51

boundary of the Children of Dan was not sufficient for them so the Children of Dan ascended and battled with Leshem, captured it, and vanquished it by the edge of the sword. They took possession of it, dwelled there, and called Leshem, Dan after the name of their ancestor. [48]*This is the inheritance of the tribe of the Children of Dan according to their families — these cities and their villages.*

[49]*And they completed apportioning the Land according to its borders; the Children of Israel gave Joshua son of Nun an inheritance within their midst.* [50] *They gave him the city which he requested according to the directive of HASHEM — Timnas Serach in Mount Ephraim. He built the city and dwelled there.*

[51] *These are the inheritances which Elazar the Kohen, Joshua son of Nun, and the leaders of the tribal families of the Children of Israel divided by*

father, and Calev were buried here *(T'vuos HaAretz).*

In *Judges* 2:9, Joshua's city, Timnas Serach, is called Timnas Cheres, because a figure of a sun appeared on his gravestone [*cheres* means, 'sun'; see *Job* 9:7] in order that each passerby should bemoan, 'Woe that the man who made the sun stand still is dead' *(Rashi).*

Others say that Timnas Cheres was the city's true name, but that it was called Timnas Serach because before Joshua lived there its fruits appeared as earthenware [*cheres* also means 'earthenware'] (devoid of juice), but after he arrived the abundance of juice in its fruits caused them to spoil [*serach* means 'rot'] if they were kept too long. Some argue that this was not a blessing. They propose that before Joshua lived there the fruits would spoil because of their over-abundance of juice, but after Joshua's arrival they would keep indefinitely [like 'earthenware'] *(Bava Basra* 122b, *Rashbam).*

וַיִּבְנֶה אֶת־הָעִיר — *He built the city.*

Joshua chose this location even though he would have to build the city because it was located in Mount Ephraim which was an environment particularly suited for prophecy. The city Ramas Tzofim (mentioned in *I Samuel* (1:1) was located in Mount Ephraim [*tzofim* means 'prophets'] *(Meam Loez).*

51. נִחֲלוּ — *Divided by lottery* [lit. *inherited*].

[Those mentioned in this verse did not inherit the portions of land, but rather] 'caused the Israelites to inherit' the Land *(Rashi).*

וְרָאשֵׁי הָאָבוֹת לְמַטּוֹת — *And the leaders of the tribal families* [lit. *leaders of the fathers of the tribes*].

The translation follows *Metzudos.*

The *Talmud (Yevamos* 89b) derives from the seemingly extra word *fathers* [*Rashi*] the legal principle, *hefker beis din hefker,* which allowed the Sages to divest an individual's

יט נא
בְּגוֹרָל | בְּשִׁלֹה לִפְנֵי יְהוָֹה פֶּתַח אֹהֶל
מוֹעֵד וַיְכַלּוּ מֵחַלֵּק אֶת־הָאָרֶץ:

proprietary rights and — according to some (see *Rashba* to *Gittin* 36b) — to transfer these rights to new owners of the same property. For example, a woman who was married by virtue of a Rabbinic enactment (but not according to the strict letter of Biblical law) is inherited by her surviving husband. Her legal heirs, in absence of a valid marriage, are thus divested of her estate in favor of her husband. See further *Davar Avraham I*, 1:5.

וַיְכַלּוּ מֵחַלֵּק אֶת־הָאָרֶץ — *And they completed the division of the Land.*

Malbim argues that the seeming repetition of this phrase (see verse 49) confirms his theory regarding the methods used to divide the Land (for a fuller explanation, see *Commentary* to 17:14). In his view, the lottery merely identified the geographical area where each tribe would receive its inheritance, not the precise boundaries. Joshua was empowered to determine the size of each territory on the basis of the population of each tribe. By mentioning this phrase twice, Scripture indicates that *both* methods of land allocation had been completed.

XX

The Talmud (Makos *10b) explains that if an individual committed a murder, he would quickly flee to a city designated as a 'city of refuge.'*[1] *Every crossroads in the Land was required to have a sign pointing to the closest city of refuge, and the roads leading there were required to be maintained in excellent repair in order to facilitate the murderer's flight to the city of refuge. If, at his subsequent trial, he was found guilty by the* beis din *(court) of willful manslaughter, he was executed. If, however, he was found guilty of unintentional manslaughter, he was sentenced to return to and remain within the confines of the city and make a new life there. This halachically imposed exile from his former environment served as an expiation for his crime, for although he had acted unpremeditatedly, he was responsible for the murder of another human being, an individual bearing the stamp of his Creator, and as such was unable to live his life as he had before. He needed to be ever mindful of the crime he had committed; if given a position of honor in his new community, he was required to declare, 'I am a murderer.' If his electory said, 'In spite of that, we nominate you,' he was permitted to take office. Upon the death of the* Kohen Gadol *(High Priest), he was granted permission to return to his city (see* Commentary *to verse 6).*

The city of refuge could not have a wall around it (Mishneh LeMelech *to* Hil. Rotzeach *8:8) and was to be of medium size. If its population decreased, all classes of Jews — Kohanim, Levites, and Israelites, — were brought in so that any murderer would be able to find a relative who lived within the city to serve as a source of*

1. The sequence of events described here follows *Rambam (Hil. Rotzeach* 5:7-8) who rules that all murderers, intentional and unintentional, go unescorted to the city of refuge after they have murdered. The court of the city in which the incident occurred then summons the murderer to trial. If he is found guilty of the type of unintentional murder whose punishment is banishment to a city of refuge, he is *then* escorted by two pious scholars to the city of refuge. Their function is to inform the 'avenger of blood' that the murderer is undeserving of their revenge because he committed the crime by accident (see *Aruch LeNer* to *Makos* 10b). According to *Ben Yehudah (Responsum* 20), *Rambam's* ruling is based on the fact that he decides according to R' Yosi bar Yehudah who states that both intentional and unintentional murderers were allowed to flee to a city of refuge before their trial. According to the *tanna kama,* however, that only unintentional murderers were allowed to flee to a city of refuge before trial, he would be escorted by the scholars before the trial, as well.

19 *lottery in Shiloh before HASHEM at the door of the*
51 *Sanctuary. And they completed the division of the*
Land.

comfort (Aruch LeNer). *Water and food markets had to be available within the city. In further fulfillment of the Torah's decree that the murderer must flee* to one of these cities and live (Deuteronomy *4:43), the* Talmud (Makos *10a) comments that the teacher of a student of Torah who was exiled to a city of refuge was obligated to follow him to his new residence and teach him there, for the Torah states that he must live, and how could he live if he could not study Torah from his teacher?*

These designated cities were called 'cities of refuge' for they served as a haven for the murderer from the גּוֹאֵל הַדָּם, avenger of blood. *This was a relative or court-appointed individual (see* Commentary *to verse 3) who was empowered by the Torah to kill the unintentional murderer if he willfully left his new community. In a sense, this relative potentially lurking outside the city limits served as a compelling motivation for the murderer to remain in the city of refuge. If, however, the avenger of blood killed his kinsman's murderer within the city limits, he was tried as a willful murderer who was liable to capital punishment.*

In several passages, the Torah mentions the significance of the cities of refuge (see Numbers *35;* Deuteronomy *4 and 19). Before the Jews crossed the Jordan River, Moses designated three cities in the Trans-Jordan to serve as cities of refuge (Betzer, Ramos Gilead, and Golan). These cities were not in effect as cities of refuge until Joshua designated the three cities on the western side of the Jordan in fulfillment of the Torah's command that there should be six cities of refuge* (Numbers *35:13). In addition to these six cities, the Torah required that the forty-two cities given to the Levites (see Chapter 21) also serve as cities of refuge. The difference between the original six and the additional forty-two is that the original six cities protected the unintentional murderer from recrimination by the avenger of blood whether or not he intended the city to protect him, whereas the forty-two cities of the Levites only protected him if protection was his intention.*[2]

Not all accidental deaths were judged unintentional. According to the oral tradition, there are three categories of accidents: (a) where the accused was so negligent in his behavior that the murder committed bordered on being intentional (e.g., he razed his wall which was adjacent to a public thoroughfare and the stones fell on a passerby); (b) where the accused was so unresponsible for the cause of the death that the murder committed bordered on being beyond his control (e.g., he razed his wall which was adjacent to a place that no one ever frequents, but unexpectedly someone passed by and was killed by the deluge of rocks); and (c) where the murder was purely accidental but the accused was somewhat responsible (e.g., during the day he razed his wall which was adjacent to a place that people frequent at night but not during the day, and the stones fell on a passerby). Only murders in this last category carry the penalty of exile to the city of refuge (Rambam, Hil. Rotzeach, *Ch. 6).*

---

2. *Minchas Chinuch* (502) interprets *Rashi (Makos* 10a) to mean that the additional forty-two Levite cities which were used as cities of refuge only protected the unintentional murderer if at the time he entered the city he intended the city to protect him. However, if he entered without such intention, but later decided to take advantage of the city's protection, these cities would not afford him protection.

Meshech Chachmah (Numbers 35:15) argues that the six cities of refuge which provide protection even without the murderer's intention only provide this benefit for a Jew. However, a *ger toshav* (see *Commentary* to verse 9) is only protected by these cities if he intends that the city should protect him.

כ
א־ג

א־ב וַיְדַבֵּר יהוה אֶל־יְהוֹשֻׁעַ לֵאמֹר׃ דַּבֵּר
אֶל־בְּנֵי יִשְׂרָאֵל לֵאמֹר תְּנוּ לָכֶם אֶת־עָרֵי
הַמִּקְלָט אֲשֶׁר־דִּבַּרְתִּי אֲלֵיכֶם בְּיַד־מֹשֶׁה׃
ג לָנוּס שָׁמָּה רוֹצֵחַ מַכֵּה־נֶפֶשׁ בִּשְׁגָגָה
בִּבְלִי־דָעַת וְהָיוּ לָכֶם לְמִקְלָט מִגֹּאֵל

The establishment of these cities as the first act of state after the division of the Land was a declaration that in Eretz Yisrael *the lives of the citizens were the holiest and most precious of all earthly treasures. It was a recognition that human beings were created in the image of God, which is the value upon which the entire Torah is predicated. If man was merely an animal, then force, selfishness, and satisfying one's desires would be the sole forces of his life, and the concepts of justice, love of one's fellow man, and moral sanctification would be irrelevant. But these concepts form the basis upon which the Torah rests.*

They assume the higher dignity and value of human beings who are created in the image of God. Justice is predicated upon one's fellow man being created in the image of God, while love and moral sanctification assume that the individual himself was created in that likeness. Indifference to the loss of innocent blood could not be tolerated for one moment in Eretz Yisrael *for it would be tantamount to open denial of the principle that man was created in God's likeness. If this principle were denied, there would be no justification for the state, for* Eretz Yisrael *was only given to the Jews on the condition that they uphold the Torah, not deny any of its fundamentals. Thus, when the avenger of blood was authorized by the court — or where necessary even appointed by it (see* Commentary *to verse 3) — it was not only done for the sake of the victim or his relative, but also for the sake of the state whose fundamental principle had been violated by the death of one of its citizens* (R' Hirsch).

1. וַיְדַבֵּר אֶל־יְהוֹשֻׁעַ — *And HASHEM spoke to Joshua.*

Scripture describes God's communication with Moses differently than it does His communication with other prophets. The verb וַיְדַבֵּר, *he spoke*, is only used when God speaks to Moses, whereas the verb וַיֹּאמֶר is typically used when God addresses the other prophets. This is the only verse [in the *Book* of *Joshua*] which describes God's speaking to Joshua with the verb וַיְדַבֵּר *(Rashi* to *Makos* 11a).

This striking exception led the *Talmud (Makos* 11a) to comment that this entire passage (Chapter 20) is 'Torah,' even though it is written in the prophets. The *Talmud's* comment has received various interpretations:

□ *Rashi (Makos* 11a) understands that this passage is different because it is the only one in which God told Joshua to fulfill a command in the Torah. The other instances in *Joshua* where the expression וַיֹּאמֶר is employed do not charge Joshua to fulfill a commandment in the Torah. (The Pentateuch specifically outlines the guidelines for the cities of refuge in *Numbers* 35:9-34.) [Thus, Scripture adopts the language of the Pentateuch when this Torah command is expressed to Joshua.]

□ *Vilna Gaon* suggests that this passage is introduced by the expression וַיְדַבֵּר because its parallel passage in *Numbers* 35:9 is introduced by the expression וַיְדַבֵּר.

□ Some commentators understand that in a certain sense this passage has the status of the Pentateuch. Whenever God spoke to Moses by the term וַיְדַבֵּר, Scripture implies that many details of

20
1-3

1 And HASHEM spoke to Joshua saying, 2 'Speak to
the Children of Israel, saying, "Designate the
cities of refuge which I mentioned to you through
Moses — 3 where a murderer may flee, one who kills a
person through carelessness, unintentionally. They
will be a haven for you from the avenger of blood.

the communication (laws) transmitted to Moses were not written down, but were kept within the Oral Tradition. According to this view, Scripture uses וַיְדַבֵּר to signify that Joshua here received an additional communication which was not recorded in the text but was added to the Oral Tradition *(Malbim* to *Leviticus* 1:1).

☐ Others understand that Joshua was similar to Moses in the sense that God could reveal details of certain commandments to him *(Meshech Chachmah,* Introduction to *Exodus).*

2. תְּנוּ לָכֶם אֶת־עָרֵי הַמִּקְלָט — *Designate* [lit. *give to you*] *the cities of refuge.*

This passage concerning the allocation of cities of refuge follows the passage which mentions the completion of the division of the Land and parallels the juxtaposition of these two topics in the Pentateuch. *Numbers* 35, in which the cities of refuge are first mentioned, also follows the passages *(Numbers* 33:50 — 34:29) which enumerate some of the details of the division of *Eretz Yisrael (Radak).*

The Jews were not required to set aside cities of refuge until the Land was divided. Thus, this passage does not appear until after *Eretz Yisrael* has been divided *(Malbim).*

Sifri (Numbers 35:10) states that the cities of refuge were to be designated after the Land has been 'conquered and settled.' *Ramban (Deuteronomy* 19:1) understands that 'settled' means by living in the cities and houses. Therefore, there must have been some delay between the conclusion of the division and the designation of the cities of refuge.

Meam Loez comments that this command needed to be given even though the people were aware of the Pentateuch's command to designate cities of refuge after the conquest of the Land, because the Land was not, in fact, entirely conquered (see *Lev Aharon* cited in *Commentary* to 13:8).

The acquisition of *Eretz Yisrael* required the spilling of much blood. This passage concerning the separation of cities of refuge also served to counteract any possible tolerance for unauthorized bloodshed by reminding the Jews of the severe penalty for even an unpremeditated murder *(Daas Sofrim).*

אֲשֶׁר־דִּבַּרְתִּי אֲלֵיכֶם — *Which I mentioned to you.*

The verb דִּבֵּר has a forceful and harsh connotation. God employed this expression to cause the people to designate these cities immediately and not to tarry as they had in the conquest of the Land [see *Commentary* to 13:1] *(Kli Yakar).*

3. בִּשְׁגָגָה בִּבְלִי־דָעַת — *Through carelessness, unintentionally.*

In describing the type of murder which incurs the penalty of exile to a city of refuge, *Numbers* 35:15 states that it was committed *through carelessness,* while *Deuteronomy* 4:42 states that it was committed *unintentionally.* This verse cites both criteria which the *Talmud (Makos* 7b) interprets as follows: (a) *through carelessness* excludes an individual from exile to a city of refuge because he killed purposely. According to *Rambam (Hil. Rotzeach* 6:10), who follows Rava's position, this refers to an individual who thought it was permissible to murder and thus committed his act. Even if such an individual seeks refuge in one of the designated cities, he may be killed by the avenger of blood. (b) *unintentionally* excludes an in-

כ
ד־ו

ד הַדָּם: וְנָס אֶל־אַחַת | מֵהֶעָרִים הָאֵלֶּה
וְעָמַד פֶּתַח שַׁעַר הָעִיר וְדִבֶּר בְּאָזְנֵי זִקְנֵי
הָעִיר־הַהִיא אֶת־דְּבָרָיו וְאָסְפוּ אֹתוֹ
הָעִירָה אֲלֵיהֶם וְנָתְנוּ־לוֹ מָקוֹם וְיָשַׁב
ה עִמָּם: וְכִי יִרְדֹּף גֹּאֵל הַדָּם אַחֲרָיו וְלֹא־
יַסְגִּרוּ אֶת־הָרֹצֵחַ בְּיָדוֹ כִּי בִבְלִי־דַעַת
הִכָּה אֶת־רֵעֵהוּ וְלֹא־שֹׂנֵא הוּא לוֹ
ו מִתְּמוֹל שִׁלְשׁוֹם: וְיָשַׁב | בָּעִיר הַהִיא עַד־
עָמְדוֹ לִפְנֵי הָעֵדָה לַמִּשְׁפָּט עַד־מוֹת

dividual who intended to kill an animal but accidentally killed a man standing next to it instead from going to a city of refuge. Or, it refers to an individual who killed a man because he mistook him for an animal (*Tosafos, Bava Kama* 26b, s.v. פרט). According to *Rambam (ibid.)* this is another example of an act of negligence which is deemed intentional.

לְמִקְלָט — *Haven.*

Only while he remained within these designated cities would the one who murdered unintentionally be protected from the relatives of the deceased who sought to avenge his kinsman's death.

מִגֹּאֵל הַדָּם — *From the avenger of blood.*

Anyone who inherits the estate of the deceased (according to the Torah's law of inheritance) is the avenger of blood (*Rambam, Hil. Rotzeach* 1:2). If the victim does not have any relatives who could serve as the avenger of the blood, then the court would appoint one (*Sanhedrin* 45b, *Rashi*; cf., however *Ramban, Aseh* 13 to *Sefer HaMitzvos* of *Rambam*).

Before the unintentional murderer permanently lives in the city of refuge (i.e., before his trial and on return from his trial), the avenger of blood may not cause him any harm. If, however, once inside the city the murderer willfully decides to leave, it is permissible, although not a mitzvah, for the avenger to kill him (*Rambam, ibid.*, 5:9-10).

4. The following procedure concerning the admittance of the murderer to the city of refuge is not mentioned in the Pentateuch.

פֶּתַח שַׁעַר הָעִיר — *At the entrance to the city gate.*

[This refers to the *beis din* (court) of the city.]

אֶת־דְּבָרָיו — *His words.*

The murderer had to explain how his murder was unintentional (*Metzudos*).

בְּאָזְנֵי זִקְנֵי הָעִיר־הַהִיא — *(In the ears of) To the elders of that city.*

Meam Loez points out that the murderer needed to explain his case before the most pious men of the city, which would undoubtedly cause him great embarrassment. Because he felt this embarrassment about his act, he was awarded entry to the city of refuge.

וְאָסְפוּ אֹתוֹ — *They shall take him into.*

Even though they do not know whether he is telling the truth, they must allow him entry to the city (*Metzudos*).

וְנָתְנוּ־לוֹ מָקוֹם — *And give him a place.*

Radak asserts that the Sages derived the law that the Levites were not allowed to charge the unintentional murderer rent for his dwelling in the city of refuge from this verse, which states that they were *to give him a place.* The word *give* implies in a gratuitous manner.

Radak is undoubtedly referring to the

[4] *He shall flee to one of these cities, stand at the
entrance to the city gate, and speak his words to the
elders of that city. They shall take him into the city
and give him a place, and he shall live among them.*
[5] *And if the avenger of blood pursues him, they shall
not deliver the murderer into his hand, for
unintentionally he killed his fellow, and he did not
hate him from before.* [6] *He shall dwell in that city
until he stands before the tribunal for judgment, until*

Mishnah (Makos 12b, 13a) which relates a dispute between R' Yehudah and R' Meir. According to *Rashi's (ibid.)* interpretation of their dispute, the issue of the *Mishnah* is whether the cities which surround the cities of refuge [*Chiddushei Raphael*] are required to pay the Levites rent for the murderer who fled there. According to *Tosafos'* interpretation, the issue of the *Mishnah* is whether the murderer himself is required to pay taxes to the Levite city. *Aruch LeNer (ibid.)* explains that there is a difference in *halachah* between the view of *Rashi* and *Tosafos.* In *Rashi's* view, all agree that no taxes have to be paid on behalf of the murderer; there is, however, a difference of opinion whether rent needs to be paid. According to *Tosafos'* view, all agree that the murderer needs to pay rent; the only difference of opinion is whether he also needs to pay tax.

The *Talmud,* however, does not cite this verse *and give him a place* as the source for the *Mishnah.*

וְיָשַׁב עִמָּם — *And he shall live among them.*

He may not be given a dwelling removed from a populated area for the avenger may come to kill him and his cries would not be heard. Therefore, he must be given a place where he can *live among them (Meam Loez).*

5. אַחֲרָיו — *Him* [lit. *after him*].

This refers to pursuing the killer to the city of refuge *(Metzudos).* [See *Commentary* to verse 3.]

וְלֹא־יַסְגִּרוּ — *They shall not deliver.*

The men in the city of refuge should aid the murderers and not deliver him to the avenger of blood *(Metzudos).*

כִּי בִבְלִי־דַעַת — *For unintentionally.*

The people in the city of refuge must protect the killer if the killing was unintentional *(Metzudos).*

וְלֹא־שֹׂנֵא הוּא לוֹ — *He did not hate him.*

Therefore, we need not suspect that [the killer] was deceiving us [about the accidental nature of the death] *(Metzudos).*

Hatred, according to *Rambam (Hil. Rotzeach* 6:10), means that he had refused to speak to the victim for the last three days. Had he 'hated' the victim, says the *Talmud,* we can never construe the death as a pure accident, and he is therefore not permitted to stay in a city of refuge.

6. עַד־עָמְדוֹ לִפְנֵי הָעֵדָה לַמִּשְׁפָּט — *Until he stands before the tribunal for judgment.*

Before a murderer was judged, he was sent to a city of refuge. He left the city when he was summoned to trial. If he deserved the death penalty, he was killed; if he was found innocent, he was released; and if he was to be punished by exile, he was returned to the city of refuge *(Makos* 9b).

A murderer exiled to a city of refuge may never leave that city, even to perform the mitzvah of saving a life. Even if the entire nation of Israel needs him, as was the case with King David's general Yoav the son of Tzruyah, he may not leave until the death of the High Priest *(Rambam, Hil. Rotzeah* 7:8).

Or Sameyach (Hil. Rotzeach 7:8) explains that the murderer may not leave the confines of the city of refuge even though the lives of

כ הַכֹּהֵן הַגָּדוֹל אֲשֶׁר יִהְיֶה בַּיָּמִים הָהֵם אָז
ז יָשׁוּב הָרוֹצֵחַ וּבָא אֶל־עִירוֹ וְאֶל־
בֵּיתוֹ אֶל־הָעִיר אֲשֶׁר־נָס מִשָּׁם׃ ז וַיַּקְדִּשׁוּ

many people may be imperiled, according to the established principle that an individual is not required to place his own life in doubtful danger even if it would mean saving others from certain danger (see *Sema, Choshen Mishpat* 426:2). Since the murderer exposes himself to attack by the avenger of blood as soon as he leaves the city, he would thus be placing his own life in jeopardy.

Kli Chemdah (Parshas Pinchas), however, argues that if the murderer was required to save the lives of other Jews, his leaving would be considered unintentional. The law clearly states that a murderer who accidentally strays from the city of refuge may not be attacked by the avenger of blood *(Rambam, Hil. Rotzeach* 5:11). He, therefore, explains that this law which restricts the murderer from leaving the city of refuge is a decree of the Torah and is unfathomable. It is plainly an exception to the principle that the saving of a life overrides the Torah's other laws.

עַד־מוֹת הַכֹּהֵן הַגָּדוֹל — *Until the death of the Kohen Gadol.*

There were three types of *Kohen Gadol* (cf., however, *Rambam, Hil. Rotzeach* 7:9 who lists four types; see *Aruch LeNer)* and the death of any of them would free the unintentional murderer from the city of refuge *(Makos* 11a): (a) a *Kohen Gadol* who was anointed with oil and wore all eight priestly garments [this type existed before the time of Yoshiyahu *(Rashi)*] (b) a *Kohen Gadol* who was not anointed with oil, but wore all eight priestly garments [this type existed from the time of Yoshiyahu *(Rashi)*] (c) a *Kohen Gadol* who served in the stead of a *Kohen Gadol* who was temporarily unable to serve, but had been replaced by the former *Kohen Gadol.*

According to *Rashi,* it would follow that types (a) and (b) were not *Kohen Gadol* at the same time. *Ritva (Makos* 11a) questions this assumption because the *Talmud* is initially uncertain if all three types need to die to free the murderer or only one of the three types. Obviously, the *Talmud* assumes that types (a) and (b) served at the same time. *Ritva* suggests that both types (a) and (b) existed before the times of Yoshiyahu in a case where the anointed *Kohen Gadol* was temporarily appointed to succeed him. Since there could never be two anointed *Kohanim Gedolim* at the same time, the replacement would not be anointed. *Ritva* concludes that *Rashi* agrees with his interpretation; *Rashi,* however, was only interested in describing the primary *Kohen Gadol. Ramban (Leviticus* 16:32) also interprets that *Rashi* would agree that an unanointed *Kohen Gadol* could exist at the same time as an anointed one, for on Yom Kippur a stand-by *Kohen Gadol* was designated in the event that the anointed *Kohen Gadol* was unable to serve. This replacement was not anointed (see *Rama MePano, Responsum* 102:6). For further elucidation see *Radak* to *I Samuel* 2:35.

Why was the murderer released from the city of refuge when the High Priest *(Kohen Gadol)* died?

□ R' Meir said that a murderer diminishes the lifespan of man and the *Kohen Gadol* increases it by atoning for the sins of his people. Thus, it is not proper that someone who decreases man's life should be free to walk around in the presence of a person who increases it *(Sifri* to *Numbers* 35:25).

□ Rebi said that a murderer defiles the Land and causes the Divine Presence to depart [see *Shabbos* 33a *(Emek Netziv)*] while the *Kohen Gadol* causes the Divine Presence to dwell on man in the Land. It is inappropriate that a man who defiled the Land should be free to walk around in the presence of one who causes the Divine Presence to dwell on man *(Sifri, ibid.)*.

□ When a calamity occurs, the people affected find solace in another person's suffering. The worst national tragedy that could occur is the loss of the nation's spiritual leader, the *Kohen Gadol.* Thus upon his death, the mourners of the slain victim would find some relief from their misery and would

20 *the death of the Kohen Gadol who will be in those*
7 *days. Then, the murderer may return and go to his*
city and his house — to the city from which he fled." '
[7] *They designated Kedesh in the Galilee in the*

no longer seek to avenge their relative's death by killing his assassin (*Moreh Nevuchim* and *Abarbanel*).

☐ There are many different levels of negligence which result in the death of an innocent person. Therefore, some unintentional murders could be construed as almost criminal. It is therefore impossible to ascribe a set time of exile for all unintentional murders. God, to whom all is revealed, sets the length of exile for each murderer by arranging for the death of the *Kohen Gadol* in a way that will be equitable for all contained in a city of refuge (*Rosh* cited by *Iturei Torah*).

According to the *Talmud* (*Makos* 11a), the *Kohen Gadol* was not guiltless, since he should have prayed for Divine mercy that no such calamity befall the Jewish people. (See *Targum Yonasson* to *Numbers* 35:25.) Therefore, if the murderer prayed for the *Kohen Gadol's* early demise, his prayer might have been answered. It was, therefore, the custom that the mother of the *Kohen Gadol* supplied these unintentional murderers with food and clothing so that they would pray that her son not die.

Chiddushei Raphael explains that the prayers of the unintentional murderers concerning the prolongation of the *Kohen Gadol's* life were more propitious than the prayers of any other men, because by offering such a prayer they demonstrated that they harbored no ill-feeling toward the *Kohen Gadol*, even though it was also through his negligence that they needed to be exiled to a city of refuge.

אֲשֶׁר יִהְיֶה בַּיָּמִים הָהֵם — *Who will be in those days.*

Even if the *Kohen Gadol* ministering at the time is not of the stature of Aaron or Elazar, his death frees the murderer from the city of refuge (see *Makos* 11a).

7. וַיַּקְדִּשׁוּ — *(And) they designated.*

The people designated these cities[1]

1. Today, if an individual accidentally kills another person, ח״ו, is he required to flee to one of the cities of refuge? In cases of deliberate murder, is the practice that the relative of the victim avenges the loss of his kinsman still applicable?

Since a *beis din* (court) of twenty-three men is required to try cases of murder, *Tur* (*Choshen Mishpat* 425) rules that we are no longer able to judge such cases [because *smichah* (the permission to judge), which makes one eligible for this *beis din*, is no longer operational]. Similarly, he states that although it is a mitzvah to banish an unintentional murderer to a city of refuge, this practice is no longer applicable. *Sefer HaChinuch* (410) explains that in order to invoke exile to a city of refuge, the Jewish nation needs to live in *Eretz Yisrael* and the High Court needs to be established in its place in Jerusalem to judge cases of murder.

Although *Urim V'Tumim* (*Choshen Mishpat* II) is certain that the institution of the 'avenger of blood' is no longer applicable today because the avenger is only given the liberty to pursue the murderer after his final judgment has been made [and we cannot judge his case as *Tur* mentions, because we do not have a *beis din* which is qualified], *Ketzos HaCohen* (*Choshen Mishpat* II) is in doubt. His doubt is based on the interpretations that *Kesef Mishnah* (*Hil. Rotzeach* 6:5) makes to *Rambam* (*ibid.*) who states that the avenger of blood is permitted to pursue the murderer, even if the act of murder was committed before only one witness. Normally two witnesses are required to establish a fact in *beis din*. *Kesef Mishnah* suggests that *Rambam* refers to a case where there were indeed two witnesses, but they did not appear in court together, in which case their testimony in cases of murder has the status of one single witness — invalid. The avenger of blood would be legally certain that the murderer did kill his relative and would therefore be justified in pursuing him, although the court would not be able to try the murderer since the testimony was inadmissible (both witnesses have to come together to *beis din*). *Kesef Mishnah* also suggests that *Rambam* refers to a case where the witnesses to the crime did not pass the scrutiny of the court. *Ketzos HaChoshen* argues that

immediately upon hearing that Joshua received his command from God *(Meam Loez).*

Although Moses designated the cities of refuge to the east of the Jordan before his death, they were not used until Joshua designated the remaining three (*Makos* 9b).

Some authorities wish to adduce evidence from Moses' action of separating three cities of refuge (even though they were not effective until Joshua separated the remaining three) that one should perform part of a mitzvah if he is unable to perform the entire one — e.g. he only has half the quantity of matzah that one is required to eat at the Passover Seder. Others argue that no evidence can be adduced from Moses' action, for although Moses' designation of the three cities of refuge did not take effect at that time, it did have the result that after Joshua designated the remaining three cities, all the cities were effective, and thus it caused the mitzvah to be performed in its entirety *(Bris Yu'akov, Orach Chaim,* Responsum 5; see also *Birkei Yosef, Orach Chaim* 482:4, *Chasam Sofer, Orach Chaim,* Responsum 49).

[It is noteworthy that Scripture lists hese three cities from north to south, vhen the reverse order would have been xpected, since Hebron was in Judah's erritory. As mentioned in the *Prefatory lemarks* to Chapter 15, the tribe of udah was always in the vanguard and ndeed it was this tribe which inherited he first territory in *Eretz Yisrael.* 'erhaps the answer lies in the fact that ities of refuge were a realistic necessity, iot a valued distinction. In the places where there were more murderers, there were more such cities (see further in this note). It is perhaps for this reason that Scripture begins the list from the north.[1] The north is symbolically considered to represent the forces of evil which God created in nature, whereas the south is associated with the more sublime — the spiritual and the holy (see *Cardinal Points and Color Schemes in Jewish Symbolism,* Dr. Paul Forcheimer, Breuer Jubilee Volume, New York, 1962). Thus when Judah received the first portion of territory in *Eretz Yisrael* on the basis of merit (see *Prefatory Remarks* to Chapter 13), he received territory in the south of the country. When, however, the cities of refuge for murderers are listed, Scripture begins with those in the north, for the conference of these cities is a concession to the evil in the world, not a reward for their beneficiaries. (Cf. *Maharsha* to *Makos* 10a.)]

These three cities divided *Eretz Yisrael* from north to south into four equal parts. Thus, the distance from the southern border of *Eretz Yisrael* to Hebron was equal to the distance from Hebron to Shechem, to the distance from Shechem to Kedesh, and to the distance from Kedesh to the northern border of *Eretz Yisrael (Makos* 9b).

This arrangement of refuge cities was done in fulfillment of the verse, *You should divide into three the border of your Land (Deuteronomy* 19:3). The question arises,

ccording to *Kesef Mishneh's* first interpretation, a qualified *beis din* is required before the venger of blood is permitted to pursue the murderer, and since we today do not have such a *eis din,* no avenger of blood would be allowed to kill him. However, according to *Kesef Iishneh's* second interpretation, *Rambam* only intended to teach that the avenger's killing of ie murderer is unpunishable because it is 'no worse than one who killed without intention.' Hence, *Ketzos* argues, today if the avenger were to kill the deliberate murderer it would be 'no orse than one who killed without intention.' He concludes in unresolved doubt. (Cf. *Or omeyach, Hil. Melachim* 3:10, who argues that the institution of גואֵל הַדָּם was intended for ie public welfare and does not function according to the normal procedures of courts and itnesses, and thus one witness is sufficient.)

Chavos Yair (Responsum 146) states that the avenger of blood may not even bring the ssassin to a non-Jewish court in order to have him killed. However, in the event that a non- w murders a Jew, *Tzemach Tzedek* (111) rules that the avenger of blood must bring the urderer to trial and bear the burden of normal court fees. Any additional expenses must be orne by the Jewish community.

The three cities Kedesh, Shechem, and Hebron, were also located in the north of their spective territories.

however, if the placement of these cities divided the Land into four equal parts, why did not the verse state, 'divide into *four* the border of your Land'?

□ *Mizrachi (ibid.)* explains that *divide into three* refers to the three sections of land that would be formed by two cuts across the width of *Eretz Yisrael.* Within each section lay a city of refuge, and this city together with its surrounding land would *divide the Land into three.*

□ *Sifsei Chachamim (ibid.)* suggests that *divide into three* refers to the number of times the Land is to be divided. The result of three divisions is four parts.

□ *Maharam Shiff (Megillah* 19a) explains that the verse implies that the *border* of the Land was to be divided into three. It was accomplished by the following method: (a) they measured half of the land, from the southern border to the place where the middle city of refuge was to be; (b) they divided that distance by two and designated the city of Hebron; (c) they measured the distance from Hebron to the site of the most northern city of refuge (which was half the distance of the Land); (d) they divided that distance by two and designated the city of Shechem; (e) they measured the distance between Shechem and the northern border (which was half the distance of the Land); and (f) they divided this distance by two and designated the city of Kadesh. Hence, the *border* was divided into *three.*

In addition, the *Talmud (Makos* 9b) relates that the three cities of refuge in *Eretz Yisrael* were located at the same latitude as the three cities of refuge in the Trans-Jordan. Thus, Hebron was across from Betzer, Shechem was across from Ramos Gilead, and Kedesh was across from Golan.

In the days of the Messiah, an additional three cities will be separated. They will appear in the lands of the Keini, Kenizzi, and Kadmoni. These lands were originally given to Abraham as a part of *Eretz Yisrael,* but were never conquered *(Rambam, Hil. Rotzeach* 8:4).

According to the *Talmud (Pesachim* 86a), death will no longer occur after the advent of the Messiah, and thus the cities of refuge would be seemingly superfluous. *Aruch LeNer (Makos* 9b) explains that only death by natural causes will cease. Death through injuries, however, will still exist.

Three cities of refuge were designated on each side of the Jordan.[1] Consequently, the two and one half tribes that were to the east of the Jordan had a relatively greater proportion of cities of refuge than the nine and one half tribes on the west of the Jordan. However, the other forty-two cities of the Levites also served as cities of refuge, which made the ratio of cities to tribes equal, for there were seven cities of Levites in addition to the three cities of refuge to the east of the Jordan. Thus, there were ten cities for two and one-half tribes, making a ratio of four cities per tribe in the Trans-Jordan. In *Eretz Yisrael* proper, there were thirty-eight cities for nine and one-half tribes, also yielding a ratio of four cities per tribe *(Malbim).*

Ramban (Numbers 35:14) argues, however, that the cities of refuge were not disproportionately distributed in Gilead, because the area of land to the west of the Jordan River approximately equaled the area of land to the east, even though it was inhabited by much fewer tribes.

Ramban also suggests that three cities were designated to the east of the Jordan River out of honor for Moses so that he could designate half of the six cities of refuge.

The *Talmud (Makos* 9b) attributes the uneven distribution of cities of refuge to the fact that there were many murderers in Gilead.

The question arises, however, why would more murderers in the Trans-Jordan require that there be a greater concentration of cities of refuge? These cities were designed to protect an individual who committed an *unintentional* murder, not a *deliberate* one.

□ *Tosafos (Makos* 9b) answers on the basis of a principle of Divine justice which the *Talmud (Makos* 10b) expresses: An individual who deliberately murders another without witnesses will ultimately die through an accidental murder. *Tosafos,* therefore, asserts that there were many people in the

1. *Sifri (Numbers* 35:13) states that these cities served as a refuge for unintentional murderers who lived outside the Land of Israel and the Trans-Jordan, as well (see *Kesef Mishneh* to *Hil. Rotzeach* 8:1).

אֶת־קֶ֤דֶשׁ בַּגָּלִיל֙ בְּהַ֣ר נַפְתָּלִ֔י וְאֶת־שְׁכֶ֖ם
בְּהַ֣ר אֶפְרָ֑יִם וְאֶת־קִרְיַ֥ת אַרְבַּ֛ע הִ֥יא
ח חֶבְר֖וֹן בְּהַ֥ר יְהוּדָֽה׃ וּמֵעֵ֜בֶר לְיַרְדֵּ֤ן
יְרִיחוֹ֙ מִזְרָ֔חָה נָתְנ֞וּ אֶת־בֶּ֥צֶר בַּמִּדְבָּ֛ר
בַּמִּישֹׁ֖ר מִמַּטֵּ֣ה רְאוּבֵ֑ן וְאֶת־רָאמֹ֤ת
°גּוֹלָן ק׳ בַּגִּלְעָד֙ מִמַּטֵּה־גָ֔ד וְאֶת־°גלון בַּבָּשָׁ֖ן
ט מִמַּטֵּ֥ה מְנַשֶּֽׁה׃ אֵ֣לֶּה הָיוּ֩ עָרֵ֨י הַמּֽוּעָדָ֜ה
לְכֹ֣ל ׀ בְּנֵ֣י יִשְׂרָאֵ֗ל וְלַגֵּר֙ הַגָּ֣ר בְּתוֹכָ֔ם
לָנ֣וּס שָׁ֔מָּה כָּל־מַכֵּה־נֶ֖פֶשׁ בִּשְׁגָגָ֑ה וְלֹ֣א
יָמ֗וּת בְּיַד֙ גֹּאֵ֣ל הַדָּ֔ם עַד־עָמְד֖וֹ לִפְנֵ֥י

Trans-Jordan who murdered intentionally, but without witnesses. God arranged that they should be killed accidentally, and thus there was a need for a greater proportion of cities of refuge (see *Maharsha*).

□ *Ramban (Numbers* 35:14) maintains that although these people committed intentional murders, they feigned having killed accidentally. It was necessary to have a greater proportion of cities of refuge, since it was not possible to determine who indeed was telling the truth.

□ *Gur Aryeh (Numbers* 35:14) explains that since Gilead was a land where intentional murder was frequent, life was not valued so highly. It, therefore, became a place where more accidental murders occurred since people did not feel the necessity of being careful in regard to another's life.

□ *Maharsha (Makos* 9b) suggests that there was a need for these cities for those individuals who committed intentional murders as well since the *Mishnah* (9b) states that both intentional and unintentional murders fled to the cities of refuge before their trial (see *Commentary* to verse 6).

□ See also *Tiferes Yisrael (Boaz)* and *Amtachas Binyamin.*

קֶדֶשׁ — *Kedesh.*
See *Commentary* to 19:37.

שְׁכֶם — *Shechem.*
This city is located between Mount Gerizim to the south and Mount Eval to the north and is the present day city of Nabulus.

As mentioned previously, the three cities of refuge in *Eretz Yisrael* divided

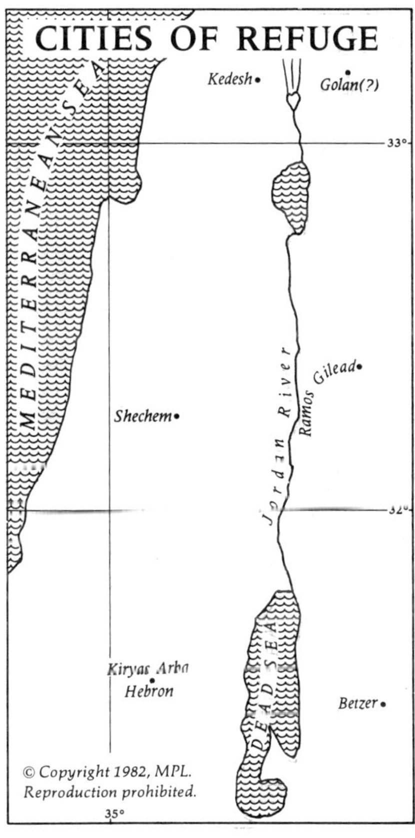

Mountain of Naftali, Shechem in the Mountain of
Ephraim, and Kiryas Arba which is Hebron in the
Mountain of Judah. 8 *And on the other side of the*
Jordan east of Jericho, they designated Betzer in the
wilderness on the plain from the tribe of Reuben, and
Ramos Gilead from the tribe of Gad, and Golan in the
Bashan from the tribe of Menashe. 9 *These were the*
cities designated for all the Children of Israel and for
the convert who dwells among them — where a
person who murders through carelessness might flee
and not die by the hand of the avenger of blood
before he stands before the tribunal for judgment.

the Land into four equal parts. However, this distribution was unequal in regard to the area of land which each city served. Since Shechem was located in the middle of the Land, it only served one quarter of the Land, whereas Kedesh and Hebron served three-eighths. The *Talmud (Makos* 10a) explains that there was a higher concentration of murderers around the city of Shechem, and therefore this city served as a refuge for as many people as the other cities of refuge, even though the murderers came from a smaller area of land. *Siach Yitzchak* explains that the Trans-Jordan had even a higher concentration of murderers than the area around Shechem because the Trans-Jordan did not have the benefit of the Divine Presence as did *Eretz Yisrael* (see *footnote* to 22:19).

חֶבְרוֹן — *Hebron.*
See *Commentary* to 10:36

8. נָתְנוּ — *They designated.*
These were designated in the days of Moses *(Rashi).*

These three cities of refuge in the Trans-Jordan are listed from south to north, unlike the three mentioned in the previous verse (see *Commentary* to verse 7). The *Talmud (Makos* 10a) explains that Reuben merited that the list of cities of refuge in the Trans-Jordan begin with his territory because he was the first brother of Joseph to suggest that the brothers not kill Joseph, but rather incarcerate him in a pit *(Genesis* 37:21).

בֶּצֶר — *Betzer.*
It was located southwest of Aro'er at the same latitude as Hebron.

רָאמוֹת בַּגִּלְעָד — *Ramos Gilead.*
It is the city called Kalet Alrabat on one of the highest peaks of Mount Gilead to the north of Wadi Zerki (Yabuk).

גּוֹלָן — *Golan.*
According to the *Talmud (Makos* 9b), it was located across from the city of Kedesh. However, its location is not known today.

9. הַמּוּעָדָה — *Designated.*
Targum renders: designated or prepared.

Metzudos asserts that this word derives from the word 'group.'

וְלַגֵּר הַגָּר בְּתוֹכָם — *And for the convert who dwells among them.*
If a *ger toshav,* one who upholds the seven Noachide laws, kills a slave or another *ger toshav,* he is exiled to a city of refuge *(Makos* 8b, *Rambam).*

See *footnote* to *Prefatory Remarks.*

א הָעֵדָה: וַיִּגְּשׁוּ רָאשֵׁי אֲבוֹת
הַלְוִיִּם אֶל־אֶלְעָזָר הַכֹּהֵן וְאֶל־יְהוֹשֻׁעַ בִּן־
נוּן וְאֶל־רָאשֵׁי אֲבוֹת הַמַּטּוֹת לִבְנֵי
ב יִשְׂרָאֵל: וַיְדַבְּרוּ אֲלֵיהֶם בְּשִׁלֹה בְּאֶרֶץ

XXI

After the Scriptural passage (Numbers *34:16-29) which describes the manner in which* Eretz Yisrael *should be divided, God commands Moses concerning the designation of cities for the Levites,* And the cities shall they have to dwell in; and their outskirts shall be for their cattle and for their goods and for their animals.

The Torah states that the six cities of refuge designated for a person who murders unintentionally are to be included among the cities given to the Levites. As Malbim *points out, this statement presumes that the six cities of refuge would be appointed first. Thus the designation of the cities of refuge took place after the division of the land, prior to the distribution of cities for the Levites.*

According to the Biblical command, every tribe was required to give cities to the Levites: And the cities which you shall give shall be of the possession of the Children of Israel; from them that have many you shall give many, and from them that have few you shall give few. Every one shall give cities to the Levites ... (Numbers *35:8). It would appear from this verse that those tribes which had more members were to give more cities to the Levites, but we find that this was not the case. For example, Judah, Simeon, and Benjamin were less numerous than Yisachar, Asher, Naftali, and half of Menashe, but gave the same number of cities (thirteen) as the latter tribes. Similarly, although Dan outnumbered Ephraim two to one, each tribe gave four cities.* Ravad (Bava Basra *117) suggests that each tribe did not receive a number of cities proportional to its population. Some tribes received more mountainous country, some received country more suitable for agriculture. The Torah's directive meant that each tribe should give cities in proportion to the number of cities it received in the division of the Land. Thus, even a numerous tribe may have received a smaller number of cities and was therefore only required to give a smaller number of cities to the Levites. Alternatively,* Ramban (Numbers *35:8) explains that the cities were not of equal worth; the disparity in quality was compensated for by quantity.*

The cities which the Levites received were spread throughout Eretz Yisrael *in fulfillment of Jacob's utterance to Levi* (Genesis *49:7),* 'I will scatter them in Israel.' [See Prefatory Remarks *to Chapter 19.*] *This geographical dispersion enabled the Levites to receive regular tithes from their fellow Jews, thereby freeing the Levites to concentrate solely on spiritual matters.*

In this chapter, Scripture mentions the forty-eight cities which were given to the Levites. They are recounted a second time in I Chronicles *6:38-66. The number of cities for the Kohanim, however, must have increased over time. For example, Nov mentioned in* I Samuel *22:19 as the city of Kohanim was not listed as one of the forty-eight cities in this chapter. Givas Pinchas* (Joshua *24:33) may have been another city for Kohanim.*

Thirteen of the Levites' forty-eight cities, more than one-fourth of the total, were given to the Kohanim. Ibn Ezra (Exodus *28:1) explains this lack of proportionality by the fact that the Kohanim greatly increased in number during Israel's journey through the Wilderness so that in terms of population, they comprised more than one-quarter of the Levites. [According to* Ramban, *however, it is not necessary to posit that the Kohanim increased to such a large extent, for the cities they received*

¹ *And the leaders of the fathers of the Levites
approached Elazar the Kohen and Joshua son of Nun
and the leaders of the fathers of the tribes of the
Children of Israel.* ² *And they spoke to them in*

may have been smaller or of poorer quality. In this way they would have received accommodations commensurate with their numbers.]

According to the Talmud (Sotah *48b*)*, these cities belonged to the Levites only until the end of the first Temple.* Meshech Chachmah (Numbers *35:13*) *conjectures that they were not reinstated when the Jews returned to the Land after the Babylonian exile because their designation may have required the* urim v'tumim, *as is suggested by the fact that Elazar was present at the first distribution of Levite cities; he donned the* urim v'tumim *(see* Commentary *to 14:2). The* urim v'tumim *did not exist during the Second Temple.*

Rambam (Hil. Shmittah V'Yovel *13:12*) *explains why the Torah prohibited the Levites from acquiring territory in the Land* (Numbers *18:20*) *and only permitted them to live in cities. The Levites were to function differently than the other tribes; they were to devote themselves exclusively to Divine service. Specifically, they were to perform the service in the Holy Temple and to teach the other tribes about the Torah's guidelines for living. Thus, they were forbidden to engage in agriculture and war, occupations which would diminish much time from their holy mission.*

1. וַיִּגְּשׁוּ — *And* [*they*] *approached.*

According to the *Midrash* (see *Yalkut* to *Genesis* 44) the word *approached* denotes appeasement, as it is used in regard to Judah in *Genesis* 44:18 when he confronted an angry Joseph. The leaders of the Levites came to Elazar, Joshua, and the leaders of the other tribes to address a claim which had been brought against them. It had been argued that since the Levites did not attempt to acquire their cities during Moses' time when the Trans-Jordan had been conquered and since they delayed their claim to these cities seven years after *Eretz Yisrael* had been conquered, it appeared that they had renounced their claim to them.

The Levites countered that since the Tabernacle had not yet been established, it was not necessary for them to have these cities, for they were intended to be in exchange for the Divine service that they would perform. Since private altars were permitted before the erection of the Tabernacle at Shiloh (see *Prefatory Remarks* to Chapter 18), there was only limited service for the Levites to perform, and they felt it inappropriate to be supplied with these cities. After the Tabernacle at Shiloh had been established, however, the Levites were charged with certifying that no unqualified or ritually unclean individual would enter its sacred halls and with opening and closing the gates; they now felt justified in receiving the Torah's compensation for their service. It is for this reason that verse 2 states that they spoke to the leaders of the other tribes in *Shiloh* to emphasize that since the service was being performed in the Sanctuary it was fitting that they be compensated for their service *(Chida; Meam Loez).*

רָאשֵׁי אֲבוֹת הַלְוִיִּם — *The leaders* [lit. *heads*] *of the fathers of the Levites.*

The Levites were composed of four families: Gershon, Kehas, Merari, and the sons of Aaron. Although Aaron descended from Kehas through his father Amram, he was accorded special status since only he and his children were Kohanim.

אֶל־אֶלְעָזָר הַכֹּהֵן... — *Elazar the Kohen ...*

[The people mentioned in this verse also distributed the other portions of

כְּנַעַן לֵאמֹר יהוה צִוָּה בְּיַד־מֹשֶׁה לָתֶת־
לָנוּ עָרִים לָשָׁבֶת וּמִגְרְשֵׁיהֶן לִבְהֶמְתֵּנוּ׃
ג וַיִּתְּנוּ בְנֵי־יִשְׂרָאֵל לַלְוִיִּם מִנַּחֲלָתָם אֶל־

territory for each tribe (see 14:1).]

2. בְּאֶרֶץ כְּנַעַן — *In the Land of Canaan.*
HaRav Gifter questions the import of this phrase, for it is common knowledge that Shiloh was in the Land of Canaan.

לָשָׁבֶת — *In which to dwell.*
Abarbanel cites the *Talmud (Makkos* 12a) as proof that the Levites did not legally own these cities even until the end of the First Temple [see *Prefatory Remarks*], but were merely permitted to dwell in them. Thus, the Levites did not bury their dead in them, and they did not change any of the cities' names. (See also *Tosefta, Bikorim* 1:4 and *Rashash* to *Berachos* 20a.)

ה׳ צִוָּה — *HASHEM commanded.*
The following cities were not distributed to the Levites earlier because the command to assign the cities applied only after the cities of refuge were designated. The commandment appears in *Numbers* 35:6, *And among the cities which you shall give to the Levites shall be six cities of refuge ... and to them you shall add forty-two cities.* The wording implies that the forty-two cities are to be given *after* the cities of refuge have been named *(Malbim).*

3. וּמִגְרְשֵׁיהֶן — *And their open lands.*
Besides the actual city which was given to the Levites, an additional tract of land surrounding the city in all directions was also given according to the command mentioned in *Numbers* 35:2. The size of this additional tract pushed the city limit *(techum)* two thousand *amos* (approximately 7/10 mile) in each direction *(Sotah* 27b; *Numbers* 35:4). This tract was concentrically sub-divided into two parts. The subdivision which belted the city proper *(migrash)* extended one thousand *amos* past the city's border. It was forbidden to plant grain or trees or to build houses in this area so that this vacant property would enhance the beauty of the city *(Rashi, Sotah* 27b). The outer belt of one thousand *amos* could be used by the Levites for fields and vineyards.

Rambam (Hil. Shmittah VeYovel 13:2), however, contends that three thousand *amos* were assigned in each direction *(techum).* The inner belt of one thousand *amos* was to remain vacant; however, the outer belt, which was to be used for fields and vineyards, extended an additional two thousand *amos.*

Ramban (Numbers 35:2) suggests that the plain wording of the verses in the Pentateuch suggest an entirely different configuration of the Levites' cities. In his view *Numbers* 35 discusses the calculations to be made for a city which is a square, one thousand *amos* on a side. Five hundred *amos* are added to each side of the square, and this additional area constitutes the vacant land around the city. (Note that the corners become *rounded* when five hundred *amos* are added to each side.) The rounded corners are then squared off and this extra area between the rounded and squared off corners may be used for planting crops or vineyards. In all, the original city with the newly added area becomes a square two thousand *amos* on a side in fulfillment of *Numbers* 35:3. *Ramban* adds that squaring off the corners enhances the beauty of the city.

HaKsav V'HaKabbalah (Ma'sey 48) questions *Ramban's* interpretation that the Levite cities mentioned in this verse were one thousand *amos* on a side. Although the *Talmud (Arachin* 33b) states that the cities were to be of medium size, no measurement is stated. [Note that according to *Rashi* and *Rambam* the city could be of any size or shape. The diagram assumes that the

21 *Shiloh in the Land of Canaan saying, 'Through*
3 *Moses HASHEM commanded you to give us cities in*
which to dwell and their open lands for our cattle.'
³ Thus, the Children of Israel gave to the Levites from

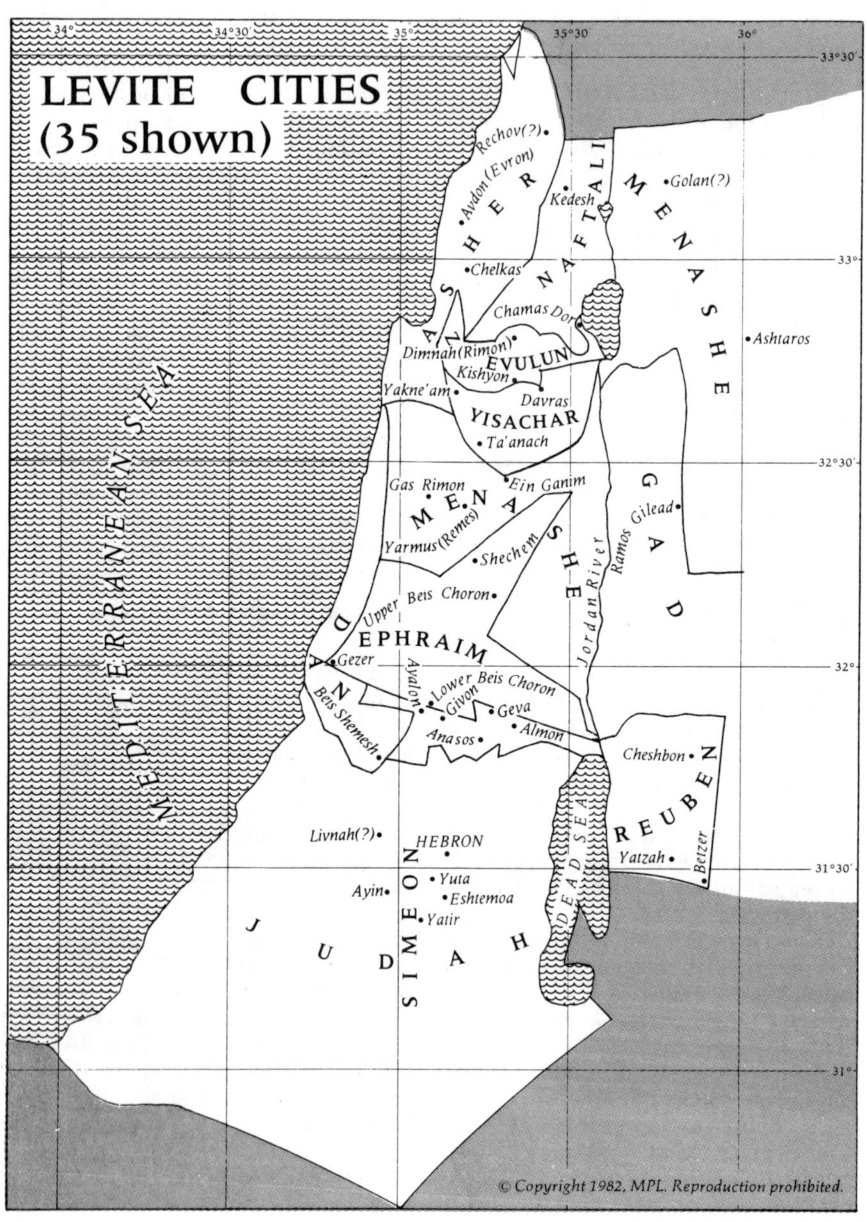

city was one thousand *amos* on a side in order to contrast the three views.]

How the open land *(migrash)* was allocated around the city is disputed in the *Talmud (Eruvin* 56b and 57a, according to *Tosafos s.v.* מאי). [According to *Rashi's* primary interpretation of that passage, however, there may be no dispute, and all would agree to view (a) stated below.]

(a) The open land *(migrash)* surrounded the city on all sides, including the corners of the city (Rava bar Ada and Abaye).

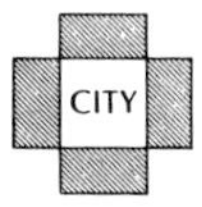

(b) The open land only surrounded the sides of the city, not the corners (Ravina).

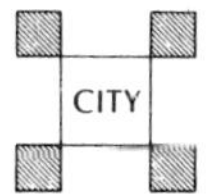

(c) The open land was allocated only on the corners of the cities, not the sides (Rav Ashi).

It would appear that *Rashi's* view in *Sotah* reflects the opinion of Rava bar Ada and Abaye, since he does not specify that any fraction of the inner one thousand *amos* is not included in the open land. Similarly, *Rambam* makes no distinction regarding the inner one thousand *amah* tract of land around the city.

Ramban's view, however, is not so clear. A diagram of *Ramban's* view

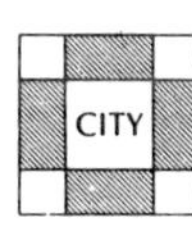

appears in *Tur Al HaTorah* and indicates that the five hundred *amah* measurement (see above) from each side of the city *(migrash)* extended only from the sides of the city, not the corners.

This seems to be in accordance with Ravina's view (b) mentioned above, but no indication is given in *Tur* or *Ramban* that they have decided according to Ravina's view.

A second diagram of *Ramban's* view appears in Rabbi C. B. Chavel's notes to *Ramban's* Commentary on the Pentateuch *(Numbers* 35:2). In his illustration, the five

hundred *amah* measurement extends only from the *middle* of the sides of the city. As one approaches the corners of the city, the measurement decreases.

Rabbi Chavel does not explain why a full five hundred *amah* measurement does not extend from the entire length of each side of the city as is indicated in *Tur's* diagram.

In our illustration and calculation (see Table below) of *Ramban's* view, we have suggested a third interpretation. According to this view the configuration of the *migrash* (open land) could be consistent with Rava bar Ada's opinion, namely, that the *migrash* was allocated on all sides of the city at an equal distance from the sides of the city.

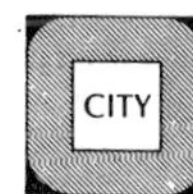

However, whereas according to Rava bar Ada more than one thousand *amos* of *migrash* was designated for each corner of the city (since the corners of the *migrash* were square, not round), *Ramban* could hold that the corners of the *migrash* were rounded so that the *migrash* abutting the corners of the city measured exactly five hundred *amos*.

◆§ Area designated for fields

The area of land between the rounded corners of the *migrash* and the squared off corners of the *techum* was the tract of land designated for fields and vineyards.

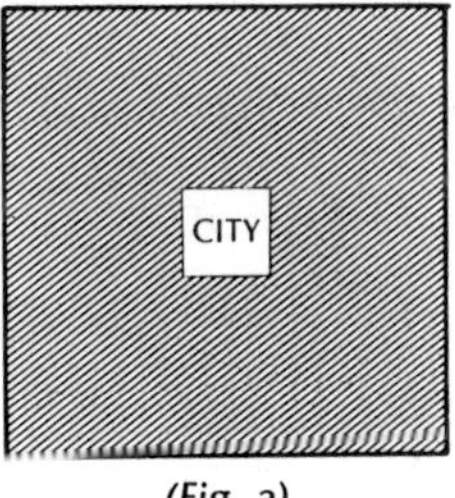

(Fig. a)

The *Talmud (Eruvin* 51a) derives that the two thousand *amah* outer border of the city *(techum)* should be squared off at the corners *(Fig. a)*, not rounded *(Fig. b)*.

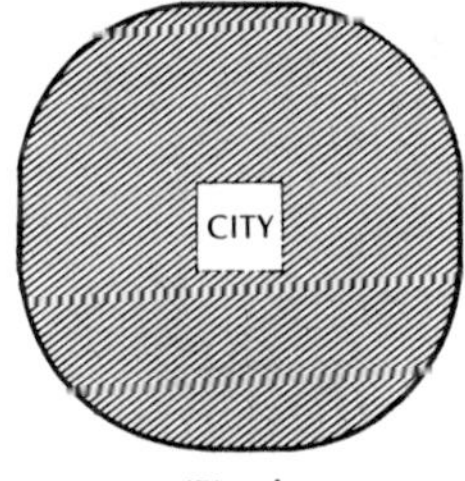

(Fig. b)

(A two thousand *amah* measurement from the corner would form the shape of a quarter-circle.) The *Talmud*, however, does not mention any source which would suggest that the vacant land *(migrash)* around the Levites' cities should also be squared off at the corners, and thus we would expect that they should be rounded. However, from the questions the *Talmud* asks in *Eruvin* (56b and 57a — אכתי תילתא הוי and תילתא הווי), the *Talmud* assumes that, indeed, even the vacant land *(migrash)* was squared off at the corner. Thus, we have assumed in the diagrams illustrating the views of *Rashi* and *Rambam* that the vacant land *(migrash)* was squared off at the corners.

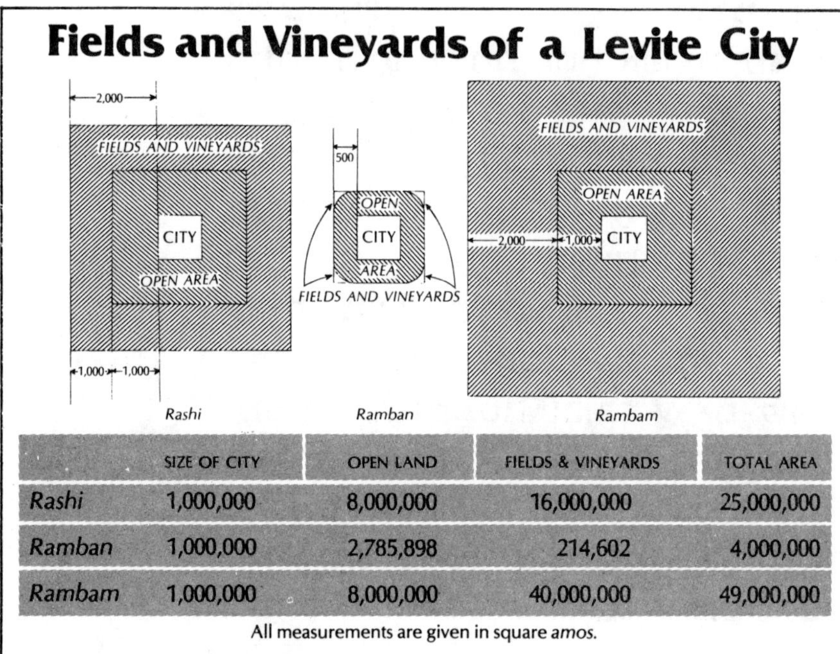

	SIZE OF CITY	OPEN LAND	FIELDS & VINEYARDS	TOTAL AREA
Rashi	1,000,000	8,000,000	16,000,000	25,000,000
Ramban	1,000,000	2,785,898	214,602	4,000,000
Rambam	1,000,000	8,000,000	40,000,000	49,000,000

All measurements are given in square *amos*.

NOTE: According to *Rashi* and *Rambam* the city could be of any size or shape. The size shown in this table was chosen to illustrate the difference among the commentators.

◂§ The Cities of the Levites

4. A lottery system was established to distribute cities to the four Levite families. The twelve tribes were divided into four groups and each group designated a number of cities to be given to the Levites. The tribes of Judah, Simeon, and Benjamin designated thirteen cities; Ephraim, Dan, and half of Menashe, ten; Yisachar, Asher, Naftali and the second half of Menashe, thirteen; and Reuben, Gad, and Zevulun, twelve. Four cards were placed in each of four containers. On one set of four was inscribed the names of the Levite families and on the second set was inscribed the four groups of tribes. One draw was made from each container to determine in which section of *Eretz Yisrael* each family would receive its cities.

Malbim perceives a correlation between the sanctity of the Levites' particular tasks and that of the lands which they acquired through the lottery. The sons of Aaron, who were occupied with the holiest of activities — the actual service within the Temple — received cities in the territories of Judah, Simeon, and Benjamin which were adjacent to the site where the Temple

פִּ֣י יְהוָ֑ה אֶת־הֶעָרִ֥ים הָאֵ֖לֶּה וְאֶת־
ד מִגְרְשֵׁיהֶֽן׃ וַיֵּצֵ֥א הַגּוֹרָ֖ל
לְמִשְׁפְּחֹ֣ת הַקְּהָתִ֑י וַיְהִ֡י לִבְנֵי֩ אַהֲרֹ֨ן הַכֹּהֵ֜ן
מִן־הַלְוִיִּ֗ם מִמַּטֵּ֣ה יְ֠הוּדָה וּמִמַּטֵּ֨ה
הַשִּׁמְעֹנִ֜י וּמִמַּטֵּ֣ה בִנְיָמִ֗ן בַּגּוֹרָ֛ל עָרִ֖ים
ה שְׁל֥שׁ עֶשְׂרֵֽה׃ וְלִבְנֵ֨י קְהָ֜ת
הַנּֽוֹתָרִ֗ם מִמִּשְׁפְּחֹ֣ת מַטֵּֽה־אֶ֠פְרַיִם וּמִמַּטֵּה־
דָ֞ן וּמֵחֲצִי֙ מַטֵּ֣ה מְנַשֶּׁ֔ה בַּגּוֹרָ֖ל עָרִ֥ים
ו עָֽשֶׂר׃ וְלִבְנֵ֣י גֵרְשׁ֗וֹן מִֽמִּשְׁפְּח֣וֹת
מַטֵּֽה־יִשָּׂשכָ֡ר וּמִמַּטֵּֽה־אָ֠שֵׁר וּמִמַּטֵּ֨ה
נַפְתָּלִ֜י וּמֵחֲצִ֨י מַטֵּ֤ה מְנַשֶּׁה֙ בַבָּשָׁ֔ן בַּגּוֹרָ֖ל
ז עָרִ֖ים שְׁל֥שׁ עֶשְׂרֵֽה׃ לִבְנֵ֤י
מְרָרִי֙ לְמִשְׁפְּחֹתָ֔ם מִמַּטֵּ֨ה רְאוּבֵ֜ן
וּמִמַּטֵּה־גָ֗ד וּמִמַּטֵּ֣ה זְבוּלֻ֔ן עָרִ֖ים שְׁתֵּ֥ים
ח עֶשְׂרֵֽה׃ וַיִּתְּנ֤וּ בְנֵֽי־
יִשְׂרָאֵל֙ לַלְוִיִּ֔ם אֶת־הֶעָרִ֥ים הָאֵ֖לֶּה וְאֶת־
מִגְרְשֵׁיהֶ֑ן כַּאֲשֶׁ֨ר צִוָּ֧ה יְהוָ֛ה בְּיַד־מֹשֶׁ֖ה
ט בַּגּוֹרָֽל׃ וַֽיִּתְּנ֗וּ מִמַּטֵּה֙ בְּנֵ֣י

would be built. The sons of Kehas, who transported the Holy Ark and other vessels used within the Temple, received cities in the territories of Ephraim, Dan and part of Menashe which surrounded the tribes in which the Temple was contained. The sons of Gershon, who transported the Tabernacle with its coverings and draperies (a task of lesser sanctity), received cities in the territories of Yisachar, Asher, and Naftali, which were the most distant of all from the Temple. The sons of Merari, who transported the walls of the Tabernacle, received their cities in the land across the Jordan, outside *Eretz Yisrael* proper. (Cf. *Meshech Chachmah* to *Deuteronomy* 10:8.)

וַיֵּצֵא הַגּוֹרָל — *And the lottery was drawn* [lit. *went out*].

Malbim explains that when each family of Levites was called, the names of the tribes which were to give them cities lighted upon Elazar's breastplate. [Etched on the twelve stones of the breastplate were the names of each tribe.]

5. וְלִבְנֵי קְהָת הַנּוֹתָרִים — *To the remaining sons of Kehas.*

The remaining sons of Kehas were the sons of Moses, Yitzhar, Hebron and Uziel *(Rashi).*

6. בַּבָּשָׁן — *In the Bashan.*

This refers to the half tribe of Menashe which received its inheritance to the west of the Jordan *(Metzudos).*

their inheritances according to the command of
HASHEM — these cities and their open lands.
4 *And the lottery was drawn for the families of*
Kehas: to the children of Aaron the Kohen from the
Levites — from the tribe of Judah, from the tribe of
Simeon, and from the tribe of Benjamin — thirteen in
the lottery of cities.
5 *To the remaining sons of Kehas — from the*
families of the tribe of Ephraim, of the tribe of Dan,
and of part of the tribe of Menashe — ten in the
lottery of cities.
6 *To the sons of Gershon — from the families of the*
tribe of Yisachar, of the tribe of Asher, of the tribe of
Naftali and of part of the tribe of Menashe in the
Bashan — thirteen in the lottery of cities.
7 *To the sons of Merari according to their families*
— from the tribe of Reuben from the tribe of Gad,
and from the tribe of Zevulun — twelve cities.
8 *And the Children of Israel gave these cities and*
their open lands to the Levites by lottery as HASHEM
had commanded through Moses.
9 *And they gave — from the tribe of the Children of*

7. מִמַּטֵּה רְאוּבֵן — *From the tribe of Reuben.*

Later in this chapter, Scripture mentions all the cities given by each tribe, but does not include the cities which were given by Reuben. Although some texts of *Joshua* do include verses which recount the cities Reuben gave, these verses should be deleted, for, according to Rav Hai Gaon, they were interpolated from *I Chronicles* 6:63-4 *(Radak).*

◆§ The Cities of the Kohanim — from Judah, Simeon and Benjamin

9-16. In the following verses Scripture recounts the cities given by each individual tribe. However, Scripture combines Judah and Simeon and does not specify which cities were given by each. *Ran (Sanhedrin* 111b) explains that since Simeon received its territory within Judah's borders, Scripture dealt with these two tribes as one unit (cf., *Commentary* to 19:1).

Of the nine cities mentioned in the following verses, eight of them, according to Chapter 15, belonged to Judah. Since Judah did not have eight times the population of Simeon, it is surprising that they gave eight times as many cities, for the Torah states, *from them that have many you shall give many and from that have few you shall give few (Numbers* 35:8). According to the opinions of *Ravad* and *Ramban* mentioned in the *Prefatory Remarks* to this chapter, it could be argued that Judah received eight times as many cities as Simeon [*Ravad*] or that the one

כא
י־יז

יְהוּדָה וּמִמַּטֵּה בְּנֵי שִׁמְעוֹן אֵת הֶעָרִים
י הָאֵלֶּה אֲשֶׁר־יִקְרָא אֶתְהֶן בְּשֵׁם׃ וַיְהִי
לִבְנֵי אַהֲרֹן מִמִּשְׁפְּחוֹת הַקְּהָתִי מִבְּנֵי לֵוִי
יא כִּי לָהֶם הָיָה הַגּוֹרָל רִאישֹׁנָה׃ וַיִּתְּנוּ לָהֶם
אֶת־קִרְיַת אַרְבַּע אֲבִי הָעֲנוֹק הִיא חֶבְרוֹן
בְּהַר יְהוּדָה וְאֶת־מִגְרָשֶׁהָ סְבִיבֹתֶיהָ׃
יב וְאֶת־שְׂדֵה הָעִיר וְאֶת־חֲצֵרֶיהָ נָתְנוּ
יג לְכָלֵב בֶּן־יְפֻנֶּה בַּאֲחֻזָּתוֹ׃ וְלִבְנֵי ׀
אַהֲרֹן הַכֹּהֵן נָתְנוּ אֶת־עִיר מִקְלַט הָרֹצֵחַ
אֶת־חֶבְרוֹן וְאֶת־מִגְרָשֶׁהָ וְאֶת־לִבְנָה
יד וְאֶת־מִגְרָשֶׁהָ׃ וְאֶת־יַתִּר וְאֶת־מִגְרָשֶׁהָ
טו וְאֶת־אֶשְׁתְּמֹעַ וְאֶת־מִגְרָשֶׁהָ׃ וְאֶת־חֹלֹן
וְאֶת־מִגְרָשֶׁהָ וְאֶת־דְּבִר וְאֶת־מִגְרָשֶׁהָ׃
טז וְאֶת־עַיִן וְאֶת־מִגְרָשֶׁהָ וְאֶת־יֻטָּה וְאֶת־
מִגְרָשֶׁהָ אֶת־בֵּית שֶׁמֶשׁ וְאֶת־מִגְרָשֶׁהָ
עָרִים תֵּשַׁע מֵאֵת שְׁנֵי הַשְּׁבָטִים
יז הָאֵלֶּה׃ וּמִמַּטֵּה בִנְיָמִן אֶת־
גִּבְעוֹן וְאֶת־מִגְרָשֶׁהָ אֶת־גֶּבַע וְאֶת־

city Simeon gave was larger or of better quality that those given by Judah [*Ramban*]. *Margolios HaYam (Sanhedrin* 111b) also suggests that the eight cities mentioned in the following verses which appear to have been given to Judah in Chapter 15 in reality did not belong to Judah. In 15:32 it is stated that there were twenty-nine cites of Judah near the border of Edom when in reality Scripture lists thirty-eight. *Rashi* comments that Scripture did not count the nine cities which were later given to Simeon. Thus, argues *Margolios HaYam,* not all the cities listed in Chapter 15 did indeed belong to Judah and therefore several of the cities found in the following verses may have belonged to Simeon. See also *Meishiv Davar* (Volume 2; 64) and *T'vuos HaAretz* (p. 278).

9. אֲשֶׁר־יִקְרָא אֶתְהֶן בְּשֵׁם — *Which will be mentioned by name.*

Until this point, the text merely stated the number of cities to be given by each group of tribes. Now, however, Scripture will enumerate the individual cities by name *(Rashi).*

10. כִּי לָהֶם הָיָה הַגּוֹרָל רִאישֹׁנָה — *For theirs was the first draw of the lottery.*

They did not receive the first group of cities because of the respect due to Kohanim, but because their name was drawn first in the lottery *(Metzudos).*

11. חֶבְרוֹן — *Hebron.*

See *Commentary* to 10:36.

21 *Judah and from the tribe of the Children of Simeon —*
10-18 *these cities which will be mentioned by name.* 10 *And*
to the sons of Aaron from the family of Kehas of the
sons of Levi — for theirs was the first draw of the
lottery. 11 *They gave them the city of Kiryas Arba,*
father of the Anak, which is Hebron in the mountain
of Judah, and the open land around it. 12 *And fields*
of the city and its village they gave to Calev the son
of Yefuneh as his inheritance.

13 *To the sons of Aaron the Kohen they gave the*
city of refuge for a murderer, Hebron and its open
land and Livnah and its open land; 14 *and Yatir and*
its open land and Eshtemoa and its open land; 15 *and*
Cholon and its open land and Devir and its open
land; 16 *and Ayin and its open land, Yutah and its*
open land, and Beis Shemesh and its open land —
nine cities from these two tribes.

17 *And from the tribe of Benjamin — Givon and its*
open land and Geva and its open land; 18 *Anasos and*

12. לְכָלֵב בֶּן־יְפֻנֶּה בַּאֲחֻזָּתוֹ — *To Calev the son of Yefuneh as his inheritance.*
See *Commentary* to 15:13-15.

13. עִיר מִקְלַט — *City of refuge.*
According to the Biblical command (*Numbers* 35:6), each city of refuge was given to the Levites. The cities of the Levites also acted as cities of refuge. However, there was one major difference between the six cities designated as places of refuge and the cities of the Levites (see also *Prefatory Remarks* to Chapter 20). While the six designated cities protected every murderer, the cities of the Levites sheltered only those murderers who realized that they were entitled to seek protection there (*Makkos* 10a, *Rashi*). [*Cf.*, however, *Ramban* to *Numbers* 35:14 and Response of *Radvaz*, Vol. 5, 2138.]

לִבְנָה — *Livnah.*
See *Commentary* to 12:15.

14. יַתִּר — *Yatir.*
See *Commentary* to 15:48.

אֶשְׁתְּמוֹעַ — *Eshtemoa.*
See *Commentary* to 15:50.

15. חלן — *Cholon.*
This city was mentioned in 15:51.

דְּבִר — *Devir.*
Although its exact location is not known, we do know that it lies in the valley southwest of Hebron (*T'vuos HaAretz*). [It is mentioned in 15:15.]

16. עַיִן — *Ayin.*
It is located approximately 15 miles south of Beis Guvin.

יֻטָּה — *Yutah.*
See *Commentary* to 15:55.

בֵּית שָׁמֶשׁ — *Beis Shemesh.*
See *Commentary* to 15:10.

17. גִּבְעוֹן — *Givon.*
See *Commentary* to 18:25.

גֶּבַע — *Geva.*
See *Commentary* to 18:24.

כא
יח־כח

יח מִגְרָשֶׁהָ: אֶת־עֲנָתוֹת וְאֶת־מִגְרָשֶׁהָ וְאֶת־
יט עַלְמוֹן וְאֶת־מִגְרָשֶׁהָ עָרִים אַרְבַּע: כָּל־
עָרֵי בְנֵי־אַהֲרֹן הַכֹּהֲנִים שְׁלֹשׁ־עֶשְׂרֵה
כ עָרִים וּמִגְרְשֵׁיהֶן: וּלְמִשְׁפְּחוֹת
בְּנֵי־קְהָת הַלְוִיִּם הַנּוֹתָרִים מִבְּנֵי קְהָת
כא וַיְהִי עָרֵי גוֹרָלָם מִמַּטֵּה אֶפְרָיִם: וַיִּתְּנוּ
לָהֶם אֶת־עִיר מִקְלַט הָרֹצֵחַ אֶת־שְׁכֶם
וְאֶת־מִגְרָשֶׁהָ בְּהַר אֶפְרָיִם וְאֶת־גֶּזֶר
כב וְאֶת־מִגְרָשֶׁהָ: וְאֶת־קִבְצַיִם וְאֶת־מִגְרָשֶׁהָ
וְאֶת־בֵּית חוֹרֹן וְאֶת־מִגְרָשֶׁהָ עָרִים
כג אַרְבַּע: וּמִמַּטֵּה־דָן אֶת־
אֶלְתְּקֵא וְאֶת־מִגְרָשֶׁהָ אֶת־גִּבְּתוֹן
כד וְאֶת־מִגְרָשֶׁהָ: אֶת־אַיָּלוֹן וְאֶת־מִגְרָשֶׁהָ
אֶת־גַּת־רִמּוֹן וְאֶת־מִגְרָשֶׁהָ עָרִים
כה אַרְבַּע: וּמִמַּחֲצִית מַטֵּה מְנַשֶּׁה
אֶת־תַּעְנַךְ וְאֶת־מִגְרָשֶׁהָ וְאֶת־גַּת רִמּוֹן
כו וְאֶת־מִגְרָשֶׁהָ עָרִים שְׁתָּיִם: כָּל־עָרִים
עֶשֶׂר וּמִגְרְשֵׁיהֶן לְמִשְׁפְּחוֹת בְּנֵי־קְהָת
כז הַנּוֹתָרִים: וְלִבְנֵי גֵרְשׁוֹן
מִמִּשְׁפְּחֹת הַלְוִיִּם מֵחֲצִי מַטֵּה מְנַשֶּׁה
°גּוֹלָן ק׳ אֶת־עִיר מִקְלַט הָרֹצֵחַ אֶת־°גלון בַּבָּשָׁן
וְאֶת־מִגְרָשֶׁהָ וְאֶת־בְּעֶשְׁתְּרָה וְאֶת־
רוו מִגְרָשֶׁהָ עָרִים שְׁתָּיִם: וּמִמַּטֵּה

18. עֲנָתוֹת — *Anasos.*

This city was not mentioned before among the cities of Benjamin in Chapter 18. It was located about four miles northeast of Jerusalem *(T'vuos HaAretz).*

Evyasar the Kohen was exiled to this city by King Solomon *(Radak* to *I Kings* 2:26). The prophet Jeremiah who was also a *Kohen* came from this city *(Radak* to *Jeremiah* 1:1).

עַלְמוֹן — *Almon.*

This city is identical with Alemes, mentioned in *I Chronicles* 6:45, and with Bachurim, mentioned in *II Samuel* 16:5 *(Rashi).*

It was located about a mile northeast of Anasos.

its open land and Almon and its open land — four
cities; 19 *all the cities of the sons of Aaron the*
Kohanim — thirteen cities and their open lands.
20 *And to the families of the sons of Kehas, the*
Levites, the remaining children of Kehas — the cities
of their draw from the tribe of Ephraim. 21 *They gave*
them the city of refuge for a murderer, Shechem and
its open land in the mountains of Ephraim and Gezer
and its open land; 22 *and Kivtzayim and its open land*
and Beis Choron and its open land — four cities.
23 *And from the tribe of Dan, Eltekai and its open*
land; Gibson and its open land; 24 *Ayalon and its*
open land, Gas Rimon and its open land — four cities.
25 *And from part of the tribe of Menashe, Ta'anach*
and its open land and Gas Rimon and its open land —
two cities. 26 *All the ten cities and their open lands*
were for the remaining families of the sons of Kehas.
27 *And to the sons of Gershon of the families of the*
Levites — from part of the tribe of Menashe — the
city of refuge for a murderer, Golan in the Bashan
and its open land, and Beshterah and its open land —
two cities.

◆§ The Cities of Kehas — from Ephraim, Dan and half of Menashe

21. שְׁכֶם — *Shechem.*
See *Commentary* to 20:7.

גֶּזֶר — *Gezer.*
See *Commentary* to 16:3.

22. קִבְצַיִם — *Kivtzaim.*
Its location is unknown.

בֵּית חֹרוֹן — *Beis Choron.*
It is not clear whether this refers to Upper Beis Choron (16:5) or Lower Beis Choron (16:3) *(T'vuos HaAretz).*

23. אֶלְתְּקֵא — *Eltekei.*
See *Commentary* to 19:44.

גִּבְּתוֹן — *Gibson.*
See *Commentary* to 19:44.

24. אַיָּלוֹן — *Ayalon.*
See *Commentary* to 19:42.

25. תַּעְנַךְ — *Ta'anach.*
See *Commentary* to 12:21.

גַּת רִמּוֹן — *Gas Rimon.*
T'vuos HaAretz identifies this city as Bilam mentioned in *I Chronicles* 6:55.

◆§ The Cities of Gershon — from half of Menashe, Yisachar, Asher, and Naftali

27. גּוֹלָן — *Golan.*
See *Commentary* to 20:8.

בְּעֶשְׁתְּרָה — *Beshterah.*
This is the city of Ashtaros [see *Commentary* to 12:4].

יִשָּׂשכָר אֶת־קִשְׁיוֹן וְאֶת־מִגְרָשֶׁהָ אֶת־
כט דָּבְרַת וְאֶת־מִגְרָשֶׁהָ׃ אֶת־יַרְמוּת וְאֶת־
מִגְרָשֶׁהָ אֶת־עֵין גַּנִּים וְאֶת־מִגְרָשֶׁהָ
ל עָרִים אַרְבַּע׃ וּמִמַּטֵּה
אָשֵׁר אֶת־מִשְׁאָל וְאֶת־מִגְרָשֶׁהָ אֶת־
לא עַבְדּוֹן וְאֶת־מִגְרָשֶׁהָ׃ אֶת־חֶלְקָת וְאֶת־
מִגְרָשֶׁהָ וְאֶת־רְחֹב וְאֶת־מִגְרָשֶׁהָ עָרִים
לב אַרְבַּע׃ וּמִמַּטֵּה נַפְתָּלִי אֶת־עִיר
מִקְלַט הָרֹצֵחַ אֶת־קֶדֶשׁ בַּגָּלִיל וְאֶת־
מִגְרָשֶׁהָ וְאֶת־חַמֹּת דֹּאר וְאֶת־מִגְרָשֶׁהָ
וְאֶת־קַרְתָּן וְאֶת־מִגְרָשֶׁהָ עָרִים שָׁלֹשׁ׃
לג כָּל־עָרֵי הַגֵּרְשֻׁנִּי לְמִשְׁפְּחֹתָם שְׁלֹשׁ־
לד עֶשְׂרֵה עִיר וּמִגְרְשֵׁיהֶן׃ וּלְמִשְׁפְּחוֹת
בְּנֵי־מְרָרִי הַלְוִיִּם הַנּוֹתָרִים מֵאֵת מַטֵּה
זְבוּלֻן אֶת־יָקְנְעָם וְאֶת־מִגְרָשֶׁהָ אֶת־
לה קַרְתָּה וְאֶת־מִגְרָשֶׁהָ׃ אֶת־דִּמְנָה וְאֶת־
מִגְרָשֶׁהָ אֶת־נַהֲלָל וְאֶת־מִגְרָשֶׁהָ עָרִים
לו אַרְבַּע׃ וּמִמַּטֵּה־גָד אֶת־עִיר
מִקְלַט הָרֹצֵחַ אֶת־רָמֹת בַּגִּלְעָד וְאֶת־
לז מִגְרָשֶׁהָ וְאֶת־מַחֲנַיִם וְאֶת־מִגְרָשֶׁהָ׃ אֶת־
חֶשְׁבּוֹן וְאֶת־מִגְרָשֶׁהָ אֶת־יַעְזֵר וְאֶת־

28. קִשְׁיוֹן — *Kishyon.*
See *Commentary* to 19:20.

דָּבְרַת — *Davras*
This city was located about one mile west of Mount Tabor.

29. יַרְמוּת — *Yarmus.*
This is the city Rames mentioned in 19:21 *(T'vuos HaAretz).*

עֵין גַּנִּים — *Ein Ganim.*
See *Commentary* to 19:21.

30. מִשְׁאָל — *Mishal.*
T'vuos HaAretz cites a source which locates this city on the Mediterranean coast near Mount Carmel, but it is presently unknown.

עַבְדּוֹן — *Avdon.*
This is the city of Evron mentioned in 19:28 *(T'vuos HaAretz).*

31. חֶלְקָת — *Chelkas.*
See *Commentary* to 19:25.

רְחֹב — *Rechov.*
It is unclear to which Rechov this verse refers, for there were two in Asher's territory (19:28; 19:30) *(T'vuos HaAretz).*

[28] *And from the tribe of Yisachar — Kishyon and
its open land, Davras and its open land;* [29] *Yarmus
and its open land, Ein Ganim and its open land —
four cities.*

[30] *And from the tribe of Asher — Mishal and its
open land, Avdon and its open land;* [31] *Chelkas and
its open land, Rechov and its open land — four cities.*

[32] *And from the tribe of Naftali — the city of
refuge for a murderer, Kedesh in the Galilee and its
open land, Chamos Dor and its open land, and
Kartan and its open land — three cities;* [33] *all the cities
of Gershon according to their families — thirteen
cities and their open land.*

[34] *And for the families of the sons of Merari the
remaining Levites — from the tribe of Zevulun —
Yakne'am and its open land. Kartah and its open
land;* [35] *Dimnah and its open land, Nahalal and its
open land — four cities.*

[36] *And from the tribe of Gad, the city of refuge for
a murderer, Ramos Gilead and its open land, and
Machanayim and its open land;* [37] *Cheshbon and its
open land, Yazer and its open land — all the cities
four.*

32. קֶדֶשׁ — *Kedesh.*
See *Commentary* to 19:37.

חַמֹּת דֹּאר — *Chamos Dor.*
This is the city of Tiberias.

קַרְתָּן — *Kartan.*
This location of this city is unknown *(T'vuos HaAretz).*

◆§ The Cities of Merari — from Zevulun, Reuben and Gad

34. יָקְנְעָם — *Yakne'am.*
See *Commentary* to 12:22.

קַרְתָּה — *Kartah.*
It was the city of Tavor mentioned among the cities of Yisachar. One half of Mount Tabor belonged to Yisachar and one half to Zevulun. The city of Tavor was located on the border between them *(T'vuos HaAretz).*

35. דִּמְנָה — *Dimnah.*
This city is identical with the city of Rimon mentioned in 19:13 *(T'vuos HaAretz).*

נַהֲלָל — *Nahalal.*
See *Commentary* to 19:15.

36. [See *Commentary* to verse 7 regarding the omission of the cities from the tribe of Reuben from these verses.]

מַחֲנַיִם — *Machanayim.*
See *Commentary* to 13:26.

37. חֶשְׁבּוֹן — *Cheshbon.*
See *Commentary* to 12:2.

יַעְזֵר — *Yazer.*
See *Commentary* to 13:25.

כא
לח־מג

לח מִגְרָשֶׁהָ כָּל־עָרִים אַרְבַּע׃ כָּל־
הֶעָרִים לִבְנֵי מְרָרִי לְמִשְׁפְּחֹתָם הַנּוֹתָרִים
מִמִּשְׁפְּחוֹת הַלְוִיִּם וַיְהִי גּוֹרָלָם עָרִים
לט שְׁתֵּים עֶשְׂרֵה׃ כֹּל עָרֵי הַלְוִיִּם בְּתוֹךְ
אֲחֻזַּת בְּנֵי־יִשְׂרָאֵל עָרִים אַרְבָּעִים
מ וּשְׁמֹנֶה וּמִגְרְשֵׁיהֶן׃ תִּהְיֶינָה הֶעָרִים
הָאֵלֶּה עִיר עִיר וּמִגְרָשֶׁיהָ סְבִיבֹתֶיהָ כֵּן
מא לְכָל־הֶעָרִים הָאֵלֶּה׃ וַיִּתֵּן
יהוה לְיִשְׂרָאֵל אֶת־כָּל־הָאָרֶץ אֲשֶׁר
נִשְׁבַּע לָתֵת לַאֲבוֹתָם וַיִּרָשׁוּהָ וַיֵּשְׁבוּ בָהּ׃
מב וַיָּנַח יהוה לָהֶם מִסָּבִיב כְּכֹל אֲשֶׁר־נִשְׁבַּע
לַאֲבוֹתָם וְלֹא־עָמַד אִישׁ בִּפְנֵיהֶם מִכָּל־
אֹיְבֵיהֶם אֵת כָּל־אֹיְבֵיהֶם נָתַן יהוה
מג בְּיָדָם׃ לֹא־נָפַל דָּבָר מִכֹּל הַדָּבָר הַטּוֹב
אֲשֶׁר־דִּבֶּר יהוה אֶל־בֵּית יִשְׂרָאֵל

כב
א

א הַכֹּל בָּא׃ אָז יִקְרָא

God's Promises Fulfilled

41-43. After the conclusion of the conquest and division of the Land, Scripture recounts the seven things which were accomplished *(Malbim).* [These seven will be explained in the following comments.]

וַיִּתֵּן ה׳ — *HASHEM gave.*

(1) HASHEM gave them the land as a gift, as He had promised the Patriarchs *(Genesis* 15:8) *(Malbim).*

[This verse also marks the fulfillment of His promise to Joshua and Israel in 1:2, *'the land which I give to ... the Children of Israel.'*]

אֲשֶׁר נִשְׁבַּע לָתֵת לַאֲבוֹתָם — *Which He swore to give to their fathers.*

[This verse marks the fulfillment of the statement God made to Joshua in 1:6: *'because you will cause this people to inherit the Land which I have sworn to their fathers.'*]

וַיִּרָשׁוּהָ — *And they inherited it.*

(2) Israel inherited the Land because God cleared it from its inhabitants and thus made it available to the Jews *(Malbim).*

וַיֵּשְׁבוּ בָהּ — *And dwelled in it.*

(3) Each tribe dwelled in the territory which had been assigned to it during the seven years of division *(Malbim).*

42. וַיָּנַח ה׳ לָהֶם — *And HASHEM gave them rest.*

(4) The war with their enemies had ended *(Malbim).*

[This verse marks the fulfillment of Joshua's prediction *'Until HASHEM gives your brothers rest'* (1:15).]

וְלֹא־עָמַד אִישׁ בִּפְנֵיהֶם — *No man stood before them.*

(5) While the actual conquest was going on, the enemy offered no resistance, but fell before the Jews *(Malbim).*

38 *All the cities for the sons of Merari according to
their families from the remaining families of the
Levites — their draw was twelve cities.*
39 *All the cities of the Levites within the inheritance
of the Children of Israel — forty-eight and their open
lands.* 40 *These cities shall be — each city with its
encircling open land; so shall it be for all these cities.*
41 *HASHEM gave to Israel the entire Land which He
swore to give to their fathers; and they inherited it
and dwelled in it.* 42 *And HASHEM gave them rest
from all sides, as all He had sworn to their fathers. No
man stood before them from all their enemies. All
their enemies HASHEM delivered into their hands.*
43 *Nothing was lacking from all the good things of
which HASHEM told the House of Israel. Everything
was fulfilled.*

אֵת כָּל־אֹיְבֵיהֶם נָתַן ה׳ בְּיָדָם — *All their enemies HASHEM delivered into their hands.*

(6) He delivered them by miracles and by Divine Providence *(Malbim).*

43. לֹא־נָפַל דָּבָר — *Nothing was lacking.*

(7) Every blessing and accomplishment which God had promised them in the Torah was fulfilled *(Malbim).*

Even though certain lands had not yet been conquered, this was due to Joshua's and Israel's lassitude *(Ralbag)* [rather than to God's failure to fulfill His promises to the Jewish people].

XXII

It was explained in the Prefatory Remarks *to 1:12-18 that the tribes of Reuben, Gad and part of Menashe pledged to Moses to assist the other tribes conquer and settle* Eretz Yisrael *proper in return for the territory they found desirable on the eastern bank of the Jordan (see* footnote *to 1:14). In addition, they volunteered to remain with their brethren on the western side of the Jordan until the Land was apportioned to all the tribes. After each tribe received its inheritance (Chapters 13-19) and the Levites received their cities (Chapter 21), the pledge made by these three tribes had been completely fulfilled and they could have immediately returned home to their families. They awaited Joshua's approval for dismissal, however, as a display of honor for their revered leader* (Lev Aharon).

Although the agreement these tribes made with Moses was initiated by them, after they agreed to Moses' conditions, they were no longer at liberty to renounce their claim to the Trans-Jordan in order to refrain from participating in the conquest, for once they had committed themselves, it became a Divinely imposed obligation for them to conquer Eretz Yisrael. *Moses admonished these tribes by saying,* 'If you will not do so [*participate in the conquest*], you will have sinned against HASHEM' (Numbers *32:23). It is evident, then, that failure to participate in the conquest was not merely the abnegation of a voluntary fulfillment of a*

יְהוֹשֻׁעַ לָרְאוּבֵנִי וְלַגָּדִי וְלַחֲצִי מַטֵּה
ב מְנַשֶּׁה׃ וַיֹּאמֶר אֲלֵיהֶם אַתֶּם שְׁמַרְתֶּם אֵת
כָּל־אֲשֶׁר צִוָּה אֶתְכֶם מֹשֶׁה עֶבֶד יהוה
וַתִּשְׁמְעוּ בְקוֹלִי לְכֹל אֲשֶׁר־צִוִּיתִי אֶתְכֶם׃
ג לֹא־עֲזַבְתֶּם אֶת־אֲחֵיכֶם זֶה יָמִים רַבִּים
עַד הַיּוֹם הַזֶּה וּשְׁמַרְתֶּם אֶת־מִשְׁמֶרֶת
ד מִצְוַת יהוה אֱלֹהֵיכֶם׃ וְעַתָּה הֵנִיחַ יהוה
אֱלֹהֵיכֶם לַאֲחֵיכֶם כַּאֲשֶׁר דִּבֶּר לָהֶם

condition for acquiring the Trans-Jordan, but was also considered a transgression against God. It was due to this Divinely imposed obligation that Joshua implored these tribes before they were about to cross the Jordan, 'Remember what Moses ... **commanded** you' (Joshua *1:13). Their participation was no longer voluntary, but obligatory.*

This dual nature of their agreement was alluded to by Moses when he blessed the tribe of Gad before his death. He executed the justice of HASHEM, and his judgments with Israel (Deuteronomy *33:21).* The justice of HASHEM *refers to their Divinely imposed obligation to participate in the conquest, and* the judgments with Israel *refers to their pledge to the Israelites to partipate in the conquest in exchange for the Trans-Jordan* (Brisker Rav *to* Deuteronomy *33:21).*

Before Joshua dismissed these tribes to return to the Trans-Jordan and begin their new lives, he extolled their virtues. Perhaps, in verse 3 Joshua praises them for fulfilling their two-fold obligation. You have not forsaken your brothers — *'you have participated in the conquest as you pledged in exchange for the Trans-Jordan.'* You have kept the charge of HASHEM — *'You have also fulfilled the Divinely imposed duty of participating in the conquest.'*

☙ Farewell to the tribes of Reuben, Gad, and Menashe.

1-9. Joshua's farewell to these tribes consisted of two parts — praises and words of encouragement and upliftment — in conformity with the *halachah* governing one's departure from his friend (see *Meiri, Berachos* 31a). Joshua identifies four noteworthy accomplishments of these tribes (see *Alshich,* verses 2 and 3) and then proceeds with a blessing that these tribes, although they will be separated from the Land and their brethren, should maintain an absolute adherence to God's law.

1. אָז — *Then.*

Then means upon completion of the division of the Land *(Mahari Kara).*

יִקְרָא — *Decided to call.*

[See *Commentary* to 10:12 where two possible translations of this 'then-future' construction are cited. According to *Ibn Ezra,* this phrase should be rendered in the past tense, *then Joshua called.*

However, according to *Rashi,* this phrase should be translated, *then* — upon completion of the division of the Land — *Joshua decided to call.* Thus, in *Rashi's* view, Joshua reviewed the efforts of these three tribes over the past fourteen years. Since he was so pleased with all their accomplishments during this time, he enumerates them as praises (see *Commentary* further) before dispatching them to return to their families across the Jordan.]

לָרְאוּבֵנִי וְלַגָּדִי וְלַחֲצִי מַטֵּה מְנַשֶּׁה — *The Reubenites, and the Gadites and part of*

*1 Then Joshua decided to call the Reubenites, and
the Gadites and part of the tribe of Menashe. 2 And
he said to them, 'You fulfilled all that Moses, servant
of HASHEM commanded you, and you have listened
to my voice, to all that I have commanded you. 3 You
have not forsaken your brothers these many days —
to this day. You have kept the charge of the
commandments of HASHEM your God. 4 And now
HASHEM your God has given rest to your brothers as*

the tribe of Menashe.

[These were the tribes who inherited the land on the eastern side of the Jordan and pledged to help the other tribes conquer and settle *Eretz Yisrael* proper (see 1:12-18).]

2. אֲשֶׁר צִוָּה אֶתְכֶם מֹשֶׁה — *That Moses ... commanded you.*

Moses had commanded them to *cross over* [the Jordan], *every man armed for war (Numbers* 32:27) [in order to receive territory east of the Jordan] *(Metzudos).*

(a) You not only fulfilled your agreement with Moses to participate in the seven year conquest of the Land ... *(Alshich).*

וַתִּשְׁמְעוּ בְּקוֹלִי — *And you have listened to my voice.*

(b) ... you also fulfilled my orders. I commanded you to make an unconventional seige of Jericho by encircling the city and trumpeting shofars, and you listened. I commanded you to ambush Ai, and you listened. You meticulously followed all my orders *(Alshich).*

3. לֹא־עֲזַבְתֶּם אֶת־אֲחֵיכֶם — *You have not forsaken your brothers.*

(c) In addition to participating in the conquest of the Land and obeying my orders, you did not forsake your brothers and you therefore remained in *Eretz Yisrael* until the division of the Land was completed. This took an additional seven years *(Alshich).*

עַד הַיּוֹם הַזֶּה — *To this day.*

(d) You remained in the Land *until this day* when I summoned you. This illustrates your eagerness to even exceed my orders *(Alshich).*

וּשְׁמַרְתֶּם אֶת־מִשְׁמֶרֶת — *You have kept the charge* [lit. *protection*].

Your remaining in the Land for seven years after the conquest was a 'fence' around your commitment to participate in the conquest. In this way you safeguarded your pledge. If you were so exacting in Your commitment to God's servant and to me, *you* [certainly] *will keep the charge of the commandments of HASHEM your God (Alshich).*

Abarbanel understands this phrase more literally that the verb is in the past tense. He suggests that this phrase refers to the fact that these tribes walked with the Holy Ark and protected it.

4. ... וְעַתָּה הֵנִיחַ ה׳ — *And now HASHEM ... has given rest* [*to your brothers*].

Do not think that you need to remain in the Land because it was not entirely conquered. Those parts which are as yet unconquered will be easily acquired, for *God has given rest to your brothers.* Thus, your participation is unnecessary and you have permission to return *(Meam Loez).*

Others suggest that Joshua intended to inform these tribes that it was not their physical assistance which brought about the victory, but their willingness to participate, which demonstrated the great unity among the Israelites. In the merit of this unity, *God has given rest to your brothers (Meam Loez).*

וְעַתָּ֗ה פְּנ֞וּ וּלְכ֣וּ לָכֶ֗ם לְאָֽהֳלֵיכֶם֮ אֶל־
אֶ֣רֶץ אֲחֻזַּתְכֶ֒ם אֲשֶׁ֣ר ׀ נָתַ֣ן לָכֶ֗ם מֹשֶׁה֙
ה עֶ֣בֶד יְהוָ֔ה בְּעֵ֖בֶר הַיַּרְדֵּֽן׃ רַ֣ק ׀ שִׁמְר֣וּ
מְאֹ֡ד לַעֲשׂ֞וֹת אֶת־הַמִּצְוָ֣ה וְאֶת־הַתּוֹרָ֗ה
אֲשֶׁ֨ר צִוָּ֣ה אֶתְכֶם֮ מֹשֶׁ֣ה עֶֽבֶד־יְהוָה֒
לְ֠אַהֲבָה אֶת־יְהוָ֨ה אֱלֹהֵיכֶ֜ם וְלָלֶ֧כֶת
בְּכָל־דְּרָכָ֛יו וְלִשְׁמֹ֥ר מִצְוֺתָ֖יו וּֽלְדָבְקָה־
ב֑וֹ וּלְעָבְד֕וֹ בְּכָל־לְבַבְכֶ֖ם וּבְכָל־נַפְשְׁכֶֽם׃
ו וַיְבָרְכֵ֖ם יְהוֹשֻׁ֑עַ וַֽיְשַׁלְּחֵ֔ם וַיֵּלְכ֖וּ אֶל־
ז אָהֳלֵיהֶֽם׃ וְלַחֲצִ֣י ׀
שֵׁ֣בֶט הַֽמְנַשֶּׁ֗ה נָתַ֣ן מֹשֶׁה֮ בַּבָּשָׁן֒ וּלְחֶצְי֗וֹ

5. רַק שִׁמְרוּ — *O that you should be* [*very*] *careful* [lit. *guard*].

The term רַק used here indicates a wish *(Ibn Janach;* see *Commentary* to 1:17).

Because these tribes would be permanently living very far from the Sanctuary, Joshua was concerned that their commitment to the observance of the *mitzvos* [precepts] would suffer. He therefore reminded them of their primary purpose in life *(Abarbanel).*

Joshua wanted to emphasize to these tribes that they were still required to firmly adhere to the Torah even though they would be living outside *Eretz Yisrael.* All the blessings and curses which were said regarding those living in *Eretz Yisrael* were also said in regard to them as well *(Lev Aharon).*

אֶת־הַמִּצְוָה — *The commandments* [lit. *the commandment*].

This refers to all the precepts, both positive and negative *(Ramban;* Introduction to *Genesis).*

וְאֶת־הַתּוֹרָה — *And the Torah.*

This refers to the narrative portions of the Pentateuch, which teach the foundations of belief in God *(Ramban,* Introduction to *Genesis).* [Perhaps this also refers to the study of Torah.]

לְאַהֲבָה אֶת־ה׳ — *To love HASHEM.*

This verse is closely patterned after *Deuteronomy* 10:12 and 11:22.

Sforno (Deuteronomy 11:22) comments that if one occupies himself with Torah *(Heed the commandments),* he will come to recognize the lovingkindness which God has shown him, and he will then come *to love HASHEM.*

וְלָלֶכֶת בְּכָל־דְּרָכָיו — *And to walk in all His ways.*

The precept of walking in God's ways *(Deuteronomy* 13:5) is interpreted by the *Talmud (Sotah* 14a) to mean that man should imitate the qualities of his Creator. Just as God clothes the naked, as it is written: *God made for Adam and his wife garments ... and He clothed them (Genesis* 3:21), so should man clothe the naked. Just as God visits the sick, as it is written: *HASHEM appeared to him* [*Abraham*] *in the plains of Mamre* [on the third day after his circumcision] *(Genesis* 18:1), so should man visit the sick.

וּלְדָבְקָה־בוֹ — *And to cling to Him.*

According to *Ibn Ezra (Deuteronomy* 11:22, as understood by *Ramban),* this phrase is not hortatory in nature, but rather expresses the result of adhering to the prescription laid down in the

He told them. Now turn and go to your dwellings, to
the land of your inheritance which Moses the servant
of HASHEM has given you across the Jordan. 5 *O that*
you should be very careful to observe the
commandments and the Torah which Moses the
servant of HASHEM has commanded you — to love
HASHEM your God and to walk in all His ways and to
observe His commandments and to cling to Him and
to serve Him with all your heart and with all your
soul.' 6 *Then Joshua blessed them and sent them*
away, and they went to their dwellings.
7 *And to part of the tribe of Menashe, Moses had*
given in the Bashan, and to part Joshua had given

beginning of the verse. If one loves God, follows in His ways, and keeps His commandments, **then** *he will cling to Him.*

Ramban (ibid.), however, contends that this phrase is another exhortation which prohibits idolatry. One may never allow his thoughts to stray from God and consider serving other gods. In his mind, he must always *cling to Him.*

Sforno (ibid.) understands 'clinging to God' as a complete submission of one's will to God's will, so that all the individual's actions will be done for the sake of Heaven.

6. אָהֳלֵיהֶם — *Their dwellings* [lit. *tents*].

Targum renders: to their cities.

[See *Commentary* to 3:14. In this context, it would appear that **אֹהֶל**, literally *tent,* means *wife,* as in *Deuteronomy* 5:27: *Return to your tents,* which the *Talmud (Beitzah* 5b) interprets as 'return to your wives.' For three days before the transmission of the Torah on Mount Sinai, husbands and wives were not permitted to live together. Afterwards, however, Moses told them: *Return to your tents.*

Similarly, in this context, Joshua charges them to return to their wives whom they had not seen for fourteen years (see *Bereishis Rabbah* 98:15), the duration of the conquest and division of the Land. During these years, the families of Reuben, Gad, and part of Menashe were located on the eastern side of the Jordan, as Joshua had commanded them in 1:14: *Your wives, your children, and your cattle will reside across the Jordan ... and the mighty warriors ... will cross over ...*]

7. וְלַחֲצִי שֵׁבֶט הַמְנַשֶּׁה — *And to part of the tribe of Menashe.*

At this point, Scripture explains why Joshua assembled only part of the tribe of Menashe, rather than the entire tribe. The reason, as explained in this verse, is that only part of the tribe of Menashe was given land to the east of the Jordan; the other part of Menashe was given land to the west of the Jordan *(Metzudos).*

Malbim, however, argues that Scripture need not repeat the fact that the tribe of Menashe was divided, for we were made aware of it previously. *Malbim* contends that Scripture mentions the fact of Menashe's division in this context in order to explain why Joshua blessed the tribe twice, once in verse 6 and once in verse 7. Since they were divided, they were in need of an extra blessing.

According to *Alshich,* Joshua was concerned that the tribe of Menashe was in need of an extra blessing for two

כב ח־ט

°בְּעֵבֶר ק׳

נָתַן יְהוֹשֻׁעַ עִם־אֲחֵיהֶם °מעֵבר הַיַּרְדֵּן
יָמָּה וְגַם כִּי שִׁלְּחָם יְהוֹשֻׁעַ אֶל־
ח אָהֳלֵיהֶם וַיְבָרְכֵם׃ וַיֹּאמֶר אֲלֵיהֶם
לֵאמֹר בִּנְכָסִים רַבִּים שׁוּבוּ אֶל־
אָהֳלֵיכֶם וּבְמִקְנֶה רַב־מְאֹד בְּכֶסֶף
וּבְזָהָב וּבִנְחֹשֶׁת וּבְבַרְזֶל וּבִשְׂלָמוֹת
הַרְבֵּה מְאֹד חִלְקוּ שְׁלַל־אֹיְבֵיכֶם
ט עִם־אֲחֵיכֶם׃ וַיָּשֻׁבוּ וַיֵּלְכוּ בְּנֵי־
רְאוּבֵן וּבְנֵי־גָד וַחֲצִי | שֵׁבֶט הַמְנַשֶּׁה מֵאֵת
בְּנֵי יִשְׂרָאֵל מִשִּׁלֹה אֲשֶׁר בְּאֶרֶץ־כְּנָעַן
לָלֶכֶת אֶל־אֶרֶץ הַגִּלְעָד אֶל־אֶרֶץ אֲחֻזָּתָם
אֲשֶׁר נֹאחֲזוּ־בָהּ עַל־פִּי יְהוָה בְּיַד־מֹשֶׁה׃

reasons: (a) since the remainder of their tribe would be settling in the holy environs of *Eretz Yisrael*, they might be grieved because they were excluded from this opportunity, (b) they did not request the Trans-Jordan along with the tribes of Reuben and Gad (see *Prefatory Remarks* to verse 1:14), but were assigned it by Moses. Therefore, Joshua spoke to them individually in order to comfort them.

שִׁלְּחָם יְהוֹשֻׁעַ ... וַיְבָרְכֵם — *Joshua sent them away ... (and) he blessed them.*

[It appears that this verse is a mere repetition of the previous one, since both verses mention Joshua's dispatching the tribes and blessing them.]

Rashi comments that this verse refers only to the dispatching of Menashe (see above comment), whereas verse 6 refers to the other two tribes.

Radak disagrees, suggesting that Joshua's blessing in this verse refers to all three tribes. Scripture repeats the fact that Joshua dispatched them and blessed them in order to introduce Joshua's statement to the three tribes in verse 8: *With much wealth return to your dwellings.*

The *Midrash (Bereishis Rabbah* 35:3) clarifies the apparent redundancy of verses 6 and 7 by explaining that Joshua actually dispatched the three tribes twice. After they asked permission to leave the first time, they were detained and could not leave for two days, at which time they again asked permission to leave. This incident is one of the sources for the *halachah* that one who asks his teacher for permission to leave town and is detained overnight, is required to ask him again (see *Rama, Yoreh Deah* 242:16; *Taz; Nekudas HaKesef).*

8. אֹיְבֵיכֶם — *Your enemies.*

The *Midrash (Bereishis Rabbah* 98:15) relates that for the fourteen years that these men were separated from their families in the Trans-Jordan both the fathers and their distant sons did not cut their hair as a sign of mourning. At that time, a group of people known as the Hagarites also allowed their hair to grow. Upon the return of these tribes to the Trans-Jordan, they witnessed a battle between their sons and the Hagarites, but were unable to identify their sons because they had not seen them for fourteen years. God intervened and motivated their sons to cry out, 'Help us, O God, help us ...,

among their brothers on the western side of the Jordan. Also, when Joshua sent them away to their dwellings he blessed them.
8 *And he said to them saying, 'With much wealth return to your dwellings, and with very much cattle, with silver, gold, copper, and iron and with very many garments. Divide the spoils of your enemies with your brothers.'*
9 *And the Children of Reuben, Gad, and part of the tribe of Menashe returned and went — from the Children of Israel — from Shiloh which is in the land of Canaan to travel to the land of Gilead, to the land of their inheritance which they took possession of in accordance with the word of HASHEM through*

whereupon the tribes came to their sons' rescue. R' Levi suggested that their sons were saved because of Joshua's blessing, *'Divide the spoils of your enemies.'* It is implied that these tribes will have future enemies whose possessions they will divide, namely the Hagarites.

עִם־אֲחֵיכֶם — *With your brothers.*

To what brothers was Joshua referring?

According to *Rashi's* view *(verse 7)* that Joshua was speaking only to the tribe of Menashe, the phrase *with your brothers* refers to the other two tribes which were traveling to the east of the Jordan — Reuben and Gad.

Joshua intended to demonstrate to the tribe of Menashe that although they were only a fraction of a tribe, they were as important as an entire tribe. He, therefore, gave them a share of the booty commensurate with the shares of Reuben and Gad *(Kli Yakar).*

Rashi notes that this phrase could also refer to the members of the tribes of Gad, Reuben, and Menashe who remained behind to protect the women, children, and cities. They would also receive a share of the booty.

Meam Loez comments that those members of Reuben and Gad who remained as the eastern side of the Jordan to guard the women, children, and chattel would have certainly been granted a share in the booty without Joshua's suggestion, for the principle that those who do not participate in the battles receive a share of the spoils had been established by Abraham. Abraham personally refused the spoils of war offered to him by the king of Sodom, but he did request a share for the young men who guarded the troops' possessions during battle. The tribe of Menashe, however, was not required to go to war (since they never requested territory in the Trans-Jordan), and they could have claimed that they would not be required to divide the spoils of their volunteer efforts with their brethren to the east of the Jordan. Therefore, Joshua exhorted them to divide their spoils with them.

Radak suggests that Joshua is telling Reuben, Gad, and Menashe they will receive a share of the booty along with the tribes who received their territories on the west bank of the Jordan.

9. וַיָּשֻׁבוּ וַיֵּלְכוּ — *And [they] returned and [they] went.*

The seeming redundancy *they returned* and *they went* can be understood in light of the *Midrash (Bereishis Rabbah* 35:3). In order to bestow honor on these three tribes, Joshua personally escorted them to the Jordan River.

כב
י־יב

י וַיָּבֹאוּ אֶל־גְּלִילוֹת הַיַּרְדֵּן אֲשֶׁר בְּאֶרֶץ
כְּנָעַן וַיִּבְנוּ בְנֵי־רְאוּבֵן וּבְנֵי־גָד וַחֲצִי
שֵׁבֶט הַמְנַשֶּׁה שָׁם מִזְבֵּחַ עַל־הַיַּרְדֵּן
יא מִזְבֵּחַ גָּדוֹל לְמַרְאֶה: וַיִּשְׁמְעוּ בְנֵי־
יִשְׂרָאֵל לֵאמֹר הִנֵּה־בָנוּ בְנֵי־רְאוּבֵן וּבְנֵי־
גָד וַחֲצִי שֵׁבֶט הַמְנַשֶּׁה אֶת־הַמִּזְבֵּחַ אֶל־
מוּל אֶרֶץ כְּנַעַן אֶל־גְּלִילוֹת הַיַּרְדֵּן אֶל־
יב עֵבֶר בְּנֵי יִשְׂרָאֵל: וַיִּשְׁמְעוּ בְּנֵי יִשְׂרָאֵל

When, however, they saw he would have to return home by himself, they escorted him to his house *(they returned)* and proceeded to the Trans-Jordan from there *(they went).*

Malbim suggests that Joshua had assembled these three tribes in his city Timnas Serach, which was located in Mount Ephraim, and had dispatched them to their homeland. However, instead of proceeding directly to the east bank of the Jordan, the tribes first traveled to Shiloh *(they returned)* in order to pray at the Sanctuary and to ask the Israelites there for permission to return home. From there they proceeded to the Trans-Jordan *(they went).*

◆§ The Suspected Rebellion

10-33. Before Reuben, Gad and Menashe departed from *Eretz Yisrael* proper, Joshua had emphatically urged them to maintain their love for God and their commitment to His commandments (verse 5). Afterwards, they went to Shiloh, the focal point of communal worship, and then traveled to the Jordan and built an altar on its west bank. When the nation heard that Gad, Reuben, and Menashe had built the altar, it thought that these tribes were rebelling against God, since it was forbidden to sacrifice on private altars after the Tabernacle was erected in Shiloh *(Rashi).*

The Israelites of the other tribes sent a representative contingent to investigate the matter and to stay civil war. Pinchas and the tribal leaders were justified in accusing these tribes of idolatry or rebellion, despite the Torah's requirement that one must judge another individual favorably even if by all indications he appears guilty. Since the tribes of Reuben, Gad, and Menashe had publicly constructed an altar, it was not unreasonable to assume that their intentions were idolatrous, for they had not fashioned it in a way which left no room for doubt *(Meam Loez).*

10. אֲשֶׁר בְּאֶרֶץ כְּנָעַן — *Which was in the land of Canaan.*

Our verse implies clearly that their motive in constructing the altar was honorable, in sharp contrast to that ascribed to them by the rest of Israel (see below). The fact that they built the altar on the west, rather than the east bank of the Jordan, indicates that they had no intention of separating themselves from the rest of the nation *(Malbim).*

Had they truly intended to offer sacrifices on this altar, they would have constructed it on the east bank of the Jordan where they were to reside.

עַל — *Near* [lit. *on*].

The translation follows *Metzudos.*

מִזְבֵּחַ גָּדוֹל — *A large altar.*

The fact that they built such a *large altar* is another indication that they did not intend to use it for sacrifices *(Meam Loez).*

לְמַרְאֶה — *As a showpiece.*

The altar was made for them to look

Moses. 10 *And they came to the region of the Jordan*
which was in the land of Canaan; the Children of
Reuben, Gad, and part of the tribe of Menashe built
an altar there, near the Jordan — a large altar as a
showpiece. 11 *And the Children of Israel heard as*
follows; 'Behold, the Children of Reuben, Gad, and
part of the tribe of Menashe have built the altar
across the land of Canaan in the region of the Jordan,
on the side of the Children of Israel.' 12 *And the*

at, not to serve as a place for sacrifices *(Metzudos).*

Mahari Kara suggests that these tribes chose the design of an altar for the monument they built in order to show that they have a share in the public sacrifices which are offered in the Sanctuary at Shiloh and that they always have the right to travel to Shiloh and offer sacrifices.

Why was it, in fact, permissible for these tribes to construct the altar in apparent violation of the command, *You shall not make with Me gods of silver (Exodus* 20:20), which the *Talmud (Avodah Zarah* 43a) interprets as a prohibition against making objects which appear similar to the vessels used in the Temple? [According to *Rambam (Beis HaBechirah* 7:10), however, the prohibition against making these objects is part of the positive commandment to revere the Holy Temple.]

Meshech Chachmah (Exodus 20:20) maintains that although there is a prohibition against fashioning objects similar to the vessels of the Temple, this prohibition does not apply to making an altar. He argues that if it were prohibited, it would never have been permissible to offer sacrifices on private altars, as indeed it was before the Sanctuary was erected in Shiloh. According to his view, construction of this altar was not forbidden.

Malbim suggests that an altar is only considered to resemble the altar of the Temple if it is made in such a way that one could offer sacrifices upon it. The altar which Reuben, Gad, and Menashe built, however, had no steps and was very high, which obviously rendered it inappropriate for offering sacrifices. This is the meaning of the verse *(Joshua* 22:10), *a large altar as a showpiece,* for their altar was intended as a monument, rather than as a place to offer sacrifices.

Similarly, *Meshech Chachmah* suggests that the prohibition against making replicas of the vessels of the Temple applies only if the one who makes them intends to use them. However, since Reuben, Gad, and Menashe intended to make a memorial which would not be used for sacrifices, their altar was permissible.

11. וַיִּשְׁמְעוּ בְנֵי־יִשְׂרָאֵל — *And the Children of Israel heard.*

They heard about the altar and assumed that these tribes had built a replica of the altar at Shiloh on the west bank of the Jordan in order to attract the nine and one half tribes living west of the Jordan to their alien form of worship *(Malbim).*

לֵאמֹר — *As follows* [lit. *saying*].

In this context, this word means that what was heard was permissible to repeat to others. According to *Alshich,* Scripture repeats, *And the Children of Israel heard* (verses 11 and 12), because there were two distinct stages of revelation of the incident with the altar. First, a small group of people *heard* about the altar (verse 11). After their story was corroborated by witnesses, they were allowed to repeat it (לֵאמֹר) to the public. As a result, the entire nation *heard* and assembled (verse 12).

הַמִּזְבֵּחַ — *The altar.*

Scripture does not say *an* altar, but rather *the* altar, for the Israelites west of the Jordan thought that Reuben, Gad, and Menashe had built a replica of the altar in Shiloh *(Malbim).*

כב
יג־טז

וַיִּקָּהֲלוּ כָּל־עֲדַת בְּנֵי־יִשְׂרָאֵל שִׁלֹה
יג לַעֲלוֹת עֲלֵיהֶם לַצָּבָא׃ וַיִּשְׁלְחוּ
בְנֵי־יִשְׂרָאֵל אֶל־בְּנֵי־רְאוּבֵן וְאֶל־בְּנֵי־גָד
וְאֶל־חֲצִי שֵׁבֶט־מְנַשֶּׁה אֶל־אֶרֶץ הַגִּלְעָד
יד אֶת־פִּינְחָס בֶּן־אֶלְעָזָר הַכֹּהֵן׃ וַעֲשָׂרָה
נְשִׂאִים עִמּוֹ נָשִׂיא אֶחָד נָשִׂיא אֶחָד לְבֵית
אָב לְכֹל מַטּוֹת יִשְׂרָאֵל וְאִישׁ רֹאשׁ בֵּית־
טו אֲבוֹתָם הֵמָּה לְאַלְפֵי יִשְׂרָאֵל׃ וַיָּבֹאוּ אֶל־
בְּנֵי־רְאוּבֵן וְאֶל־בְּנֵי־גָד וְאֶל־חֲצִי שֵׁבֶט־
מְנַשֶּׁה אֶל־אֶרֶץ הַגִּלְעָד וַיְדַבְּרוּ אִתָּם
טז לֵאמֹר׃ כֹּה אָמְרוּ כֹּל ׀ עֲדַת יהוה מָה־
הַמַּעַל הַזֶּה אֲשֶׁר מְעַלְתֶּם בֵּאלֹהֵי

12. וַיִּשְׁמְעוּ בְּנֵי יִשְׂרָאֵל — *And the Children of Israel heard.*

Scripture repeats this phrase to emphasize that immediately upon hearing of the episode of the altar, the people assembled without delay to determine the appropriate response *(Poras Yosef).*

They were so enraged that they mistakenly failed to consult Joshua and the Sanhedrin, a prerequisite for waging war. This explains why Scripture does not mention Joshua's inclusion in the assembly. After they assembled, however, they realized that they were obligated to make a gesture of peace before waging war, for this practice was required for even non-Jewish enemies *(Alshich).*

לַצָּבָא — *With an army.*

The translation follows *Radak.*

The nation was planning to wage war against these tribes because it was forbidden to build other altars after the altar at Shiloh had been erected *(Rashi).*

The nation did not intend to wage war immediately against Reuben, Gad, and Menashe, for they hoped to persuade these tribes to repent. Only if they were not successful, did they plan to wage war *(Alshich).*

Had Reuben, Gad, and Menashe been guilty and unwilling to repent, would the Israelites have been justified in waging war against them? May one Jew kill another without due process? *Rambam (Moreh Nevuchim* 3:41) asserts that any Jew who flagrantly violates a law in the Torah to demonstrate his denial of its veracity is considered a heretic, and as such deserves the death penalty regardless of the specific infraction he committed. Similarly, if a group of Jews who are knowledgeable of the Torah rebels and behaves in a heretical manner, they, too, deserve the death penalty. Thus, if Reuben, Gad, and Menashe had indeed violated the prohibition of sacrificing on the altar and had not repented, the other Israelites would have been justified in going to war against them.

13. וַיִּשְׁלְחוּ בְנֵי־יִשְׂרָאֵל — *The Children of Israel sent.*

Before they advanced to wage war, they sent a contingent to convince Reuben, Gad, and Menashe to repent *(Metzudos).*

פִּינְחָס בֶּן־אֶלְעָזָר הַכֹּהֵן — *Pinchas the son*

Children of Israel heard. The entire congregation of
the Children of Israel assembled at Shiloh to advance
upon them with an army.
13 *The Children of Israel sent Pinchas the son of*
Elazar the Kohen to the land of Gilead — to the
Children of Reuben, Gad, and half of the tribe of
Menashe. 14 *And ten leaders with him, one leader of a*
father's house for each of the tribes of Israel; the men
were the heads of their patriarchal houses of the
thousands of Israel. 15 *They came to the Children of*
Reuben, to Gad and to part of the tribe of Menashe in
the land of Gilead, and they spoke with them saying,
16 *'Thus said the entire congregation of HASHEM,*
"What is this betrayal that you have committed

of Elazar the Kohen.

Pinchas the High Priest was sent to admonish these tribes about the sacrifices they allegedly offered on the unauthorized altar *(Abarbanel,* continued from verse 12).

Alshich suggests that Pinchas was particularly appropriate for this mission because he represented שָׁלוֹם, *peace.* The Israelites truly wished to avoid war with what they thought were their estranged brethren [see *Numbers* 25:12, which explains why Pinchas represented peace].

Others suggest that Pinchas was dispatched, not as a gesture of peace, but as a symbol of war. Pinchas was the priest anointed for war, as the Torah relates in *Deuteronomy (Kli Yakar).*

Daas Sofrim adds that Pinchas had also demonstrated his zealotry in regard to the episode with Kazbi daughter of Tzur (see *Numbers* 25:6). Thus, he embodied two qualities which were essential in this mission: zeal in the safeguarding of God's precepts and love of peace.

14. וַעֲשָׂרָה נְשִׂאִים — *And ten leaders.*

In order to end the tribes' supposed rebellion against the as emissaries to the tribes *(Abarbanel).*

Alshich suggests that the Israelites sent these ten princes — who were also the military heads of the tribes — as a counterpoise to Pinchas, who represented peace. Thus, Reuben, Gad, and Menashe could clearly see that the alternative to repenting and acceding to Pinchas' plea for peace, was war.

15. אֶל ... וְאֶל ... וְאֶל — *To ... and to ... and to ...*

Scripture interjects the word 'to' before each tribe to indicate that the princes spoke to each one separately. They were ordered to do this by the assembly in order to determine if the tribes' explanations were consistent with one another *(Kli Yakar).*

16. מָה־הַמַּעַל — *What is this betrayal?*

The Israelites were not certain whether the altar was built for idolatry or for offering sacrifices to God. The former would indicate that they were betraying God, in spite of His miraculous help, whereas the latter would suggest that they were unmindful of the centralization of spiritual authority of Shiloh.

Verses 16-18 refer to the idolatry of which Reuben, Gad, and Menashe were suspected. In verse 19 the princes urge the tribes not to violate the prohibition

יִשְׂרָאֵל לָשׁוּב הַיּוֹם מֵאַחֲרֵי יְהוָה
בִּבְנוֹתְכֶם לָכֶם מִזְבֵּחַ לִמְרָדְכֶם הַיּוֹם
יז בַּיהוָה׃ הַמְעַט־לָנוּ אֶת־עֲוֺן פְּעוֹר אֲשֶׁר
לֹא־הִטַּהַרְנוּ מִמֶּנּוּ עַד הַיּוֹם הַזֶּה
יח וַיְהִי הַנֶּגֶף בַּעֲדַת יְהוָה׃ וְאַתֶּם תָּשֻׁבוּ
הַיּוֹם מֵאַחֲרֵי יְהוָה וְהָיָה אַתֶּם תִּמְרְדוּ
הַיּוֹם בַּיהוָה וּמָחָר אֶל־כָּל־עֲדַת
יט יִשְׂרָאֵל יִקְצֹף׃ וְאַךְ אִם־טְמֵאָה אֶרֶץ
אֲחֻזַּתְכֶם עִבְרוּ לָכֶם אֶל־אֶרֶץ אֲחֻזַּת

of sacrificing on an unauthorized altar *(Malbim)*.

לָשׁוּב הַיּוֹם מֵאַחֲרֵי ה׳ — *To turn away from HASHEM this day.*

Pinchas and the princes asked 'How could you possibly turn away from God *this day* while His miracles are still fresh in your mind? How could you actively rebel against Him by building this altar?' *(Malbim)*.

בִּבְנוֹתְכֶם לָכֶם מִזְבֵּחַ — *By your building an altar.*

Here they hypothesize that the altar was built for idol worship *(Malbim)*.

17. הַמְעַט — *Is* [*it*] ... *not enough* [lit. *is it small*]?

Malbim explains that Pinchas is justifying his intrusion into the affairs of Reuben, Gad, and Menashe on the grounds that two negative consequences could result from the erection of the altar, just as two tragedies were caused by the sin of Ba'al Peor (see *Malbim* further).

Abarbanel suggests that Pinchas' remonstrance was intended to protect the ten tribes to the west of the Jordan from Divine punishment, for if no Jew protested against Reuben, Gad, and Menashe's activity, God would hold the entire nation responsible for their sin. Such an incident occurred in the time of Yeravam son of Nevat, who began to do things which resembled idol worship. Because no one protested, God decreed that the Israelites would be exiled.

עֲוֺן פְּעוֹר — *Sin of Peor.*

In the last year of the Israelites' journey through the wilderness, in the city of Shittim, they were approached by the daughters of Moab, who enticed the men to immorality. Before the Moabite women allowed the men to sin with them, however, they insisted that the men worship their idol, Ba'al Peor.

God then punished the Jews with a plague in which 24,000 were killed (see *Numbers* 25:1-6).

אֲשֶׁר לֹא־הִטַּהַרְנוּ מִמֶּנּוּ עַד הַיּוֹם הַזֶּה — *From which we have not become cleansed until this day.*

Malbim continues: This sin could be to our eternal discredit as a nation, as was the sin of Ba'al Peor.

The *Midrash* states that Moses was buried across from Beis Peor, the place of this disgusting form of idolatry, so that he could atone for the sin Israel committed there. Each year, at the time the Israelites sinned with the daughters of Moab, a destructive angel created by the Israelites' sin with Peor *(Maharsha)* rises to heaven to accuse Israel of this sin. When it views the gravesite of Moses, however, it sinks, not to be heard from until the following year *(Tosafos, Sotah 14a; see Maharsha)*.

וַיְהִי הַנֶּגֶף בַּעֲדַת ה׳ — *Resulting in* [lit. *there*] *the plague in the congregation of HASHEM.*

against the God of Israel — to turn away from
HASHEM this day by your building an altar for your
rebellion this day against HASHEM. 17 *Is the sin of*
Peor, from which we have not become cleansed until
this day, not enough for us, resulting in the plague in
the congregation of HASHEM. — 18 *and today you*
would turn away from HASHEM? If you rebel against
HASHEM today, in the future He will be angry with
the entire congregation of Israel. 19 *But, if the land of*
your inheritance is unhallowed, cross over to the land

Just as some of the Israelites who were innocent of sinning with Baal Peor were among those killed in the plague, some of us who are innocent of this sin could also be punished on your account *(Malbim;* cf. *footnote to verse 18).*

18. וּמָחָר — *In the future* [lit. *tomorrow*].

Metzudos explains that this word can also mean *in the future.*

We must protest now, lest, in the future God will punish us for failing to oppose your actions *(Abarbanel).*

19. וְאַךְ — *But.*

Pinchas' second argument begins in this verse. If the tribes of Reuben, Gad, and Menashe intended to build this altar to serve God, they should know that after the Tabernacle was erected in Shiloh, it was no longer permissible to build additional altars *(Malbim).*

אִם־טְמֵאָה אֶרֶץ אֲחֻזַּתְכֶם — *If the land of your inheritance is unhallowed.*

It is unhallowed because God does not choose to allow His Divine Presence to dwell there *(Rashi).*[1]

1. The Sages have enumerated many benefits which accrue to people living in the Land of Israel. These include:

☐ The air of *Eretz Yisrael* causes one to be wise *(Bava Basra* 158b);
☐ Prophecy only occurs in the Land of Israel *(Moed Katan* 25a);
☐ One who is not able to have children should move to *Eretz Yisrael (Yevamos* 64a);
☐ One who lives in *Eretz Yisrael* lives without sin *(Kesubos* 111a);
☐ One who is buried in *Eretz Yisrael* receives atonement for his sins *(Kesubos* 111a).

In light of these facts, did the tribes of Reuben, Gad, and part of Menashe act wisely in choosing to settle in the land to the east of the Jordan River (Trans-Jordan)? Is this land considered an integral part of *Eretz Yisrael?*

Eretz Yisrael is defined by the borders of the Land which God promised to Abraham in the Covenant of the Parts: *'To your descendants have I given this Land, from the river of Egypt to the great river, the Euphrates River ...' (Genesis* 15:18). This territory acquired sanctity and became a resting place for the Divine Presence as soon as it was given to Abraham *(Kresi U'Pleisi,* Chapter 10). This sanctity can never become nullified, despite the destruction of the Temple and the Exile *(Chasam Sofer,* Responsum 234, *Yoreh Deah).* The commentators disagree as to whether the Trans-Jordan was included in this promise. Essentially, their dispute centers around the interpretation of two primary sources.

One source is *Sifri's* comment to *Deuteronomy* 26:3, which describes the recitation made by an individual who brings his first fruits to the Kohen in the Temple. He begins, *'I profess this day to HASHEM, your God, that I have come to the Land which HASHEM swore to our Fathers to give us' (Deuteronomy* 26:3). *Sifri* states that the phrase, *the Land which HASHEM swore to our Fathers,* implicitly excludes the Trans-Jordan, for that land was not given to the Israelites, but taken by them. It would appear from *Sifri* that the land of Reuben, Gad, and Menashe was not included in God's promise to Abraham.

The second source, however, seems to imply the contrary. When Moses describes the lands

כב
כ־כב

יהוה אֲשֶׁר שָׁכַן־שָׁם מִשְׁכַּן יהוה
וְהֵאָחֲזוּ בְּתוֹכֵנוּ וּבַיהוָה אַל־תִּמְרֹדוּ
וְאוֹתָנוּ אַל־תִּמְרֹדוּ בִּבְנֹתְכֶם לָכֶם מִזְבֵּחַ
כ מִבַּלְעֲדֵי מִזְבַּח יְהוָה אֱלֹהֵינוּ: הֲלוֹא |
עָכָן בֶּן־זֶרַח מָעַל מַעַל בַּחֵרֶם וְעַל־כָּל־
עֲדַת יִשְׂרָאֵל הָיָה קָצֶף וְהוּא אִישׁ אֶחָד
כא לֹא גָוַע בַּעֲוֹנוֹ: וַיַּעֲנוּ בְנֵי־
רְאוּבֵן וּבְנֵי־גָד וַחֲצִי שֵׁבֶט הַמְנַשֶּׁה
כב וַיְדַבְּרוּ אֶת־רָאשֵׁי אַלְפֵי יִשְׂרָאֵל: אֵל |
אֱלֹהִים | יהוה אֵל | אֱלֹהִים | יהוה הוּא

Radak understands this statement in a subjective manner. 'If you feel that your land has no sanctity because the Tabernacle is not present there, then cross the Jordan and take your territory among us.'

וְאוֹתָנוּ אַל־תִּמְרֹדוּ — *And do not rebel against us.*

Because we will be punished on your account, it is as if you are also rebelling against us (*Metzudos*).

20. עָכָן בֶּן־זֶרַח — *Achan the son of Zerach.*

See *Commentary* to 7:24 for the reason Achan is called by his great-grandfather's name.

which he gave to Reuben, Gad, and part of Menashe, he identifies them as *the land of Rephaim* (*Deuteronomy* 3:13). As *Rashi* notes, Rephaim was one of the ten nations promised to Abraham in the Covenant (*Genesis* 15:20), and thus it would appear that the Trans-Jordan was truly an integral part of *Eretz Yisrael.*

Or HaChaim (*Numbers* 32:7) reconciles these two sources by suggesting that the *land of the Rephaim* mentioned by Moses was not the same land promised to Abraham, but another land by the same name. Thus, in his view, the three tribes were not living in *Eretz Yisrael* proper. (See *Otzar HaSifri,* who suggests that this is the opinion of *Ran* in *Nedarim.*)

Or HaChaim (*Deuteronomy* 3:13), however, reverses his interpretation of these two sources; he agrees with *Rashi* that the *land of the Rephaim* does indeed refer to the Rephaim mentioned in God's promise to Abraham and that the Trans-Jordan is an integral part of *Eretz Yisrael.* He maintains, however, that the Trans-Jordan does not have the same sanctity as the land to the west of the Jordan. Although the Jews were given full legal claim to this region by virtue of their inheritance from Abraham, it was not intended to be the residence of the Israelites. According to *Or HaChaim,* this is why the *Sifri* excludes the Trans-Jordan from *Eretz Yisrael.*

Ramban (*Numbers* 21:21) agrees that the Trans-Jordan was included in the promise to Abraham. He cites the *Midrash* (*Bamidbar Rabbah* 7:8) which states, 'the land of Canaan has a greater sanctity than the Trans-Jordan'; an altar may be built in *Eretz Yisrael* (see *Kli Chemdah, Numbers* 21:21) [at the time when altars were permissible], but not in the Trans-Jordan. In addition, the Trans-Jordan is not considered as a land flowing with milk and honey, while the rest of *Eretz Yisrael* is (*Ramban to Deuteronomy* 18:1). Thus, even according to the opinions that the Trans-Jordan is considered part of *Eretz Yisrael,* the nature of this land is much different than the land lying to the west of the Jordan.

Tashbatz (Vol. 3, ch. 198, 200) asserts that although all the commandments which may only be performed in *Eretz Yisrael* are required to be done in the Trans-Jordan (e.g., *terumah, ma'aser,* etc.), the benefits of living in *Eretz Yisrael* which were enumerated by the Sages do not apply to this region.

22
20-22

of HASHEM's possession where the Sanctuary of HASHEM is and take your territory among us. But do not rebel against HASHEM and do not rebel against us by building yourselves an altar other than the altar of HASHEM our God. 20 *Did not Achan the son of Zerach violate the proscription, and wrath fell upon the entire community of Israel? That man was not the only one to perish for his sin."'*

21 *And the Children of Reuben, Gad, and half the tribe of Menashe responded and spoke to the leaders of the thousands of Israel,* 22 *'Almighty, God, HASHEM; Almighty, God, HASHEM, He knows and*

הָיָה קָצֶף — *Wrath fell.*

[See *Malbim* cited in *Commentary* to 7:1 s.v. 'Achan ... took.']

לֹא גָוַע בַּעֲוֹנוֹ — *Was not the only one to perish for his sin.*

Radak interpolates: He *alone* did not perish for his sin. *Mahari Kara* amplifies: In Achan's case, the sin of one individual caused thirty-six men to die. Certainly many more would die in your case because a whole group sinned.

☙ The Explanation

21. וַיְדַבְּרוּ אֶת־רָאשֵׁי אַלְפֵי יִשְׂרָאֵל — *And spoke to the leaders of the thousands of Israel.*

Reuben, Gad, and Menashe only responded to the leaders, not to Pinchas, for they felt that their answer to the leaders which explained why they were not rebelling against their fellow Israelites also included the answer to Pinchas why they were not rebelling against God *(Malbim).*

Abarbanel remarks that Reuben, Gad, and Menashe did not feel they needed to respond to Pinchas because God, Who is omniscient, knew that they had no idolatrous intentions. Their fellow Israelites, however, did need to hear that they had no plans of seceding from the nation.

22. אֵל אֱלֹהִים ה׳ — *Almighty, God, HASHEM.*

The translation, which assumes that all three words mentioned here are names of God, follows the *Midrash* cited in the *footnote.* Both *Rashi* and *Radak,* however, understand אֱלֹהִים in a profane sense. According to *Rashi,* it means 'powerful ones,' i.e. *God of the powerful ones.*

Radak renders: 'HASHEM is the supreme God of all the angels.' The phrase is repeated for emphasis. *Rashi,* however, comments that they repeated this phrase to affirm that He is the supreme Master both in this world and in the world to come.

Malbim interprets this statement as a response to the princes' assertion that the altar was for idolatrous purposes.[1] They were affirming that there is only one God, and that their intentions were

1. The *Midrash (Shochar Tov, Tehillim* 50) states that Reuben, Gad, and Menashe twice uttered these three names of God because with these names, God created the world and gave the Torah. He created the world, as it says, *Almighty God, HASHEM has spoken and summoned the earth (Psalms* 50:1) and He gave the Torah, as Scripture states in the Ten Commandments, *'For I, HASHEM your God, am a jealous God'* [ה׳ אֱלֹהֶיךָ אֵל] *(Exodus* 20:5).

The Israelites had assumed that these tribes were guilty either of idolatry or of transgressing the Torah's prohibition against the building of private sacrificial altars after the Tabernacle

יֹדֵעַ וְיִשְׂרָאֵל הוּא יֵדָע אִם־בְּמֶרֶד וְאִם־
בְּמַעַל בַּיהוָה אַל־תּוֹשִׁיעֵנוּ הַיּוֹם הַזֶּה׃
כג לִבְנוֹת לָנוּ מִזְבֵּחַ לָשׁוּב מֵאַחֲרֵי יְהוָה
וְאִם־לְהַעֲלוֹת עָלָיו עוֹלָה וּמִנְחָה וְאִם־
לַעֲשׂוֹת עָלָיו זִבְחֵי שְׁלָמִים יְהוָה הוּא
כד יְבַקֵּשׁ׃ וְאִם־לֹא מִדְּאָגָה מִדָּבָר עָשִׂינוּ
אֶת־זֹאת לֵאמֹר מָחָר יֹאמְרוּ בְנֵיכֶם
לְבָנֵינוּ לֵאמֹר מַה־לָּכֶם וְלַיהוָה אֱלֹהֵי
כה יִשְׂרָאֵל׃ וּגְבוּל נָתַן־יְהוָה בֵּינֵנוּ וּבֵינֵיכֶם
בְּנֵי־רְאוּבֵן וּבְנֵי־גָד אֶת־הַיַּרְדֵּן אֵין־לָכֶם
חֵלֶק בַּיהוָה וְהִשְׁבִּיתוּ בְנֵיכֶם אֶת־בָּנֵינוּ
כו לְבִלְתִּי יְרֹא אֶת־יְהוָה׃ וַנֹּאמֶר נַעֲשֶׂה־נָּא
לָנוּ לִבְנוֹת אֶת־הַמִּזְבֵּחַ לֹא לְעוֹלָה וְלֹא

not idolatrous. The repetition of this phrase was their response to the charge that they had built a sacrificial altar to God outside of Shiloh. Their response implies that just as God always knew that the altar was intended solely as a memorial, so will the princes realize when they see the altar that it was not designed for sacrifices.

הוּא יֹדֵעַ — *He knows.*

He knows our motives and intentions *(Radak).*

Just as *He knows* that our intentions were worthy, so we pray that you come to such a firm belief *(Alshich).*

וְיִשְׂרָאֵל הוּא יֵדָע — *And Israel too shall know.*

From this point on, the Israelites shall know that our intentions were honorable; we were not rebelling *(Radak).*

מֶרֶד — *Rebellion.*

Rebellion refers to their denial of centralized religious authority by sacrificing on this altar.

מַעַל — *Betrayal.*

Betrayal refers to their denial of God through idol worship.

אַל־תּוֹשִׁיעֵנוּ — *Save us not.*

This was addressed to God *(Rashi).*

23. לִבְנוֹת לָנוּ מִזְבֵּחַ — *[If it were our intention] to build an altar.*

The interpolation follows *Metzudos.*

They made this statement in reference to the leaders' claim that they had committed idolatry, as the verse continues, *to turn away from HASHEM (Abarbanel).*

וְאִם־לְהַעֲלוֹת עָלָיו עוֹלָה — *Or (if) to offer burnt offerings.*

Similarly, *Metzudos* interpolates: [if it were our intention] to offer burnt offerings.

They made this statement in reference to the leaders' claim that they were

was erected at Shiloh. By using the names of God found in these passages of Scripture the three tribes were rebutting both charges. They would not have practiced idolatry, because they believed in God as the Creator, and they would not have violated the law concerning private sacrificial altars, because they believed in God as the Lawgiver *(Alshich).*

Israel too shall know. If it was in rebellion or betrayal
of HASHEM, save us not this day. 23 *If it were our in-*
tention to build an altar to turn away from HASHEM,
or to offer burnt offerings or meal offerings upon it
or to offer peace offerings upon it, let HASHEM
Himself exact punishment, 24 *if we did not do this out*
of fear of the following thing: In the future your
children might say to our children, "What have you
to do with HASHEM the God of Israel. 25 *HASHEM has*
made a border between us and you, O Children of
Reuben and Children of Gad — the Jordan! You have
no share in HASHEM." And so your children will
cause our children to stop fearing HASHEM.
26 *Therefore, we said, "Let us prepare to build an*
altar, not for burnt offerings and not for sacrifices —

offering sacrifices on the altar *(Abarbanel).*

ה׳ הוּא יְבַקֵּשׁ — *Let HASHEM Himself exact punishment.*

Rashi renders: God will punish us.

24. וְאִם־לֹא מִדְּאָגָה — *If* [*we did not do this*] *out of fear.*

This verse refers to the decree which they imposed upon themselves in the preceding verse. They said: 'If we were not motivated by fear, then God Himself should exact punishment from us' *(Metzudos).*

מִדְּאָגָה — *Fear.*

This means *fear* for what your children will say to our children when they go to Shiloh to offer sacrifices *(Rashi).*

25. אֵין־לָכֶם חֵלֶק בַּה׳ — *You have no share in HASHEM.*

Words such as these will affect our children, and they will lose their fear of God[1] *(Malbim).*

Daas Sofrim explains that if a person has the opportunity to be closer to God and he rejects it, he demonstrates the weakness of his faith. This is what the sages meant when they said: One who lives outside the Land of Israel is as if he has no God *(Kesubos* 112a).

וְהִשְׁבִּיתוּ — *Cause ... to stop.*

They will cause our children to think that because they are geographically removed from God's Sanctuary, they do not have as intimate a relationship with Him as their brethren do, and they may conclude that their obligation to fear Him is less *(Daas Sofrim).*

26. וַנֹּאמֶר — [*Therefore,*] *we said.*

We spoke in order to prevent this possibility from occurring *(Malbim).*

נַעֲשֶׂה־נָּא לָנוּ — *Let us prepare* [lit. *make*].

Let us make a permanent testimony to the fact that we and you are equal in that we are *both* forbidden to offer sacrifices on an altar other than the one

1. [It is interesting that the tribes of Reuben, Gad, and Menashe had become so concerned about the spiritual welfare of their children, for as noted in *Commentary* to 1:14, their children's welfare had not always been of utmost importance to them as indicated by the fact that they had mentioned the needs of their cattle before those of their children. Apparently these tribes heeded Moses' chastisement (see *Numbers* 32:24) and correctly reordered their priorities.]

כז לִזְבַּח׃ כִּי עֵד הוּא בֵּינֵינוּ וּבֵינֵיכֶם וּבֵין
דֹּרוֹתֵינוּ אַחֲרֵינוּ לַעֲבֹד אֶת־עֲבֹדַת יְהוָה
לְפָנָיו בְּעֹלוֹתֵינוּ וּבִזְבָחֵינוּ וּבִשְׁלָמֵינוּ
וְלֹא־יֹאמְרוּ בְנֵיכֶם מָחָר לְבָנֵינוּ אֵין־לָכֶם
כח חֵלֶק בַּיהוָה׃ וַנֹּאמֶר וְהָיָה כִּי־יֹאמְרוּ
אֵלֵינוּ וְאֶל־דֹּרֹתֵינוּ מָחָר וְאָמַרְנוּ רְאוּ
אֶת־תַּבְנִית מִזְבַּח יְהוָה אֲשֶׁר־עָשׂוּ
אֲבוֹתֵינוּ לֹא לְעוֹלָה וְלֹא לְזֶבַח כִּי־עֵד
כט הוּא בֵּינֵינוּ וּבֵינֵיכֶם׃ חָלִילָה לָּנוּ מִמֶּנּוּ
לִמְרֹד בַּיהוָה וְלָשׁוּב הַיּוֹם מֵאַחֲרֵי יְהוָה
לִבְנוֹת מִזְבֵּחַ לְעֹלָה לְמִנְחָה וּלְזָבַח
מִלְּבַד מִזְבַּח יְהוָה אֱלֹהֵינוּ אֲשֶׁר לִפְנֵי
ל מִשְׁכָּנוֹ׃ וַיִּשְׁמַע פִּינְחָס הַכֹּהֵן
וּנְשִׂיאֵי הָעֵדָה וְרָאשֵׁי אַלְפֵי יִשְׂרָאֵל
אֲשֶׁר אִתּוֹ אֶת־הַדְּבָרִים אֲשֶׁר דִּבְּרוּ בְּנֵי־
רְאוּבֵן וּבְנֵי־גָד וּבְנֵי מְנַשֶּׁה וַיִּיטַב
לא בְּעֵינֵיהֶם׃ וַיֹּאמֶר פִּינְחָס בֶּן־אֶלְעָזָר
הַכֹּהֵן אֶל־בְּנֵי־רְאוּבֵן וְאֶל־בְּנֵי־גָד וְאֶל־
בְּנֵי מְנַשֶּׁה הַיּוֹם יָדַעְנוּ כִּי־בְתוֹכֵנוּ יְהוָה
אֲשֶׁר לֹא־מְעַלְתֶּם בַּיהוָה הַמַּעַל הַזֶּה אָז

in the Tabernacle at Shiloh. Thus, *your children will not say to our children ... (Malbim).*

When our children see the altar they will think that their forefathers built it in order to demonstrate that we have a share in the Tabernacle at Shiloh *(Meam Loez).*

27. כִּי — *[But that it] only.*
The translation follows *Metzudos.*

לְפָנָיו — *Before Him.*
This altar will bear testimony to the fact that the only valid altar upon which sacrifices may be offered is the altar which is *before Him* in the Tabernacle. Thus, your children will not ridicule ours *(Malbim).*

28. וְאָמַרְנוּ — *They* [lit. *we*] *will say.*
Although literally, this phrase means 'we will say,' Scripture means *our children* will say. It refers to them as *we,* because they will take the place of this generation *(Radak).*

עָשׂוּ אֲבוֹתֵינוּ — *(Which) our fathers made.*
Our fathers refers to all the Israelites of that generation. The children will reason that the very existence of the altar proves that no one opposed its construction. Thus, it serves as a

[27] *but that it only be a witness between us and you
and between our generations after us — to perform
the service of HASHEM before Him with our burnt
offerings, and with our sacrifices, and with our peace
offerings." Then your children will not say to our
children in the future, "You have no share in
HASHEM."* [28] *Thus, we said, "When they will say
this to us or to our generations in time to come, they
will say, 'See the form of the altar of HASHEM which
our fathers made, not for burnt offerings and not for
sacrifices, only as a witness between us and you.' "*
[29] *Far be it from us to rebel against HASHEM and turn
away this day from HASHEM to build an altar for
burnt offerings, meal offerings and sacrifices —
besides the altar of HASHEM our God which is before
His Sanctuary.'*

[30] *And Pinchas the Kohen and the leaders of the
congregation and the heads of the thousands of Israel
that were with him heard the explanation of the
Children of Reuben, Gad, and Menashe, and it was
good in their eyes.* [31] *And Pinchas the son of Elazar
the Kohen said to the Children of Reuben, Gad, and
Menashe, 'Today we know that HASHEM is in our
midst since you did not commit this betrayal against*

testimonial for all later generations *(Malbim).*

כִּי־עֵד הוּא — *Only as a witness.*

It bears testimony to the fact that we have not lost our portion in the altar [at Shiloh] *(Rashi).*

29. חָלִילָה לָּנוּ מִמֶּנּוּ — *Far be it from us.*

Even before your rebuke, we realized that rebellion against God is reprehensible *(Metzudos).*

וְלָשׁוּב הַיּוֹם מֵאַחֲרֵי ה׳ — *And to turn away this day from HASHEM.*

How could we ever consider rebelling against God after He has performed so many miracles on our behalf — the splitting of the Jordan River, the destruction of Jericho's walls, the stopping of the sun, etc. *(Meam Loez).*

30. וַיִּיטַב בְּעֵינֵיהֶם — *And it was good in their eyes.*

It was apparent from the way they expressed themselves that they were speaking the truth. In addition their versions were consistent with one another [see *Kli Yakar* to verse 15] *(Meam Loez).*

31. ... הַיּוֹם יָדַעְנוּ — *Today we know ...*

We know that God is in our midst, for He gave us the inspiration to discuss our suspicions about this matter with you instead of immediately going to war against you *(Metzudos).*

כב
לב־לד

הִצַּלְתֶּם אֶת־בְּנֵי יִשְׂרָאֵל מִיַּד יְהוָה:
לב וַיָּשָׁב פִּינְחָס בֶּן־אֶלְעָזָר הַכֹּהֵן |
וְהַנְּשִׂיאִים מֵאֵת בְּנֵי־רְאוּבֵן וּמֵאֵת בְּנֵי־
גָד מֵאֶרֶץ הַגִּלְעָד אֶל־אֶרֶץ כְּנַעַן אֶל־בְּנֵי
לג יִשְׂרָאֵל וַיָּשִׁבוּ אוֹתָם דָּבָר: וַיִּיטַב הַדָּבָר
בְּעֵינֵי בְּנֵי יִשְׂרָאֵל וַיְבָרְכוּ אֱלֹהִים בְּנֵי
יִשְׂרָאֵל וְלֹא אָמְרוּ לַעֲלוֹת עֲלֵיהֶם לַצָּבָא
לְשַׁחֵת אֶת־הָאָרֶץ אֲשֶׁר בְּנֵי־רְאוּבֵן וּבְנֵי־
לד גָד יֹשְׁבִים בָּהּ: וַיִּקְרְאוּ בְּנֵי־רְאוּבֵן וּבְנֵי־
גָד לַמִּזְבֵּחַ כִּי־עֵד הוּא בֵּינֹתֵינוּ כִּי יְהוָה
הָאֱלֹהִים:

כג
א־ב

א וַיְהִי מִיָּמִים רַבִּים אַחֲרֵי אֲשֶׁר־הֵנִיחַ
יְהוָה לְיִשְׂרָאֵל מִכָּל־אֹיְבֵיהֶם מִסָּבִיב
ב וִיהוֹשֻׁעַ זָקֵן בָּא בַּיָּמִים: וַיִּקְרָא יְהוֹשֻׁעַ

אֲשֶׁר לֹא־מְעַלְתֶּם בַּה׳ — *Since you did not commit this betrayal.*

We realize today that you *always intended* to make the altar for the purposes you stated today and that you did not change your intention because you were threatened by our presence *(Alshich).*

אָז הִצַּלְתֶּם — *[From] then you had saved.*

From then, i.e., from your first thought of building the altar you intended it to be a vehicle which would *save* the Israelites from God's wrath. If our sons would have in the future said these things to your children, they all would have been liable to Divine punishment *(Alshich).*

32. דָּבָר — *A report* [lit. *a word*].

Pinchas and the leaders gave the Israelites a report on their mission *(Metzudos).*

33. וַיְבָרְכוּ אֱלֹהִים — *And [they] blessed God.*

They blessed God for the fact that they were inspired to think of sending a group of emissaries before waging war *(Metzudos).*

Malbim comments that they blessed God because they did not need to wage war against their brethren. Their blessing shows that they had not reproached the tribes out of vindictiveness, but out of the purest motivation — the desire to protect their fellow Jews from the consequences of sin.

לְשַׁחֵת אֶת־הָאָרֶץ — *To destroy the land.*

From this statement, it is evident that if the ten tribes west of the Jordan had found Reuben, Gad, and Menashe guilty, they would have destroyed their land.

34. וַיִּקְרְאוּ ... לַמִּזְבֵּחַ — *[They] named the altar.*

Rashi explains that this is one of the verses which has to be understood by the mental addition of a word. Here the word *witness,* should be added after *altar.* They called the altar *Witness* because it bore testimony.

22 *HASHEM. Then you had saved the Israelites from the*
32-34 *hand of HASHEM.'* 32 *and Pinchas the son of Elazar*
the Kohen and the leaders returned from the
Children of Reuben and Gad in the land of Gilead to
the land of Canaan — to the Children of Israel — and
they gave them a report. 33 *And the Children of Israel*
were pleased. And the Children of Israel blessed God
and no longer spoke of advancing upon them with an
army — to destroy the land where the Children of
Reuben and Gad resided. 34 *And the Children of*
Reuben and the Children of Gad named the altar so it
would be a witness between us that HASHEM is God.

23 1 *And it was many days after HASHEM had given*
1 *rest to Israel from all its surrounding enemies*
that Joshua was old and well advanced in years.

XXIII

At the end of his life, Joshua was acutely aware that many Canaanites remained within the borders of Eretz Yisrael. *He understood clearly that these idolaters were a threat to the existence of the Israelites, and he envisioned two ways in which the Jews might deal with these adversaries after his death. The Israelites might make peace with the Canaanites, intermarry with them, and gradually assimilate into their culture, thus forfeiting their eternal mission (see* footnote *to 2:10). Or, the Jews might attempt to summon another military effort to eradicate these idolaters from their midst (see* Introduction, *'Amalek and the Seven Nations'). Without Joshua's presence, however, the Israelites might lose confidence in their worthiness to the Divine protection which assured their previous victories, and they might then take the first course and assimilate* (Malbim).

Joshua explained to them that his presence was unnecessary for their success; their success was entirely dependent upon their faithfulness to the Torah. If they will be scrupulous in their observance, then God, who was the source of all their previous successes, will continue to make them victorious. If, however, they fail in their observance, then the Canaanites will become a lash in [their] sides *(verse 13).*

In order to stir the Israelites to maintain their degree of righteousness in the idolatrous environment in which they were about to be surrounded, Joshua employed all his skills of rhetoric to move the nation's leaders to fulfill God's plan for the Jews and for Eretz Yisrael. *His words are reminiscent of Moses' address in the* Book *of* Deuteronomy *to the Israelites who were about to cross the Jordan and undoubtedly he learned from his revered leader that the leader of the generation should admonish his people before his death (see* Rashi *to* Deuteronomy *1:3).*

1. אַחֲרֵי — *After.*
See *Commentary* to 1:1.

אַחֲרֵי אֲשֶׁר־הֵנִיחַ ה׳ לְיִשְׂרָאֵל — *After HASHEM had given rest to Israel.*

[This chapter begins after the seven years of conquest and the seven years of division had been completed. It is perplexing that Scripture notes Joshua's aging condition at this time when 13:1

כג
ג־ו

לְכָל־יִשְׂרָאֵל לִזְקֵנָיו וּלְרָאשָׁיו וּלְשֹׁפְטָיו
וּלְשֹׁטְרָיו וַיֹּאמֶר אֲלֵהֶם אֲנִי זָקַנְתִּי בָּאתִי
ג בַּיָּמִים׃ וְאַתֶּם רְאִיתֶם אֵת כָּל־אֲשֶׁר
עָשָׂה יְהוָה אֱלֹהֵיכֶם לְכָל־הַגּוֹיִם הָאֵלֶּה
מִפְּנֵיכֶם כִּי יְהוָה אֱלֹהֵיכֶם הוּא הַנִּלְחָם
ד לָכֶם׃ רְאוּ הִפַּלְתִּי לָכֶם אֶת־הַגּוֹיִם
הַנִּשְׁאָרִים הָאֵלֶּה בְּנַחֲלָה לְשִׁבְטֵיכֶם מִן־
הַיַּרְדֵּן וְכָל־הַגּוֹיִם אֲשֶׁר הִכְרַתִּי וְהַיָּם
ה הַגָּדוֹל מְבוֹא הַשָּׁמֶשׁ׃ וַיהוָה אֱלֹהֵיכֶם
הוּא יֶהְדֳּפֵם מִפְּנֵיכֶם וְהוֹרִישׁ אֹתָם
מִלִּפְנֵיכֶם וִירִשְׁתֶּם אֶת־אַרְצָם כַּאֲשֶׁר
ו דִּבֶּר יְהוָה אֱלֹהֵיכֶם לָכֶם׃ וַחֲזַקְתֶּם מְאֹד
לִשְׁמֹר וְלַעֲשׂוֹת אֵת כָּל־הַכָּתוּב בְּסֵפֶר
תּוֹרַת מֹשֶׁה לְבִלְתִּי סוּר־מִמֶּנּוּ יָמִין

relates that, at least seven years earlier, Joshua was very aged.]

זָקֵן — *Old.*

He was advanced in years *(Abarbanel).*

בָּא בַּיָּמִים — *Well advanced in years.*

He had aged because of the stress of battle *(Abarbanel).*

According to *Ibn Ezra,* Joshua was 110 at this time; according to *Seder HaDoros,* he was 108.

Joshua had been promised, *As I had been with Moses so will I be with you* (1:5). This promise implied that Joshua would live 120 years, as did his predecessor, and that he would be vigorous and healthy until his last day. Joshua did not see fulfillment of this promise for he was dilatory in the conquest of the Land (see *Commentary* to 11:18) and as a result, he lived only 110 years and in a weakened condition during his old age *(Meam Loez).*

2. לְכָל־יִשְׂרָאֵל — *All Israel.*

It is unreasonable to assume that Joshua spoke to all the Israelites. Rather, he spoke to the leaders. The word *leaders* should be interpolated *(Ralbag).*

לִזְקֵנָיו — *Its elders.*

These formed the Sanhedrin, the Supreme Court *(Ralbag).*

וּלְרָאשָׁיו — *Its leaders.*

These were the leaders of each tribe *(Ralbag).*

וּלְשֹׁפְטָיו וּלְשֹׁטְרָיו — *Its judges and its marshals.*

Judges and marshals served in each city *(Ralbag).*

אֲנִי זָקַנְתִּי — *I am old.*

Because I am old, I am no longer capable of going out to war *(Malbim).*

However, you should not feel grief for me that I am close to death, for I have already lost my strength. In regard to your personal safety, you have nothing to fear, since I was not the source of your military victories, but God. *You have seen all that ... (Kli Yakar).*

3. וְאַתֶּם רְאִיתֶם — *You have seen.*

*[2] Joshua summoned all Israel — its elders, its leaders,
its judges, and its marshals — and said to them, 'I am
old and advanced in years. [3] You have seen all that
HASHEM your God has done to all these nations
because of you; HASHEM your God has fought for
you. [4] See, I have allotted to you as an inheritance
according to your tribes these remaining nations —
and all the nations which I have destroyed — from the
Jordan to the Mediterranean Sea in the west.
[5] HASHEM your God will push them out because of
you and drive them out from before you. You will
acquire their land as HASHEM your God has told you.
[6] Strengthen yourselves very much to keep and
observe all which is written in the book of the Torah
of Moses so that you do not deviate from it to the*

You know that I [Joshua] did not crush the enemy with my personal strength. *You have seen all that HASHEM your God has done to all these nations.* The signs and wonders which accompanied the battles prove that I was not the one who brought victory *(Malbim).*

לְכָל־הַגּוֹיִם הָאֵלֶּה — *To all these nations.*

This refers to the nations which the Jews had already conquered *(Metzudos).*

4. רְאוּ הִפַּלְתִּי לָכֶם — *See, I have allotted* [lit. *cast*] *to you.*

I have already accomplished that which I was personally required to do — i.e., to supervise the lottery which apportioned the territories. (God had told Joshua, *'You will cause this people to inherit the Land'* [1:6].)

Meam Loez interprets this statement as a second proof that Joshua was not the source of their victories, but God. The division of the Land was completed before it was entirely conquered (see *Commentary* to 13:8). This could only be done with certainty if this was a Divine guarantee that the Israelites would ultimately be victorious.

וְהַיָּם הַגָּדוֹל — [*To*] *the Mediterranean Sea.*

Radak interpolates the word *to.*

5. וַה' אֱלֹהֵיכֶם — *HASHEM your God.*

If you are afraid that the other nations will hear of my death and will no longer have any compunction to attack you, know that *HASHEM your God will push them out and drive them out from before you (Kli Yakar).*

Since I have already allotted the territories of these remaining Canaanites, all that is left is to conquer them. When I die, the eternal God will drive them out *(Malbim).*

יֶהְדֳּפֵם ... וְהוֹרִישׁ — *Will push them out ... and drive them out.*

Push them out means to prevent those who fled from the areas you conquered from returning. *Drive out* means to conquer those who have not yet been conquered *(Malbim).*

6. וַחֲזַקְתֶּם — *Strengthen yourselves.*

God will drive out your enemies only on the condition that you tenaciously observe the Torah. Thus Joshua counsels, *'Strengthen yourselves' (Malbim).* [Note that this exhortation is

ז וּשְׂמֹאול: לְבִלְתִּי־בוֹא בַּגּוֹיִם הָאֵלֶּה
הַנִּשְׁאָרִים הָאֵלֶּה אִתְּכֶם וּבְשֵׁם אֱלֹהֵיהֶם
לֹא־תַזְכִּירוּ וְלֹא תַשְׁבִּיעוּ וְלֹא תַעַבְדוּם
ח וְלֹא תִשְׁתַּחֲווּ לָהֶם: כִּי אִם־בַּיהוָה
אֱלֹהֵיכֶם תִּדְבָּקוּ כַּאֲשֶׁר עֲשִׂיתֶם עַד
ט הַיּוֹם הַזֶּה: וַיּוֹרֶשׁ יהוה מִפְּנֵיכֶם גּוֹיִם
גְּדֹלִים וַעֲצוּמִים וְאַתֶּם לֹא־עָמַד אִישׁ
י בִּפְנֵיכֶם עַד הַיּוֹם הַזֶּה: אִישׁ־אֶחָד מִכֶּם
יִרְדָּף־אָלֶף כִּי | יהוָה אֱלֹהֵיכֶם הוּא
הַנִּלְחָם לָכֶם כַּאֲשֶׁר דִּבֶּר לָכֶם:
יא וְנִשְׁמַרְתֶּם מְאֹד לְנַפְשֹׁתֵיכֶם לְאַהֲבָה

similar to the charge which God had given Joshua in 1:7.]

תּוֹרַת מֹשֶׁה — *Torah of Moses.*

Because Moses underwent so much self-sacrifice in order to acquire the Torah from God, it was called by his name, *the Torah of Moses.* Similarly, we find in *Malachi* 3:22, *Remember the Torah of Moses, My servant.* So it is with any Torah scholar. If he toils over the study of Torah day and night, the Torah becomes his, as it says *(Psalms* 1:2): *and in his* [the scholar's] *Torah he meditates day and night (Kiddushim* 32b).

יָמִין וּשְׂמֹאול — *To the right or to the left.*

See *Commentary* to 1:7.

7. לְבִלְתִּי־בוֹא בַּגּוֹיִם — *So that you do not come into* [*these*] *nations.*

Here Joshua warns the Israelites not to assimilate and become as the Canaanites *(Metzudos).*

Malbim understands this as a warning against intermarriage with the Canaanites.

Meam Loez remarks, however, that there is a seeming redundancy in this verse, *these nations, these remaining among you.* He thus interprets that *these nations* refers to the Gibeonites whom the Israelites were forbidden to marry (see *Commentary* to 9:23) and *these remaining among you* refers to the other Canaanites in the Land.

וּבְשֵׁם אֱלֹהֵיהֶם לֹא־תַזְכִּירוּ ... — *The name of their gods you may not mention.*

We can deduce from the converse of Joshua's admonition that if the Jews do begin to intermarry, they will first mention the names of Canaanite deities, then swear by them, serve them, and finally, they will bow down to them *(Malbim).* Each of these sins is worse than the previous one *(Daas Sofrim).*

וְלֹא תַשְׁבִּיעוּ — *Nor may you cause another to swear.*

One man should not make another swear by the names of the pagan deities *(Radak).*

If one takes an oath in the name of a pagan deity, he had transgressed, *and the name of gods of others you may not mention (Exodus* 23:13). This prohibition is one of forty-four transgressions in the Torah which serve to distance a Jew from idolatry *(Sefer HaChinuch,* 86).

8. כִּי אִם — *Only.*

This verse should not be understood as referring to the previous one, in which case the sense would be, 'Do not serve their gods, but serve HASHEM.' It

23
7-11

right or to the left, [7] *so that you do not come into*
these nations — these still remaining with you. The
name of their gods you may not mention, nor may
you cause another to swear by them. Do not serve
them nor bow down to them. [8] *Only to HASHEM your*
God shall you cling, as you have done to this day.
[9] *HASHEM has driven out great and powerful nations*
from before you; but you — not a man has withstood
you to this day. [10] *One man of yours chased a*
thousand, because it was HASHEM your God Who
fought for you, as He told you. [11] *Most carefully*
protect yourselves — to love HASHEM your God.

should be understood in reference to the next verse: 'If you cling to HASHEM, you will receive His assistance in your future conquests, just as you received Divine aid in the past' *(Abarbanel).*

תִּדְבָּקוּ — *Shall you cling.*

Joshua felt that it was now necessary to command the Israelites to cling to God although previously they had clung to Him of their own volition. In the Wilderness, when they were constantly surrounded by miracles such as the manna which fell from heaven every day and the well which traveled with them to provide them with water, the Israelites were constantly aware of God. Once they were established in *Eretz Yisrael,* however, and they no longer experienced daily miracles, the Jews needed to be reminded that they should cleave to God *(Ramban, Deuteronomy* 11:22).

כַּאֲשֶׁר עֲשִׂיתֶם עַד הַיּוֹם הַזֶּה — *As you have done to this day.*

Joshua bears witness to the fact that until this time the Jews had had the most intimate relationship with God — that of clinging to Him *(Daas Sofrim).*

9. וַיּוֹרֶשׁ — [*He*] *has driven out.*

Metzudos interpolates: [because of your clinging to HASHEM,] *He has driven out ...*

10. יִרְדָּף־אֶלֶף — *Chased* [lit. *will chase*] *a thousand.*

This verb is written in the future tense but really refers to the past. There are many such instances in Scripture *(Radak).*

Abarbanel, however, contends that this verb should be understood in the future tense, in which case the verse would mean that one Israelite *will chase a thousand* Canaanites, if only, as verse 8 stipulates, the Jews cleave to God. This future predication can be proven from the past, for *HASHEM your God fought for you ...*

[See *Leviticus* 26:8, וצ״ע.]

11. וְנִשְׁמַרְתֶּם מְאֹד לְנַפְשֹׁתֵיכֶם — *Most carefully protect yourselves.*

Meam Loez suggests: Even though I guaranteed you success if you heed the commandments, do not observe them for their benefit, but *most carefully protect yourselves* that you are only motivated out of love of God. This is consistent with the *Mishnah (Avos* 1:3) which states: Do not be servants who serve their master in order to receive reward, but be as servants who serve their master without the desire to receive reward [out of love for Him]. This is the highest form of service *(Maharal).*

Abarbanel interprets: Protect yourselves so that your love is directed solely towards God.

יב אֶת־יהוָה אֱלֹהֵיכֶם: כִּי | אִם־שׁוֹב תָּשׁוּבוּ
וּדְבַקְתֶּם בְּיֶתֶר הַגּוֹיִם הָאֵלֶּה הַנִּשְׁאָרִים
הָאֵלֶּה אִתְּכֶם וְהִתְחַתַּנְתֶּם בָּהֶם וּבָאתֶם
יג בָּהֶם וְהֵם בָּכֶם: יָדוֹעַ תֵּדְעוּ כִּי לֹא יוֹסִיף
יהוָה אֱלֹהֵיכֶם לְהוֹרִישׁ אֶת־הַגּוֹיִם
הָאֵלֶּה מִלִּפְנֵיכֶם וְהָיוּ לָכֶם לְפַח וּלְמוֹקֵשׁ
וּלְשֹׁטֵט בְּצִדֵּיכֶם וְלִצְנִנִים בְּעֵינֵיכֶם עַד
אֲבָדְכֶם מֵעַל הָאֲדָמָה הַטּוֹבָה הַזֹּאת
יד אֲשֶׁר נָתַן לָכֶם יהוָה אֱלֹהֵיכֶם: וְהִנֵּה
אָנֹכִי הוֹלֵךְ הַיּוֹם בְּדֶרֶךְ כָּל־הָאָרֶץ
וִידַעְתֶּם בְּכָל־לְבַבְכֶם וּבְכָל־נַפְשְׁכֶם כִּי
לֹא־נָפַל דָּבָר אֶחָד מִכֹּל | הַדְּבָרִים
הַטּוֹבִים אֲשֶׁר דִּבֶּר יהוָה אֱלֹהֵיכֶם
עֲלֵיכֶם הַכֹּל בָּאוּ לָכֶם לֹא־נָפַל מִמֶּנּוּ
טו דָּבָר אֶחָד: וְהָיָה כַּאֲשֶׁר־בָּא עֲלֵיכֶם כָּל־
הַדָּבָר הַטּוֹב אֲשֶׁר דִּבֶּר יהוָה אֱלֹהֵיכֶם
אֲלֵיכֶם כֵּן יָבִיא יהוָה עֲלֵיכֶם אֵת כָּל־
הַדָּבָר הָרָע עַד־הַשְׁמִידוֹ אוֹתְכֶם מֵעַל
הָאֲדָמָה הַטּוֹבָה הַזֹּאת אֲשֶׁר נָתַן לָכֶם

12. שׁוֹב תָּשׁוּבוּ — *Should you turn away.*

Until this point Joshua explained to the people all the benefits which would accrue to them if they observed the Torah. At this point, he explains the misery which will befall them if they forsake God's will and intermingle among the gentiles. *Should you turn away* just a little, you will end up cleaving to *these remaining nations* (*Meam Loez*).

This means: If you turn away from God (*Metzudos*).

Malbim interprets: If you turn away your love for Him.

13. יָדוֹעַ תֵּדְעוּ — [*You*] *surely know.*

This you yourselves understand (*Malbim*).

וְהָיוּ לָכֶם לְפַח — *They will be a snare to you.*

Joshua lists several dangers which will befall the Israelites if they are not prudent with regard to their relationships with the Canaanites.

A פַּח is a concealed obstacle and is symbolic of the tragedy which could ensue if the Israelites were to marry the native non-Jews even if they convert. [According to Torah law, a born Jew is prohibited to marry a Canaanite who descends from one of the Seven Nations, even if he or she converts to Judaism (see *R' Tam, Kesubos* 29a; cf.

[12] *For if you should turn away and cling to these*
remaining nations — these remaining with you — you
will intermarry with them and mingle with them and
they with you. [13] *Surely know that HASHEM your*
God will not continue to drive these nations out
before you; they will be a snare and an obstacle to
you — a lash in your sides and thorns in your eyes —
until you perish from this good land which HASHEM
your God has given to you. [14] *Behold, this day I am*
going the way of all the earth; you know with all
your heart and with all your soul that not one of all
the good things that HASHEM your God has told you
has fallen short. All have come about for you, not one
word of it has fallen short. [15] *And it shall be that just*
as every good thing which HASHEM your God has
told you has been fulfilled so will HASHEM bring
upon you every evil thing until He has dashed you
from this good land which HASHEM your God has

Commentary to 6:25).] Although the danger in this is not immediately apparent this warning should be heeded, for ultimately the peril will become obvious, and then it may be too late to avoid stumbling *(Daas Sofrim)*.

לְפַח וּלְמוֹקֵשׁ — *A snare and an obstacle.*

The translation follows *Metzudos*.

First they will have you transgress the seemingly less important mitzvos which has the hidden danger (פַּח) that it will cause you to transgress the more serious *obstacles* (מוֹקֵשׁ), those which you would never have been able to transgress *(Meam Loez)*.

וּלְשֹׁטֵט בְּצִדֵּיכֶם — *A lash in your sides.*

Rashi explains this expression to mean 'they will roam around, pillage, and loot your belongings.'

Metzudos, however, understands this expression to mean 'they will inflict pain upon you as with a whip on the flesh.'

וְלִצְנִנִים — *And thorns.*

The translation follows *Metzudos*.

Rashi renders: Camps, meaning something which will surround you from all sides.

עַד אֲבָדְכֶם מֵעַל הָאֲדָמָה — *Until you perish from* [*this good*] *land.*

According to *Rashi* and *Ibn Ezra (Deuteronomy* 11:17), perish here means 'exile.' However, *Sforno (ibid.)* understands this literally as physical destruction.

14. אָנֹכִי הוֹלֵךְ הַיּוֹם בְּדֶרֶךְ כָּל־הָאָרֶץ — *This day I am going the way of all the earth.*

I am going to die as all men do, and I will not be witness to what will happen to you in the future *(Metzudos)*.

וִידַעְתֶּם — *You know.*

Examine and scrutinize all the good things which happened to you, and you will realize that none occurred by accident. They are all part of a larger design which God constructed for your welfare *(Radak)*.

15. וְהָיָה — *And it shall be.*

Just as every good thing was fulfilled,

כג טז

טז יהוה אֱלֹהֵיכֶם: בְּעָבְרְכֶם אֶת־בְּרִית יהוה
אֱלֹהֵיכֶם אֲשֶׁר צִוָּה אֶתְכֶם וַהֲלַכְתֶּם
וַעֲבַדְתֶּם אֱלֹהִים אֲחֵרִים וְהִשְׁתַּחֲוִיתֶם
לָהֶם וְחָרָה אַף־יהוה בָּכֶם וַאֲבַדְתֶּם
מְהֵרָה מֵעַל הָאָרֶץ הַטּוֹבָה אֲשֶׁר נָתַן

כד א־ב

א לָכֶם: וַיֶּאֱסֹף יְהוֹשֻׁעַ אֶת־כָּל־
שִׁבְטֵי יִשְׂרָאֵל שְׁכֶמָה וַיִּקְרָא לְזִקְנֵי
יִשְׂרָאֵל וּלְרָאשָׁיו וּלְשֹׁפְטָיו וּלְשֹׁטְרָיו
ב וַיִּתְיַצְּבוּ לִפְנֵי הָאֱלֹהִים: וַיֹּאמֶר יְהוֹשֻׁעַ
אֶל־כָּל־הָעָם כֹּה־אָמַר יהוה אֱלֹהֵי

so will every bad thing come to pass *(Metzudos).*

16. וַהֲלַכְתֶּם וַעֲבַדְתֶּם — *And you will go and serve.*

In the second paragraph of the Shema, we say וְסַרְתֶּם וַעֲבַדְתֶּם אֱלֹהִים אֲחֵרִים, *that you turn aside and worship gods of others (Deuteronomy* 11:16), which implies an unpremeditated initiation into idol worship. In this verse, however, Joshua implies that the Jews will purposely worship pagan gods. *Daas Sofrim* comments that after all the good things which God did for the Israelites during this period of time, it would be considered as willful idol worship if they strayed from their faith in God.

XXIV

This final chapter of Joshua *essentially comprises three parts. The first two parts function together and the third part forms the conclusion for the entire book.*

In verses 1 through 13, we read that Joshua convoked a second assembly of the Israelites before his death. He delivered a panorama of Jewish history until his time and recounted the manifold acts of kindness which God had bestowed upon the Jewish people. Joshua's purpose for citing God's acts of kindness to them is a key issue discussed among the commentators. All agree that Joshua intended these remarks as a preface for the second part of the chapter as verse 14 clearly indicates (And now, *i.e., because of the aforesaid,* you should therefore fear HASHEM ...).

Verses 14 through 24 which form the heart of Joshua's discourse are interpreted in three different ways by the commentators. Each approach will be summarized so that the reader will have a coherent picture before him prior to reading the verses and Commentary.

1. וַיֶּאֱסֹף יְהוֹשֻׁעַ אֶת־כָּל־שִׁבְטֵי יִשְׂרָאֵל — *And Joshua assembled all the tribes.*

Joshua assembled the Israelites in order to admonish them a second time to obey the teachings of the Torah. The first assembly was mentioned in the beginning of Chapter 23 *(Radak).*

Since the people did not respond to Joshua's first discourse, he assembled them a second time and asked them questions. Their answers would reveal their true thoughts about his words *(Aburbanel).*

Kli Yakar, however, suggests that the main purpose of Joshua's first assembly was to exhort the nation to annihilate the remaining Canaanites, while the purpose of this assembly was to warn

23 *given you.* [16] *If you break the covenant of HASHEM*
16 *your God which He has commanded you, and you*
will go and serve gods of others and bow down to
them, the wrath of HASHEM will burn against you,
and you will quickly perish from the good land
which He has given you.'

24 [1] *And Joshua assembled all the tribes of Israel at*
1-2 *Shechem, and he summoned the elders of Israel and*
their leaders and their judges and their marshals and
they stood before God. [2] *Joshua said to the entire*
nation, 'Thus has HASHEM God of Israel spoken,

the people against any participation in idol worship.

שְׁכֶמָה — *At* [lit. *to*] *Shechem.*
Scripture did not specify where the first assembly was held, but it is reasonable to assume that it was held in Shiloh since the Sanctuary and the Holy Ark were there. The question therefore arises, why was Shechem chosen as the site for the second assembly?

☐ *Radak* notes that Shechem was a particularly appropriate setting for Joshua's exhortation against idol worship, because it was there that Jacob had said to his household and to all that were with him, *'Put away the strange gods that are among you' (Genesis* 35:2). Joshua, too, planned to admonish the people about idolatry *(Abarbanel).*

☐ *Radak* notes other distinctions of Shechem which made it appropriate for the covenant to be made there: (a) it was the first place that Abraham stationed himself upon entering *Eretz Yisrael (Genesis* 12:6), (b) here Jacob experienced a great miracle *(Genesis* 35:5) (c) it was the first piece of real estate Jacob acquired in *Eretz Yisrael (Genesis* 33:19).

☐ Others suggest that Shechem was an appropriate site for the assembly because it was located near Mount Gerizim and Mount Eval, where the nation had been strengthened in its commitment to Torah [and against idolatry] *(Kli Yakar).* (See 8:30 and *footnote* to 8:33.)

☐ *Meam Loez* advances that Shechem was near Joshua's home city of Timnas Serach (see *Commentary* to 19:50). When Joshua saw he was about to die he did not want to travel far from home and thus he called the people together at Shechem. As mentioned at the end of this chapter, he was buried in Timnas Serach.

לְזִקְנֵי יִשְׂרָאֵל — *The elders of Israel.*
The elders represented the entire nation *(Metzudos).*

לִפְנֵי הָאֱלֹהִים — *Before God.*
This phrase refers to the Holy Ark. Even though the Holy Ark was stationed in the Tabernacle in Shiloh, God commanded that it be brought to Shechem so that a covenant could be sealed before it *(Radak).*

2-4. These verses are quoted in the beginning of the *Haggadah* to fulfill the requirement that we begin the Passover story by mentioning our sullied origins. (See ArtScroll *Haggadah* pp. 90-93.)

2. כֹּה־אָמַר ה׳ — *Thus has HASHEM ... spoken.*
Joshua attempted to explain to the assembly the origins of Godliness in Israel. From Adam until Abraham, only select individuals strove to fulfill God's will. In establishing His Covenant with Abraham, however, God sought to

יִשְׂרָאֵל בְּעֵבֶר הַנָּהָר יָשְׁבוּ אֲבוֹתֵיכֶם
מֵעוֹלָם תֶּרַח אֲבִי אַבְרָהָם וַאֲבִי נָחוֹר
ג וַיַּעַבְדוּ אֱלֹהִים אֲחֵרִים: וָאֶקַּח אֶת־
אֲבִיכֶם אֶת־אַבְרָהָם מֵעֵבֶר הַנָּהָר וָאוֹלֵךְ
אוֹתוֹ בְּכָל־אֶרֶץ כְּנָעַן וָאַרְבֶּ אֶת־זַרְעוֹ
ד וָאֶתֶּן־לוֹ אֶת־יִצְחָק: וָאֶתֵּן לְיִצְחָק אֶת־

make His will known to a group, rather than to scattered individuals. Thus, the sons of Jacob and their descendants became the standard-bearers of God's will. In order to accomplish this transition from an individual to a national relationship with God, it was necessary that God purify the souls of the Patriarchs through trials of faith, since their ancestors were not worthy of this mission of Godliness. Thus Joshua begins, *'Your fathers always dwelt beyond the river.'*

According to the interpretation of *Daas Sofrim,* however, God commanded Joshua to remind the Israelites at this glorious point in their history that their successes were due solely to Divine Providence. No 'natural' interpretation of the Jewish nation's recent history could account for all their victories and accomplishments.

בְּעֵבֶר הַנָּהָר — *Beyond the river.*

This refers to the Euphrates River *(Meam Loez).*

The prophet begins to recount all the acts of kindness that God performed for the Jews; the first of these was that God redeemed the ancestors of the Israelites, despite the fact that they were bound in the morass of paganism *(Abarbanel)*

אֲבוֹתֵיכֶם מֵעוֹלָם — *Your fathers always* [lit. *Your fathers from old* or *Your worldly fathers*].

Joshua is not referring to the Patriarchs Abraham, Isaac, and Jacob, for Isaac and Jacob did not dwell *beyond the river.* Rather, he was referring to the Israelites' genealogical ancestors, and it was for this reason that he employed the term אֲבוֹתֵיכֶם מֵעוֹלָם, which implied 'natural parents' as opposed to 'spiritual parents.' The Israelites should not feel that it would be impossible for them to worship idols, for their own flesh and blood had indeed been idolaters *(Alshich).*

תֶּרַח אֲבִי ... — *Terach the father of ...*

The worship of idols, however, is not an inherited inclination. The proof of this is that Terach was both the father of Abraham who recognized his Creator and of Nachor who was a pagan. Joshua did not mention Haran, although he too was a son of Terach, because he was neither a pagan nor a man committed to God. When Nimrod forced Haran to declare his religious posture, he replied that if Abraham remained unharmed after being thrown into the fiery furnace, then he also believed in God, and if not, he believed in idolatry *(Alshich).*

וַיַּעַבְדוּ — *And they served.*

Terach and Nachor served idols. However, *I took your forefather Abraham from beyond the river ... (Alshich).*

אֱלֹהִים אֲחֵרִים — *Gods of others* [lit. *other gods*].

According to *Rashi (Exodus* 20:3), this phrase should not be translated as 'other gods,' which implies that there *are* gods other than the Almighty. Rather, the proper translation is *gods of others,* i.e., of other nations. Alternatively, *Rashi* renders this term as 'stranger-like gods,' because the idols are like strangers to their worshipers — they do not and cannot respond to those who appeal to them. (Cf. *Ramban, ibid.*

*"Your fathers always dwelt beyond the river —
Terach the father of Abraham and the father of
Nachor — and they served gods of others.* 3 *But, I
took your forefather Abraham from beyond the river
and led him throughout all the land of Canaan, and I
multiplied his seed and gave him Isaac.* 4 *And to Isaac*

and also *The Ten Commandments*, ArtScroll edition, pp. 28-29.)

3. וָאֶקַּח — *But I took.*

Just as a wise farmer transplants a sturdy seedling from a barren plot with little nutrients to a location more conducive to its growth, so did God take Abraham from beyond the Jordan to *Eretz Yisrael.* This was the first attempt to bring Godliness to Israel *(Malbim).*

From the wellsprings of My kindness, I influenced Abraham so that he would not necessarily be affected by the pernicious culture of idolatry in which he was raised *(Ralbag).*

אֶת־אֲבִיכֶם אֶת־אַבְרָהָם — *Your forefather Abraham.*

Only Abraham do I call your forefather, not Terach, for I do not trace the genealogy of a person through his natural antecedents, but through his spiritual antecedents. Abraham is considered your first spiritual father because he passed two tests of faith. [He was, however, given eight additional tests. The first two, in *Alshich's* opinion, had the effect of making Abraham into a Patriarch.] It is for this reason that Scripture employs the seemingly redundant phraseology *Your forefather, Abraham.* The first test was when he was told *Leave your country (Genesis* 12:1) and the second when he was told to circumcise himself *(Genesis* 17:11) at which time God renamed him Abraham. He became elevated through both tests until he became the Patriarch and acquired the sanctity of Abraham *(Alshich).*

וָאולֵךְ אותו — *And [I] led him.*

God brought Abraham to *Eretz Yisrael* because it is a land which is fertile for spiritual growth. This is evidenced by the fact that every place in *Eretz Yisrael* where Abraham traveled he received prophetic visions *(Abarbanel).*

וָאַרְבֶּ — *And I multiplied.*

The second act of kindness God showed to Abraham was that He gave him children and grandchildren through Sarah and Rebecca, even though they were barren. He gave him Isaac through Sarah, and Jacob and Esau through Rebecca *(Abarbanel).*

This word is written וארב but is pronounced וָאַרְבֶּה as if ה were the last letter. Since it is written without the ה it appears as the word וָאָרִב, *I contended.* God, in effect, is saying about Abraham, 'Before I granted him children, I made him endure many quarrels and tests' *(Rashi).* Abraham passed every one of these tests *(Radak).* [Abraham's trials are counted in *Avos* 5:3 and explained in the Commentaries. See ArtScroll *Genesis*, Vol. 2, pp. 385-399 and p. 424.]

By multiplying Abraham's seed, God provided for the purification of Abraham's offspring, for all the impurities which Abraham received from Terach were inherited by the line of Ishmael *(Malbim).*

וָאֶתֵּן־לו אֶת־יִצְחָק — *And (I) gave him Isaac.*

No mention is made of Ishmael, because he was the son of a maidservant and Abraham banished him *(Radak).*

The fact that Ishmael was the son of a maidservant made Ishmael Hagar's son, *not* Abraham's, because according to Jewish law, a child born from a non-Jewish woman is considered as having

כד
ה־ז

יַעֲקֹב וְאֶת־עֵשָׂו וָאֶתֵּן לְעֵשָׂו אֶת־הַר
שֵׂעִיר לָרֶשֶׁת אוֹתוֹ וְיַעֲקֹב וּבָנָיו יָרְדוּ
ה מִצְרָיִם׃ וָאֶשְׁלַח אֶת־מֹשֶׁה וְאֶת־אַהֲרֹן
וָאֶגֹּף אֶת־מִצְרַיִם כַּאֲשֶׁר עָשִׂיתִי בְּקִרְבּוֹ
ו וְאַחַר הוֹצֵאתִי אֶתְכֶם׃ וָאוֹצִיא אֶת־
אֲבוֹתֵיכֶם מִמִּצְרַיִם וַתָּבֹאוּ הַיָּמָּה וַיִּרְדְּפוּ
מִצְרַיִם אַחֲרֵי אֲבוֹתֵיכֶם בְּרֶכֶב וּבְפָרָשִׁים
ז יַם־סוּף׃ וַיִּצְעֲקוּ אֶל־יהוה וַיָּשֶׂם מַאֲפֵל
בֵּינֵיכֶם | וּבֵין הַמִּצְרִים וַיָּבֵא עָלָיו אֶת־

descended from the mother, not the father *(Alshich).*

Abarbanel explains that Ishmael is not mentioned here because his birth did not require Divine intervention. In this passage the prophet is recounting instances of miraculous Divine compassion; Sarah and Rebecca were physically incapable of having children, yet God gave them Isaac, Jacob, and Esau. Since Hagar, Ishmael's mother, *was* capable of having children, Ishmael's birth did not constitute an outstanding act of Divine kindness.

Isaac was a purified derivative of Abraham's strengths. However, Isaac's line required further purification; the refining process was completed with the birth of Esau, who inherited Isaac's taints *(Malbim).* [Thus Jacob's patrimony was perfectly pure.]

4. אֶת־יַעֲקֹב וְאֶת־עֵשָׂו — *Jacob and Esau.*

Since the holy Isaac could father such diametrically opposite children, it is clear that genetic inheritance does not determine whether one of Abraham's descendants will resemble him spiritually *(Alshich).*

It was to Jacob's great benefit that he shared his mother's womb with Esau, for this facilitated Esau's absorption of all the placular influences [stemming from Terach, and Jacob's acquisition of the pure and holy paternal influences] *(Metzudos).*

וָאֶתֵּן לְעֵשָׂו אֶת־הַר שֵׂעִיר — *And to Esau I gave Mount Seir.*

Either Jacob or Esau could have been the inheritor of Isaac's mission which he received from Abraham. However, since Esau was immediately given his portion in Mount Seir, his offspring did not suffer the tribulations of bondage in Egypt with Jacob's descendants. Esau was thereby excluded from Abraham's lineage, for God had told Abraham, *'Know that your seed shall be a stranger in a land that is not theirs and shall serve them' (Genesis* 15:13). Although Jacob and Esau were both Abraham's grandsons, only Jacob was considered as Abraham's *seed (Brisker Rav* to *Genesis).*

יָרְדוּ מִצְרָיִם — *Went down to Egypt.*

The Egyptian bondage was like a smelting furnace which further refined the Jewish soul. Previously, God's Presence had dwelled on select individuals, but now it would envelop an entire nation *(Malbim).*

[See ArtScroll *Haggadah,* p.93.]

5. וָאֶגֹּף — *And I plagued.*

The Egyptians were plagued through Moses and Aaron *(Metzudos).*

Alshich, however, interprets that three were responsible for the plagues in Egypt — Moses, Aaron, and God. This is consistent with the *Midrash* which states that the first three plagues were performed by Aaron (blood, frogs, lice),

I gave Jacob and Esau; and to Esau I gave Mount
Seir, to possess it, and Jacob and his sons went down
to Egypt. 5 *I sent Moses and Aaron, and I plagued*
Egypt with that which I did in their midst.
Afterwards, I brought you out. 6 *And I brought your*
forefathers out of Egypt, and you came to the sea; the
Egyptians pursued your forefathers with chariots
and horsemen to the Sea of Reeds. 7 *And they cried*
out to HASHEM, and He put darkness between you
and the Egyptians and brought the sea upon them

the last three by Moses (hail, locusts, darkness) and three by God (wild beasts, pestilence, and slaying of the first born). The plague of boils was performed by all three.

אֶתְכֶם — *You.*

Even though the people Joshua was addressing were not those who left Egypt, but rather their offspring, he employed the word *you* instead of 'them,' because, as the Passover *Haggadah* explains, each Jew in every generation is required to see himself as if he personally had left Egypt *(Meam Loez).* [See next comment.].

6. וָאוֹצִיא אֶת־אֲבוֹתֵיכֶם מִמִּצְרַיִם — *And I brought your forefathers out of Egypt.*

[This is another act of kindness which God performed for the Israelites.]

וַתָּבֹאוּ הַיָּמָּה — *And you came to the sea.*

The use of the second person, 'you,' implies that Joshua was addressing people who themselves had experienced the crossing of the Red Sea. Among the Children of Israel were a number of very elderly people [who were at least sixty years old at the time of the Reconnaissance Mission and were therefore not sentenced to die in the Wilderness. Consequently, at this time they were at least 114. In addition, there were also Jews who had crossed the Red Sea but who had been under twenty years old at the time of the spies' mission; they were also spared the Divine punishment of death in the Wilderness.] *(Radak).*

וַיִּרְדְּפוּ מִצְרַיִם — *The Egyptians pursued.*

God planned the Exodus in this way in order to increase the Israelites' faith in Him; immediately after this episode, Scripture states *(Exodus* 14:31): *And the people feared HASHEM and believed in HASHEM (Malbim).*

7. וַיָּשֶׂם מַאֲפֵל — *And He put darkness.*

This refers to the Clouds of Glory which protected the Israelites from any external dangers in the Wilderness, as Scripture states, *And the pillar of the cloud went from before them and stood behind them; and it came between the camp of the Egyptians and the camp of Israel; and it was a cloud and darkness to them* [*the Egyptians*], *but it gave light by night to these* [*the Israelites*] *(Exodus* 14:20) *(Metzudos).*

Abarbanel comments that this darkness was an important element of God's plan to drown the Egyptians at the Red Sea, for if the Egyptians had been permitted to witness the miracle by which the Jews were enabled to cross the Sea, they would have realized that they could not expect a similar miracle to facilitate *their* crossing, and they would have refrained from entering the Sea.

וַיָּבֵא עָלָיו אֶת־הַיָּם — *And He brought the sea upon them* [lit. *him*].

From the phrase *upon him* it would appear that the waters submerged only one individual. *Radak* comments that

הַיָּם וַיְכַסֵּהוּ וַתִּרְאֶינָה עֵינֵיכֶם אֵת אֲשֶׁר־
עָשִׂיתִי בְּמִצְרָיִם וַתֵּשְׁבוּ בַמִּדְבָּר יָמִים
ח רַבִּים׃ °ואביאה אֶתְכֶם אֶל־אֶרֶץ הָאֱמֹרִי (°וָאָבִיא ק׳)
הַיּוֹשֵׁב בְּעֵבֶר הַיַּרְדֵּן וַיִּלָּחֲמוּ אִתְּכֶם
וָאֶתֵּן אוֹתָם בְּיֶדְכֶם וַתִּירְשׁוּ אֶת־אַרְצָם
ט וָאַשְׁמִידֵם מִפְּנֵיכֶם׃ וַיָּקָם בָּלָק בֶּן־צִפּוֹר
מֶלֶךְ מוֹאָב וַיִּלָּחֶם בְּיִשְׂרָאֵל וַיִּשְׁלַח
וַיִּקְרָא לְבִלְעָם בֶּן־בְּעוֹר לְקַלֵּל אֶתְכֶם׃
י וְלֹא אָבִיתִי לִשְׁמֹעַ לְבִלְעָם וַיְבָרֶךְ בָּרוֹךְ
יא אֶתְכֶם וָאַצִּל אֶתְכֶם מִיָּדוֹ׃ וַתַּעַבְרוּ אֶת־
הַיַּרְדֵּן וַתָּבֹאוּ אֶל־יְרִיחוֹ וַיִּלָּחֲמוּ בָכֶם
בַעֲלֵי־יְרִיחוֹ הָאֱמֹרִי וְהַפְּרִזִּי וְהַכְּנַעֲנִי

him refers to Pharoah. Alternatively, *Radak* suggests that Scripture may be referring to all the Egyptians collectively as *him;* in this case, the phrase would actually mean, 'upon them.' The translation follows this latter interpretation.

This verse recounts another great act of kindness which God performed for the Israelites by allowing them to experience the revenge of their enemy as the verse states, *the righteous shall rejoice when he sees the vengeance, he shall wash his feet in the blood of the wicked (Psalms 58:11) (Abarbanel).*

It was most appropriate that the Egyptians died by drowning because they decided to kill all the Israelites' new born males by drowning. Thus, they were requited measure for measure *(Meam Loez).*

If any Egyptian attempted to flee in order to avoid entering the water, a wave pursued him and drowned him *(Rashi).*

[From this verse, it would appear that the Egyptians drowned in the water. See, however, *R' Bachaya* to *Exodus* 14:21 who argues that they drowned in the mud of the Sea's floor.]

וַתֵּשְׁבוּ בַמִּדְבָּר יָמִים רַבִּים — *There you dwelled in the Wilderness many days.*

This forty year period served to purify the Jews of the pernicious effects of the Egyptian bondage *(Malbim).*

8. אֶרֶץ הָאֱמֹרִי — *Land of the Emorites.*

This is the land of Sichon and Og, the two Emorite kings *(Poras Yosef).*

וַיִּלָּחֲמוּ אִתְּכֶם — *And they fought with you.*

The verse implies: *They* started to fight with *you;* you did not initiate an attack. Had they allowed you to pass through their land, you would not have engaged in battle *(Poras Yosef).*

וָאֶתֵּן אוֹתָם בְּיֶדְכֶם — *I delivered them into your hand.*

The fact that the Israelites were forced to remain in the Wilderness for forty years was really to their advantage for they came to the Emorites' land, fought them, and annexed their territory *(Abarbanel).*

9. וַיִּלָּחֶם בְּיִשְׂרָאֵל — *And waged war against Israel.*

It is never recorded in the Pentateuch that Balak waged war against Israel. However, from the fact that he engaged

and covered them. Your eyes have seen what I have
done in Egypt; there you dwelled in the Wilderness
many days. 8 *And I brought you to the land of the*
Emorites who lived across the Jordan, and they
fought with you. I delivered them into your hand,
and you took possession of their land, and I
destroyed them from before you. 9 *Then Balak the*
son of Tzipor, the king of Moab, arose and waged
war against Israel; he sent, and he summoned Bilaam,
the son of Beor to curse you. 10 *But I refused to listen*
to Bilaam, and he pronounced a blessing upon you. I
saved you from his hand. 11 *Then you crossed the*
Jordan and came to Jericho. The inhabitants of
Jericho fought against you — the Emorites, Perizzites,

Bilaam to curse Israel, it is evident that he would have fought Israel had the opportunity presented itself *(Radak).*

Abarbanel, however, comments that Balak did not intend to fight a conventional war against the Israelites. Rather, he intended to fight them by employing Bilaam to curse Israel. It is in this sense that Scripture means he *waged war against Israel.*

10. וָאַצִּל אֶתְכֶם מִיָּדוֹ — *I saved you from his hand.*

This is yet another act of kindness performed by God for the Israelites *(Abarbanel).*

Balak is mentioned in this passage to remind the Israelites that all his machinations did not affect their efforts to destroy the Emorites *(Abarbanel).*

11. וַתַּעַבְרוּ — *Then you crossed.*

Since the following three events occurred to the people Joshua was addressing, he briefly alluded to them and did not mention the details of the miracles which were involved. *You crossed the Jordan* refers to the miracle of the Israelites crossing on dry land. [*You*] *came to Jericho* refers to the miracle of the Jews' entry into the fortified city. The miracle of the sun stopping at Gibeon was alluded to by the phrase, *the inhabitants of Jericho fought against you* [see *Abarbanel's* explanation of this phrase in the next comment that *the inhabitants of Jericho* refers to the five monarchs who fought against the Israelites after the fall of Jericho. It was during this battle mentioned in Chapter 10 that the miracles occurred.] *(Abarbanel).*

Abarbanel also suggests that Joshua does not intend to refer to the miracles performed for the Israelites, for Joshua did not explicitly mention the parting of the Red Sea or the Jordan River. Rather, Joshua intended to recount more acts of kindness which God performed for the Israelites, such as the victories over the Seven Canaanite nations.

וַיִּלָּחֲמוּ בָכֶם בַּעֲלֵי־יְרִיחוֹ — *The inhabitants* [lit. *owners*] *of Jericho fought against you.*

Scripture did not previously mention this battle between the Israelites and the Canaanites at Jericho. Perhaps some men left Jericho before the Israelites' siege (in order to warn the other Canaanite kings of the impending danger) and later aided these kings in their subsequent battles against Joshua *(Radak).*

Malbim suggests that they should be called 'avengers of Jericho' rather than

וְהַחִתִּי וְהַגִּרְגָּשִׁי הַחִוִּי וְהַיְבוּסִי וָאֶתֵּן
יב אוֹתָם בְּיֶדְכֶם: וָאֶשְׁלַח לִפְנֵיכֶם אֶת־
הַצִּרְעָה וַתְּגָרֶשׁ אוֹתָם מִפְּנֵיכֶם שְׁנֵי
מַלְכֵי הָאֱמֹרִי לֹא בְחַרְבְּךָ וְלֹא בְקַשְׁתֶּךָ:
יג וָאֶתֵּן לָכֶם אֶרֶץ | אֲשֶׁר לֹא־יָגַעְתָּ בָּהּ
וְעָרִים אֲשֶׁר לֹא־בְנִיתֶם וַתֵּשְׁבוּ בָּהֶם
כְּרָמִים וְזֵיתִים אֲשֶׁר לֹא־נְטַעְתֶּם אַתֶּם

inhabitants of Jericho. He maintains that the verse is referring to the other monarchs who later fought against Joshua to avenge his victory over Jericho. They fought with such fury because of Jericho's capture that it *was as if* they themselves were the *inhabitants of Jericho (Abarbanel).*

... הָאֱמֹרִי וְהַפְּרִזִּי — *The Emorites, Perrizites ...*

Scripture mentions all seven nations — even though they did not all live in Jericho — for all the nations had troops stationed in Jericho, since that city was a key stronghold for the protection of the entire country *(Rashi).*

וְהַגִּרְגָּשִׁי — *Girgashites.*

Although this nation fled from *Eretz Yisrael* and settled in Africa, it is still mentioned among the nations which battled against Israel, because it had originally joined the forces of the other six nations. Later, it became frightened and fled *(Daas Sofrim).*

12. הַצִּרְעָה — *The hornet.*

This word is commonly translated as *hornet.* According to the *Mishnah (Machshirim* 6:4), the צִרְעָה was a honey-producing insect.

This is in fulfillment of the Torah's promise, *And I will send hornets before you, which shall drive out the Hivvites, Canannites, and Hittites from before you (Exodus* 23:28).

According to *Radak,* there were two hornets, one belonging to Moses and one to Joshua. The hornets would attack Israel's foes and blind them, rendering them defenseless. The Israelites would then proceed to kill them.

There are two opinions mentioned in the *Talmud (Sotah* 36a) concerning this matter. According to Reish Lakish, there was only one hornet. It did not cross the Jordan River and enter *Eretz Yisrael,* but rather remained in the Trans-Jordan and ejected its poison into the Canaanites, which both blinded and sterilized them. Rav Pappa maintains that there were two hornets, one belonging to Moses and one to Joshua.

Others understand צִרְעָה as a type of plague *(Ibn Janach). Lev Aharon* also maintains that צִרְעָה in this context does not mean *hornet,* but rather refers to a type of disease which significantly weakens its victims. This disease preceded Israel's entry into *Eretz Yisrael* and simplified their conquest of its inhabitants.

Ibn Ezra (Exodus 23:28) relates this to the disease called *Tzaraas* [see *Leviticus,* ch. 13; צָרַעַת, *tzaraas* derives from the same root as צִרְעָה, *hornet*].

Abarbanel, however, understands this phrase more figuratively. He contends that when the Canaanites heard that the Jews defeated Sichon and Og through God's intervention, they (Girgashites) fled as if they had been stung by hornets. This is what Rachav had told the two spies in 2:10-11, *we heard ... what you did to the Emorite kings ... and our hearts melted.*

לֹא בְחַרְבְּךָ וְלֹא בְקַשְׁתֶּךָ — *Not by your sword and not by your bow.*

Israel's success was attributable solely to God's intervention *(Abarbanel).*

13. וָאֶתֵּן לָכֶם אֶרֶץ — *I have given you a land.*

This was in fulfillment of His promise, [*He will*] *give you great and*

Canaanites, Hittites, Girgashites, Hivvites, and
Jebusites — and I delivered them into your hand.
12 *And I sent the hornet ahead of you, and it drove*
them out from before you — the two Emorite kings —
not by your sword and not by your bow. 13 *I have*
given you a land in which you did not labor and cities
which you did not build and you have occupied
them; you eat from vineyards and olive groves which

good cities which you did not build ... vineyards ... which you did not plant (Deuteronomy 6:11).

[See *footnote* to 7:5.]

וְעָרִים אֲשֶׁר לֹא־בְנִיתֶם — *And cities which you did not build.*

God detained the Israelites in the Wilderness for forty years in order to give the Canaanites enough time to build these houses and plant these vineyards *(Poras Yosef).*

In this way, the Jews could occupy themselves with the study of Torah immediately upon their settlement *(Meam Loez).*

JOSHUA'S DISCOURSE

◆§ Approach I

Although Joshua implored the nation, Remove the gods which your fathers served ... *(verse 14), he did not suspect them of idol worship, for they were on a lofty spiritual level as verse 31 attests,* And Israel served HASHEM all the days of Joshua, *and which is reiterated in* Judges 2:7. *However, they were guilty of failing to destroy the gold and silver objects used for idol worship which they had inherited from their idolatrous ancestors and which they had acquired in Egypt.*[1] *It was expressly forbidden to benefit from these objects because of their association with idol worship. In regard to them the Torah states,* The carvings of their gods you shall burn with fire; you shall not desire the silver or gold that is on them, or take it, lest you will be snared with it (Deuteronomy *7:25).*

Joshua knew that to persuade the Israelites to relinquish their possession of these

1. Throughout this chapter, mention is made of the idols the Israelites acquired in Egypt. The question arises, however, how could the Israelites, who came to such a supreme understanding of monotheism during the Exodus, the crossing of the Red Sea, and their experience at Mount Sinai, still be in *possession* of pagan idols? *Toras Moshe (Achron Shel Pesach),* commenting on a verse in *Songs of Songs* (1:8), explains that the Israelites acquired idols at two different times in their history: during their confiscation of the Egyptian wealth just before they left Egypt (see *Exodus* 12:35) and during the crossing of the Red Sea. Although the gold and silver objects of both acquisitions contained pagan inscriptions, those objects gained while the Israelites were still in Egypt had entirely lost their engravings and inscriptions and were totally unidentifiable as works of idol worship. The gold and silver articles amassed from the Red Sea, on the other hand, retained their vestiges of idolatry, although their pagan status had been nullified by the Egyptians. Even though this nullification completely removes the pagan nature of these objects according to the strict letter of Jewish law, *Toras Moshe* argues that the Israelites should not have relied on this leniency when they approached the holy event at Mount Sinai, but should rather have abandoned these objects as Jacob did when he ascended to Beth El *(Genesis* 35:2). Similarly, it could be argued that it was these objects which the Jews found at the Red Sea which no longer had any legal link to idolatry that Joshua beseeched the people to abandon, because they were inappropriate to the Israelites' elevated spiritual status now that they were dwelling in the Holy Land.

יד אֹכְלִים׃ וְעַתָּה יְראוּ אֶת־יְהוָה וְעִבְדוּ
אֹתוֹ בְּתָמִים וּבֶאֱמֶת וְהָסִירוּ אֶת־אֱלֹהִים
אֲשֶׁר עָבְדוּ אֲבוֹתֵיכֶם בְּעֵבֶר הַנָּהָר
טו וּבְמִצְרַיִם וְעִבְדוּ אֶת־יְהוָה׃ וְאִם רַע
בְּעֵינֵיכֶם לַעֲבֹד אֶת־יְהוָה בַּחֲרוּ לָכֶם
הַיּוֹם אֶת־מִי תַעֲבֹדוּן אִם אֶת־אֱלֹהִים
אֲשֶׁר־עָבְדוּ אֲבוֹתֵיכֶם אֲשֶׁר °בעבר (°מֵעֵבֶר ק׳)
הַנָּהָר וְאִם אֶת־אֱלֹהֵי הָאֱמֹרִי אֲשֶׁר אַתֶּם
יֹשְׁבִים בְּאַרְצָם וְאָנֹכִי וּבֵיתִי נַעֲבֹד אֶת־
טז יְהוָה׃ וַיַּעַן הָעָם וַיֹּאמֶר חָלִילָה
לָּנוּ מֵעֲזֹב אֶת־יְהוָה לַעֲבֹד אֱלֹהִים
יז אֲחֵרִים׃ כִּי יְהוָה אֱלֹהֵינוּ הוּא הַמַּעֲלֶה
אֹתָנוּ וְאֶת־אֲבוֹתֵינוּ מֵאֶרֶץ מִצְרַיִם מִבֵּית
עֲבָדִים וַאֲשֶׁר עָשָׂה לְעֵינֵינוּ אֶת־הָאֹתוֹת

valuables would not be a simple task, since man's desire for wealth is so strong. He therefore assembled the people and attempted to anticipate their overwhelming feelings of financial sacrifice by reminding them of the occasions in which God beneficently intervened on their behalf. In this way Joshua hoped that the people would feel that God could also help them be successful in Eretz Yisrael *without the wealth of these objects. Their service of God at this point in history was to rid themselves of these objects. The people replied (verse 16) that they were certain that the retention of these objects would never lead to idolatry, but Joshua responded that idolatry was inevitable and to God it would be intolerable. As a result, the people recanted and declared they would serve God by destroying their idolatrous belongings* (Alshich).

◆§ Approach II

According to Kli Yakar, *Joshua convened this assembly in order to reaffirm the Israelites' adherence to the Torah before his death, just as Moses had done in the* Book of Deuteronomy. Rashi *comments that through prophecy, Joshua knew that in the times of* Ezekiel *the Jews would argue that they were no longer required to observe the Torah since they had only accepted it on the condition that they could enter* Eretz Yisrael. *Joshua, therefore, anticipated their argument by having them reaffirm the authority of the Torah* **after** *they entered the Land, thus implying that their acceptance was unconditional.*

Joshua recounted the many acts of Divine kindness in order to awaken a feeling of gratitude so that the Jews would want to serve Him. The Midrash (Mechilta, Yisro) *explains by way of a parable why the Ten Commandments were not recounted in the first passage of the Torah* (Genesis). *A distant monarch once entered a city and told the townspeople that he wished to be their king. The citizens replied, 'Did you ever do anything for us that we should accept your sovereignty?'*

you did not plant." [14] *And now, fear* HASHEM *and*
serve Him with perfection and truth; remove the
gods which your fathers served on the other side of
the river and in Egypt, and serve HASHEM. [15] *If it is*
evil in your eyes to serve HASHEM, *choose this day*
whom you will serve — the gods your forefathers
served, who were across the Jordan or the gods of the
Emorites in whose land you dwell. But as for me and
my household, we will serve HASHEM.'

[16] *And the nation responded and said, 'Far be it*
from us to forsake HASHEM *to serve gods of others.*
[17] *For it was* HASHEM *our God Who brought us and*
our fathers out of the land of Egypt, from the house
of bondage; Who performed these wondrous signs in

In response, the monarch provided for their defense by building a wall around their city, by establishing the town's water supply, and by successfully fighting a battle against the town's enemies. When he returned to the townspeople and asked to be instated as their king, they joyously accepted. So it was with God. He informed the Jews that He created the earth and heavens and when he requested to rule over them, he recounted all the acts of kindness which He had performed — the Exodus, the splitting of the Red Sea, the drowning of their pursuers, and the manna — and afterwards He presented the Torah. Having been engendered with an overwhelming feeling of gratitude, the Jews accepted the authority of the Torah in order to 'repay' to some degree their debt of gratitude.

Similarly, Joshua recounted all God's kindness to the Israelites and then requested, 'Now ... fear HASHEM and serve Him' *(verse 14)* (Meam Loez). *He told them that if they felt that their service of God was difficult and they could not perform it with a fullness of heart, then they would eventually turn away from the Torah and worship idols. To this the people responded,* 'Far be it from us to forsake HASHEM' *(verse 16). Joshua further strengthened their allegiance to the Torah by denying their ability to remain faithful to the Torah. At this suggestion the people accepted the entire Torah by declaring,* 'No, we will serve only HASHEM' *(verse 21).*

◆§ Approach III

According to Lev Aharon, *Joshua called the people together to implore them to perfect their service of God by coming to a personal understanding of Him, as King David told his son Solomon,* 'Know the God of your father and serve him' (I Chronicles *28:9). It is this principle which underlies the first blessing of the* Shemoneh Esrei *(silent prayer) when we recite, 'God of Abraham, God of Isaac, and God of Jacob.' Even though Isaac and Jacob learned about God through their fathers, they each came to their own personal recognition of Him. Had they merely received a tradition from their fathers and not expanded it for themselves, the prayer would have read, 'God of Abraham, Isaac, and Jacob.'*

Chovos HaLevavos (Sha'ar Avodas HaElokim, *Chapter 3) writes: when one serves God out of his personal understanding of Him, he can rise to the level where*

he serves God for His own sake, not prompted by reward and punishment. It is to this level of service that the Sages referred: Do not be as servants who minister to their master in order to receive a reward ... rather ... let the fear of Heaven be upon you (Avos *1:3).*

Thus Joshua assembled the people and recounted God's many acts of kindness which they personally witnessed. Through their recognition of His kindness to them, the Israelites could attain their own understanding of Him, besides the understanding they were taught by their fathers. As a result, they could serve God with perfection and truth *(verse 14), i.e., for His own sake. Joshua's command to* remove the gods which your fathers served *(verse 14) is to be understood figuratively — each individual must remove any heretical thoughts he may have in order to achieve a clear recognition of God's kindness to him. When the nation responded that they would never serve idols, Joshua was displeased with their explanation, for they implied that they would serve God because of the kindnesses which He had done for them, not purely because He is intrinsically worthy of being served. Joshua retorted that they could never serve God on that basis, because they would eventually reject his sovereignty if He ever meted out punishments. The people answered that they, therefore, would only serve Him for His own sake, not because of His kindness to them (verse 21).*

Approach I

14. וְעַתָּה — *And now.*

Now implies 'since I have performed so many acts of kindness for you' *(Metzudos).*

יְראוּ אֶת־ה׳ — *Fear HASHEM.*

Fear HASHEM by observing all the prohibitions of the Torah and serve Him by performing all the positive commandments so that God will continue to bestow his beneficence upon us *(Alshich).*

בְּתָמִים וּבֶאֱמֶת — *With perfection and truth.*

Observe the prohibitions with a *perfect* heart and perform the positive commandments in *truth,* i.e., for their own sake, unconcerned about reward and punishment *(Alshich).*

וְהָסִירוּ אֶת־אֱלֹהִים — *Remove the gods.*

[These were Jacob's words to his household when he exhorted them to eschew idol worship.]

Joshua did not suspect them of idolatry. Their possession of these gods was a result of their failure to destroy the gold and silver objects used for idol worship which they had inherited from their idolatrous ancestors and which they had acquired in *Egypt.* It was expressly forbidden to benefit from these objects, because of their association with idol worship. In regard to them the Torah states: *'The carvings of their gods you shall burn with fire, you shall not desire the silver or gold that is on them or take it, lest you will be snared with it' (Deuteronomy* 7:25). Your service to God requires you remove these idols *(Alshich).*

וּבְמִצְרַיִם — *And in Egypt.*

Many of them worshiped idols in Egypt, as *Ezekiel* 20:8 states, *the idols of Egypt they did not forsake (Metzudos).*

וְעִבְדוּ אֶת־ה׳ — *And serve HASHEM.*

Serve God at this point by destroying these valuable objects associated with idol worship *(Alshich).*

15. וְאִם רַע בְּעֵינֵיכֶם — *If it is evil in your eyes.*

If it is evil in your eyes which see the silver and gold of your idolatrous objects, *to serve HASHEM, then choose this day whom you will serve.* As a result of your failure to remove these gods, you will gradually become insensitive to the abomination of idolatry and will eventually serve idols *(Alshich).*

בַּחֲרוּ לָכֶם הַיּוֹם אֶת־מִי תַעֲבֹדוּן — *Choose this day whom you will serve.*

If you retain these objects, it is inevitable that you will eventually become idolaters, as the verse testifies,

lest you will be snared with it (Deuteronomy 7:25). The course of your future religious commitment is before you today *(Alshich).*

וְאָנֹכִי וּבֵיתִי — *But as for me and my household.*

We will not be drawn after your decision *(Metzudos).*

16. חָלִילָה לָּנוּ מֵעֲזֹב אֶת־ה׳ — *Far be it from us to forsake HASHEM.*

Even if we do not rid ourselves of these molten figures, we are strong enough in our convictions that we will never serve idols in the future *(Alshich).*

17. כִּי ה׳ אֱלֹהֵינוּ הוּא הַמַּעֲלֶה אֹתָנוּ — *For it was HASHEM our God Who brought us.*

Our God has brought us out of Egypt and answered us in our times of need. How could we ever serve any deity but the true God? *(Alshich).*

וַאֲשֶׁר עָשָׂה לְעֵינֵינוּ אֶת־הָאֹתוֹת הַגְּדֹלוֹת הָאֵלֶּה — *Who performed these wondrous signs.*

These miracles inspired an overwhelming awe of God *(Malbim).*

Approach II

14. יְראוּ אֶת־ה׳ — *Fear HASHEM.*

After having experienced all God's kindness, you are obliged to serve Him *(Abarbanel).*

בְּתָמִים וּבֶאֱמֶת — *With perfection and truth.*

Your service to God should be performed with a *true* conviction and with a *sincere* heart *(Kli Yakar).*

15. וְאִם רַע בְּעֵינֵיכֶם — *If it is evil in your eyes.*

If you feel it is so difficult to observe all 613 commandments and you observe them under duress without a fullness of heart, then you will eventually serve idols. Therefore, *choose this day ... (Kli Yakar).*

16. חָלִילָה לָּנוּ מֵעֲזֹב אֶת־ה׳ — *Far be it from us to forsake HASHEM.*

The people impulsively reacted to Joshua's accusation, not allowing their leaders and justices to respond first *(Abarbanel).* They were disturbed that Joshua thought they might ever worship idols *(Meam Loez).*

Joshua was not giving the Israelites license to abrogate the covenant they made at Mount Sinai. He said this only to strengthen their conviction and to indicate the alternative to complete devotion to God *(Abarbanel).*

17. The Israelites affirm their allegiance to God and cite four reasons which obligate them to serve Him. They note: (a) He took us and our fathers out of Egypt; (b) He performed miracles in our midst; (c) He protected us in our travels; and (d) [verse 18] He drove out all the nations from before us *(Abarbanel).*

כִּי ה׳ אֱלֹהֵינוּ הוּא הַמַּעֲלֶה אֹתָנוּ — *For it was HASHEM our God Who brought us.*

By liberating us from the Egyptian bondage, God acquired us as His servants. It is for this reason that many commandments are designated, 'a remembrance of the Exodus from Egypt' *(Malbim).*

Approach III

14. יְראוּ אֶת־ה׳ — *Fear HASHEM.*

Besides your understanding of God which you received from your fathers, you came to your personal understanding of God by reflecting upon all those wonderful things He did for you *(Lev Aharon).*

וְהָסִירוּ אֶת־אֱלֹהִים — *Remove the gods.*

Before you attempt to arrive at your own understanding of God you must rid yourselves of any heretical thoughts and then recognize all God's beneficence *(Lev Aharon).*

וְעִבְדוּ אֶת־ה׳ — *And serve HASHEM.*

After you recognize God from your own efforts, then you can *serve Him* with *perfection and truth,* i.e., for His own sake, not prompted by reward and punishment *(Lev Aharon).*

16. חָלִילָה לָּנוּ מֵעֲזֹב אֶת־ה׳ — *Far be it from us to forsake HASHEM.*

See Approach II.

הַגְּדֹלוֹת הָאֵלֶּה וַיִּשְׁמְרֵנוּ בְּכָל־הַדֶּרֶךְ
אֲשֶׁר הָלַכְנוּ בָהּ וּבְכֹל הָעַמִּים אֲשֶׁר
יח עָבַרְנוּ בְּקִרְבָּם: וַיְגָרֶשׁ יהוה אֶת־כָּל־
הָעַמִּים וְאֶת־הָאֱמֹרִי יֹשֵׁב הָאָרֶץ מִפָּנֵינוּ
גַּם־אֲנַחְנוּ נַעֲבֹד אֶת־יהוה כִּי־הוּא
יט אֱלֹהֵינוּ: וַיֹּאמֶר יְהוֹשֻׁעַ אֶל־הָעָם
לֹא תוּכְלוּ לַעֲבֹד אֶת־יהוה כִּי־אֱלֹהִים
קְדֹשִׁים הוּא אֵל־קַנּוֹא הוּא לֹא־יִשָּׂא
כ לְפִשְׁעֲכֶם וּלְחַטֹּאותֵיכֶם: כִּי תַעַזְבוּ אֶת־
יהוה וַעֲבַדְתֶּם אֱלֹהֵי נֵכָר וְשָׁב וְהֵרַע
לָכֶם וְכִלָּה אֶתְכֶם אַחֲרֵי אֲשֶׁר־הֵיטִיב
כא לָכֶם: וַיֹּאמֶר הָעָם אֶל־יְהוֹשֻׁעַ לֹא כִּי
כב אֶת־יהוה נַעֲבֹד: וַיֹּאמֶר יְהוֹשֻׁעַ אֶל־הָעָם

Approach I

18. גַּם־אֲנַחְנוּ — *We too* [*will*] ...

Just as you and your household will serve God, so will we *(Metzudos)*.

Since we have a clear understanding of God, we can retain possession of these idolatrous objects and still be secure that we will never serve idols *(Alshich)*.

19. לֹא תוּכְלוּ לַעֲבֹד אֶת־ה׳ — *You will not be able to serve HASHEM.*

If you do not remove these objects of idolatry, *you will not be able to serve HASHEM*, because you will eventually come to worship idols *(Alshich)*.

כִּי־אֱלֹהִים קְדֹשִׁים הוּא — *For He is a holy God.*

He is holy and abhors idolatry. Therefore, He will not hold you guiltless, but will mete out punishment *(Alshich)*.

לְפִשְׁעֲכֶם — *Your transgressions.*

He will consider any future sins of idolatry as intentional, because you have the opportunity at this time to insure that they will never come about by ridding yourselves of those idolatrous objects *(Alshich)*.

20. אַחֲרֵי אֲשֶׁר־הֵיטִיב לָכֶם — *After having done good with you.*

The punishment will seem twice as great, since you were accustomed to receiving such goodness from Him *(Metzudos)*.

21. לֹא כִּי אֶת־ה׳ נַעֲבֹד — *No, we will serve only HASHEM.*

The translation follows *Metzudos*.

It is not as we said before, that we could serve God without ridding ourselves of the objects in question. *We will serve HASHEM completely by removing them from our midst (Alshich)*.

Approach II

18. כִּי־הוּא אֱלֹהֵינוּ — *For He is our God.*

It appears that the people accepted the service of God only because of the specific acts of kindness which He performed, rather than because He is intrinsically worth serving. In the following verses, Joshua reacts sharply against this misconception concerning

24
18-21 *our sight; and protected us on all the paths we*
traveled and among the peoples through whom we
passed. [18] *HASHEM drove out all the peoples and the*
Emorites who inhabited the Land before us. We too
will serve HASHEM, for He is our God.'
[19] *And Joshua said to the people, 'You will not be*
able to serve HASHEM, for He is a holy God. He is a
jealous God; He will not forgive your transgressions
or your sins. [20] *If you forsake HASHEM and serve*
strange gods, He will turn and do evil to you and
destroy you after having done good with you.'
[21] *And the people said to Joshua, 'No, we will serve*
only HASHEM.'

the basis of our obligation to serve God *(Poras Yosef).*

19. לא תוכלו לַעֲבֹד אֶת־ה׳ — *You will not be able to serve HASHEM.*

In order to elicit a clearer revelation of the people's intent to adhere to the Torah and in order to strengthen their commitment to the covenant which was about to be made, Joshua challenged them by saying, *'You will not be able to serve HASHEM.'* He offered two reasons *(Abarbanel)* [see further].

כִּי־אֱלֹהִים קְדֹשִׁים הוּא — *For He is a holy God.*

The first reason is that since *He is* [*so*] *holy,* who *could possibly serve Him?' (Abarbanel).*

אֵל־קַנּוֹא הוּא — *He is a jealous God.*

The second reason is that since *He is* [such] *a jealous God,* he will not forgive your transgressions. The people knew that both of Joshua's claims were obviously untrue. Serving God is not impossible, and He is quick to forgive sins *(Abarbanel).*

21. לֹא כִּי אֶת־ה׳ נַעֲבֹד — *No, we will serve only HASHEM.*

[No, in spite of the obstacles to God's service that you mentioned, we will serve Him.]

Approach III

18. כִּי־הוּא אֱלֹהֵינוּ — *For He is our God.*

It appears that the people accepted the service of God only because of the specific acts of kindness which He performed, rather than because He is intrinsically worth serving. In the following verses, Joshua reacts sharply against this misconception concerning the basis of our obligation to serve God *(Poras Yosef).*

19. לא תוכלו לַעֲבֹד אֶת־ה׳ — *You will not be able to serve HASHEM.*

Joshua perceived from their response that the service to God was based on the benefits which they had received from Him. Joshua was attempting to inform them that their devotion must be unconditional, rather than dependent on any benefits which they might receive *(Malbim).*

כִּי־אֱלֹהִים קְדֹשִׁים הוּא — *For He is a holy God.*

If your service is based on reward, then you will rebel from Him if He punishes you. It is likely that He will mete out punishments because *He is holy* and His standards are exacting *(Lev Aharon).*

20. כִּי תַעַזְבוּ אֶת־ה׳ — *If you forsake HASHEM.*

It is possible to forsake God if you

עֵדִים אַתֶּם בָּכֶם כִּי־אַתֶּם בְּחַרְתֶּם לָכֶם
אֶת־יְהוָה לַעֲבֹד אוֹתוֹ וַיֹּאמְרוּ עֵדִים׃
כג וְעַתָּה הָסִירוּ אֶת־אֱלֹהֵי הַנֵּכָר אֲשֶׁר
בְּקִרְבְּכֶם וְהַטּוּ אֶת־לְבַבְכֶם אֶל־יְהוָה
כד אֱלֹהֵי יִשְׂרָאֵל׃ וַיֹּאמְרוּ הָעָם אֶל־יְהוֹשֻׁעַ
אֶת־יְהוָה אֱלֹהֵינוּ נַעֲבֹד וּבְקוֹלוֹ נִשְׁמָע׃
כה וַיִּכְרֹת יְהוֹשֻׁעַ בְּרִית לָעָם בַּיּוֹם
הַהוּא וַיָּשֶׂם לוֹ חֹק וּמִשְׁפָּט בִּשְׁכֶם׃

Approach I

22. עֵדִים אַתֶּם בָּכֶם — *You are witnesses upon yourselves.*

Joshua was very pleased with their response and immediately asked them to bear witness to their statement *(Alshich).*

23. וְעַתָּה — *And now.*

Joshua was not able to finish his words before the nation impulsively affirmed his request stating, *'We are witnesses.'* Following their interruption, Joshua resumed his remarks with, *'And now ...' (Metzudos).*

הָסִירוּ אֶת־אֱלֹהֵי הַנֵּכָר — *Remove the strange gods.*

Rid yourselves of these objects of silver and gold which had once been used for idolatrous purposes *(Alshich).*

Approach II

22. עֵדִים אַתֶּם בָּכֶם — *You are witnesses upon yourselves.*

Through prophecy, Joshua knew that in the times of Ezekiel, the Jews would demand to be indistinguishable from the other nations (see *Ezekiel* 20:32). He was careful, therefore, to anticipate and to rebut any arguments that the Jews might later advance to rationalize their disloyalty to God. Lest they later claim that they had forsworn idol worship in Moses' times only in order to gain possession of *Eretz Yisrael,* Joshua had them renounce idolatry a second time after they had already occupied the land *(Rashi).*

23. הָסִירוּ אֶת־אֱלֹהֵי הַנֵּכָר — *Remove the strange gods.*

Remove any heretical thoughts that you may harbor, since you have chosen to serve God *(Abarbanel).*

Approach III

serve Him in order to receive rewards, but if you serve Him out of love, then your relationship with Him will be everlasting *(Poras Yosef).*

21. לֹא כִּי אֶת־ה׳ נַעֲבֹד — *No, we will serve only HASHEM.*

We did not imply that we would serve God out of fear of punishment or desire for reward. *We will serve HASHEM* because of His intrinsic worth *(Malbim).*

24
22-25 ²² *Then Joshua said to the people, 'You are witnesses upon yourselves that you have chosen HASHEM, to serve Him.'*

They answered, 'We are witnesses.'

²³ *'And now, remove the strange gods which are among you and direct your hearts to HASHEM, the God of Israel.'*

²⁴ *And the people replied to Joshua, 'HASHEM our God we will serve, and His voice we will heed.'*

²⁵ *Joshua made a covenant with the people that day and enumerated the statutes and laws in Shechem.*

◆§The Covenant and Conclusion

24. ה׳ אֱלֹהֵינוּ — *HASHEM our God.*

In verse 22 the Israelites declared they would serve HASHEM, whereas in this verse they stated they would serve HASHEM אֱלֹהֵינוּ [ELOHEINU], *our God.* God's name HASHEM connotes His attribute of mercy and His name ELOHEINU implies His attribute of strict justice. In this verse the people pledged they would serve God not only if He dealt with them through His attribute of mercy, but even if He dealt with them through His attribute of strict justice *(Alshich).*

וּבְקוֹלוֹ נִשְׁמָע — *And His voice we will heed.*

As soon as we hear what He desires of us, we will obey *(Meam Loez).*

25. וַיִּכְרֹת יְהוֹשֻׁעַ בְּרִית — *Joshua made a covenant.*

Tosafos, (Shabbos 88a, *s.v.* מודעא רבה) comments that in this covenant the Israelites only pledged not to involve themselves in idolatry as they said in verse 16: *Far be it from us to forsake HASHEM.*

According to *Alshich,* this covenant which Joshua made with the Israelites now was different than the covenant Moses made with them in Arvos-Moav and the one Joshua himself made with them at Mount Eval (see 8:33-35). In this covenant the people pledged to serve God even if He acts with them in what they feel is an unfair manner. (For example, He wreaks punishment upon them when their behavior is righteous.) It is for this reason that the terms חֹק and מִשְׁפָּט are used. The word חֹק (literally *statute)* connotes unfathomable behavior or legislation, whereas מִשְׁפָּט (literally *justice)* connotes reasonable behavior or legislation. Whether God deals with Israelites in a reasonable or unfathomable manner, they pledge to uphold the Torah.

וַיָּשֶׂם לוֹ חֹק וּמִשְׁפָּט בִּשְׁכֶם — *And enumerated the statutes and laws in Shechem.*

Joshua enumerated the statutes of the Torah in Shechem, and the people reaccepted them as binding *(Rashi).*

Ramban (Exodus 15:25), however, contends that the laws mentioned here were not laws of the Torah, but enactments which Joshua promulgated for the public well-being. The *Talmud (Bava Kama* 80b) lists Joshua's ordinances:

(a) It is permissible to graze one's flocks in privately owned forests;

(b) it is permissible to gather twigs and grass in privately owned fields except where tilsan beans are grown, since the growth of grass promotes their growth;

(c) it is permissible to prune branches

כו וַיִּכְתֹּב יְהוֹשֻׁעַ אֶת־הַדְּבָרִים הָאֵלֶּה
בְּסֵפֶר תּוֹרַת אֱלֹהִים וַיִּקַּח אֶבֶן גְּדוֹלָה
וַיְקִימֶהָ שָּׁם תַּחַת הָאַלָּה אֲשֶׁר בְּמִקְדַּשׁ
כז יְהוָה׃ וַיֹּאמֶר יְהוֹשֻׁעַ אֶל־כָּל־
הָעָם הִנֵּה הָאֶבֶן הַזֹּאת תִּהְיֶה־בָּנוּ לְעֵדָה
כִּי־הִיא שָׁמְעָה אֵת כָּל־אִמְרֵי יהוה אֲשֶׁר
דִּבֶּר עִמָּנוּ וְהָיְתָה בָכֶם לְעֵדָה פֶּן־
כח תְּכַחֲשׁוּן בֵּאלֹהֵיכֶם׃ וַיְשַׁלַּח יְהוֹשֻׁעַ אֶת־
כט הָעָם אִישׁ לְנַחֲלָתוֹ׃ וַיְהִי אַחֲרֵי
הַדְּבָרִים הָאֵלֶּה וַיָּמָת יְהוֹשֻׁעַ בִּן־נוּן עֶבֶד

for the purpose of grafting, except from the bottom two hand-breaths [approx. 7 inches] of an olive tree trunk;

(d) a new spring which gushes may be used by the entire city;

(e) all tribes may fish in the Sea of Tiberias (Kineret Sea) as long as their nets do not impede the passage of ships;

(f) it is permissible to relieve oneself behind a fence, even in a field of saffron;

(g) it is permissible to walk through fields after the grain has been collected until the new seeds begin to germinate, which occurs at the second rain;

(h) it is permissible to walk on the side of the road — even if it is private property — when the mud on the road hardens and potholes form;

(i) it is permissible to break vines in a vineyard, if necessary, when one has lost his way; and

(j) when a corpse is found, and no relatives can be traced, the body must be buried in the place it is found, even if this is private property.

For the specific conditions under which these enactments are applicable, see *Rambam (Hil. Nizkei Mamon* 5:3).

See also *Eruvin* 22b.

26. וַיִּכְתֹּב יְהוֹשֻׁעַ אֶת־הַדְּבָרִים הָאֵלֶּה — *And Joshua wrote these words.*

Targum renders: Joshua wrote these words and hid them in the Pentateuch. *Metzudos* explains that they were hidden in the place where the Pentateuch was stored, the Holy Ark.

What were *these words?*

On a literal level, the verse refers to the conversation that Joshua had just concluded with the nation *(Metzudos).*

Some commentators maintain that they were the words of the last eight verses in *Deuteronomy* which Moses could not have written, since his death had already been mentioned in the eighth verse from the end of *Deuteronomy (Makkos* 11a).

Others assert that they were the words that Joshua spoke concerning the cities of refuge (see *Commentary* to 20:1) which were also mentioned in the Pentateuch *(Makkos* 11a).

וַיִּקַּח אֶבֶן גְּדוֹלָה — *And (he) took a large stone.*

Joshua hollowed out the rock, and it served as a container for his book *(Malbim).*

Daas Sofrim suggests that this rock merely served as a monument to the day's events at Shechem.

תַּחַת הָאַלָּה — *Beneath the doorpost.*

The translation follows *Targum.* [Perhaps a record of the covenant was placed under the doorpost as a reminder to those entering the Sanctuary that their service to God is predicated on their agreement to forswear idolatry.]

26 *And Joshua wrote these words in the Book of the*
law of God and took a large stone and placed it there
beneath the doorpost which was in the Sanctuary of
HASHEM.
27 *And Joshua declared to all the people, 'Behold,*
this stone shall be a witness upon us, for it has heard
all the words HASHEM spoke to us. It shall be a wit-
ness against you if you deny your God.' 28 *And*
Joshua sent the people away, each man to his
inheritance.
29 *After these events Joshua son of Nun, the*

Rashi cites other commentators who suggest that this refers to the terebinth tree [אֵלָה] in Shechem under which Jacob buried idols; Scripture states, *And they gave Jacob all the strange gods which were in their hand and their earrings which were in their ears, and Jacob hid them under the terebinth near Shechem (Genesis* 35:4).

בְּמִקְדַּשׁ ה׳ — *In the Sanctuary of HASHEM.*

Because the Holy Ark was then at Shechem, that city was referred to as the place of *the Sanctuary (Metzudos).*

Malbim understands this as a reference to the Sanctuary at Shiloh.

27. הָאֶבֶן הַזֹּאת — *This stone.*

Targum interprets: This stone shall be as the stone tablets of the Decalogue, for they both bear witness, and they are inscribed with similar messages.

תִּהְיֶה־בָּנוּ לְעֵדָה — *Shall be a witness upon us.*

Just as Moses took the Torah Scroll and placed it in the Holy Ark to bear witness to the Jews' commitment to Torah observance, Joshua took his Book and placed it in the stone to bear witness *upon us* and *against you.* By saying *upon us,* Joshua includes himself and the entire Jewish people, for the stone will bear witness to all that God communicated to *us* in this Book. He also says *against you* — lest the people renege on their promise to serve only God *(Malbim).*

כִּי־הִיא שָׁמְעָה — *For it has heard.*

Figuratively speaking, the rock 'heard' these words *(Radak).*

אֲשֶׁר דִּבֶּר עִמָּנוּ — [*HASHEM*] *spoke to us.*

This refers to the words which He spoke to us on Mount Sinai *(Radak).*

[Cf., however, *Malbim* cited in the above note].

28. וַיְשַׁלַּח — *And* [*Joshua*] *sent.*

According to *Seder HaDoros,* each tribe went to its own territory and buried its progenitor, the son of Jacob from whom it descended. Reuben and Gad were buried in the Trans-Jordan in the city of Romia. Simeon and Levi were buried in Mondo. This city was given to Simeon and its outskirts were given to Levi. Judah was buried in Babia across from Beis Lechem. The bones of Yisachar and Zevulun were buried in Tzidon Rabbah. Dan was buried in Ashtal; Naftali and Asher in Kedesh. The bones of Joseph were buried in Shechem (see v. 32) and Benjamin was buried in Jerusalem across from the Jebusites. [See *Rashi* to *Exodus* 13:19.]

29. וַיָּמָת יְהוֹשֻׁעַ — *Joshua died.*

Joshua, of course, could not have written this verse, nor the four remaining verses of the book. Elazar authored verses 29 to 32, and Pinchas authored verse 33 *(Bava Basra* 15a).

ל יְהוָה בֶּן־מֵאָה וָעֶשֶׂר שָׁנִים׃ וַיִּקְבְּרוּ אוֹתוֹ
בִּגְבוּל נַחֲלָתוֹ בְּתִמְנַת־סֶרַח אֲשֶׁר בְּהַר־
לא אֶפְרָיִם מִצְּפוֹן לְהַר־גָּעַשׁ׃ וַיַּעֲבֹד יִשְׂרָאֵל
אֶת־יהוה כֹּל יְמֵי יְהוֹשֻׁעַ וְכֹל | יְמֵי
הַזְּקֵנִים אֲשֶׁר הֶאֱרִיכוּ יָמִים אַחֲרֵי
יְהוֹשֻׁעַ וַאֲשֶׁר יָדְעוּ אֵת כָּל־מַעֲשֵׂה יהוה
לב אֲשֶׁר עָשָׂה לְיִשְׂרָאֵל׃ וְאֶת־עַצְמוֹת יוֹסֵף
אֲשֶׁר־הֶעֱלוּ בְנֵי־יִשְׂרָאֵל | מִמִּצְרַיִם קָבְרוּ
בִשְׁכֶם בְּחֶלְקַת הַשָּׂדֶה אֲשֶׁר קָנָה יַעֲקֹב
מֵאֵת בְּנֵי־חֲמוֹר אֲבִי־שְׁכֶם בְּמֵאָה
קְשִׂיטָה וַיִּהְיוּ לִבְנֵי־יוֹסֵף לְנַחֲלָה׃
לג וְאֶלְעָזָר בֶּן־אַהֲרֹן מֵת וַיִּקְבְּרוּ אֹתוֹ
בְּגִבְעַת פִּינְחָס בְּנוֹ אֲשֶׁר נִתַּן־לוֹ בְּהַר
אֶפְרָיִם׃

According to *Ibn Ezra (Exodus* 33:11), Joshua died within the year that he made a covenant with the nation. According to *Seder HaDoros*, he died two years after the covenant.

עֶבֶד ה׳ — *The servant of HASHEM.*

Alshich interprets that Joshua acquired this title only *after these events*, i.e., all the events recounted in this book. In the beginning of *Joshua* he was not referred to by this title. However, after performing miracles, conquering the Land for God, dividing the Land, and establishing a new covenant between the Israelites and God, he earned this new appellation.

[See *Commentary* to 1:1.]

בֶּן־מֵאָה וָעֶשֶׂר שָׁנִים — *At the age of one hundred ten years.*

Joshua should have lived as long as Moses, 120 years. Ten years were deducted from his life, however, because he was not alacritous enough in the conquest of the Land *(Bamidbar Rabbah* 22:6). [See *Commentary* to 11:18.]

30. בִּגְבוּל נַחֲלָתוֹ — *In the border of his inheritance.*

From here we learn that it is an act of kindness to bury a dead person in his own land among his relatives *(Abarbanel)*. [See *Commentary* to 24:28.]

בְּתִמְנַת־סֶרַח — *In Timnas Serach.*

See *Commentary* to 19:50.

לְהַר־גָּעַשׁ — *Mount Ga'ash.*

Since Scripture never mentions the existence of this mountain in any other place, R' Yehoshua ben Levi inferred that this name should be understood homiletically. Because the nation was lax and did not eulogize Joshua in a manner befitting his stature, God caused the mountain to erupt on the day of his burial (גָּעַשׁ means *to erupt) (Radak).*

[Scripture does not mention that a thirty day mourning period was held for Joshua, although it did mention one for Moses.]

Why was it that the nation failed to properly eulogize Joshua, who was

24
30-33 *servant of HASHEM, died at the age of one hundred ten years.* [30] *And they buried him in the border of his inheritance in Timnas Serach which is in Mount Ephraim, north of Mount Ga'ash.* [31] *And Israel served HASHEM all the days of Joshua and all the days of the Elders whose days were lengthened after Joshua's death and who had known all the deeds of HASHEM which He had done for Israel.* [32] *And Joseph's bones which the Children of Israel brought up from Egypt they buried in Shechem, in the portion of field which Jacob acquired from the children of Chamor, the father of Shechem, for a* kesitah. *It was for the Children of Joseph as an inheritance.* [33] *And Elazar the son of Aaron died, and they buried him in the knoll of Pinchas his son which he gave him on Mount Ephraim.*

Moses' foremost student, performed wondrous miracles, and conquered the thirty-one powerful kings of *Eretz Yisrael?* The Jews' failure to honor Joshua properly is especially perplexing, for at that time the nation was at the highest level of spirituality. This is evident from the next verse, which states, *And (they) served HASHEM all the days of Joshua* (24:31).

Or HaYashar (Zevachim 116b) suggests that the nation had never sanctioned Joshua's marriage to Rachav, who had been a harlot for forty years before she converted to Judaism (see *Commentary* to 2:1). Actually, Joshua had married Rachav at God's command *(Tosafos, Sotah* 35b) and eight prophets descended from their union. Nevertheless, the nation always doubted the propriety of the marriage and expressed their disapproval after Joshua's death. The mountain threatened to erupt as a sign to the people that God Himself had sanctioned Joshua's marriage to Rachav.

The *Talmud (Shabbos* 105b) deduces from here that anyone who does not properly eulogize a *talmid chacham* (pious scholar) deserves to be buried alive.

31. הֶאֱרִיכוּ יָמִים — *Days were lengthened.*

Their *days* were lengthened, but not their *years,* for they were punished [for not eulogizing Joshua appropriately] *(Rashi).*

Rashi (Shabbos 105b) explains that 'lengthened days' means days of good quality. (Cf., however, *Maharsha, ibid.)*

The elders lived for only twenty-eight years after Joshua became leader *(Metzudos* citing *Seder Olam).*

32. אֲשֶׁר־הֶעֱלוּ בְנֵי־יִשְׂרָאֵל — *Which the Children of Israel brought up.*

The verse in *Exodus* (13:19) specifically states that it was Moses — not the Children of Israel — who brought Joseph's bones from Egypt. *Radak* explains that although Moses issued the command to transport Joseph's body, it was the Israelites who actually fulfilled the act.

The *Talmud (Sotah* 13b) derives a general principle from the disparity

between these two verses. If one person begins a mitzvah and another completes it, the second person is credited with its performance. Although Moses originally brought Joseph's bones from Egypt, he was unable to enter *Eretz Yisrael.* Thus, our verse credits the Israelites, who completed Moses' task by transporting Joseph's bones into *Eretz Yisrael,* with the entire mitzvah.

קָבְרוּ בִשְׁכֶם — *They buried in Shechem.*

Why was Joseph buried in Shechem?

As a mark of respect, Joseph was buried in the first plot of land which Jacob acquired in *Eretz Yisrael (Radak).*

Because Joseph bore the responsibility for Jacob's burial, Jacob gave him the city of Shechem for his burial site as Scripture states, *'I* [Jacob] *have given you one portion* [Shechem — see *Rashi*] *more than your brothers' (Rashi* to *Genesis* 48:22).

On a Midrashic level, Joseph was buried in Shechem because it was from there that his brothers had kidnapped him. Thus it was proper that his bones should be returned there (*Sotah* 13b).

אֲשֶׁר קָנָה יַעֲקֹב מֵאֵת בְּנֵי־חֲמוֹר — *Which* [*Jacob*] *acquired from the children of Chamor.*

[See *Genesis* 33:19.]

קְשִׂיטָה — *Kesitah.*

This was a certain type of coin *(Metzudos).*

23:16, Abraham paid 400 shekalim of silver.

וַיִּהְיוּ לִבְנֵי־יוֹסֵף לְנַחֲלָה — *It was for the Children of Joseph as an inheritance.*

Having Joseph's remains in their territory made it into a good inheritance *(Radak).*

33. וְאֶלְעָזָר בֶּן־אַהֲרֹן מֵת — *And Elazar the son of Aharon died.*

This verse was written by Pinchas *(Bava Basra* 15a).

Elazar died as a result of Joshua's death. Since he was the leader of the generation which did not eulogize Joshua properly, he was held responsible, and thus his *days were lengthened,* but not his years (see *Commentary* to verse 31). Scripture used the past perfect tense in regard to Joshua's death, and the past tense in regard to Elazar's death in order to connote that Elazar's death was a consequence of Joshua's death *(Meam Loez).*

בְּגִבְעַת פִּינְחָס בְּנוֹ — *In the knoll of Pinchas his son.*

If his father Elazar had not owned this land, how did his son Pinchas gain ownership of it? The *Talmud (Bava Basra* 111b) explains that Pinchas's wife had inherited land from her family. When she died, the property passed to her husband.

Others suggest that the knoll was given as a gift to Pinchas by the nation, just as Calev and Joshua had received land (*Radak*).

תם ונשלם שבח לאל בורא עולם

חזק

INDICES

SUBJECT INDEX

(PR=Prefatory Remarks; ft.=footnote)

GEOGRAPHICAL INDEX

The following is a transliterated listing of the geographical names found in the *Book of Joshua* followed by the verse numbers where they appear. Verse numbers in **bold faced type** indicate that a discussion of the **location** of the geographical name may be found in the *Commentary* to that verse. [E.g. — "Cheshbon **9:10, 12:2,** 13:17" indicates that Cheshbon is mentioned in three verses, 9:10, 12:2, and 13:17; and its geographical location is discussed in the *Commentary* to 12:2.]